PEARSON CUSTOM LIBRARY

MARKETING METRICS
MARK 314
School of Business
MacEwan University

PEARSON

V092

ISBN 10: 1-269-83412-6
ISBN 13: 978-1-269-83412-4

PEARSON

Table of Contents

INTRODUCTION

In recent years, data-based marketing has swept through the business world. In its wake, measurable performance and accountability have become the keys to marketing success. However, few managers appreciate the range of metrics by which they can evaluate marketing strategies and dynamics. Fewer still understand the pros, cons, and nuances of each.

In this environment, we have come to recognize that marketers, general managers, and business students need a comprehensive, practical reference on the metrics used to judge marketing programs and quantify their results. In this book, we seek to provide that reference. We wish our readers great success with it.

1   What Is a Metric?

A metric is a measuring system that quantifies a trend, dynamic, or characteristic.[1] In virtually all disciplines, practitioners use metrics to explain phenomena, diagnose causes, share findings, and project the results of future events. Throughout the worlds of science, business, and government, metrics encourage rigor and objectivity. They make it possible to compare observations across regions and time periods. They facilitate understanding and collaboration.

2   Why Do You Need Metrics?

"When you can measure what you are speaking about, and express it in numbers, you know something about it; but when you cannot measure it, when you cannot express it in numbers, your knowledge is of a meager and unsatisfactory kind: it may be the beginning of knowledge, but you have scarcely, in your thoughts, advanced to the stage of science."—William Thomson, Lord Kelvin, Popular Lectures and Addresses (1891–94)[2]

Lord Kelvin, a British physicist and the manager of the laying of the first successful transatlantic cable, was one of history's great advocates for quantitative investigation. In his day, however, mathematical rigor had not yet spread widely beyond the worlds of science, engineering, and finance. Much has changed since then.

Today, numerical fluency is a crucial skill for every business leader. Managers must quantify market opportunities and competitive threats. They must justify the financial risks and benefits of their decisions. They must evaluate plans, explain variances, judge performance, and identify leverage points for improvement—all in numeric terms. These responsibilities require a strong command of measurements and of the systems and formulas that generate them. In short, they require metrics.

Managers must select, calculate, and explain key business metrics. They must understand how each is constructed and how to use it in decision-making. Witness the following, more recent quotes from management experts:

> "... *every metric, whether it is used explicitly to influence behavior, to evaluate future strategies, or simply to take stock, will affect actions and decisions.*"[3]

> "*If you can't measure it, you can't manage it.*"[4]

3   Marketing Metrics: Opportunities, Performance, and Accountability

Marketers are by no means immune to the drive toward quantitative planning and evaluation. Marketing may once have been regarded as more an art than a science. Executives may once have cheerfully admitted that they knew they wasted half the money they spent on advertising, but they didn't know which half. Those days, however, are gone.

Today, marketers must understand their addressable markets quantitatively. They must measure new opportunities and the investment needed to realize them. Marketers must quantify the value of products, customers, and distribution channels—all under various pricing and promotional scenarios. Increasingly, marketers are held accountable for the financial ramifications of their decisions. Observers have noted this trend in graphic terms:

> "*For years, corporate marketers have walked into budget meetings like neighborhood junkies. They couldn't always justify how well they spent past handouts or what difference it all made. They just wanted more money—for flashy TV ads, for big-ticket events, for, you know, getting out the message and building up the brand. But those heady days of blind budget increases are fast being replaced with a new mantra: measurement and accountability.*"[5]

4 Choosing the Right Numbers

The numeric imperative represents a challenge, however. In business and economics, many metrics are complex and difficult to master. Some are highly specialized and best suited to specific analyses. Many require data that may be approximate, incomplete, or unavailable.

Under these circumstances, no single metric is likely to be perfect. For this reason, we recommend that marketers use a portfolio or "dashboard" of metrics. By doing so, they can view market dynamics from various perspectives and arrive at "triangulated" strategies and solutions. Additionally, with multiple metrics, marketers can use each as a check on the others. In this way, they can maximize the accuracy of their knowledge.[6] They can also estimate or project one data point on the basis of others. Of course, to use multiple metrics effectively, marketers must appreciate the relations between them and the limitations inherent in each.

When this understanding is achieved, however, metrics can help a firm maintain a productive focus on customers and markets. They can help managers identify the strengths and weaknesses in both strategies and execution. Mathematically defined and widely disseminated, metrics can become part of a precise, operational language within a firm.

Data Availability and Globalization of Metrics

A further challenge in metrics stems from wide variations in the availability of data between industries and geographies. Recognizing these variations, we have tried to suggest alternative sources and procedures for estimating some of the metrics in this book.

Fortunately, although both the range and type of marketing metrics may vary between countries,[7] these differences are shrinking rapidly. Ambler,[8] for example, reports that performance metrics have become a common language among marketers, and that they are now used to rally teams and benchmark efforts internationally.

5 Mastering Metrics

Being able to "crunch the numbers" is vital to success in marketing. Knowing which numbers to crunch, however, is a skill that develops over time. Toward that end, managers must practice the use of metrics and learn from their mistakes. By working through the examples in this book, we hope our readers will gain both confidence and a firm understanding of the fundamentals of data-based marketing. With time and experience, we trust that you will also develop an intuition about metrics, and learn to dig deeper when calculations appear suspect or puzzling.

Ultimately, with regard to metrics, we believe many of our readers will require not only familiarity but also fluency. That is, managers should be able to perform relevant calculations on the fly—under pressure, in board meetings, and during strategic deliberations and negotiations. Although not all readers will require that level of fluency, we believe it will be increasingly expected of candidates for senior management positions, especially those with significant financial responsibility. We anticipate that a mastery of data-based marketing will become a means for many of our readers to differentiate and position themselves for career advancement in an ever more challenging environment.

Reference Materials

Throughout this text, we have highlighted formulas and definitions for easy reference. We have also included outlines of key terms at the beginning of each chapter and section. Within each formula, we have followed this notation to define all inputs and outputs.

$—(**Dollar Terms**): *A monetary value. We have used the dollar sign and "dollar terms" for brevity, but any other currency, including the euro, yen, dinar, or yuan, would be equally appropriate.*

%—(**Percentage**): *Used as the equivalent of fractions or decimals. For readability, we have intentionally omitted the step of multiplying decimals by 100 to obtain percentages.*

#—(**Count**): *Used for such measures as unit sales or number of competitors.*

R—(**Rating**): *Expressed on a scale that translates qualitative judgments or preferences into numeric ratings. Example: A survey in which customers are asked to assign a rating of "1" to items that they find least satisfactory and "5" to those that are most satisfactory. Ratings have no intrinsic meaning without reference to their scale and context.*

I—(**Index**): *A comparative figure, often linked to or expressive of a market average. Example: the consumer price index. Indexes are often interpreted as a percentage.*

$—Dollar. %—Percentage. #—Count. R—Rating. I—Index.

References and Suggested Further Reading

Abela, Andrew, Bruce H. Clark, and Tim Ambler. "Marketing Performance Measurement, Performance, and Learning," working paper, September 1, 2004.

Ambler, Tim, and Chris Styles. (1995). "Brand Equity: Toward Measures That Matter," working paper No. 95-902, London Business School, Centre for Marketing.

Barwise, Patrick, and John U. Farley. (2003). "Which Marketing Metrics Are Used and Where?" Marketing Science Institute, (03-111), working paper, Series issues two 03-002.

Clark, Bruce H., Andrew V. Abela, and Tim Ambler. "Return on Measurement: Relating Marketing Metrics Practices to Strategic Performance," working paper, January 12, 2004.

Hauser, John, and Gerald Katz. (1998). "Metrics: You Are What You Measure," *European Management Journal*, Vo. 16, No. 5, pp. 517–528.

Kaplan, R. S., and D. P. Norton. (1996). *The Balanced Scorecard: Translating Strategy into Action*, Boston, MA: Harvard Business School Press.

Table 1   Major Metrics List

Section	Metric	Section	Metric
Share of Hearts, Minds, and Markets		2	Channel Margins
1	Revenue Market Share	3	Average Price per Unit
1	Unit Market Share	3	Price Per Statistical Unit
2	Relative Market Share	4	Variable and Fixed Costs
3	Brand Development Index	5	Marketing Spending
3	Category Development Index	6	Contribution per Unit
		6	Contribution Margin (%)
4–6	Decomposition of Market Share	6	Break-Even Sales
4	Market Penetration	7	Target Volume
4	Brand Penetration	7	Target Revenues
4	Penetration Share	*Product and Portfolio Management*	
5	Share of Requirements	1	Trial
6	Heavy Usage Index	1	Repeat Volume
7	Hierarchy of Effects	1	Penetration
7	Awareness	1	Volume Projections
7	Top of Mind	2	Year-on-Year Growth
7	Ad Awareness	2	Compound Annual Growth Rate (CAGR)
7	Knowledge		
7	Consumer Beliefs	3	Cannibalization Rate
7	Purchase Intentions	3	Fair Share Draw Rate
7	Purchase Habits	4	Brand Equity Metrics
7	Loyalty	5	Conjoint Utilities
7	Likeability	6	Segment Utilities
8	Willingness to Recommend	7	Conjoint Utilities and Volume Projections
8	Customer Satisfaction		
9	Net Promoter	*Customer Profitability*	
10	Willingness to Search	1	Customers
Margins and Profits		1	Recency
		1	Retention Rate
1	Unit Margin	2	Customer Profit
1	Margin (%)	3	Customer Lifetime Value

Table 1 *Continued*

Section	Metric	Section	Metric
4	Prospect Lifetime Value	3	Price Elasticity of Demand
5	Average Acquisition Cost	4	Optimal Price
5	Average Retention Cost	5	Residual Elasticity
Sales Force and Channel Management		*Promotion*	
1	Workload	1	Baseline Sales
1	Sales Potential Forecast	1	Incremental Sales/Promotion Lift
2	Sales Goal		
3	Sales Force Effectiveness	2	Redemption Rates
4	Compensation	2	Costs for Coupons and Rebates
4	Break-Even Number of Employees	2	Percentage Sales with Coupon
5	Sales Funnel, Sales Pipeline	3	Percent Sales on Deal
6	Numeric Distribution	3	Pass-Through
6	All Commodity Volume (ACV)	4	Price Waterfall
6	Product Category Volume (PCV)	*Advertising Media and Web Metrics*	
6	Total Distribution	1	Impressions
6	Category Performance Ratio	1	Gross Rating Points (GRPs)
7	Out of Stock	2	Cost per Thousand Impressions (CPM)
7	Inventories	3	Net Reach
8	Markdowns	3	Average Frequency
8	Direct Product Profitability (DPP)	4	Frequency Response Functions
8	Gross Margin Return on Inventory Investment (GMROII)	5	Effective Reach
		5	Effective Frequency
Pricing Strategy		6	Share of Voice
1	Price Premium	7	Pageviews
2	Reservation Price	8	Rich Media Display Time
2	Percent Good Value		*Continues*

Table 1 *Continued*

Section	Metric	Section	Metric
9	Rich Media Interaction Rate	*Marketing and Finance*	
10	Clickthrough Rate	1	Net Profit
11	Cost per Click	1	Return on Sales (ROS)
11	Cost per Order	1	Earnings Before Interest, Taxes, Depreciation, and Amortization (EBITDA)
11	Cost per Customer Acquired		
12	Visits	2	Return on Investment (ROI)
12	Visitors	3	Economic Profit (aka EVA®)
12	Abandonment Rate	4	Payback
13	Bounce Rate	4	Net Present Value (NPV)
14	Friends/Followers/Supporters	4	Internal Rate of Return (IRR)
15	Downloads	5	Return on Marketing Investment (ROMI); Revenue

6 Marketing Metrics Survey

Why Do a Survey of Which Metrics Are Most Useful?

From the beginning of our work on this book, we have fielded requests from colleagues, editors, and others to provide a short list of the "key" or "top ten" marketing metrics. The intuition behind this request is that readers (managers and students) ought to be able to focus their attention on the "most important" metrics. Until now we have resisted that request.

Our reasons for not providing the smaller, more concentrated list of "really important" metrics are as follows. First, we believe that any ranking of marketing metrics from most to least useful will depend on the type of business under consideration. For example, marketers of business-to-business products and services that go to market through a direct sales force don't need metrics that measure retail availability or dealer productivity.

The second reason we believe that different businesses will have different rankings is that metrics tend to come in matched sets. For example, if customer lifetime value is important to your business (let's say, financial services), then you are likely to value measures of retention and acquisition costs as well. The same notion applies to retail, media, sales force, and Web traffic metrics. If some of these are important to you, others in the same general categories are likely to be rated as useful, too.

Third, businesses don't always have access (at a reasonable cost) to the metrics they would like to have. Inevitably, some of the rankings presented will reflect the cost of obtaining the data that underlie the particular metrics.

Fourth, some metrics might be ranked lower, but ultimately prove to be useful, after managers fully understand the pros and cons of a particular metric. For example, many believe that Economic Value Added (EVA) is the "gold standard" of profitability metrics, but it ranks far below other financial performance measures such as ROI. We believe one reason for the low ranking of EVA is that this metric is less applicable at the "operating level" than for overall corporate performance. The other reason is that the measure is relatively new, and many managers don't understand it as well. Customer Lifetime Value is another metric that is gaining acceptance, but is still unfamiliar to many managers. If all these metrics were well understood, there would be no need for a book of this type.

In summary, while we believe the rankings resulting from our survey can be useful, we ask readers to keep the above points in mind. We report in Tables 2 and 3 the overall ranking of the usefulness of various metrics as well as the different rankings for different types of businesses and different categories of metrics. Although no business is likely to be exactly like yours, we thought readers might find it useful to see what other marketers thought which metrics were most useful in monitoring and managing their businesses.

Survey Sample

Our survey was completed by 194 senior marketing managers and executives. More than 100 held the title of Vice President/Director/Manager or "Head" of Marketing, some with global responsibility. Most held titles such as VP of Marketing, Marketing Director, and Director Sales and Marketing. There were 10 presidents and C-level managers with heavy marketing responsibilities, and the remaining respondents included product/ project/category managers, trade marketing managers, pricing managers, key account managers, development managers, and assistant/associate vice presidents.

Industries represented in our survey are too diverse to easily summarize. No more than 10 responses from a single industry were recorded, and the respondents listed their markets as aerospace, automobiles, banking, chemicals, consumer goods, construction, computers, consulting, education, industrial distribution, investments, government, health care, housing, insurance, information technology, manufacturing, materials, medical devices, paints, pharmaceuticals, retailing, software, telecommunications, and transportation. Roughly 20% of respondents did not provide a specific industry.

Survey questions asked respondents to rate the usefulness of particular metrics in monitoring and managing their businesses. Note that this survey asks managers to give ratings with respect to how these metrics are actually used but does not inquire about the reason. Nor did the survey offer guidance concerning the meaning of "useful"—that was left as a matter of interpretation for survey participants.

Financial metrics are generally rated very high in usefulness compared to any true marketing metrics. This is not surprising given that financial metrics are common to almost every business.

Table 2 Survey of Senior Marketing Managers on the Perceived Usefulness of Various Marketing Metrics (n = 194)

Group / Metric	Question Number	Chapter in Book	All Who Responded to Question — % Saying Very Useful	All Who Responded to Question — Rank	Customer Relationship — Contract Rank	Customer Relationship — Frequent Purchase Rank	Customer Relationship — Infrequent Purchase Rank	What Does Your Business Sell? — Products Rank	What Does Your Business Sell? — Services Rank	What Does Your Business Sell? — Mixed Rank	Who Are Your Customers? — End Consumers Rank	Who Are Your Customers? — Business Rank	Who Are Your Customers? — Mixed Rank
# of People in Group			194		65	69	41	105	36	31	44	85	48
Net Profit	Q8.10#1	10	91%	1	1	1	1	1	1	1	1	1	1
Margin %	Q8.3#2	3	78%	2	10	2	3	2	6	2	2	3	6
Return on Investment	Q8.10#3	10	77%	3	4	5	2	3	5	3	3	2	8
Customer Satisfaction	Q8.2#12	2	71%	4	2	17	11	13	3	5	19	6	4
Target Revenues	Q8.4#2	3	71%	5	8	12	5	12	8	3	13	7	6
Sales Total	Q8.6#3	6	70%	6	7	10	8	10	8	8	16	3	12
Target Volumes	Q8.4#1	3	70%	7	5	6	11	8	13	10	8	7	10
Return on Sales	Q8.10#2	10	69%	8	12	12	3	9	17	8	4	17	2
Loyalty	Q8.2#8	2	69%	9	70	71	98	4	11	17	13	5	16
Annual Growth %	Q8.4#7	4	69%	10	13	3	11	7	11	15	8	10	10
Dollar Market Share	Q8.1#1	2	67%	11	13	7	7	5	13	21	8	11	13

Continues

Table 2   *Continued*

Group			All Who Responded to Question		Customer Relationship			What Does Your Business Sell?			Who Are Your Customers?		
# of People in Group			194		Contract 65	Frequent Purchase 69	Infrequent Purchase 41	Products 105	Services 36	Mixed 31	End Consumers 44	Business 85	Mixed 48
Metric	Question Number	Chapter in Book	% Saying Very Useful	Rank	Rank	Rank	Rank	Rank	Rank	Rank	Rank	Rank	Rank
Customers	Q8.5#1	5	67%	12	5	16	11	19	4	5	26	13	3
Unit Margin	Q8.3#1	3	65%	13	17	9	5	11	21	10	13	12	13
Retention Rate	Q8.5#3	5	63%	14	3	26	26	28	2	5	76	9	5
Sales Potential Forecast	Q8.6#2	6	62%	15	11	18	11	17	18	10	23	14	18
Unit Market Share	Q8.1#2	2	61%	16	23	4	16	5	54	30	8	18	17
Brand Awareness	Q8.2#1	2	61%	17	23	7	16	14	33	10	4	25	9
Variable and Fixed Costs	Q8.3#6	3	60%	18	15	11	32	15	8	30	19	21	13
Willingness to Recommend	Q8.2#10	2	57%	19	9	32	26	30	6	19	36	16	29
Volume Projections	Q8.4#6	4	56%	20	23	14	21	16	31	24	45	15	27
Sales Force Effective	Q8.6#4	6	54%	21	21	22	21	25	31	15	42	23	18
Price Premium	Q8.8#1	7	54%	22	28	27	8	23	33	17	56	19	25

Metric												
Marketing Spending	Q8.3#7	3	52%	23	51	15	16	18	67	21	6	46	21
Average Price per Unit	Q8.3#4	3	51%	24	23	23	32	21	33	38	27	26	25
Penetration	Q8.4#5	4	50%	25	39	19	21	22	54	24	39	24	32
Top of Mind	Q8.2#2	2	50%	26	33	25	26	30	33	30	39	27	21
Compensation	Q8.6#5	6	49%	27	17	30	52	32	18	46	42	20	58
Return on Marketing Investment (ROMI)	Q8.10#8	10	49%		47	32	8	26	45	24	19	39	24
Consumer Beliefs	Q8.2#5	2	48%	29	33	35	21	47	21	10	30	29	36
Contribution Margin %	Q8.3#9	3	47%	30	56	21	21	29	46	24	45	32	21
Net Present Value	Q8.10#6	10	46%	31	31	37	26	39	27	20	39	41	20
Market Penetration	Q8.1#6	2	45%	32	17	41	58	38	41	38	45	35	33
Sales Funnel, Sales Pipeline	Q8.6#7	6	44%	33	17	60	32	54	21	21	74	21	58
Relative Market Share	Q8.1#3	2	44%	34	36	38	40	32	33	65	58	41	27
Purchase Habits	Q8.2#7	2	43%	35	39	35	43	27	41	80	30	29	69
Inventories	Q8.7#7	6	43%	36	62	20	48	20	109	59	24	45	46
Likeability	Q8.2#9	2	43%	37	28	54	38	47	21	46	45	37	39
Effective Reach	Q8.9#6	9	42%	38	48	40	32	37	46	44	7	61	46
Economic Profit (EVA)	Q8.10#4	10	41%	39	31	63	26	50	27	30	71	36	38
Impressions	Q8.9#1	9	41%	40	36	61	26	50	41	24	19	64	29
Customer Profit	Q8.5#4	5	41%	41	16	69	52	59	18	54	73	28	46
Optimal Price	Q8.8#5	7	41%	42	39	47	36	36	46	46	45	49	36

Continues

Table 2   *Continued*

Group	Question Number	Chapter in Book	All Who Responded to Question 194		Customer Relationship			What Does Your Business Sell?			Who Are Your Customers?		
# of People in Group					Contract 65	Frequent Purchase 69	Infrequent Purchase 41	Products 105	Services 36	Mixed 31	End Consumers 44	Business 85	Mixed 48
Metric			% Saying Very Useful	Rank	Rank	Rank	Rank	Rank	Rank	Rank	Rank	Rank	Rank
Payback	Q8.10#5	10	41%	42	51	51	20	54	27	43	67	34	44
Incremental Sales or Promotional Lift	Q8.8#8	8	41%	44	66	24	52	24	96	65	24	50	51
Consumer Knowledge	Q8.2#4	2	40%	45	36	57	43	64	21	30	58	37	51
Contribution per Unit	Q8.3#8	3	40%	46	71	29	48	39	62	46	63	54	29
Break-Even Sales	Q8.3#10	3	40%	46	51	39	43	43	40	59	58	41	46
Customer Lifetime Value	Q8.5#5	5	39%	48	23	77	40	69	21	30	76	46	33
Price Elasticity	Q8.8#4	7	39%	48	71	31	38	35	72	54	34	56	39
Purchase Intentions	Q8.2#6	2	39%	50	54	67	19	62	41	30	45	32	79
Growth CAGR	Q8.4#8	4	38%	51	45	32	74	41	54	72	83	31	45
Internal Rate of Return	Q8.10#7	10	38%	52	44	63	36	66	27	29	71	53	35
Effective Frequency	Q8.9#7	9	37%	53	56	52	43	45	67	44	12	74	46

Visitors	Q8.9#15	9	37%	54	39	58	58	60	46	38	53	51	62
Average Acquisition Cost	Q8.5#7	5	36%	55	21	95	43	77	13	38	83	41	43
Share of Voice	Q8.9#8	9	36%	55	66	43	52	45	62	64	33	72	39
Visits	Q8.9#14	9	36%	57	39	58	66	61	46	38	53	55	51
Workload	Q8.6#1	6	36%	58	50	48	66	53	54	59	79	40	58
Repeat Volume	Q8.4#4	4	36%	59	56	46	58	50	54	65	64	52	58
Clickthrough Rate	Q8.9#10	9	35%	60	33	61	77	63	33	54	29	67	51
Baseline Sales	Q8.8#7	8	34%	61	71	42	56	42	72	80	45	56	69
Total Distribution	Q8.7#4	6	34%	62	84	43	48	44	96	59	28	66	69
Net Reach	Q8.9#4	9	34%	62	62	48	66	58	72	51	37	62	62
Brand Penetration	Q8.1#7	2	34%	64	62	54	62	47	62	75	30	69	62
Out of Stock %	Q8.7#6	6	33%	65	86	27	88	34	109	86	18	64	85
Average Retention Cost	Q8.5#8	5	33%	66	30	98	40	82	13	51	91	48	51
Product Category Volume	Q8.7#3	6	33%	67	84	45	57	57	92	58	62	62	51
Cost per Customer Acquired	Q8.9#13	9	32%	68	48	72	66	70	54	51	74	60	51
Average Frequency	Q8.9#5	9	31%	69	76	48	71	54	83	75	16	77	86
Channel Margin	Q8.3#3	3	30%	70	66	80	48	70	83	37	67	82	39
Direct Product Profitability	Q8.7#9	6	30%	71	76	56	62	67	72	54	66	69	62
Recency	Q8.5#2	5	29%	72	56	74	71	75	33	80	94	59	62
Cost per Thousand Impression	Q8.9#3	9	28%	73	62	81	62	70	62	75	38	83	75

Continues

Table 2   *Continued*

Group		Metric	Question Number	Chapter in Book	% Saying Very Useful	All Who Responded to Question	Customer Relationship			What Does Your Business Sell?			Who Are Your Customers?		
# of People in Group						Rank	Contract	Frequent Purchase	Infrequent Purchase	Products	Services	Mixed	End Consumers	Business	Mixed
						194	65	69	41	105	36	31	44	85	48
						Rank	Rank	Rank	Rank	Rank	Rank	Rank	Rank	Rank	Rank
		Pageview	Q8.9#9	9	28%	74	45	84	88	87	54	46	56	83	69
		Cost per Click	Q8.9#11	9	27%	75	56	86	77	79	46	65	53	88	75
		Brand Equity Metrics	Q8.4#10	4	26%	76	76	76	77	68	72	89	58	90	74
		Markdowns	Q8.7#8	6	26%	77	96	52	84	65	106	80	34	90	86
		Cannibalization Rate	Q8.4#9	4	24%	78	88	65	95	74	83	97	78	76	91
		Abandonment Rate	Q8.9#16	9	24%	79	56	90	95	90	62	71	81	87	68
		Ad Awareness	Q8.2#3	2	23%	80	76	88	77	78	72	80	64	104	75
		Cost per Order	Q8.9#12	9	23%	81	71	91	74	90	67	65	95	73	75
		Gross Rating Points	Q8.9#2	9	23%	82	88	91	58	84	67	80	42	99	92
		Break-Even Number of Employees	Q8.6#6	6	23%	83	66	96	71	100	46	59	85	69	96
		Hierarchy of Effects	Q8.1#11	2	23%	84	81	83	84	80	72	86	92	83	69

Numeric Distribution %	Q8.7#1	6	22%	85	108	75	62	73	106	103	69	89	97
All Commodity Volume	Q8.7#2	6	22%	85	96	67	93	75	83	89	69	78	104
Penetration Share	Q8.1#8	2	22%	87	76	93	74	84	72	75	95	75	79
Brand Development Index	Q8.1#4	2	21%	88	91	79	94	89	83	75	80	94	79
Prospect Lifetime Value	Q8.5#6	5	21%	89	81	106	66	95	46	104	98	67	97
Percentage Sales on Deal	Q8.8#12	8	21%	89	91	82	87	92	83	72	87	79	92
Willingness to Search	Q8.2#13	2	20%	91	71	102	77	86	72	107	85	79	100
Trial Volume	Q8.4#3	4	19%	92	90	72	108	82	96	97	90	79	103
Net Promoter Score	Q8.2#11	2	19%	93	55	101	103	94	61	107	106	58	109
Facings	Q8.7#5	6	19%	94	99	66	105	81	72	107	45	99	110
Redemption Rates	Q8.8#9	8	19%	95	102	69	100	92	96	104	82	94	92
Cost of Coupons/ Rebates	Q8.8#10	8	19%	95	102	77	90	87	96	97	87	102	79
Category Development Index	Q8.1#5	2	18%	97	95	87	103	97	83	86	99	92	79
Reservation Price	Q8.8#2	7	17%	98	99	93	84	96	72	89	100	86	99
GMROII	Q8.7#10	6	16%	99	102	84	99	98	96	89	87	94	100
Percent Good Value	Q8.8#3	7	16%	99	91	108	77	107	67	72	100	109	62
Percentage Sales with Coupon	Q8.8#11	8	16%	99	109	88	90	98	96	89	93	105	86
Price per Statistical Unit	Q8.3#5	3	16%	102	91	102	90	104	83	65	104	94	79
Conjoint Utilities	Q8.4#11	4	14%	103	81	99	108	101	92	89	107	94	89
Residual Elasticity	Q8.8#6	7	14%	104	98	109	77	102	92	97	109	92	92

Continues

18

Table 2 *Continued*

Group / Metric	Question Number	Chapter in Book	All Who Responded to Question (194)		Customer Relationship			What Does Your Business Sell?			Who Are Your Customers?		
			% Saying Very Useful	Rank	Contract (65)	Frequent Purchase (69)	Infrequent Purchase (41)	Products (105)	Services (36)	Mixed (31)	End Consumers (44)	Business (85)	Mixed (48)
					Rank	Rank	Rank	Rank	Rank	Rank	Rank	Rank	Rank
Percent Time on Deal	Q8.8#13	8	14%	105	102	96	95	105	96	89	97	102	104
Conjoint Utilities & Volume Projection	Q8.4#12	4	13%	106	87	99	108	103	92	89	103	105	89
Pass-Through	Q8.8#15	8	11%	107	102	107	100	108	83	97	102	108	100
Share of Requirements	Q8.1#9	2	10%	108	102	102	105	106	106	106	108	99	108
Average Deal Depth	Q8.8#14	8	10%	109	110	105	100	109	96	97	105	107	104
Heavy Usage Index	Q8.1#10	2	6%	110	101	110	107	110	96	110	110	110	104

Table 3   Ranking of Metrics by Category

Metric	Section in Survey	% Saying Very Useful	Ranking in Survey Section
Dollar Market Share	1	67%	1
Unit Market Share	1	61%	2
Market Penetration	1	45%	3
Relative Market Share	1	44%	4
Brand Penetration	1	34%	5
Hierarchy of Effects	1	23%	6
Penetration Share	1	22%	7
Brand Development Index	1	21%	8
Category Development Index	1	18%	9
Share of Requirements	1	10%	10
Heavy Usage Index	1	6%	11
Customer Satisfaction	2	71%	1
Loyalty	2	69%	2
Brand Awareness	2	61%	3
Willingness to Recommend	2	57%	4
Top of Mind	2	50%	5
Consumer Beliefs	2	48%	6
Purchase Habits	2	43%	7
Likeability	2	43%	8
Consumer Knowledge	2	40%	9
Purchase Intentions	2	39%	10
Ad Awareness	2	23%	11
Willingness to Search	2	20%	12
Net Promoter Score	2	19%	13
Margin %	3	78%	1
Unit Margin	3	65%	2
Variable and Fixed Costs	3	60%	3

Continues

Table 3 *Continued*

Metric	Section in Survey	% Saying Very Useful	Ranking in Survey Section
Marketing Spending	3	52%	4
Average Price per Unit	3	51%	5
Contribution Margin %	3	47%	6
Contribution per Unit	3	40%	7
Break-Even Sales	3	40%	8
Channel Margin	3	30%	9
Price per Statistical Unit	3	16%	10
Target Revenues	4	71%	1
Target Volumes	4	70%	2
Annual Growth %	4	69%	3
Volume Projections	4	56%	4
Penetration	4	50%	5
Growth CAGR	4	38%	6
Repeat Volume	4	36%	7
Brand Equity Metrics	4	26%	8
Cannibalization Rate	4	24%	9
Trial Volume	4	19%	10
Conjoint Utilities	4	14%	11
Conjoint Utilities & Volume Projection	4	13%	12
Customers	5	67%	1
Retention Rate	5	63%	2
Customer Profit	5	41%	3
Customer Lifetime Value	5	39%	4
Average Acquisition Cost	5	36%	5
Average Retention Cost	5	33%	6
Recency	5	29%	7
Prospect Lifetime Value	5	21%	8
Sales Total	6	70%	1

Metric	Section in Survey	% Saying Very Useful	Ranking in Survey Section
Sales Potential Forecast	6	62%	2
Sales Force Effective	6	54%	3
Compensation	6	49%	4
Sales Funnel, Sales Pipeline	6	44%	5
Workload	6	36%	6
Break-Even Number of Employees	6	23%	7
Inventories	7	43%	1
Total Distribution	7	34%	2
Out of Stock % (OOS)	7	33%	3
Product Category Volume (PCV)	7	33%	4
Direct Product Profitability (DPP)	7	30%	5
Markdowns	7	26%	6
Numeric Distribution %	7	22%	7
All Commodity Volume (ACV)	7	22%	8
Facings	7	19%	9
Gross Margin Return on Inventory Investment (GMROII)	7	16%	10
Price Premium	8	54%	1
Optimal Price	8	41%	2
Incremental Sales or Promotional Lift	8	41%	3
Price Elasticity	8	39%	4
Baseline Sales	8	34%	5
Percentage Sales on Deal	8	21%	6
Redemption Rates	8	19%	7

Continues

Table 3 *Continued*

Metric	Section in Survey	% Saying Very Useful	Ranking in Survey Section
Cost of Coupons/ Rebates	8	19%	8
Reservation Price	8	17%	9
Percent Good Value	8	16%	10
Percentage Sales with Coupon	8	16%	11
Residual Elasticity	8	14%	12
Percent Time on Deal	8	14%	13
Pass-Through	8	11%	14
Average Deal Depth	8	10%	15
Effective Reach	9	42%	1
Impressions	9	41%	2
Effective Frequency	9	37%	3
Visitors	9	37%	4
Share of Voice	9	36%	5
Visits	9	36%	6
Clickthrough Rate	9	35%	7
Net Reach	9	34%	8
Cost per Customer Acquired	9	32%	9
Average Frequency	9	31%	10
Cost per Thousand Impression (CPM)	9	28%	11
Pageview	9	28%	12
Cost per Click (CPC)	9	27%	13
Abandonment Rate	9	24%	14
Cost per Order	9	23%	15
Gross Rating Points	9	23%	16
Net Profit	10	91%	1
Return on Investment (ROI)	10	77%	2

■

Metric	Section in Survey	% Saying Very Useful	Ranking in Survey Section
Return on Sales (ROS)	10	69%	3
Return on Marketing Investment (ROMI)	10	49%	4
Net Present Value (NPV)	10	46%	5
Economic Profit (EVA)	10	41%	6
Payback	10	41%	7
Internal Rate of Return (IRR)	10	38%	8

ENDNOTES

1. Word Reference, www.wordreference.com. Accessed 22 April 2005.

2. Bartlett, John. (1992). *Bartlett's Familiar Quotations*, 16th edition; Justin Kaplan, general editor.

3. Hauser, John, and Gerald Katz. "Metrics: You are What You Measure," *European Management Journal*, Volume 16 No 5 October 1998.

4. Kaplan, Robert S., and David P. Norton. (1996). *Balanced Scorecard*, Boston, MA: Harvard Business School Press.

5. Brady, Diane, with David Kiley and Bureau Reports, "Making Marketing Measure Up," *Business Week*.

6. Strictly speaking, all the numbers can contain some error. Share may be estimated, for example, from retail sales to consumers. Sales might come from shipment to retailers.

7. Barwise, Patrick, and John U. Farley. (2003). "Which Marketing Metrics Are Used and Where?" Marketing Science Institute (03-111), working paper, Series issues two 03-002.

8. Ambler, Tim, Flora Kokkinaki, and Stefano Puntoni. (2004). "Assessing Marketing Performance: Reasons for Metrics Selection," *Journal of Marketing Management*, 20, 475–498.

MARGINS AND PROFITS

Introduction

Key concepts covered:

Margins

Selling Prices and Channel Margins

Average Price per Unit and Price per Statistical Unit

Variable Costs and Fixed Costs

Marketing Spending—Total, Fixed, and Variable

Break-Even Analysis and Contribution Analysis

Target Volume

Peter Drucker has written that the purpose of a business is to create a customer. As marketers, we agree. But we also recognize that a business can't survive unless it makes a margin as well as a customer. At one level, margins are simply the difference between a product's price and its cost. This calculation becomes more complicated, however, when multiple variations of a product are sold at multiple prices, through multiple channels, incurring different costs along the way. For example, a recent *Business Week* article noted that less "than two-thirds of GM's sales are retail. The rest go to rental-car agencies or to company employees and their families—sales that provide lower gross margins."[1] Although it is still the case that a business can't survive unless it earns a positive margin, it can be a challenge to determine precisely what margin the firm actually does earn.

In the first section of this chapter, we'll explain the basic computation of unit and percentage margins, and we'll introduce the practice of calculating margins as a percentage of selling price.

Next, we'll show how to "chain" this calculation through two or more levels in a distribution channel and how to calculate end-user purchase price on the basis of a

From Chapter 3 of *Marketing Metrics: The Definitive Guide to Measuring Marketing Performance*, 2/e.
Paul W. Farris. Neil T. Bendle. Phillip E. Pfeifer. David J. Reibstein. Copyright © 2010 by Pearson Education.
Published by Wharton School Publishing.

marketer's selling price. We'll explain how to combine sales through different channels to calculate average margins and how to compare the economics of different distribution channels.

In the third section, we'll discuss the use of "statistical" and standard units in tracking price changes over time.

We'll then turn our attention to measuring product costs, with particular emphasis on the distinction between fixed and variable costs. The margin between a product's unit price and its variable cost per unit represents a key calculation. It tells us how much the sale of each unit of that product will contribute to covering a firm's fixed costs. "Contribution margin" on sales is one of the most useful marketing concepts. It requires, however, that we separate fixed from variable costs, and that is often a challenge. Frequently, marketers must take "as a given" which of their firm's operating and production costs are fixed and which are variable. They are likely, however, to be responsible for making these fixed versus variable distinctions for marketing costs. That is the subject of the fifth section of this chapter.

In the sixth section, we'll discuss the use of fixed- and variable-cost estimates in calculating the break-even levels of sales and contribution. Finally, we'll extend our calculation of break-even points, showing how to identify sales and profit targets that are mutually consistent.

	Metric	Construction	Considerations	Purpose
1	Unit Margin	Unit price less the unit cost.	What are the standard units in the industry? May not reflect contribution margin if some fixed costs are allocated.	Determine value of incremental sales. Guide pricing and promotion.
1	Margin (%)	Unit margin as a percentage of unit price.	May not reflect contribution margin if some fixed costs are allocated.	Compare margins across different products/sizes/ forms of product. Determine value of incremental sales. Guide pricing and promotion decisions.

	Metric	Construction	Considerations	Purpose
2	Channel Margins	Channel profits as percentage of channel selling price.	Distinguish margin on sales (usual) from markup on cost (also encountered).	Evaluate channel value added in context of selling price. Calculate effect of price changes at one level of channel on prices and margins at other levels in the same channel (supply chain).
3	Average Price per Unit	Can be calculated as total revenue divided by total unit sales.	Some units may have greater relevance from producers' perspective than consumers' (e.g., ounces of shampoo vs. bottles). Changes may not be result of pricing decisions.	Understand how average prices are affected by shifts in pricing and product mix.
3	Price per Statistical Unit	SKU prices weighted by relevant percentage of each SKU in a statistical unit.	Percentage SKU mix should correspond over medium-term to actual mix of sales.	Isolate effect of price changes from mix changes by standardizing the SKU mix of a standard unit.
4	Variable and Fixed Costs	Divide costs into two categories: those that vary with volume (variable) and those that do not (fixed).	Variable costs may include production, marketing, and selling expenses. Some variable costs depend on units sold; others depend on revenue.	Understand how costs are affected by changes in sales volume.
5	Marketing Spending	Analyze costs that comprise marketing spending.	Can be divided into fixed and variable marketing costs.	Understand how marketing spending changes with sales.

Continues

	Metric	Construction	Considerations	Purpose
6	Contribution per Unit	Unit price less unit variable cost.	Ensure that marketing variable costs have not already been deducted from price.	Understand profit impact of changes in volume. Calculate break-even level of sales.
6	Contribution Margin (%)	Contribution per unit divided by unit price.	Ensure that variable costs are consistently based on units or revenue, as appropriate.	Same as above, but applies to dollar sales.
6	Break-Even Sales Level	For unit break-even, divide fixed costs by contribution per unit. For revenue break-even, divide fixed costs by contribution margin (%).	Variable and fixed cost estimates may be valid only over certain ranges of sales and production.	Rough indicator of project attractiveness and ability to earn profit.
7	Target Volume	Adjust break-even calculation to include profit target.	Variable marketing costs must be reflected in contribution margins. Sales increases often require increased investment or working capital.	Ensure that unit sales objectives will enable firm to achieve financial hurdle rates for profit, ROS, or ROI.
7	Target Revenues	Convert target volume to target revenues by using average prices per unit. Alternatively, combine cost and target data with knowledge of contribution margins.	Same as above.	Same as above, applied to revenue objectives.

1 Margins

Margin (on sales) is the difference between selling price and cost. This difference is typically expressed either as a percentage of selling price or on a per-unit basis.

Unit Margin ($) = Selling Price per Unit ($) − Cost per Unit ($)

$$\text{Margin (\%)} = \frac{\text{Unit Margin (\$)}}{\text{Selling Price per Unit (\$)}}$$

Managers need to know margins for almost all marketing decisions. Margins represent a key factor in pricing, return on marketing spending, earnings forecasts, and analyses of customer profitability.

Purpose: To determine the value of incremental sales, and to guide pricing and promotion decisions.

Margin on sales represents a key factor behind many of the most fundamental business considerations, including budgets and forecasts. All managers should, and generally do, know their approximate business margins. Managers differ widely, however, in the assumptions they use in calculating margins and in the ways they analyze and communicate these important figures.

Percentage Margins and Unit Margins: A fundamental variation in the way people talk about margins lies in the difference between percentage margins and unit margins on sales. The difference is easy to reconcile, and managers should be able to switch back and forth between the two.

What is a unit? Every business has its own notion of a "unit," ranging from a ton of margarine, to 64 ounces of cola, to a bucket of plaster. Many industries work with multiple units and calculate margin accordingly. The cigarette industry, for example, sells "sticks," "packs," "cartons," and 12M "cases" (which hold 1,200 individual cigarettes). Banks calculate margin on the basis of accounts, customers, loans, transactions, households, and branch offices. Marketers must be prepared to shift between such varying perspectives with little effort because decisions can be grounded in any of these perspectives.

Construction

Unit Margin ($) = Selling Price per Unit ($) − Cost per Unit ($)

$$\text{Margin (\%)} = \frac{\text{Unit Margin (\$)}}{\text{Selling Price per Unit (\$)}}$$

Percentage margins can also be calculated using total sales revenue and total costs.

$$\text{Margin (\%)} = \frac{[\text{Total Sales Revenue (\$)} - \text{Total Cost (\$)}]}{\text{Total Sales Revenue (\$)}}$$

When working with either percentage or unit margins, marketers can perform a simple check by verifying that the individual parts sum to the total.

To Verify a Unit Margin ($): **Selling Price per Unit = Unit Margin + Cost per Unit**

To Verify a Margin (%): **Cost as % of Sales = 100% − Margin %**

EXAMPLE: A company markets sailcloth by the lineal yard. Its cost basis and selling price for standard cloth are as follows:

Unit Selling Price (Selling Price per Unit) = $24 per Lineal Yard

Unit Cost (Cost per Unit) = $18 per Lineal Yard

To calculate unit margin, we subtract the cost from the selling price:

Unit Margin = $24 per Yard − $18 per Yard

= $6 per Yard

To calculate the percentage margin, we divide the unit margin by the selling price:

$$\text{Margin (\%)} = \frac{(\$24 - \$18) \text{ per Yard}}{\$24}$$

$$= \frac{\$6}{\$24} = 25\%$$

Let's verify that our calculations are correct:

Unit Selling Price = Unit Margin + Unit Cost

$24 per Yard = $6 per Yard + $18 per Yard   **correct**

A similar check can be made on our calculations of percentage margin:

100% − Margin on Sales (%) = Cost as % of Selling Price

$$100\% - 25\% = \frac{\$18}{\$24}$$

75% = 75%   **correct**

When considering multiple products with different revenues and costs, we can calculate overall margin (%) on either of two bases:

- Total revenue and total costs for all products, or
- The dollar-weighted average of the percentage margins of the different products

EXAMPLE: The sailcloth company produces a new line of deluxe cloth, which sells for $64 per lineal yard and costs $32 per yard to produce. The margin on this item is 50%.

$$\text{Unit Margin (\$)} = \$64 \text{ per Yard} - \$32 \text{ per Yard}$$

$$= \$32 \text{ per Yard}$$

$$\text{Margin (\%)} = \frac{(\$64 - \$32)}{\$64}$$

$$= \frac{\$32}{\$64}$$

$$= 50\%$$

Because the company now sells two different products, its average margin can only be calculated when we know the volume of each type of goods sold. It would not be accurate to take a simple average of the 25% margin on standard cloth and the 50% margin on deluxe cloth, unless the company sells the same dollar volume of both products.

If, one day, the company sells 20 yards of standard cloth and two yards of deluxe cloth, we can calculate its margins for that day as follows (see also Table 1):

$$\text{Total Sales} = 20 \text{ Yards at } \$24, \text{ and } 2 \text{ Yards at } \$64$$

$$= \$608$$

$$\text{Total Costs} = 20 \text{ Yards at } \$18, \text{ and } 2 \text{ Yards at } \$32$$

$$= \$424$$

$$\text{Margin (\$)} = \$184$$

$$\text{Margin (\%)} = \frac{\text{Margin (\$184)}}{\text{Total Sales (\$608)}}$$

$$= 30\%$$

Because dollar sales differ between the two products, the company margin of 30% is not a simple average of the margins of those products.

Table 1   Sales, Costs, and Margins

	Standard	Deluxe	Total
Sales in Yards	20	2	22
Selling Price per Yard	$24.00	$64.00	
Total Sales $	$480.00	$128.00	$608.00
Cost per Yard	$18.00	$32.00	
Total Costs $	$360.00	$64.00	$424.00
Total Dollar Margin ($)	$120.00	$64.00	$184.00
Unit Margin	$6.00	$32.00	$8.36
Margin (%)	25%	50%	30%

Data Sources, Complications, and Cautions

After you determine which units to use, you need two inputs to determine margins: *unit costs* and *unit selling prices.*

Selling prices can be defined before or after various "charges" are taken: Rebates, customer discounts, brokers' fees, and commissions can be reported to management either as costs or as deductions from the selling price. Furthermore, external reporting can vary from management reporting because accounting standards might dictate a treatment that differs from internal practices. Reported margins can vary widely, depending on the calculation technique used. This can result in deep organizational confusion on as fundamental a question as what the price of a product actually is.

Price waterfalls show cautions on deducting certain discounts and allowances in calculating "net prices." Often, there is considerable latitude on whether certain items are subtracted from list price to calculate a net price or are added to costs. One example is the retail practice of providing gift certificates to customers who purchase certain amounts of goods. It is not easy to account for these in a way that avoids confusion among prices, marketing costs, and margins. In this context, two points are relevant: (1) Certain items can be treated either as deductions from prices or as increments to cost, but not both. (2) The treatment of such an item will not affect the unit margin, but will affect the percentage margin.

Margin as a percentage of costs: Some industries, particularly retail, calculate margin as a percentage of costs, not of selling prices. Using this technique in the previous example, the percentage margin on a yard of standard sailcloth would be reckoned as the

Table 2   Relationship Between Margins and Markups

Price	Cost	Margin	Markup
$10	$9.00	10%	11%
$10	$7.50	25%	33%
$10	$6.67	33.3%	50%
$10	$5.00	50%	100%
$10	$4.00	60%	150%
$10	$3.33	66.7%	200%
$10	$2.50	75%	300%

$6.00 unit margin divided by the $18.00 unit cost, or 33%. This can lead to confusion. Marketers must become familiar with the practices in their industry and stand ready to shift between them as needed.

Markup or margin? Although some people use the terms "margin" and "markup" interchangeably, this is not appropriate. The term "markup" commonly refers to the practice of adding a percentage to costs in order to calculate selling prices.

To get a better idea of the relationship between margin and markup, let's calculate a few. For example, a 50% markup on a variable cost of $10 would be $5, yielding a retail price of $15. By contrast, the margin on an item that sells at a retail price of $15 and that carries a variable cost of $10 would be $5/$15, or 33.3%. Table 2 shows some common margin/markup relationships.

One of the peculiarities that can occur in retail is that prices are "marked up" as a percentage of a store's purchase price (its variable cost for an item) but "marked down" during sales events as a percentage of retail price. Most customers understand that a 50% "sale" means that retail prices have been marked down by 50%.

EXAMPLE: An apparel retailer buys t-shirts for $10 and sells them at a 50% markup. As noted previously, a 50% markup on a variable cost of $10 yields a retail price of $15. Unfortunately, the goods don't sell, and the store owner wants to sell them at cost to clear shelf space. He carelessly asks a sales assistant to mark the goods down by 50%. This 50% markdown, however, reduces the retail price to $7.50. Thus, a 50% markup followed by a 50% markdown results in a loss of $2.50 on each unit sold.

It is easy to see how confusion can occur. We generally prefer to use the term margin to refer to margin on sales. We recommend, however, that all managers clarify with their colleagues what is meant by this important term.

EXAMPLE: A wireless provider sells a handset for $100. The handset costs $50 to manufacture and includes a $20 mail-in rebate. The provider's internal reports add this rebate to the cost of goods sold. Its margin calculations therefore run as follows:

$$\text{Unit Margin (\$)} = \text{Selling Price} - \text{Cost of Goods Sold and Rebate}$$

$$= \$100 - (\$50 + \$20) = \$30$$

$$\text{Margin (\%)} = \frac{\$30}{\$100} = 30\%$$

Accounting standards mandate, however, that external reports deduct rebates from sales revenue (see Table 3). Under this construction, the company's margin calculations run differently and yield a different percentage margin:

$$\text{Unit Margin (\$)} = \text{Selling Price, Net of Rebate} - \text{Cost of Goods Sold}$$

$$= (\$100 - \$20) - \$50 = \$30$$

$$\text{Margin (\%)} = \frac{\$30}{(\$100 - \$20)}$$

$$= \frac{\$30}{\$80} = 37.5\%$$

Table 3 Internal and External Reporting May Vary

	Internal Reporting	External Reporting
Dollars Received from Customer	$100	$100
Rebate	—	$20
Sales	$100	$80
Manufacturing Cost	$50	$50
Rebate	$20	—
Cost of Goods Sold	$70	$50
Unit Margin ($)	$30	$30
Margin (%)	30.0%	37.5%

In this example, managers add the rebate to cost of goods sold for the sake of internal reports. In contrast, accounting regulations require that the rebate be deducted from sales for the purpose of external reports. This means that the percentage margin varies between the internal and external reports. This can cause considerable angst within the company when quoting a percentage margin.

As a general principle, we recommend that internal margins follow formats mandated for external reporting in order to limit confusion.

Various costs may or may not be included: The inclusion or exclusion of costs generally depends on the intended purpose of the relevant margin calculations. We'll return to this issue several times. At one extreme, if all costs are included, then margin and net profit will be equivalent. On the other hand, a marketer may choose to work with "contribution margin" (deducting only variable costs), "operating margin," or "margin before marketing." By using certain metrics, marketers can distinguish fixed from variable costs and can isolate particular costs of an operation or of a department from the overall business.

Related Metrics and Concepts

Gross Margin: *This is the difference between revenue and cost before accounting for certain other costs. Generally, it is calculated as the selling price of an item, less the cost of goods sold (production or acquisition costs, essentially). Gross margin can be expressed as a percentage or in total dollar terms. If the latter, it can be reported on a per-unit basis or on a per-period basis for a company.*

2   Prices and Channel Margins

Channel margins can be expressed on a per-unit basis or as a percentage of selling price. In "chaining" the margins of sequential distribution channels, the selling price of one channel member becomes the "cost" of the channel member for which it serves as a supplier.

$$\text{Supplier Selling Price (\$)} = \text{Customer Selling Price (\$)} - \text{Customer Margin (\$)}$$

$$\text{Customer Selling Price (\$)} = \frac{\text{Supplier Selling Price (\$)}}{[1 - \text{Customer Margin (\%)}]}$$

When there are several levels in a distribution chain—including a manufacturer, distributor, and retailer, for example—one must not simply add all channel margins as reported in order to calculate "total" channel margin. Instead, use the selling prices at the beginning and end of the distribution chain (that is, at the levels of the manufacturer and the retailer) to calculate total channel margin. Marketers should be able to work forward from their own selling price to the consumer's purchase price and should understand channel margins at each step.

Purpose: To calculate selling prices at each level in the distribution channel.

Marketing often involves selling through a series of "value-added" resellers. Sometimes, a product changes form through this progression. At other times, its price is simply "marked up" along its journey through the distribution channel (see Figure 1).

In some industries, such as imported beer, there may be as many as four or five channel members that sequentially apply their own margins before a product reaches the consumer. In such cases, it is particularly important to understand channel margins and pricing practices in order to evaluate the effects of price changes.

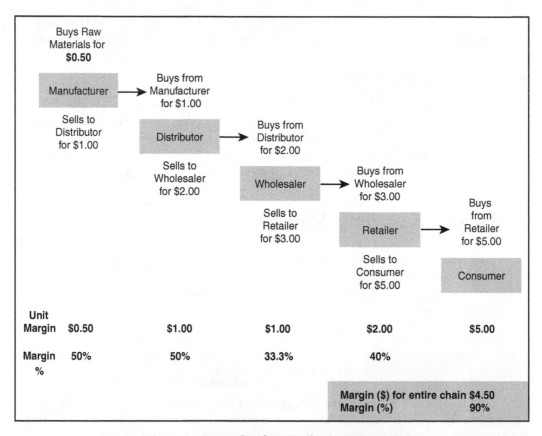

Figure 1   Example of a Distribution Channel

Remember: Selling Price = Cost + Margin

Construction

First, decide whether you want to work "backward," from customer selling prices to supplier selling prices, or "forward." We provide two equations to use in working backward, one for dollar margins and the other for percentage margins:

Supplier Selling Price ($) = Customer Selling Price ($) − Customer Margin ($)

Supplier Selling Price ($) = Customer Selling Price ($) ∗ [1 − Customer Margin (%)]

EXAMPLE: Aaron owns a small furniture store. He buys BookCo brand bookcases from a local distributor for $200 per unit. Aaron is considering buying directly from BookCo, and he wants to calculate what he would pay if he received the same price that BookCo charges his distributor. Aaron knows that the distributor's percentage margin is 30%.

The manufacturer supplies the distributor. That is, in this link of the chain, the manufacturer is the supplier, and the distributor is the customer. Thus, because we know the customer's percentage margin, in order to calculate the manufacturer's price to Aaron's distributor, we can use the second of the two previous equations.

Supplier Selling Price ($) = Customer Selling Price ($) ∗ [1 − Customer Margin (%)]

$$= \$200 * 70\% = \$140$$

Aaron's distributor buys each bookcase for $140 and sells it for $200, earning a margin of $60 (30%).

Although the previous example may be the most intuitive version of this formula, by rearranging the equation, we can also work forward in the chain, from supplier prices to customer selling prices. In a forward-looking construction, we can solve for the customer selling price, that is, the price charged to the next level of the chain, moving toward the end consumer.[2]

$$\text{Customer Selling Price (\$)} = \frac{\text{Supplier Selling Price (\$)}}{[1 - \text{Customer Margin (\%)}]}$$

Customer Selling Price ($) = Supplier Selling Price ($) + Customer Margin ($)

EXAMPLE: Clyde's Concrete sells 100 cubic yards of concrete for $300 to a road construction contractor. The contractor wants to include this in her bill of materials, to be charged to a local government (see Figure 2). Further, she wants to earn a 25% margin. What is the contractor's selling price for the concrete?

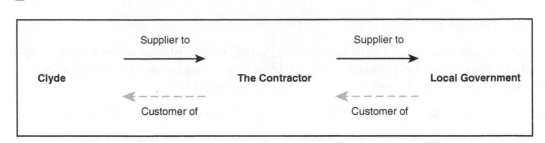

Figure 2   Customer Relationships

This question focuses on the link between Clyde's Concrete (supplier) and the contractor (customer). We know the supplier's selling price is $300 and the customer's intended margin is 25%. With this information, we can use the first of the two previous equations.

$$\text{Customer Selling Price} = \frac{\text{Supplier Selling Price}}{(1 - \text{Customer Margin \%})}$$

$$= \frac{\$300}{(1 - 25\%)}$$

$$= \frac{\$300}{75\%} = \$400$$

To verify our calculations, we can determine the contractor's percentage margin, based on a selling price of $400 and a cost of $300.

$$\text{Customer Margin} = \frac{(\text{Customer Selling Price} - \text{Supplier Selling Price})}{\text{Customer Selling Price}}$$

$$= \frac{(\$400 - \$300)}{\$400}$$

$$= \frac{\$100}{\$400} = 25\%$$

First Channel Member's Selling Price: Equipped with these equations and with knowledge of all the margins in a chain of distribution, we can work all the way back to the selling price of the first channel member in the chain.

First Channel Member's Selling Price ($) = Last Channel Member's Selling Price ($) ∗ [1 − Last Channel Margin (%)] ∗ [1 − Next-to-last Channel Margin (%)] ∗ [1 − Next-to-next-to-last Channel Margin (%)] . . . and so on

EXAMPLE: The following margins are received at various steps along the chain of distribution for a jar of pasta sauce that sells for a retail price of $5.00 (see Table 4).

What does it cost the manufacturer to produce a jar of pasta sauce? The retail selling price ($5.00), multiplied by 1 less the retailer margin, will yield the wholesaler selling price. The wholesaler selling price can also be viewed as the cost to the retailer. The *cost* to the wholesaler (distributor selling price) can be found by multiplying the wholesaler selling price by 1 less the wholesaler margin, and so forth. Alternatively, one might follow the next procedure, using a channel member's percentage margin to calculate its dollar margin, and then subtracting that figure from the channel member's selling price to obtain its cost (see Table 5).

Thus, a jar of pasta that sells for $5.00 at retail actually costs the manufacturer 50 cents to make.

Table 4   Example—Pasta Sauce Distribution Margins

Distribution Stage	Margin
Manufacturer	50%
Distributor	50%
Wholesaler	33%
Retailer	40%

Table 5   Cost (Purchase Price) of Retailer

Stage	Margin %	$
Cost to Consumer		$5.00
Retailer Margin	40%	$2.00
Cost to Retailer		$3.00
Wholesaler Margin	33%	$1.00
Cost to Wholesaler		$2.00
Distributor Margin	50%	$1.00
Cost to Distributor		$1.00
Manufacturer Margin	50%	$0.50
Manufacturer's Cost		$0.50

The margins taken at multiple levels of a distribution process can have a dramatic effect on the price paid by consumers. To work backward in analyzing these, many people find it easier to convert markups to margins. Working forward does not require this conversion.

EXAMPLE: To show that margins and markups are two sides of the same coin, let's demonstrate that we can obtain the same sequence of prices by using the markup method here. Let's look at how the pasta sauce is marked up to arrive at a final consumer price of $5.00.

As noted previously, the manufacturer's cost is $0.50. The manufacturer's percentage markup is 100%. Thus, we can calculate its dollar markup as $0.50 * 100% = $0.50. Adding the manufacturer's markup to its cost, we arrive at its selling price: $0.50 (cost) + $0.50 (markup) = $1.00. The manufacturer sells the sauce for $1.00 to a distributor. The distributor applies a markup of 100%, taking the price to $2.00, and sells the sauce to a wholesaler. The wholesaler applies a markup of 50% and sells the sauce to a retailer for $3.00. Finally, the retailer applies a markup of 66.7% and sells the pasta sauce to a consumer for $5.00. In Table 6, we track these markups to show the pasta sauce's journey from a manufacturer's cost of $0.50 to a retail price (consumer's cost) of $5.00.

Table 6   Markups Along the Distribution Channel

Stage	Markup %	$	Margin
Manufacturer's Cost		$0.50	
Manufacturer Markup	100%	$0.50	50%
Cost to Distributor		$1.00	
Distributor Markup	100%	$1.00	50%
Cost to Wholesaler		$2.00	
Wholesaler Markup	50%	$1.00	33.3%
Cost to Retailer		$3.00	
Retailer Markup	67%	$2.00	40%
Cost to Consumer		$5.00	

Data Sources, Complications, and Cautions

The information needed to calculate channel margins is the same as for basic margins. Complications arise, however, because of the layers involved. In this structure, the selling price for one layer in the chain becomes the cost to the next layer. This is clearly visible in consumer goods industries, where there are often multiple levels of distribution between the manufacturer and the consumer, and each channel member requires its own margin.

Cost and selling price depend on location within the chain. One must always ask, "Whose cost is this?" and "Who sells at this price?" The process of "chaining" a sequence of margins is not difficult. One need only clarify who sells to whom. In tracking this, it can help first to draw a horizontal line, labeling all the channel members along the chain, with the manufacturer at the far left and the retailer on the right. For example, if a beer exporter in Germany sells to an importer in the U.S., and that importer sells to a distributor in Virginia, who sells the beer to a retailer, then four distinct selling prices and three channel margins will intervene between the exporter and retail store customer. In this scenario, the exporter is the first supplier. The importer is the first customer. To avoid confusion, we recommend mapping out the channel and calculating margins, purchase prices, and selling prices at each level.

Throughout this section, we've assumed that all margins are "gross margins," calculated as selling price minus cost of goods sold. Of course, channel members will incur other costs in the process of "adding value." If a wholesaler pays his salespeople a commission on sales, for example, that would be a cost of doing business. But it would not be a part of the cost of goods sold, and so it is not factored into gross margin.

Related Metrics and Concepts

HYBRID (MIXED) CHANNEL MARGINS

> **Hybrid Channel:** *The use of multiple distribution systems to reach the same market. A company might approach consumers through stores, the Web, and telemarketing, for example. Margins often differ among such channels. Hybrid channels may also be known as mixed channels.*

Increasingly, businesses "go to market" in more than one way. An insurance company, for example, might sell policies through independent agents, toll-free telephone lines, and the Web. Multiple channels often generate different channel margins and cause a supplier to incur different support costs. As business migrates from one channel to another, marketers must adjust pricing and support in economically sensible ways. To make appropriate decisions, they must recognize the more profitable channels in their mix and develop programs and strategies to fit these.

When selling through multiple channels with different margins, it is important to perform analyses on the basis of *weighted* average channel margins, as opposed to a simple average. Using a simple average can lead to confusion and poor decision-making.

As an example of the variations that can occur, let's suppose that a company sells 10 units of its product through six channels. It sells five units through one channel at a 20% margin, and one unit through each of the other five channels at a 50% margin. Calculating its average margin on a weighted basis, we arrive at the following figure:

$$\text{Percentage Margin (\%)} = \frac{[(5 * 20\%) + (5 * 50\%)]}{10} = 35\%$$

By contrast, if we calculate the average margin among this firm's six channels on a simple basis, we arrive at a very different figure:

$$\text{Percentage Margin (\%)} = \frac{[(1 * 20\%) + (5 * 50\%)]}{6} = 45\%$$

This difference in margin could significantly blur management decision-making.

AVERAGE MARGIN

When assessing margins in dollar terms, use percentage of unit sales.

> Average Margin ($) = [Percentage of Unit Sales through Channel 1 (%) * Margin Earned in Channel 1 ($)] + [Percentage of Unit Sales through Channel 2 (%) * Margin Earned in Channel 2 ($)] + Continued to Last Channel

When assessing margin in percentage terms, use percentage of dollar sales.

> Average Margin (%) = [Percentage of Dollar Sales through Channel 1 (%) * Margin Earned in Channel 1 (%)] + [Percentage of Dollar Sales through Channel 2 (%) * Margin Earned in Channel 2 (%)] + Continued to Last Channel

EXAMPLE: Gael's Glass sells through three channels: phone, online, and store. These channels generate the following margins: 50%, 40%, and 30%, respectively. When Gael's wife asks what his average margin is, he initially calculates a simple margin and says it's 40%. Gael's wife investigates further, however, and learns that her husband answered too quickly. Gael's company sells a total of 10 units. It sells one unit by phone at a 50% margin, four units online at a 40% margin, and five units in the store at a 30% margin.

To determine the company's average margin among these channels, the margin in each must be weighted by its relative sales volume. On this basis, Gael's wife calculates the weighted average margin as follows:

Average Channel Margin = (Percentage of Unit Sales by Phone * Phone Channel Margin)
+ (Percentage of Unit Sales Online * Online Channel Margin)
+ (Percentage of Unit Sales through Store * Store Channel Margin)

$$= (1/10 * 50\%) + (4/10 * 40\%) + (5/10 * 30\%)$$

$$= 5\% + 16\% + 15\%$$

Average Channel Margin = 36%

EXAMPLE: Sadetta, Inc. has two channels—online and retail—which generate the following results:

One customer orders online, paying $10 for one unit of goods that costs the company $5. This generates a 50% margin for Sadetta. A second customer shops at the store, buying two units of product for $12 each. Each costs $9. Thus, Sadetta earns a 25% margin on these sales. Summarizing:

Online Margin (1) = 50%. Selling Price (1) = $10. Supplier Selling Price (1) = $5.

Store Margin (2) = 25%. Selling Price (2) = $12. Supplier Selling Price (2) = $9.

In this scenario, the relative weightings are easy to establish. In unit terms, Sadetta sells a total of three units: one unit (33.3%) online, and two (66.6%) in the store. In dollar terms, Sadetta generates a total of $34 in sales: $10 (29.4%) online, and $24 (70.6%) in the store.

Thus, Sadetta's average unit margin ($) can be calculated as follows: The online channel generates a $5.00 margin, while the store generates a $3.00 margin. The relative weightings are online 33.3% and store 66.6%.

Average Unit Margin ($) = [Percentage Unit Sales Online (%) * Unit Margin Online ($)]
+ [Percentage Unit Sales in Store (%) * Unit Margin in Store ($)]

$$= 33.3\% * \$5.00 + 66.6\% * \$3.00$$

$$= \$1.67 + \$2.00$$

$$= \$3.67$$

Sadetta's average margin (%) can be calculated as follows: The online channel generates a 50% margin, while the store generates a 25% margin. The relative weightings are online 29.4% and store 70.6%.

■————————————————————————————————————

Average Margin (%) = [Percentage Dollar Sales Online (%) * Margin Online (%)]
      + [Percentage Dollar Sales in Store (%) * Margin in Store (%)]

= 29.4% * 50% + 70.6% * 25%

= 14.70% + 17.65%

= 32.35%

Average margins can also be calculated directly from company totals. Sadetta, Inc. generated a total gross margin of $11 by selling three units of product. Its average unit margin was thus $11/3, or $3.67. Similarly, we can derive Sadetta's average percentage margin by dividing its total margin by its total revenue. This yields a result that matches our weighted previous calculations: $11/$34 = 32.35%.

————————————————————————————————————

The same weighting process is needed to calculate average selling prices.

**Average Selling Price ($) = [Percentage Unit Sales through Channel 1 (%)
      * Selling Price in Channel 1 ($)] + [Percentage Unit Sales
      through Channel 2 (%) * Selling Price in Channel 2 ($)]
      + Continued to [Percentage Unit Sales through the Last
      Channel (%) * the Last Channel's Selling Price ($)]**

————————————

EXAMPLE: Continuing the previous example, we can see how Sadetta, Inc. calculates its average selling price.

Sadetta's online customer pays $10 per item. Its store customer pays $12 per item. Weighting each channel by unit sales, we can derive Sadetta's average selling price as follows:

Average Selling Price ($) = [Percentage Unit Sales Online (%) * Selling Price Online ($)]
      + [Percentage Unit Sales in Store (%) * Selling Price in Store ($)]

= 33.3% * $10 + 66.7% * $12

= $3.33 + $8

= $11.33

————————————————————————————————————

The calculation of average supplier selling price is conceptually similar.

**Average Supplier Selling Price ($) = [Percentage Unit Sales through Channel 1 (%)
      * Supplier Selling Price in Channel 1 ($)] + [Percentage
      Unit Sales through Channel 2 (%) * Supplier Selling
      Price in Channel 2 ($)] + Continued to [Percentage Unit
      Sales through the Last Channel (%) * the Last Channel
      Supplier's Selling Price ($)]**

EXAMPLE: Now, let's consider how Sadetta, Inc. calculates its average supplier selling price.

Sadetta's online merchandise cost the company $5 per unit. Its in-store merchandise cost $9 per unit. Thus:

$$\begin{aligned}
\text{Average Supplier Selling Price (\$)} &= [\text{Percentage Unit Sales Online (\%)} * \text{Supplier Selling Price Online (\$)}] + [\text{Percentage Unit Sales through Store (\%)} * \text{Supplier Selling Price in Store (\$)}] \\
&= 33.3\% * \$5 + 66.7\% * \$9 \\
&= \$1.67 + \$6 = \$7.67
\end{aligned}$$

With all these pieces of the puzzle, we now have much greater insight into Sadetta, Inc.'s business (see Table 7).

Table 7   Sadetta's Channel Measures

	Online	In Store	Average/Total
Selling Price (SP)	$10.00	$12.00	
Supplier Selling Price (SSP)	$5.00	$9.00	
Unit Margin ($)	$5.00	$3.00	
Margin (%)	50%	25%	
Units Sold	1	2	3
% Unit Sales	33.3%	66.7%	
Dollar Sales	$10.00	$24.00	$34.00
% Dollar Sales	29.4%	70.6%	
Total Margin	$5.00	$6.00	$11.00
Average Unit Margin ($)			$3.67
Average Margin (%)			32.4%
Average Selling Price			$11.33
Average Supplier Selling Price			$7.67

3   Average Price per Unit and Price per Statistical Unit

Average prices represent, quite simply, total sales revenue divided by total units sold. Many products, however, are sold in multiple variants, such as bottle sizes. In these cases, managers face a challenge: They must determine "comparable" units.

Average prices can be calculated by weighting different unit selling prices by the percentage of unit sales (mix) for each product variant. If we use a standard, rather than an actual mix of sizes and product varieties, the result is price per statistical unit. Statistical units are also known as equivalent units.

$$\text{Average Price per Unit (\$)} = \frac{\text{Revenue (\$)}}{\text{Units Sold (\#)}}$$

or

$$= [\text{Price of SKU 1 (\$)} \star \text{SKU 1 Percentage of Sales (\%)}]$$
$$+ [\text{Price of SKU 2 (\$)} \star \text{SKU 2 Percentage of Sales (\%)}]$$

$$\text{Price per Statistical Unit (\$)} = \text{Total Price of a Bundle of SKUs Comprising a Statistical Unit (\$)}$$

$$\text{Unit Price per Statistical Unit (\$)} = \frac{\text{Price per Statistical Unit (\$)}}{\substack{\text{Total Units in the Bundle of SKUs} \\ \text{Comprising that Statistical Unit (\#)}}}$$

Average price per unit and prices per statistical unit are needed by marketers who sell the same product in different packages, sizes, forms, or configurations at a variety of different prices. As in analyses of different channels, these product and price variations must be reflected accurately in overall average prices. If they are not, marketers may lose sight of what is happening to prices and why. If the price of each product variant remained unchanged, for example, but there was a shift in the mix of volume sold, then the average price per unit would change, but the price per statistical unit would not. Both of these metrics have value in identifying market movements.

Purpose: To calculate meaningful average selling prices within a product line that includes items of different sizes.

Many brands or product lines include multiple models, versions, flavors, colors, sizes, or—more generally—stock keeping units (SKUs). Brita water filters, for example, are sold in a number of SKUs. They are sold in single-filter packs, double-filter packs, and special banded packs that may be restricted to club stores. They are sold on a standalone basis and in combination with pitchers. These various packages and product forms may be known as SKUs, models, items, and so on.

> **Stock Keeping Unit (SKU):** *A term used by retailers to identify individual items that are carried or "stocked" within an assortment. This is the most detailed level at which the inventory and sales of individual products are recorded.*

Marketers often want to know both their own average prices and those of retailers. By reckoning in terms of SKUs, they can calculate an average price per unit at any level in the distribution chain. Two of the most useful of these averages are

1. A unit price average that includes all sales of all SKUs, expressed as an average price per defined unit. In the water filter industry, for example, these might include such figures as $2.23/filter, $0.03/filtered ounce, and so on.

2. A price per statistical unit that consists of a fixed bundle (number) of individual SKUs. This bundle is often constructed so as to reflect the actual mix of sales of the various SKUs.

The average price per unit will change when there is a shift in the percentage of sales represented by SKUs with different unit prices. It will also change when the prices of the individual SKUs are modified. This contrasts with price per statistical unit, which, by definition, has a fixed proportion of each SKU. Consequently, a price per statistical unit will change only when there is a change in the price of one or more of the SKUs included in it.

The information gleaned from a price per statistical unit can be helpful in considering price movements within a market. Price per statistical unit, in combination with unit price averages, provides insight into the degree to which the average prices in a market are changing as a result of shifts in "mix"—proportions of sales generated by differently priced SKUs—versus price changes for individual items. Alterations in mix—such as a relative increase in the sale of larger versus smaller ice cream tubs at retail grocers, for example—will affect average unit price, but not price per statistical unit. Pricing changes in the SKUs that make up a statistical unit, however, will be reflected by a change in the price of that statistical unit.

Construction

As with other marketing averages, average price per unit can be calculated either from company totals or from the prices and shares of individual SKUs.

$$\textbf{Average Price per Unit (\$)} = \frac{\textbf{Revenue (\$)}}{\textbf{Units Sales (\#)}}$$

or

$$= [\textbf{Unit Price of SKU 1 (\$)} * \textbf{SKU 1 Percentage of Sales (\%)}]$$
$$+ [\textbf{Unit Price of SKU 2 (\$)} * \textbf{SKU 2 Percentage of Sales (\%)}]$$
$$+ \textbf{and so forth}$$

The average price per unit depends on both unit prices and unit sales of individual SKUs. The average price per unit can be driven upward by a rise in unit prices, or by an increase in the unit shares of higher-priced SKUs, or by a combination of the two.

An "average" price metric that is not sensitive to changes in SKU shares is the price per statistical unit.

Price per Statistical Unit

Procter & Gamble and other companies face a challenge in monitoring prices for a wide variety of product sizes, package types, and product formulations. There are as many as 25 to 30 different SKUs for some brands, and each SKU has its own price. In these situations, how do marketers determine a brand's overall price level in order to compare it to competitive offerings or to track whether prices are rising or falling? One solution is the "statistical unit," also known as the "statistical case" or—in volumetric or weight measures—the statistical liter or statistical ton. A statistical case of 288 ounces of liquid detergent, for example, might be defined as comprising

Four 4-oz bottles = 16 oz

Twelve 12-oz bottles = 144 oz

Two 32-oz bottles = 64 oz

One 64-oz bottle = 64 oz

Note that the contents of this statistical case were carefully chosen so that it contains the same number of ounces as a standard case of 24 12-ounce bottles. In this way, the statistical case is comparable in size to a standard case. The advantage of a statistical case is that its contents can approximate the mix of SKUs the company actually sells.

Whereas a statistical case of liquid detergent will be filled with whole bottles, in other instances a statistical unit might contain fractions of certain packaging sizes in order for its total contents to match a required volumetric or weight total.

Statistical units are composed of fixed proportions of different SKUs. These fixed proportions ensure that changes in the prices of the statistical unit reflect only changes in the *prices* of the SKUs that comprise it.

The price of a statistical unit can be expressed either as a total price for the bundle of SKUs comprising it, or in terms of that total price divided by the total volume of its contents. The former might be called the "price per statistical unit"; the latter, the "unit price per statistical unit."

EXAMPLE: Carl's Coffee Creamer (CCC) is sold in three sizes: a one-liter economy size, a half-liter "fridge-friendly" package, and a 0.05-liter single serving. Carl defines a 12-liter statistical case of CCC as

Two units of the economy size = 2 liters (2 * 1.0 liter)

19 units of the fridge-friendly package = 9.5 liters (19 * 0.5 liter)

Ten single servings = 0.5 liter (10 * .05)

Prices for each size and the calculation of total price for the statistical unit are shown in the following table:

SKU Names	Size	Price of Item	Number in Statistical Case	Liters in Statistical Case	Total Price
Economy	1 Liter	$8.00	2	2.0	$16.00
Fridge-Friendly	0.5 Liter	$6.00	19	9.5	$114.00
Single Serving	0.05 Liter	$1.00	10	0.5	$10.00
TOTAL				12	$140.00

Thus, the total price of the 12-liter statistical case of CCC is $140. The per-liter price within the statistical case is $11.67.

Note that the $140 price of the statistical case is higher than the $96 price of a case of 12 economy packs. This higher price reflects the fact that smaller packages of CCC command a higher price per liter. If the proportions of the SKUs in the statistical case exactly match the actual proportions sold, then the per-liter price of the statistical case will match the per-liter price of the actual liters sold.

EXAMPLE: Carl sells 10,000 one-liter economy packs of CCC, 80,000 fridge-friendly half liters, and 40,000 single servings. What was his average price per liter?

$$\text{Average Price per Unit (\$)} = \frac{\text{Revenue (\$)}}{\text{Unit Sales (\#)}}$$

$$= \frac{(\$8 * 10k + \$6 * 80k + \$1 * 40k)}{(1 * 10k + 0.5 * 80k + 0.05 * 40k)}$$

$$= \frac{\$600k}{52k} = \$11.54$$

Note that Carl's average price per liter, at $11.54, is less than the per-liter price in his statistical case. The reason is straightforward: Whereas fridge-friendly packs outnumber economy packs by almost ten to one in the statistical case, the actual sales ratio of these SKUs was only eight to one. Similarly, whereas the ratio of single-serving items to economy items in the statistical case is five to one, their actual sales ratio was only four to one. Carl's company sold a smaller percentage of the higher (per liter) priced items than was represented in its statistical case. Consequently, its actual average price per liter was less than the per-liter price within its statistical unit.

In the following table, we illustrate the calculation of the average price per unit as the weighted average of the unit prices and unit shares of the three SKUs of Carl's Coffee Creamer. Unit prices and unit (per-liter) shares are provided.

SKU Name	Size	Price	SKUs Sold	Units Sold (Liters)	Unit Price (per Liter)	Unit Share
Economy	1 Liter	$8	10k	10k	$8	19.23%
Fridge-Friendly	0.5 Liter	$6	80k	40k	$12	76.92%
Single Serving	0.05 Liter	$1	40k	2k	$20	3.85%
TOTAL			130k	52k		100%

On this basis, the average price per unit ($) = ($8 * 0.1923) + ($12 * 0.7692) + ($20 * 0.0385) = $11.54.

Data Sources, Complications, and Cautions

With complex and changing product lines, and with different selling prices charged by different retailers, marketers need to understand a number of methodologies for calculating average prices. Merely determining how many units of a product are sold, and at what price, throughout the market is a major challenge. As a standard method of tracking prices, marketers use statistical units, which are based on constant proportions of sales of different SKUs in a product line.

Typically, the proportions of SKUs in a statistical unit correspond—at least approximately—to historical market sales. Sales patterns can change, however. In consequence, these proportions need to be monitored carefully in evolving markets and changing product lines.

Calculating a meaningful average price is complicated by the need to differentiate between changes in sales mix and changes in the prices of statistical units. In some industries, it is difficult to construct appropriate units for analyzing price and sales data. In the chemical industry, for example, an herbicide might be sold in a variety of different sizes, applicators, and concentration levels. When we factor in the complexity of different prices and different assortments offered by competing retail outlets, calculating and tracking average prices becomes a non-trivial exercise.

Similar challenges arise in estimating inflation. Economists calculate inflation by using a basket of goods. Their estimates might vary considerably, depending on the goods included. It is also difficult to capture quality improvements in inflation figures. Is a 2009 car, for example, truly comparable to a car built 30 years earlier?

In evaluating price increases, marketers are advised to bear in mind that a consumer who shops for large quantities at discount stores may view such increases very differently from a pensioner who buys small quantities at local stores. Establishing a "standard" basket for such different consumers requires astute judgment. In seeking to summarize the aggregate of such price increases throughout an economy, economists may view inflation as, in effect, a statistical unit price measure for that economy.

4   Variable Costs and Fixed Costs

Variable costs can be aggregated into a "total" or expressed on a "per-unit" basis. Fixed costs, by definition, do not change with the number of units sold or produced. Variable costs are assumed to be relatively constant on a per-unit basis. Total variable costs increase directly and predictably with unit sales volume. Fixed costs, on the other hand, do not change as a direct result of short-term unit sales increases or decreases.

Total Costs ($) = Fixed Costs ($) + Total Variable Costs ($)

Total Variable Costs ($) = Unit Volume (#) ∗ Variable Cost per Unit ($)

Marketers need to have an idea of how costs divide between variable and fixed. This distinction is crucial in forecasting the earnings generated by various changes in unit sales and thus the financial impact of proposed marketing campaigns. It is also fundamental to an understanding of price and volume trade-offs.

Purpose: To understand how costs change with volume.

At first glance, this appears to be an easy subject to master. If a marketing campaign will generate 10,000 units of additional sales, we need only know how much it will cost to supply that additional volume.

The problem, of course, is that no one really knows how changes in quantity will affect a firm's total costs—in part because the workings of a firm can be so complex. Companies simply can't afford to employ armies of accountants to answer every possible expense question precisely. Instead, we often use a simple model of cost behavior that is good enough for most purposes.

Construction

The standard linear equation, $Y = mX + b$, helps explain the relationship between total costs and unit volume. In this application, Y will represent a company's total cost, m will be its variable cost per unit, X will represent the quantity of products sold (or produced), and b will represent the fixed cost (see Figure 3).

Total Cost ($) = Variable Cost per Unit ($) ∗ Quantity (#) + Fixed Cost ($)

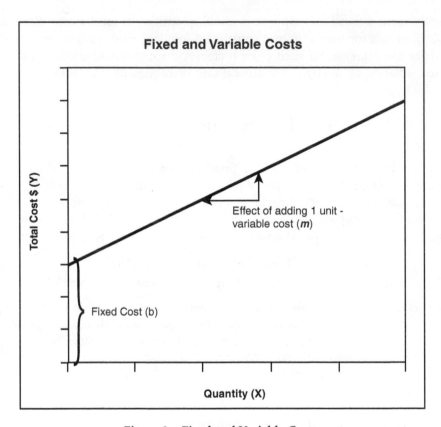

Figure 3   Fixed and Variable Costs

On this basis, to determine a company's total cost for any given quantity of products, we need only multiply its variable cost per unit by that quantity and add its fixed cost.

To communicate fully the implications of fixed costs and variable costs, it may help to separate this graph into two parts (see Figure 4).

By definition, fixed costs remain the same, regardless of volume. Consequently, they are represented by a horizontal line across the graph in Figure 4. Fixed costs do not increase vertically—that is, they do not add to the total cost—as quantity rises.

The result of multiplying variable cost per unit by quantity is often called the total variable cost. Variable costs differ from fixed costs in that, when there is no production, their total is zero. Their total increases in a steadily rising line, however, as quantity increases.

We can represent this model of cost behavior in a simple equation.

Total Cost ($) = Total Variable Cost ($) + Fixed Cost ($)

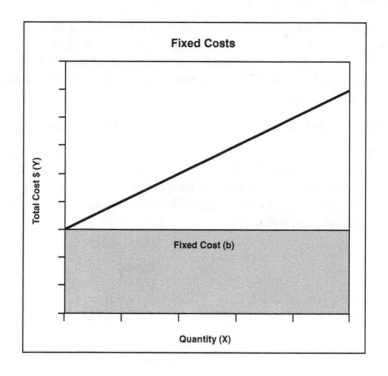

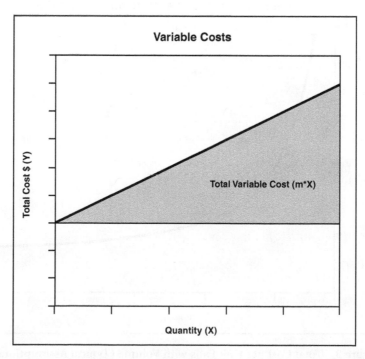

Figure 4   Total Cost Consists of Fixed and Variable Costs

To use this model, of course, we must place each of a firm's costs into one or the other of these two categories. If an expense does not change with volume (rent, for example), then it is part of fixed costs and will remain the same, regardless of how many units the firm produces or sells. If a cost *does* change with volume (sales commissions, for example), then it is a variable cost.

$$\text{Total Variable Costs (\$)} = \text{Unit Volume (\#)} * \text{Variable Cost per Unit (\$)}$$

Total Cost per Unit: It is also possible to express the total cost for a given quantity on a per-unit basis. The result might be called total cost per unit, unit total cost, average cost, full cost, or even fully loaded cost. For our simple linear cost model, the total cost per unit can be calculated in either of two ways. The most obvious would be to divide the total cost by the number of units.

$$\text{Total Cost per Unit (\$)} = \frac{\text{Total Cost (\$)}}{\text{Quantity (\#)}}$$

This can be plotted graphically, and it tells an interesting tale (see Figure 5). As the quantity rises, the total cost per unit (average cost per unit) declines. The shape of this

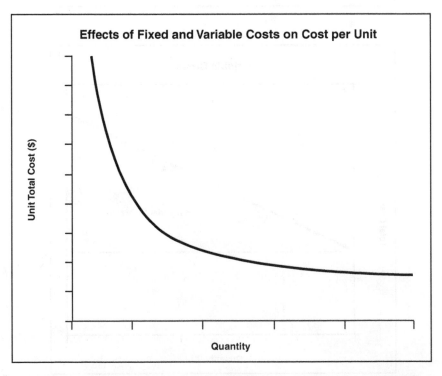

Figure 5   Total Cost per Unit Falls with Volume (Typical Assumptions)

curve will vary among firms with different cost structures, but wherever there are both fixed and variable costs, the total cost per unit will decline as fixed costs are spread across an increasing quantity of units.

The apportionment of fixed costs across units produced leads us to another common formula for the total cost per unit.

Total Cost per Unit (\$) = Variable Cost per Unit (\$) + [Fixed Cost (\$)/Quantity (#)]

As the quantity increases—that is, as fixed costs are spread over an increasing number of units—the total cost per unit declines in a non-linear way.[3]

EXAMPLE: As a company's unit sales increase, its fixed costs hold steady at \$500. The variable cost per unit remains constant at \$10 per unit. Total variable costs increase with each unit sold. The total cost per unit (also known as average total cost) decreases as incremental units are sold and as fixed costs are spread across this rising quantity. Eventually, as more and more units are produced and sold, the company's total cost per unit approaches its variable cost per unit (see Table 8).

Table 8   Fixed and Variable Costs at Increasing Volume Levels

Units Sold	1	10	100	1,000
Fixed Costs	\$500	\$500	\$500	\$500
Variable Costs	\$10	\$100	\$1,000	\$10,000
Total Costs	\$510	\$600	\$1,500	\$10,500
Total Cost per Unit	\$510.00	\$60.00	\$15.00	\$10.50
Variable Cost per Unit	\$10	\$10	\$10	\$10

In summary, the simplest model of cost behavior is to assume total costs increase linearly with quantity supplied. Total costs are composed of fixed and variable costs. Total cost per unit decreases in a non-linear way with rising quantity supplied.

Data Sources, Complications, and Cautions

Total cost is typically assumed to be a linear function of quantity supplied. That is, the graph of total cost versus quantity will be a straight line. Because some costs are fixed, total cost starts at a level above zero, even when no units are produced. This is because fixed costs include such expenses as factory rent and salaries for full-time employees, which must be paid regardless of whether any goods are produced and sold. Total variable costs, by contrast, rise and fall with quantity. Within our model, however, variable cost *per unit* is assumed to hold constant—at $10 per unit for example—regardless of whether one unit or 1,000 units are produced. This is a useful model. In using it, however, marketers must recognize that it fails to account for certain complexities.

The linear cost model does not fit every situation: Quantity discounts, expectations of future process improvements, and capacity limitations, for example, introduce dynamics that will limit the usefulness of the fundamental linear cost equation: Total Cost = Fixed Cost + Variable Cost per Unit * Quantity. Even the notion that quantity determines the total cost can be questioned. Although firms pay for *inputs*, such as raw materials and labor, marketers want to know the cost of the firm's *outputs*, that is, finished goods sold. This distinction is clear in theory. In practice, however, it can be difficult to uncover the precise relationship between a quantity of outputs and the total cost of the wide array of inputs that go into it.

The classification of costs as fixed or variable depends on context: Even though the linear model may not work in all situations, it does provide a reasonable approximation for cost behavior in many contexts. Some marketers have trouble, however, with the fact that certain costs can be considered fixed in some contexts and variable in others. In general, for shorter time frames and modest changes in quantity, many costs are fixed. For longer time frames and larger changes in quantity, most costs are variable. Let's consider rent, for example. Small changes in quantity do not require a change in workspace or business location. In such cases, rent should be regarded as a fixed cost. A major change in quantity, however, would require more or less workspace. Rent, therefore, would become variable over that range of quantity.

Don't confuse Total Cost per Unit with Variable Cost per Unit: In our linear cost equation, the variable cost per unit is the amount by which total costs increase if the firm increases its quantity by one unit. This number should not be confused with the total cost per unit, calculated as *Variable Cost per Unit + (Fixed Cost/Quantity)*. If a firm has fixed costs, then its total cost per unit will always be greater than the variable cost per unit. Total cost per unit represents the firm's average cost per unit at the current quantity—and *only* at the current quantity. Do not make the mistake of thinking of total cost per unit as a figure that applies to changing quantities. Total cost per unit only applies at the volume at which it was calculated.

A related misunderstanding may arise at times from the fact that total cost per unit generally decreases with rising quantity. Some marketers use this fact to argue for aggressively increasing quantity in order to "bring our costs down" and improve profitability. Total cost, by contrast with total cost *per unit*, almost always increases with quantity. Only with certain quantity discounts or rebates that "kick in" when target volumes are reached can total cost decrease as volume increases.

5 Marketing Spending—Total, Fixed, and Variable

To predict how selling costs change with sales, a firm must distinguish between fixed selling costs and variable selling costs.

$$\text{Total Selling (Marketing) Costs (\$)} = \text{Total Fixed Selling Costs (\$)} \\ + \text{Total Variable Selling Costs (\$)}$$

$$\text{Total Variable Selling Costs (\$)} = \text{Revenue (\$)} * \text{Variable Selling Cost (\%)}$$

Recognizing the difference between fixed and variable selling costs can help firms account for the relative risks associated with alternative sales strategies. In general, strategies that incur variable selling costs are less risky because variable selling costs will remain lower in the event that sales fail to meet expectations.

Purpose: To forecast marketing spending and assess budgeting risk.

Marketing Spending: *Total expenditure on marketing activities. This typically includes advertising and non-price promotion. It sometimes includes sales force spending and may also include price promotions.*

Marketing costs are often a major part of a firm's overall discretionary expenditures. As such, they are important determinants of short-term profits. Of course, marketing and selling budgets can also be viewed as investments in acquiring and maintaining customers. From either perspective, however, it is useful to distinguish between fixed marketing costs and variable marketing costs. That is, managers must recognize which marketing costs will hold steady, and which will change with sales. Generally, this classification will require a "line-item by line-item" review of the entire marketing budget.

In prior sections, we have viewed total variable costs as expenses that vary with unit sales volume. With respect to selling costs, we'll need a slightly different conception. Rather than varying with unit sales, total variable selling costs are more likely to vary directly with the monetary value of the units sold—that is, with revenue. Thus, it is more likely that variable selling costs will be expressed as a percentage of revenue, rather than a certain monetary amount per unit.

The classification of selling costs as fixed or variable will depend on an organization's structure and on the specific decisions of management. A number of items, however, typically fall into one category or the other—with the proviso that their status as fixed or variable can be time-specific. In the long run, all costs eventually become variable.

Over typical planning periods of a quarter or a year, fixed marketing costs might include

- Sales force salaries and support.

- Major advertising campaigns, including production costs.

- Marketing staff.

- Sales promotion material, such as point-of-purchase sales aids, coupon production, and distribution costs.

- Cooperative advertising allowances based on prior-period sales.

Variable marketing costs might include

- Sales commissions paid to sales force, brokers, or manufacturer representatives.

- Sales bonuses contingent on reaching sales goals.

- Off-invoice and performance allowances to trade, which are tied to current volume.

- Early payment terms (if included in sales promotion budgets).

- Coupon face-value payments and rebates, including processing fees.

- Bill-backs for local campaigns, which are conducted by retailers but reimbursed by national brand and cooperative advertising allowances, based on current period sales.

Marketers often don't consider their budgets in fixed and variable terms, but they can derive at least two benefits by doing so.

First, if marketing spending is in fact variable, then budgeting in this way is more accurate. Some marketers budget a *fixed* amount and then face an end-of-period discrepancy or "variance" if sales miss their declared targets. By contrast, a flexible budget—that is, one that takes account of its genuinely variable components—will reflect actual results, regardless of where sales end up.

Second, the short-term risks associated with fixed marketing costs are greater than those associated with variable marketing costs. If marketers expect revenues to be sensitive to factors outside their control—such as competitive actions or production shortages—they can reduce risk by including more variable and less fixed spending in their budgets.

A classic decision that hinges on fixed marketing costs versus variable marketing costs is the choice between engaging third-party contract sales representatives versus an in-house sales force. Hiring a salaried—or predominantly salaried—sales force entails more risk than the alternative because salaries must be paid even if the firm fails to achieve its revenue targets. By contrast, when a firm uses third-party brokers to sell its goods on commission, its selling costs decline when sales targets are not met.

Construction

Total Selling (Marketing) Costs ($) = Total Fixed Selling Costs ($)
+ Total Variable Selling Costs ($)

Total Variable Selling Costs ($) = Revenue ($) * Variable Selling Cost (%)

Commissioned Sales Costs: Sales commissions represent one example of selling costs that vary in proportion to revenue. Consequently, any sales commissions should be included in variable selling costs.

EXAMPLE: Henry's Catsup spends $10 million a year to maintain a sales force that calls on grocery chains and wholesalers. A broker offers to perform the same selling tasks for a 5% commission.

At $100 million in revenue,

$$\text{Total Variable Selling Cost} = \$100 \text{ million} * 5\% = \$5 \text{ million}$$

At $200 million in revenue,

$$\text{Total Variable Selling Cost} = \$200 \text{ million} * 5\% = \$10 \text{ million}$$

At $300 million in revenue,

$$\text{Total Variable Selling Cost} = \$300 \text{ million} * 5\% = \$15 \text{ million}$$

If revenues run less than $200 million, the broker will cost less than the in-house sales force. At $200 million in revenue, the broker will cost the same as the sales force. At revenue levels greater than $200 million, the broker will cost more.

Of course, the transition from a salaried sales staff to a broker may itself cause a change in revenues. Calculating the revenue level at which selling costs are equal is only a starting point for analysis. But it is an important first step in understanding the trade-offs.

There are many types of variable selling costs. For example, selling costs could be based upon a complicated formula, specified in a firm's contracts with its brokers and dealers. Selling costs might include incentives to local dealers, which are tied to the achievement of specific sales targets. They might include promises to reimburse retailers for spending on cooperative advertising. By contrast, payments to a Web site for a fixed number of impressions or click-throughs, in a contract that calls for specific dollar compensation, would more likely be classified as fixed costs. On the other hand, payments for conversions (sales) would be classified as variable marketing costs.

EXAMPLE: A small manufacturer of a regional food delicacy must select a budget for a television advertising campaign that it plans to launch. Under one plan, it might pay to create a commercial and air it in a certain number of time slots. Its spending level would thus be fixed. It would be selected ahead of time and would not vary with the results of the campaign.

Under an alternative plan, the company could produce the advertisement—still a fixed cost—but ask retailers to air it in their local markets and pay the required media fees to television stations as part of a cooperative advertising arrangement. In return for paying the media fees, local stores would receive a discount (a bill-back) on every unit of the company's product that they sell.

Under the latter plan, the product discount would be a variable cost, as its total amount would depend on the number of units sold. By undertaking such a cooperative advertising campaign, the manufacturer would make its marketing budget a mix of fixed and variable costs. Is such cooperative advertising a good idea? To decide this, the company must determine its expected sales under both arrangements, as well as the consequent economics and its tolerance for risk.

Data Sources, Complications, and Cautions

Fixed costs are often easier to measure than variable costs. Typically, fixed costs might be assembled from payroll records, lease documents, or financial records. For variable costs, it is necessary to measure the rate at which they increase as a function of activity level. Although variable selling costs often represent a predefined percentage of revenue, they may alternatively vary with the number of *units* sold (as in a dollar-per-case discount). An additional complication arises if some variable selling costs apply to only a portion of total sales. This can happen, for example, when some dealers qualify for cash discounts or full-truckload rates and some do not.

In a further complication, some expenses may appear to be fixed when they are actually stepped. That is, they are fixed to a point, but they trigger further expenditures beyond that point. For example, a firm may contract with an advertising agency for up to three campaigns per year. If it decides to buy more than three campaigns, it would incur an incremental cost. Typically, stepped costs can be treated as fixed—provided that the boundaries of analysis are well understood.

Stepped payments can be difficult to model. Rebates for customers whose purchases exceed a certain level, or bonuses for salespeople who exceed quota, can be challenging functions to describe. Creativity is important in designing marketing discounts. But this creativity can be difficult to reflect in a framework of fixed and variable costs.

In developing their marketing budgets, firms must decide which costs to expense in the current period and which to amortize over several periods. The latter course is appropriate for expenditures that are correctly viewed as investments. One example of such an investment would be a special allowance for financing receivables from new distributors. Rather than adding such an allowance to the current period's budget, it would be better viewed as a marketing item that increases the firm's investment in working capital. By contrast, advertising that is projected to generate long-term impact may be loosely called an investment, but it would be better treated as a marketing expense. Although there may be a valid theoretical case for amortizing advertising, that discussion is beyond the scope of this book.

Related Metrics and Concepts

Levels of marketing spending are often used to compare companies and to demonstrate how heavily they "invest" in this area. For this purpose, marketing spending is generally viewed as a percentage of sales.

Marketing As a Percentage of Sales: *The level of marketing spending as a fraction of sales. This figure provides an indication of how heavily a company is marketing. The appropriate level for this figure varies among products, strategies, and markets.*

$$\text{Marketing As a Percentage of Sales (\%)} = \frac{\text{Marketing Spending (\$)}}{\text{Revenue (\$)}}$$

Variants on this metric are used to examine components of marketing in comparison with sales. Examples include trade promotion as a percentage of sales, or sales force as a percentage of sales. One particularly common example is:

Advertising As a Percentage of Sales: *Advertising expenditures as a fraction of sales. Generally, this is a subset of marketing as a percentage of sales.*

Before using such metrics, marketers are advised to determine whether certain marketing costs have already been subtracted in the calculation of sales revenue. Trade allowances, for example, are often deducted from "gross sales" to calculate "net sales."

Slotting Allowances: These are a particular form of selling costs encountered when new items are introduced to retailers or distributors. Essentially, they represent a charge made by retailers for making a "slot" available for a new item in their stores and warehouses. This charge may take the form of a one-time cash payment, free goods, or a special discount. The exact terms of the slotting allowance will determine whether it constitutes a fixed or a variable selling cost, or a mix of the two.

6   Break-Even Analysis and Contribution Analysis

The break-even level represents the sales amount—in either unit or revenue terms—that is required to cover total costs (both fixed and variable). Profit at break-even is zero. Break-even is only possible if a firm's prices are higher than its variable costs per unit. If so, then each unit of product sold will generate some "contribution" toward covering fixed costs. The difference between price per unit and variable cost per unit is defined as Contribution per Unit.

$$\text{Contribution per Unit (\$) = Selling Price per Unit (\$) − Variable Cost per Unit (\$)}[4]$$

$$\text{Contribution Margin (\%)} = \frac{\text{Contribution per Unit (\$)}}{\text{Selling Price per Unit (\$)}}$$

$$\text{Break-Even Volume } (\#) = \frac{\text{Fixed Costs } (\$)}{\text{Contribution per Unit } (\$)}$$

$$\text{Break-Even Revenue } (\$) = \text{Break-Even Volume (Units) } (\#) * \text{Price per Unit } (\$)$$

or

$$= \frac{\text{Fixed Costs } (\$)}{\text{Contribution Margin } (\%)}$$

Break-even analysis is the Swiss Army knife of marketing economics. It is useful in a variety of situations and is often used to evaluate the likely profitability of marketing actions that affect fixed costs, prices, or variable costs per unit. Break-even is often derived in a "back-of-the-envelope" calculation that determines whether a more detailed analysis is warranted.

Purpose: To provide a rough indicator of the earnings impact of a marketing activity.

The break-even point for any business activity is defined as the level of sales at which neither a profit nor a loss is made on that activity—that is, where Total Revenues = Total Costs. Provided that a company sells its goods at a price per unit that is greater than its variable cost per unit, the sale of each unit will make a "contribution" toward covering some portion of fixed costs. That contribution can be calculated as the difference between price per unit (revenue) and variable cost per unit. On this basis, break-even constitutes the minimum level of sales at which total contribution fully covers fixed costs.

Construction

To determine the break-even point for a business program, one must first calculate the fixed costs of engaging in that program. For this purpose, managers do not need to estimate projected volumes. Fixed costs are constant, regardless of activity level. Managers do, however, need to calculate the difference between revenue per unit and variable costs per unit. This difference represents contribution per unit ($). Contribution rates can also be expressed as a percentage of selling price.

EXAMPLE: Apprentice Mousetraps wants to know how many units of its "Magic Mouse Trapper" it must sell to break even. The product sells for $20. It costs $5 per unit to make. The company's fixed costs are $30,000. Break-even will be reached when total contribution equals fixed costs.

$$\text{Break-Even Volume} = \frac{\text{Fixed Costs}}{\text{Contribution per Unit}}$$

$$\text{Contribution per Unit} = \text{Sale Price per Unit} - \text{Variable Cost per Unit}$$

$$= \$20 - \$5 = \$15$$

$$\text{Break-Even Volume} = \frac{\$30,000}{\$15} = 2,000 \text{ mousetraps}$$

This dynamic can be summarized in a graph that shows fixed costs, variable costs, total costs, and total revenue (see Figure 6). Below the break-even point, total costs exceed total revenue, creating a loss. Above the break-even point, a company generates profits.

Break-Even: *Break-even occurs when the total contribution equals the fixed costs. Profits and losses at this point equal zero.*

One of the key building blocks of break-even analysis is the concept of contribution. Contribution represents the portion of sales revenue that is not consumed by variable costs and so contributes to the coverage of fixed costs.

Contribution per Unit ($) = Selling Price per Unit ($) − Variable Cost per Unit ($)

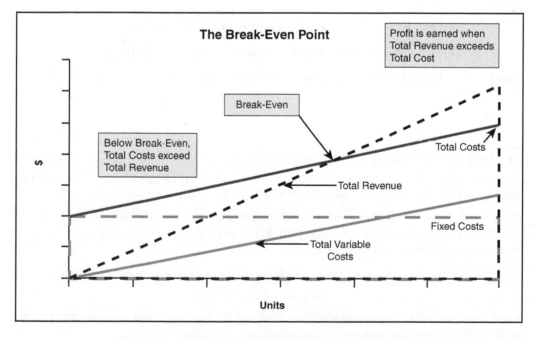

Figure 6   At Break-Even, Total Costs = Total Revenues

Contribution can also be expressed in percentage terms, quantifying the fraction of the sales price that contributes toward covering fixed costs. This percentage is often called the contribution margin.

$$\text{Contribution Margin (\%)} = \frac{\text{Contribution per Unit (\$)}}{\text{Selling Price per Unit (\$)}}$$

Formulas for total contribution include the following:

Total Contribution (\$) = Units Sold (#) * Contribution per Unit (\$)

Total Contribution (\$) = Total Revenues (\$) − Total Variable Costs (\$)

As previously noted,

Total Variable Costs = Variable Costs per Unit * Units Sold

Total Revenues = Selling Price per Unit * Units Sold

Break-Even Volume: *The number of units that must be sold to cover fixed costs.*

$$\text{Break-Even Volume (#)} = \frac{\text{Fixed Costs (\$)}}{\text{Contribution per Unit (\$)}}$$

Break-even will occur when an enterprise sells enough units to cover its fixed costs. If the fixed costs are \$10 and the contribution per unit is \$2, then a firm must sell five units to break even.

Break-Even Revenue: *The level of dollar sales required to break even.*

Break-Even Revenue (\$) = Break-Even Volume (Units) (#) * Price per Unit (\$)

This formula is the simple conversion of volume in units to the revenues generated by that volume.

EXAMPLE: Apprentice Mousetraps wants to know how many dollars' worth of its "Deluxe Mighty Mouse Trapper" it must sell to break even. The product sells for \$40 per unit. It costs \$10 per unit to make. The company's fixed costs are \$30,000.

With fixed costs of \$30,000, and a contribution per unit of \$30, Apprentice must sell \$30,000/\$30 = 1,000 deluxe mousetraps to break even. At \$40 per trap, this corresponds to revenues of 1,000 * \$40 = \$40,000.

Break-Even Revenue (\$) = Break-Even Volume (#) * Price per Unit (\$)

= 1,000 * \$40 = \$40,000

Break-even in dollar terms can also be calculated by dividing fixed costs by the fraction of the selling price that represents contribution.

$$\text{Break-Even Revenue} = \frac{\text{Fixed Costs}}{[(\text{Selling Price} - \text{Variable Costs})/\text{Selling Price}]}$$

$$= \frac{\$30,000}{[(\$40 - \$10)/\$40]}$$

$$= \frac{\$30,000}{75\%} = \$40,000$$

BREAK-EVEN ON INCREMENTAL INVESTMENT

Break-even on incremental investment is a common form of break-even analysis. It examines the additional investment needed to pursue a marketing plan, and it calculates the additional sales required to cover that expenditure. Any costs or revenues that would have occurred regardless of the investment decision are excluded from this analysis.

EXAMPLE: John's Clothing Store employs three salespeople. It generates annual sales of $1 million and an average contribution margin of 30%. Rent is $50,000. Each sales person costs $50,000 per year in salary and benefits. How much would sales have to increase for John to break even on hiring an additional salesperson?

If the additional "investment" in a salesperson is $50,000, then break-even on the new hire will be reached when sales increase by $50,000/30%, or $166,666.67.

Data Sources, Complications, and Cautions

To calculate a break-even sales level, one must know the revenues per unit, the variable costs per unit, and the fixed costs. To establish these figures, one must classify all costs as either fixed (those that do not change with volume) or variable (those that increase linearly with volume).

The time scale of the analysis can influence this classification. Indeed, one's managerial intent can be reflected in the classification. (Will the company fire employees and sublet factory space if sales turn down?) As a general rule, all costs become variable in the long term. Firms generally view rent, for example, as a fixed cost. But in the long term, even rent becomes variable as a company may move into larger quarters when sales grow beyond a certain point.

Before agonizing over these judgments, managers are urged to remember that the most useful application of the break-even exercise is to make a rough judgment about whether more detailed analyses are likely to be worth the effort. The break-even calculation enables managers to judge various options and proposals quickly. It is not, however, a substitute for more detailed analyses, including projections of target profits, risk, and the time value of money.

Related Metrics and Concepts

Payback Period: *The period of time required to recoup the funds expended in an investment. The payback period is the time required for an investment to reach break-even (see previous sections).*

7   Profit-Based Sales Targets

In launching a program, managers often start with an idea of the dollar profit they desire and ask what sales levels will be required to reach it. Target volume (#) is the unit sales quantity required to meet an earnings goal. Target revenue ($) is the corresponding figure for dollar sales. Both of these metrics can be viewed as extensions of break-even analysis.

$$\text{Target Volume (\#)} = \frac{[\text{Fixed Costs (\$)} + \text{Target Profits (\$)}]}{\text{Contribution per Unit (\$)}}$$

$$\text{Target Revenue (\$)} = \text{Target Volume (\#)} * \text{Selling Price per Unit (\$)}$$

or

$$= \frac{[\text{Fixed Costs (\$)} + \text{Target Profits (\$)}]}{\text{Contribution Margin (\%)}}$$

Increasingly, marketers are expected to generate volumes that meet the target profits of their firm. This will often require them to revise sales targets as prices and costs change.

Purpose: To ensure that marketing and sales objectives mesh with profit targets.

In the previous section, we explored the concept of break-even, the point at which a company sells enough to cover its fixed costs. In target volume and target revenue calculations, managers take the next step. They determine the level of unit sales or revenues needed not only to cover a firm's costs but also to attain its profit targets.

Construction

Target Volume: *The volume of sales necessary to generate the profits specified in a company's plans.*

The formula for target volume will be familiar to those who have performed break-even analysis. The only change is to add the required profit target to the fixed costs. From another perspective, the break-even volume equation can be viewed as a special case of the general target volume calculation—one in which the profit target is zero, and a company seeks only to cover its fixed costs. In target volume calculations, the company broadens this objective to solve for a desired profit.

$$\textbf{Target Volume (\#)} = \frac{[\textbf{Fixed Costs (\$) + Target Profits (\$)}]}{\textbf{Contribution per Unit (\$)}}$$

EXAMPLE: Mohan, an artist, wants to know how many caricatures he must sell to realize a yearly profit objective of $30,000. Each caricature sells for $20 and costs $5 in materials to make. The fixed costs for Mohan's studio are $30,000 per year:

$$\text{Target Volume} = \frac{(\text{Fixed Costs + Target Profits})}{(\text{Sales Price} - \text{Variable Costs})}$$

$$= \frac{(\$30{,}000 + \$30{,}000)}{(\$20 - \$5)}$$

$$= 4{,}000 \text{ caricatures per year}$$

It is quite simple to convert unit target volume to target revenues. One need only multiply the volume figure by an item's price per unit. Continuing the example of Mohan's studio,

$$\text{Target Revenue (\$)} = \text{Target Volume (\#)} * \text{Selling Price (\$)}$$

$$= 4{,}000 * \$20 = \$80{,}000$$

Alternatively, we can use a second formula:

$$\text{Target Revenue} = \frac{[\text{Fixed Costs (\$) + Target Profits (\$)}]}{\text{Contribution Margin (\%)}}$$

$$= \frac{(\$30{,}000 + \$30{,}000)}{(\$15/\$20)}$$

$$= \frac{\$60{,}000}{0.75} = \$80{,}000$$

Data Sources, Complications, and Cautions

The information needed to perform a target volume calculation is essentially the same as that required for break-even analysis—fixed costs, selling price, and variable costs. Of course, before determining target volume, one must also set a profit target.

The major assumption here is the same as in break-even analysis: Costs are linear with respect to unit volume over the range explored in the calculation.

Related Metrics and Concepts

Target Volumes *not* based on Target Profit: In this section, we have assumed that a firm starts with a *profit* target and seeks to determine the volume required to meet it. In certain instances, however, a firm might set a volume target for reasons other than short-term profit. For example, firms sometimes adopt top-line growth as a goal. Please do not confuse this use of target volume with the profit-based target volumes calculated in this section.

Returns and Targets: Companies often set hurdle rates for return on sales and return on investment and require that projections achieve these before any plan can be approved. Given these targets, we can calculate the sales volume required for the necessary return.

EXAMPLE: Niesha runs business development at Gird, a company that has established a return on sales target of 15%. That is, Gird requires that all programs generate profits equivalent to 15% of sales revenues. Niesha is evaluating a program that will add $1,000,000 to fixed costs. Under this program, each unit of product will be sold for $100 and will generate a contribution margin of 25%. To reach break-even on this program, Gird must sell $1,000,000/$25 = 40,000 units of product. How much must Gird sell to reach its target return on sales (ROS) of 15%?

To determine the revenue level required to achieve a 15% ROS, Niesha can use either a spreadsheet model and trial and error, or the following formula:

$$\text{Target Revenue} = \frac{\text{Fixed Costs (\$)}}{[\text{Contribution Margin (\%)} - \text{Target ROS (\%)}]}$$

$$= \frac{\$1,000,000}{(0.25 - 0.15)}$$

$$= \frac{\$1,000,000}{0.1} = \$10,000,000$$

Thus, Gird will achieve its 15% ROS target if it generates $10,000,000 in sales. At a selling price of $100 per unit, this is equivalent to unit sales of 100,000.

ENDNOTES

1. "Running Out of Gas," *Business Week*, March 28th, 2005.

2. This formula should be familiar if we consider that the supplier selling price is merely the cost to that layer of the chain. So this becomes Selling Price = Cost/(1 − Margin %). This is the same as Sale $ = Cost $ + Margin $.

3. Those familiar with basic economics use the term "marginal cost" to refer to the cost of an additional unit of output. In this linear cost model, marginal cost is the same for all units and is equal to the variable cost per unit.

4. Both contribution per unit ($) and contribution margin (%) are closely related to unit margin ($) and margin (%). The difference is that contribution margins (whether unit- or percentage-based) result from a more careful separation of fixed and variable costs.

SHARE OF HEARTS, MINDS, AND MARKETS

Introduction

Key concepts covered:

Market Share	Heavy Usage Index
Relative Market Share	Awareness, Attitudes, and Usage (AAU)
Market Concentration	Customer Satisfaction
Brand Development Index (BDI)	Willingness to Recommend
Category Development Index (CDI)	Net Promoter
Penetration	Willingness to Search
Share of Requirements	

"As Wal-Mart aggressively rolls out more stores, it continues to capture an increasing share of wallet. Three out of five consumers shopped for gifts at Wal-Mart this past holiday season. U.S. households now buy, on average, 22% of their groceries at Wal-Mart. A quarter of all shoppers indicate that they are spending more of their clothing budget at Wal-Mart now compared with a year ago. These ShopperScape findings lend credence to Retail Forward's premise that Wal-Mart will continue to push the boundaries of what consumers will allow it to be."[1]

From Chapter 2 of *Marketing Metrics: The Definitive Guide to Measuring Marketing Performance*, 2/e.
Paul W. Farris. Neil T. Bendle. Phillip E. Pfeifer. David J. Reibstein. Copyright © 2010 by Pearson Education.
Published by Wharton School Publishing.

At first glance, market share appears to involve a relatively simple calculation: "us/(us + them)." But this raises a host of questions. Who, for example, are "they?" That is, how broadly do we define our competitive universe? Which units are used? Where in the value chain do we capture our information? What time frame will maximize our signal-to-noise ratio? In a metric as important as market share, and in one as closely monitored for changes and trends, the answers to such questions are crucial. In this chapter, we will address them and also introduce key components of market share, including penetration share, heavy usage index, and share of requirements.

Probing the dynamics behind market share, we'll explore measures of awareness, attitude, and usage—major factors in the decision-making process by which customers select one brand over another. We'll discuss customer satisfaction with products and dealers, the quantification of which is growing in importance among marketing professionals. Finally, we'll consider metrics measuring the depth of consumer preference and satisfaction, including customers' willingness to search if a brand is unavailable and their disposition to recommend that brand to others. Increasingly, marketers rely on these as leading indicators of future changes in share.

	Metric	Construction	Considerations	Purpose
1	Revenue Market Share	Sales revenue as a percentage of market sales revenue.	Scope of market definition. Channel level analyzed. Before/after discounts. Time period covered.	Measure of competitiveness.
1	Unit Market Share	Unit sales as a percentage of market unit sales.	Scope of market definition. Channel level analyzed. Time period covered.	Measure of competitiveness.
2	Relative Market Share	Brand market share divided by largest competitor's market share.	Can use either unit or revenue shares.	Assesses comparative market strength.

	Metric	Construction	Considerations	Purpose
3	Brand Development Index	Brand sales in a specified segment, compared with sales of that brand in the market as a whole.	Can use either unit or revenue sales.	Regional or segment differences in brand purchases and consumption.
3	Category Development Index	Category sales in a specified segment, compared with sales of that category in the market as a whole.	Can use either unit or revenue sales.	Regional or segment differences in category purchases and consumption.
4 5 6	Decomposition of Market Share	Penetration Share * Share of Requirements * Heavy Usage Index.	Can be based on unit or revenue shares. Time period covered.	Calculation of market share. Competitive analysis. Historical trends analysis. Formulation of marketing objectives.
4	Market Penetration	Purchasers of a product category as a percentage of total population.	Based on population. Therefore, unit/revenue consideration not relevant.	Measures category acceptance by a defined population. Useful in tracking acceptance of new product categories.
4	Brand Penetration	Purchasers of a brand as a percentage of total population.	Based on population. Therefore, unit/revenue consideration not relevant.	Measures brand acceptance by a defined population.

Continues

	Metric	Construction	Considerations	Purpose
4	Penetration Share	Brand penetration as a percentage of market penetration.	A component of the market share formula.	Comparative acceptance of brand within category.
5	Share of Requirements	Brand purchases as a percentage of total category purchases by buyers of that brand.	Can use either unit or revenue shares. May rise even as sales decline, leaving only most loyal customers.	Level of commitment to a brand by its existing customers.
6	Heavy Usage Index	Category purchases by customers of a brand, compared with purchases in that category by average customers in the category.	Can use either unit or revenue sales.	Measures relative usage of a category by customers for a specific brand.
7	Hierarchy of Effects	Awareness; attitudes, beliefs; importance; intentions to try; buy; trial, repeat.	Strict sequence is often violated and can be reversed.	Set marketing and advertising objectives. Understand progress in stages of customer decision process.
7	Awareness	Percentage of total population that is aware of a brand.	Is this prompted or unprompted awareness?	Consideration of who has heard of the brand.
7	Top of Mind	First brand to consider.	May be subject to most recent advertising or experience.	Saliency of brand.
7	Ad Awareness	Percentage of total population that is aware of a brand's advertising.	May vary by schedule, reach, and frequency of advertising.	One measure of advertising effects. May indicate "stopping power" of ads.

	Metric	Construction	Considerations	Purpose
7	Knowledge	Percentage of population with knowledge of product, recollection of its advertising.	Not a formal metric. Is this prompted or unprompted knowledge?	Extent of familiarity with product beyond name recognition.
7	Consumer Beliefs	Customers/consumers view of product, generally captured via survey responses, often through ratings on a scale.	Customers/consumers may hold beliefs with varying degrees of conviction.	Perception of brand by attribute.
7	Purchase Intentions	Probability of intention to purchase.	To estimate probability of purchase, aggregate and analyze ratings of stated intentions (for example, top two boxes).	Measures pre-shopping disposition to purchase.
7	Purchase Habits	Frequency of purchase. Quantity typically purchased.	May vary widely among shopping trips.	Helps identify heavy users.
7	Loyalty	Measures include share of requirements, willingness to pay premium, willingness to search.	"Loyalty" itself is not a formal metric, but specific metrics measure aspects of this dynamic. New product entries may alter loyalty levels.	Indication of base future revenue stream.
7	Likeability	Generally measured via ratings across a number of scales.	Often believed to correlate with persuasion.	Shows overall preference prior to shopping.

Continues

	Metric	Construction	Considerations	Purpose
8	Willingness to Recommend	Generally measured via ratings across a 1–5 scale.	Nonlinear in impact.	Shows strength of loyalty, potential impact on others.
8	Customer Satisfaction	Generally measured on a 1–5 scale, in which customers declare their satisfaction with brand in general or specific attributes.	Subject to response bias. Captures views of current customers, not lost customers. Satisfaction is a function of expectations.	Indicates likelihood of repurchase. Reports of dissatisfaction show aspects that require improvement to enhance loyalty.
9	Net Promoter	Percentage of customers willing to recommend to others less the percentage unwilling to recommend the product or service.	Requires a survey of intentions.	Some claim it to be the single best metric for marketers.
10	Willingness to Search	Percentage of customers willing to delay purchases, change stores, or reduce quantities to avoid switching brands.	Hard to capture.	Indicates importance of distribution coverage.

1 Market Share

Market share is the percentage of a market (defined in terms of either units or revenue) accounted for by a specific entity.

$$\text{Unit Market Share (\%)} = \frac{\text{Unit Sales (\#)}}{\text{Total Market Unit Sales (\#)}}$$

$$\text{Revenue Market Share (\%)} = \frac{\text{Sales Revenue (\$)}}{\text{Total Market Revenue (\$)}}$$

Marketers need to be able to translate sales targets into market share because this will demonstrate whether forecasts are to be attained by growing with the market or by capturing share from competitors. The latter will almost always be more difficult to achieve. Market share is closely monitored for signs of change in the competitive landscape, and it frequently drives strategic or tactical action.

Purpose: Key indicator of market competitiveness.

Market share is an indicator of how well a firm is doing against its competitors. This metric, supplemented by changes in sales revenue, helps managers evaluate both primary and selective demand in their market. That is, it enables them to judge not only total market growth or decline but also trends in customers' selections among competitors. Generally, sales growth resulting from primary demand (total market growth) is less costly and more profitable than that achieved by capturing share from competitors. Conversely, losses in market share can signal serious long-term problems that require strategic adjustments. Firms with market shares below a certain level may not be viable. Similarly, within a firm's product line, market share trends for individual products are considered early indicators of future opportunities or problems.

Construction

Market Share: *The percentage of a market accounted for by a specific entity.*

Unit Market Share: *The units sold by a particular company as a percentage of total market sales, measured in the same units.*

$$\text{Unit Market Share (\%)} = \frac{\text{Unit Sales (\#)}}{\text{Total Market Unit Sales (\#)}}$$

This formula, of course, can be rearranged to derive either unit sales or total market unit sales from the other two variables, as illustrated in the following:

$$\text{Unit Sales (\#)} = \text{Unit Market Share (\%)} * \text{Total Market Unit Sales (\#)}$$

$$\text{Total Market Unit Sales (\#)} = \frac{\text{Unit Sales (\#)}}{\text{Unit Market Share (\%)}}$$

Revenue Market Share: *Revenue market share differs from unit market share in that it reflects the prices at which goods are sold. In fact, a relatively simple way to calculate relative price is to divide revenue market share by unit market share.*

$$\text{Revenue Market Share (\%)} = \frac{\text{Sales Revenue (\$)}}{\text{Total Market Sales Revenue (\$)}}$$

As with the unit market share, this equation for revenue market share can be rearranged to calculate either sales revenue or total market sales revenue from the other two variables.

Data Sources, Complications, and Cautions

Market definition is never a trivial exercise: If a firm defines its market too broadly, it may dilute its focus. If it does so too narrowly, it will miss opportunities and allow threats to emerge unseen. To avoid these pitfalls, as a first step in calculating market share, managers are advised to define the served market in terms of unit sales or revenues for a specific list of competitors, products, sales channels, geographic areas, customers, and time periods. They might posit, for example, that "Among grocery stores, we are the revenue market share leader in sales of frozen Italian food entrées in the Northeastern U.S."

Data parameters must be carefully defined: Although market share is likely the single most important marketing metric, there is no generally acknowledged best method for calculating it. This is unfortunate, as different methods may yield not only different computations of market share at a given moment, but also widely divergent trends over time. The reasons for these disparities include variations in the lenses through which share is viewed (units versus dollars), where in the channel the measurements are taken (shipments from manufacturers versus consumer purchases), market definition (scope of the competitive universe), and measurement error. In the situation analysis that underlies strategic decisions, managers must be able to understand and explain these variations.

Competitive dynamics in the automobile industry, and at General Motors in particular, illustrate the complexities involved in quantifying market share:

"With market share sliding in the first two months of the year, from 27.2% to 24.9%—the lowest level since a two-month strike shut the company down in 1998—GM as a whole expects a net loss of $846 million the first quarter."[2]

Reviewing this statement, drawn from *Business Week* in 2005, a marketing manager might immediately pose a number of questions:

- Do these figures represent unit (auto) or revenue (dollar) market shares?
- Does this trend hold for both unit and revenue market shares at GM?
- Was revenue market share calculated before or after rebates and discounts?
- Do the underlying sales data reflect factory shipments, which relate directly to the manufacturer's current income statement, or sales to consumers, which are buffered by dealer inventories?

- Does the decline in market share translate to an equivalent percentage decrease in sales, or has the total market size changed?

Managers must determine whether a stated market share is based on shipment data, channel shipments, retail sales, customer surveys, or some other source. On occasion, share figures may represent combinations of data (a firm's actual shipments, for example, set against survey estimates of competitors' sales). If necessary, managers must also adjust for differences in channels.

The time period measured will affect the signal-to-noise ratio: In analyzing short-term market dynamics, such as the effects of a promotion or a recent price change, managers may find it useful to measure market share over a brief period of time. Short-term data, however, generally carry a low signal-to-noise ratio. By contrast, data covering a longer time span will be more stable but may obscure important, recent changes in the market. Applied more broadly, this principle also holds in aggregating geographic areas, channel types, or customers. When choosing markets and time periods for analysis, managers must optimize for the type of signal that is most important.

Potential bias in reported shares: One way to find data for market sizing is through surveys of customer usage. In interpreting these data, however, managers must bear in mind that shares based on reported (versus recorded) sales tend to be biased toward well-known brands.

Related Metrics and Concepts

Served Market: *That portion of the total market for which the firm competes. This may exclude geographic regions or product types. In the airline industry, for example, as of mid 2009, Ryan Air did not fly to the United States. Consequently, the U.S. would not be considered part of its served market.*

2 Relative Market Share and Market Concentration

Relative market share indexes a firm's or a brand's market share against that of its leading competitor.

$$\text{Relative Market Share (I) (\%)} = \frac{\text{Brand's Market Share (\$,\#)}}{\text{Largest Competitor's Market Share (\$,\#)}}$$

Market concentration, a related metric, measures the degree to which a comparatively small number of firms accounts for a large proportion of the market.

These metrics are useful in comparing a firm's or a brand's relative position across different markets and in evaluating the type and degree of competition in those markets.

Purpose: To assess a firm's or a brand's success and its position in the market.

A firm with a market share of 25% would be a powerful leader in many markets but a distant "number two" in others. Relative market share offers a way to benchmark a firm's or a brand's share against that of its largest competitor, enabling managers to compare relative market positions across different product markets. Relative market share gains some of its significance from studies—albeit controversial ones—suggesting that major players in a market tend to be more profitable than their competitors. This metric was further popularized by the Boston Consulting Group in its famous matrix of relative share and market growth (see Figure 1).

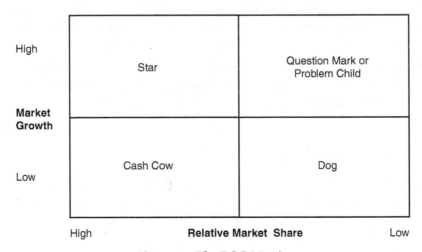

Figure 1   The BCG Matrix

In the BCG matrix, one axis represents relative market share—a surrogate for competitive strength. The other represents market growth—a surrogate for potential. Along each dimension, products are classified as high or low, placing them in one of four quadrants. In the traditional interpretation of this matrix, products with high relative market shares in growing markets are deemed stars, suggesting that they should be supported with vigorous investment. The cash for that investment may be generated by cash cows, products with high relative shares in low-growth markets. Problem child products may have potential for future growth but hold weak competitive positions. Finally, dogs have neither strong competitive position nor growth potential.

Construction

$$\text{Relative Market Share (I)} = \frac{\text{Brand's Market Share (\$,\#)}}{\text{Largest Competitor's Market Share (\$,\#)}}$$

Relative market share can also be calculated by dividing brand sales (#,$) by largest competitor's sales (#,$) because the common factor of total market sales (or revenue) cancels out.

EXAMPLE: The market for small urban cars consists of five players (see Table 1).

Table 1 Market for Small Urban Cars

	Units Sold (Thousands)	Revenue (Thousands)
Zipper	25	€375,000
Twister	10.0	€200,000
A-One	7.5	€187,500
Bowlz	5	€125,000
Chien	2.5	€50,000
Market Total	50.0	€937,500

In the market for small urban cars, managers at A-One want to know their firm's market share relative to its largest competitor. They can calculate this on the basis of revenues or unit sales.

In unit terms, A-One sells 7,500 cars per year. Zipper, the market leader, sells 25,000. A-One's relative market share in unit terms is thus 7,500/25,000 or 0.30. We arrive at the same number if we first calculate A-One's share (7,500/50,000 = .15) and Zipper's share (25,000/50,000 = .50) and then divide A-One's share by Zipper's share (.15/.50 = .30).

In revenue terms, A-One generates €187.5 million in car sales each year. Zipper, the market leader, generates €375 million. A-One's relative market share in revenue terms is thus €187.5m/€375m, or 0.5. Due to its comparatively high average price per car, A-One's relative market share is greater in revenue than in unit terms.

Related Metrics and Concepts

Market Concentration: *The degree to which a relatively small number of firms accounts for a large proportion of the market. This is also known as the concentration ratio. It is usually calculated for the largest three or four firms in a market.*[3]

Three (Four) Firm Concentration Ratio: *The total (sum) of the market shares held by the leading three (four) competitors in a market.*

EXAMPLE: In the small urban car market, the three firm concentration ratio is comprised of the market shares of the top three competitors—Zipper, Twister, and A-One (see Table 2).

Table 2   Market Share—Small Urban Cars

	Units Sold (Thousands)	Unit Share	Revenue (Thousands)	Revenue Share
Zipper	25.0	50%	€375,000	40.0%
Twister	10.0	20%	€200,000	21.3%
A-One	7.5	15%	€187,500	20.0%
Bowlz	5.0	10%	€125,000	13.3%
Chien	2.5	5%	€50,000	5.3%
Market Total	50.0	100%	€937,500	100%

In unit terms, the three firm concentration ratio is 50% + 20% + 15% = 85%.

In revenue terms, it is 40% + 21.3% + 20% = 81.3%.

Herfindahl Index: *A market concentration metric derived by adding the squares of the individual market shares of all the players in a market. As a sum of squares, this index tends to rise in markets dominated by large players.*

EXAMPLE: The Herfindahl Index dramatically highlights market concentration in the small urban car market (see Table 3).

Table 3 Calculation of the Herfindahl Index for Small Urban Cars

	Units Sold (Thousands)	Unit Share	Herfindahl Index	Revenue (Thousands)	Revenue Share	Herfindahl Index
Zipper	25.0	50%	0.25	€375,000	40%	0.16
Twister	10.0	20%	0.04	€200,000	21%	0.0455
A-One	7.5	15%	0.0225	€187,500	20%	0.04
Bowlz	5.0	10%	0.01	€125,000	13%	0.0178
Chien	2.5	5%	0.0025	€50,000	5%	0.0028
Market Total	50.0	100%	0.325	€937,500	100%	0.2661

On a unit basis, the Herfindahl Index is equal to the square of the unit market share of Zipper (50% ^ 2 = 0.25), plus that of Twister (20% ^ 2 = 0.04), plus those of A-One, Bowlz, and Chien = 0.325.

On a revenue basis, the Herfindahl Index comprises the square of the revenue market share of Zipper (40% ^ 2 = 0.16), plus those of all its competitors = 0.2661.

As demonstrated by the Herfindahl Index, the market for small urban cars is slightly more concentrated in unit terms than in revenue terms. The reason for this is straightforward: Higher-priced cars in this market sell fewer units.

Note: For a given number of competitors, the Herfindahl Index would be lowest if shares were equally distributed. In a five-firm industry, for example, equally distributed shares would yield a Herfindahl Index of 5 * (20% ^ 2) = 0.2.

Data Sources, Complications, and Cautions

As ever, appropriate market definition and the use of comparable figures are vital prerequisites to developing meaningful results.

Related Metrics and Concepts

Market Share Rank: *The ordinal position of a brand in its market, when competitors are arranged by size, with 1 being the largest.*

Share of Category: *This metric is derived in the same manner as market share, but is used to denote a share of market within a certain retailer or class of retailers (for example, mass merchandisers).*

3 Brand Development Index and Category Development Index

The brand development index (BDI) quantifies how well a brand is performing within a specific group of customers, compared with its average performance among all consumers.

$$\text{Brand Development Index (I)} = \frac{[\textbf{Brand Sales to Group (\#)/Households (\#)} \text{ in the Group}]}{[\textbf{Total Brand Sales (\#)/Total Household (\#)}]}$$

The category development index (CDI) measures the sales performance of a category of goods or services within a specific group, compared with its average performance among all consumers.

$$\text{Category Development Index (I)} = \frac{[\textbf{Category Sales to Group (\#)/Households in Group (\#)}]}{[\textbf{Total Category Sales (\#)/Total Household (\#)}]}$$

The brand and category development indexes are useful for understanding specific customer segments relative to the market as a whole. Although defined here with respect to households, these indexes could also be calculated for customers, accounts, businesses, or other entities.

Purpose: To understand the relative performance of a brand or category within specified customer groups.

The brand and category development indexes help identify strong and weak segments (usually, demographic or geographic) for particular brands or categories of goods and services. For example, by monitoring the CDI (category development index), marketers might determine that Midwesterners buy twice as many country-western music CDs per capita as Americans in general, while consumers living on the East Coast buy less than the national average. This would be useful information for targeting the launch campaign for a new country-western performer. Conversely, if managers found that a particular product had a low brand development index in a segment that carried a high CDI for its category, they might ask why that brand suffered relatively poor performance in such a promising segment.

Construction

Brand Development Index—BDI (I): *An index of how well a brand performs within a given market group, relative to its performance in the market as a whole.*

$$\text{Brand Development Index—BDI (I)} = \frac{[\text{Brand Sales to Group (\#) / Households in Group (\#)}]}{[\text{Total Brand Sales (\#) / Total Household (\#)}]}$$

The BDI (brand development index) is a measure of brand sales per person or per household within a specified demographic group or geography, compared with its average sales per person or household in the market as a whole. To illustrate its use: One might hypothesize that sales per capita of Ben & Jerry's brand ice cream would be greater in the brand's home state, Vermont, than in the rest of the country. By calculating Ben & Jerry's BDI for Vermont, marketers could test this hypothesis quantitatively.

EXAMPLE: Oaties is a minor brand of breakfast cereal. Among households without children, its sales run one packet per week per 100 households. In the general population, Oaties' sales run one packet per week per 80 households. This translates to 1/100 of a packet per household in the childless segment, versus 1/80 of a packet in the general populace.

$$\text{BDI} = \frac{(\text{Brand Sales / Household})}{(\text{Total Brand Sales / Household})}$$

$$= \frac{1/100}{1/80} = 0.8$$

Oaties performs slightly less well in the childless segment than in the market as a whole.

Category Development Index—CDI: *An index of how well a category performs within a given market segment, relative to its performance in the market as a whole.*

$$\text{Category Development Index (I)} = \frac{[\text{Category Sales to Group (\#) / Households in Group (\#)}]}{[\text{Total Category Sales (\#) / Total Household (\#)}]}$$

Similar in concept to the BDI, the category development index demonstrates where a category shows strength or weakness relative to its overall performance. By way of example, Boston enjoys high per-capita consumption of ice cream. Bavaria and Ireland both show higher per-capita consumption of beer than Iran.

Data Sources and Complications

In calculating BDI or CDI, a precise definition of the segment under study is vital. Segments are often bounded geographically, but they can be defined in any way for which data can be obtained.

Related Metrics and Concepts

The term category development index has also been applied to retail organizations. In this application, it measures the extent to which a retailer emphasizes one category versus others.

$$\text{Category Development Index (I)} = \frac{\text{Retailer's Share of Category Sales (\%)}}{\text{Retailer's Total Share of Market (\%)}}$$

This use of the term is similar to the category performance ratio.

4 Penetration

Penetration is a measure of brand or category popularity. It is defined as the number of people who buy a specific brand or a category of goods at least once in a given period, divided by the size of the relevant market population.

$$\text{Market Penetration (\%)} = \frac{\text{Customers Who Have Purchased a Product in the Category (\#)}}{\text{Total Population (\#)}}$$

$$\text{Brand Penetration (\%)} = \frac{\text{Customers Who Have Purchased the Brand (\#)}}{\text{Total Population (\#)}}$$

$$\text{Penetration Share (\%)} = \frac{\text{Brand Penetration (\%)}}{\text{Market Penetration (\%)}}$$

$$\text{Penetration Share (\%)} = \frac{\text{Customers Who Have Purchased the Brand (\#)}}{\text{Customers Who Have Purchased a Product in the Category (\#)}}$$

Often, managers must decide whether to seek sales growth by acquiring existing category users from their competitors or by expanding the total population of category users, attracting new customers to the market. Penetration metrics help indicate which of these strategies would be most appropriate and help managers to monitor their success. These equations might also be calculated for usage instead of purchase.

Construction

Penetration: *The proportion of people in the target who bought (at least once in the period) a specific brand or a category of goods.*

$$\text{Market Penetration (\%)} = \frac{\text{Customers Who Have Purchased a Product in the Category (\#)}}{\text{Total Population (\#)}}$$

$$\text{Brand Penetration (\%)} = \frac{\text{Customers Who Have Purchased the Brand (\#)}}{\text{Total Population (\#)}}$$

Two key measures of a product's "popularity" are penetration rate and penetration share. The penetration rate (also called penetration, brand penetration, or market penetration as appropriate), is the percentage of the relevant population that has purchased a given brand or category at least once in the time period under study.

EXAMPLE: Over a period of a month, in a market of 10,000 households, 500 households purchased Big Bomb brand flea foggers.

$$\text{Brand Penetration, Big Bomb} = \frac{\text{Big Bomb Customers}}{\text{Total Population}}$$

$$= \frac{500}{10,000} = 5\%$$

A brand's penetration share, in contrast to penetration rate, is determined by comparing that brand's customer population to the number of customers *for its category* in the relevant market as a whole. Here again, to be considered a customer, one must have purchased the brand or category at least once during the period.

$$\text{Penetration Share (\%)} = \frac{\text{Brand Penetration (\%)}}{\text{Market Penetration (\%)}}$$

EXAMPLE: Returning to the flea fogger market, during the month in which 500 households purchased Big Bomb, 2,000 households bought at least one product of any brand in this category. This enables us to calculate Big Bomb's penetration share.

$$\text{Penetration Share, Big Bomb} = \frac{\text{Big Bomb Customers}}{\text{Category Customers}}$$

$$= \frac{500}{20,000} = 25\%$$

DECOMPOSING MARKET SHARE

Relationship of Penetration Share to Market Share: *Market share can be calculated as the product of three components: penetration share, share of requirements, and heavy usage index.*

Market Share (%) = Penetration Share (%) ∗ Share of Requirements (%)
∗ Heavy Usage Index (I)

Share of Requirements: *The percentage of customers' needs in a category that are served by a given brand or product.*

Heavy Usage Index: *A measure of how heavily the people who use a specific product use the entire category of such products.*

In light of these relationships, managers can use this decomposition of market share to reveal penetration share, given the other inputs.

$$\textbf{Penetration Share (\%)} = \frac{\textbf{Market Share (\%)}}{[\textbf{Heavy Usage Index (I)} \ast \textbf{Share of Requirements (\%)}]}$$

EXAMPLE: Eat Wheats brand cereal has a market share in Urbanopolis of 6%. The heavy usage index for Eat Wheats cereal is 0.75 in Urbanopolis. Its share of requirements is 40%. From these data, we can calculate the penetration share for Eat Wheats brand cereal in Urbanopolis:

$$\text{Penetration Share} = \frac{\text{Market Share}}{(\text{Heavy Usage Index} \ast \text{Share of Requirements})}$$

$$= \frac{6\%}{(0.75 \ast 40\%)} = \frac{6\%}{.30} = 20\%$$

Data Sources, Complications, and Cautions

The time period over which a firm measures penetration can have a significant impact on the penetration rate. For example, even among the most popular detergent brands, many are not purchased weekly. As the time period used to define penetration becomes shorter, managers can expect penetration rates to decline. By contrast, penetration share may be less subject to this dynamic because it represents a comparison between brands, among which the effects of shorter periods may fall approximately evenly.

RELATED METRICS AND CONCEPTS

Total Number of Active Customers: *The customers (accounts) who purchased at least once in a given time period. When assessed at a brand level, this is equivalent to brand penetration. This term is often used in shorthand form—total number of customers—though this would not be appropriate when a distinction must be made for ex-customers.*

Accepters: *Customers who are disposed to accept a given product and its benefits: the opposite of rejecters.*

Ever-tried: *The percentage of a population that has tried a given brand at any time.*

5 Share of Requirements

Share of requirements, also known as share of wallet, is calculated solely among buyers of a specific brand. Within this group, it represents the percentage of purchases within the relevant category, accounted for by the brand in question.

$$\text{Unit Share of Requirements (\%)} = \frac{\text{Brand Purchases (\#)}}{\text{Total Category Purchases by Brand Buyers (\#)}}$$

$$\text{Revenue Share of Requirements (\%)} = \frac{\text{Brand Purchases (\$)}}{\text{Total Category Purchases by Brand Buyers (\$)}}$$

Many marketers view share of requirements as a key measure of loyalty. This metric can guide a firm's decisions on whether to allocate resources toward efforts to expand a category, to take customers from competitors, or to increase share of requirements among its established customers. Share of requirements is, in essence, the market share for a brand within a market narrowly defined as the people who have already purchased that brand.

Purpose: To understand the source of market share in terms of breadth and depth of consumer franchise, as well as the extent of relative category usage (heavy users/larger customers versus light users/smaller customers).

Construction

Share of Requirements: *A given brand's share of purchases in its category, measured solely among customers who have already purchased that brand. Also known as share of wallet.*

When calculating share of requirements, marketers may consider either dollars or units. They must ensure, however, that their heavy usage index is consistent with this choice.

$$\text{Unit Share of Requirements (\%)} = \frac{\text{Brand Purchases (\#)}}{\text{Total Category Purchases by Brand Buyers (\#)}}$$

$$\text{Revenue Share of Requirements (\%)} = \frac{\text{Brand Purchases (\$)}}{\text{Total Category Purchases by Brand Buyers (\$)}}$$

The best way to think about share of requirements is as the average market share enjoyed by a product among the customers who buy it.

EXAMPLE: In a given month, the unit purchases of AloeHa brand sunscreen ran 1,000,000 bottles. Among the households that bought AloeHa, total purchases of sunscreen came to 2,000,000 bottles.

$$\text{Share of Requirements} = \frac{\text{AloeHa Purchases}}{\text{Category Purchases by AloeHa Customers}}$$

$$= \frac{1,000,000}{2,000,000} = 50\%$$

Share of requirements is also useful in analyzing overall market share. As previously noted, it is part of an important formulation of market share.

Market Share = Penetration Share * Share of Requirements * Heavy Usage Index

Share of requirements can thus be calculated indirectly by decomposing market share.

$$\text{Share of Requirements (\%)} = \frac{\text{Market Share (\%)}}{[\text{Penetration Share (\%)} * \text{Heavy Usage Index (I)}]}$$

EXAMPLE: Eat Wheats brand cereal has a market share in Urbanopolis of 8%. The heavy usage index for Eat Wheats in Urbanopolis is 1. The brand's penetration share in Urbanopolis is 20%. On this basis, we can calculate Eat Wheats' share of requirements in Urbanopolis:

$$\text{Share of Requirements} = \frac{\text{Market Share}}{(\text{Heavy Usage Index} * \text{Penetration Share})}$$

$$= \frac{8\%}{(1 * 20\%)} = \frac{8\%}{20\%} = 40\%$$

Note that in this example, market share and heavy usage index must both be defined in the same terms (units or revenue). Depending on the definition of these two metrics, the calculated share of requirements will be either unit share of requirements (%) or revenue share of requirements (%).

Data Sources, Complications, and Cautions

Double Jeopardy: Some marketers strive for a "niche" positioning that yields high market share through a combination of low penetration and high share of requirements. That is, they seek relatively few customers but very loyal ones. Before embarking on this strategy, however, a phenomenon known as "double jeopardy" should be considered. Generally, the evidence suggests that it's difficult to achieve a high share of requirements without also attaining a high penetration share. One reason is that products with high market share generally have high availability, whereas those with low market share may not. Therefore, it can be difficult for customers to maintain loyalty to brands with low market share.

Related Metrics and Concepts

Sole Usage: *The fraction of a brand's customers who use only the brand in question.*

Sole Usage Percentage: *The proportion of a brand's customers who use only that brand's products and do not buy from competitors. Sole users may be die-hard, loyal customers. Alternatively, they may not have access to other options, perhaps because they live in remote areas. Where sole use is 100%, the share of wallet is 100%.*

$$\text{Sole Usage (\%)} = \frac{\text{Customers Who Buy Only the Brand in Question (\#)}}{\text{Total Brand Customers (\#)}}$$

Number of Brands Purchased: During a given period, some customers may buy only a single brand within a category, whereas others buy two or more. In evaluating loyalty to a given brand, marketers can consider the average number of brands purchased by consumers of that brand versus the average number purchased by all customers in that category.

EXAMPLE: Among 10 customers for cat food, 7 bought the Arda brand, 5 bought Bella, and 3 bought Constanza. Thus, the 10 customers made a total of 15 brand purchases (7 + 5 + 3), yielding an average of 1.5 brands per customer.

Seeking to evaluate customer loyalty, a Bella brand manager notes that of his firm's five customers, 3 bought only Bella, whereas two bought both Arda and Bella. None of Bella's customers bought Constanza. Thus, the five Bella customers made seven brand purchases (1 + 1 + 1 + 2 + 2), yielding an average of 1.4 (that is, 7/5) brands per Bella customer. Compared to the average category purchaser, who buys 1.5 brands, Bella buyers are slightly more loyal.

Repeat Rate: *The percentage of brand customers in a given period who are also brand customers in the subsequent period.*

Repurchase Rate: *The percentage of customers for a brand who repurchase that brand on their next purchase occasion.*

Confusion abounds in this area. In these definitions, we have tried to distinguish a metric based on calendar time (repeat rate) from one based on "customer time" (repurchase rate). A related metric, retention, is used in contractual situations in which the first non-renewal (non-purchase) signals the end of a customer relationship. Although we suggest that the term retention be applied only in contractual situations, you will often see repeat rates and repurchase rates referred to as "retention rates." Due to a lack consensus on the use of these terms, marketers are advised not to rely on the names of these metrics as perfect indicators of how they are calculated.

The importance of repeat rate depends on the time period covered. Looking at one week's worth of purchases is unlikely to be very illuminating. In a given category, most consumers only buy one brand in a week. By contrast, over a period of years, consumers may buy several brands that they do not prefer, on occasions when they can't find the brand to which they seek to be loyal. Consequently, the right period to consider depends on the product under study and the frequency with which it is bought. Marketers are advised to take care to choose a meaningful period.

6   Heavy Usage Index

The heavy usage index is a measure of the relative intensity of consumption. It indicates how heavily the customers for a given brand use the product category to which that brand belongs, compared with the average customer for that category.

$$\text{Heavy Usage Index (I)} = \frac{\text{Average Total Purchases in Category by Brand Customers (\#,\$)}}{\text{Average Total Purchases in Category by All Customers for That Category (\#,\$)}}$$

or

$$\text{Heavy Usage Index (I)} = \frac{\text{Market Share (\%)}}{[\text{Penetration Share (\%)} * \text{Share of Requirements (\%)}]}$$

The heavy usage index, also called the weight index, yields insight into the source of volume and the nature of a brand's customer base.

Purpose: To define and measure whether a firm's consumers are "heavy users."

The heavy usage index answers the question, "How heavily do our customers use the category of our product?" When a brand's heavy usage index is greater than 1.0, this signifies that its customers use the category to which it belongs more heavily than the average customer for that category.

Construction

Heavy Usage Index: *The ratio that compares the average consumption of products in a category by customers of a given brand with the average consumption of products in that category by all customers for the category.*

The heavy usage index can be calculated on the basis of unit or dollar inputs. For a given brand, if the heavy usage index is greater than 1.0, that brand's customers consume an above-average quantity or value of products in the category.

$$\text{Heavy Usage Index (I)} = \frac{\text{Average Total Purchases in Category by Brand Customers (\#,\$)}}{\text{Average Total Purchases in Category by All Customers for That Category (\#,\$)}}$$

EXAMPLE: Over a period of one year, the average shampoo purchases by households using Shower Fun brand shampoo totaled six 15-oz bottles. During the same period, average shampoo consumption by households using any brand of shampoo was four 15-oz bottles.

The heavy usage index for households buying Shower Fun is therefore 6/4, or 1.5. Customers of Shower Fun brand shampoo are disproportionately heavy users. They buy 50% more shampoo than the average shampoo consumer. Of course, because Shower Fun buyers are part of the overall market average, when compared with non-users of Shower Fun, their relative usage is even higher.

As previously noted, market share can be calculated as the product of three components: penetration share, share of requirements, and heavy usage index. Consequently, we can calculate a brand's heavy usage index if we know its market share, penetration share, and share of requirements, as follows:

$$\text{Heavy Usage Index (I)} = \frac{\text{Market Share (\%)}}{[\text{Penetration Share (\%)} * \text{Share of Requirements (\%)}]}$$

This equation works for market shares defined in either unit or dollar terms. As noted earlier, the heavy usage index can measure either unit or dollar usage. Comparing a brand's unit heavy usage index to its dollar heavy usage index, marketers can determine whether category purchases by that brand's customers run above or below the average category price.

Data Sources, Complications, and Cautions

The heavy usage index does not indicate how heavily customers use a specific brand, only how heavily they use the category. A brand can have a high heavy usage index, for example, meaning that its customers are heavy category users, even if those customers use the brand in question to meet only a small share of their needs.

7   Awareness, Attitudes, and Usage (AAU): Metrics of the Hierarchy of Effects

Studies of awareness, attitudes, and usage (AAU) enable marketers to quantify levels and trends in customer knowledge, perceptions, beliefs, intentions, and behaviors. In some companies, the results of these studies are called "tracking" data because they are used to track long-term changes in customer awareness, attitudes, and behaviors.

AAU studies are most useful when their results are set against a clear comparator. This benchmark may comprise the data from prior periods, different markets, or competitors.

Purpose: To track trends in customer attitudes and behaviors.

Awareness, attitudes, and usage (AAU) metrics relate closely to what has been called the Hierarchy of Effects, an assumption that customers progress through sequential stages from lack of awareness, through initial purchase of a product, to brand loyalty (see Figure 2). AAU metrics are generally designed to track these stages of knowledge, beliefs, and behaviors. AAU studies also may track "who" uses a brand or product—in which customers are defined by category usage (heavy/light), geography, demographics, psychographics, media usage, and whether they purchase other products.

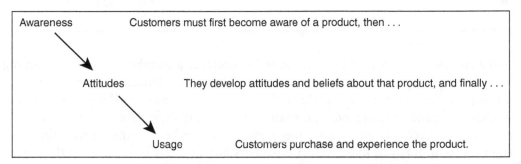

Figure 2   Awareness, Attitudes, and Usage: Hierarchy of Effects

Information about attitudes and beliefs offers insight into the question of why specific users do, or do not, favor certain brands. Typically, marketers conduct surveys of large samples of households or business customers to gather these data.

Construction

Awareness, attitudes, and usage studies feature a range of questions that aim to shed light on customers' relationships with a product or brand (see Table 4). For example, who are the acceptors and rejecters of the product? How do customers respond to a replay of advertising content?

Table 4 Awareness, Attitudes, and Usage: Typical Questions

Type	Measures	Typical Questions
Awareness	Awareness and Knowledge	Have you heard of Brand X?
		What brand comes to mind when you think "luxury car?"
Attitudes	Beliefs and Intentions	Is Brand X for me?
		On a scale of 1 to 5, is Brand X for young people?
		What are the strengths and weaknesses of each brand?
Usage	Purchase Habits and Loyalty	Did you use Brand X this week?
		What brand did you last buy?

Marketers use answers to these questions to construct a number of metrics. Among these, certain "summary metrics" are considered important indicators of performance. In many studies, for example, customers' "willingness to recommend" and "intention to purchase" a brand are assigned high priority. Underlying these data, various diagnostic metrics help marketers understand *why* consumers may be willing—or unwilling—to recommend or purchase that brand. Consumers may not have been aware of the brand, for example. Alternatively, they may have been aware of it but did not subscribe to one of its key benefit claims.

AWARENESS AND KNOWLEDGE

Marketers evaluate various levels of awareness, depending on whether the consumer in a given study is prompted by a product's category, brand, advertising, or usage situation.

> **Awareness:** *The percentage of potential customers or consumers who recognize—or name—a given brand. Marketers may research brand recognition on an "aided" or*

"prompted" level, posing such questions as, "Have you heard of Mercedes?" Alternatively, they may measure "unaided" or "unprompted" awareness, posing such questions as, "Which makes of automobiles come to mind?"

Top of Mind: *The first brand that comes to mind when a customer is asked an unprompted question about a category. The percentage of customers for whom a given brand is top of mind can be measured.*

Ad Awareness: *The percentage of target consumers or accounts who demonstrate awareness (aided or unaided) of a brand's advertising. This metric can be campaign- or media-specific, or it can cover all advertising.*

Brand/Product Knowledge: *The percentage of surveyed customers who demonstrate specific knowledge or beliefs about a brand or product.*

ATTITUDES

Measures of attitude concern consumer response to a brand or product. Attitude is a combination of what consumers believe and how strongly they feel about it. Although a detailed exploration of attitudinal research is beyond the scope of this book, the following summarizes certain key metrics in this field.

Attitudes/Liking/Image: *A rating assigned by consumers—often on a scale of 1–5 or 1–7—when survey respondents are asked their level of agreement with such propositions as, "This is a brand for people like me," or "This is a brand for young people." A metric based on such survey data can also be called relevance to customer.*

Perceived Value for Money: *A rating assigned by consumers—often on a scale of 1–5 or 1–7—when survey respondents are asked their level of agreement with such propositions as, "This brand usually represents a good value for the money."*

Perceived Quality/Esteem: *A consumer rating—often on a scale of 1–5 or 1–7—of a given brand's product when compared with others in its category or market.*

Relative Perceived Quality: *A consumer rating (often from 1–5 or 1–7) of brand product compared to others in the category/market.*

Intentions: *A measure of customers' stated willingness to behave in a certain way. Information on this subject is gathered through such survey questions as, "Would you be willing to switch brands if your favorite was not available?"*

Purchase Intentions: *A specific measure or rating of consumers' stated purchase intentions. Information on this subject is gathered through survey respondents' reactions to such propositions as, "It is very likely that I will purchase this product."*

USAGE

Measures of usage concern such market dynamics as purchase frequency and units per purchase. They highlight not only what was purchased, but also when and where it was purchased. In studying usage, marketers also seek to determine how many people have tried a brand. Of those, they further seek to determine how many have "rejected" the brand, and how many have "adopted" it into their regular portfolio of brands.

> **Usage:** *A measure of customers' self-reported behavior.*

In measuring usage, marketers pose such questions as the following: What brand of toothpaste did you last purchase? How many times in the past year have you purchased toothpaste? How many tubes of toothpaste do you currently have in your home? Do you have any Crest toothpaste in your home at the current time?

In the aggregate, AAU metrics concern a vast range of information that can be tailored to specific companies and markets. They provide managers with insight into customers' overall relationships with a given brand or product.

Data Sources, Complications, and Cautions

Sources of AAU data include

- Warranty cards and registrations, often using prizes and random drawings to encourage participation.

- Regularly administered surveys, conducted by organizations that interview consumers via telephone, mail, Web, or other technologies, such as hand-held scanners.

Even with the best methodologies, however, variations observed in tracking data from one period to the next are not always reliable. Managers must rely on their experience to distinguish seasonality effects and "noise" (random movement) from "signal" (actual trends and patterns). Certain techniques in data collection and review can also help managers make this distinction.

1. **Adjust for periodic changes** in how questions are framed or administered. Surveys can be conducted via mail or telephone, for example, among paid or unpaid respondents. Different data-gathering techniques may require adjustment in the norms used to evaluate a "good" or "bad" response. If sudden changes appear in the data from one period to the next, marketers are advised to determine whether methodological shifts might play a role in this result.

2. Try to **separate customer from non-customer responses;** they may be very different. Causal links among awareness, attitudes, and usage are rarely clear-cut.

Though the hierarchy of effects is often viewed as a one-way street, on which awareness leads to attitudes, which in turn determine usage, the true causal flow might also be reversed. When people own a brand, for example, they may be predisposed to like it.

3. **Triangulate customer survey data** with sales revenue, shipments, or other data related to business performance. Consumer attitudes, distributor and retail sales, and company shipments may move in different directions. Analyzing these patterns can be a challenge but can reveal much about category dynamics. For example, toy shipments to retailers often occur well in advance of the advertising that drives consumer awareness and purchase intentions. These, in turn, must be established before retail sales. Adding further complexity, in the toy industry, the purchaser of a product might not be its ultimate consumer. In evaluating AAU data, marketers must understand not only the drivers of demand but also the logistics of purchase.

4. **Separate leading from lagging indicators** whenever possible. In the auto industry, for example, individuals who have just purchased a new car show a heightened sensitivity to advertisements for its make and model. Conventional wisdom suggests that they're looking for confirmation that they made a good choice in a risky decision. By helping consumers justify their purchase at this time, auto manufacturers can strengthen long-term satisfaction and willingness to recommend.

Related Metrics and Concepts

Likeability: *Because AAU considerations are so important to marketers, and because there is no single "right" way to approach them, specialized and proprietary systems have been developed. Of these, one of the best known is the Q scores rating of "likeability." A Q Score is derived from a general survey of selected households, in which a large panel of consumers share their feelings about brands, celebrities, and television shows.*[4]

Q Scores rely upon responses reported by consumers. Consequently, although the system used is sophisticated, it is dependent on consumers understanding and being willing to reveal their preferences.

Segmentation by Geography, or Geo-clustering: *Marketers can achieve insight into consumer attitudes by separating their data into smaller, more homogeneous groups of customers. One well-known example of this is Prizm. Prizm assigns U.S. households to clusters based on ZIP Code,[5] with the goal of creating small groups of similar households. The typical characteristics of each Prizm cluster are known, and these are used to assign a name to each group. "Golden Ponds" consumers, for* *example, comprise elderly singles and couples leading modest lifestyles in small towns. Rather than monitoring AAU statistics for the population as a whole, firms often find it useful to track these data by cluster.*

8   Customer Satisfaction and Willingness to Recommend

Customer satisfaction is generally based on survey data and expressed as a rating. For example, see Figure 3.

Very Dissatisfied	Somewhat Dissatisfied	Neither Satisfied nor Dissatisfied	Somewhat Satisfied	Very Satisfied
1	2	3	4	5

Figure 3   Ratings

Within organizations, customer satisfaction ratings can have powerful effects. They focus employees on the importance of fulfilling customers' expectations. Furthermore, when these ratings dip, they warn of problems that can affect sales and profitability.

A second important metric related to satisfaction is willingness to recommend. When a customer is satisfied with a product, he or she might recommend it to friends, relatives, and colleagues. This can be a powerful marketing advantage.

Purpose: Customer satisfaction provides a leading indicator of consumer purchase intentions and loyalty.

Customer satisfaction data are among the most frequently collected indicators of market perceptions. Their principal use is twofold.

1.   Within organizations, the collection, analysis, and dissemination of these data send a message about the importance of tending to customers and ensuring that they have a positive experience with the company's goods and services.

2.   Although sales or market share can indicate how well a firm is performing *currently*, satisfaction is perhaps the best indicator of how likely it is that the firm's customers will make further purchases *in the future*. Much research has focused on the relationship between customer satisfaction and retention.

Studies indicate that the ramifications of satisfaction are most strongly realized at the extremes. On the scale in Figure 3, individuals who rate their satisfaction level as "5" are likely to become return customers and might even evangelize for the firm. Individuals who rate their satisfaction level as "1," by contrast, are unlikely to return. Further, they can hurt the firm by making negative comments about it to prospective customers. Willingness to recommend is a key metric relating to customer satisfaction.

Construction

Customer Satisfaction: *The number of customers, or percentage of total customers, whose reported experience with a firm, its products, or its services (ratings) exceeds specified satisfaction goals.*

Willingness to Recommend: *The percentage of surveyed customers who indicate that they would recommend a brand to friends.*

These metrics quantify an important dynamic. When a brand has loyal customers, it gains positive word-of-mouth marketing, which is both free and highly effective.

Customer satisfaction is measured at the individual level, but it is almost always reported at an aggregate level. It can be, and often is, measured along various dimensions. A hotel, for example, might ask customers to rate their experience with its front desk and check-in service, with the room, with the amenities in the room, with the restaurants, and so on. Additionally, in a holistic sense, the hotel might ask about overall satisfaction "with your stay."

Customer satisfaction is generally measured on a five-point scale (see Figure 4).

Very Dissatisfied	Somewhat Dissatisfied	Neither Satisfied nor Dissatisfied	Somewhat Satisfied	Very Satisfied
1	2	3	4	5

Figure 4   A Typical Five-Point Scale

Satisfaction levels are usually reported as either "top box" or, more likely, "top two boxes." Marketers convert these expressions into single numbers that show the percentage of respondents who checked either a "4" or a "5." (This term is the same as that commonly used in projections of trial volumes.)

EXAMPLE: The general manager of a hotel in Quebec institutes a new system of customer satisfaction monitoring (see Figure 5). She leaves satisfaction surveys at checkout. As an incentive to respond, all respondents are entered into a drawing for a pair of free airline tickets.

	Very Dissatisfied	Somewhat Dissatisfied	Neither Satisfied nor Dissatisfied	Somewhat Satisfied	Very Satisfied
Score	1	2	3	4	5
Responses (200 useable)	3	7	40	100	50
%	2%	4%	20%	50%	25%

Figure 5   Hotel Customer Survey Response

The manager collects 220 responses, of which 20 are unclear or otherwise unusable. Among the remaining 200, 3 people rate their overall experience at the hotel as very unsatisfactory, 7 deem it somewhat unsatisfactory, and 40 respond that they are neither satisfied nor dissatisfied. Of the remainder, 50 customers say they are very satisfied, while the rest are somewhat satisfied.

The top box, comprising customers who rate their experience a "5," includes 50 people or, as a percentage, 50/200 = 25%. The top two boxes comprise customers who are "somewhat" or "very" satisfied, rating their experience a "4" or "5." In this example, the "somewhat satisfied" population must be calculated as the total usable response pool, less customers accounted for elsewhere, that is, 200 − 3 − 7 − 40 − 50 = 100. The sum of the top two boxes is thus 50 + 100 = 150 customers, or 75% of the total.

Customer satisfaction data can also be collected on a 10-point scale. Regardless of the scale used, the objective is to measure customers' perceived satisfaction with their experience of a firm's offerings. Marketers then aggregate these data into a percentage of top-box responses.

In researching satisfaction, firms generally ask customers whether their product or service has met or exceeded expectations. Thus, expectations are a key factor behind satisfaction. When customers have high expectations and the reality falls short, they will be disappointed and will likely rate their experience as less than satisfying. For this reason, a luxury resort, for example, might receive a lower satisfaction rating than a budget motel—even though its facilities and service would be deemed superior in "absolute" terms.

Data Sources, Complications, and Cautions

Surveys constitute the most frequently used means of collecting satisfaction data. As a result, a key risk of distortion in measures of satisfaction can be summarized in a single question: Who responds to surveys?

"Response bias" is endemic in satisfaction data. Disappointed or angry customers often welcome a means to vent their opinions. Contented customers often do not. Consequently, although many customers might be happy with a product and feel no need to complete a survey, the few who had a bad experience might be disproportionately represented among respondents. Most hotels, for example, place response cards in their rooms, asking guests, "How was your stay?' Only a small percentage of guests ever bother to complete those cards. Not surprisingly, those who do respond probably had a bad experience. For this reason, marketers can find it difficult to judge the true level of customer satisfaction. By reviewing survey data over time, however, they may discover important trends or changes. If complaints suddenly rise, for example, that may constitute early warning of a decline in quality or service. (See number of complaints in the following section.)

Sample selection may distort satisfaction ratings in other ways as well. Because only *customers* are surveyed for customer satisfaction, a firm's ratings may rise artificially as deeply dissatisfied customers take their business elsewhere. Also, some populations may be more frank than others, or more prone to complain. These normative differences can affect perceived satisfaction levels. In analyzing satisfaction data, a firm might interpret rating differences as a sign that one market is receiving better service than another, when the true difference lies only in the standards that customers apply. To correct for this issue, marketers are advised to review satisfaction measures over time *within the same market*.

A final caution: Because many firms define customer satisfaction as "meeting or exceeding expectations," this metric may fall simply because expectations have risen. Thus, in interpreting ratings data, managers may come to believe that the quality of their offering has declined when that is not the case. Of course, the reverse is also true. A firm might boost satisfaction by lowering expectations. In so doing, however, it might suffer a decline in sales as its product or service comes to appear unattractive.

Related Metrics and Concepts

Trade Satisfaction: *Founded upon the same principles as consumer satisfaction, trade satisfaction measures the attitudes of trade customers.*

Number of Complaints: *The number of complaints lodged by customers in a given time period.*

9 Net Promoter[6]

> Net promoter is a measure of the degree to which current customers will recommend a product, service, or company.
>
> **Net Promoter Score (I) = Percentage of Promoters (%) − Percentage of Detractors (%)**
>
> Net promoter is claimed to be a particularly useful measure of customer satisfaction and/or loyalty.

Purpose: To measure how well the brand or company is succeeding in creating satisfied, loyal customers.

Net Promoter Score[7] (NPS) is a registered trademark of Frederick R. Reichheld, Bain & Company, and Satmetrix that is a particularly simple measure of the satisfaction/loyalty of current customers. Customers are surveyed and asked (on a ten-point scale) how likely they are to recommend the company or brand to a friend or colleague. Based on their answers to this single question, customers are divided into

- **Promoters:** Customers who are willing to recommend the company to others (who gave the company a rating of 9 or 10).

- **Passives:** Satisfied but unenthusiastic customers (ratings of 7 or 8).

- **Detractors:** Customers who are unwilling to recommend the company to others (ratings of 0 to 6).

High NPSs generally mean that a company is doing a good job of securing their customers' loyalty and active evangelism. Low and negative Net Promoter Scores are important early warning signals for the firm. Because the metric is simple and easy to understand, it provides a stable measure companies use to motivate employees and monitor progress.

Construction

The Net Promoter Score (NPS) is created by subtracting the percentage of detractors among current customers from the percentage of promoters among current customers.

Net Promoter Score (I) = Percentage of Promoters (%) − Percentage of Detractors (%)

For example if a survey of a company's customers reports that there were 20% promoters, 70% passives, and 10% detractors, the company would have a Net Promoter Score of 20–10 =10.

Data Sources, Complications and Cautions

Although the trademarked NPS asks a specific question, uses a 10-point scale, and defines promoters, passives, and detractors in a particular way (detractors are those giving ratings of 0 through 6), it is easy to imagine other versions of NPS that differ with respect to the wording of the question, the scale used (1 through 5 rather than 0 through 10), and the definitions (and labels) of the resulting groups of responders. The defining features of NPS are that it is constructed from responses to a question about willingness to recommend and is a net measure found by subtracting the fraction unwilling to recommend from the fraction willing to recommend and leaving out those in the middle.

The same NPS score can indicate different business circumstances. For instance, a Net Promoter Score of zero can indicate highly polarized customers, 50% promoters, 50% detractors, or a totally ambivalent customer base, 100% passives. Getting the NPS score may be a good way of starting a discussion about customer perceptions of the brand. As it is an average of current customers' responses, managers must drill down to the data to understand the precise situation their business faces.

This score in specific circumstances can generate results that could mislead a manager who is not being careful. For example, consider a company whose current customers are 30% promoters, 30% detractors, and 40% passives. This company's NPS is an unimpressive zero, or 30%-30%.

Suppose next that a new competitor steals two-thirds of the company's detractors, and because these detractors immediately defect to the new competitor, they cease to be customers of the company. The NPS is remeasured.

Promoters are now 30% / (100% − 20% = 80%) = 37.5% of the customers that remain.

Passives are now 40% / (100% − 20% = 80%) = 50% of the customers that remain.

Detractors are now only (30% − 20% = 10%) / (100% − 20% = 80%) = 12.5% of the customers that remain.

The NPS is now 37.5% − 12.5% = a very healthy looking + 25.

The defection of the most vulnerable and unhappy customers led directly to an increase in NPS. Managers should make sure they fully understand what has happened.

While benchmarking is often a useful exercise, it is inappropriate to directly apply this measure across categories. Some products are in categories that are more likely to gain engagement both positive and negative than others.

A high Net Promoter Score while generally desirable does beg the question whether the company is properly monetizing the value they are providing to the consumer. The easiest way to develop a high Net Promoter Score is to provide a highly valued product free to customers. Why wouldn't they be happy to recommend you? While there may be strategic reasons for situations like this to be acceptable to the company in the short or medium term, this probably won't be a viable long-term strategy.

The Net Promoter Score is calculated from survey data. As such it may suffer from the problems common to most surveys, and the results should be interpreted in light of other data, such as sales trends. Is increased customer satisfaction leading to increased sales? If so, fine; if not, why not?

Although the Net Promoter Score has received much attention and relatively rapid adoption, it has also been the target of a recent award-winning article. Consultant Timothy Keiningham and his co-authors claim the benefits of the measure have been overstated relative to other measures of loyalty and satisfaction.[8]

10   Willingness to Search

Although many metrics explore brand loyalty, one has been called the "acid test." That is,

Willingness to Search (%) = Percentage of Customers Willing to Delay Purchases, Change Stores, or Reduce Purchase Quantities to Avoid Switching Brands

This metric can tell a company much about the attitudes of its customers and whether its position in the market is likely to be defensible against sustained pressure from a competitor.

Purpose: To assess the commitment of a firm's or a brand's customer base.

Brand or company loyalty is a key marketing asset. Marketers evaluate aspects of it through a number of metrics, including repurchase rate, share of requirements, willingness to pay a price premium, and other AAU measures. Perhaps the most fundamental test of loyalty, however, can be captured in a simple question: When faced with a situation in which a brand is not available, will its customers search further or substitute the best available option?

When a brand enjoys loyalty at this level, its provider can generate powerful leverage in trade negotiations. Often, such loyalty will also give providers time to respond to a competitive threat. Customers will stay with them while they address the threat.

Loyalty is grounded in a number of factors, including

- Satisfied and influential customers who are willing to recommend the brand.

- Hidden values or emotional benefits, which are effectively communicated.

- A strong image for the product, the user, or the usage experience.

Purchase-based loyalty metrics are also affected by whether a product is broadly and conveniently available for purchase, and whether customers enjoy other options in its category.

Construction

Willingness to Search: *The likelihood that customers will settle for a second-choice product if their first choice is not available. Also called "accept no substitutes."*

Willingness to search represents the percentage of customers who are willing to leave a store without a product if their favorite brand is unavailable. Those willing to substitute constitute the balance of the population.

Data Sources, Complications, and Cautions

Loyalty has multiple dimensions. Consumers who are loyal to a brand in the sense of rarely switching may or may not be willing to pay a price premium for that brand or recommend it to their friends. Behavioral loyalty may also be difficult to distinguish from inertia or habit. When asked about loyalty, consumers often don't know what they will do in new circumstances. They may not have accurate recall about past behavior, especially in regard to items with which they feel relatively low involvement.

Furthermore, different products generate different levels of loyalty. Few customers will be as loyal to a brand of matches, for example, as to a brand of baby formula. Consequently, marketers should exercise caution in comparing loyalty rates across products. Rather, they should look for category-specific norms.

Degrees of loyalty also differ between demographic groups. Older consumers have been shown to demonstrate the highest loyalty rates.

Even with these complexities, however, customer loyalty remains one of the most important metrics to monitor. Marketers should understand the worth of their brands in the eyes of the customer—and of the retailer.

ENDNOTES

1. "Wal-Mart Shopper Update," *Retail Forward*, February 2005.

2. "Running Out of Gas," *Business Week*, March 28th, 2005.

3. American Marketing Association definition. Accessed 06/08/2005. http://www .marketingpower.com/live/mg-dictionary.php?SearchFor=market+concentration& Searched=1.

4. Check the Marketing Evaluations, Inc., Web site for more detail: http://www.qscores .com/. Accessed 03/03/05.

5. Claritas provides the Prizm analysis. For more details, visit the company Web site: http://www.clusterbigip1.claritas.com/claritas/Default.jsp. Accessed 03/03/05.

6. Reichheld, Fred, *The Ultimate Question: Driving Good Profits and True Growth* (Boston: Harvard Business School Publishing Corporation, 2006.)

7. http://www.theultimatequestion.com/theultimatequestion/measuring_netpro-moter.asp?groupCode=2

8. Timothy Keiningham, Bruce Cooil, Tor Wallin Andreassen and Lerzan Aksoy (2007) "A Longitudinal Examination of Net Promoter and Firm Revenue Growth." *Journal of Marketing*, Volume 71, July 2007.

PRODUCT AND PORTFOLIO MANAGEMENT

Introduction

Key concepts covered:

Trial, Repeat, Penetration, and Volume Projections

Growth: Percentage and CAGR

Cannibalization Rate and Fair Share Draw Rate

Brand Equity Metrics

Conjoint Utilities and Consumer Preference

Segmentation and Conjoint Utilities

Conjoint Utilities and Volume Projection

Effective marketing comes from customer knowledge and an understanding of how a product fits customers' needs. In this chapter, we'll describe metrics used in product strategy and planning. These metrics address the following questions: What volumes can marketers expect from a new product? How will sales of existing products be affected by the launch of a new offering? Is brand equity increasing or decreasing? What do customers really want, and what are they willing to sacrifice to obtain it?

We'll start with a section on trial and repeat rates, explaining how these metrics are determined and how they're used to generate sales forecasts for new products. Because forecasts involve growth projections, we'll then discuss the difference between year-on-year growth and compound annual growth rates (CAGR). Because growth of one product sometimes comes at the expense of an existing product line, it is important to

From Chapter 4 of *Marketing Metrics: The Definitive Guide to Measuring Marketing Performance*, 2/e. Paul W. Farris. Neil T. Bendle. Phillip E. Pfeifer. David J. Reibstein. Copyright © 2010 by Pearson Education. Published by Wharton School Publishing.

understand cannibalization metrics. These reflect the impact of new products on a portfolio of existing products.

Next, we'll cover selected metrics associated with brand equity—a central focus of marketing. Indeed, many of the metrics throughout this book can be useful in evaluating brand equity. Certain metrics, however, have been developed specifically to measure the "health" of brands. This chapter will discuss them.

Although branding strategy is a major aspect of a product offering, there are others, and managers must be prepared to make trade-offs among them, informed by a sense of the "worth" of various features. Conjoint analysis helps identify customers' valuation of specific product attributes. Increasingly, this technique is used to improve products and to help marketers evaluate and segment new or rapidly growing markets. In the final sections of this chapter, we'll discuss conjoint analysis from multiple perspectives.

	Metric	Construction	Considerations	Purpose
1	Trial	First-time users as a percentage of the target population.	Distinguish "ever-tried" from "new" triers in current period.	Over time, sales should rely less on trial and more on repeat purchasers.
1	Repeat Volume	Repeat buyers, multiplied by the number of products they buy in each purchase, multiplied by the number of times they purchase per period.	Depending on when trial was achieved, not all triers will have an equal opportunity to make repeat purchases.	Measure of the stability of a brand franchise.
1	Penetration	Users in the previous period, multiplied by repeat rate for the current period, plus new triers in the current period.	The length of the period will affect norms, that is, more customers buy in a year than in a month.	Measure of the population buying in the current period.
1	Volume Projections	Combine trial volume and repeat volume.	Adjust trial and repeat rates for time frame. Not all triers will have time or opportunity to repeat.	Plan production and inventories for both trade sales and consumer off-take.

	Metric	Construction	Considerations	Purpose
2	Year-on-Year Growth	Percentage change from one year to the next.	Distinguish unit and dollar growth rates.	Plan production and budgeting.
2	Compound Annual Growth Rate (CAGR)	Ending value divided by starting value to the power of 1/N, in which N is the number of periods.	May not reflect individual year-on-year growth rates.	Useful for averaging growth rates over long periods.
3	Cannibalization Rate	Percentage of new product sales taken from existing product line.	Market expansion effects should also be considered.	Useful to account for the fact that new products often reduce the sales of existing products.
3	Fair Share Draw	Assumption that new entrants in a market capture sales from established competitors in proportion to established market shares.	May not be a reasonable assumption if there are significant differences among competing brands.	Useful to generate an estimate of sales and shares after entry of new competitor.
4	Brand Equity Metrics	Numerous measures, for example, Conjoint utility attributed to brand.	Metrics tracking essence of brand may not track health and value.	Monitor health of a brand. Diagnose weaknesses, as needed.
5	Conjoint Utilities	Regression coefficients for attribute levels derived from conjoint analysis.	May be function of number, level, and type of attributes in study.	Indicates the relative values that customers place on attributes of which product offerings are composed.

Continues

	Metric	Construction	Considerations	Purpose
6	Segment Utilities	Clustering of individuals into market segments on the basis of sum-of-squares distance between regression coefficients drawn from conjoint analysis.	May be function of number, level, and type of attributes in conjoint study. Assumes homogeneity within segments.	Uses customer valuations of product attributes to help define market segments.
7	Conjoint Utilities and Volume Projection	Used within conjoint simulator to estimate volume.	Assumes awareness and distribution levels are known or can be estimated.	Forecast sales for alternative products, designs, prices, and branding strategies.

1   Trial, Repeat, Penetration, and Volume Projections

Test markets and volume projections enable marketers to forecast sales by sampling customer intentions through surveys and market studies. By estimating how many customers will try a new product, and how often they'll make repeat purchases, marketers can establish the basis for such projections.

$$\text{Trial Rate (\%)} = \frac{\text{First-time Triers in Period } t \text{ (\#)}}{\text{Total Population (\#)}}$$

First-time Triers in Period t (#) = Total Population (#) * Trial Rate (%)

Penetration t (#) = [Penetration in t-1 (#) * Repeat Rate Period t (%)] + First-time Triers in Period t (#)

Projection of Sales t (#) = Penetration t (#) * Average Frequency of Purchase (#) * Average Units per Purchase (#)

Projections from customer surveys are especially useful in the early stages of product development and in setting the timing for product launch. Through such projections, customer response can be estimated without the expense of a full product launch.

Purpose: To understand volume projections.

When projecting sales for relatively new products, marketers typically use a system of trial and repeat calculations to anticipate sales in future periods. This works on the principle that everyone buying the product will either be a new customer (a "trier") or a repeat customer. By adding new and repeat customers in any period, we can establish the penetration of a product in the marketplace.

It is challenging, however, to project sales to a large population on the basis of simulated test markets, or even full-fledged regional rollouts. Marketers have developed various solutions to increase the speed and reduce the cost of test marketing, such as stocking a store with products (or mock-ups of new products) or giving customers money to buy the products of their choice. These simulate real shopping conditions but require specific models to estimate full-market volume on the basis of test results. To illustrate the conceptual underpinnings of this process, we offer a general model for making volume projection on the basis of test market results.

Construction

The penetration of a product in a future period can be estimated on the basis of population size, trial rates, and repeat rates.

Trial Rate (%): *The percentage of a defined population that purchases or uses a product for the first time in a given period.*

EXAMPLE: A cable TV company keeps careful records of the names and addresses of its customers. The firm's vice president of marketing notes that 150 households made first-time use of his company's services in March 2009. The company has access to 30,000 households. To calculate the trial rate for March, we can divide 150 by 30,000, yielding 0.5%.

First-time Triers in Period *t* (#): *The number of customers who purchase or use a product or brand for the first time in a given period.*

$$\text{Penetration } t \text{ (\#)} = [\text{Penetration in } t\text{-1 (\#)} * \text{Repeat Rate Period } t \text{ (\%)}] + \text{First-time Triers in Period } t \text{ (\#)}$$

EXAMPLE: A cable TV company started selling a monthly sports package in January. The company typically has an 80% repeat rate and anticipates that this will continue for the new offering. The company sold 10,000 sports packages in January. In February, it expects to add 3,000 customers for the package. On this basis, we can calculate expected penetration for the sports package in February.

$$\text{Penetration in February} = (\text{Penetration January} * \text{Repeat Rate})$$
$$+ \text{First-time Triers in February}$$
$$= (10{,}000 * 80\%) + 3{,}000 = 11{,}000$$

Later that year, in September, the company has 20,000 subscribers. Its repeat rate remains 80%. The company had 18,000 subscribers in August. Management wants to know how many new customers the firm added for its sports package in September:

$$\text{First-time Triers} = \text{Penetration} - \text{Repeat Customers}$$
$$= 20{,}000 - (18{,}000 * 80\%) = 5{,}600$$

From penetration, it is a short step to projections of sales.

$$\textbf{Projection of Sales (\#)} = \textbf{Penetration (\#)} * \textbf{Frequency of Purchase (\#)}$$
$$* \textbf{ Units per Purchase (\#)}$$

Simulated Test Market Results and Volume Projections

TRIAL VOLUME

Trial rates are often estimated on the basis of surveys of potential customers. Typically, these surveys ask respondents whether they will "definitely" or "probably" buy a product. As these are the strongest of several possible responses to questions of purchase intentions, they are sometimes referred to as the "top two boxes." The less favorable responses in a standard five-choice survey include "may or may not buy," "probably won't buy," and "definitely won't buy."

Because not all respondents follow through on their declared purchase intentions, firms often make adjustments to the percentages in the top two boxes in developing sales projections. For example, some marketers estimate that 80% of respondents who say they'll "definitely buy" and 30% of those who say that they'll "probably buy" will in fact purchase a product when given the opportunity.[1] (The adjustment for customers following through is used in the following model.) Although some respondents in the bottom three boxes might buy a product, their number is assumed to be insignificant. By reducing the score for the top two boxes, marketers derive a more realistic estimate of the number of potential customers who will try a product, given the right circumstances. Those circumstances are often shaped by product awareness and availability.

Awareness: Sales projection models include an adjustment for lack of awareness of a product within the target market (see Figure 1). Lack of awareness reduces the trial rate because it excludes some potential customers who might try the product but don't

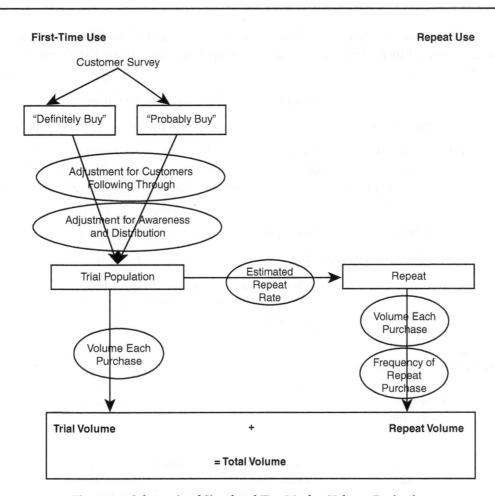

First-Time Use   **Repeat Use**

Figure 1   Schematic of Simulated Test Market Volume Projection

know about it. By contrast, if awareness is 100%, then all potential customers know about the product, and no potential sales are lost due to lack of awareness.

Distribution: Another adjustment to test market trial rates is usually applied—accounting for the estimated availability of the new product. Even survey respondents who say they'll "definitely" try a product are unlikely to do so if they can't find it easily. In making this adjustment, companies typically use an estimated distribution, a percentage of total stores that will stock the new product, such as ACV % distribution.

Adjusted Trial Rate (%) = Trial Rate (%) ∗ Awareness (%) ∗ ACV (%)

After making these modifications, marketers can calculate the number of customers who are expected to try the product, simply by applying the adjusted trial rate to the target population.

$$\textbf{Trial Population (\#) = Target Population (\#)} * \textbf{Adjusted Trial Rate (\%)}$$

Estimated in this way, trial population (#) is identical to penetration (#) in the trial period.

To forecast trial volume, multiply trial population by the projected average number of units of a product that will be bought in each trial purchase. This is often assumed to be one unit because most people will experiment with a single unit of a new product before buying larger quantities.

$$\textbf{Trial Volume (\#) = Trial Population (\#)} * \textbf{Units per Purchase (\#)}$$

Combining all these calculations, the entire formula for trial volume is

$$\textbf{Trial Volume (\#) = Target Population (\#)} * [(80\% * \textbf{Definitely Buy (\#)})$$
$$+ (30\% * \textbf{Probably Buy (\#)}) * \textbf{Awareness (\%)} * \textbf{ACV (\%)}]$$
$$* \textbf{Units per Purchase (\#)}$$

EXAMPLE: The marketing team of an office supply manufacturer has a great idea for a new product—a safety stapler. To sell the idea internally, they want to project the volume of sales they can expect over the stapler's first year. Their customer survey yields the following results (see Table 1).

Table 1   Customer Survey Responses

	% of Customers Responding
Definitely Will Buy	20%
Probably Will Buy	50%
May/May Not Buy	15%
Probably Won't Buy	10%
Definitely Won't Buy	5%
Total	100%

On this basis, the company estimates a trial rate for the new stapler by applying the industry-standard expectation that 80% of "definites" and 30% of "probables" will in fact buy the product if given the opportunity.

$$\text{Trial Rate} = 80\% \text{ of "Definites"} + 30\% \text{ of "Probables"}$$
$$= (80\% * 20\%) + (30\% * 50\%)$$
$$= 31\%$$

Thus, 31% of the population is expected to try the product if they are aware of it and if it is available in stores. The company has a strong advertising presence and a solid distribution network. Consequently, its marketers believe they can obtain an ACV of approximately 60% for the stapler and that they can generate awareness at a similar level. On this basis, they project an adjusted trial rate of 11.16% of the population:

$$\text{Adjusted Trial Rate} = \text{Trial Rate} * \text{Awareness} * \text{ACV}$$
$$= 31\% * 60\% * 60\% = 11.16\%$$

The target population comprises 20 million people. The trial population can be calculated by multiplying this figure by the adjusted trial rate.

$$\text{Trial Population} = \text{Target Population} * \text{Adjusted Trial Rate}$$
$$= 20 \text{ million} * 11.16\% = 2.232 \text{ million}$$

Assuming that each person buys one unit when trying the product, the trial volume will total 2.232 million units.

We can also calculate the trial volume by using the full formula:

$$\text{Trial Volume} = \text{Target Population}$$
$$* [((80\% * \text{Definites}) + (30\% * \text{Probables})) * \text{Awareness} * \text{ACV}]$$
$$* \text{Units per purchase}$$
$$= 20\text{m} * [((80\% * 20\%) + (30\% * 50\%)) * 60\% * 60\%)] * 1$$
$$= 2.232 \text{ million}$$

REPEAT VOLUME

The second part of projected volume concerns the fraction of people who try a product and then repeat their purchase decision. The model for this dynamic uses a single estimated repeat rate to yield the number of customers who are expected to purchase again after their initial trial. In reality, initial repeat rates are often lower than subsequent repeat rates. For example, it is not uncommon for 50% of trial purchasers to make a first repeat purchase, but for 80% of those who purchase a second time to go on to purchase a third time.

Repeat Buyers (#) = Trial Population (#) * Repeat Rate (%)

To calculate the repeat volume, the repeat buyers figure can then be multiplied by an expected volume per purchase among repeat customers and by the number of times these customers are expected to repeat their purchases within the period under consideration.

$$\textbf{Repeat Volume (\#)} = \textbf{Repeat Buyers (\#)} * \textbf{Repeat Unit Volume per Customer (\#)}$$
$$* \textbf{Repeat Occasions (\#)}$$

This calculation yields the total volume that a new product is expected to generate among repeat customers over a specified introductory period. The full formula can be written as

$$\textbf{Repeat Volume (\#)} = [\textbf{Trial Population (\#)} * \textbf{Repeat Rate (\%)}]$$
$$* \textbf{Repeat Unit Volume per Customer (\#)} * \textbf{Repeat Occasions (\#)}$$

EXAMPLE: Continuing the previous office supplies example, the safety stapler has a trial population of 2.232 million. Marketers expect the product to be of sufficient quality to generate a 10% repeat rate in its first year. This will yield 223,200 repeat buyers:

$$\text{Repeat Buyers} = \text{Trial Population} * \text{Repeat Rate}$$
$$= 2.232 \text{ million} * 10\%$$
$$= 223,200$$

On average, the company expects each repeat buyer to purchase on four occasions during the first year. On average, each purchase is expected to comprise two units.

$$\text{Repeat Volume} = \text{Repeat Buyers} * \text{Repeat Unit Volume per Customer} * \text{Repeat Occasions}$$
$$= 223,200 * 2 * 4$$
$$= 1,785,600 \text{ units}$$

This can be represented in the full formula:

$$\text{Repeat Volume (\#)} = [\text{Repeat Rate (\%)} * \text{Trial Population (\#)}]$$
$$* \text{Repeat Volume per Customer (\#)}$$
$$* \text{Repeat Occasions (\#)}$$
$$= (10\% * 2,232,000) * 2 * 4$$
$$= 1,785,600 \text{ units}$$

TOTAL VOLUME

Total volume is the sum of trial volume and repeat volume, as all volume must be sold to either new customers or returning customers.

$$\textbf{Total Volume (\#)} = \textbf{Trial Volume (\#)} + \textbf{Repeat Volume (\#)}$$

To capture total volume in its fully detailed form, we need only combine the previous formulas.

Total Volume (#) = [Target Population * ((0.8 * Definitely Buy + 0.3 * Probably Buy)
* Awareness * ACV) * Units per Trial Purchase]
+ [(Trial Population * Repeat Rate)
* Repeat Volume per Customer * Repeat Occasions]

Example: Total volume in year one for the stapler is the sum of trial volume and repeat volume.

$$\text{Total Volume} = \text{Trial Volume} + \text{Repeat Volume}$$
$$= 2,232,000 + 1,785,600$$
$$= 4,017,600 \text{ Units}$$

A full calculation of this figure and a template for a spreadsheet calculation are presented in Table 2.

Table 2   Volume Projection Spreadsheet

Preliminary Data	Source	
Definitely Will Buy	Customer Survey	20%
Probably Will Buy	Customer Survey	50%
Likely Buyers		
Likely Buyers from Definites	= Definitely Buy * 80%	16%
Likely Buyers from Probables	= Probably Buy * 30%	15%
Trial Rate (%)	Total of Likely Buyers	31%
Marketing Adjustments		
Awareness	Estimated from Marketing Plan	60%
ACV	Estimated from Marketing Plan	60%
Adjusted Trial Rate (%)	= Trial Rate * Awareness * ACV	11.2%
Target Population (#) (thousands)	Marketing Plan Data	20,000
Trial Population (#) (thousands)	= Target Population * Adjusted Trial Rate	2,232

Continues

119

	Table 2 *Continued*	
Preliminary Data	**Source**	
Unit Volume Purchased per Trial (#)	Estimated from Marketing Plan	1
Trial Volume (#) (Thousands)	**= Trial Population * Volume per Trier**	**2,232**
Repeat Rate (%)	Estimated from Marketing Plan	10%
Repeat Buyers (#)	= Repeat Rate * Trial Population	223,200
Avg. Volume per Repeat Purchase (#)	Estimated from Marketing Plan	2
Repeat Purchase Frequency ** (#)	Estimated from Marketing Plan	4
Repeat Volume (Thousands) Frequency	**= Repeat Buyers * Repeat Volume per Purchase * Repeat Purchase**	**1,786**
Total Volume (Thousands)		**4,018**

**Note: The average frequency of repeat purchases per repeat purchaser should be adjusted to reflect the time available for first-time triers to repeat, the purchase cycle (frequency) for the category, and availability. For example, if trial rates are constant over the year, the number of repeat purchases would be about 50% of what it would have been if all had tried on day 1 of the period.

Data Sources, Complications, and Cautions

Sales projections based on test markets will always require the inclusion of key assumptions. In setting these assumptions, marketers face tempting opportunities to make the assumptions fit the desired outcome. Marketers must guard against that temptation and perform sensitivity analysis to establish a range of predictions.

Relatively simple metrics such as trial and repeat rates can be difficult to capture in practice. Although strides have been made in gaining customer data—through customer loyalty cards, for example—it will often be difficult to determine whether customers are new or repeat buyers.

Regarding awareness and distribution: Assumptions concerning the level of public awareness to be generated by launch advertising are fraught with uncertainty. Marketers are advised to ask: What sort of awareness does the product need? What complementary promotions can aid the launch?

Trial and repeat rates are both important. Some products generate strong results in the trial stage but fail to maintain ongoing sales. Consider the following example.

EXAMPLE: Let's compare the safety stapler with a new product, such as an enhanced envelope sealer. The envelope sealer generates less marketing buzz than the stapler but enjoys a greater repeat rate. To predict results for the envelope sealer, we have adapted the data from the safety stapler by reducing the top two box responses by half (reflecting its lower initial enthusiasm) and raising the repeat rate from 10% to 33% (showing stronger product response after use).

At the six-month mark, sales results for the safety stapler (Product A) are superior to those for the envelope sealer (Product B). After one year, sales results for the two products are equal. On a three-year time scale, however, the envelope sealer—with its loyal base of customers—emerges as the clear winner in sales volume (see Figure 2).

The data for the graph is derived as shown in Table 3.

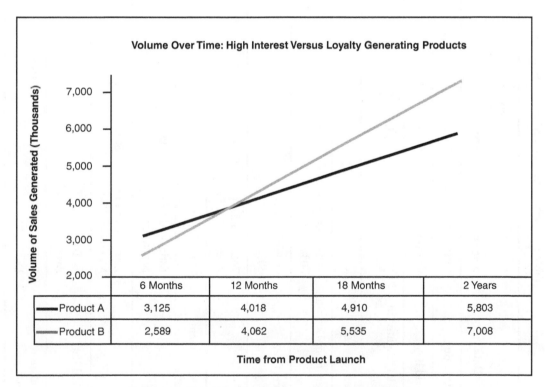

Figure 2   Time Horizon Influences Perceived Results

Table 3 High Initial Interest or Long-Term Loyalty—Results over Time

Preliminary Data	Source	6 Months Prod A	6 Months Prod B	12 Months Prod A	12 Months Prod B	18 Months Prod A	18 Months Prod B	2 Years Prod A	2 Years Prod B
Definitely Will Buy	Customer Survey	20%	10%	20%	10%	20%	10%	20%	10%
Probably Will Buy	Customer Survey	50%	25%	50%	25%	50%	25%	50%	25%
Differences Highlighted in Yellow									
Likely Buyers									
Likely Buyers from Definites	= Definitely Buy * 80%	16%	8%	16%	8%	16%	8%	16%	8%
Likely Buyers from Probables	= Probably Buy * 30%	15%	8%	15%	8%	15%	8%	15%	8%
Trial Rate	Total of Likely Buyers	31%	16%	31%	16%	31%	16%	31%	16%
Marketing Adjustments									
Awareness	Estimated from Marketing Plan	60%	60%	60%	60%	60%	60%	60%	60%
ACV	Estimated from Marketing Plan	60%	60%	60%	60%	60%	60%	60%	60%
Adjusted Trial Rate	= Trial Rate * Awareness * ACV	11.2%	5.6%	11.2%	5.6%	11.2%	5.6%	11.2%	5.6%
Target Population (Thousands)	Marketing Plan Data	20,000	20,000	20,000	20,000	20,000	20,000	20,000	20,000

	Formula								
Trial Population (Thousands)	= Target Population * Adjusted Trial Rate	2,232	1,116	2,232	1,116	2,232	1,116	2,232	1,116
Unit Volume Purchased at Trial	Estimated from Marketing Plan	1	1	1	1	1	1	1	1
Trial Volume (Thousands)	= Trial Population * Volume bought	2,232	1,116	2,232	1,116	2,232	1,116	2,232	1,116
Repeat Rate	Estimated from Marketing Plan	10%	33%	10%	33%	10%	33%	10%	33%
Repeat Buyers	= Repeat Rate * Trial Population	223.20	368.28	223.20	368.28	223.20	368.28	223.20	368.28
Repeat Purchase Unit Volume	Estimated from Marketing Plan	2	2	2	2	2	2	2	2
Number of Repeat Purchases	Estimated from Marketing Plan	2	2	4	4	6	6	8	8
Repeat Volume (Thousands)	= Repeat Buyers * Repeat Volume * Number of Repeat Purchases	893	1,473	1,786	2,946	2,678	4,419	3,571	5,892
Total Volume		3,125	2,589	4,018	4,062	4,910	5,535	5,803	7,008

Repeating and Trying: Some models assume that customers, after they stop repeating purchases, are lost and do not return. However, customers may be acquired, lost, reacquired, and lost again. In general, the trial-repeat model is best suited to projecting sales over the first few periods. Other means of predicting volume include share of requirements and penetration metrics. Those approaches may be preferable for products that lack reliable repeat rates.

	Market Size	Penetration Share	Share of Requirements	Heavy Usage Index	Market Share	Units Sold
New Product	1,000,000	5%	80%	1.2	4.8%	48,000
Source	Estimated	Estimated	Estimated	Estimated	Penetration Share * Share of Requirements * Heavy Usage Index	Share * Market Size

Related Metrics and Concepts

Ever-Tried: This is slightly different from trial in that it measures the percentage of the target population that has "ever" (in any previous period) purchased or consumed the product under study. Ever-tried is a cumulative measure and can never add up to more than 100%. Trial, by contrast, is an incremental measure. It indicates the percentage of the population that tries the product for the first time in a given period. Even here, however, there is potential for confusion. If a customer stops buying a product but tries it again six months later, some marketers will categorize that individual as a returning purchaser, others as a new customer. By the latter definition, if individuals can "try" a product more than once, then the sum of all "triers" could equal more than the total population. To avoid confusion, when reviewing a set of data, it's best to clarify the definitions behind it.

Variations on Trial: Certain scenarios reduce the barriers to trial but entail a lower commitment by the customer than a standard purchase.

- **Forced Trial:** No other similar product is available. For example, many people who prefer Pepsi-Cola have "tried" Coca-Cola in restaurants that only serve the latter, and vice versa.

- **Discounted Trial:** Consumers buy a new product but at a substantially reduced price.

Forced and discounted trials are usually associated with lower repeat rates than trials made through volitional purchase.

Evoked Set: The set of brands that consumers name in response to questions about which brands they consider (or might consider) when making a purchase in a specific category. Evoked Sets for breakfast cereals, for example, are often quite large, while those for coffee may be smaller.

Number of New Products: The number of products introduced for the first time in a specific time period.

Revenue from New Products: Usually expressed as the percentage of sales generated by products introduced in the current period or, at times, in the most recent three to five periods.

Margin on New Products: The dollar or percentage profit margin on new products. This can be measured separately but does not differ mathematically from margin calculations.

Company Profit from New Products: The percentage of company profits that is derived from new products. In working with this figure, it is important to understand how "new product" is defined.

Target Market Fit: Of customers purchasing a product, target market fit represents the percentage who belong in the demographic, psychographic, or other descriptor set for that item. Target market fit is useful in evaluating marketing strategies. If a large percentage of customers for a product belongs to groups that have not previously been targeted, marketers may reconsider their targets—and their allocation of marketing spending.

2 Growth: Percentage and CAGR

There are two common measures of growth. Year-on-year percentage growth uses the prior year as a base for expressing percentage change from one year to the next. Over longer periods of time, compound annual growth rate (CAGR) is a generally accepted metric for average growth rates.

$$\textbf{Year-on-Year Growth (\%)} = \frac{\textbf{Value (\$,\#,\%)}\ t - \textbf{Value (\$,\#,\%)}\ t - 1}{\textbf{Value (\$,\#,\%)}\ t - 1}$$

Compound Annual Growth Rate, or $= \{[\textbf{Ending Value (\$,\#,\%)/Starting Value (\$,\#,\%)}]$
CAGR (%) $\wedge\ [\textbf{1/Number of Years (\#)}]\} - 1$

Same stores growth = Growth calculated only on the basis of stores that were fully established in both the prior and current periods.

Purpose: To measure growth.

Growth is the aim of virtually all businesses. Indeed, perceptions of the success or failure of many enterprises are based on assessments of their growth. Measures of year-on-year growth, however, are complicated by two factors:

1. Changes over time in the base from which growth is measured. Such changes might include increases in the number of stores, markets, or salespeople generating sales. This issue is addressed by using "same store" measures (or corollary measures for markets, sales personnel, and so on).

2. Compounding of growth over multiple periods. For example, if a company achieves 30% growth in one year, but its results remain unchanged over the two subsequent years, this would not be the same as 10% growth in each of three years. CAGR, the compound annual growth rate, is a metric that addresses this issue.

Construction

Percentage growth is the central plank of year-on-year analysis. It addresses the question: What has the company achieved this year, compared to last year? Dividing the results for the current period by the results for the prior period will yield a comparative figure. Subtracting one from the other will highlight the increase or decrease between periods. When evaluating comparatives, one might say that results in Year 2 were, for example, 110% of those in Year 1. To convert this figure to a growth rate, one need only subtract 100%.

The periods considered are often years, but any time frame can be chosen.

$$\text{Year-on-Year Growth (\%)} = \frac{\text{Value (\$,\#,\%)} \, t - \text{Value (\$,\#,\%)} \, t - 1}{\text{Value (\$,\#,\%)} \, t - 1}$$

EXAMPLE: Ed's is a small deli, which has had great success in its second year of operation. Revenues in Year 2 are $570,000, compared with $380,000 in Year 1. Ed calculates his second-year sales results to be 150% of first-year revenues, indicating a growth rate of 50%.

$$\text{Year-on-Year Sales Growth} = \frac{\$570,000 - \$380,000}{\$380,000} = 50\%$$

Same Stores Growth: This metric is at the heart of retail analysis. It enables marketers to analyze results from stores that have been in operation for the entire period under consideration. The logic is to eliminate the stores that have not been open for the full period to ensure comparability. Thus, same stores growth sheds light on the effectiveness with which equivalent resources were used in the period under study versus the prior period. In retail, modest same stores growth and high general growth rates would indicate a rapidly expanding organization, in which growth is driven by investment. When both same stores growth and general growth are strong, a company can be viewed as effectively using its existing base of stores.

EXAMPLE: A small retail chain in Bavaria posts impressive percentage growth figures, moving from €58 million to €107 million in sales (84% growth) from one year to the next. Despite this dynamic growth, however, analysts cast doubt on the firm's business model, warning that its same stores growth measure suggests that its concept is failing (see Table 4).

Table 4   Revenue of a Bavarian Chain Store

Store	Opened	Revenue First Year (m)	Revenue Second Year (m)
A	Year 1	€10	€9
B	Year 1	€19	€20
C	Year 1	€20	€15
D	Year 1	€9	€11
E	Year 2	n/a	€52
		€58	€107

Same stores growth excludes stores that were not open at the beginning of the first year under consideration. For simplicity, we assume that stores in this example were opened on the first day of Years 1 and 2, as appropriate. On this basis, same stores revenue in Year 2 would be €55 million—that is, the €107 million total for the year, less the €52 million generated by the newly opened Store E. This adjusted figure can be entered into the same stores growth formula:

$$\text{Same Stores Growth} = \frac{(\text{Stores A-D Sales Year 2}) - (\text{Stores A-D Sales Year 1})}{\$\text{Stores A-D Sales Year 1}}$$

$$= \frac{€55m - €58m}{€58} = -5\%$$

As demonstrated by its negative same stores growth figure, sales growth at this firm has been fueled entirely by a major investment in a new store. This suggests serious doubts about its existing store concept. It also raises a question: Did the new store "cannibalize" existing store sales? (See the next section for cannibalization metrics.)

Compounding Growth, Value at Future Period: By compounding, managers adjust growth figures to account for the iterative effect of improvement. For example, 10% growth in each of two successive years would not be the same as a total of 20% growth over the two-year period. The reason: Growth in the second year is built upon the elevated base achieved in the first. Thus, if sales run $100,000 in Year 0 and rise by 10% in Year 1, then Year 1 sales come to $110,000. If sales rise by a further 10% in Year 2, however, then Year 2 sales do not total $120,000. Rather, they total $110,000 + (10% * $110,000) = $121,000.

The compounding effect can be easily modeled in spreadsheet packages, which enable you to work through the compounding calculations one year at a time. To calculate a value in Year 1, multiply the corresponding Year 0 value by one plus the growth rate. Then use the value in Year 1 as a new base and multiply it by one plus the growth rate to determine the corresponding value for Year 2. Repeat this process through the required number of years.

EXAMPLE: Over a three-year period, $100 dollars, compounded at a 10% growth rate, yields $133.10.

Year 0 to Year 1 $100 + 10% Growth (that is, $10) = $110

Year 1 to Year 2 $110 + 10% Growth ($11) = $121

Year 2 to Year 3 $121 + 10% Growth ($12.10) = $133.10

There is a mathematical formula that generates this effect. It multiplies the value at the beginning—that is, in Year 0—by one plus the growth rate to the power of the number of years over which that growth rate applies.

Value in Future Period ($,#,%) = Current Value ($,#,%) * [(1 + CAGR (%)) ^ Number of Periods (#)]

EXAMPLE: Using the formula, we can calculate the impact of 10% annual growth over a period of three years. The value in Year 0 is $100. The number of years is 3. The growth rate is 10%.

Value in Future Period = Value in Year 0 $*$ (1 + Growth Rate) $\wedge$ Number of Years

= $100 $*$ (100% + 10%) $\wedge$ 3

= $100 $*$ 133.1% = $133.10

Compound Annual Growth Rate (CAGR): The CAGR is a constant year-on-year growth rate applied over a period of time. Given starting and ending values, and the length of the period involved, it can be calculated as follows:

CAGR (%) = {[Ending Value ($,#)/Starting Value ($,#)] $\wedge$ 1/Number of Periods (#)} $-$ 1

EXAMPLE: Let's assume we have the results of the compounding growth observed in the previous example, but we don't know what the growth rate was. We know that the starting value was $100, the ending value was $133.10, and the number of years was 3. We can simply enter these numbers into the CAGR formula to derive the CAGR.

CAGR = [(Ending Value/Starting Value) $\wedge$ (1/Number of Years)] $-$ 1

= [($133.10/$100) $\wedge$ 1/3] $-$ 1

= [1.331 (The Increase) $\wedge$ 1/3 (Cube Root)] $-$ 1 = 1.1 $-$ 1 = 10%

Thus, we determine that the growth rate was 10%.

Data Sources, Complications, and Cautions

Percentage growth is a useful measure as part of a package of metrics. It can be deceiving, however, if not adjusted for the addition of such factors as stores, salespeople, or products, or for expansion into new markets. "Same store" sales, and similar adjustments for other factors, tell us how effectively a company uses comparable resources. These very adjustments, however, are limited by their deliberate omission of factors that weren't in operation for the full period under study. Adjusted figures must be reviewed in tandem with measures of total growth.

Related Metrics and Concepts

Life Cycle: Marketers view products as passing through four stages of development:

- **Introductory:** Small markets not yet growing fast.

- **Growth:** Larger markets with faster growth rates.

- **Mature:** Largest markets but little or no growth.

- **Decline:** Variable size markets with negative growth rates.

This is a rough classification. No generally accepted rules exist for making these classifications.

3   Cannibalization Rates and Fair Share Draw

Cannibalization is the reduction in sales (units or dollars) of a firm's existing products due to the introduction of a new product. The cannibalization rate is generally calculated as the percentage of a new product's sales that represents a loss of sales (attributable to the introduction of the new entrant) of a specific existing product or products.

$$\text{Cannibalization Rate (\%)} = \frac{\text{Sales Lost from Existing Products (\#,\$)}}{\text{Sales of New Product (\#,\$)}}$$

Cannibalization rates represent an important factor in the assessment of new product strategies.

Fair share draw constitutes an assumption or expectation that a new product will capture sales (in unit or dollar terms) from existing products in proportion to the market shares of those existing products.

Cannibalization is a familiar business dynamic. A company with a successful product that has strong market share is faced by two conflicting ideas. The first is that it wants to maximize profits on its existing product line, concentrating on the current strengths that promise success in the short term. The second idea is that this company—or its competitors—may identify opportunities for new products that better fit the needs of certain segments. If the company introduces a new product in this field, however, it may "cannibalize" the sales of its existing products. That is, it may weaken the sales of its proven, already successful product line. If the company declines to introduce the new product, however, it will leave itself vulnerable to competitors who *will* launch such a product, and may thereby capture sales and market share from the company. Often, when new segments are emerging and there are advantages to being early to market, the key factor becomes timing. If a company launches its new product too early, it may lose too much income on its existing line; if it launches too late, it may miss the new opportunity altogether.

Cannibalization: *A market phenomenon in which sales of one product are achieved at the expense of some of a firm's other products.*

The cannibalization rate is the percentage of sales of a new product that come from a specific set of existing products.

$$\text{Cannibalization Rate (\%)} = \frac{\text{Sales Lost from Existing Products (\#,\$)}}{\text{Sales of New Product (\#,\$)}}$$

EXAMPLE: A company has a single product that sold 10 units in the previous period. The company plans to introduce a new product that will sell 5 units with a cannibalization rate of 40%. Thus 40% of the sales of the new product (40% * 5 units = 2 units) come at the expense of the old product. Therefore, after cannibalization, the company can expect to sell 8 units of the old product and 5 of the new product, or 13 units in total.

Any company considering the introduction of a new product should confront the potential for cannibalization. A firm would do well to ensure that the amount of cannibalization is estimated beforehand to provide an idea of how the product line's contribution as a whole will change. If performed properly, this analysis will tell a company whether overall profits can be expected to increase or decrease with the introduction of the new product line.

EXAMPLE: Lois sells umbrellas on a small beach where she is the only provider. Her financials for last month were as follows:

Umbrella Sales Price:	$20
Variable Cost per Umbrella:	$10
Umbrella Contribution per Unit:	$10
Total Unit Sales per Month:	100
Total Monthly Contribution:	**$1,000**

Next month, Lois plans to introduce a bigger, lighter-weight umbrella called the "Big Block." Projected financials for the Big Block are as follows:

Big Block Sales Price:	$30
Variable Cost per Big Block:	$15
Big Block Contribution per Unit:	$15
Total Unit Sales per Month (Big Block):	50
Total Monthly Contribution (Big Block):	**$750**

If there is no cannibalization, Lois thus expects her total monthly contribution will be $1,000 + $750, or $1,750. Upon reflection, however, Lois thinks that the unit cannibalization rate for Big Block will be 60%. Her projected financials after accounting for cannibalization are therefore as follows:

Big Block Unit Sales:	50
Cannibalization Rate:	60%
Regular Umbrella Sales Lost:	50 * 60% = 30

New Regular Umbrella Sales:	$100 - 30 = 70$
New Total Contribution (Regular):	70 Units * $10 Contribution per Unit = $700
Big Block Total Contribution:	50 Units * $15 Contribution per Unit = $750
Lois' Total Monthly Contribution:	**$1,450**

Under these projections, total umbrella sales will increase from 100 to 120, and total contribution will increase from $1,000 to $1,450. Lois will replace 30 regular sales with 30 Big Block sales and gain an extra $5 unit contribution on each. She will also sell 20 more umbrellas than she sold last month and gain $15 unit contribution on each.

In this scenario, Lois was in the enviable position of being able to cannibalize a lower-margin product with a higher-margin one. Sometimes, however, new products carry unit contributions lower than those of existing products. In these instances, cannibalization reduces overall profits for the firm.

An alternative way to account for cannibalization is to use a weighted contribution margin. In the previous example, the weighted contribution margin would be the unit margin Lois receives for Big Block after accounting for cannibalization. Because each Big Block contributes $15 directly and cannibalizes the $10 contribution generated by regular umbrellas at a 60% rate, Big Block's weighted contribution margin is $15 − (0.6 * $10), or $9 per unit. Because Lois expects to sell 50 Big Blocks, her total contribution is projected to increase by 50 * $9, or $450. This is consistent with our previous calculations.

If the introduction of Big Block requires some fixed marketing expenditure, then the $9 weighted margin can be used to find the break-even number of Big Block sales required to justify that expenditure. For example, if the launch of Big Block requires $360 in one-time marketing costs, then Lois needs to sell $360/$9, or 40 Big Blocks to break even on that expenditure.

If a new product has a margin lower than that of the existing product that it cannibalizes, and if its cannibalization rate is high enough, then its weighted contribution margin might be negative. In that case, company earnings will decrease with each unit of the new product sold.

Cannibalization refers to a dynamic in which one product of a firm takes share from one or more other products of *the same firm*. When a product takes sales from a competitor's product, that is not cannibalization . . . though managers sometimes incorrectly state that their new products are "cannibalizing" sales of a competitor's goods.

Though it is not cannibalization, the impact of a new product on the sales of competing goods is an important consideration in a product launch. One simple assumption about how the introduction of a new product might affect the sales of existing products is called "fair share draw."

Fair Share Draw: *The assumption that a new product will capture sales (in unit or dollar terms) from existing products in direct proportion to the market shares held by those existing products.*

EXAMPLE: Three rivals compete in the youth fashion market in a small town. Their sales and market shares for last year appear in the following table.

Firm	Sales	Share
Threadbare	$500,000	50%
Too Cool for School	$300,000	30%
Tommy Hitchhiker	$200,000	20%
Total	$1,000,000	100%

A new entrant is expected to enter the market in the coming year and to generate $300,000 in sales. Two-thirds of those sales are expected to come at the expense of the three established competitors. Under an assumption of fair share draw, how much will each firm sell next year?

If the new firm takes two-thirds of its sales from existing competitors, then this "capture" of sales will total (2/3) * $300,000, or $200,000. Under fair share draw, the breakdown of that $200,000 will be proportional to the shares of the current competitors. Thus 50% of the $200,000 will come from Threadbare, 30% from Too Cool, and 20% from Tommy. The following table shows the projected sales and market shares next year of the four competitors under the fair share draw assumption:

Firm	Sales	Share
Threadbare	$400,000	36.36%
Too Cool for School	$240,000	21.82%
Tommy Hitchhiker	$160,000	14.55%
New Entrant	$300,000	27.27%
Total	$1,100,000	100%

■───

Notice that the new entrant expands the market by $100,000, an amount equal to the sales of the new entrant that *do not* come at the expense of existing competitors. Notice also that under fair share draw, the relative shares of the existing competitors remain unchanged. For example, Threadbare's share, relative to the total of the original three competitors, is 36.36/(36.36 + 21.82 + 14.55), or 50%—equal to its share before the entry of the new competitor.

───

Data Sources, Complications, and Cautions

As noted previously, in cannibalization, one of a firm's products takes sales from one or more of *that* firm's other products. Sales taken from the products of competitors are not "cannibalized" sales, though some managers label them as such.

Cannibalization rates depend on how the features, pricing, promotion, and distribution of the new product compare to those of a firm's existing products. The greater the similarity of their respective marketing strategies, the higher the cannibalization rate is likely to be.

Although cannibalization is always an issue when a firm launches a new product that competes with its established line, this dynamic is particularly damaging to the firm's profitability when a low-margin entrant captures sales from the firm's higher-margin offerings. In such cases, the new product's weighted contribution margin can be negative. Even when cannibalization rates are significant, however, and even if the net effect on the bottom line is negative, it may be wise for a firm to proceed with a new product if management believes that the original line is losing its competitive strength. The following example is illustrative.

───────

EXAMPLE: A producer of powdered-milk formula has an opportunity to introduce a new, improved formula. The new formula has certain attributes not found in the firm's existing products. Due to higher costs, however, it will carry a contribution margin of only $8, compared with the $10 margin of the established formula. Analysis suggests that the unit cannibalization rate of the new formula will be 90% in its initial year. If the firm expects to sell 300 units of the new formula in its first year, should it proceed with the introduction?

Analysis shows that the new formula will generate $8 * 300, or $2,400 in direct contribution. Cannibalization, however, will reduce contribution from the established line by $10 * 0.9 * 300, or $2,700. Thus, the company's overall contribution will decline by $300 with the introduction of the new formula. (Note also that the weighted unit margin

■

for the new product is −$1.) This simple analysis suggests that the new formula should not be introduced.

The following table, however, contains the results of a more detailed four-year analysis. Reflected in this table are management's beliefs that without the new formula, sales of the regular formula will decline to 700 units in Year 4. In addition, unit sales of the new formula are expected to increase to 600 in Year 4, while cannibalization rates decline to 60%.

	Year 1	Year 2	Year 3	Year 4	Total
Unit Sales of Regular Formula *Without* New Product Launch	1,000	900	800	700	3,400
		—		—	
Unit Sales of New Formula	300	400	500	600	1,800
Cannibalization Rate	90%	80%	70%	60%	—
Unit Sales of Regular Formula *with* New Product Launch	730	580	450	340	2,100

Without the new formula, total four-year contribution is projected as $10 * 3,400, or $34,000. With the new formula, total contribution is projected as ($8 * 1,800) + ($10 * 2,100), or $35,400. Although forecast contribution is lower in Year 1 with the new formula than without it, total four-year contribution is projected to be higher with the new product due to increases in new-formula sales and decreases in the cannibalization rate.

4   Brand Equity Metrics

Brand equity is strategically crucial, but famously difficult to quantify. Many experts have developed tools to analyze this asset, but there's no universally accepted way to measure it. In this section, we'll consider the following techniques to gain insight in this area:

Brand Equity Ten (Aaker)

Brand Asset® Valuator (Young & Rubicam)

Brand Equity Index (Moran)

Brand Valuation Model (Interbrand)

Purpose: To measure the value of a brand.

A brand encompasses the name, logo, image, and perceptions that identify a product, service, or provider in the minds of customers. It takes shape in advertising, packaging, and other marketing communications, and becomes a focus of the relationship with consumers. In time, a brand comes to embody a promise about the goods it identifies— a promise about quality, performance, or other dimensions of value, which can influence consumers' choices among competing products. When consumers trust a brand and find it relevant, they may select the offerings associated with that brand over those of competitors, even at a premium price. When a brand's promise extends beyond a particular product, its owner may leverage it to enter new markets. For all these reasons, a brand can hold tremendous value, known as *brand equity*.

Yet this value can be remarkably difficult to measure. At a corporate level, when one company buys another, marketers might analyze the goodwill component of the purchase price to shed light on the value of the brands acquired. As goodwill represents the excess paid for a firm—beyond the value of its tangible, measurable assets, and as a company's brands constitute important intangible assets—the goodwill figure may provide a useful indicator of the value of a portfolio of brands. Of course, a company's brands are rarely the only intangible assets acquired in such a transaction. Goodwill more frequently encompasses intellectual property and other intangibles in addition to brand. The value of intangibles, as estimated by firm valuations (sales or share prices), is also subject to economic cycles, investor "exuberance," and other influences that are difficult to separate from the intrinsic value of the brand.

From a consumer's perspective, the value of a brand might be the amount she would be willing to pay for merchandise that carries the brand's name, over and above the price she'd pay for identical unbranded goods.[2] Marketers strive to estimate this premium in order to gain insight into brand equity. Here again, however, they encounter daunting complexities, as individuals vary not only in their awareness of different brands, but in the criteria by which they judge them, the evaluations they make, and the degree to which those opinions guide their purchase behavior.

Theoretically, a marketer might aggregate these preferences across an entire population to estimate the total premium its members would pay for goods of a certain brand. Even that, however, wouldn't fully capture brand equity. What's more, the value of a brand encompasses not only the premium a customer will pay for each unit of merchandise associated with that brand, but also the incremental volume it generates. A successful brand will shift outward the demand curve for its goods or services; that is, it not only will enable a provider to charge a higher price (P' rather than P, as seen in Figure 3), but it will also sell an increased quantity (Q' rather than Q). Thus, brand equity in this example can be viewed as the difference between the revenue with the brand (P' × Q') and the revenue without the brand (P × Q)—depicted as the shaded area in Figure 3.

(Of course, this example focuses on revenue, when, in fact, it is profit or present value of profits that matters more.)

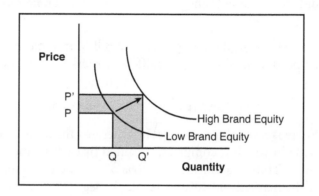

Figure 3   Brand Equity—Outward Shift of Demand Curve

In practice, of course, it's difficult to measure a demand curve, and few marketers do so. Because brands are crucial assets, however, both marketers and academic researchers have devised means to contemplate their value. David Aaker, for example, tracks 10 attributes of a brand to assess its strength. Bill Moran has formulated a brand equity index that can be calculated as the product of effective market share, relative price, and customer retention. Kusum Ailawadi and her colleagues have refined this calculation, suggesting that a truer estimate of a brand's value might be derived by multiplying the Moran index by the dollar volume of the market in which it competes. Young & Rubicam, a marketing communications agency, has developed a tool called the Brand Asset Valuator©, which measures a brand's power on the basis of differentiation, relevance, esteem, and knowledge. An even more theoretical conceptualization of brand equity is the difference of the firm value with and without the brand. If you find it difficult to imagine the firm without its brand, then you can appreciate how difficult it is to quantify brand equity. Interbrand, a brand strategy agency, draws upon its own model to separate tangible product value from intangible brand value and uses the latter to rank the top 100 global brands each year. Finally, conjoint analysis can shed light on a brand's value because it enables marketers to measure the impact of that brand on customer preference, treating it as one among many attributes that consumers trade off in making purchase decisions (see section 5).

Construction

Brand Equity Ten (Aaker): David Aaker, a marketing professor and brand consultant, highlights 10 attributes of a brand that can be used to assess its strength. These include Differentiation, Satisfaction or Loyalty, Perceived Quality, Leadership or Popularity, Perceived Value, Brand Personality, Organizational Associations, Brand Awareness,

Market Share, and Market Price and Distribution Coverage. Aaker doesn't weight the attributes or combine them in an overall score, as he believes any weighting would be arbitrary and would vary among brands and categories. Rather, he recommends tracking each attribute separately.

Brand Equity Index (Moran): Marketing executive Bill Moran has derived an index of brand equity as the product of three factors: Effective Market Share, Relative Price, and Durability.

Brand Equity Index (I) = Effective Market Share (%) * Relative Price (I) * Durability (%)

Effective Market Share is a weighted average. It represents the sum of a brand's market shares in all segments in which it competes, weighted by each segment's proportion of that brand's total sales. Thus, if a brand made 70% of its sales in Segment A, in which it had a 50% share of the market, and 30% of its sales in Segment B, in which it had a 20% share, its Effective Market Share would be $(0.7 * 0.5) + (0.3 * 0.2) = 0.35 + 0.06 = 0.41$, or 41%.

Relative Price is a ratio. It represents the price of goods sold under a given brand, divided by the average price of comparable goods in the market. For example, if goods associated with the brand under study sold for $2.50 per unit, while competing goods sold for an average of $2.00, that brand's Relative Price would be 1.25, and it would be said to command a price premium. Conversely, if the brand's goods sold for $1.50, versus $2.00 for the competition, its Relative Price would be 0.75, placing it at a discount to the market. Note that this measure of relative price is not the same as dividing the brand price by the market average price. It does have the advantage that, unlike the latter, the calculated value is not affected by the market share of the firm or its competitors.

Durability is a measure of customer retention or loyalty. It represents the percentage of a brand's customers who will continue to buy goods under that brand in the following year.

EXAMPLE: ILLI is a tonic drink that focuses on two geographic markets—eastern and western U.S. metropolitan areas. In the western market, which accounts for 60% of ILLI's sales, the drink has a 30% share of the market. In the East, where ILLI makes the remaining 40% of its sales, it has a 50% share of the market.

Effective Market Share is equal to the sum of ILLI's shares of the segments, weighted by the percentage of total brand sales represented by each.

$$West = 30\% * 60\% = 0.18$$

$$East = 50\% * 40\% = 0.20$$

$$\textbf{Effective Market Share} = 0.38$$

The average price for tonic drinks is $2.00, but ILLI enjoys a premium. It generally sells for $2.50, yielding a Relative Price of $2.50 / $2.00, or 1.25.

Half of the people who purchase ILLI this year are expected to repeat next year, generating a Durability figure of 0.5. (See section 1 for a definition of repeat rates.)

With this information, ILLI's Brand Equity Index can be calculated as follows:

Brand Equity = Effective Market Share * Relative Price * Durability = 0.38 * 1.25 * 0.5

$$= 0.2375$$

Clearly, marketers can expect to encounter interactions among the three factors behind a Brand Equity Index. If they raise the price of a brand's goods, for example, they may increase its Relative Price but reduce its Effective Market Share and Durability. Would the overall effect be positive for the brand? By estimating the Brand Equity Index before and after the price increase under consideration, marketers may gain insight into that question.

Notice that two of the factors behind this index, Effective Market Share and Relative Price, draw upon the axes of a demand curve (quantity and price). In constructing his index, Moran has taken those two factors and combined them, through year-to-year retention, with the dimension of time.

Ailawadi, et al suggested that the equity index of a brand can be enhanced by multiplying it by the dollar volume of the market in which the brand competes, generating a better estimate of its value. Ailawadi also contends that the equity of a brand is better captured by its overall revenue premium (relative to generic goods) rather than its price per unit alone, as the revenue figure incorporates both price and quantity and so reflects a jump from one demand curve to another rather than a movement along a single curve.

Brand Asset Valuator (Young & Rubicam): Young & Rubicam, a marketing communications agency, has developed the Brand Asset Valuator, a tool to diagnose the power and value of a brand. In using it, the agency surveys consumers' perspectives along four dimensions:

- **Differentiation:** The defining characteristics of the brand and its distinctiveness relative to competitors.

- **Relevance:** The appropriateness and connection of the brand to a given consumer.

- **Esteem:** Consumers' respect for and attraction to the brand.

- **Knowledge:** Consumers' awareness of the brand and understanding of what it represents.

Young & Rubicam maintains that these criteria reveal important factors behind brand strength and market dynamics. For example, although powerful brands score high on all four dimensions, growing brands may earn higher grades for Differentiation and Relevance, relative to Knowledge and Esteem. Fading brands often show the reverse pattern, as they're widely known and respected but may be declining toward commoditization or irrelevance (see Figure 4).

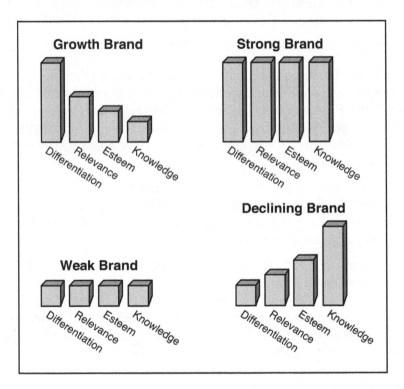

Figure 4   Young & Rubicam Brand Asset Valuator Patterns of Brand Equity

The Brand Asset Valuator is a proprietary tool, but the concepts behind it have broad appeal. Many marketers apply these concepts by conducting independent research and exercising judgment about their own brands relative to the competition. Leon Ramsellar[3] of Philips Consumer Electronics, for example, has reported using four key measures in evaluating brand equity and offered sample questions for assessing them.

- **Uniqueness:** Does this product offer something new to me?

- **Relevance:** Is this product relevant for me?

- **Attractiveness:** Do I want this product?

- **Credibility:** Do I believe in the product?

Clearly Ramsellar's list is not the same as Y&R's BAV, but the similarity of the first two factors is hard to miss.

Brand Valuation Model (Interbrand): Interbrand, a brand strategy agency, draws upon financial results and projections in its own model for brand valuation. It reviews a company's financial statements, analyzes its market dynamics and the role of brand in income generation, and separates those earnings attributable to tangible assets (capital, product, packaging, and so on) from the residual that can be ascribed to a brand. It then forecasts future earnings and discounts these on the basis of brand strength and risk. The agency estimates brand value on this basis and tabulates a yearly list of the 100 most valuable global brands.

Conjoint Analysis: Marketers use conjoint analysis to measure consumers' preference for various attributes of a product, service, or provider, such as features, design, price, or location (see section 5). By including brand and price as two of the attributes under consideration, they can gain insight into consumers' valuation of a brand—that is, their willingness to pay a premium for it.

Data Sources, Complications, and Cautions

The methods described previously represent experts' best attempts to place a value on a complex and intangible entity. Almost all of the metrics in this book are relevant to brand equity along one dimension or another.

Related Metrics and Concepts

Brand strategy is a broad field and includes several concepts that at first may appear to be measurable. Strictly speaking, however, brand strategy is not a metric.

Brand Identity: This is the marketer's vision of an ideal brand—the company's goal for perception of that brand by its target market. All physical, emotional, visual, and verbal messages should be directed toward realization of that goal, including name, logo, signature, and other marketing communications. Brand Identity, however, is not stated in quantifiable terms.

Brand Position and **Brand Image:** These refer to consumers' actual perceptions of a brand, often relative to its competition. Brand Position is frequently measured along product dimensions that can be mapped in multi-dimensional space. If measured consistently over time, these dimensions may be viewed as metrics—as coordinates on a perceptual map.

Product Differentiation: This is one of the most frequently used terms in marketing, but it has no universally agreed-upon definition. More than mere "difference," it generally refers to distinctive attributes of a product that generate increased customer preference or demand. These are often difficult to view quantitatively because they may be actual or perceived, as well as non-monotonic. In other words, although certain attributes such as price can be quantified and follow a linear preference model (that is, either more or less is always better), others can't be analyzed numerically or may fall into a sweet spot, outside of which neither more nor less would be preferred (the spiciness of a food, for example). For all these reasons, Product Differentiation is hard to analyze as a metric and has been criticized as a "meaningless term."

Additional Citations

Simon, Julian, "Product Differentiation": A Meaningless Term and an Impossible Concept, *Ethics*, Vol. 79, No. 2 (Jan., 1969), pp. 131-138. Published by The University of Chicago Press.

5   Conjoint Utilities and Consumer Preference

Conjoint utilities measure consumer preference for an attribute level and then—by combining the valuations of multiple attributes—measure preference for an overall choice. Measures are generally made on an individual basis, although this analysis can also be performed on a segment level. In the frozen pizza market, for example, conjoint utilities can be used to determine how much a customer values superior taste (one attribute) versus paying extra for premium cheese (a second attribute).

Conjoint utilities can also play a role in analyzing compensatory and non-compensatory decisions. Weaknesses in compensatory factors can be made up in other attributes. A weakness in a non-compensatory factor cannot be overcome by other strengths.

Conjoint analysis can be useful in determining what customers really want and—when price is included as an attribute—what they'll pay for it. In launching new products, marketers find such analyses useful for achieving a deeper understanding of the values that customers place on various product attributes. Throughout product management, conjoint utilities can help marketers focus their efforts on the attributes of greatest importance to customers.

━━━ ■

Purpose: To understand what customers want.

Conjoint analysis is a method used to estimate customers' preferences, based on how customers weight the attributes on which a choice is made. The premise of conjoint analysis is that a customer's preference between product options can be broken into a set of attributes that are weighted to form an overall evaluation. Rather than asking people directly what they want and why, in conjoint analysis, marketers ask people about their overall preferences for a set of choices described on their attributes and then decompose those into the component dimensions and weights underlying them. A model can be developed to compare sets of attributes to determine which represents the most appealing bundle of attributes for customers.

Conjoint analysis is a technique commonly used to assess the attributes of a product or service that are important to targeted customers and to assist in the following:

- Product design
- Advertising copy
- Pricing
- Segmentation
- Forecasting

Construction

> **Conjoint Analysis:** *A method of estimating customers by assessing the overall preferences customers assign to alternative choices.*

An individual's preference can be expressed as the total of his or her baseline preferences for any choice, plus the partworths (relative values) for that choice expressed by the individual.

In linear form, this can be represented by the following formula:

Conjoint Preference Linear Form (I) = [Partworth of Attribute1 to Individual (I) * Attribute Level (1)] + [Partworth of Attribute2 to Individual (I) * Attribute Level (2)] + [Partworth of Attribute3 to Individual (I) * Attribute Level (3)] + etc.

───────────

EXAMPLE: Two attributes of a cell phone, its price and its size, are ranked through conjoint analysis, yielding the results shown in Table 5.

This could be read as follows:

Table 5   Conjoint Analysis: Price and Size of a Cell Phone

Attribute	Rank	Partworth
Price	$100	0.9
Price	$200	0.1
Price	$300	−1
Size	Small	0.7
Size	Medium	−0.1
Size	Large	−0.6

A small phone for $100 has a partworth to customers of 1.6 (derived as 0.9 + 0.7). This is the highest result observed in this exercise. A small but expensive ($300) phone is rated as −0.3 (that is, −1 + 0.7). The desirability of this small phone is offset by its price. A large, expensive phone is least desirable to customers, generating a partworth of −1.6 (that is, (−1) + (−0.6)).

On this basis, we determine that the customer whose views are analyzed here would prefer a medium-size phone at $200 (utility = 0) to a small phone at $300 (utility = −0.3). Such information would be instrumental to decisions concerning the trade-offs between product design and price.

This analysis also demonstrates that, within the ranges examined, price is more important than size from the perspective of this consumer. Price generates a range of effects from 0.9 to −1 (that is, a total spread of 1.9), while the effects generated by the most and least desirable sizes span a range only from 0.7 to −0.6 (total spread = 1.3).

COMPENSATORY VERSUS NON-COMPENSATORY CONSUMER DECISIONS

A compensatory decision process is one in which a customer evaluates choices with the perspective that strengths along one or more dimensions can compensate for weaknesses along others.

In a non-compensatory decision process, by contrast, if certain attributes of a product are weak, no compensation is possible, even if the product possesses strengths along other dimensions. In the previous cell phone example, for instance, some customers may feel that if a phone were greater than a certain size, no price would make it attractive.

In another example, most people choose a grocery store on the basis of proximity. Any store within a certain radius of home or work may be considered. Beyond that distance, however, all stores will be excluded from consideration, and there is nothing a store can do to overcome this. Even if it posts extraordinarily low prices, offers a stunningly wide assortment, creates great displays, and stocks the freshest foods, for example, a store will not entice consumers to travel 400 miles to buy their groceries.

Although this example is extreme to the point of absurdity, it illustrates an important point: When consumers make a choice on a non-compensatory basis, marketers need to define the dimensions along which certain attributes *must* be delivered, simply to qualify for consideration of their overall offering.

One form of non-compensatory decision-making is elimination-by-aspect. In this approach, consumers look at an entire set of choices and then eliminate those that do not meet their expectations in the order of the importance of the attributes. In the selection of a grocery store, for example, this process might run as follows:

- Which stores are within 5 miles of my home?
- Which ones are open after 8 p.m.?
- Which carry the spicy mustard that I like?
- Which carry fresh flowers?

The process continues until only one choice is left.

In the ideal situation, in analyzing customers' decision processes, marketers would have access to information on an individual level, revealing

- Whether the decision for each customer is compensatory or not
- The priority order of the attributes
- The "cut-off" levels for each attribute
- The relative importance weight of each attribute if the decision follows a compensatory process

More frequently, however, marketers have access only to past behavior, helping them make inferences regarding these items.

In the absence of detailed, individual information for customers throughout a market, conjoint analysis provides a means to gain insight into the decision-making processes of a sampling of customers. In conjoint analysis, we generally assume a compensatory process. That is, we assume utilities are additive. Under this assumption, if a choice is weak along one dimension (for example, if a store does not carry spicy mustard), it can compensate for this with strength along another (for example, it does carry fresh-cut flowers) at least in part. Conjoint analyses can approximate a non-compensatory model by assigning non-linear weighting to an attribute across certain levels of its value. For example, the weightings for distance to a grocery store might run as follows:

Within 1 mile:	0.9
1-5 miles away:	0.8
5-10 miles away:	−0.8
More than 10 miles away:	−0.9

In this example, stores outside a 5-mile radius cannot practically make up the loss of utility they incur as a result of distance. Distance becomes, in effect, a non-compensatory dimension.

By studying customers' decision-making processes, marketers gain insight into the attributes needed to meet consumer expectations. They learn, for example, whether certain attributes are compensatory or non-compensatory. A strong understanding of customers' valuation of different attributes also enables marketers to tailor products and allocate resources effectively.

Several potential complications arise in considering compensatory versus non-compensatory decisions. Customers often don't know whether an attribute is compensatory or not, and they may not be readily able to explain their decisions. Therefore, it is often necessary either to infer a customer's decision-making process or to determine that process through an evaluation of choices, rather than a description of the process.

It is possible, however, to uncover non-compensatory elements through conjoint analysis. Any attribute for which the valuation spread is so high that it cannot practically be made up by other features is, in effect, a non-compensatory attribute.

EXAMPLE: Among grocery stores, Juan prefers the Acme market because it's close to his home, despite the fact that Acme's prices are generally higher than those at the local Shoprite store. A third store, Vernon's, is located in Juan's apartment complex. But Juan avoids it because Vernon's doesn't carry his favorite soda.

From this information, we know that Juan's shopping choice is influenced by at least three factors: price, distance from his home, and whether a store carries his favorite soda. In Juan's decision process, price and distance seem to be compensating factors. He trades price for distance. Whether the soda is stocked seems to be a non-compensatory factor. If a store doesn't carry Juan's favorite soda, it will not win his business, regardless of how well it scores on price and location.

Data Sources, Complications, and Cautions

Prior to conducting a conjoint study, it is necessary to identify the attributes of importance to a customer. Focus groups are commonly used for this purpose. After attributes and levels are determined, a typical approach to Conjoint Analysis is to use a fractional factorial orthogonal design, which is a partial sample of all possible combinations of attributes. This is to reduce the total number of choice evaluations required by the respondent. With an orthogonal design, the attributes remain independent of one another, and the test doesn't weigh one attribute disproportionately to another.

There are multiple ways to gather data, but a straightforward approach would be to present respondents with choices and to ask them to rate those choices according to their preferences. These preferences then become the dependent variable in a regression, in which attribute levels serve as the independent variables, as in the previous equation. Conjoint utilities constitute the weights determined to best capture the preference ratings provided by the respondent.

Often, certain attributes work in tandem to influence customer choice. For example, a fast *and* sleek sports car may provide greater value to a customer than would be suggested by the sum of the fast and sleek attributes. Such relationships between attributes are not captured by a simple conjoint model, unless one accounts for interactions.

Ideally, conjoint analysis is performed on an individual level because attributes can be weighted differently across individuals. Marketers can also create a more balanced view by performing the analysis across a sample of individuals. It is appropriate to perform the analysis within consumer segments that have similar weights. Conjoint analysis can be viewed as a snapshot in time of a customer's desires. It will not necessarily translate indefinitely into the future.

It is vital to use the correct attributes in any conjoint study. People can only tell you their preferences within the parameters you set. If the correct attributes are not included in a study, while it may be possible to determine the relative importance of those attributes that *are* included, and it may technically be possible to form segments on the basis of the resulting data, the analytic results may not be valid for forming *useful* segments. For example, in a conjoint analysis of consumer preferences regarding colors and styles of cars, one may correctly group customers as to their feelings about these attributes. But if consumers really care most about engine size, then those segmentations will be of little value.

6 Segmentation Using Conjoint Utilities

Understanding customers' desires is a vital goal of marketing. Segmenting, or clustering similar customers into groups, can help managers recognize useful patterns and identify attractive subsets within a larger market. With that understanding, managers can select target markets, develop appropriate offerings for each, determine the most effective ways to reach the targeted segments, and allocate resources accordingly. Conjoint analysis can be highly useful in this exercise.

Purpose: To identify segments based on conjoint utilities.

As described in the previous section, conjoint analysis is used to determine customers' preferences on the basis of the attribute weightings that they reveal in their decision-making processes. These weights, or utilities, are generally evaluated on an individual level.

Segmentation entails the grouping of customers who demonstrate similar patterns of preference and weighting with regard to certain product attributes, distinct from the patterns exhibited by other groups. Using segmentation, a company can decide which group(s) to target and can determine an approach to appeal to the segment's members. After segments have been formed, a company can set strategy based on their attractiveness (size, growth, purchase rate, diversity) and on its own capability to serve these segments, relative to competitors.

Construction

To complete a segmentation based on conjoint utilities, one must first determine utility scores at an individual customer level. Next, one must cluster these customers into segments of like-minded individuals. This is generally done through a methodology known as cluster analysis.

> **Cluster Analysis:** *A technique that calculates the distances between customer and forms groups by minimizing the differences within each group and maximizing the differences between groups.*

Cluster analysis operates by calculating a "distance" (a sum of squares) between individuals and, in a hierarchical fashion, starts pairing those individuals together. The process of pairing minimizes the "distance" within a group and creates a manageable number of segments within a larger population.

EXAMPLE: The Samson-Finn Company has three customers. In order to help manage its marketing efforts, Samson-Finn wants to organize like-minded customers into segments. Toward that end, it performs a conjoint analysis in which it measures its customers' preferences among products that are either reliable or very reliable, either fast or very fast (see Table 6). It then considers the conjoint utilities of each of its customers to see which of them demonstrate similar wants. When clustering on conjoint data, the distances would be calculated on the partworths.

Table 6   Customer Conjoint Utilities

	Very Reliable	Reliable	Very Fast	Fast
Bob	0.4	0.3	0.6	0.2
Erin	0.9	0.1	0.2	0.7
Yogesh	0.3	0.3	0.5	0.2

The analysis looks at the difference between Bob's view and Erin's view on the importance of reliability on their choice. Bob's score is 0.4 and Erin's is 0.9. We can square the difference between these to derive the "distance" between Bob and Erin.

Using this methodology, the distance between each pair of Samson-Finn's customers can be calculated as follows:

Distances	Very Reliable		Reliable		Very Fast		Fast
Bob and Erin:	$= (0.4 - 0.9)^2$	$+$	$(0.3 - 0.1)^2$	$+$	$(0.6 - 0.2)^2$	$+$	$(0.2 - 0.7)^2$
	$= 0.25$	$+$	0.04	$+$	0.16	$+$	0.25
	$= 0.7$						
Bob and Yogesh:	$= (0.4 - 0.3)^2$	$+$	$(0.3 - 0.3)^2$	$+$	$(0.6 - 0.5)^2$	$+$	$(0.2 - 0.2)^2$
	$= 0.01$	$+$	0.0		$+ 0.01$	$+$	0.0
	$= 0.02$						
Erin and Yogesh:	$= (0.9 - 0.3)^2$	$+$	$(0.1 - 0.3)^2$	$+$	$(0.2 - 0.5)^2$	$+$	$(0.7 + 0.2)^2$
	$= 0.36$		$+ 0.04$		$+ 0.09$	$+$	0.25
	$= 0.74$						

On this basis, Bob and Yogesh appear to be very close to each other because their sum of squares is 0.02. As a result, they should be considered part of the same segment. Conversely, in light of the high sum-of-squares distance established by her preferences, Erin should not be considered a part of the same segment with either Bob or Yogesh.

Of course, most segmentation analyses are performed on large customer bases. This example merely illustrates the process involved in the cluster analysis calculations.

Data Sources, Complications, and Cautions

As noted previously, a customer's utilities may not be stable, and the segment to which a customer belongs can shift over time or across occasions. An individual might belong to one segment for personal air travel, in which price might be a major factor, and another for business travel, in which convenience might become more important. Such a customer's conjoint weights (utilities) would differ depending on the purchase occasion.

Determining the appropriate *number* of segments for an analysis can be somewhat arbitrary. There is no generally accepted statistical means for determining the "correct" number of segments. Ideally, marketers look for a segment structure that fulfills the following qualifications:

- Each segment constitutes a homogeneous group, within which there is relatively little variance between attribute utilities of different individuals.

- Groupings are heterogeneous across segments; that is, there is a wide variance of attribute utilities *between* segments.

7   Conjoint Utilities and Volume Projection

The conjoint utilities of products and services can be used to forecast the market share that each will achieve and the volume that each will sell. Marketers can project market share for a given product or service on the basis of the proportion of individuals who select it from a relevant choice set, as well as its overall utility.

Purpose: To use conjoint analysis to project the market share and the sales volume that will be achieved by a product or service.

Conjoint analysis is used to measure the utilities for a product. The combination of these utilities, generally additive, represents a scoring of sorts for the expected popularity of that product. These scores can be used to rank products. However, further information is needed to estimate market share. One can anticipate that the top-ranked product in a selection set will have a greater probability of being chosen by an individual than products ranked lower for that individual. Adding the number of customers who rank the brand first should allow the calculation of customer share.

Data Sources, Complications, and Cautions

To complete a sales volume projection, it is necessary to have a full conjoint analysis. This analysis must include all the important features according to which consumers make their choice. Defining the "market" is clearly crucial to a meaningful result.

To define a market, it is important to identify all the choices in that market. Calculating the percentage of "first choice" selections for each alternative merely provides a "share of preferences." To extend this to market share, one must estimate (1) the volume of sales per customer, (2) the level of distribution or availability for each choice, and (3) the percentage of customers who will defer their purchase until they can find their first choice.

The greatest potential error in this process would be to exclude meaningful attributes from the conjoint analysis.

Network effects can also distort a conjoint analysis. In some instances, customers do not make purchase decisions purely on the basis of a product's attributes but are also affected by its level of acceptance in the marketplace. Such network effects, and the importance of harnessing or overcoming them, are especially evident during shifts in technology industries.

References and Suggested Further Reading

Aaker, D.A. (1991). *Managing Brand Equity: Capitalizing on the Value of a Brand Name*, New York: Free Press; Toronto; New York: Maxwell Macmillan; Canada: Maxwell Macmillan International.

Aaker, D.A. (1996). *Building Strong Brands*, New York: Free Press.

Aaker, D.A., and J.M. Carman. (1982). "Are You Overadvertising?" *Journal of Advertising Research*, 22(4), 57–70.

Aaker, D.A., and K.L. Keller. (1990). "Consumer Evaluations of Brand Extensions," *Journal of Marketing*, 54(1), 27–41.

Ailawadi, Kusum, and Kevin Keller. (2004). "Understanding Retail Branding: Conceptual Insights and Research Priorities," *Journal of Retailing*, Vol. 80, Issue 4, Winter, 331–342.

Ailawadi, Kusum, Donald Lehman, and Scott Neslin. (2003). "Revenue Premium As an Outcome Measure of Brand Equity," *Journal of Marketing*, Vol. 67, No. 4, 1–17.

Burno, Hernan A., Unmish Parthasarathi, and Nisha Singh, eds. (2005). "The Changing Face of Measurement Tools Across the Product Lifecycle," *Does Marketing Measure Up? Performance Metrics: Practices and Impact*, Marketing Science Institute, No. 05-301.

Harvard Business School Case: Nestlé Refrigerated Foods Contadina Pasta & Pizza (A) 9-595-035. Rev Jan 30 1997.

Moran, Bill. Personal communication with Paul Farris.

ENDNOTES

1. Harvard Business School Case: Nestlé Refrigerated Foods Contadina Pasta & Pizza (A) 9-595-035. Rev Jan 30 1997.

2. Kusum Ailawadi, Donald Lehmann, and Scott Neslin (2003), "Revenue Premium as an Outcome Measure of Brand Equity," *Journal of Marketing*, Vol. 67, No. 4, 1-17.

3. Bruno, Hernan, Unmish Parthasarathi, and Nisha Singh, eds. (2005). "The Changing Face of Measurement Tools Across the Product Lifecycle," *Does Marketing Measure Up? Performance Metrics: Practices and Impact*, Marketing Science Conference Summary, No. 05-301.

4. Young and Rubicam can be found at: http://www.yr.com/yr/. Accessed 03/03/05.

5. Bruno, Hernan, Unmish Parthasarathi, and Nisha Singh, eds. (2005). "The Changing Face of Measurement Tools Across the Product Lifecycle," *Does Marketing Measure Up? Performance Metrics: Practices and Impact*, Marketing Science Conference Summary, No. 05-301.

6. See Darden technical note and original research.

7. The information from Bill Moran comes from personal communications with the authors.

8. Interbrand can be contacted at: http://www.interbrand.com/. Accessed 03/03/05.

Developing a Brand Equity Measurement and Management System

Learning Objectives

After reading this chapter, you should be able to

1. Describe the new accountability in terms of ROMI.
2. Outline the two steps in conducting a brand audit.
3. Describe how to design, conduct, and interpret a tracking study.
4. Identify the steps in implementing a brand equity management system.

Marketers must adopt research methods and procedures so they understand when, where, how, and why consumers buy.

Source: David Noton Photography/Alamy

From Chapter 8 of *Strategic Brand Management: Building, Measuring, and Managing Brand Equity*, Fourth Edition. Kevin Lane Keller.

Preview

The customer-based brand equity (CBBE) concept provides guidance about how we can measure brand equity. Given that customer-based brand equity is the differential effect that knowledge about the brand has on customer response to the marketing of that brand, two basic approaches to measuring brand equity present themselves. An *indirect approach* can assess potential sources of customer-based brand equity by identifying and tracking consumers' brand knowledge—all the thoughts, feelings, images, perceptions, and beliefs linked to the brand. A *direct approach,* on the other hand, can assess the actual impact of brand knowledge on consumer response to different aspects of the marketing program.

The two approaches are complementary, and marketers can and should use both. In other words, for brand equity to provide a useful strategic function and guide marketing decisions, marketers must fully understand the sources of brand equity, how they affect outcomes of interest such as sales, and how these sources and outcomes change, if at all, over time.

Before we get into specifics of measurement, this chapter offers some big-picture perspectives of how to think about brand equity measurement and management. Specifically, we'll consider how to develop and implement a brand equity measurement system. A *brand equity measurement system* is a set of research procedures designed to provide marketers with timely, accurate, and actionable information about brands so they can make the best possible tactical decisions in the short run and strategic decisions in the long run. The goal is to achieve a full understanding of the sources and outcomes of brand equity and to be able to relate the two as much as possible.

The ideal brand equity measurement system would provide complete, up-to-date, and relevant information about the brand and its competitors to the right decision makers at the right time within the organization. After providing some context about the heightened need for marketing accountability, we'll look in detail at three steps toward achieving that ideal—conducting brand audits, designing brand tracking studies, and establishing a brand equity management system.

THE NEW ACCOUNTABILITY

Although senior managers at many firms have embraced the marketing concept and the importance of brands, they often struggle with questions such as: How strong is our brand? How can we ensure that our marketing activities create value? How do we measure that value?

Virtually every marketing dollar spent today must be justified as both effective and efficient in terms of *return of marketing investment* (ROMI).[1] This increased accountability has forced marketers to address tough challenges and develop new measurement approaches.

Complicating matters is that, depending on the particular industry or category, some observers believe up to 70 percent (or even more) of marketing expenditures may be devoted to programs and activities that improve brand equity but cannot be linked to short-term incremental profits.[2] Measuring the long-term value of marketing in terms of both its full short-term and long-term impact on consumers is thus crucial for accurately assessing return on investment.

Clearly marketers need new tools and procedures that clarify and justify the value of their expenditures, beyond ROMI measures tied to short-term changes in sales.

In the remainder of this chapter, we offer several additional concepts and perspectives to help in that pursuit.

CONDUCTING BRAND AUDITS

To learn how consumers think, feel, and act toward brands and products so the company can make informed strategic positioning decisions, marketers should first conduct a brand audit. A *brand audit* is a comprehensive examination of a brand to discover its sources of brand equity. In accounting, an audit is a systematic inspection by an outside firm of accounting records including analyses, tests, and confirmations.[3] The outcome is an assessment of the firm's financial health in the form of a report.

A similar concept has been suggested for marketing. A *marketing audit* is a "comprehensive, systematic, independent, and periodic examination of a company's—or business unit's—marketing environment, objectives, strategies, and activities with a view of determining problem areas and opportunities and recommending a plan of action to improve the company's marketing performance."[4] The process is a three-step procedure in which the first step is agreement on objectives, scope, and approach; the second is data collection; and the third and final step is report preparation and presentation. This is an internally, company-focused exercise to make sure marketing operations are efficient and effective.

A brand audit, on the other hand, is a more externally, consumer-focused exercise to assess the health of the brand, uncover its sources of brand equity, and suggest ways to improve and leverage its equity. A brand audit requires understanding the sources of brand equity from the perspective of both the firm and the consumer. From the perspective of the firm, what products and services are currently being offered to consumers, and how they are being marketed and branded? From the perspective of the consumer, what deeply held perceptions and beliefs create the true meaning of brands and products?

The brand audit can set strategic direction for the brand, and management should conduct one whenever important shifts in strategic direction are likely.[5] Are the current sources of brand equity satisfactory? Do certain brand associations need to be added, subtracted, or just strengthened? What brand opportunities exist and what potential challenges exist for brand equity? With answers to these questions, management can put a marketing program into place to maximize sales and long-term brand equity.

Conducting brand audits on a regular basis, such as during the annual planning cycle, allows marketers to keep their fingers on the pulse of their brands. Brand audits are thus particularly useful background for managers as they set up their marketing plans and can have profound implications on brands' strategic direction and resulting performance.

DOMINO'S PIZZA

In late 2009, Domino's was a struggling business in a declining market. Pizza sales were slumping as consumers defected to healthier and fresher dining options at one end or to less expensive burger or sandwich options at the other end. Caught in the middle, Domino's also found its heritage in "speed" and "best in delivery" becoming less important; even worse, it was undermining consumer's perceptions of the brand's taste, the number-one driver of choice in the pizza category. To address the problem, Domino's decided to conduct a detailed brand audit with extensive qualitative and quantitative research. Surveys, focus groups, intercept interviews, social media conversations, and ethnographic research generated a number of key insights. The taste problem was severe—some consumers bluntly said that Domino's tasted more like the box than the pizza. Research also revealed that consumers felt betrayed by a company they felt they no longer knew. A focus on impersonal, efficient service meant that in consumers' minds, there was no Domino's kitchens, no chefs, not even ingredients. Consumers were skeptical of "new and improved" claims and felt companies never admitted they were wrong. Based on these and other insights, Domino's began its brand comeback. Step one—new recipes for crust, sauce, and cheese that resulted in substantially better taste-test scores. Next, Domino's decided not to run from criticism and launched the "Oh Yes We Did" campaign. Using traditional TV and print media and extensive online components, the company made clear that it had listened and responded by creating a better pizza. Documentary-type filming showed Domino's CEO and other executives observing the original consumer research and describing how they took it to heart. Surprise visits were made to harsh critics from the focus groups, who tried the new pizza on camera and enthusiastically praised it. Domino's authentic, genuine approach paid off. Consumer perceptions dramatically improved and growth in sales in 2010 far exceeded the competitors'.[6]

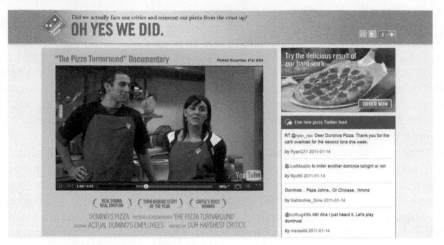

A thorough, insightful brand audit helped to convince Domino's they needed to confront their perceived flaws head on.

Source: Domino's Pizza LLC

The brand audit consists of two steps: the brand inventory and the brand exploratory. We'll discuss each in turn. The Brand Focus illustrates a sample brand audit using the Rolex brand as an example.

Brand Inventory

The purpose of the **brand inventory** is to provide a current, comprehensive profile of how all the products and services sold by a company are marketed and branded. Profiling each product or service requires marketers to catalogue the following in both visual and written form for each product or service sold: the names, logos, symbols, characters, packaging, slogans, or other trademarks used; the inherent product attributes or characteristics of the brand; the pricing, communications, and distribution policies; and any other relevant marketing activity related to the brand.

Often firms set up a "war room" where all the various marketing activities and programs can be displayed or accessed. Visual and verbal information help to provide a clearer picture. Figure 1 shows a wall that software pioneer Red Hat created of all its various ads, brochures, and other marketing materials. Managers were pleasantly surprised when they saw

FIGURE 1

Red Hat Brand Wall

Source: Photo courtesy of Red Hat, Inc.

how consistent all the various items were in form, look, and content, although they were left scratching their heads as to why the Red Hat office in Australia had created branded underwear as a promotional gift. Needless to say, the "tighty whities" were dropped after being deemed off-brand.[7]

The outcome of the brand inventory should be an accurate, comprehensive, and up-to-date profile of how all the products and services are branded in terms of which brand elements are employed and how, and the nature of the supporting marketing program. Marketers should also profile competitive brands in as much detail as possible to determine points-of-parity and points-of-difference.

Rationale. The brand inventory is a valuable first step for several reasons. First, it helps to suggest what consumers' current perceptions may be based on. Consumer associations are typically rooted in the *intended* meaning of the brand elements attached to them—but not always. The brand inventory therefore provides useful information for interpreting follow-up research such as the brand exploratory we discuss next.

Although the brand inventory is primarily a descriptive exercise, it can supply some useful analysis too, and initial insights into how brand equity may be better managed. For example, marketers can assess the consistency of all the different products or services sharing a brand name. Are the different brand elements used on a consistent basis, or are there many different versions of the brand name, logo, and so forth for the same product—perhaps for no obvious reason—depending on which geographic market it is being sold in, which market segment it is being targeted to, and so forth? Similarly, are the supporting marketing programs logical and consistent across related brands?

As firms expand their products geographically and extend them into other categories, deviations—sometimes significant in nature—commonly emerge in brand appearance and marketing. A thorough brand inventory should be able to reveal the extent of brand consistency. At the same time, a brand inventory can reveal a lack of perceived differences among different products sharing the brand name—for example, as a result of line extensions—that are designed to differ on one or more key dimensions. Creating sub-brands with distinct positions is often a marketing priority, and a brand inventory may help to uncover undesirable redundancy and overlap that could lead to consumer confusion or retailer resistance.

Brand Exploratory

Although the supply-side view revealed by the brand inventory is useful, actual consumer perceptions, of course, may not necessarily reflect those the marketer intended. Thus, the second step of the brand audit is to provide detailed information about what consumers actually think of the brand by means of the **brand exploratory**. The brand exploratory is research directed to understanding what consumers think and feel about the brand and act toward it in order to better understand sources of brand equity as well as any possible barriers.

Preliminary Activities. Several preliminary activities are useful for the brand exploratory. First, in many cases, a number of prior research studies may exist and be relevant. It is important to dig through company archives to uncover reports that may have been buried, and perhaps even long forgotten, but that contain insights and answers to a number of important questions or suggest new questions that may still need to be posed.

Second, it is also useful to interview internal personnel to gain an understanding of their beliefs about consumer perceptions for the brand and competitive brands. Past and current marketing managers may be able to share some wisdom not necessarily captured in prior research reports. The diversity of opinion that typically emerges from these internal interviews serves several functions, increasing the likelihood that useful insights or ideas will be generated, as well as pointing out any inconsistencies or misconceptions that may exist internally for the brand.

Although these preliminary activities are useful, additional research is often required to better understand how customers shop for and use different brands and what they think and feel about them. To allow marketers to cover a broad range of issues and to pursue some in greater depth, the brand exploratory often employs qualitative research techniques as a first step, as summarized in Figure 2, followed by more focused and definitive survey-based quantitative research.

Free association	Day/Behavior reconstruction
Adjective ratings and checklists	Photo/Written journal
Confessional interviews	Participatory design
Projective techniques	Consumer-led problem solving
Photo sorts	Real-life experimenting
Archetypal research	Collaging and drawing
Bubble drawings	Consumer shadowing
Store telling	Consumer–product interaction
Personification exercises	Video observation
Role playing	
Metaphor elicitation*	

*ZMET trademark

FIGURE 2

Summary of Qualitative
Techniques

Interpreting Qualitative Research. There are a wide variety of qualitative research techniques. Marketers must carefully consider which ones to employ.

Criteria. Levy identifies three criteria by which we can classify and judge any qualitative research technique: direction, depth, and diversity.[8] For example, any projective research technique varies in terms of the nature of the stimulus information (is it related to the person or the brand?), the extent to which responses are superficial and concrete as opposed to deeper and more abstract (and thus requiring more interpretation), and the way the information relates to information gathered by other projective techniques.

In Figure 2, the tasks at the top of the left-hand list ask very specific questions whose answers may be easier to interpret. The tasks on the bottom of the list ask questions that are much richer but also harder to interpret. Tasks on the top of the right-hand list are elaborate exercises that consumers undertake themselves and that may be either specific or broadly directed. Tasks at the bottom of the right-hand list consist of direct observation of consumers as they engage in various behaviors.

According to Levy, the more specific the question, the narrower the range of information given by the respondent. When the stimulus information in the question is open-ended and responses are freer or less constrained, the respondent tends to give more information. The more abstract and symbolic the research technique, however, the more important it is to follow up with probes and other questions that explicitly reveal the motivation and reasons behind consumers' responses.

Ideally, qualitative research conducted as part of the brand exploratory should vary in direction and depth as well as in technique. The challenge is to provide accurate interpretation—going beyond what consumers explicitly state to determine what they implicitly mean.

Mental Maps and Core Brand Associations. One useful outcome of qualitative research is a mental map. A *mental map* accurately portrays in detail all salient brand associations and responses for a particular target market. One of the simplest means to get consumers to create a mental map is to ask them for their top-of-mind brand associations ("When you think of this brand, what comes to mind?").

It is sometimes useful to group brand associations into related categories with descriptive labels. *Core brand associations* are those abstract associations (attributes and benefits) that characterize the 5–10 most important aspects or dimensions of a brand. They can serve as the basis of brand positioning in terms of how they create points-of-parity and points-of-difference. For example, in response to a Nike brand probe, consumers may list LeBron James, Tiger Woods, Roger Federer, or Lance Armstrong, whom we could call "top athletes." The challenge is to include all relevant associations while making sure each is as distinct as possible. Figure 3 displays a hypothetical mental map and some core brand associations for MTV.

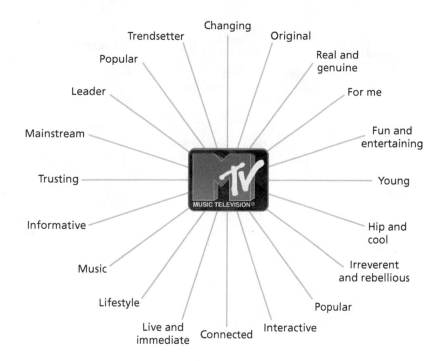

FIGURE 3a

Classic MTV Mental Map

Source: MTV logo, MCT/Newscom

Music
What's hot and what's new

Credibility
Expert, trusting, reality

Personality
Irreverent, hip, cool

Accessibility
Relevant, for everyone

Interactivity
Connected and participatory

Community
Shared experience (literally and talk value)

Modern
Hip, cool

Spontaneity
Up-to the-minute, immediate

Originality
Genuine, creative

Fluidity
Always changing and evolving

FIGURE 3b

Possible MTV Core Brand Associations

A related methodology, brand concept maps (BCM), elicits brand association networks (brand maps) from consumers and aggregates individual maps into a consensus map.[9] This approach structures the brand elicitation stage of identifying brand associations by providing survey respondents with a set of brand associations used in the mapping stage. The mapping stage is also structured and has respondents use the provided set of brand associations to build an individual brand map that shows how brand associations are linked to each other and to the brand, as well as how strong these linkages are. Finally, the aggregation stage is also structured and analyzes individual brand maps step by step, uncovering the common thinking involved. Figure 4 displays a brand concept map for the Mayo Clinic (the subject of Branding Brief 2) provided by a sample of patients.

One goal from qualitative, as well as quantitative, research in the brand exploratory is a clear, comprehensive profile of the target market. As part of that process, many firms are literally creating personas to capture their views as to the target market, as summarized in The Science of Branding 1.

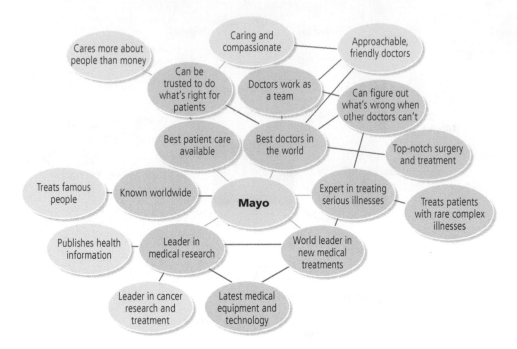

FIGURE 4

Sample Mayo Clinic
Brand Concept Map

Conducting Quantitative Research. Qualitative research is suggestive, but a more definitive assessment of the depth and breadth of brand awareness and the strength, favorability, and uniqueness of brand associations often requires a quantitative phase of research.

The guidelines for the quantitative phase of the exploratory are relatively straightforward. Marketers should assess all potentially salient associations identified by the qualitative research phase according to their strength, favorability, and uniqueness. They should examine both specific brand beliefs and overall attitudes and behaviors to reveal potential sources and outcomes of brand equity. And they should assess the depth and breadth of brand awareness by employing various cues. Typically, marketers will also need to conduct similar types of research for competitors to better understand their sources of brand equity and how they compare with the target brand.

Much of the above discussion of qualitative and quantitative measures has concentrated on associations to the brand name—for example, what do consumers think about the brand when given its name as a probe? Marketers should study other brand elements in the brand exploratory as well, because they may trigger other meanings and facets of the brand.

For instance, we can ask consumers what inferences they make about the brand on the basis of the product packaging, logo, or other attribute alone, such as, "What would you think about the brand just on the basis of its packaging?" We can explore specific aspects of the brand elements—for example, the label on the package or the shape of the package itself—to uncover their role in creating brand associations and thus sources of brand equity. We should also determine which of these elements most effectively represents and symbolizes the brand as a whole.

Brand Positioning and the Supporting Marketing Program

The brand exploratory should uncover the current knowledge structures for the core brand and its competitors, as well as determining the desired brand awareness and brand image and points-of-parity and points-of-difference. Moving from the current brand image to the desired brand image typically means adding new associations, strengthening existing ones, or weakening or eliminating undesirable ones in the minds of consumers.

John Roberts, one of Australia's top marketing academics, sees the challenge in achieving the ideal positioning for a brand as being able to achieve congruence among four key considerations: (1) what customers currently believe about the brand (and thus find credible), (2) what customers will value in the brand, (3) what the firm is currently saying about the brand, and (4) where the firm would like to take the brand (see Figure 5).[10] Because each of the four considerations may suggest or reflect different approaches to positioning, finding a positioning that balances the four considerations as much as possible is key.

A number of different internal management personnel can be part of the planning and positioning process, including brand, marketing research, and production managers, as can relevant outside

THE SCIENCE OF BRANDING 1

The Role of Brand Personas

To crystalize all the information and insights they have gained about their target market(s), researchers can employ personas. **Personas** are detailed profiles of one, or perhaps a few, target market consumers. They are often defined in terms of demographic, psychographic, geographic, or other descriptive attitudinal or behavioral information. Researchers may use photos, images, names, or short bios to help convey the particulars of the persona.

The rationale behind personas is to provide exemplars or archetypes of how the target customer looks, acts, and feels that are as true-to-life as possible, to ensure marketers within the organization fully understand and appreciate their target market and therefore incorporate a nuanced target customer point of view in all their marketing decision-making. Personas are fundamentally designed to bring the target consumer to life.

A good brand persona can guide all marketing activities. Burger King's brand persona is a cool, youngish uncle, who—although somewhat older than the chain's early-teens male target—is younger than their parents. The corresponding brand voice appears online, in ads and promotions, and wherever the brand expresses itself.

Although personas can provide a very detailed and accessible perspective on the target market, it can come at a cost. Overly focusing on a narrow slice of the target market can lead to oversimplification and erroneous assumptions about how the target market as a whole thinks, feels, or acts. The more heterogeneity in the target market, the more problematic the use of personas can be.

To overcome the potential problem of overgeneralization, some firms are creating multiple personas to provide a richer tapestry of the target market. There can also be varying levels of personas, such as primary (target consumer), secondary (target consumer with differing needs, targets, goals), and negative (false stereotypes of users).

Burger King adopted a persona as the "cool youngish uncle" to help guide the irreverent tone and personality of its marketing communications.

Source: Charles Harris/AdMedia/Newscom

Sources: Allen P. Adamson, *Brand Digital: Simple Ways Top Brands Succeed in the Digital Age* (New York: Palgrave-MacMillan, 2008); Lisa Sanders, "Major Marketers Get Wise to the Power of Assigning Personas," *Advertising Age*, 9 April 2007, 36; Stephen Herskovitz and Malcolm Crystal, "The Essential Brand Persona: Storytelling and Branding," *Journal of Business Strategy* 31, no. 3 (2010): 21. For additional information on storytelling, see Edward Wachtman and Sheree Johnson, "Discover Your Persuasive Story," *Marketing Management* (March/April 2009): 22–27.

marketing partners like the marketing research suppliers and ad agency team. Once marketers have a good understanding from the brand audit of current brand knowledge structures for their target consumers and have decided on the desired brand knowledge structures for optimal positioning, they may still want to do additional research testing alternative tactical programs to achieve that positioning.

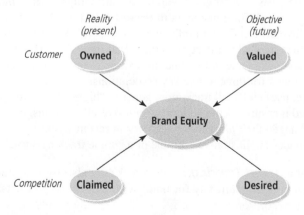

FIGURE 5

John Roberts's Brand Positioning Considerations

Source: Used with permission of John Roberts, ANU College of Business and Economics, The Australian National University.

DESIGNING BRAND TRACKING STUDIES

Brand audits are a means to provide in-depth information and insights essential for setting long-term strategic direction for the brand. But to gather information for short-term tactical decisions, marketers will typically collect less detailed brand-related information through on-going tracking studies.

Brand tracking studies collect information from consumers on a routine basis over time, usually through quantitative measures of brand performance on a number of key dimensions that marketers can identify in the brand audit or other means. They apply components from the brand value chain to better understand where, how much, and in what ways brand value is being created, offering invaluable information about how well the brand has achieved its positioning.

As more marketing activity surrounds the brand—as the firm introduces brand extensions or incorporates an increasing variety of communication options in support of the brand—it becomes difficult and expensive to research each one. Regardless of how few or how many changes are made in the marketing program over time, however, marketers need to monitor the health of the brand and its equity so they can make adjustments if necessary.

Tracking studies thus play an important role by providing consistent baseline information to facilitate day-to-day decision making. A good tracking system can help marketers better understand a host of important considerations such as category dynamics, consumer behavior, competitive vulnerabilities and opportunities, and marketing effectiveness and efficiency.

What to Track

It is usually necessary to customize tracking surveys to address the specific issues faced by the brand or brands in question. Each brand faces a unique situation that the different types of questions in its tracking survey should reflect.

Product–Brand Tracking.   Tracking an individual branded product requires measuring brand awareness and image, using both recall and recognition measures and moving from more general to more specific questions. Thus, it may make sense to first ask consumers what brands come to mind in certain situations, to next ask for recall of brands on the basis of various product category cues, and to then finish with tests of brand recognition (if necessary).

Moving from general to more specific measures is also a good idea in brand tracking surveys to measure brand image, especially specific perceptions like what consumers think characterizes the brand, and evaluations such as what the brand means to consumers. A number of specific brand associations typically exist for the brand, depending on the richness of consumer knowledge structures, which marketers can track over time.

Given that brands often compete at the augmented product level, it is important to measure all associations that may distinguish competing brands. Thus, measures of specific, "lower-level" brand associations should include all potential sources of brand equity such as performance and imagery attributes and functional and emotional benefits. Benefit associations often represent key points-of-parity or points-of-difference, so it is particularly important to track them as well. To better understand any changes in benefit beliefs for a brand, however, marketers may also want to measure the attribute beliefs that underlie those benefit beliefs. In other words, changes in descriptive attribute beliefs may help to explain changes in more evaluative benefit beliefs for a brand.

Marketers should assess those key brand associations that make up the potential sources of brand equity on the basis of strength, favorability, and uniqueness *in that order.* Unless associations are strong enough for consumers to recall them, their favorability does not matter, and unless they are favorable enough to influence consumers' decisions, their uniqueness does not matter. Ideally, marketers will collect measures of all three dimensions, but perhaps for only certain associations and only some of the time; for example, favorability and uniqueness may be measured only once a year for three to five key associations.

At the same time, marketers will track more general, "higher-level" judgments, feelings, and other outcome-related measures. After soliciting their overall opinions, consumers can be asked whether they have changed their attitudes or behavior in recent weeks or months and, if so, why. Branding Brief 1 provides an illustrative example of a simple tracking survey for McDonald's.

Corporate or Family Brand Tracking.   Marketers may also want to track the corporate or family brand separately or concurrently (or both) with individual products. Besides measures

BRANDING BRIEF 1

Sample Brand Tracking Survey

Assume McDonald's is interested in designing a short online tracking survey. How might you set it up? Although there are a number of different types of questions, your tracking survey might take the following form.

Introduction: We're conducting a short online survey to gather consumer opinions about quick-service or "fast-food" restaurant chains.

Brand Awareness and Usage

a. What brands of quick-service restaurant chains are you aware of?

b. At which brands of quick-service restaurant chains would you consider eating?

c. Have you eaten in a quick-service restaurant chain in the last week? Which ones?

A whole range of questions can be used to understand McDonald's sources and outcomes of brand equity in a tracking survey.

Source: Kim Karpeles/Alamy

d. If you were to eat in a quick-service restaurant tomorrow for lunch, which one would you go to?

e. What if you were eating dinner? Where would you go?

f. Finally, what if you were eating breakfast? Where would you go?

g. What are your favorite quick-service restaurant chains?

We want to ask you some general questions about a particular quick-service restaurant chain, McDonald's.

Have you heard of this restaurant? [Establish familiarity.]

Have you eaten at this restaurant? [Establish trial.]

When I say McDonald's, what are the first associations that come to your mind? Anything else? [List all.]

Brand Judgments

We're interested in your overall opinion of McDonald's.

a. How favorable is your attitude toward McDonald's?

b. How well does McDonald's satisfy your needs?

c. How likely would you be to recommend McDonald's to others?

d. How good a value is McDonald's?

e. Is McDonald's worth a premium price?

f. What do you like best about McDonald's? Least?

g. What is most unique about McDonald's?

h. To what extent does McDonald's offer advantages that other similar types of quick-service restaurants cannot?

i. To what extent is McDonald's superior to other brands in the quick-service restaurant category?

j. Compared to other brands in the quick-service restaurant category, how well does McDonald's satisfy your basic needs?

We now want to ask you some questions about McDonald's as a company. Please indicate your agreement with the following statements.

McDonald's is . . .

a. Innovative

b. Knowledgeable

c. Trustworthy

d. Likable

e. Concerned about their customers

f. Concerned about society as a whole

g. Likable

h. Admirable

Brand Performance

We now would like to ask some specific questions about McDonald's. Please indicate your agreement with the following statements.

McDonald's . . .

a. Is convenient to eat at

b. Provides quick, efficient service

c. Has clean facilities

d. Is ideal for the whole family

e. Has delicious food

f. Has healthy food

g. Has a varied menu

h. Has friendly, courteous staff

i. Offers fun promotions

j. Has a stylish and attractive look and design

k. Has high-quality food

Brand Imagery

a. To what extent do people you admire and respect eat at McDonald's?

b. How much do you like people who eat at McDonald's?

c. How well do each of the following words describe McDonald's?

Down-to-earth, honest, daring, up-to-date, reliable, successful, upper class, charming, outdoorsy

d. Is McDonald's a restaurant that you can use in a lot of different meal situations?

e. To what extent does thinking of McDonald's bring back pleasant memories?

f. To what extent do you feel that you grew up with McDonald's?

Brand Feelings

Does McDonald's give you a feeling of . . .

a. Warmth?

b. Fun?

c. Excitement?

d. Sense of security or confidence?

e. Social approval?

f. Self-respect?

Brand Resonance

a. I consider myself loyal to McDonald's.

b. I buy McDonald's whenever I can.

c. I would go out of my way to eat at McDonald's.

d. I really love McDonald's.

e. I would really miss McDonald's if it went away.

f. McDonald's is special to me.

g. McDonald's is more than a product to me.

h. I really identify with people who eat at McDonald's.

i. I feel a deep connection with others who eat at McDonald's.

j. I really like to talk about McDonald's to others.

k. I am always interested in learning more about McDonald's.

l. I would be interested in merchandise with the McDonald's name on it.

m. I am proud to have others know I eat at McDonald's.

n. I like to visit the McDonald's Web site.

o. Compared to other people, I follow news about McDonald's closely.

of corporate credibility, you can consider other measures of corporate brand associations including the following (illustrated with the GE corporate brand):

- How well managed is GE?
- How easy is it to do business with GE?
- How concerned is GE with its customers?
- How approachable is GE?
- How accessible is GE?
- How much do you like doing business with GE?
- How likely are you to invest in GE stock?
- How would you feel if a good friend accepted employment with GE?

The actual questions should reflect the level and nature of experience your respondents are likely to have had with the company.

When a brand is identified with multiple products, as in a corporate or family branding strategy, one important issue is which particular products the brand reminds consumers of. At the same time, marketers also want to know which particular products are most influential in affecting consumer perceptions about the brand.

To identify these more influential products, ask consumers which products they associate with the brand on an unaided basis ("What products come to mind when you think of the Nike brand?") or an aided basis by listing sub-brand names ("Are you aware of Nike Air Force basketball shoes? Nike Sphere React tennis apparel? Nike Air Max running shoes?"). To better understand the dynamics between the brand and its corresponding products, also ask consumers about their relationship between them ("There are many different products associated with Nike. Which ones are most important to you in formulating your opinion about the brand?").

Global Tracking. If your tracking covers diverse geographic markets—especially in both developing and developed countries—then you may need a broader set of background measures to

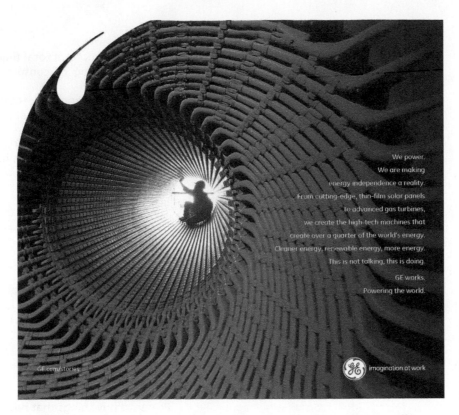

We power.
We are making
energy independence a reality.
From cutting-edge, thin-film solar panels
to advanced gas turbines,
we create the high-tech machines that
create over a quarter of the world's energy.
Cleaner energy, renewable energy, more energy.
This is not talking, this is doing.
GE works.
Powering the world.

GE.com/stories

imagination at work

It is perhaps no coincidence that one of the strongest B-to-B brands—GE—is also one of the best-managed.
Source: Courtesy of GE

put the brand development in those markets in the right perspective. You would not need to collect them frequently, but they could provide useful explanatory information (see Figure 6 for some representative measures).

How to Conduct Tracking Studies

Which elements of the brand should you use in tracking studies? In general, marketers use the brand name, but it may also make sense to use a logo or symbol in probing brand structures, especially if these elements can play a visible and important role in the decision process.

You also need to decide whom to track, as well as when and where to track.

Whom to Track. Tracking often concentrates on current customers, but it can also be rewarding to monitor nonusers of the brand or even of the product category as a whole, for example, to suggest potential segmentation strategies. Marketers can track those customers loyal to the brand against those loyal to other brands, or against those who switch brands. Among current customers, marketers can distinguish between heavy and light users of the brand. Dividing up the market typically requires different questionnaires (or at least sections of a basic questionnaire) to better capture the specific issues of each segment.

It's often useful to closely track other types of customers, too, such as channel members and other intermediaries, to understand their perceptions and actions toward the brand. Of particular interest is their image of the brand and how they feel they can help or hurt its equity. Retailers can answer direct questions such as, "Do you feel that products in your store sell faster if they have [the brand name] on them? Why or why not?" Marketers might also want to track employees such as salespeople, to better understand their beliefs about the brand and how they feel they're contributing to its equity now or could do so in the future. Such tracking may be especially important with service organizations, where employees play profound roles in affecting brand equity.

When and Where to Track. How often should you collect tracking information? One useful approach for monitoring brand associations is continuous tracking studies, which collect information from consumers continually over time. The advantage of continuous tracking is that it smoothes out aberrations or unusual marketing activities or events like a high profile new digital campaign or an unlikely occurrence in the marketing environment to provide a more representative set of baseline measures.

The frequency of such tracking studies, in general, depends on the frequency of product purchase (marketers typically track durable goods less frequently because they are purchased less

Economic Indicators
Gross domestic product
Interest rates
Unemployment
Average wage
Disposable income
Home ownership and
  housing debt
Exchange rates, share markets,
  and balance of payments

Retail
Total spent in supermarkets
Change year to year
Growth in house brand

Technology
Computer at home
DVR
Access to and use of Internet
Phones
PDA
Microwaves
Television

Personal Attitudes and Values
Confidence
Security
Family
Environment
Traditional values
Foreigners vs. sovereignty

Media Indicators
Media consumption: total time
  spent watching TV, consuming
  other media
Advertising expenditure: total, by
  media and by product category

Demographic Profile
Population profile: age, sex, income,
  household size
Geographic distribution
Ethnic and cultural profile

Other Products and Services
Transport: own car—how many
Best description of car
Motorbike
Home ownership or renting
Domestic trips overnight in last year
International trips in last two years

Attitude to Brands and Shopping
Buy on price
Like to buy new things
Country of origin or manufacture
Prefer to buy things that have been
  advertised
Importance of familiar brands

FIGURE 6
Brand Context Measures

often), and on the consumer behavior and marketing activity in the product category. Many companies conduct a certain number of interviews of different consumers every week—or even every day—and assemble the results on a rolling or moving average basis for monthly or quarterly reports.

MILLWARD BROWN

Millward Brown has led the innovation and implementation of tracking studies for the last 30 years. In general, the firm interviews 50–100 people a week and looks at the data with moving averages trended over time. Then it relates specific marketing activity and events to the trend data to understand their impact. Client brands are typically compared to a competitive set to determine relative performance within the product category. Millward Brown collects data on a variety of topics as dictated by the client needs. Modules include brand equity (current and future potential), brand positioning, value perceptions, awareness and response to marketing communications and in-store promotions, consumer profiles, and so on. The survey data is analyzed in conjunction with a variety of other data sources (traditional and social media, search data, sales data, etc.) to provide guidance on improving marketing ROI. Interviews on average run from 15 to 20 minutes in length (on the Web, the phone—both landline and mobile—and in-person in emerging markets). A 20-minute weekly interview with 50 nationally representative consumers can cost roughly $300,000 annually for a typical consumer product, depending on modality.[11]

When the brand has more stable and enduring associations, tracking on a less frequent basis can be enough. Nevertheless, even if the marketing of a brand does not appreciably change over time, competitive entries can change consumer perceptions of the dynamics within the market, making tracking critical. Finally, the stage of the product or brand life cycle will affect your decision about the frequency of tracking: Opinions of consumers in mature markets may not change much, whereas emerging markets may shift quickly and perhaps unpredictably.

How to Interpret Tracking Studies

To yield actionable insights and recommendations, tracking measures must be as reliable and sensitive as possible. One problem with many traditional measures of marketing phenomena is that they don't change much over time. Although this stability may mean the data haven't changed much, it may also be that one or more brand dimensions have changed to some extent but the measures themselves are not sensitive enough to detect subtle shifts. To develop sensitive tracking measures, marketers might need to phrase questions in a comparative way—"compared to other brands, how much . . ." or in terms of time periods—"compared to one month or one year ago, how much . . ."

Another challenge in interpreting tracking studies is deciding on appropriate benchmarks. For example, what is a sufficiently high level of brand awareness? When are brand associations sufficiently strong, favorable, and unique? How positive should brand judgments and feelings be? What are reasonable expectations for the amount of brand resonance? The cutoffs must not be unreasonable and must properly reflect the interests of the intended internal management audience. Appropriately defined and tested targets can help management benchmark against competitors and assess the productivity of brand marketing teams.

Marketers may also have to design these targets with allowance for competitive considerations and the nature of the category. In some low-involvement categories like, say, lightbulbs, it may be difficult to carve out a distinct image, unlike the case for higher-involvement products like cars or computers. Marketers must allow for and monitor the number of respondents who indicate they "don't know" or have "no response" to the brand tracking measures: the more of these types of answers collected, the less consumers would seem to care.

One of the most important tasks in conducting brand tracking studies is to identify the determinants of brand equity.[12] Which brand associations actually influence consumer attitudes and behavior and create value for the brand? Marketers must identify the real value drivers for a brand—that is, those tangible and intangible points-of-difference that influence and determine consumers' product and brand choices. Similarly, marketers must identify the marketing activities that have the most effective impact on brand knowledge, especially consumer exposure to advertising and other communication mix elements.

Carefully monitoring and relating key sources and outcome measures of brand equity should help to address these issues. The brand resonance and brand value chain models suggest many possible links and paths to explore for their impact on brand equity.

ESTABLISHING A BRAND EQUITY MANAGEMENT SYSTEM

Brand tracking studies, as well as brand audits, can provide a huge reservoir of information about how best to build and measure brand equity. To get the most value from these research efforts, firms need proper internal structures and procedures to capitalize on the usefulness of the brand equity concept and the information they collect about it. Although a brand equity measurement system does not ensure that managers will always make "good" decisions about the brand, it should increase the likelihood they do and, if nothing else, decrease the likelihood of "bad" decisions.

Embracing the concept of branding and brand equity, many firms constantly review how they can best factor it into the organization. Interestingly, perhaps one of the biggest threats to brand equity comes from *within* the organization, and the fact that too many marketing managers remain on the job for only a limited period of time. As a result of these short-term assignments, marketing managers may adopt a short-term perspective, leading to an overreliance on quick-fix sales-generating tactics such as line and category extensions, sales promotions, and so forth. Because these managers lack an understanding and appreciation of the brand equity concept, some critics maintain, they are essentially running the brand "without a license."

To counteract these and other potential forces within an organization that may lead to ineffective long-term management of brands, many firms have made internal branding a top priority. As part of these efforts, they must put a brand equity management system into place. A ***brand equity management system*** is a set of organizational processes designed to improve the understanding and use of the brand equity concept within a firm. Three major steps help to implement a brand equity management system: creating brand charters, assembling brand equity reports, and defining brand equity responsibilities. The following subsections discuss each of these in turn. Branding Brief 2 describes how the Mayo Clinic has developed a brand equity measurement and management system.

BRANDING BRIEF 2

Understanding and Managing the Mayo Clinic Brand

Mayo Clinic was founded in the late 1800s by Dr. William Worral Mayo and his two sons, who later pioneered the "group practice of medicine" by inviting other physicians to work with them in Rochester, Minnesota. The Mayos believed that "two heads are better than one, and three are even better." From this beginning on the frontier, Mayo Clinic grew to be a worldwide leader in patient care, research, and education and became renowned for its world-class specialty care and medical research. In addition to the original facilities in Rochester, Mayo later built clinics in Jacksonville, Florida, and Scottsdale, Arizona, during the 1980s. More than 500,000 patients are cared for in Mayo's inpatient and outpatient practice annually.

In 1996, Mayo undertook its first brand equity study and since then has conducted regular, national qualitative and quantitative studies. Mayo's research identifies seven key brand attributes or values, including (1) integration, (2) integrity, (3) longevity, (4) exclusivity, (5) leadership, (6) wisdom, and (7) dedication. Although some of these values also characterize other high-quality medical centers, integration and integrity are more nearly unique to Mayo.

In terms of integration, respondents described Mayo as bringing together a wealth of resources to provide the best possible care. They perceived Mayo to be efficient, organized, harmonious, and creating a sense of participation and partnership. For example, one person described Mayo as "A well conducted symphony . . . works harmoniously . . . One person can't do it alone . . . Teamwork, cooperation, compatibility."

For integrity, respondents placed great value on the fact that Mayo is noncommercial and committed to health and healing over profit. One participant said, "The business element is taken out of Mayo. . . . Their ethics are higher . . . which gives me greater faith in their diagnosis."

Although none of Mayo Clinic's brand attributes are solely negative, perceptions of exclusivity pose some specific challenges. This attribute was sometimes described positively, in perceptions that Mayo offers the highest quality care and elite doctors, but inaccurate beliefs that it serves only the rich and famous and the sickest of the sick were emotionally distancing and made Mayo seem inaccessible.

In a more recent quantitative study, overall awareness of Mayo Clinic in the United States was 90.2 percent, and a remarkable one-third knew at least one Mayo patient. One of the key questions in the survey asked, "Suppose your health plan or personal finances permitted you to go anywhere in the U.S. for a serious medical condition which required highly specialized care, to which one institution would you prefer to go?" Mayo Clinic was the most popular choice, earning 18.6 percent of the responses, compared with 5.0 percent for the next most frequently mentioned medical center. Word-of-mouth has the most influence on these preferences for highly specialized medical care.

From its research, Mayo Clinic understands that its brand "is precious and powerful." Mayo realized that while it had an overwhelmingly positive image, it was vital to develop guidelines to protect the brand. In 1999, the clinic created a brand

The Mayo Clinic knows the importance and value of its brand and carefully monitors and manages its image and equity.
Source: Courtesy Mayo Clinic

management infrastructure to be the "institutional clearinghouse for ongoing knowledge about external perceptions of Mayo Clinic and its related activities." Mayo Clinic also established guidelines for applying the brand to products and services. Its brand management measures work to ensure that the clinic preserves its brand equity, as well as allowing Mayo to continue to accomplish its mission:

> *To inspire hope and contribute to health and well-being by providing the best care to every patient through integrated clinical practice, education and research.*

Sources: Thanks to Mayo Clinic's John La Forgia, Kent Seltman, Scott Swanson, and Amy Davis for assistance and cooperation, including interviews in October 2011; www.mayoclinic.org; "Mayo Clinic Brand Management," internal document, 1999; Leonard L. Berry and Neeli Bendapudi, "Clueing in Customers," *Harvard Business Review* (February 2003): 100–106; Paul Roberts, "The Agenda—Total Teamwork," *Fast Company*, April 1999, 148; Leonard L. Berry and Kent D. Seltman, *Management Lessons from Mayo Clinic: Inside One of the World's Most Admired Service Organizations* (New York: McGraw Hill, 2008).

Brand Charter

The first step in establishing a brand equity management system is to formalize the company view of brand equity into a document, the *brand charter*, or brand bible as it is sometimes called, that provides relevant guidelines to marketing managers within the company as well as to key marketing partners outside the company such as marketing research suppliers or ad agency staff. This document should crisply and concisely do the following:

- Define the firm's view of branding and brand equity and explain why it is important.
- Describe the scope of key brands in terms of associated products and the manner by which they have been branded and marketed (as revealed by historical company records as well as the most recent brand audit).
- Specify what the actual and desired equity is for brands at all relevant levels of the brand hierarchy, for example, at both the corporate and the individual product level. The charter should define and clarify points-of-parity, points-of-difference, and the brand mantra.
- Explain how brand equity is measured in terms of the tracking study and the resulting brand equity report (described shortly).
- Suggest how marketers should manage brands with some general strategic guidelines, stressing clarity, consistency, and innovation in marketing thinking over time.
- Outline how to devise marketing programs along specific tactical guidelines, satisfying differentiation, relevance, integration, value, and excellence criteria. Guidelines for specific brand management tasks such as ad campaign evaluation and brand name selection may also be offered.
- Specify the proper treatment of the brand in terms of trademark usage, design considerations, packaging, and communications. As these types of instructions can be long and detailed, it is often better to create a separate *Brand or Corporate Identity Style Manual* or guide to address these more mechanical considerations.

Although parts of the brand charter may not change from year to year, the firm should nevertheless update it on an annual basis to provide decision makers with a current brand profile and to identify new opportunities and potential risks for the brand. As marketers introduce new products, change brand programs, and conduct other marketing initiatives, they should reflect these adequately in the brand charter. Many of the in-depth insights that emerge from brand audits also belong in the charter.

Skype's brand bible, for example, outlines the branding and image of its products and services.[13] The document clearly states how Skype wants to be seen by consumers, how the firm uses its branding to achieve that, and why this is important. It also explains how Skype's logo of clouds and the vivid blue color are designed to make clean lines and foster a creative and simple look. The brand bible explains the "do's and don'ts" of marketing Skype's products and services and the dangers for the company image of working outside the brand guidelines.

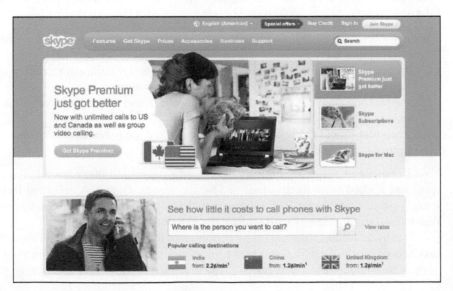

Skype's brand bible provides important guidelines about how the brand should look and behave.

Source: Skype

Brand Equity Report

The second step in establishing a successful brand equity management system is to assemble the results of the tracking survey and other relevant performance measures for the brand into a brand equity report or scorecard to be distributed to management on a regular basis (weekly, monthly, quarterly, or annually). Much of the information relevant to the report may already exist within the organization. Yet it may have been presented to management in disjointed chunks so that no one has a holistic understanding of it. The brand equity report attempts to effectively integrate all these different measures.[14]

Contents. The brand equity report should describe *what* is happening with the brand as well as *why* it is happening. It should include all relevant internal measures of operational efficiency and effectiveness and external measures of brand performance and sources and outcomes of brand equity.[15]

In particular, one section of the report should summarize consumers' perceptions of key attribute or benefit associations, preferences, and reported behavior as revealed by the tracking study. Another section of the report should include more descriptive market-level information such as the following:

- Product shipments and movement through channels of distribution
- Retail category trends
- Relevant cost breakdowns
- Price and discount schedules where appropriate
- Sales and market share information broken down by relevant factors (such as geographic region, type of retail account, or customer)
- Profit assessments

These measures can provide insight into the market performance component of the brand value chain. Management can compare them to various frames of reference—performance last month/quarter/year—and color code them green, yellow, or red, depending on whether the trends are positive, neutral, or negative, respectively. Internal measures might focus on how much time, money, and labor was being spent on various marketing activities.[16]

Dashboards. As important as the information making up the brand equity report is the *way* the information is presented. Thus firms are now also exploring how best to display the right data to influence marketing decision makers. Top digital agency R/GA, for example, has created a data-visualization department to reflect the growing importance of presenting information to its clients.[17]

A number of firms have implemented *marketing dashboards* to provide comprehensive but actionable summaries of brand-related information. A marketing dashboard functions just like the dashboard of a car. Although they can be valuable tools for companies, if not designed and implemented properly dashboards also can be a big waste of time and money. An early leader on the subject, Pat LaPointe has identified four success factors in developing a successful dashboard:[18]

1. Senior-level executives must devote the necessary resources to its development and stay actively involved—delegating the task to lower levels of the organization rarely pays off.
2. The investment in resources doesn't stop with launch. Additional resources are required to gather, align, and properly interpret the right information.
3. Graphics and analytics matter. Excel may be cheap and easy to use, but it can also constrain thinking.
4. Executives should focus on what can be measured today but also learn more about how to improve the dashboard in the future.

IT company Unisys successfully developed a dashboard that covered all its geographical areas and applied to all its divisions and business units. Data was collected from a variety of sources—brand tracking, CRM programs, tradeshows, media reports, satisfaction studies, and Web logs—offering views for all levels right up to the CMO.[19]

To provide feedback on marketing performance to boards of directors, former Harvard Business School faculty Gail McGovern and John Quelch advocate quarterly tracking reports of the three or four marketing or customer-related metrics that truly drive and predict the company's

Harrah's has an extensive customer information system that helps the company track key metrics.
Source: Craig Moran/ Rapport Press/Newscom

business performance—the behavioral measures specific to a company's business model.[20] As an example, they note how the board of casino operator Harrah's focuses on three metrics: share of its customer's gaming dollars (share of wallet), loyalty program updates (an indicator of increased concentration of a customer's gaming at Harrah's), and percent of revenue from customers visiting more than one of Harrah's 30 casinos (an indicator of cross-selling). To support its tracking, Harrah's has spent $50 million annually on a customer information system.

Similarly, Ambler and Clark offer three recommendations.[21] First, marketers must work with their CFO to develop marketing dashboards and to shift metrics and forecasting responsibilities to the finance department. Second, marketers should develop with each agency a detailed brief with measurable objectives and a results-driven compensation component (for agencies). Third, marketers need to dedicate extra time to securing buy-in from colleagues on their business model, strategy, and metrics.

In terms of choosing specific metrics for a brand equity report or dashboard, Ambler and Clark offer three additional guidelines.[22] First, marketers must select metrics that suit their business model and strategy. Two, they need to balance their metrics portfolio across audiences, comprehensiveness, efficiency, and other considerations. Three, marketers should review and modify their metrics portfolio as their needs change.

With advances in computer technology, it will be increasingly easy for firms to place the information that makes up the brand equity report online, so managers can access it through the firm's intranet or some other means. For example, early research pioneer NFO MarketMind developed a brand management database system that integrated continuous consumer tracking survey data, media weight (or cost) data, warehouse sales and retail scan data, and PR and editorial content.

Brand Equity Responsibilities

To develop a brand equity management system that will maximize long-term brand equity, managers must clearly define organizational responsibilities and processes with respect to the brand. Brands need constant, consistent nurturing to grow. Weak brands often suffer from a lack of discipline, commitment, and investment in brand building. In this section, we consider internal issues of assigning responsibilities and duties for properly managing brand equity, as well as external issues related to the proper roles of marketing partners. The Science of Branding 2 describes some important principles in building a brand-driven organization.

THE SCIENCE OF BRANDING 2

Maximizing Internal Branding

Internal branding doesn't always receive as much time, money, or effort as external branding programs receive. But although it may require significant resources, it generates a number of benefits. Internal branding creates a positive and more productive work environment. It can also be a platform for change and help foster an organization's identity. For example, after employee turnover became too high, Yahoo! created the "What Sucks" program in which employees could send their concerns straight to the CEO.

Branding expert Scott Davis offers a number of insights into what it takes to make a brand-driven organization. According to Davis, for employees to become passionate brand advocates, they must understand what a brand is, how it is built, what their organization's brand stands for, and what their role is in delivering on the brand promise. Formally, he sees the process of helping an organization's employees assimilate the brand as three stages:

Part of the success of Nordstrom's legendary customer service is that it empowers employees to take brand-consistent actions.
Source: REUTERS/Rick Wilking

1. *Hear It:* How do we best get it into their hands?

2. *Believe It:* How do we best get it into their heads?

3. *Live It:* How do we best get it into their hearts?

Davis also argues that six key principles should guide the brand assimilation process within an organization, offering the following examples.

1. *Make the brand relevant.* Each employee must understand and embrace the brand meaning. Nordstrom, whose brand relies on top-notch customer service, empowers sales associates to approve exchanges without manager approval.

2. *Make the brand accessible.* Employees must know where they can get brand knowledge and answers to their brand-related questions. Ernst & Young launched "The Branding Zone" on its intranet to provide employees easy access to information about its branding, marketing, and advertising programs.

3. *Reinforce the brand continuously.* Management must reinforce the brand meaning with employees beyond the initial rollout of an internal branding program. Southwest Airlines continually reinforces its brand promise of "a symbol of freedom" through ongoing programs and activities with a freedom theme.

4. *Make brand education an ongoing program.* Provide new employees with inspiring and informative training. Ritz-Carlton ensures that each employee participates in an intensive orientation called "The Gold Standard" that includes principles to improve service delivery and maximize guest satisfaction.

5. *Reward on-brand behaviors.* An incentive system to reward employees for exceptional support of the brand strategy should coincide with the roll-out of an internal branding program. Prior to its merger with United, Continental Airlines rewarded employees with cash bonuses each month that the airline ranked in the top five of on-time airlines.

6. *Align hiring practices.* HR and marketing must work together to develop criteria and screening procedures to ensure that new hires are good fits for the company's brand culture. Pret A Manger sandwich shops has such a carefully honed screener that only 20 percent of applicants end up being hired.

Davis also emphasizes the role of senior management in driving internal branding, noting that the CEO ultimately sets the tone and compliance with a brand-based culture and determines whether proper resources and procedures are put into place.

Sources: Scott M. Davis, *Building the Brand-Driven Business: Operationalize Your Brand to Drive Profitable Growth* (San Francisco, CA: Jossey-Bass, 2002); Scott M. Davis, "Building a Brand-Driven Organization," in *Kellogg on Branding*, eds. Alice M. Tybout and Tim Calkins (Hoboken, NJ: John Wiley & Sons, 2005); Scott M. Davis, *The Shift: The Transformation of Today's Marketers into Tomorrow's Growth Leaders* (San Francisco, CA: Jossey-Bass, 2009).

Overseeing Brand Equity. To provide central coordination, the firm should establish a position responsible for overseeing the implementation of the brand charter and brand equity reports, to ensure that product and marketing actions across divisions and geographic boundaries reflect their spirit as closely as possible and maximize the long-term equity of the brand. A natural place to house such oversight duties and responsibilities is in a corporate marketing group that has a senior management reporting relationship.

Scott Bedbury, who helped direct the Nike and Starbucks brands during some of their most successful years, is emphatic about the need for "top-down brand leadership."[23] He advocates the addition of a chief brand officer (CBO) who reports directly to the CEO of the company and who:

- *Is an omnipresent conscience whose job is to champion and protect the brand—the way it looks and feels—both inside and outside the company.* The CBO recognizes that the brand is the sum total of everything a company does and strives to ensure that all employees understand the brand and its values, creating "brand disciples" in the process.
- *Is an architect and not only helps build the brand but also plans, anticipates, researches, probes, listens, and informs.* Working with senior leadership, the CBO helps envision not just what works best for the brand today but also what can help drive it forward in the future.
- *Determines and protects the voice of the brand over time by taking a long-term (two to three years) perspective.* The CBO can be accountable for brand-critical and corporate-wide activities such as advertising, positioning, corporate design, corporate communications, and consumer or market insights.

Bedbury also advocates periodic brand development reviews (full-day meetings quarterly, or even half-day meetings monthly) for brands in difficult circumstances. As part of a brand development review, he suggests the following topics and activities:[24]

- *Review brand-sensitive material:* For example, review brand strength monitors or tracking studies, brand audits, and focus groups, as well as less formal personal observations or "gut feelings."
- *Review the status of key brand initiatives:* Because brand initiatives include strategic thrusts to either strengthen a weakness in the brand or exploit an opportunity to grow the brand in a new direction, customer perceptions may change and marketers therefore need to assess them.
- *Review brand-sensitive projects:* For example, evaluate advertising campaigns, corporate communications, sales meeting agendas, and important human resources programs (recruitment, training, and retention that profoundly affect the organization's ability to embrace and project brand values).
- *Review new product and distribution strategies with respect to core brand values:* For example, evaluate licensing the brand to penetrate new markets, forming joint ventures to develop new products or brands, and expanding distribution to nontraditional platforms such as large-scale discount retailers.
- *Resolve brand positioning conflicts:* Identify and resolve any inconsistencies in positioning across channels, business units, or markets.

Even strong brands need careful watching to prevent managers from assuming it's acceptable to "make one little mistake" with brand equity or to "let it slide." A number of top companies like Colgate-Palmolive, Canada Dry, Quaker Oats, Pillsbury, Coca-Cola, and Nestlé Foods have created brand equity gatekeepers for some or all their brands at one time.[25] Branding Brief 3 contains a checklist by which firms can assess their marketing skills and performance.

One of senior management's important roles is to determine marketing budgets and decide where and how to allocate company resources within the organization. The brand equity management system must be able to inform and provide input to decision makers so that they can recognize the short-term and long-term ramifications of their decisions for brand equity. Decisions about which brands to invest in, and whether to implement brand-building marketing programs or leverage brand equity through brand extensions instead, should reflect the current and desired state of the brand as revealed through brand tracking and other measures.

Organizational Design and Structures. The firm should organize its marketing function to optimize brand equity. Several trends have emerged in organizational design and structure

How Good Is Your Marketing? Rating a Firm's Marketing Assessment System

Famed former London Business School professor Tim Ambler has a wealth of experience in working with companies. He notes that in his interactions, "most companies do not have a clear picture of their own marketing performance which may be why they cannot assess it." To help companies evaluate if their marketing assessment system is good enough, he suggests that they ask the following 10 questions—the higher the score, the better the assessment system.

1. Does the senior executive team regularly and formally assess marketing performance?

   a. Yearly—10

   b. Six-monthly—10

   c. Quarterly—5

   d. More often—0

   e. Rarely—0

   f. Never—0

2. What does the senior executive team understand by "customer value"?

   a. Don't know. We are not clear about this—0

   b. Value of the customer to the business (as in "customer lifetime value")—5

   c. Value of what the company provides from the customers' point of view—10

   d. Sometimes one, sometimes the other—10

3. How much time does the senior executive team give to marketing issues?

   a. >30%—10

   b. 20–30%—6

   c. 10–20%—4;

   d. <10%—0

4. Does the business/marketing plan show the non-financial corporate goals and link them to market goals?

   a. No/no plan—0

   b. Corporate no, market yes—5

   c. Yes to both—10

5. Does the plan show the comparison of your marketing performance with competitors or the market as a whole?

   a. No/no plan—0

   b. Yes, clearly—10

   c. In between—5

6. What is your main marketing asset called?

   a. Brand equity—10

   b. Reputation—10

   c. Other term—5

   d. We have no term—0

7. Does the senior executive team's performance review involve a quantified view of the main marketing asset and how it has changed?

   a. Yes to both—10

   b. Yes but only financially (brand valuation)—5

   c. Not really—0

8. Has the senior executive team quantified what "success" would look like 5 or 10 years from now?

   a. No—0

   b. Yes—10

   c. Don't know—0

9. Does your strategy have quantified milestones to indicate progress toward that success?

   a. No—0

   b. Yes—10

   c. What strategy?—0

10. Are the marketing performance indicators seen by the senior executive team aligned with these milestones?

    a. No—0

    b. Yes, external (customers and competitors)—7

    c. Yes, internal (employees and innovativeness)—5

    d. Yes, both—10

Sources: Adapted from Tim Ambler, "10 Ways to Rate Your Firm's Marketing Assessment System," www.zibs.com, September 2005; Tim Ambler, *Marketing and the Bottom Line*, 2nd ed. (London: FT Prentice Hall, 2004).

Many leading manufacturers such as Procter & Gamble are assuming the role of category captain to help retailers manage sections of their stores.
Source: HolgerBurmeister/ Alamy

that reflect the growing recognition of the importance of the brand and the challenges of managing brand equity carefully. For example, an increasing number of firms are embracing brand management. Firms from more and more industries—such as the automobile, health care, pharmaceutical, and computer software and hardware industries—are introducing brand managers into their organizations. Often, they have hired managers from top packaged-goods companies, adopting some of the same brand marketing practices as a result.

Interestingly, packaged-goods companies, such as Procter & Gamble, continue to evolve the brand management system. With category management, manufacturers offer retailers advice about how to best stock their shelves. An increasing number of retailers are also adopting category management principles. Although manufacturers functioning as category captains can improve sales, experts caution retailers to exercise their own insights and values to retain their distinctiveness in the marketplace.

Many firms are thus attempting to redesign their marketing organizations to better reflect the challenges faced by their brands. At the same time, because of changing job requirements and duties, the traditional marketing department is disappearing from a number of companies that are exploring other ways to conduct their marketing functions through business groups, multidisciplinary teams, and so on.[26]

The goal in these new organizational schemes is to improve internal coordination and efficiencies as well as external focus on retailers and consumers. Although these are laudable goals, clearly one of the challenges with these new designs is to ensure that brand equity is preserved and nurtured, and not neglected due to a lack of oversight.

With a multiple-product, multiple-market organization, the difficulty often lies in making sure that both product and place are in balance. As in many marketing and branding activities, achieving the proper balance is the goal, in order to maximize the advantages and minimize the disadvantages of both approaches.

Managing Marketing Partners. Because the performance of a brand also depends on the actions taken by outside suppliers and marketing partners, firms must manage these relationships carefully. Increasingly, firms have been consolidating their marketing partnerships and reducing the number of their outside suppliers.

This trend has been especially apparent with global advertising accounts, where a number of firms have placed most, if not all, their business with one agency. For example, Colgate-Palmolive has worked largely with just Young & Rubicam, and American Express and IBM with Ogilvy & Mather.

Factors like cost efficiencies, organizational leverage, and creative diversification affect the number of outside suppliers the firm will hire in any one area. From a branding perspective, one advantage of dealing with a single major supplier such as an ad agency is the greater consistency in understanding and treatment of a brand that can result.

Other marketing partners can also play an important role. For example, channel members and retailers are important in enhancing brand equity and cleverly designed push programs can be critical. One important function of having a brand charter or bible is to inform and educate marketing partners so that they can provide more brand-consistent support.

REVIEW

A brand equity measurement system is defined as a set of research procedures designed to provide timely, accurate, and actionable information for marketers regarding brands so that they can make the best possible tactical decisions in the short run as well as strategic decisions in the long run. Implementing a brand equity measurement system involves two steps: conducting brand audits, designing brand tracking studies, and establishing a brand equity management system.

A brand audit is a consumer-focused exercise to assess the health of the brand, uncover its sources of brand equity, and suggest ways to improve and leverage its equity. It requires understanding brand equity from the perspective of both the firm and the consumer. The brand audit consists of two steps: the brand inventory and the brand exploratory.

The purpose of the brand inventory is to provide a complete, up-to-date profile of how all the products and services sold by a company are marketed and branded. Profiling each product or service requires us to identify the associated brand elements as well as the supporting marketing program. The brand exploratory is research activity directed to understanding what consumers think and feel about the brand to identify sources of brand equity.

Brand audits can be used to set the strategic direction for the brand. As a result of this strategic analysis, a marketing program can be put into place to maximize long-term brand equity. Tracking studies employing quantitative measures can then be conducted to provide marketers with current information as to how their brands are performing on the basis of a number of key dimensions identified by the brand audit.

Tracking studies involve information collected from consumers on a routine basis over time and provide valuable tactical insights into the short-term effectiveness of marketing programs and activities. Whereas brand audits measure "where the brand has been," tracking studies measure "where the brand is now" and whether marketing programs are having their intended effects.

Three major steps must occur as part of a brand equity management system. First, the company view of brand equity should be formalized into a document, the brand charter. This document serves a number of purposes: It chronicles the company's general philosophy with respect to brand equity; summarizes the activity and outcomes related to brand audits, brand tracking, and so forth; outlines guidelines for brand strategies and tactics; and documents proper treatment of the brand. The charter should be updated annually to identify new opportunities and risks and to fully reflect information gathered by the brand inventory and brand exploratory as part of any brand audits.

Second, the results of the tracking surveys and other relevant outcome measures should be assembled into a brand equity report that is distributed to management on a regular basis (monthly, quarterly, or annually). The brand equity report should provide descriptive information as to *what* is happening to a brand as well as diagnostic information as to *why* it is happening. These reports are often being displayed in marketing dashboards for ease of review.

Finally, senior management must be assigned to oversee how brand equity is treated within the organization. The people in that position would be responsible for overseeing the implementation of the brand charter and brand equity reports to make sure that, as much as possible, product and marketing actions across divisions and geographic boundaries are performed in a way that reflects the spirit of the charter and the substance of the report so as to maximize the long-term equity of the brand.

DISCUSSION QUESTIONS

1. What do you see as the biggest challenges in conducting a brand audit? What steps would you take to overcome them?
2. Pick a brand. See if you can assemble a brand inventory for it.
3. Consider the McDonald's tracking survey presented in Branding Brief 3. What might you do differently? What questions would you change or drop? What questions might you add? How might this tracking survey differ from those used for other products?
4. Can you develop a tracking survey for the Mayo Clinic? How might it differ from the McDonald's tracking survey?
5. Critique the Rolex brand audit in the Brand Focus. How do you think it could be improved?

BRAND FOCUS

Rolex Brand Audit

For over a century, Rolex has remained one of the most recognized and sought-after luxury brands in the world. In 2009, *Businessweek*/Interbrand ranked Rolex as the 71st most valuable global brand, with an estimated brand value of $5 billion.[27] A thorough audit can help pinpoint opportunities and challenges for Rolex, whose brand equity has been historically strong, as much is at stake.

"The name of Rolex is synonymous with quality. Rolex—with its rigorous series of tests that intervene at every stage—has redefined the meaning of quality."

—www.rolex.com

BACKGROUND

History

Rolex was founded in 1905 by a German named Hans Wilsdorf and his brother-in-law, William Davis, as a watch-making company, Wilsdorf & Davis, with headquarters in London, England. Wilsdorf, a self-proclaimed perfectionist, set out to improve the mainstream pocket watch right from the start. By 1908, he had created a timepiece that kept accurate time but was small enough to be worn on the wrist. That same year, Wilsdorf trademarked the name "Rolex" because he thought it sounded like the noise a watch made when it was wound. Rolex was also easy to pronounce in many different languages.

In 1912, Rolex moved its headquarters to Geneva, Switzerland, and started working on improving the reliability of its watches. Back then, dust and moisture could enter the watch case and cause damage to the movement or internal mechanism of the watch. As a result, Wilsdorf invented a screw crown and waterproof casebook mechanism that revolutionized the watch industry. In 1914, the Rolex wristwatch obtained the first Kew "A" certificate after passing the world's toughest timing test, which included testing the watch at extreme temperature levels.

Twelve years later, Wilsdorf developed and patented the now famous Oyster waterproof case and screw crown. This mechanism became the first true protection against water, dust, and dirt. To generate publicity for the watch, jewelry stores displayed fish tanks in their windows with the Oyster watch

completely submerged in it. The Oyster was put to the test on October 7, 1927, when Mercedes Gleitze swam the English Channel wearing one. She emerged 15 hours later with the watch functioning perfectly, much to the amazement of the media and public. Gleitze became the first of a long list of "ambassadors" that Rolex has used to promote its wristwatches.

Over the years, Rolex has pushed innovation in watches to new levels. In 1931, the firm introduced the Perpetual self-winding rotor mechanism, eliminating the need to wind a watch. In 1945, the company invented the first watch to display a number date at the 3 o'clock position and named it the Datejust. In 1953, Rolex launched the Submariner—the first diving watch that was water-resistant and pressure-resistant to 100 meters. The sporty watch appeared in various James Bond movies in the 1950s and became an instant symbol of prestige and durability.

For decades, Swiss-made watches owned the middle and high-end markets, remaining virtually unrivaled until the invention of the quartz watch in 1969. Quartz watches kept more accurate time, were less expensive to make, and quickly dominated the middle market. Within 10 years, quartz watches made up approximately half of all watch sales worldwide.[28] Joe Thompson, editor of *Modern Jeweler*, a U.S. trade publication, explained, "By 1980, people thought the mechanical watch was dead."[29]

Rolex proved the experts wrong. The company would not give in to the quartz watch rage. In order to survive, however, Rolex was forced to move into the high-end market exclusively—leaving the middle to the quartz people—and create a strategy to defend and build its position there.

Private Ownership

Rolex is a privately owned company and has been controlled by only three people in its 100-year history. Before Wilsdorf died, he set up the Hans Wilsdorf Foundation, ensuring that some of the company's income would go to charity and that control of the company lay with the foundation.[30] This move was a critical step toward the long-term success of Rolex as a high-end brand. Over the years, many luxury brands have been forced to

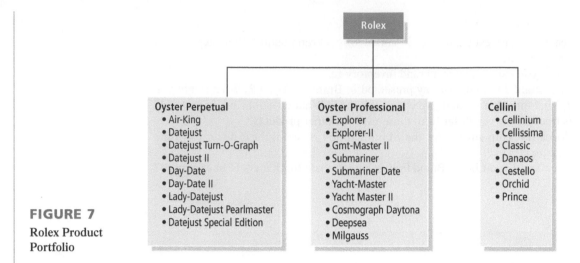

FIGURE 7
Rolex Product
Portfolio

affiliate with conglomerates in order to compete, but by staying an independent entity, Rolex has remained focused on its core business. André Heiniger, managing chairman of Rolex through the 1980s, explained, "Rolex's strategy is oriented to marketing, maintaining quality, and staying out of fields where we are not prepared to compete effectively."

Brand Portfolio

Rolex includes three family brands of wristwatches, called "collections"; each has a subset of brands (see Figure 7).

- The *Oyster Perpetual Collection* includes the "traditional" Rolex wristwatch, and has eight sub-brands that are differentiated by features and design. The Perpetual Collection targets affluent men and women.

- The *Professional Collection* targets specific athletic and adventurer user groups through its features and imagery. The Oyster Professional Collection includes seven sub-brands.

- The *Cellini Collection* focuses on formal occasions through its elegant designs, and encompasses seven sub-brands. These watches incorporate fashion and style features like colored leather bands and an extensive use of diamonds.

In addition to the three collections, Rolex owns a separate "fighter" brand called Tudor, developed in 1946 to stave off competition from mid-range watches such as Tag Heuer, Citizen, and Rado. Tudor has its own range of family brands, or collections, namely Prince, Princess, Monarch, and Sport, each of which encompasses a number of sub-brands. Tudor watches are sold at own-brand specialty stores and through the network of exclusive Rolex dealers. Although they are no longer for sale in the United States, there are many outlets in Europe and Asia. Tudor targets younger consumers and offers watches at a lower price range. The brand is distinctly separate, and the Rolex name does not appear on Tudor watches.

BRAND INVENTORY

Rolex's success as the largest single luxury watch brand can be credited to several factors. The company not only produces extremely high-quality timepieces, but also tightly controls how its watches are sold, ensuring high demand and premium prices. In addition, Rolex's sophisticated marketing strategy has created an exclusive and premium brand that many aspire to own. The brand inventory will describe each of these factors in more depth.

Brand Elements

Rolex's most distinguishable brand element is its Crown logo. Trademarked in 1925, the Crown made its appearance on the watches in 1939. The logo has undergone few revisions, keeping its signature five-point crown intact over the years. Rolex watches feature the name "Rolex" on the dial, a tradition dating to 1926. This development initially helped increase brand recognition. Many Rolex watches also have a distinct look, including a big round face and wide wrist band.

Rolex watches have a classic design and look.
Source: Lee Hacker/Alamy

Product

Throughout the years, Rolex timepieces have maintained the high quality, durability, and prestige on which the company built its name. In particular, the firm has maintained a keen focus on delivering a highly accurate watch of superior craftsmanship, using only the finest premium materials such as gold, platinum, and jewels. It continually works on improving the functionality of its watches with better movements and new, sophisticated features. As a result, Rolex watches are complex mechanisms compared to most mass-produced watches. A quartz watch, for example, has between 50 and 100 parts; a Rolex Oyster chronometer has 220.[31]

Each Rolex watch consists of 10 unique features identified as the company's "10 Golden Rules:"

1. A waterproof case
2. The Perpetual rotor
3. The case back
4. The Oyster case
5. The winding crown
6. The finest and purest materials
7. Quality control
8. Rolex self-winding movement
9. Testing from the independent Controle Official Suisse des Chronometres
10. Rolex testing

The company does not license its brand or produce any other product besides watches. Its product portfolio is clear, concise, and focused.

Rolex spends more time and money than any other watch company fighting counterfeiters. Today, it is often hard to spot the differences between a $25 counterfeit and a $10,000 authentic Rolex watch. Counterfeiting Rolex watches has become a sophisticated industry, with sales exceeding $1.8 billion per year.

Pricing

By limiting production to approximately 2,000 watches a day, Rolex keeps consumer demand high and prices at a premium.

Prices start around $2,500 for the basic Oyster Perpetual and can reach $200,000, depending on the specific materials used such as steel, yellow gold, or platinum. Scarcity also helps positively influence the resale value of Rolex watches. One report indicated that "almost all older Rolex models are valued above their initial selling price."[32]

Distribution

Rolex carefully monitors how its timepieces are sold, distributing them only through its approximately 60,000 "Official Rolex Dealers" worldwide. Official dealers must meet several criteria, including a high-end image, adequate space, attractive location, and outstanding service. In addition, a large secondary market exists for Rolex, both through online auction sites such as eBay and at live auctions run by Christies and Sotheby's.

Communications

Rolex's marketing and communications strategy strives to create a high-quality, exclusive brand image. The company associates itself with "ambassadors"—established artists, top athletes, rugged adventurers, and daring explorers—to help create this imagery. Rolex also sponsors various sports and cultural events as well as philanthropy programs to help align with targeted demographics as well as create positive associations in consumers' minds.

Advertising. Rolex is the number-one watch advertiser in the world. In 2008, the firm spent over $49 million on advertising, $20 million more than the number-two contender, Breitling.[33] One of the company's largest expenditures is for magazine advertising. Rolex's print ads are often simple and austere, usually featuring one of its many brand ambassadors or a close-up photo of one of its watches with the tagline "Rolex. A Crown for Every Achievement." Rolex does not advertise extensively on television, but does sponsor some events that are televised.

Ambassadors. Rolex's celebrity endorsers are continuously added and dropped depending on their performance. These ambassadors fall into four categories: athletes, artists, explorers,

Rolex sponsors a number of different sporting events, including sailing races.
Source: AP Photo/J Pat Carter

Artists	Explorers	Golfers	Racing
Cecilia Bartoli	David Doubilet	Paul Casey	Sir Jackie Stewart
Michael Buble	Sylvia Earle	Luke Donald	Tom Kristensen
Placido Domingo	Alain Hubert	Ricky Fowler	Rolex 24 at Daytona
Gustavo Dudamel	Jean Troillet	Retief Goosen	Goodwood Revival
Renee Fleming	Ed Viesturs	Charles Howell	24 Hours at Le Mans
Sylvie Guillem	Chuck Yeager	Trevor Immelman	
Jonas Kaufmann	Setting Out to Conquer the World	Martin Kaymer	Tennis
Diana Krall	Deepsea Under the Pole	Matteo Manassero	Roger Federer
Yo-Yo Ma	The Deep	Phil Mickelson	Justine Henin
Anoushka Shankar	The Deepest Dive	Jack Nicklaus	Ana Ivanovic
Bryn Terfel		Lorena Ochoa	Zheng Jie
Rolando Villazon	Yachting	Arnold Palmer	Juan Martín del Potro
Yuja Wang	Robert Scheidt	Gary Player	Li Na
Royal Opera House	Paul Cayard	Adam Scott	Jo-Wilfried Tsonga
Teatro Alla Scalla	Rolex Sydney Hobart	Annika Sorenstam	Caroline Wosniacki
Wiener Philharmoniker	Maxi Yacht Rolex Cup	Camilo Villegas	Wimbledon
	Rolex Fastnet Race	Tom Watson	Australian Open
	Rolex Farr 40 World Championship	U.S. Open Championship	Monte-Carlo Rolex Masters
	Rolex Swan Cup	The Open Championship	Shanghai Rolex Masters
		The Ryder Cup	
	Equestrian	The President's Cup	Skiing
	Rodrigo Pessoa	Evian Masters	Hermann Maier
	Gonzalo Pieres, Jr.	The Solheim Cup	Lindsay Vonn
			Carlo Janka
			The Hahnenkamm Races

FIGURE 8 2011 Rolex Ambassadors

and yachtsmen (see Figure 8). Aligning with acclaimed artists symbolizes the pursuit of perfection. Association with elite sports figures is meant to signify the company's quest for excellence. Its support of sailing events, for example, highlights the company's core values: excellence, precision, and team spirit.[34] Explorers also test the excellence and innovation of Rolex's watches at extreme conditions. Rolex ambassadors have scaled Mt. Everest, broken the speed of sound, reached the depths of the ocean, and traveled in space. A print ad will usually feature one ambassador and one specific watch, with the goal of targeting a very specific demographic or consumer group.

In 2011, much to the surprise of industry experts, Rolex signed golfer Tiger Woods as a Rolex ambassador. Woods has had a long and complicated history as a celebrity endorser of watches. In 1997, just after he turned pro, Rolex's Tudor watch signed him to a partnership that lasted almost five years. Woods backed out of the contract in 2002 to sign with rival Tag Heuer, which paid him approximately $2 million annually. Woods rationalized his decision to end ties with Tudor by explaining, "My tastes have changed," and that he didn't "feel a connection with that company."[35] In 2009, the tables turned when Tag Heuer announced it had ended the relationship following Woods's involvement in a sex scandal.

Rolex's sponsorship marked the golfer's first celebrity endorsement since 2009. The company said it was "convinced that Tiger Woods still has a long career ahead of him and that he has all the qualities required to continue to mark the history of golf. The brand is committed to accompanying him in his new challenges . . . This association pays tribute to the exceptional stature of Tiger Woods and the leading role he plays in forging the sport's global appeal. It also constitutes a joint commitment to the future."[36]

Sports and Culture. Rolex sponsors a variety of elite athletic and cultural events to reinforce the same messages, values, and associations as it does through its ambassador endorsements. These include a quest for excellence, pursuit of perfection, teamwork, and ruggedness. Rolex sponsors sporting events in golf (U.S. Open Championship, the Open Championship, and the Ryder Cup), tennis (Wimbledon and the Australian Open), skiing (the Hahnenkamm Races), racing (Rolex 24 at Daytona), and equestrian events.

Rolex also sponsors several sailing races, including the Rolex Sydney, Rolex Fastnet Race, and Maxi Yacht Rolex Cup. The company has partnered with extreme exploration expeditions, including The Deepest Dive and Deepsea Under the Pole. It is a major contributor to establishments such as the Royal Opera House in London and the Teatro alla Scala in Milan to align with a more cultural audience.

Philanthropy. Rolex gives back through three established philanthropic programs:

1. The *Awards for Enterprise* program supports individuals whose work focuses on benefiting their communities and the world. These projects are focused on science and health, applied technology, exploration and discovery, the environment, and cultural heritage.[37]

2. The *Young Laureates Programme* is part of the Awards for Enterprise program, providing support for outstanding innovators between the ages of 18 and 30.[38]

3. The *Rolex Mentor and Protégé Arts Initiative* seeks out extraordinarily gifted young artists around the world and pairs them with established masters. Young artists have been paired with accomplished filmmakers, dancers, artists, composers, and actors.[39]

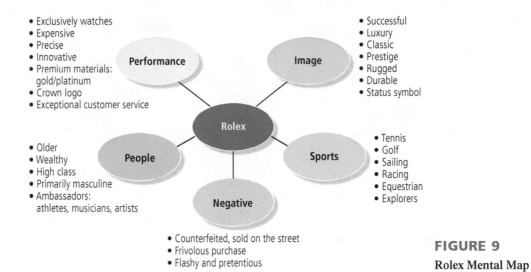

FIGURE 9
Rolex Mental Map

BRAND EXPLORATORY

Consumer Knowledge

Rolex has successfully leveraged its history and tradition of excellence along with innovation to become the most powerful and recognized watchmaker in the world. Some positive consumer brand associations for Rolex might be "sophisticated," "prestigious," "exclusive," "powerful," "elegant," "high quality." Some negative brand associations that some consumers may link to the brand, however, could include "flashy" or "snobby." Figure 9 displays a hypothetical Rolex mental map.

In one report by the Luxury Institute research group in New York, consumers had positive attitudes in terms of purchase intent toward Rolex. Wealthy people said they were more likely to buy a Rolex than any other brand for their next watch. The Rolex brand was far more recognizable (84 percent knew it) than Bulgari (39 percent) and even Cartier (63 percent), although several rivals outranked Rolex for perceived quality and exclusivity.[40]

A 2008 Mintel survey on the watch industry revealed that "women are still likely to view watches as an accessory, with many buyers choosing their watch based on looks alone. However, at the top end of the luxury market there is a growing number of women who are interested in mechanical watches. The study also found that women are increasingly choosing androgynous or unisex watches."[41]

Many older, affluent people place a high value on owning a Rolex, whether new or collectible. In 2011, a Rolex sold for $1 million for the first time. The watch—an oversized stainless-steel split-second chronograph wristwatch manufactured in 1942—was purchased at Christie's Geneva auction for $1,163,340, an all-time high price paid for any Rolex.[42]

While the brand and product line seem to resonant well with older, wealthy individuals, Rolex struggles somewhat to connect with younger consumers. In a NPD Group poll, 36 percent of people under the age of 25 didn't wear a watch.[43] Another study by Piper Jaffray revealed that 59 percent of teenagers said they never wear a watch and 82 percent said they didn't plan to buy one in the next six months.

Brand Resonance Pyramid

The Rolex brand resonance model pyramid is equally strong on the left-hand and right-hand sides. There is great synergy between the two sides of the pyramid; the functional and emotional benefits Rolex strives to deliver are in harmony with consumers' imagery and feelings about the brand. The pyramid is also strong from bottom to top, enjoying the highest brand awareness of any luxury brand as well as high repeat purchase rates and high customer loyalty. Rolex has successfully focused on both the superior product attributes and the imagery associated with owning and wearing a Rolex. Figure 10 highlights some key aspects of the Rolex brand resonance pyramid.

Competitive Analysis

Rolex has many competitors in the $26.5 billion watch industry; however, only a few brands compete in the very high-end market.[44] Through its pricing and distribution strategies, Rolex has positioned itself as a high-end luxury watch brand. On the lower end of the spectrum it competes with companies such as TAG Heuer and OMEGA, and on the high end with brands such as Patek Philippe, maker of the world's most expensive wristwatch.

TAG Heuer. A leader in the luxury watch industry, the Swiss firm TAG Heuer distinguishes itself by focusing on extreme chronograph precision in its watches, and on sports and auto-racing sponsorship in its advertising. Founded by Edouard Heuer in 1876, TAG Heuer has been a mainstay in the luxury watch business. In 1887, the firm created the first oscillating pinion, a technology that significantly improved the chronograph industry and is still used in many of its watches today. In 1895, it developed and patented the first water-resistant case for pocket watches. TAG Heuer expanded into the United States in 1910, introduced a chronograph wristwatch in 1914, and has continued to focus on chronograph innovation ever since.

TAG's image and positioning is inextricably connected to chronograph precision. Its timepieces were the official stopwatches of the Olympic Games in 1920, 1924, and 1928. The firm was a Ferrari team sponsor of Formula 1 from 1971 to 1979 and was part of the TAG-McLaren racing team from 1985 to 2002. It was also the official timekeeper of the F-1 race series for much of the 1990s and early 2000s.[45] TAG Heuer has sponsored numerous Americas Cup teams and other yacht racing teams over the years.

TAG Heuer uses officially licensed retailers to sell its watches both in stores and online. These licensed retailers range from exclusive jewelers to department stores such as Nordstrom and Macy's. The watchmaker generates brand awareness through

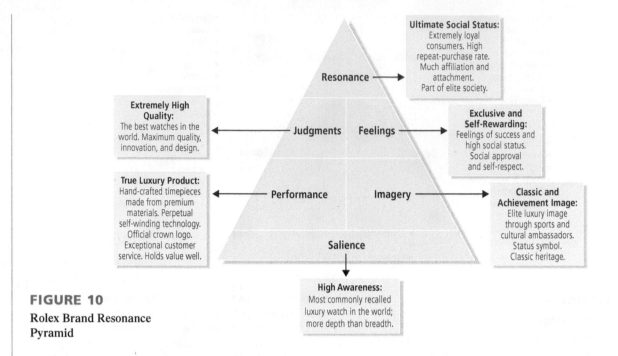

FIGURE 10
Rolex Brand Resonance
Pyramid

brand ambassadors and sponsoring sporting events and advertises extensively in magazines. In 1999, TAG Heuer was purchased by luxury goods conglomerate LVHM.

OMEGA. Founded in 1848 by Louis Brandt, OMEGA has long prided itself on the precision of its watches and timing devices. It built what was Amelia Earhart's watch of choice during one of her transatlantic flights and has been involved in aviation and athletic timing ever since. OMEGA was the time equipment selected for the 1936 Winter Olympics, which saw the first use of synchronized chronographs. By 1937, the company had launched its first waterproof wristwatch, and in 1967 it invented the first underwater touchpad timing equipment, which was used in Olympic swimming competitions. OMEGA watches accompanied the expedition to locate the exact position of the North Pole, and boarded the Apollo 11 mission to become the first and only watch ever to land on the moon. OMEGA is now owned by watch conglomerate, Swatch Group.

Like Rolex and TAG Heuer, OMEGA employs ambassadors to generate brand awareness, including athletes Michael Phelps, Alexander Popov, Ernie Els, and race car driver Michael Schumacher as well as Hollywood stars Nicole Kidman and Cindy Crawford. In 1995, OMEGA became the official watch of the *James Bond* film franchise.

OMEGA watches are offered in both women's and men's styles in four different collections: Constellation, Seamaster, Speedmaster, and De Ville. Prices vary greatly even within individual collections. Watches in the De Ville collection range from $1,650 to over $100,000.

Patek Philippe. In 1839, Antoine Norbert de Patek and François Czapek started a Swiss-based watch company built upon 10 values: independence, innovation, tradition, quality and workmanship, rarity, value, aesthetics, service, emotion, and heritage. After several name changes during its formative years, the company was finally named Patek Philippe. The innovator of many technologies found in today's high-end watch, it represents the absolute pinnacle of luxury timepieces.

In particular, the firm prides itself on creating many of the world's most complicated watches through innovations with split-second chronograph and perpetual date technology.

Unlike other leading luxury watchmakers, Patek Philippe does not rely on event sponsorship or brand ambassadors to generate name recognition. However, since 1851, the firm has made watches for royalty throughout Europe. Its watches are only sold through authorized retailers, of which there are 600 worldwide. In 1996, the brand started its "Generations" campaign, building on its values of heritage and tradition and featuring the tag line, "You Never Actually Own a Patek Philippe, You Merely Look After It for the Next Generation."

Patek Philippe evaluates every authorized dealer's storefront to ensure that it meets the watchmaker's quality standards. It also separates itself from other watchmakers on price, with its least expensive noncustomized watch retailing at $11,500 and its most expensive at over $600,000.

STRATEGIC RECOMMENDATIONS
Positioning

Figure 11 summarizes some positioning analysis and possible points-of-parity and points-of-difference, as described below.

Brand Mantra:
"Classic Designs, Timeless Status"

Points-of-Parity	Points-of-Difference
• Swiss watchmaker	• Innovative products
• Durable	• Unique appearance
• Fine materials	Big face; wide wrist band
• Quality craftsmanship	• Iconic crown logo
• Accurate	• Exclusive, prestigious imagery
• Attractive	• Rich history and heritage
	• Enduring premium value

FIGURE 11
Possible Rolex Brand Positioning

Points-of-Parity. Rolex is similar to other watchmakers in the high-end luxury watch market on several levels. They all make their watches in Switzerland, which is renowned for superior craftsmanship in watch making, and they all deliver high quality. All pride themselves on their attention to detail and ongoing innovation in the watch industry.

Points-of-Difference. Rolex separates itself from the competition in several ways. One, Rolex watches have a distinct look with their Crown logo, big face, and wide band. Two, Rolex has kept a strategically tight control on its distribution channel and production levels, creating a sense of prestige, importance, and exclusivity in the minds of consumers. Three, it has kept the brand pure, remaining focused only on watches and never licensing its name. Through careful selection of event sponsorships and brand ambassadors, Rolex has cut through the clutter, resonated with consumers around the world, and maintained an air of prestige.

Brand Mantra. Rolex has been extremely successful in building a global name through clever marketing and communications, without compromising the integrity of the brand. It has nurtured the belief that acquiring a Rolex represents a milestone in one's life and has built a well-known brand recognized for its elegance and status throughout the entire world. A brand mantra that captures these ideas might be, "Classic Designs, Timeless Status."

TACTICAL RECOMMENDATIONS

The Rolex brand audit proved that Rolex is a very strong brand with significant brand equity. It also identified a few opportunities and challenges:

Leverage the Company's Independent, Continuous Heritage and Focus

- Rolex is the largest and most successful watch company in the world. As a result, many consumers don't realize it is privately owned and competes against major conglomerates such as TAG Heuer's parent company, LVMH, and OMEGA's parent company, Swatch Group. While being privately owned is a good thing for many reasons, it also brings up several challenges. For example, Rolex has to compete against companies that are 10 times its size. Larger companies have lower labor costs, wider distribution, and significant advertising synergies.

- Rolex may want to leverage and promote the fact that in some ways it has to work harder to succeed. It is doing what it has done for 100 years—making durable, reliable, premium watches on its own. Due to the currently popular anti-Wall Street vibe, this positioning may resonant well with consumers.

Leverage the Company's Elite Craftsmanship and Innovation

- Research from the Luxury Institute group suggested that consumers do not consider Rolex the top brand in quality and exclusivity. History has proved that Rolex watches are in fact leaders in both craftsmanship and innovation and Rolex may want to run a campaign focused more on these aspects.

Connect with the Female Consumer

- Women make up the majority of jewelry and watch purchases. However, as Mintel's 2008 study revealed, women are more and more interested in purchasing unisex mechanical watches rather than feminine-styled watches. This is a great opportunity for Rolex, whose watches are primarily masculine in design. The firm could move away from its decorative, jeweled watches and introduce more powerful, gender-neutral watches. Its 2009 Oyster Perpetual Datejust Rolesor 36 mm is one example—robust, with large utilitarian numbers, and waterproof to a depth of 100 meters.[46] However, its floral dial design and diamond-set bezel possibly give it an unnecessary feminine angle.

- Rolex may want to tweak its female ambassador list to coincide with a more unisex product line. Women who have succeeded in a male-dominated environment such as Condoleezza Rice or Katie Couric could be powerful brand endorsers.

Attack the Online Counterfeit Industry

- Counterfeits damage the company's brand equity and present a huge risk to the brand. The boom in e-commerce has taken counterfeit Rolexes from the street corner to the Internet, where fakes can reach far more consumers. Consequently, the age-old problem of counterfeiting is a bigger threat than ever before. To maintain its limited distribution, Rolex does not authorize any of its watches to be sold on the Internet. In order to combat the online sale of counterfeits, however, Rolex might consider building an exclusive online store, or an exclusive distribution site to which all official e-retailers must link. In fact, Rolex dedicates extensive resources to fight the illegal use of the brand, including sponsoring the International Anti-Counterfeiting Coalition and suing companies that allow the sale of counterfeit Rolexes.

Use Marketing to Reach Younger Consumers

- Research has shown that younger consumers do not value watches the same way older generations did. As a result, Rolex should be researching the questions: How will prestige be defined in the twenty-first century? Who or what symbolizes prestige, ruggedness, precision? Will the same formula work for the millennial generation as they age and move into the Rolex target market?

Communicate Long-Term Value

- Rolex competes for a share of the luxury buyer's wallet with a host of other types of goods, such as clothes, shoes, and handbags. Many are less durable over time than a Rolex watch and are susceptible to falling out of fashion. Rolex should leverage its superior value retention—both in its resale value and in its "heirloom" quality—in order to better compete for luxury spending with brands outside its category.

- Swiss luxury watch competitor Patek Philippe used print advertising to communicate the heirloom quality of its watches. Rolex could pursue a similar approach, perhaps using its more visible ambassadors, to communicate its own heirloom quality.

Notes

1. Frederick E. Webster, Jr., Alan J. Malter, and Shankar Ganesan, "Can Marketing Regain Its Seat at the Table?" *Marketing Science Institute Report* No. 03–113, Cambridge, MA, 2003. See also Frederick E. Webster Jr., Alan J. Malter, and Shankar Ganesan, "The Decline and Dispersion of Marketing Competence," *MIT Sloan Management Review* 46, no. 4 (Summer 2005): 35–43.

2. Patrick LaPointe, *Marketing by the Dashboard Light— How to Get More Insight, Foresight, and Accountability from Your Marketing Investment* (New York: Association of National Advertisers, 2005).

3. Clyde P. Stickney, Roman L. Weil, Katherine Schipper, and Jennifer Francis, *Financial Accounting: An Introduction to Concepts, Methods, and Uses* (Mason, OH: Southwestern Cengage Learning, 2010).

4. Phillip Kotler, William Gregor, and William Rogers, "The Marketing Audit Comes of Age," *Sloan Management Review* 18, no. 2 (Winter 1977): 25–43.

5. Laurel Wentz, "Brand Audits Reshaping Images," *Ad Age International* (September 1996): 38–41.

6. Grand Ogilvy Winner, "Pizza Turnaround: Speed Kills. Good Taste Counts," *Journal of Advertising Research* (September 2011): 463–466; Seth Stevenson, "Like Cardboard," *Slate*, 11 January 2010; Ashley M. Heher, "Domino's Comes Clean With New Pizza Ads," *Associated Press*, 11 January 2010; Bob Garfield, "Domino's Does Itself a Disservice by Coming Clean About Its Pizza," *Advertising Age*, 11 January 2010; www.pizzaturnaround.com.

7. Private correspondence with Chris Grams and John Adams from Red Hat.

8. Sidney J. Levy, "Dreams, Fairy Tales, Animals, and Cars," *Psychology and Marketing* 2 (Summer 1985): 67–81.

9. Deborah Roeddder John, Barbara Loken, Kyeongheui Kim, and Alokparna Basu Monga, "Brand Concept Maps: A Methodology for Identifying Brand Association Networks," *Journal of Marketing Research* 43 (November 2006): 549–563.

10. John Roberts, professor of marketing, Australian National University, personal correspondence, 23 June 2011.

11. Nigel Hollis, executive vice president and chief global analyst at Millward Brown, personal correspondence, 6 October 2011.

12. Na Woon Bong, Roger Marshall, and Kevin Lane Keller, "Measuring Brand Power: Validating a Model for Optimizing Brand Equity," *Journal of Product and Brand Management* 8, no. 3 (1999): 170–184.

13. http://download.skype.com/share/brand/Skype BrandBook.zip.

14. Joel Rubinson, "Brand Strength Means More Than Market Share," paper presented at the ARF Fourth Annual Advertising and Promotion Workshop, New York, 1992.

15. Tim Ambler, *Marketing and the Bottom Line*, 2nd ed. (London: FT Prentice Hall, 2004).

16. Michael Krauss, "Marketing Dashboards Drive Better Decisions," *Marketing News*, 1 October 2005.

17. Kunur Patel, "Data Moves From Research to Consumer Lure," *Advertising Age*, 6 June 2011, 4.

18. Pat LaPointe, "Dashboards—Huge Value or Big Expense," www.marketingNPV.com, 10 August 2010; see also, Koen Pauwels, Tim Ambler, Bruce Clark, Pat LaPointe, David Reibstein, Bernd Skiera, Berend Wierenga, Thorsten Wiesel, *Dashboards & Marketing: Why, What, How and What Research Is Needed?*, Report no. 08-203, Marketing Science Institute Electronic Working Paper series, 2008.

19. Amy Miller and Jennifer Cloffi, "Measuring Marketing Effectiveness and Value: The Unisys Marketing Dashboard," *Journal of Advertising Research* 44 (September 2004): 237–243; "Unisys Overcomes 6 Common Dashboard Mistakes," www.marketingnpv.com, 4 October 2004.

20. Gail McGovern and John Quelch, "Sarbox Still Putting the Squeeze on Marketing," *Advertising Age*, 19 September 2005, 28.

21. Tim Ambler and Bruce Clark, "What Will Matter Most to Marketers Three Years from Now?" paper presented at Marketing Science Institute Conference, *Does Marketing Measure Up? Performance Metrics: Practices and Impacts*, 21–22 June 2004, London, United Kingdom. See also Bruce H. Clark and Tim Ambler, "Marketing Performance Measurement: Evolution of Research and Practice," *International Journal of Business Performance Management* 3, nos. 2/3/4 (2001): 231–244; and Bruce H. Clark, Andrew Abela, and Tim Ambler, "Organizational Motivation, Opportunity and Ability to Measure Marketing Performance," *Journal of Strategic Marketing* 13 (December 2005): 241–259.

22. Bruce Clark and Tim Ambler, "Managing the Metrics Portfolio," *Marketing Management* (Fall 2011): 16–21.

23. Scott Bedbury, *A New Brand World* (New York: Viking Press, 2002).

24. Bedbury, *A New Brand World*.

25. Betsy Spethman, "Companies Post Equity Gatekeepers," *Brandweek*, 2 May 1994, 5.

26. "The Death of the Brand Manager," *The Economist*, 9 April 1994, 67–68.

27. www.businessweek.com; www.interbrand.com; "Best Global Brands 2010."

28. David Liebeskind, "What Makes Rolex Tick?" *Stern Business*, Fall/Winter 2004.

29. Peter Passell, "Watches That Time Hasn't Forgotten?" *New York Times*, 24 November 1995.

30. Gene Stone, *The Watch* (New York: ABRAMS, 2006).

31. David Liebeskind, "What Makes Rolex Tick?" *Stern Business*, Fall/ Winter 2004.

32. Ibid.

33. Joe Thomas, "Rolex Leads U.S. Watch Advertiser Pack." *Watch Time Magazine*, 12 July 2009.

34. www.rolex.com, accessed 15 November 2011.

35. Suzanne Vranica and Sam Walker, "Some Find Tiger's Move Untimely—Golfer Switches Watches to TAG

Heuer From Rolex; Brand Experts Disapprove," *Wall Street Journal*, 7 October 2002.

36. "Tiger Woods Signs Endorsement Deal with Tiger," *Watch Time Magazine*, October 2011.

37. www.rolex.com, accessed November 15, 2011.

38. Ibid.

39. Ibid.

40. Christina Binkley, "Fashion Journal: Celebrity Watch: Are You a Brad or a James?" *Wall Street Journal*, 11 January 2007.

41. Jemima Sissons, "Haute Couture Takes On Horlogerie: Fashion's Big Guns Continue to Impress in the Battle for Women's Wrists," *Wall Street Journal*, 19 March 2010.

42. "Christie's Achieves World Record Price for Any Rolex Sold at Auction," *Watch Time Magazine*, 27 May 2011.

43. Hurt Harry, "The 12-Watches-a-Year Solution," *New York Times*, 1 July 2006.

44. Women's Wear Daily, July 2005; www.fashion products.com; Federation of Swiss Watch Industry, 2010.

45. http://www.f1scarlet.com/historyoftag_f1.html.

46. Sissons, "Haute Couture Takes on Horlogerie."

Measuring Sources of Brand Equity: Capturing Customer Mind-Set

Measuring Sources of Brand Equity: Capturing Customer Mind-Set

Learning Objectives

After reading this chapter, you should be able to

1. Describe effective qualitative research techniques for tapping into consumer brand knowledge.

2. Identify effective quantitative research techniques for measuring brand awareness, image, responses, and relationships.

3. Profile and contrast some popular brand equity models.

Marketers strive to learn everything about how consumers use the products they sell. For pillow manufacturers, that might mean knowing how many consumers fold, stack, or just hug their pillows.

Source: Jose Luis Pelaez/Stone/Getty Images

Preview

Understanding the current and desired brand knowledge structures of consumers is vital to effectively building and managing brand equity. Ideally, marketers would be able to construct detailed "mental maps" to understand exactly what exists in consumers' minds—all their thoughts, feelings, perceptions, images, beliefs, and attitudes toward different brands. These mental blueprints would then provide managers with the insights to develop a solid brand positioning with the right points-of-parity and points-of-difference and the strategic guidance to help them make good brand decisions. Unfortunately, such brand knowledge structures are not easily measured because they reside only in consumers' minds.

Nevertheless, effective brand management requires us to thoroughly understand the consumer. Often a simple insight into how consumers think of or use products and the particular brands in a category can help create a profitable change in the marketing program. That's why many large companies conduct exhaustive research studies (or brand audits) to learn as much as possible about consumers.

A number of detailed, sophisticated research techniques and methods now exist to help marketers better understand consumer knowledge structures. A host of primary and secondary data sources exist online. Many industry or company studies can be accessed and surveys can be efficiently distributed and collected. This chapter highlights some of the important considerations critical to the measurement of brand equity.[1] Figure 1 outlines general considerations in understanding consumer behavior, and Branding Brief 1 describes the lengths to which marketers have gone in the past to learn about consumers.

According to the brand value chain, sources of brand equity arise from the customer mind-set. In general, measuring sources of brand equity requires that the brand manager fully understand how customers shop for and use products and services and, most important, what customers know, think, and feel about and act toward various brands. In particular, measuring sources of customer-based brand equity requires us to measure various aspects of brand awareness and brand image that can lead to the differential customer response making up brand equity.

Consumers may have a holistic view of brands that is difficult to divide into component parts. But many times we can, in fact, isolate perceptions and assess them in greater detail. The remainder of this chapter describes qualitative and quantitative approaches to identifying potential sources of brand equity—that is, capturing the customer mind-set.

QUALITATIVE RESEARCH TECHNIQUES

There are many different ways to uncover the types of associations linked to the brand and their corresponding strength, favorability, and uniqueness. *Qualitative research techniques* often identify possible brand associations and sources of brand equity. These are relatively unstructured measurement approaches that permit a range of both questions and answers and so can often be a useful first step in exploring consumer brand and product perceptions.

Who buys our product or service?
Who makes the decision to buy the product?
Who influences the decision to buy the product?
How is the purchase decision made? Who assumes what role?
What does the customer buy? What needs must be satisfied?
Why do customers buy a particular brand?
Where do they go or look to buy the product or service?
When do they buy? Any seasonality factors?
What are customers' attitudes toward our product?
What social factors might influence the purchase decision?
Does the customers' lifestyle influence their decisions?
How is our product perceived by customers?
How do demographic factors influence the purchase decision?

FIGURE 1

Understanding
Consumer Behavior

Source: Based on a list from George Belch and Michael Belch, *Advertising and Communication Management*, 3rd ed. (Homewood, IL: Irwin, 1995).

BRANDING BRIEF 1

Digging Beneath the Surface to Understand Consumer Behavior

Because the consumer behavior we observe can differ from the behavior consumers report in surveys, useful marketing insights sometimes emerge from unobtrusively observing consumers rather than talking to them. For example, Hoover became suspicious when people claimed in surveys that they vacuumed their houses for an hour each week. To check, the company installed timers in certain models and exchanged them for the same models in consumers' homes. The timers showed that people actually spent only a little over *half* an hour vacuuming each week. One researcher analyzed household trash to determine the types and quantities of food people consumed, finding that people really don't have a very good idea of how much and what types of food they eat. Similarly, much research has shown that people report they eat healthier food than would appear to be case if you opened their cabinets!

DuPont commissioned marketing studies to uncover personal pillow behavior for its Dacron polyester unit, which supplies filling to pillow makers and sells its own Comforel brand (now part of INVISTA). One challenge: people don't give up their old pillows. Thirty-seven percent of one sample described their relationship with their pillow as like "an old married couple," and an additional 13 percent characterized their pillow like a "childhood friend." The researchers found that people fell into distinct groups in terms of pillow behavior: stackers (23 percent), plumpers (20 percent), rollers or folders (16 percent), cuddlers (16 percent), and smashers, who pound their pillows into a more comfy shape (10 percent). Women were more likely to plump, while men were more likely to fold. The prevalence of stackers led the company to sell more pillows packaged as pairs, as well as to market different levels of softness or firmness.

Much of this type of research has its roots in *ethnography*, the anthropological term for the study of cultures in their natural surroundings. The intent behind these in-depth, observational studies is for consumers to drop their guard and provide a more realistic portrayal of who they are rather than who they would like to be. On the basis of ethnographic research that uncovered consumers' true feelings, ad campaigns have been created for a Swiss chocolate maker with the theme "The True Confessions of a Chocoholic" (because chocolate lovers often hid stashes all though the house), for Tampax tampons with the theme "More Women Trust Their Bodies to Tampax" (because teen users wanted the freedom to wear body-conscious clothes), and for Crisco shortening with the theme "Recipe for Success" (because people often baked pies and cookies in a celebratory fashion).

Sources: Russell Belk, ed., *Handbook of Qualitative Research Method in Marketing* (Northampton, MA: Edward Elgar Publishing, 2006); Eric J. Arnould and Amber Epp, "Deep Engagement with Consumer Experience: Listening and Learning with Qualitative Data," in *The Handbook of Marketing Research: Uses, Misuses, and Future Advances*, eds. Rajiv Grover and Marco Vriens (Thousand Oaks, CA: Sage Press, 2006): 51–58; Jennifer Chang Coupland, "Invisible Brands: An Ethnography of Households and the Brands in Their Kitchen Pantries," *Journal of Consumer Research* 32 (June 2005): 106–118; John Koten, "You Aren't Paranoid If You Feel Someone Eyes You Constantly," *Wall Street Journal*, 2 March 1985; Susan Warren, "Pillow Talk: Stackers Outnumber Plumpers; Don't Mention Drool," *Wall Street Journal*, 8 January 1998, B1.

Qualitative research has a long history in marketing. Ernest Dichter, one of the early pioneers in consumer psychoanalytic research, first applied these research principles in a study for Plymouth automobiles in the 1930s.[2] His research revealed the important—but previously overlooked—role that women played in the automobile purchase decision. Based on his consumer analysis, Plymouth adopted a new print ad strategy that highlighted a young couple gazing admiringly at a Plymouth automobile under the headline "Imagine Us in a Car Like That." Dichter's subsequent work had an important impact on a number of different ad campaigns.[3]

Some of his assertions were fairly controversial. For instance, he equated convertibles with youth, freedom, and the secret wish for mistresses; argued that women used Ivory soap to wash away their sins before a date; and maintained that baking was an expression of femininity and pulling a cake or loaf out of an oven for women was "in a sense like giving birth." His suggested tagline "Putting a Tiger in the Tank" for Exxon resulting in a long-running and successful ad campaign, however.[4]

This section next reviews a number of qualitative research techniques for identifying sources of brand equity such as brand awareness, brand attitudes, and brand attachment. These techniques also can identify outcomes of brand equity such as price elasticities and brand choice and preference.

Free Association

The simplest and often the most powerful way to profile brand associations is free association tasks, in which subjects are asked what comes to mind when they think of the brand, without any more specific probe or cue than perhaps the associated product category. ("What does the Rolex name mean to you?" or "Tell me what comes to mind when you think of Rolex watches.")

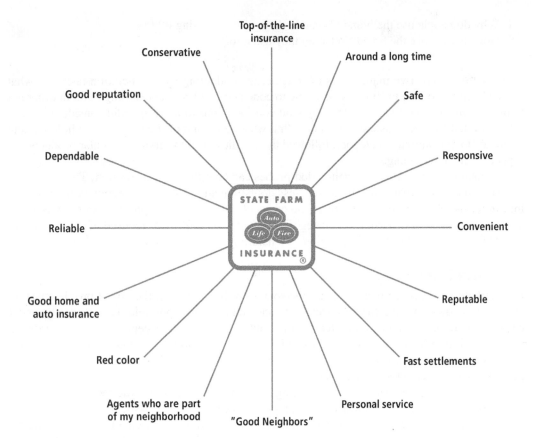

FIGURE 2

Sample State Farm Mental Map

Source: Logo used with permission of State Farm Insurance

Marketers can use the resulting associations to form a rough mental map for the brand (see Figure 2 for a sample mental map for State Farm insurance).

Marketers use free association tasks mainly to identify the range of possible brand associations in consumers' minds, but free association may also provide some rough indication of the relative strength, favorability, and uniqueness of brand associations.[5] Coding free association responses in terms of the order of elicitation—whether they are early or late in the sequence—at least gives us a rough measure of their strength.[6] For example, if many consumers mention "fast and convenient" as one of their first associations when given "McDonald's restaurants" as a probe, then the association is probably a relatively strong one and likely able to affect consumer decisions. Associations later in the list may be weaker and thus more likely to be overlooked during consumer decision making. Comparing associations with those elicited for competitive brands can also tell us about their relative uniqueness. Finally, we can discern even favorability, to some extent, on the basis of how consumers phrase their associations.

Answers to free-association questions help marketers clarify the range of possible associations and assemble a brand profile.[7] To better understand the favorability of associations, we can ask consumers follow-up questions about the favorability of associations they listed or, more generally, what they like best about the brand. Similarly, we can ask them follow-up questions about the uniqueness of associations they listed or, more generally, about what they find unique about the brand. Useful questions include the following:

1. What do you like best about the brand? What are its positive aspects or advantages?
2. What do you like least about the brand? What are its negative aspects or disadvantages?
3. What do you find unique about the brand? How is it different from other brands?

These simple, direct measures can be extremely valuable for determining core aspects of a brand image. To elicit more structure and guidance, consumers can be asked further follow-up questions about what the brand means to them in terms of the classic journalism "who, what, when, where, why, and how" questions:

1. Who uses the brand? What kind of person?
2. What types of situations do they use the brand?
3. When and where do they use the brand?

4. Why do people use the brand? What do they get out of using it?

5. How do they use the brand? What do they use it for?

Guidelines. The two main issues to consider in conducting free association tasks are what types of probes to give to subjects, and how to code and interpret the resulting data. In order not to bias results, it is best to move from general considerations to more specific considerations, as we illustrated earlier. Thus, ask consumers first what they think of the brand as a whole without reference to any particular category, followed by specific questions about particular products and aspects of the brand image.

Consumers' responses to open-ended probes can be either oral or written. The advantage of oral responses is that subjects may be less deliberate and more spontaneous in their reporting. In terms of coding the data, divide the protocols each consumer provides into phrases and aggregate them across consumers in categories. Because of their more focused nature, responses to specific probes and follow-up questions are naturally easier to code.

Projective Techniques

For marketers to succeed in uncovering the sources of brand equity, they must profile consumers' brand knowledge structures as accurately and completely as possible. Unfortunately, under certain situations, consumers may feel that it would be socially unacceptable or undesirable to express their true feelings—especially to an interviewer they don't even know! As a result, they may find it easier to fall back on stereotypical, pat answers they believe would be acceptable or perhaps even expected by the interviewer.

Consumers may be particularly unwilling or unable to reveal their true feelings when marketers ask about brands characterized by a preponderance of imagery associations. For example, it may be difficult for consumers to admit that a certain brand name product has prestige and enhances their self-image. They may instead refer to some particular product feature as the reason they like or dislike the brand. Or they may simply find it difficult to identify and express their true feelings when asked directly, *even if they attempt to do so.* For either of these reasons, it might be impossible to obtain an accurate portrayal of brand knowledge structures without some rather unconventional research methods.

Projective techniques are diagnostic tools to uncover the true opinions and feelings of consumers when they are unwilling or otherwise unable to express themselves on these matters.[8] Marketers present consumers with an incomplete stimulus and ask them to complete it, or they give consumers an ambiguous stimulus and ask them to make sense of it. The idea is that in the process consumers will reveal some of their true beliefs and feelings. Thus, projective techniques can be especially useful when deeply rooted personal motivations or personally or socially sensitive subjects are at issue.

In psychology, the most famous example of a projective technique is the *Rorschach test*, in which experimenters present ink blots to subjects and ask them what the ink blots remind them of. In responding, subjects may reveal certain facets of their own, perhaps subconscious, personality. Psychologists also use dream analysis or probe the earliest and most defining memories a person has on a topic.[9]

Projective techniques have a long history in marketing, beginning with the motivation research of the late 1940s and 1950s.[10] A classic example is an experiment exploring hidden feelings toward instant coffee conducted by Mason Haire in the late 1940s, summarized in Branding Brief 2.[11] Although projective techniques don't always yield results as powerful as in that example, they often provide useful insights that help to assemble us a more complete picture of consumers and their relationships with brands. Many kinds of projective techniques are possible. We'll highlight a few here.[12]

Completion and Interpretation Tasks. Classic projective techniques use incomplete or ambiguous stimuli to elicit consumer thoughts and feelings. One approach is "bubble exercises," which depict different people buying or using certain products or services. Empty bubbles, as in cartoons, are placed in the scenes to represent the thoughts, words, or actions of one or more of the participants. Marketers then ask consumers to "fill in the bubble" by indicating what they believe is happening or being said in the scene. The stories and conversations told this way can be especially useful for assessing user and usage imagery for a brand.

BRANDING BRIEF 2

Once Upon a Time . . . You Were What You Cooked

One of the most famous applications of psychographic techniques was made by Mason Haire in the 1940s. The purpose of the experiment was to uncover consumers' true beliefs and feelings toward Nescafé instant coffee.

The impetus for the experiment was a survey conducted to determine why the initial sales of Nescafé instant coffee were so disappointing. The majority of the people who reported they didn't like the product stated that the reason was the flavor. On the basis of consumer taste tests, however, Nescafé's management knew consumers found the taste of instant coffee acceptable when they didn't know what type of coffee they were drinking. Suspecting that consumers were not expressing their true feelings, Haire designed a clever experiment to discover what was really going on.

Haire set up two shopping lists containing the same six items. Shopping List 1 specified Maxwell House drip ground coffee, whereas Shopping List 2 specified Nescafé instant coffee, as follows:

Shopping List 1	Shopping List 2
Pound and a half of hamburger	Pound and a half of hamburger
2 loaves Wonder bread	2 loaves Wonder bread
Bunch of carrots	Bunch of carrots
1 can Rumford's Baking Powder	1 can Rumford's Baking Powder
Maxwell House coffee (drip ground)	Nescafé instant coffee
2 cans Del Monte peaches	2 cans Del Monte peaches
5 lbs. potatoes	5 lbs. potatoes

Two groups of matched subjects were each given one of the lists and asked to "Read the shopping list. . . . Try to project yourself into the situation as far as possible until you can more or less characterize the woman who bought the groceries." Subjects then wrote a brief description of the personality and character of that person.

After coding the responses into frequently mentioned categories, Haire found that two starkly different profiles emerged:

	List 1 (Maxwell House)	List 2 (Nescafé)
Lazy	4%	48%
Fails to plan household purchases and schedules well	12%	48%
Thrifty	16%	4%
Not a good wife	0%	16%

Haire interpreted these results as indicating that instant coffee represented a departure from homemade coffee and traditions

Marketers of Nescafé instant coffee had to go to great lengths when the product was introduced to figure out what consumers really thought of it.

Source: Helen Sessions/Alamy

with respect to caring for one's family. In other words, at that time, the "labor-saving" aspect of instant coffee, rather than being an asset, was a liability in that it violated consumer traditions. Consumers were evidently reluctant to admit this fact when asked directly but were better able to express their true feelings when asked to project to another person.

The strategic implications of this new research finding were clear. Based on the original survey results, the obvious positioning for instant coffee with respect to regular coffee would have been to establish a point-of-difference on "convenience" and a point-of-parity on the basis of "taste." Based on the projective test findings, however, it was obvious that there also needed to be a point-of-parity on the basis of user imagery. As a result, a successful ad campaign was launched that promoted Nescafé coffee as a way for housewives to free up time so they could devote additional time to more important household activities.

Sources: Mason Haire, "Projective Techniques in Marketing Research," *Journal of Marketing* (April 1950): 649–652; J. Arndt, "Haire's Shopping List Revisited," *Journal of Advertising Research* 13 (1973): 57–61; G. S. Lane and G. L. Watson, "A Canadian Replication of Mason Haire's 'Shopping List' Study," *Journal of the Academy of Marketing Science* 3 (1975): 48–59; William L. Wilkie, *Consumer Behavior*, 3rd ed. (New York: John Wiley and Sons, 1994).

Comparison Tasks.   Another useful technique is comparison tasks, in which we ask consumers to convey their impressions by comparing brands to people, countries, animals, activities, fabrics, occupations, cars, magazines, vegetables, nationalities, or even other brands.[13] For example, we might ask consumers, "If Dannon yogurt were a car, which one would it be? If it were an animal, which one might it be? Looking at the people depicted in these pictures, which ones do you think would be most likely to eat Dannon yogurt?" In each case, we would ask a follow-up question about why subjects made the comparison they did. The objects people choose to represent the brand and their reasons can provide glimpses into the psyche of the consumer with respect to a brand, particularly useful in understanding imagery associations.

By examining the answers to probes, researchers may be better able to assemble a rich image for the brand, for example, identifying key brand personality associations. Branding Brief 3 outlines how hotel chain Joie de Vivre uses magazine imagery to clarify its brand positions.

Archetypes.   Archetype research is one technique for eliciting deeply held consumer attitudes and feelings. According to cultural anthropologist G. C. Rapaille, consumers often make purchase decisions based on factors of which they are only subconsciously aware. Conventional market research typically does not uncover these motivations, so Rapaille employs the archetype research technique to find them.[14]

Rapaille believes children experience a significant initial exposure to an element of their world called the "imprinting moment." The pattern that emerges when we generalize these imprinting moments for the entire population is the *archetype*, a fundamental psychological association, shared by the members of the culture, with a given cultural object. Different cultures have dramatically different archetypes for the same objects. In France, the archetype for cheese is "alive" because age is its most important trait. By contrast, the U.S. archetype for cheese is "dead"; it is wrapped in plastic ("a body-bag"), put in the refrigerator ("a morgue"), and pasteurized ("scientifically dead").

Rapaille uses relaxation exercises and visualization with consumers to find the imprinting moments appropriate to the product he is researching. For example, at a focus group, he will dim the lights, play soothing music, and coax the subjects into a meditative state. He will then elicit stories about the product from the subjects and analyze these stories to illuminate the archetype.

Zaltman Metaphor Elicitation Technique

One interesting approach to better understand how consumers view brands is the Zaltman Metaphor Elicitation Technique (ZMET).[15] ZMET is based on a belief that consumers often have subconscious motives for their purchasing behavior. "A lot goes on in our minds that we're not aware of," said former Harvard Business School professor Gerald Zaltman. "Most of what influences what we say and do occurs below the level of awareness. That's why we need new techniques to get at hidden knowledge—to get at what people don't know they know."

To access this hidden knowledge, he developed the Zaltman Metaphor Elicitation Technique. As described in its U.S. patent, ZMET is "a technique for eliciting interconnected constructs that influence thought and behavior." The word *construct* refers to "an abstraction created by the researcher to capture common ideas, concepts, or themes expressed by customers." For example, the construct "ease of use" might capture the statements "simple to operate," "works without hassle," and "you don't really have to do anything."

ZMET stems from knowledge and research from varied fields such as "cognitive neuroscience, neurobiology, art critique, literary criticism, visual anthropology, visual sociology, semiotics . . . art therapy, and psycholinguistics." The technique is based on the idea that "most social communication is nonverbal" and, as a result, approximately two-thirds of all stimuli received by the brain are visual. Using ZMET, Zaltman teases out consumers' hidden thoughts and feelings about a particular topic, which often can be expressed best using metaphors.

Zaltman defines a metaphor as "a definition of one thing in terms of another, [which] people can use . . . to represent thoughts that are tacit, implicit, and unspoken." ZMET focuses on surface, thematic, and deep metaphors. Some common deep metaphors include "transformation," "container," "journey," "connection," and "sacred and profane."

A ZMET study starts with a group of participants who are asked in advance to think about the research topic at hand and collect a set of images from their own sources (magazines, catalogs, and family photo albums) that represent their thoughts and feelings about the research topic. The participants bring these images with them for a personal one-on-one two-hour interview

BRANDING BRIEF 3

Brand Imagery at Joie de Vivre

Joie de Vivre Hospitality LLC operates a chain of boutique hotels, restaurants, and resorts in California, Arizona, and Chicago. Chip Conley founded the company in 1987 when he purchased a rundown motel in a seedy area of San Francisco and converted it into the Phoenix, a fashionable destination popular among entertainment celebrities. In establishing Joie de Vivre, Conley's goal was "to create a company with hip hotel concepts that appealed to a younger consumer base."

Since launching the Phoenix, the company has grown to a total of 34 hotels, the largest group of boutique hotels in California, and is now going national. "Each hotel is a specific world of style and service catering to the needs and wishes of like-minded travelers." Each property's unique décor, quirky amenities, and thematic style are loosely based on a popular magazine. Conley explains the design choices for the hotels and resorts as follows:

> What we've learned over time is that people choose their hotels based on the brand as a mirror. So every time we create a new hotel, spa, or resort, we imagine a magazine that defines the hotel. We choose five words that define the magazine, and by doing that, we get the psychographic fit.

For example, the Phoenix is represented by *Rolling Stone*. The five words used by Conley to describe the magazine are "adventurous, hip, irreverent, funky, and young at heart." The Hotel del Sol—a converted motel bearing a yellow exterior and surrounded by palm trees wrapped with festive lights—is described as "kind of *Martha Stewart Living* meets *Islands* magazine."

Joie de Vivre hotels strive to combine style and flavor with comfort and service. The boutique concept enables the hotels to offer personal touches for its clients, such as LCD flat-screen TVs with HD channels in rooms, billiards tables, and complimentary Wi-Fi, morning coffee, afternoon tea service, and wine hour. The Rex Hotel has a library and a literary flavor. One of the newer offerings, the Hotel Vitale, showcases yoga classes in the rooftop penthouse of its Financial District building. It is described as *Real Simple* magazine meets *Dwell* magazine; the five words that define it are "nurturing, fresh, modern, urbane, and revitalizing."

In addition to providing comfort considerations, Joie de Vivre creates loyalty among its customers with a dedication to customer service. The company condenses all pertinent service information onto a small laminated card that all employees carry with them while they work. By way of introducing the staff to the guests, the company displays "Host Profiles" at the check-in desk that give useful and interesting information about the employees. Various hotel staff contributed to a set of 20 free guides to San Francisco that guests can use to find out about the city from a local's perspective. Joie de Vivre also developed a loyalty program, called the Joy of Life Club, whereby frequent guests earn redeemable points based on what they spend during each stay at one of the company's properties.

The personal touches and unique personality offered by Joie de Vivre hotels have helped the company build a loyal customer

All Joie de Vivre's properties have a unique brand personality. Hotel Rex is sophisticated with a literary theme; Hotel del Sol is fun, colorful and casual.
Source: Joie de Vivre Hotels

base (see the accompanying photos). One repeat customer referred to the company's Hotel Rex as "a home away from home." To help first-time visitors choose the right hotel for them, the company's Web site includes a Hotel Matchmaker personality test offered by a fictional character, "Yvette," that offers recommendations based on answers to five key questions.

Sources: Neal Templin, "Boutique-Hotel Group Thrives on Quirks," *Wall Street Journal*, 18 March 1999; Clifford Carlsen, "Joie de Vivre Resorts to New Hospitality Strategy," *San Francisco Business Times*, 18 June 1999; Chip Conley, *The Rebel Rules* (New York: Fireside, 2001); "On the Record," *San Francisco Chronicle*, 7 August 2005; Tom Osborne, "What Is Your Brand Personality?," *Viget Inspire*, www.viget.com, 2 February 2009; www.jdvhospitality.com, accessed 20 December 2011.

with a study administrator, who uses advanced interview techniques to explore the images with the participant and reveal their deep ideas, archetypes, themes, and emotions through a "guided conversation."

The interview consists of a series of steps, each with a specific purpose in mind:

1. *Storytelling:* Exploring individual visual metaphors
2. *Expand the Frame:* Expanding the metaphoric meaning of images
3. *Sensory Metaphor:* Eliciting metaphors about the research topic from each sensory modality
4. *Vignette:* Using the mind's eye to create a short story about the research topic
5. *Digital Image:* Integrating the images to create a visual summary of the research topic

Once the participants' interviews have been completed, researchers identify key themes or constructs, code the data, and assemble a consensus map of the most important constructs. Quantitative analyses of the data can provide information for advertising, promotions, and other marketing decisions.

ZMET has been applied in a variety of different ways, including as a means to help understand consumers' images of brands, products, and companies. Marketers can employ ZMET for a variety of consumer-insight research topics. Zaltman lists several of these:

> ZMET is useful in understanding consumers' images of brands, products, companies, brand equity, product concepts and designs, product usage and purchase experiences, life experiences, consumption context, and attitudes toward business.

For example, DuPont enlisted Zaltman to research women's attitudes toward hosiery. Conventional research yielded the conclusion that "women mostly hated wearing pantyhose," but DuPont market researchers were not convinced that this conclusion provided a complete picture. Zaltman used ZMET with 20 subjects in order to uncover deeper answers to the question, "What are your thoughts and feelings about buying and wearing pantyhose?" He discovered that women had a "like–hate" relationship with pantyhose; they disliked the discomfort and run-proneness of pantyhose but liked the feel of elegance and sexiness they got from wearing it. This discovery prompted a number of hosiery manufacturers to include more sexy and alluring imagery in their advertising. Figure 3 displays a consensus map that emerged from a study of intimate apparel.

Neural Research Methods

Taking ZMET one step further to dig even deeper into the subconscious, some marketing researchers are bypassing any verbal response from consumers to literally get inside the minds of consumers through various neural research methods. *Neuromarketing* is the study of how the

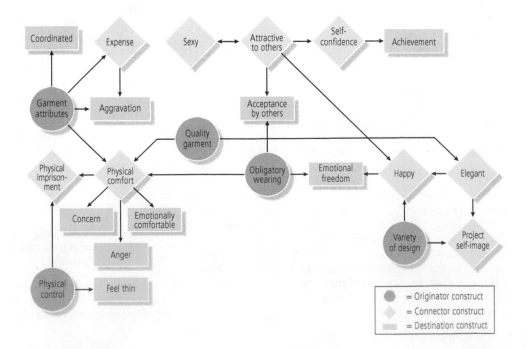

FIGURE 3

Application of ZMET to Intimate Apparel Market

brain responds to marketing stimuli, including brands.[16] For example, some firms are applying sophisticated techniques such as EEG (elector encephalograph) technology to monitor brain activity and better gauge consumer responses to marketing.

Neurological research has been applied many ways in marketing.[17] It has been used to measure the type of emotional response consumers exhibit when presented with marketing stimuli. Neurological research has shown that people activate different regions of the brain in assessing the personality traits of people than they do when assessing brands.

One major research finding to emerge from neurological consumer research is that many purchase decisions appear to be characterized less by the logical weighing of variables and more "as a largely unconscious habitual process, as distinct from the rational, conscious, information-processing model of economists and traditional marketing textbooks." Even basic decisions, such as the purchase of gasoline, seem to be influenced by brain activity at the subrational level.

Firms as varied as Intel, Paypal, Google, HP, Citi, and Microsoft have employed neurological marketing research studies. Frito-Lay hired neuromarketing firm NeuroFocus to study how consumers responded to their Cheetos cheese-flavored snack. Scanning the brains of a carefully chosen group of consumers revealed that their most powerful response was to the product's messy outer coating. The research study's insight led to an award-winning ad campaign.[18]

By adding neurological techniques to their research arsenal, marketers are trying to move toward a more complete picture of what goes on inside consumers' heads.[19] Although it may be able to offer different insights from conventional techniques, neurological research at this point is very costly, running as much as $100,000 or even more per project. Given the complexity of the human brain, however, many researchers caution that neurological research should not form the sole basis for marketing decisions. These research activities have not been universally accepted. The measurement devices to capture brain activity can be highly obtrusive, such as with skull caps studded with electrodes, creating artificial exposure conditions. Others question whether they offer unambiguous implications for marketing strategy. Brian Knutson, a professor of neuroscience and psychology at Stanford University, compares the use of EEG to "standing outside a baseball stadium and listening to the crowd to figure out what happened."

Brand Personality and Values

Brand personality is the human characteristics or traits that consumers can attribute to a brand. We can measure it in different ways. Perhaps the simplest and most direct way is to solicit open-ended responses to a probe such as the following:

> If the brand were to come alive as a person, what would it be like? What would it do? Where would it live? What would it wear? Who would it talk to if it went to a party (and what would it talk about)?

If consumers have difficulty getting started in their descriptions, an easily understood example or prompt serves as a guide. For example, if Campbell's soup were to be described as a person, one possible response might be as follows:[20]

> Mrs. Campbell is a rosy-cheeked and plump grandmother who lives in a warm, cozy house and wears an apron as she cooks wonderful things for her grandchildren.

Other means are possible to capture consumers' points of view. For example, marketers can give consumers a variety of pictures or a stack of magazines and ask them to assemble a profile of the brand. Ad agencies often conduct "picture sorting" studies to clarify who are typical users of a brand.

Brand personality and user imagery may not always agree. When *USA Today* was first introduced, a research study exploring consumer opinions of the newspaper indicated that the benefits readers and nonreaders perceived were highly consistent. Perceptions of the *USA Today* brand personality—as colorful, friendly, and simple—were also highly related. User imagery, however, differed dramatically: Nonreaders viewed a typical *USA Today* reader as a shallow "air head"; readers, on the other hand, saw a typical *USA Today* reader as a well-rounded person interested in a variety of issues. Based on these findings, an advertising campaign was introduced to appeal to nonreaders that showed how prominent people endorsed the newspaper.[21]

When *USA Today* launched, readers and nonreaders had very different brand imagery perceptions.
Source: Keri Miksza

The Big Five. We can assess brand personality more definitively through adjective checklists or ratings. Jennifer Aaker conducted a research project that provides an interesting glimpse into the personality of a number of well-known brands, as well as a methodology to examine the personality of any one brand. Based on an extensive data collection of ratings of 114 personality traits on 37 brands in various product categories by over 600 individuals representative of the U.S. population, she created a brand personality scale that reflected the following five factors (with underlying facets) of brand personality:[22]

1. Sincerity (down-to-earth, honest, wholesome, and cheerful)
2. Excitement (daring, spirited, imaginative, and up-to-date)
3. Competence (reliable, intelligent, and successful)
4. Sophistication (upper class and charming)
5. Ruggedness (outdoorsy and tough)

Figure 4 depicts the specific trait items that make up the Aaker brand personality scale. Respondents in her study rated how descriptive each personality trait was for each brand according to a seven-point scale (1 = not at all descriptive; 7 = extremely descriptive). Aaker averaged responses to provide summary measures. Some brands tend to be strong on one particular factor; some brands like Nike are high on more than one factor; some brands score poorly on all factors.

A cross-cultural study exploring the generalizability of this scale outside the United States found that three of the five factors applied in Japan and Spain, but that a "peacefulness" dimension replaced "ruggedness" both in Japan and Spain, and a "passion" dimension emerged in Spain instead of "competency."[23] Research on brand personality in Korea revealed that two culture-specific factors emerge ("passive likeableness" and "ascendancy"), reflecting the importance of Confucian values in Korea's social and economic systems.[24]

Ethnographic and Experiential Methods

More than ever, researchers are working to improve the effectiveness of their qualitative approaches, as well as to go beyond traditional qualitative techniques to research consumers in their natural environment.[25] The rationale is that no matter how clever the research design, consumers may not be able to fully express their true selves as part of a formalized research study. By tapping more directly into consumers' actual home, work, or shopping behaviors, researchers might be able to elicit more meaningful responses.[26] As markets become more competitive

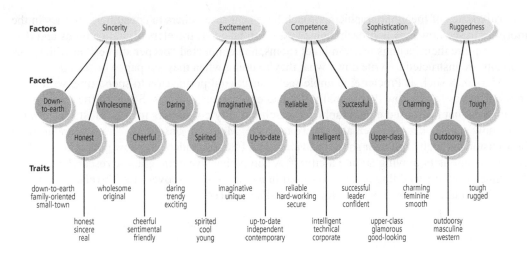

FIGURE 4
Brand Personality Scale Measures

and many brand differences are threatened, any insight that helps to support a stronger brand positioning or create a stronger link to consumers is valuable (see Branding Brief 4).

We've noted that much of this type of research has its roots in ethnographic research originally used by anthropologists. Ethnographic research uses "thick description" based on participant observation. In marketing, the goal of ethnographic research is to extract and interpret the deep cultural meaning of events and activities through various research techniques such as consumer immersion, site visits, shop-alongs, embedded research, etc.[27]

BRANDING BRIEF 4

Making the Most of Consumer Insights

Consumer research plays a significant role in uncovering information valuable to consumer-focused companies. David Taylor, founder of the Brand Gym consultancy, cautions that not all findings from consumer research can be considered insights. He defines an insight as "a penetrating, discerning understanding that unlocks an opportunity."

According to Taylor, an insight holds far more potential than a finding. Using Microsoft as an example, Taylor draws the contrast between the finding that "people need to process more and more information and data" and the insight that "information is the key to power and freedom." This insight might help Microsoft develop products that appeal to a larger consumer base than if the company relied solely on the finding.

Taylor developed a set of criteria to evaluate insights:

- *Fresh:* An insight might be obvious and, in fact, be overlooked or forgotten as a result. Check again.

- *Relevant:* An insight when played back to other target consumers should strike a chord.

- *Enduring:* By building on a deep understanding of consumers' beliefs and needs, a true consumer insight should have potential to remain relevant over time.

- *Inspiring:* All the team should be excited by the insight and see different but consistent applications.

Insights can come from consumer research such as focus groups, but also from using what Taylor describes

as the "core insight drills." A sample of these drills follows:

- How could the brand/category do more to help improve people's lives?

- What do people really value in the category? What would they not miss?

- What conflicting needs do people have? How can these tradeoffs be solved?

- What bigger market is the brand really competing in from a consumer viewpoint? What could the brand do more of to better meet these "higher-order" needs?

- What assumptions do people make about the market that could be challenged?

- How do people think the product works, and how does it work in reality?

- How is the product used in reality? What other products are used instead of the brand, where the brand could do a better job?

These "drills" can help companies unearth consumer insights that lead to better products and services, and ultimately to stronger brands.

Source: David Taylor, "Drilling for Nuggets: How to Use Insight to Inspire Innovation," *Brand Strategy*, March 2000. Used with permission of Brand Strategy, www.brandstrategy.co.uk.

Advocates of the ethnographic approach have sent researchers to consumers' homes in the morning to see how they approach their days, given business travelers digital cameras and diaries to capture their feelings when in hotel rooms, and conducted "beeper studies" in which participants are instructed to write down what they're doing when they are paged or texted.[28]

Marketers such as Procter & Gamble seek consumers' permission to spend time with them in their homes to see how they actually use and experience products. Some of the many other companies that have used ethnographic research to study consumers include Best Western (to learn how seniors decide when and where to shop), Moen (to observe over an extended time how customers really use their shower devices), and Intel (to understand how people use mobile communications in moving around a city).[29] A comprehensive ethnographic research study for JCPenney on their wedding registry resulted in a complete makeover at all levels.[30] Consider how ethnographic research paid off for Hewlett-Packard (HP).

HEWLETT-PACKARD (HP)

To better understand how surgeons operate, HP's medical products division sent a set of researchers into hospitals to observe. Surgeons need to carefully monitor their scalpel movements on a video monitor. During an operation, however, the researchers observed that many other staff members would cross in front of the monitor, obscuring the surgeon's line of sight. Because these staff members were going about their duties, the surgeons had failed to complain and prior research had failed to uncover the problem. Based on this research insight, HP developed a surgical helmet with goggles that cast images right in front of a surgeon's eyes, circumventing the problem.[31]

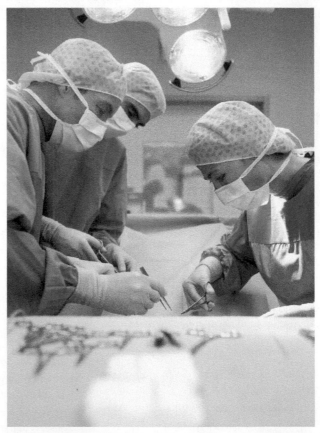

An ethnographic research study by HP led to a breakthrough new medical product.
Source: moodboard/Alamy

Business-to-business firms can also benefit from company visits that help to cement relationships and supplement research efforts. Technology firms such as Hewlett-Packard use cross-functional customer visits as a market research tool to gain a competitive advantage.

1. Send an advance letter of confirmation with an agenda so customers know what to expect and can be prepared.
2. Send small cross-functional teams.
3. Select customers according to a plan and visit at least a dozen.
4. Don't keep going back to the same small group of favorite customers.
5. Interview people at each site who represent each stage of the purchasing decision.
6. Get support from local account management.
7. Use a two- to three-page discussion guide in outline form.
8. Assign roles to team members (moderator, listener, note taker, etc.).
9. Use open-ended questions.
10. Don't ask customers to give solutions—get them to identify problems.
11. Don't talk too much and don't show off your expertise.
12. Probe deeper by using follow-up questions.
13. Debrief immediately.
14. Highlight verbatim quotes in reports.
15. A summary report should emphasize big news and be organized by major themes.
16. Archive the report online with other marketing research and intelligence.

FIGURE 5

Tips for Conducting Good Customer Visits

Figure 5 offers advice from one expert on the subject, Ed McQuarrie, about best practices for an outbound or inbound customer visit.[32]

Service companies often employ *mystery shoppers*, paid researchers who pose as customers to learn about the service experience provided by a company. Sometimes the results can be eye-opening. When the president of Office Depot decided to pose as a mystery shopper himself, he found that employees were spending too much time keeping stores clean and well-stocked and not enough time actually building relationships with customers. As a result, the company reduced the size of stores, retrained and incentivized employees to focus more on customers, and added other products and services that customers wanted that were not currently available.[33]

Through the years, companies have changed the way they gain customer insights. Microsoft employs ethnographic research with in-depth studies of consumer online search attitudes and behavior. Observing consumers inside and outside the home in a series of research studies, the company learned of changes over time in the way consumers explore and learn about new things online.[34]

- An initial study in 2004 revealed that consumers were just trying to find out what experts say, because they felt that experts "knew it all."
- A follow-up study in 2007 showed that consumers believed all the information they needed to learn was actually available through search engines—they just needed to figure out how to use the search engines.
- By 2010, however, ethnographic research showed that people felt they actually created their own knowledge. Search engines were just enablers.

Of special research importance to many companies are lead or leading users. Many firms ask online groups of their most progressive consumers to give feedback via instant-messages or chat rooms. PepsiCo's DEWmocracy 2 program, launched in July 2009, was a 12-month, seven-stage campaign to create another consumer-generated version of its Mountain Dew soft drink, as had happened when the first DEWmocracy produced the highly successful Mountain Dew Voltage. The new campaign tapped into DEW labs, the brand's private online community of its most loyal customers, but also Facebook, Twitter, USTREAM, a 12-second TV video contest, and a dedicated YouTube channel.[35] Another company with close ties to leading-edge users is Burton Snowboards.

BURTON SNOWBOARDS

The best-known snowboard brand, Burton Snowboards, saw its market share increase from 30 percent to 40 percent by focusing on one objective—providing the best equipment to the largest number of snowboarders. To accomplish this goal, Burton engages in a number of activities. Burton puts much emphasis on its many professional riders worldwide, including a smaller percentage who are on its sponsored team. Staff members talk to the riders—on the slopes or on the phone—almost every day, and riders help to design virtually every Burton product. Company researchers immerse themselves in the riders' lives, watching where they shop, what they buy, and what they think about the sport and the equipment. To make sure it doesn't lose touch with its rank-and-file consumers, however, the company makes sure its sales representatives hit the slopes on the weekend to interact with amateur snowboarders. All employees also get a free season pass for the slopes and are allowed to use any new Burton gear for a few days to test and promote it. In 2010, the Burton Demo Tour became the largest consumer interactive product demo in the snowboard world, with over 2,000 riders testing Burton gear on slopes all over North America. Burton also has the eTeam—an online community of 25,000 kids who provide real-time feedback in exchange for free product trials. All of this information is fed into Burton's state-of-the-art innovation center, "Craig's," named after the late snowboarding pioneer Craig Kelly, where advanced prototypes are developed and tested almost daily.[36]

Burton collects information from casual and professional riders to help it design innovative snowboards and other products.

Source: Olivier Maire/EPA/Newscom

Compact video cameras make capturing participants' words and actions easier, and short films are often part of the research output that is reported to help bring the research to life.[37] Every research method, however, has its advantages and disadvantages.[38] Two of the more significant downsides to ethnographic research are that it is time-consuming and expensive. Moreover, because it is based on subjective interpretation, multiple points of view may prevail.

Summary

Qualitative research techniques are a creative means of ascertaining consumer perceptions that may otherwise be difficult to uncover. The range of possible qualitative research techniques is limited only by the creativity of the marketing researcher.

Qualitative research, however, also has its drawbacks. The in-depth insights that emerge have to be tempered by the realization that the samples are often very small and may not necessarily generalize to broader populations. Moreover, given the qualitative nature of the data, there may be questions of interpretation. Different researchers examining the same results from a qualitative research study may draw different conclusions.

QUANTITATIVE RESEARCH TECHNIQUES

Although qualitative measures are useful in identifying the range of possible associations with a brand and some initial insights into their strength, favorability, and uniqueness, marketers often want a more definitive portrait of the brand to allow them to make more confident and defensible strategic and tactical recommendations.

Some say qualitative research strives to uncover and discover, while quantitative research aims to prove or disprove. Whereas qualitative research typically elicits some type of verbal response from consumers, *quantitative research* typically employs various types of scale questions from which researchers can draw numerical representations and summaries.

Quantitative measures of brand knowledge can help to more definitively assess the depth and breadth of brand awareness; the strength, favorability, and uniqueness of brand associations; the positivity of brand judgments and feelings; and the extent and nature of brand relationships. Quantitative measures are often the primary ingredient in tracking studies that monitor brand knowledge structures of consumers over time.

Brand Awareness

Brand awareness is related to the strength of the brand in memory, as reflected by consumers' ability to identify various brand elements like the brand name, logo, symbol, character, packaging, and slogan under different conditions. Brand awareness describes the likelihood that a brand will come to mind in different situations, and the ease with which it does so given different types of cues.

Marketers use several measures of awareness of brand elements.[39] Choosing the right one is a matter of knowing the relative importance of brand awareness for consumer behavior in the category and the role it plays in the success of the marketing program. Let's look at some of these awareness issues.

Recognition. Brand recognition requires consumers to identify the brand under a variety of circumstances and can rest on the identification of any of the brand elements. The most basic recognition test gives consumers a set of individual items visually or orally and asks them whether they think they've previously seen or heard of these items. To provide a more sensitive test, it is often useful to include decoys or lures—items consumers could not possibly have seen. In addition to "yes" or "no" responses, consumers can also rate how confident they are in their recognition of an item.

Other, somewhat more subtle, recognition measures test "perceptually degraded" versions of the brand, which are masked or distorted in some way or shown for extremely brief duration. For example, we can test brand name recognition with missing letters. Figure 6 tests your ability to recognize brand names with less than full information. These more subtle measures may be particularly important for brands that have a high level of recognition, in order to provide more sensitive assessments.[40]

A brand name with a high level of awareness will be recognized under less than ideal conditions. Consider the following list of incomplete names (i.e., word fragments). Which ones do you recognize? Compare your answers to the answer key in the footnote to see how well you did.

1. D _ _ N E _
2. K O _ _ K
3. D U _ A C _ _ _
4. H Y _ T _
5. A D _ _ L
6. M _ T _ E L
7. D _ L T _
8. N _ Q U _ L
9. G _ L L _ T _ _
10. H _ _ S H _ Y
11. H _ L L _ _ R K
12. M _ C H _ _ I N
13. T _ P P _ R W _ _ E
14. L _ G _
15. N _ K _

Answers: (1) Disney; (2) Kodak; (3) Duracell; (4) Hyatt; (5) Advil; (6) Mattel; (7) Delta; (8) NyQuil; (9) Gillette; (10) Hershey; (11) Hallmark; (12) Michelin; (13) Tupperware; (14) Lego; (15) Nike.

FIGURE 6

Don't Tell Me, It's On the Tip of My Tongue

Brand recognition is especially important for packaging, and some marketing researchers have used creative means to assess the visibility of package design. As a starting point, they consider the benchmark or "best case" of the visibility of a package when a consumer (1) with 20–20 vision (2) is face-to-face with a package (3) at a distance of less than five feet (4) under ideal lighting conditions.

A key question then is whether the package design is robust enough to be still recognizable if one or more of these four conditions are not present. Because shopping is often not conducted under "ideal" conditions, such insights are important. For example, many consumers who wear eyeglasses do not wear them when shopping in a supermarket. Is the package still able to effectively communicate to consumers under such conditions?

Research methods using tachistoscopes (T-scopes) and eye tracking techniques exist to test the effectiveness of alternative package designs according to a number of specific criteria:

- Degree of shelf impact
- Impact and recall of specific design elements
- Perceived package size
- Copy visibility and legibility
- Distance at which the package can first be identified
- Angle at which the package can first be identified
- Speed with which the package can be identified

These additional measures can provide more sensitive measures of recognition than simple "yes" or "no" tasks. By applying these direct and indirect measures of brand recognition, marketers can determine which brand elements exist in memory and, to some extent, the strength of their association. One advantage that brand recognition measures have over recall measures is the chance to use visual recognition. It may be difficult for consumers to describe a logo or symbol in a recall task; it's much easier for them to assess the same elements visually in a recognition task.

Nevertheless, brand recognition measures provide only an approximation of *potential* recallability. To determine whether consumers will actually recall the brand elements under various circumstances, we need measures of brand recall.

Recall.   To demonstrate brand recall, consumers must retrieve the actual brand element from memory when given some related probe or cue. Thus, brand recall is a more demanding memory task than brand recognition because consumers are not just given a brand element and asked to say whether they've seen it before.

Different measures of brand recall are possible depending on the type of cues provided to consumers. *Unaided recall* on the basis of "all brands" provided as a cue is likely to identify

Before a new package ever hits the shelf, marketers often conduct research to understand its likely impact even in the store itself.
Source: Paul Burns Cultura/ Newscom

only the very strongest brands. *Aided recall* uses various types of cues to help consumer recall. One possible sequence of aided recall might use progressively narrower cues—such as product class, product category, and product type labels—to provide insight into the organization of consumers' brand knowledge structures.

For example, if recall of the Porsche 911—a high-performance German sports car—in non-German markets were of interest, recall probes could begin with "all cars" and move to more and more narrowly defined categories such as "sports cars," "foreign sports cars," or even "high-performance German sports cars." Marketers could ask consumers: "When you think of foreign sports cars, which brands come to mind?"

Other types of cues can help measure brand recall. For example, marketers can ask about product attributes ("When you think of chocolate, which brands come to mind?) or usage goals ("If you were thinking of having a healthy snack, which brands come to mind?"). Often, to capture the breadth of brand recall and to assess brand salience, we might need to examine the context of the purchase decision or consumption situation, such as different times and places. The stronger the brand associations to these non-product considerations, the more likely it is that consumers will recall them when given those situational cues.

When combined, measures of recall based on product attribute or category cues and situational or usage cues give an indication of breadth and depth of recall. We can further distinguish brand recall according to the order as well as the latency or speed of recall. In many cases, people will recognize a brand when it is shown to them and will recall it if they are given a sufficient number of cues. Thus, potential recallability is high. The more important issue is the salience of the brand: Do consumers think of the brand under the right circumstances, for example, when they could be either buying or using the product? How quickly do they think of the brand? Is it automatically or easily recalled? Is it the first brand they recall?

Corrections for Guessing. Any research measure must consider the issue of consumers making up responses or guessing. That problem may be especially evident with certain types of aided awareness or recognition measures for the brand. Spurious awareness occurs when consumers erroneously claim they recall something they really don't and that may not even exist. For example, one market research firm, Oxtoby-Smith, conducted a benchmark study of awareness of health and beauty products.[41] In the study, the firm asked consumers questions like this:

> "The following is a list of denture adhesive brand names. Please answer yes if you've heard the name before and no if you haven't. Okay? Orafix? Fasteeth? Dentu-Tight? Fixodent?"

Although 16 percent of the sample reported that they had heard of Dentu-Tight, there was one problem: it didn't exist! Similarly high levels of reported recall were reported for plausible-sounding but fictitious brands such as Four O'Clock Tea (8 percent), Leone Pasta (16 percent), and Mrs. Smith's Cake Mix (31 percent). On the basis of this study, Oxtoby-Smith found that spurious awareness was about 8 percent for new health and beauty products and even higher in some other product categories. In one case, a proposed line extension was mistakenly thought to already exist by about 50 percent of the sample (a finding that no doubt sent a message to the company that it should go ahead and introduce the product!).

From a marketing perspective, the problem with spurious awareness is that it may send misleading signals about the proper strategic direction for a brand. For example, Oxtoby-Smith reported that one of its clients was struggling with a 5 percent market share despite the fact that 50 percent of survey respondents reported they were aware of the brand. On the surface, it would seem a good idea to improve the image of the brand and attitudes toward it in some way. Upon further examination, marketers determined that spurious awareness accounted for *almost half* the survey respondents who reported brand awareness, suggesting that a more appropriate solution to the true problem would be to first build awareness to a greater degree. Marketers should be sensitive to the possibilities of misleading signals because of spurious brand awareness, especially with new brands or ones with plausible-sounding names.

Strategic Implications. The advantage of aided recall measures is that they yield insight into how brand knowledge is organized in memory and what kind of cues or reminders may be necessary for consumers to be able to retrieve the brand from memory. Understanding recall when

For a unique sports car like Porsche, it is important for marketers to understand the breadth and depth of its brand awareness.

Source: Hand-out/PORSCHE CANADA/Newscom

we use different levels of product category specificity as cues is important, because it has implications for how consumers form consideration sets and make product decisions.

For example, again consider the Porsche 911. Assume consumer recall of this particular car model was fairly low when all cars were considered but very high when foreign sports cars were considered. In other words, consumers strongly categorized the Porsche 911 as a prototypical sports car but tended to think of it in only that way. If that were the case, for more consumers to entertain the possibility of buying a Porsche 911, we might need to broaden the meaning of Porsche so that it has a stronger association to cars in general. Of course, such a strategy risks alienating existing customers who had been initially attracted by the "purity" and strong identification of the Porsche 911 as a sports car. The choice of appropriate strategy would depend on the relative costs and benefits of targeting the two different segments.

The point is that the category structure that exists in consumers' minds—as reflected by brand recall performance—can have profound implications for consumer choice and marketing strategy, as demonstrated by The Science of Branding 1. The insights gleaned from measuring brand recall are also valuable for developing brand identity and integrated marketing communication programs. For example, we can examine brand recall for each brand element to explore the extent to which any one of these (name, symbol, or logo) suggests any other. Are consumers aware of all the different brand elements and how they relate?

We also need a complete understanding of brand image, as covered in the following section.

Brand Image

One vitally important aspect of the brand is its image, as reflected by the associations that consumers hold for it. It is useful for marketers to make a distinction between lower-level considerations, related to consumer perceptions of specific performance and imagery attributes and benefits, and higher-level considerations related to overall judgments, feelings, and relationships. There is an obvious connection between the two levels, because consumers' overall responses and relationship with a brand typically depend on perceptions of specific attributes and benefits of that brand. This section considers some issues in measuring lower-level brand performance and imagery associations.

Beliefs are descriptive thoughts that a person holds about something (for instance, that a particular software package has many helpful features and menus and is easy to use).[42] Brand association beliefs are those specific attributes and benefits linked to the brand and its competitors.

THE SCIENCE OF BRANDING 1

Understanding Categorical Brand Recall

A classic experiment by Prakash Nedungadi provides a compelling demonstration of the importance of understanding the category structure that exists in consumer memory as well as the value of strategies for increasing the recallability or accessibility of brands during choice situations. As a preliminary step in his research study, Nedungadi first examined the category structure for fast-food restaurants that existed in consumers' minds. He found that a "major subcategory" was "hamburger chains" and a "minor subcategory" was "sandwich shops." He also found, on the basis of usage and linking surveys, that within the major subcategory of national hamburger chains, a major brand was McDonald's and a minor brand was Wendy's, and within the minor subcategory of local sandwich shops, a major brand was Joe's Deli (a brand in his survey area) and a minor brand was Subway. Consistent with this reasoning, in an unaided recall and choice task, consumers were more likely to remember and select a brand from a major subcategory than from a minor subcategory and, within a subcategory, a major brand rather than a minor brand.

Nedungadi next looked at the effects of different brand "primes" on subsequent choices among the four fast-food restaurants. Brands were primed by having subjects in the experiment first answer a series of seemingly unrelated questions—including some about the brand to be primed—before making their brand selections. Two key findings emerged. First, a major brand that was primed was more likely to be selected in the later choice task even though attitudes toward the brand were no different from those of a control group. In other

words, merely making the brand more accessible in memory increased the likelihood that it would be chosen *independent of any differences in brand attitude*. Second, priming a minor brand in a minor subcategory actually benefited the *major* brand in that subcategory more. In other words, by drawing attention to the minor subcategory of sandwich shops—which could easily be overlooked—the minor brand, Subway, indirectly primed the major brand, Joe's Deli, in the subcategory. The implications of Nedungadi's research are that marketers must understand how consumers' memory is organized and, as much as possible, ensure that the proper cues and primes are evident to prompt brand recall.

In sum, brand recall provides insight into category structure and brand positioning in consumers' minds. Brands tend to be recalled in categorical clusters when consumers are given a general probe. Certain brands are grouped together in memory because they share certain associations and are thus likely to cue and remind consumers of each other if one is recalled.

Sources: Prakash Nedungadi, "Recall and Consumer Consideration Sets: Influencing Choice Without Altering Brand Evaluations," *Journal of Consumer Research* 17 (December 1990): 263–276; Joseph W. Alba and J. Wesley Hutchinson, "Dimensions of Consumer Expertise," *Journal of Consumer Research* 13 (March 1987): 411–454; Kalpesh Kaushik Desai and Wayne D. Hoyer, "Descriptive Characteristics of Memory-Based Consideration Sets: Influence of Usage Occasion Frequency and Usage Location Familiarity," *Journal of Consumer Research* 27 (2000): 309–323.

For example, consumers may have brand association beliefs for Sony PlayStation 3 entertainment system such as "fun and exciting," "cool and hip," "colorful," "great graphics," "advanced technology," "variety of game titles," and "sometimes violent." They may also have associations to the brand logo and the slogan, "It Only Does Everything." PlayStation 3 user imagery may be "used by teenagers or 20-something males who are serious about playing video games, especially sports games."

The qualitative research approaches we described earlier are useful in uncovering the different types of specific brand associations making up the brand image. To better understand their potential ability to serve as basis for brand positioning and how they might contribute to brand equity, we can assess belief associations on the basis of one or more of the three key dimensions—strength, favorability, and uniqueness—making up the sources of brand equity.

As a first cut, we can use open-ended measures that tap into the strength, favorability, and uniqueness of brand associations, as follows:

1. What are the strongest associations you have to the brand? What comes to mind when you think of the brand? (Strength)
2. What is good about the brand? What do you like about the brand? What is bad about the brand? What do you dislike about the brand? (Favorability)
3. What is unique about the brand? What characteristics or features does the brand share with other brands? (Uniqueness)

1. To what extent do you feel the following product characteristics are descriptive of Lipton iced tea (where 1 = strongly disagree and 7 = strongly agree)?

_____ convenient
_____ refreshing and thirst quenching
_____ real and natural
_____ good-tasting
_____ contemporary and relevant
_____ used by young professionals

2. How good or bad is it for iced tea to have the following product characteristics (where 1 = very bad and 7 = very good)?

_____ convenient
_____ refreshing and thirst quenching
_____ real and natural
_____ good-tasting
_____ contemporary and relevant
_____ used by young professionals

3. How unique is Lipton iced tea in terms of the following product characteristics (where 1 = not at all unique and 7 = highly unique)?

_____ convenient
_____ refreshing and thirst quenching
_____ real and natural
_____ good-tasting
_____ contemporary and relevant
_____ used by young professionals

FIGURE 7

Example of Brand Association Ratings in Terms of Strength, Favorability, and Uniqueness

To gain more specific insights, we could rate these belief associations according to strength, favorability, and uniqueness, as Figure 7 illustrates with Lipton iced tea. Indirect tests also can assess the derived importance and favorability of these brand associations (through multivariate regression techniques).

Other Approaches. A more complicated quantitative technique to assess overall brand uniqueness is multidimensional scaling, or perceptual maps. *Multidimensional scaling* (MDS) is a procedure for determining the perceived relative images of a set of objects, such as products or brands. MDS transforms consumer judgments of similarity or preference into distances represented in perceptual space. For example, if brands A and B are judged by respondents to be the most similar of a set of brands, the MDS algorithm will position brands A and B so that the distance between them in multidimensional space is smaller than the distance between any other two pairs of brands. Respondents may base their similarity between brands on any basis—tangible or intangible.[43]

Figure 8 displays a hypothetical perceptual map of restaurants in a particular market. Segment 1 is more concerned with health than taste and is well targeted by Brand B; segment 2 is more concerned with taste and is well targeted by Brand C. Brand A is trapped in the middle. It either must improve taste to provide a healthy alternative to Brand C for segment 2, or it must improve healthiness to prove a tastier alternative to Brand B for segment 1.

Brand Responses

The purpose of measuring more general, higher-level considerations is to find out how consumers combine all the more specific, lower-level considerations about the brand in their minds to form different types of brand responses and evaluations.

Purchase Intentions. Another set of measures closely related to brand attitudes and consideration looks at purchase intentions[44] and focus on the likelihood of buying the brand or of switching to another brand. Research in psychology suggests that purchase intentions are most likely to

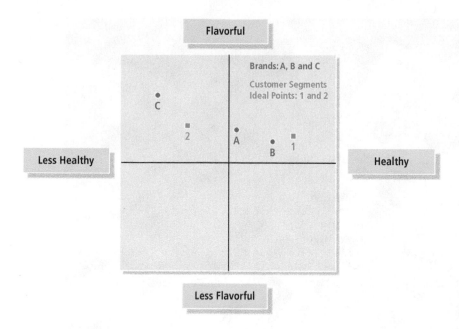

FIGURE 8

Hypothetical Restaurant
Perceptual Map

be predictive of actual purchase when there is correspondence between the two in the following dimensions:[45]

- Action (buying for own use or to give as a gift)
- Target (specific type of product and brand)
- Context (in what type of store based on what prices and other conditions)
- Time (within a week, month, or year)

In other words, when asking consumers to forecast their likely purchase of a product or a brand, we want to specify *exactly* the circumstances—the purpose of the purchase, the location of the purchase, the time of the purchase, and so forth. For example, we could ask consumers:

> "Assume your refrigerator broke down over the next weekend and could not be inexpensively repaired. If you went to your favorite appliance store and found all the different brands competitively priced, how likely would you be to buy a General Electric refrigerator?"

Consumers could indicate their purchase intention on an 11-point probability scale that ranges from 0 (definitely would not buy) to 10 (definitely would buy).

Likelihood to Recommend. Bain's Frederick Reichheld suggests there is only one customer question that really matters: "How likely is it that you would recommend this product or service to a friend or colleague?" According to Reichheld, a customer's willingness to recommend results from all aspects of a customer's experience.[46]

Reicheld uses answers to this question to create what he calls a Net Promoter Score (NPS). Specifically, in a survey, customers are asked to rate their likelihood to recommend on a 0–10-point scale. Marketers then subtract *detractors* (those who gave a 0–6) from *promoters* (those who gave a 9 or 10) to arrive at the NPS score. Customers who rate the brand with a 7 or 8 are deemed *passively satisfied* and are not included. A typical set of NPS scores falls in the 10–30 percent range, but world-class companies can score over 50 percent. Some firms with top NPS scores include USAA (89 percent), Apple (77 percent), Amazon.com (74 percent), and Google (71 percent).

Several companies have seen benefits from adopting NetPromoter scores as a means of tracking brand health. When the European unit of GE Healthcare overhauled its call center and put more specialists in the field, GE Healthcare's Net Promoter scores jumped 10–15 points. BearingPoint found clients who gave it high Net Promoter scores showed the highest revenue growth. When Intuit applied Net Promoter to its TurboTax product, feedback revealed dissatisfaction with the software's rebate procedure. After Intuit dropped the proof-of-purchase requirement, sales jumped 6 percent.

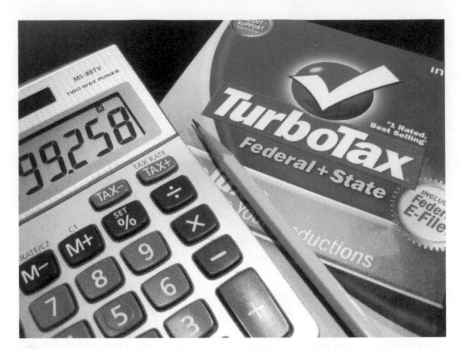

TurboTax used NetPromoter scores to help fine-tune its marketing program.
Source: AP Photo/ RIGELHAUPT SAMUEL/SIPA

Brand Relationships

Brand relationships can be characterized in terms of brand resonance; there are possible measures for each of the four key dimensions: behavioral loyalty, attitudinal attachment, sense of community, and active engagement. This section considers additional considerations with respect to each of those four dimensions. Figure 9 displays a scale, although developed by its authors to measure overall brand engagement, could easily be adapted to measure brand resonance by replacing mentions of brands with a specific brand. For example, instead of saying, "I have a special bond with the brands I like," it could say, "I have a special bond with my Saab automobile," and so on.

Behavioral Loyalty. To capture reported brand usage and behavioral loyalty, we could ask consumers several questions directly. Or we could ask them what percentage of their last purchases in the category went to the brand (past purchase history) and what percentage of their planned next purchases will go to the brand (intended future purchases). For example, the marketers or brand managers of Duracell batteries might ask the following questions:

- Which brand of batteries do you usually buy?
- Which brand of batteries did you buy last time?
- Do you have any batteries on hand? Which brand?
- Which brands of batteries did you consider buying?
- Which brand of batteries will you buy next time?

These types of questions can provide information about brand attitudes and usage for Duracell, including potential gaps with competitors and the names of other brands that might be in the consideration set at the time of purchase.

Marketers can make their measures open ended, force consumers to choose one of two brands, or offer multiple choice or rating scales. They can compare the answers with actual measures of consumer behavior to assess whether consumers are accurate in their predictions. For example, if 30 percent of consumers reported, on average, that they thought they would take their vitamins daily over the next two weeks, but only 15 percent of consumers reported two weeks later that they actually had done so during that period, then Centrum brand managers might need to devise strategies to better convert intentions to actual behavior.

In a business-to-business setting, Narayandas advocates analyzing sales records, talking to sales teams, and conducting surveys to assess where customers stand on a "loyalty ladder."[47]

1. I have a special bond with the brands I like.
2. I consider my favorite brands to be part of myself.
3. I often feel a personal connection between my brands and me.
4. Part of me is defined by important brands in my life.
5. I feel as if I have a close personal connection with the brands I most prefer.
6. I can identify with important brands in my life.
7. There are links between the brands that I prefer and how I view myself.
8. My favorite brands are an important indication of who I am.

FIGURE 9

A Brand Engagement Scale

Source: David Sprott, Sandor Czellar, and Eric Spangenberg, "The Importance of a General Measure of Brand Engagement on Market Behaviour: Development and Validation of a Scale," *Journal of Marketing Research* 46 (February 2009): 92–104.

Attitudinal Attachment. Several different approaches have been suggested to measure the second component of brand resonance—brand attachment.[48] Some researchers like to characterize it in terms of brand love.[49] One study proposed a brand love scale that consists of 10 items: (1) This is a wonderful brand; (2) This brand makes me feel good; (3) This brand is totally awesome; (4) I have neutral feelings about this brand (reverse-coded item); (5) This brand makes me very happy; (6) I love this brand; (7) I have no particular feelings about this brand (reverse-coded item); (8) This brand is a pure delight; (9) I am passionate about this brand; and (10) I am very attached to this brand.[50]

Another study found 11 dimensions that characterized brand love:[51]

1. Passion (for the brand).
2. Duration of the relationship (the relationship with the brand exists for a long time).
3. Self-congruity (congruity between self-image and product image).
4. Dreams (the brand favors consumer dreams).
5. Memories (evoked by the brand).
6. Pleasure (that the brand provides to the consumer).
7. Attraction (feel toward the brand).
8. Uniqueness (of the brand and/or of the relationship).
9. Beauty (of the brand).
10. Trust (the brand has never disappointed).
11. Declaration of affect (feel toward the brand).

One promising approach defines brand attachment in terms of two underlying constructs—brand-self connections and brand prominence—where each of those two dimensions have two subdimensions, suggesting the following sets of measures:[52]

1. **Brand-Self Connection**
   a. *Connected*: "To what extent do you feel that you are personally connected to (Brand)?"
   b. *Part of Who You Are*: "To what extent is (Brand) part of you and who you are?"

2. **Brand Prominence**
   a. *Automatic*: "To what extent are your thoughts and feelings towards (Brand) often automatic, coming to mind seemingly on their own?"
   b. *Naturally*: "To what extent do your thoughts and feelings towards (Brand) come to you naturally and instantly?"

Sense of Community. Although measuring behavioral loyalty and attitudinal attachment may require a fairly structured set of questions, both sense of community and active engagement could call for more varied measures because of their diverse set of issues.

One interesting concept that has been proposed with respect to community is *social currency*, developed by brand consultants Vivaldi Partners. They define social currency as "the extent to which people share the brand or information about the brand as part of their everyday social lives at work or at home." Figure 10 displays the different dimensions that make up the social currency concept according to Vivaldi Partners.

Dimension	Key Question	Value of Dimension
Conversation	What share of your brand users recognizes and stirs buzz?	Customers proactively talk about a brand.
Advocacy	How many act as disciples and stand up for your brand?	Customers are willing to tell others about a brand or recommend it further.
Information	How many feel they exchange fruitful information with others?	The more information customers have about a brand the more likely they are to develop preferences for the brand.
Affiliation	What share of users has a sense of community?	Value of brand is closely related to sense of community it creates among other like-minded people.
Utility	How much value do consumers derive from interacting with others?	Social exchange with others involving a brand is an integral part of people's lives.
Identity	How many of your users can identify with other users?	Customers develop strong sense of identity and ability to express themselves to others by using a brand.

FIGURE 10

Vivaldi Partners' Social Currency Model

Source: Used with permission from Erich Joachimsthaler at Vivaldi Partners.

Active Engagement.   According to the brand resonance model, *active engagement* for a brand is defined as the extent to which consumers are willing to invest their own personal resources—time, energy, money, and so on—on the brand beyond those resources expended during purchase or consumption of the brand.

For example, in terms of engagement, in-depth measures could explore word-of-mouth behavior, online behavior, and so forth. For online behavior, measures could explore the extent of customer-initiated versus firm-initiated interactions, the extent of learning and teaching by the customer versus by the firm, the extent of customers teaching other customers, and so on.[53]

The key to such metrics is the qualitative nature of the consumer-brand interaction and how well it reflects intensity of feelings. One mistake many Internet firms made was to put too much emphasis on "eyeballs" and "stickiness"—the number and duration of page views at a Web site, respectively. The depth of the underlying brand relationships of the customers making those visits, however, and the manner in which those relationships manifest themselves in brand-beneficial actions, will typically be more important.

Accordingly, researchers are attempting to determine the brand value of different on-line and social media activities.[54] For example, how important is a "like" from a user on Facebook? One firm estimated that bringing a user on as a fan could be worth between 44 cents and $3.60 in equivalent media value from increased impressions generated from the Facebook newsfeed. Critics of the study, however, pointed out that not all fans are created equal.[55]

Several different specific approaches have been suggested to measure brand engagement. The Science of Branding 2 provides a detailed breakdown of the concept.

Fournier's Brand Relationship Research.   Boston University's Susan Fournier argues that brands can and do serve as viable relationship partners, and she suggests a reconceptualization of the notion of brand personality within this framework.[56] Specifically, the everyday execution of marketing mix decisions constitutes a set of behaviors enacted on the part of the brand. These actions trigger a series of inferences regarding the implicit *contract* that appears to guide the engagement of the consumer and brand and, hence, the type of relationship formed.

Brand personality as conceptualized within this framework describes the *relationship role* enacted by the brand in its partnership capacity. For example, if the brand expresses behaviors that signal commitment to the consumer, and further if it sends gifts as symbols of affection, the consumer may infer a courtship or marriage type of engagement with the brand.

Fournier identifies a typology of 15 different relationship types characterizing consumers' engagement with brands (see Figure 11). Fournier argues that this relationship role view of brand personality provides more actionable guidance to managers who wish to create and manage their brand personalities in line with marketing actions than does the trait-based

THE SCIENCE OF BRANDING 2

Understanding Brand Engagement

There are several different ways to think of brand engagement. *Actual brand engagement* is the activities with which the consumer currently is engaged with the brand and is typically what is measured with the brand resonance model. Two other approaches provide interesting contrasts. *Ideal brand engagement* is the activities the brand consumer wishes they could do with the brand. *Market brand engagement* is the activities the consumer believes other consumers are doing with the brand.

Market brand engagement will be closely related to measures of *brand momentum*—how much progress the brand appears to be making with consumers in the marketplace. Both sets of measures deal with consumer perceptions of how other consumers are connecting to a brand.

Measures of actual brand engagement can take two forms—more general, macro measures or more specific, micro measures. Macro measures focus on the types of resources expended, for example:

Time: "It is worth spending more time on the brand (or going out of the way for it)."
Energy: "It is worth investing extra effort on the brand."
Money: "It is worth spending more money on the brand."

Micro sets of measures focus on specific categories of brand-related activities. These activities fall into three categories depending on whether they relate to: (1) collecting brand information, (2) participating in brand marketing activities, or (3) interacting with other people and having a sense of community. Here are some possible questions.

Collecting Brand Information

I like learning about this brand.
If this brand has any new products or services, I tend to notice it.
If I see a newspaper or magazine article about this brand, I tend to read it.
If I hear a TV or radio story about this brand, I tend to listen to it.
If I see a news story online about this brand, I tend to open and read it.

I like to visit this brand's Web site.
I like to read online blogs about this brand.

Participating in Brand Marketing Activities

If I notice an ad for this brand, I tend to pay attention to it.
If I notice a sales promotion from this brand, I tend to pay attention to it.
If I get something in the mail from this brand, I tend to open it.
If this brand sponsors a sports, entertainment or arts event, I tend to notice it.
If I see a billboard or any outdoor type ad for this brand, I tend to notice it.
If this brand has a display or demonstration in the store, I tend to notice it.
If this brand shows up in a movie or television show, I tend to notice it.
If I get a chance to sample one of this brand's new products, I tend to try it.
I like to buy licensed products from this brand.

Interacting with Other People

I like to talk to others about this brand.
I like to talk to people at work about this brand.
I like to talk to my friends and family about this brand.
I like to seek out others who use this brand.
I have joined or would like to join an online community with other users of this brand.
I have joined or would like to join an online community with others who like this brand.
I have joined or would like to join an online community with people from the company who makes this brand.
I am active in a loyalty program for this brand.
I tend to notice when other people are using this brand.

These are only some representative examples of the types of survey measures that could be employed to assess brand engagement. Depending on the category and circumstances, a variety of other questions could be devised and fruitfully applied.

view, which identifies general personality tendencies that might or might not be connected to marketing strategies and goals.

Fournier has conducted fascinating research that reframes the conceptualization and measurement of brand strength strictly in relationship terms. It defines a brand's strength in terms of the strength, depth, and durability of the consumer-brand relational bond using the multi-faceted concept of **brand relationship quality**, or BRQ. Extensive validation work supported a multifaceted hierarchical structure for the BRQ construct that includes six main dimensions of relationship strength, many with important subfacets. The main facets are (1) interdependence, (2) self-concept connection, (3) commitment, (4) love/passion, (5) intimacy, and (6) brand partner quality.

Relationship Form	Case Examples
Arranged marriage: Nonvoluntary union imposed by preferences of third party. Intended for long-term, exclusive commitment.	Karen's husband's preferred brands (e.g., Mop'n Glo, Palmolive, Hellman's); Karen's Esteé Lauder, imposed through gift-giving; Jean's use of Murphy's Oil Soap as per manufacturer recommendation.
Casual friend/buddy: Friendship low in affect and intimacy, characterized by infrequent or sporadic engagement and few expectations of reciprocity or reward.	Karen and her household cleaning brands.
Marriage of convenience: Long-term, committed relationship precipitated by environmental influence rather than deliberate choice, and governed by satisfying rules.	Vicki's switch to regional Friend's Baked Beans brand from favored B&M brand left behind; Jean's loyalty to DeMoulas salad dressing brand left behind by client at the bar.
Committed partnership: Long-term, voluntarily imposed, socially supported union high in love, intimacy, trust, and commitment to stay together despite adverse circumstances. Adherence to exclusivity rules expected.	Jean and virtually all her cooking, cleaning, and household appliance brands; Karen and Gatorade.
Best friendship: Voluntary union based on reciprocity principle, the endurance of which is ensured through continued provision of positive rewards. Characterized by revelation of true self, honesty, and intimacy. Congruity in partner images and personal interests common.	Karen and Reebok running shoes; Vicki and Crest or Ivory.
Compartmentalized friendship: Highly specialized, situationally confined, enduring friendship characterized by lower intimacy than other friendship forms but higher socio-emotional rewards and interdependence. Easy entry and exit.	Vicki and her stable of shampoos, perfumes, and lingerie brands.
Kinship: Nonvoluntary union with lineage ties.	Vicki's preferences for Tetley tea or Karen's for Ban, Joy, and Miracle Whip, all of which were inherited through their mothers.
Rebound relationship: Union precipitated by desire to replace prior partner, as opposed to attraction to replacement partner.	Karen's use of Comet, Gateway, and Success Rice.
Childhood friendship: Infrequently engaged, affective relation reminiscent of childhood times. Yields comfort and security of past self.	Jean and Jell-O pudding.
Courtship: Interim relationship state on the road to committed partnership contract.	Vicki and her Musk scent brands.
Dependency: Obsessive, highly emotional, selfish attractions cemented by feeling that the other is irreplaceable. Separation from other yields anxiety. High tolerance of other's transgressions results.	Karen and Mary Kay; Vicki and Soft 'n Dry.
Fling: Short-term, time-bounded engagement of high emotional reward. Devoid entirely of commitment and reciprocity demands.	Vicki's trial-size shampoo brands.
Enmity: Intensely involving relationship characterized by negative affect and desire to inflict pain or revenge on the other.	Karen and her husband's brands, postdivorce; Jean and her other-recommended-but-rejected brands (e.g., ham, peanut butter, sinks).
Enslavement: Nonvoluntary relationship union governed entirely by desires of the relationship partner.	Karen and Southern Bell, Cable Vision. Vicki and Playtex, a bra for large-breasted women.
Secret affair: Highly emotive, privately held relationship considered risky if exposed to others.	Karen and the Tootsie Pops she sneaks at work.

FIGURE 11

A Typology of Consumer-Brand Relationships

Fournier argues that these facets and their subfacets (such as trust within the partner quality facet or consumer-to-firm and firm-to-consumer intimacy) have superior diagnostic value over competing strength measures, and she suggests they have greater managerial utility in their application. In her experience, BRQ measures have been successfully incorporated in brand tracking studies, where they provide profiles of brand strength versus competitors, useful ties to marketplace performance indicators, and specific guidance for the enhancement and dilution of brand equity through managerial actions in the marketplace. Although brand relationship quality shares some characteristics with brand resonance, it provides valuable additional perspectives and insights.

The six main facets of brand relationship quality are as follows:

- *Interdependence:* The degree to which the brand is ingrained in the consumer's daily course of living, both behaviorally (in terms of frequency, scope, and strength of interactions) and cognitively (in terms of longing for and preoccupation with anticipated brand interactions). Interdependence is often revealed through the presence of routinized behavioral rituals surrounding brand purchase and use, and through separation anxiety experienced during periods of product deprivation. At its extremes, interdependence becomes dependency and addiction.

- *Self-concept connection:* The degree to which the brand delivers on important identity concerns, tasks, or themes, thereby expressing a significant part of the self-concept, both past (including nostalgic references and brand memories) and present, and personal as well as social. Grounding of the self provides feelings of comfort, connectedness, control, and security. In its extreme form, self-connection reflects integration of concepts of brand and self.

- *Commitment:* Dedication to continued brand association and betterment of the relationship, despite circumstances foreseen and unforeseen. Commitment includes professed faithfulness and loyalty to the other, often formalized through stated pledges and publicized intentions. Commitment is not defined solely by sunk costs and irretrievable investments that pose barriers to exit.

- *Love/passion:* Affinity toward and adoration of the brand, particularly with respect to other available alternatives. The intensity of the emotional bonds joining relationship partners may range from feelings of warmth, caring, and affection to those of true passion. Love includes the belief that the brand is irreplaceable and uniquely qualified as a relationship partner.

- *Intimacy:* A sense of deep familiarity with and understanding of both the essence of the brand as a partner in the relationship and the nature of the consumer-brand relationship itself. Intimacy is revealed in the presence of a strong consumer-brand relationship culture, the sharing of little-known personal details of the self, and an elaborate brand memory containing significant experiences or associations. Intimacy is a two-dimensional concept: the consumer develops intimate knowledge of the brand, and also feels a sense of intimacy exhibited on the part of the brand toward the individual as a consumer.

- *Partner quality:* Perceived partner quality involves a summary judgment of the caliber of the role enactments performed by the brand in its partnership role. Partner quality includes three central components: (1) an empathic orientation toward the other (ability of the partner to make the other feel wanted, cared for, respected, noticed, and important; responsiveness to needs); (2) a character of reliability, dependability, and predictability in the brand; and (3) trust or faith in the belief that the brand will adhere to established relationship rules and be held accountable for its actions.

COMPREHENSIVE MODELS OF CONSUMER-BASED BRAND EQUITY

The customer-based brand equity model presented in this text provides a comprehensive, cohesive overview of brand building and brand equity. Other researchers and consultants have also put forth consumer-based brand equity models that share some of the same principles and philosophy as the CBBE model, although developed in a different way. The Brand Focus presents a detailed account of arguably the most successful and influential industry branding model, Young and Rubicam's BrandAsset Valuator. Another influential model is Millward Brown's BrandDynamics.[57]

BrandDynamics

Marketing research agency Millward Brown's BrandDynamics model offers a graphical model to represent the emotional and functional strength of relationship consumers have with

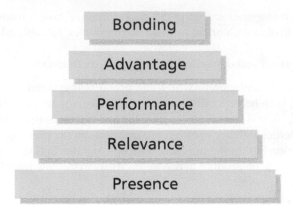

FIGURE 12

BrandDynamics™
from Millward Brown

Source: Reproduced with
permission courtesy of
Millward Brown. www.
millwardbrown.com.

a brand. As Figure 12 shows, the BrandDynamics model adopts a hierarchical approach to determine the strength of relationship a consumer has with a brand. The five levels of the model, in ascending order of an increasingly intense relationship, are presence, relevance, performance, advantage, and bonding. Consumers are placed into one of the five levels depending on their brand responses. By comparing the pattern across brands, we can uncover relative strengths and weaknesses and see where brands can focus their efforts to improve their loyalty relationships.

Relationship to the CBBE Model

We can easily relate the five sequenced stages of Millward Brown's BrandDynamics model—presence, relevance, performance, advantage, and bonding—to the four ascending steps of the CBBE model (identity, meaning, responses, and relationships) and specific CBBE model concepts (such as salience, consideration, performance or quality, superiority, and resonance).

Thus, the CBBE model synthesizes the concepts and measures from a leading industry model and at the same time provides much additional substance and insight. Several particularly noteworthy aspects of the CBBE model are (1) its emphasis on brand salience and breadth and depth of brand awareness as the foundation of brand building; (2) its recognition of the dual nature of brands and the significance of both rational and emotional considerations in brand building; and (3) the importance it places on brand resonance as the culmination of brand building and a more meaningful way to view brand loyalty.

REVIEW

According to the brand value chain, sources of brand equity arise from the customer mind-set. In general, measuring sources of brand equity requires that the brand manager fully understand how customers shop for and use products and services and, most important, what customers know, think, and feel about various brands. In particular, measuring sources of customer-based brand equity requires measuring various aspects of brand awareness and brand image that lead to the customer response that creates brand equity.

This chapter described both qualitative and quantitative approaches to measure consumers' brand knowledge structures and identify potential sources of brand equity—that is, measures to capture the customer mind-set. Qualitative research techniques are a means to identify possible brand associations. Quantitative research techniques are a means to better approximate the breadth and depth of brand awareness; the strength, favorability, and uniqueness of brand associations; the favorability of brand responses; and the nature of brand relationships. Because of their unstructured nature, qualitative measures are especially well suited to provide an in-depth glimpse of what brands and products mean to consumers. To obtain more precise and generalizable information, however, marketers typically use quantitative scale measures.

Figure 13 summarizes some of the different types of measures that were discussed in the chapter.

I. **Qualitative Research Techniques**
   Free association
   Adjective ratings and checklists
   Projective techniques
   Photo sorts
   Bubble drawings
   Story telling
   Personification exercises
   Role playing
   Experiential methods
II. **Quantitative Research Techniques**
   A. Brand Awareness
      Direct and indirect measures of brand recognition
      Aided and unaided measures of brand recall
   B. Brand Image
      Open-ended and scale measures of specific brand attributes and benefits
         Strength
         Favorability
         Uniqueness
      Overall judgments and feelings
      Overall relationship measures
         Intensity
         Activity

FIGURE 13
Summary of Qualitative
and Quantitative
Measures

DISCUSSION QUESTIONS

1. Pick a brand. Employ projective techniques to attempt to identify sources of its brand equity. Which measures work best? Why?
2. Run an experiment to see whether you can replicate Mason Haire's instant coffee experiment (see Branding Brief 2). Do the same attributions still hold? If not, can you replace coffee with a brand combination from another product category that would produce pronounced differences?
3. Pick a product category. Can you profile the brand personalities of the leading brands in the category using Aaker's brand personality inventory?
4. Pick a brand. How would you best profile consumers' brand knowledge structures? How would you use quantitative measures?
5. Think of your brand relationships. Can you find examples of brands that fit into Fournier's different categories?

BRAND FOCUS

Young & Rubicam's BrandAsset Valuator

This appendix summarizes BrandAsset® Valuator (BAV), originally developed by Young & Rubicam, now overseen and expanded by BAV Consulting.[58] It is the world's largest database of consumer-derived information on brands. The BAV model is developmental in that it explains how brands grow, how they get into trouble, and how they recover.

BAV measures brands on four fundamental measures of equity value plus a broad array of perceptual dimensions. It provides comparative measures of the equity value of thousands of brands across hundreds of different categories, as well as a set of strategic brand management tools for planning: brand positioning, brand extensions, joint branding ventures, and other strategies designed to assess and direct brands and their growth. BAV is also linked to financial metrics and is used to determine a brand's contribution to a company's valuation.

Since 1993, BAV has carried out research with almost 800,000 consumers in 51 countries, enabling BAV to follow truly global brand trends. Consumers' perceptions of approximately 45,000 brands have been collected across the same set of 72 dimensions, including 48 image attributes, usage, consideration, and cultural and customer values. These elements are incorporated into a specially developed set of brand loyalty measures.

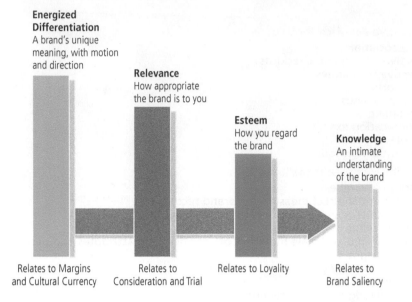

FIGURE 14

Four Pillars Assess
Brand Health,
Development, and
Momentum

Source: BrandAsset
Consulting. Used with
permission.

BAV represents a unique brand equity research tool. Unlike most conventional brand image surveys that adhere to a narrowly defined product category, respondents evaluate brands in a category-agnostic context. Brands are percentile ranked against *all* brands in the study for each brand metric. Thus, by comparing brands across as well as within categories, BAV is able to draw the broadest possible conclusions about how consumer-level brand equity is created and built—or lost. In the United States for the past 10 years, data has been collected quarterly from an 18,000-person panel, which enables the identification and analysis of short-term branding trends and phenomena.

Four Pillars

There are four key components of brand health in BAV (see Figure 14). Each pillar is derived from various measures that relate to different aspects of consumers' brand perceptions. Taken together, the four pillars trace the progression of a brand's development.

- *Energized Differentiation* measures the degree to which a brand is seen as different from others, and captures the brand's direction and momentum. This is a necessary condition for profitable brand building. It relates to pricing power and is often the key brand pillar in explaining valuation multiples like market value to sales.

- *Relevance* measures the appropriateness of the brand to consumers and the overall size of a brand's potential franchise or penetration.

- *Esteem* measures how well the brand is regarded and respected—in short, how well it's liked. Esteem is related to loyalty.

- *Knowledge* measures how intimately familiar consumers are with a brand, related to the saliency of the brand. Interestingly, high knowledge is inversely related to a brand's potential.

Relationship Among the Pillars

Examining the relationships between these four dimensions—a brand's "pillar patterns"—reveals much about a brand's current and future status (see Figure 15). It is not enough to look at each brand pillar in isolation; it is the relationships between the pillars that tell a story about brand health and opportunities. Here are some key relationships:

- When Energized Differentiation is greater than Relevance, the brand is standing out and receiving attention in the marketplace. It now has the potential to channel this point of difference and energy into building meaningfulness for consumers by driving Relevance.

- But if a brand is more Relevant than Differentiated, this suggests commoditization. While the brand is appropriate and meaningful within the lives of consumers, it is perceived as interchangeable with other players in the category. Therefore, consumers will not go out of their way for this brand, remain loyal to it, or pay a premium for it, since it lacks that special something we quantify as Energized Differentiation. Convenience, habit and price become drivers of brand choice in this scenario.

- Leadership brands are strong on both pillars, resulting in consumer passion as well as market penetration.

Brands often strive to build awareness, but if the brand's pillars are not in the proper alignment, then consumer knowledge of a brand becomes an obstacle that may need to be surmounted before the brand can continue to build healthy momentum.

- When a brand's Esteem is greater than its Knowledge, this tells us that consumers like what they know about the brand so far, and typically want to find out more, suggesting growth potential.

- But if brand Knowledge is greater than Esteem, then consumers feel that they know more than enough about the brand and they are not interested in getting to know it any better. In this case, Knowledge is an impediment that the brand must try to overcome if it wishes to attract more consumers.

Energized Differentiation > Relevance

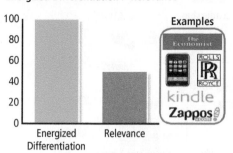

Brand has captured attention and now
has potential to grow and to build
Relevance: Brand has momentum

Energized Differentiation < Relevance

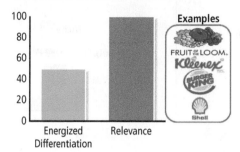

Uniqueness has faded, price or convenience
has become dominant reason to buy:
Brand has lost pricing power

Esteem > Knowledge

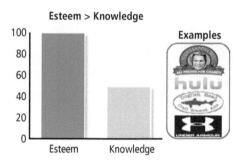

Brand is better liked than known:
Desire to find out more

Esteem < Knowledge

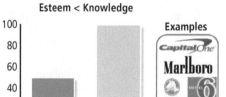

Brand is better known than liked:
Too much knowledge is becoming
a dangerous thing

FIGURE 15

Pillar Patterns Tell a Story

Source: BrandAsset Consulting. Used with permission.

The Powergrid

BrandAsset® Valuator has integrated the two macro dimensions of Brand Strength (Energized Differentiation and Relevance) and Brand Stature (Esteem and Knowledge) into a visual analytical representation known as the PowerGrid (see Figure 16). The PowerGrid depicts the stages in the cycle of brand development—each with its characteristic pillar patterns—in successive quadrants.

Brands generally begin their life in the lower left quadrant, where they first need to develop Relevant Differentiation and establish their reason for being. Most often, the movement from there is "up" into the top left quadrant. Increased Differentiation, followed by Relevance, initiates growth in Brand Strength. These developments occur before the brand has acquired significant Esteem or is widely known.

This quadrant represents two types of brands. For brands destined for a mass target, like Yelp and Kindle, this is the stage of emerging potential. Specialized or narrowly targeted brands, however, tend to remain in this quadrant (when viewed from the perspective of a mass audience) and can use their strength to occupy a profitable niche. This incudes brands like Method and W Hotels. From the point of view of brand leaders, new potential competitors will emerge from this quadrant.

The upper right quadrant, the Leadership Quadrant, is populated by brand leaders—those that have high levels of both Brand Strength and Brand Stature. Both older and relatively new brands can be in this quadrant, meaning that brand leadership is truly a function of the pillar measures, not of longevity. When properly managed, a brand can build and maintain a leadership position indefinitely. Examples of brands in the leadership position include Facebook, Levi's, and Nike.

Although declining brand equity is not inevitable, brands for whom strength has declined (usually driven by declining Energized Differentiation) can also be seen in this same quadrant. Brands whose Strength has started to dip below the level of their Stature display the first signs of weakness, which may well be masked by their still-buoyant sales and wide penetration. Examples include such brands as Macy's and Visa.

Brands that fail to maintain their Brand Strength—their Relevant Differentiation—begin to fade and move "down" into the bottom right quadrant. These brands become vulnerable not just to existing competitors, but also to the depredations of discount price brands, and they frequently end up being drawn into heavy and continuous price promotion in order to defend their consumer franchise and market share. American Airlines and TV Guide fall into this category.

Significant investigation has been done on relating BAV metrics to financial performance and stock price. First, the position of a brand on the PowerGrid indicates the level of intangible value (market value of brand or company-invested capital) per dollar of sale. The leadership quadrant produces brands with the largest intangible value per dollar of sale. Next, through extensive modeling, BAV has shown that a change in brand assets impacts stock price. From a macro perspective, two-thirds of the change in brand assets directly impacts stock price and the expectation for future returns. One-third of the change in brand assets impacts curent earnings. The importance of brand assets on stock price and company valuation is highly dependent on the category or economic sector.

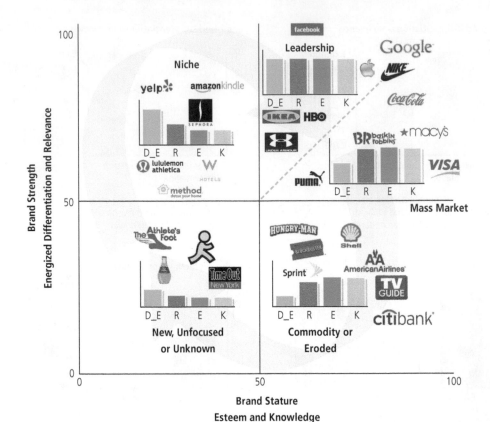

FIGURE 16

Brand Development Cycle as Illustrated by the Power Grid

Source: BrandAsset Consulting. Used with permission.

Applying BAV to Google

The best way to understand the BAV model is to apply it to a brand and category. Google is a dramatic example. Google achieved leadership status faster than any other brand measured in BAV. Google built each brand pillar, beginning with Energized Differentiation, both quickly and strongly. After rapidly establishing Energized Differentiation, Google built the other three pillars. It took only three years for Google's percentile-ranking on all four pillars to reach the high 90s.

At the same time, AOL began to falter, losing first Energized Differentiation, then Relevance and Esteem. For a while, AOL's Knowledge remained high, but with declining Relevance, eroding Differentiation and less Esteem, consumers began to lose interest until finally, AOL's Knowledge pillar followed the other pillars and began to decline. Figure 17 displays the sharp contrast in brand development between the two.

How has Google developed and maintained brand leadership? From the BAV perspective, there are three main contributing factors: (1) consistently strong brand attributes that translate into competitive advantages, (2) successful brand extensions into new categories, and (3) successful expansion into global markets and the fast establishment of brand leadership.

Competitive Advantages on Brand Attributes

Google's leadership is supported by competitive advantages on the factors that contribute to the strength of the key pillars. The BAV factors are created from the 48 brand image attributes, using data compiled from Google and its competitor brands. The individual attributes within each factor are the dimensions most correlated with each other through the eyes of consumers when

considering Google and its competitive set; thus, factors define how consumers view the category and the brands within it.

As shown in Figure 18, Google is stonger than the competitive average on the *Cutting Edge* (innovation) factor and the *Bold* personality factor. Both of these factors build Google's Energized Differentiation. Google's advantage on the *Dependability* (trust) factor helps keep the Relevance pillar strong, and Google's strength on the *Superiority* (best brand) factor supports both the Relevance and the Esteem pillars.

Successful Category Extensions

Google has done a masterful job of entering new categories with sub-brands. In many of these categories—such as Google Maps, Android by Google, and Gmail—the Google entrant has become the category leader. Most of the sub-brands also have very high Brand Strength, which helps replenish the Brand Strength of the Google corporate brand (see Figure 19). In this way, the leadership of the sub-brands helps support the parent brand, a common theme among strong parent brands with sub-brands.

The significant strength of Google's image profile has made entrance into new categories easier. Google does not face the entrance issues that weaker brands have when their image profiles are not robust enough to create differentiation in the new category, a key condition for a successful extension.

Successful Global Expansion

BAV metrics uniquely gauge the nature of international marketing opportunties. BAV shows global brands must build consistently strong Brand Strength, Brand Stature, and power on key factors that drive brand pillars and meaning *in each market*.

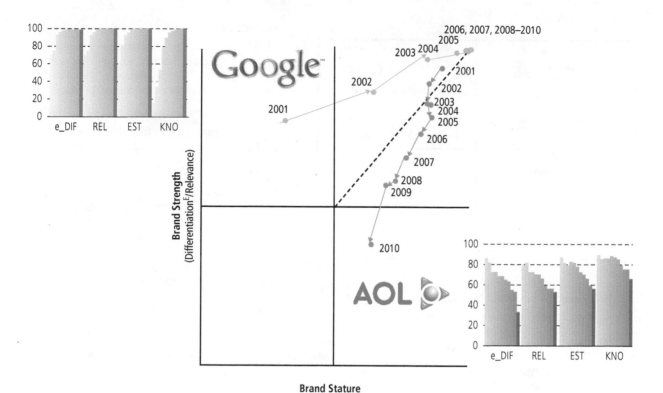

FIGURE 17 Google vs. AOL Brand Development

Source: BrandAsset Consulting. Used with permission.

Key Category Factors

CUTTING EDGE
(Drives DIF and ENE)

Innovative
Progressive
Visionary

BOLD
(Drives ENE)

Fun
Dynamic
Social

DEPENDABLE
(Drives REL)

Reliable
Intelligent
Trustworthy

SUPERIOR
(Drives REL and EST)

Best Brand
Leader
Worth More

Factor and Attribute Percentile Rank

	Competitor's Avg	Google
CUTTING EDGE	65.7	72.2
Innovative	92.0	99.5
Progressive	9.9	17.5
Visionary	95.2	99.5
BOLD	82.8	93.8
Fun	70.2	87.1
Dynamic	90.2	98.3
Social	88.0	96.0
DEPENDABLE	81.6	97.4
Reliable	76.1	98.3
Intelligent	93.7	99.0
Trustworthy	75.1	94.8
SUPERIOR	70.7	81.1
Best Brand	68.1	98.5
Leader	88.8	99.3
Worth More	55.9	44.6

FIGURE 18

Google Maintains Competitive Superiority on Key Factors Driving Brand Pillars

Source: BrandAsset Consulting. Used with permission.

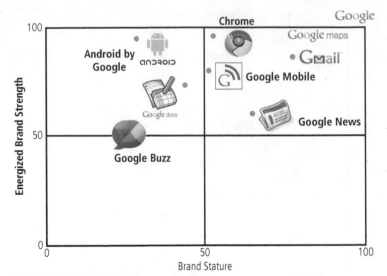

FIGURE 19 Google's Successful New Product Introductions

Source: BrandAsset Consulting. Used with permission.

Summary

There is a lot of commonality between the basic BAV model and the brand resonance model. The four factors in the BAV model can easily be related to specific components of the brand resonance model:

- BAV's Differentiation relates to brand superiority.
- BAV's Relevance relates to brand consideration.
- BAV's Esteem relates to brand credibility.
- BAV's Knowledge relates to brand resonance.

Note that brand awareness and familiarity are handled differently in the two approaches. The brand resonance framework maintains that brand salience and breadth and depth of awareness is a necessary *first* step in building brand equity. The BAV model treats familiarity in a more affective manner—almost in a warm feeling or friendship sense—and thus sees it as the *last* step in building brand equity, more akin to the resonance component itself.

The main advantage of the BAV model is that it provides rich category-agnostic descriptions and profiles across a large number of brands. It also provides focus on four key branding dimensions. It provides a brand landscape in which marketers can see where their brands stand relative to other prominent brands in many different markets.

The descriptive nature of the BAV model does mean, however, that there is potentially less insight as to exactly *how* a brand could rate highly on those factors. Because the measures underlying the four factors have to be relevant across a very disparate range of product categories, the measures (and, consequently, the factors) tend to be abstract in nature and not related directly to product attributes and benefits, or more specific marketing concerns. Nevertheless, the BAV model represents a landmark study in terms of its ability to enhance marketers' understanding of what drives top brands and where their brands fit in a vast brandscape.

Specifically, financial analysis of global brands has shown that brands that have consistently high Brand Strength and consistently high common meaning (attribute factor scores) will deliver better margin growth rates and are more efficient at producing higher pretax margins.

Google has achieved leadership status in global markets the same way it achieved leadership status in the USA—by quickly "maxing out" on Brand Strength and Brand Stature. In all countries recently surveyed, Google is a super-leadership brand on the PowerGrid (see Figure 20). Reviewing the key image factors across countries shows that Google ranks in the high 90s on each factor and each dimension, *according to consumers in each local market*. This is true consistency, which Google has built by focusing on the important factors within each local market.

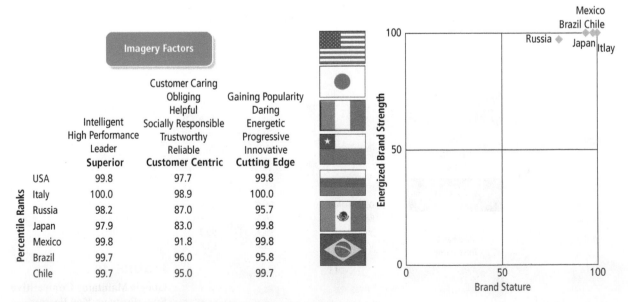

	Intelligent High Performance Leader **Superior**	Customer Caring Obliging Helpful Socially Responsible Trustworthy Reliable **Customer Centric**	Gaining Popularity Daring Energetic Progressive Innovative **Cutting Edge**
USA	99.8	97.7	99.8
Italy	100.0	98.9	100.0
Russia	98.2	87.0	95.7
Japan	97.9	83.0	99.8
Mexico	99.8	91.8	99.8
Brazil	99.7	96.0	95.8
Chile	99.7	95.0	99.7

FIGURE 20 Google Is Consistently a Global Brand Leader

Source: BrandAsset Consulting. Used with permission.

Notes

1. Some leading textbooks in this area are J. Paul Peter and Jerry C. Olson, *Consumer Behavior and Marketing Strategy*, 8th ed. (Homewood, IL: McGraw-Hill/Irwin, 2007); Wayne D. Hoyer and Deborah J. MacInnis, *Consumer Behavior*, 5th ed. (Mason, OH: South-Western, 2010); and Michael R. Solomon, *Consumer Behavior: Buying, Having, and Being*, 9th ed. (Upper Saddle River, NJ: Prentice Hall, 2011).

2. John Motavalli, "Probing Consumer Minds," *Adweek*, 7 December 1987, 4–8.

3. Ernest Dichter, *Handbook of Consumer Motivations* (New York: McGraw-Hill, 1964).

4. "Retail Therapy: How Ernest Dichter, An Acolyte of Sigmund Freud, Revolutionized Marketing," *The Economist*, 17 December 2011.

5. H. Shanker Krishnan, "Characteristics of Memory Associations: A Consumer-Based Brand Equity Perspective," *International Journal of Research in Marketing* (October 1996): 389–405; Geraldine R. Henderson, Dawn Iacobucci, and Bobby J. Calder, "Using Network Analysis to Understand Brands," in *Advances in Consumer Research* 29, eds. Susan M. Broniarczyk and Kent Nakamoto (Valdosta, GA: Association for Consumer Research, 2002): 397–405.

6. J. Wesley Hutchinson, "Expertise and the Structure of Free Recall," in *Advances in Consumer Research* 10, eds. Richard P. Bagozzi and Alice M. Tybout (Ann Arbor, MI: Association of Consumer Research, 1983): 585–589; see also Chris Janiszewski and Stijn M. J. van Osselaer, "A Connectionist Model of Brand–Quality Associations," *Journal of Marketing Research* 37 (August 2000): 331–350.

7. Yvan Boivin, "A Free Response Approach to the Measurement of Brand Perceptions," *International Journal of Research in Marketing* 3 (1986): 11–17; Jeffrey E. Danes, Jeffrey S. Hess, John W. Story, and Keith Vorst, "On the Validity of Measuring Brand Images by Rating Concepts and Free Associations," *Journal of Brand Management*, 2012, in press.

8. Jean Bystedt, Siri Lynn, and Deborah Potts, *Moderating to the Max* (Ithaca, NY: Paramount Market Publishing, 2003).

9. For an application in marketing, see Kathryn A. Braun-LaTour, Michael S. LaTour, and George M. Zinkhan, "Using Childhood Memories to Gain Insight Into Brand Meaning," *Journal of Marketing* 71 (April 2007): 45–60.

10. Sydney J. Levy, "Dreams, Fairy Tales, Animals, and Cars," *Psychology and Marketing* 2, no. 2 (1985): 67–81.

11. Mason Haire, "Projective Techniques in Marketing Research, *Journal of Marketing* (April 1950): 649–656. Interestingly, a follow-up study conducted several decades later suggested that instant coffee users were no longer perceived as psychologically different from drip grind users. See Frederick E. Webster Jr. and Frederick Von Pechmann, "A Replication of the 'Shopping List' Study," *Journal of Marketing* 34 (April 1970): 61–63.

12. Levy, "Dreams, Fairy Tales."

13. Jeffrey Durgee and Robert Stuart, "Advertising Symbols and Brand Names That Best Represent Key Product Meanings," *Journal of Consumer Marketing* 4, no. 3 (1987): 15–24.

14. Clotaire Rapaille, *Culture Code* (New York: Broadway, 2006); Alexandra Harrington, "G. C. Rapaille: Finding the Keys in the Cultural Unconscious," *Response TV*, 1 September 2001; Jeffrey Ball, "'But How Does It Make You Feel?'" *Wall Street Journal*, 3 May 1999; Jack Hitt, "Does the Smell of Coffee Brewing Remind You of Your Mother?" *New York Times Magazine*, 7 May 2000.

15. Gerald Zaltman and Robin Higie, "Seeing the Voice of the Customer: Metaphor-Based Advertising Research," *Journal of Advertising Research* (July/August 1995): 35–51; Daniel H. Pink, "Metaphor Marketing," *Fast Company*, April 1998; Gerald Zaltman, "Metaphorically Speaking," *Marketing Research* (Summer 1996); www.olsonzaltman.com; Gerald Zaltman, "How Customers Think: Essential Insights into the Mind of the Market," *Harvard Business School Press* (2003); Wendy Melillo, "Inside the Consumer Mind: What Neuroscience Can Tell Us About Marketing," *Adweek*, 16 January 2006; Torsten Ringberg, Gaby Odekerken-Schröder, and Glenn L. Christensen, "A Cultural Models Approach to Segmenting Consumer Recovery Expectations," *Journal of Marketing* 71 (July 2007): 194–214; Gerald Zaltman and Lindsay Zaltman, *Marketing Metaphoria: What Deep Metaphors Reveal About the Minds of Consumers* (Boston: Harvard Business School Press, 2008).

16. For some provocative research, see Carolyn Yoon, Angela H. Gutchess, Fred M. Feinberg, and Thad A. Polk, "A Functional Magnetic Resonance Imaging Study of Neural Dissociations between Brand and Person Judgments," *Journal of Consumer Research* 33 (June 2006): 31–40; Samuel M. McClure, Jian Li, Damon Tomlin, Kim S. Cypert, Latané M. Montague, and P. Read Montague, "Neural Correlates of Behavioral Preference for Culturally Familiar Drinks," *Neuron* 44, no. 2 (October 2004): 379–387; Hilke Plassmann, Carolyn Yoon, Fred M. Feinberg, and Baba Shiv, "Consumer Neuroscience," in *Wiley International Encyclopedia of Marketing, Volume 3: Consumer Behavior*, eds. Richard P. Bagozzi and Ayalla Ruvio (West Sussex, UK: John Wiley, 2010). Martin Lindstrom, *Buyology: Truth and Lies About Why We Buy* (New York: Doubleday, 2008).

17. For foundational research, see Giovanna Egidi, Howard C. Nusbaum, and John T. Cacioppo, "Neuroeconomics," in *The Handbook of Consumer Psychology*, eds. Curtis Haugvedt, Paul Herr, and Frank Kardes, Vol. 57 (Mahwah, NJ: Lawrence Erlbaum Associates, 2007): 1177–1214.

18. Adam Penenberg, "They Have Hacked Your Brain," *Fast Company*, September 2011.

19. Tom Abate, "Coming to a Marketer Near You: Brain Scanning," *San Francisco Chronicle*, 19 May 2008; Brian Sternberg, "How Coach Potatoes Watch TV

Could Hold Clues for Advertisers," *Boston Globe*, 6 September 2009, G1, G3.

20. Jennifer Aaker, "Dimensions of Brand Personality," *Journal of Marketing Research* 34, no. 8 (1997): 347–356.

21. Jay Dean, "A Practitioner's Perspective on Brand Equity," in *Proceedings of the Society for Consumer Psychology*, eds. Wes Hutchinson and Kevin Lane Keller (Clemson, SC: CtC Press, 1994), 56–62.

22. Aaker, "Dimensions of Brand Personality." See also Jennifer Aaker, "The Malleable Self: The Role of Self-Expression in Persuasion," *Journal of Marketing Research* 36, no. 2 (1999): 45–57; Joseph T. Plummer, "Brand Personality: A Strategic Concept for Multinational Advertising," in *Marketing Educators' Conference* (New York: Young & Rubicam 1985): 1–31.

23. Jennifer L. Aaker, Veronica Benet-Martinez, and Jordi Garolera, "Consumption Symbols as Carriers of Culture: A Study of Japanese and Spanish Brand Personality Constructs," *Journal of Personality and Social Psychology* 81, no. 3 (2001): 492–508.

24. Yongjun Sung and Spencer F. Tinkham, "Brand Personality Structures in the United States and Korea: Common and Culture-Specific Factors," *Journal of Consumer Psychology* 15, no. 4 (2005): 334–350.

25. Gil Ereaut and Mike Imms, "'Bricolage': Qualitative Market Research Redefined," *Admap*, December 2002, 16–18.

26. Jennifer Chang Coupland, "Invisible Brands: An Ethnography of Households and the Brands in Their Kitchen Pantries," *Journal of Consumer Research* 32 (June 2005): 106–118; Mark Ritson and Richard Elliott, "The Social Uses of Advertising: An Ethnographic Study of Adolescent Advertising Audiences," *Journal of Consumer Research* 26 (December 1999): 260–277.

27. Donna Kelly and Michael Gibbons, "Ethnography: The Good, the Bad, and the Ugly," *Journal of Medical Marketing* 8, no. 4 (2008): 279–285; Special Issue on Ethnography, *International Journal of Marketing Research* 49, no. 6 (2007).

28. Melanie Wells, "New Ways to Get into Our Heads," *USA Today*, 2 March 1999, B1–B2.

29. Gerry Kermouch, "Consumers in the Mist," *Business Week*, 26 February 2001, 92–94; Alfred Hermida, "Bus Ride to the Future," www.bbc.co.uk, 3 December 2001.

30. Eric J. Arnould and Amber Epp, "Deep Engagement with Consumer Experience: Listening and Learning with Qualitative Data," in *The Handbook of Marketing Research: Uses, Misuses, and Future Advances*, eds. Rajiv Grover and Marco Vriens (Thousand Oaks, CA: Sage Press, 2006): 51–58.

31. Dev Patnik and Robert Becker, "Direct Observation: Some Practical Advice," *Marketing News*, Fall 1999; A. Parasuraman, Dhruv Grewal, and R. Krishnan, *Marketing Research*, 2nd ed. (Boston: Houghton Mifflin, 2007).

32. Edward F. McQuarrie, "Taking a Road Trip," *Marketing Management* 3 (Winter 1995): 9–21; Edward F. McQuarrie, *Customer Visits: Building a Better Market Focus*, 3rd ed. (Armonk, NY: M. E. Sharpe, 2008);

"How to Conduct Good Customer Visits: 16 Tips from Ed McQuarrie," www.managementroundtable.com.

33. Kevin Peters, "How 'Mystery Shopping' Helped Spark a Turnaround," *Harvard Business Review* (November 2011): 47–50.

34. Gord Hotchkiss, "Exploring the Shift in Search Behaviors with Microsoft's Jacquelyn Krones," www.searchengineland.com, 15 July 2011.

35. Jennifer Cirillo, "DEWmocracy 2 Continues to Buzz," *Beverage World*, 11 March 2010.

36. Rekha Balu, "Listen Up! (It Might Be Your Customer Talking)," *Fast Company*, May 2000, 304–316; Joseph Manez and Jennifer Reingold, "Burton Snowboards," *Fast Company*, September 2006, 58–59; www.burton.com; Justin Gural, "Craig's: Burton Snowboards' Future Lab," *USA Today*, 14 January 2011; Roger Brooks, "Jake Burton Charts a New Course in Snowboarding," *Success*, February 2010; Russ Edelman, "Burton Snowboards: Passion, Innovation and Profit," www.cnbc.com, 22 November 2011.

37. Russell W. Belk and Robert V. Kozinets, "Videography in Marketing and Consumer Research," *Qualitative Market Research* 8, no. 2 (2005): 128–142.

38. Louella Miles, "Market Research: Living Their Lives," www.brandrepublic.com, 11 December 2003.

39. Judith A. Howard and Daniel G. Renfrow, "Social Cognition," in *Handbook of Social Psychology*, ed. John Delamater (New York: Springer Science+Business, 2006), 259–282; Robert S. Wyer, "The Role of Information Accessibility in Cognition and Behavior: Implications for Consumer Information Processing," in *The Handbook of Consumer Psychology*, eds. Curtis Haugvedt, Paul Herr, and Frank Kardes, Vol. 57 (Mahwah, NJ: Lawrence Erlbaum Associates, 2007), 31–76; Barbara Loken, Larry Barsalou, and Christopher Joiner, "Categorization Theory and Research in Consumer Psychology: Category Representation and Category-Based Inference," in *The Handbook of Consumer Psychology*, eds. Curtis Haugvedt, Paul Herr, and Frank Kardes, Vol. 57 (Mahwah, NJ: Lawrence Erlbaum Associates, 2007), 453–485.

40. For an interesting related topic, see Henrik Hagtvedt, "The Impact of Incomplete Typeface Logos on Perceptions of the Firm," *Journal of Marketing* 75 (July 2011): 86–93.

41. Raymond Gordon, "Phantom Products," *Forbes*, 21 May 1984, 202–204.

42. Philip Kotler and Kevin Lane Keller, *Marketing Management: Analysis, Planning, Implementation, and Control*, 14th ed. (Upper Saddle River, NJ: Prentice Hall, 2012).

43. Joseph F. Hair Jr., Rolph E. Anderson, Ronald Tatham, and William C. Black, *Multivariate Data Analysis*, 4th ed. (Englewood Cliffs, NJ: Prentice Hall, 1995); James Lattin, Douglas Carrol, and Paul Green, *Analyzing Multivariate Data*, 5th ed. (Pacific Grove, CA: Duxbury Press, 2003).

44. J. Scott Armstrong, Vicki G. Morwitz, and V. Kumar, "Sales Forecasts for Existing Consumer Products and Services: Do Purchase Intentions Contribute to Accuracy?" *International Journal of Forecasting* 16 (2000): 383–397.

45. Icek Ajzen and Martin Fishbein, *Understanding Attitudes and Predicting Social Behavior* (Englewood Cliffs, NJ: Prentice Hall, 1980); Vicki G. Morwitz, Joel Steckel, and Alok Gupta, "When Do Purchase Intentions Predict Sales?," *International Journal of Forecasting* 23, no. 3, (2007): 347–364; Pierre Chandon, Vicki G. Morwitz, and Werner J. Reinartz, "Do Intentions Really Predict Behavior? Self-Generated Validity Effects in Survey Research," *Journal of Marketing* 69 (April 2005): 1–14.

46. Fred Reichheld, *Ultimate Question: For Driving Good Profits and True Growth* (Cambridge, MA: Harvard Business School Press, 2006); Jena McGregor, "Would You Recommend Us?" *BusinessWeek*, 30 January 2006, 94–95; Kathryn Kranhold, "Client-Satisfaction Tool Takes Root," *Wall Street Journal*, 10 July 2006; Timothy L. Keiningham, Bruce Cooil, Tor Wallin Andreassen, and Lerzan Aksoy, "A Longitudinal Examination of Net Promoter and Firm Revenue Growth," *Journal of Marketing* 71 (July 2007): 39–51; Neil A. Morgan and Lopo Leotte Rego, "The Value of Different Customer Satisfaction and Loyalty Metrics in Predicting Business Performance," *Marketing Science* 25 (September–October 2006): 426–439; Timothy L. Keiningham, Lerzan Aksoy, Bruce Cooil, and Tor W. Andreassen, "Linking Customer Loyalty to Growth," *MIT Sloan Management Review* (Summer 2008): 51–57.

47. Das Narayandas, "Building Loyalty in Business Markets," *Harvard Business Review* (September 2005): 131–138.

48. For more general discussion of consumer attachment, see Susan S. Kleine and Stacy M. Baker, "An Integrative Review of Material Possession Attachment," *Academy of Marketing Science Review* 8, no. 4 (2004): 1–39; Rosellina Ferraro, Jennifer Edson Escalas, and James R. Bettman, "Our Possessions, Our Selves: Domains of Self-Worth and the Possession-Self Link," *Journal of Consumer Psychology* 21, no. 2 (2011): 169–177.

49. See, for example, Lars Bergkvist and Tino Bech-Larsen, "Two Studies of Consequences and Actionable Antecedents of Brand Love," *Journal of Brand Management* 17 (June 2010): 504–518.

50. Barbara A. Carroll and Aaron C. Ahuvia, "Some Antecedents and Outcomes of Brand Love," *Marketing Letters* 17 (2006): 79–89.

51. Rajeev Batra, Aaron Ahuvia, and Richard P Bagozzi, "Brand Love," *Journal of Marketing* (2012), in press.

52. C.W. Park, Deborah J. Macinnis, Joseph Priester, Andreas B. Eisingerich, and Dawn Iacobucci, "Brand Attachment and Brand Attitude Strength: Conceptual and Empirical Differentiation of Two Critical Brand Equity Drivers," *Journal of Marketing* 74 (November 2010): 1–17.

53. Vikas Mittal and Mohanbir S. Sawhney, "Managing Customer Retention in the Attention Economy," working paper, University of Pittsburgh, 2001.

54. For a broad overview, see "Digital Marketing: Special Advertising Section," *Adweek*, 28 October 2011.

55. Jon Bruner, "What's a 'Like' Worth?," *Forbes*, 8 August 2011; Brian Morrisey, "Value of a 'Fan' on Social Media: $3.60," *Adweek*, 13 April 2010; www.vitrue.com, accessed 23 June 2011.

56. Susan M. Fournier, "Consumers and Their Brands: Developing Relationship Theory in Consumer Research," *Journal of Consumer Research* 24 (March 1998): 343–373; Susan M. Fournier, Susan Dobscha, and David G. Mick, "Preventing the Premature Death of Relationship Marketing," *Harvard Business Review* (January–February 1998): 42–51; Susan M. Fournier and Julie L. Yao, "Reviving Brand Loyalty: A Reconceptualization Within the Framework of Consumer–Brand Relationships," *International Journal of Research in Marketing* 14 (1997): 451–472; Susan Fournier, "Lessons Learned About Consumers' Relationships with Their Brands," in *Handbook of Brand Relationships*, eds. Joseph Priester, Deborah MacInnis, and C. W. Park (NY: Society for Consumer Psychology and M.E. Sharp, 2009), 5–23; Susan Fournier, Michael Breazeale, Marc Fetscherin, and T. C. Melewar, eds., *Consumer–Brand Relationships: Theory and Practice* (London: Routledge Taylor & Francis Group, 2012).

57. For a helpful review of different perspectives, see Jonathan Knowles, "In Search of a Reliable Measure of Brand Equity," *MarketingNPV* 2, no. 3 (July 2005).

58. This section greatly benefited from helpful and insightful contributions by Ed Lebar, John Gerzama, Scott Stiff, and Paul Fox.

Measuring Outcomes of Brand Equity: Capturing Market Performance

From Chapter 10 of *Strategic Brand Management: Building, Measuring, and Managing Brand Equity*, Fourth Edition. Kevin Lane Keller.

Measuring Outcomes of Brand Equity: Capturing Market Performance

Learning Objectives

After reading this chapter, you should be able to

1. Recognize the multidimensionality of brand equity and the importance of multiple methods to measure it.

2. Contrast different comparative methods to assess brand equity.

3. Explain the basic logic of how conjoint analysis works.

4. Review different holistic methods for valuing brand equity.

5. Describe the relationship between branding and finance.

Intel tracks the price premiums it enjoys over competitors as a measure of its brand strength.
Source: Intel Corporation

Preview

Ideally, to measure brand equity, we would create a "brand equity index"—one easily calculated number that summarizes the health of the brand and completely captures its brand equity. But just as a thermometer measuring body temperature provides only one indication of how healthy a person is, so does any one measure of brand equity provide only one indication of the health of a brand. Brand equity is a multidimensional concept, and complex enough to require many different types of measures. Applying multiple measures increases the diagnostic power of marketing research and the likelihood that managers will better understand what is happening to their brands and, perhaps more important, why.[1]

In arguments suggesting that researchers should employ multiple measures of brand equity, writers have drawn interesting comparisons between measuring brand equity and assessing the performance of an aircraft in flight or a car on the road; for example:

> The pilot of the plane has to consider a number of indicators and gauges as the plane is flown. There is the fuel gauge, the altimeter, and a number of other important status indicators. All of these dials and meters tell the pilot different things about the health of the plane. There is no one gauge that summarizes everything about the plane. The plane needs the altimeter, compass, radar, and the fuel gauge. As the pilot looks at the instrument cluster, he has to take all of these critical indicators into account as he flies.[2]

The dashboard of a car or the gauges on the plane, which together measure its "health" while being driven or flown, are analogous to the multiple measures of brand equity necessary to assess the health of a brand.

By applying measurement techniques, we should gain a good understanding of the depth and breadth of brand awareness; the strength, favorability, and uniqueness of brand associations; the positivity of brand responses; and the nature of brand relationships for their brands. A product with positive brand equity can enjoy the following six important customer-related benefits:

1. Perception of better product or service performance
2. Greater loyalty and less vulnerability to competitive marketing actions and marketing crises
3. Larger margins and more inelastic responses to price increases and elastic responses to price decreases
4. Greater trade cooperation and support
5. Increased marketing communication effectiveness
6. Opportunity for successful licensing and brand extension

The customer-based brand equity model maintains that these benefits, and thus the ultimate value of a brand, depend on the underlying components of brand knowledge and sources of brand equity. We can measure these individual components; however, to provide more direct estimates, we still must assess their resulting value in some way. This chapter examines measurement procedures to assess the effects of brand knowledge structures on these and other measures that capture market performance for the brand.[3]

First, we review comparative methods, which are means to better assess the effects of consumer perceptions and preferences on consumer response to the marketing program and the specific benefits of brand equity. Next, we look at holistic methods, which attempt to estimate the overall or summary value of a brand.[4] Some of the interplay between branding and financial considerations is included in the Brand Focus.

COMPARATIVE METHODS

Comparative methods are research studies or experiments that examine consumer attitudes and behavior toward a brand to directly estimate specific benefits arising from having a high level of awareness and strong, favorable, and unique brand associations. There are two types of comparative methods.

- *Brand-based comparative approaches* use experiments in which one group of consumers responds to an element of the marketing program or some marketing activity when it is attributed to the target brand, and another group responds to that same element or activity when it is attributed to a competitive or fictitiously named brand.
- *Marketing-based comparative approaches* use experiments in which consumers respond to changes in elements of the marketing program or marketing activity for the target brand or competitive brands.

The brand-based approach holds the marketing program fixed and examines consumer response based on changes in brand identification, whereas the marketing-based approach holds the brand fixed and examines consumer response based on changes in the marketing program. We'll look at each of these two approaches in turn and then describe conjoint analysis as a technique that, in effect, combines the two.

Brand-Based Comparative Approaches

Competitive brands can be useful benchmarks in brand-based comparative approaches. Although consumers may interpret marketing activity for a fictitiously named or unnamed version of the product or service in terms of their general product category knowledge, they may also have a particular brand, or *exemplar*, in mind. This exemplar may be the category leader or some other brand that consumers feel is representative of the category, like their most preferred brand. Consumers may make inferences to supply any missing information based on their knowledge of this particular brand. Thus, it may be instructive to examine how consumers evaluate a proposed new ad campaign, new promotion offering, or new product when it is also attributed to one or more major competitors.

Applications.   The classic example of the brand-based comparative approach is "blind testing" research studies in which different consumers examine or use a product with or without brand identification. Invariably, differences emerge. For example, in one study, people who were asked to blind test Coca-Cola and two store brands of cola split their preferences almost evenly among the three—31 percent for Coke and 33 percent and 35 percent for the others. But when the samples were identified, 50 percent of other participants in the experiment said they preferred Coke.[5]

One natural application of the brand-based comparative approach is product purchase or consumption research for new or existing products, as long as the brand identification can be hidden in some way for the "unbranded" control group. Brand-based comparative approaches are also useful to determine brand equity benefits related to price margins and premiums.

T-MOBILE

Deutsche Telecom invested much time and money in recent years in building its T-Mobile mobile communication brand. In the United Kingdom, however, the company has leased or shared its network lines with competitor Virgin Mobile. As a result, the audio quality of the signal that a T-Mobile customer received in making a call should have been virtually identical to the audio quality of the signal for a Virgin Mobile customer. After all, the same network was being used to send the signal. Despite that fact, research showed that Virgin Mobile customers rated their signal quality significantly higher than did T-Mobile customers. The strong Virgin brand image appeared to cast a halo over its different service offerings, literally causing consumers to change their impressions of product performance.[6]

Virgin's brand is so strong that consumers may evaluate the same product or service more favorably if they think it comes from Virgin.
Source: AP Photo/Jacques Brinon

Critique. The main advantage of a brand-based comparative approach is that because it holds all aspects of the marketing program fixed for the brand, it isolates the value of a brand in a very real sense. Understanding exactly how knowledge of the brand affects consumer responses to prices, advertising, and so forth is extremely useful in developing strategies in these different areas. At the same time, we could study an almost infinite variety of marketing activities, so what we learn is limited only by the number of different applications we examine.

Brand-based comparative methods are particularly applicable when the marketing activity under consideration represents a change from past marketing of the brand, for example, a new sales or trade promotion, ad campaign, or proposed brand extension. If the marketing activity under consideration is already strongly identified with the brand—like an ad campaign that has been running for years—it may be difficult to attribute some aspect of the marketing program to a fictitiously named or unnamed version of the product or service in a believable fashion.

Thus, a crucial consideration with the brand-based comparative approach is the realism we can achieve in the experiment. We usually have to sacrifice some realism in order to gain sufficient control to isolate the effects of brand knowledge. When it is too difficult for consumers to examine or experience some element of the marketing program without being aware of the brand, we can use detailed concept statements of that element instead. For example, we can ask consumers to judge a proposed new product when it is either introduced by the firm as a brand extension or introduced by an unnamed firm in that product market. Similarly, we can ask about acceptable price ranges and store locations for the brand name product or a hypothetical unnamed version.

One concern about brand-based comparative approaches is that the simulations and concept statements may highlight the particular product characteristics enough to make them more salient than they would otherwise be, distorting the results.

Marketing-Based Comparative Approaches

Marketing-based comparative approaches hold the brand fixed and examine consumer response based on changes in the marketing program.

Applications. There is a long academic and industry tradition of exploring price premiums using marketing-based comparative approaches. In the mid-1950s, Edgar Pessemier developed a dollar-metric measure of brand commitment that relied on a step-by-step increase of the price difference between the brand normally purchased and an alternative brand.[7] To reveal brand-switching and loyalty patterns, Pessemier plotted the percentage of consumers who switched from their regular brand as a function of the brand price increases.

A number of marketing research suppliers have adopted variations of this approach to derive similar types of demand curves, and many firms now try to assess price sensitivity and willingness-to-pay thresholds for different brands.[8] For example, Intel would routinely survey computer shoppers to find out how much of a discount they would require before switching to a personal computer that did not have an Intel microprocessor in it (say, an AMD chip) or, conversely, what premium they would be willing to pay to buy a personal computer that did have an Intel microprocessor in it.

We can apply marketing-based comparative approaches in other ways, assessing consumer response to different advertising strategies, executions, or media plans through multiple test markets. For example, SymphonyIRI's electronic test markets and similar research methodologies can permit tests of different advertising weights or repetition schedules as well as ad copy tests. By controlling for other factors, we can isolate the effects of the brand and product. Anheuser-Busch conducted an extensive series of test markets that revealed that Budweiser beer had such a strong image with consumers that advertising could be cut, at least in the short run, without hurting sales performance.

Marketers can also explore potential brand extensions by collecting consumer evaluations of a range of concept statements describing brand extension candidates. For example, Figure 1 displays the results of a consumer survey conducted at one time to examine reactions to hypothetical extensions of the Planters nuts brand. Contrasting those extensions provides some indication of the equity of the brand.

In this example, the survey results suggested that consumers expected any Planters brand extension to be "nut-related." Appropriate product characteristics for a possible Planters brand extension seemed to be "crunchy," "sweet," "salty," "spicy," and "buttery." In terms of where in the store consumers would have expected to find new Planters products, the snack and candy sections seemed most likely. On the other hand, consumers did not seem to expect to find new Planters products in the breakfast food aisle, bakery product section, refrigerated section, or frozen food section.

Average Scale Rating[a]	Proposed Extensions
10	Peanuts
9	Snack mixes, nuts for baking
8	—
7	Pretzels, chocolate nut candy, caramel corn
6	Snack crackers, potato chips, nutritional granola bars
5	Tortilla chips, toppings (ice cream/dessert)
4	Lunchables/lunch snack packs, dessert mixes (cookie/cake/brownie)
3	Ice cream/ice cream bars, toppings (salad/vegetable)
2	Cereal, toaster pastries, Asian entrees/sauces, stuffing mix, refrigerated dough, jams/jellies
1	Yogurt

[a]Consumers rated hypothetical proposed extensions on an 11-point scale anchored by 0 (definitely would *not* expect Planter's to sell it) and 10 (definitely would expect Planter's to sell it).

FIGURE 1

Reactions to Proposed
Planters Extensions

A brand like Planters
has many extension
opportunities that it
should research carefully.
Source: Jarrod Weaton/
Weaton Digital, Inc.

Consistent with these survey results, besides selling a variety of nuts (peanuts, mixed nuts, cashews, almonds, pistachios, walnuts, and so on), Planters now sells trail mix, sunflower seeds, peanut bars, and peanut butter.

Critique. The main advantage of the marketing-based comparative approach is ease of implementation. We can compare virtually any proposed set of marketing actions for the brand. At the same time, the main drawback is that it may be difficult to discern whether consumer responses to changes in the marketing stimuli are being caused by brand knowledge or by more generic product knowledge. In other words, it may be that for *any* brand in the product category, consumers would be willing to pay certain prices, accept a particular brand extension, and so forth. One way to determine whether consumer response is specific to the brand is to conduct similar tests of consumer response with competitive brands. A statistical technique well suited to do just that is described next.

Conjoint Analysis

Conjoint analysis is a survey-based multivariate technique that enables marketers to profile the consumer decision process with respect to products and brands.[9] Specifically, by asking consumers to express preferences or choose among a number of carefully designed product profiles, researchers can determine the trade-offs consumers are making between various brand attributes, and thus the importance they are attaching to them.[10]

Each profile consumers see is made up of a set of attribute levels chosen on the basis of experimental design principles to satisfy certain mathematical properties. The value consumers attach to each attribute level, as statistically derived by the conjoint formula, is called a *part worth*. We can use the part worths in various ways to estimate how consumers would value a new combination of the attribute levels. For example, one attribute is the brand name. The part worth for the "brand name" attribute reflects its value.

One classic study of conjoint analysis, reported by Green and Wind, examined consumer evaluations of a spot-remover product on five attributes: package design, brand name, price, *Good Housekeeping seal*, and money-back guarantee.[11] These same authors also applied conjoint analysis in a landmark research study to arrive at the design that became the Courtyard by Marriott hotel chain.[12]

Applications. Conjoint analysis has a number of possible applications. In the past, Ogilvy & Mather ad agency used a brand/price trade-off methodology as a means of assessing advertising effectiveness and brand value.[13] Brand/price trade-off is a simplified version of

A comprehensive conjoint analysis project helped design Courtyard by Marriott to better satisfy consumer needs and desires.

Source: AP Photo/ PRNewsFoto/Marriott International, Inc.

conjoint measurement with just two variables—brand and price. Consumers make a series of simulated purchase choices between different combinations of brands and prices. Each choice triggers an increase in the price of the selected brand, forcing the consumer to choose between buying a preferred brand and paying less. In this way, consumers reveal how much their brand loyalty is worth and, conversely, which brands they would relinquish for a lower price.

Academic researchers with an interest in brand image and equity have used other variations and applications of conjoint analysis. For example, Rangaswamy, Burke, and Oliva use conjoint analysis to explore how brand names interact with physical product features to affect the extendability of brand names to new product categories.[14] Barich and Srinivasan apply conjoint analysis to corporate image programs, to show how it can determine the company attributes relevant to customers, rank the importance of those attributes, estimate the costs of making improvements (or correcting customer perceptions), and prioritize image goals to obtain the maximum benefit, in terms of improved perceptions, for the resources spent.[15]

Critique. The main advantage of the conjoint-based approach is that it allows us to study different brands and different aspects of the product or marketing program (product composition, price, distribution outlets, and so on) simultaneously. Thus, we can uncover information about consumers' responses to different marketing activities for both the focal and competing brands.

One of the disadvantages of conjoint analysis is that marketing profiles may violate consumers' expectations based on what they already know about brands. Thus, we must take care that consumers do not evaluate unrealistic product profiles or scenarios. It can also be difficult to specify and interpret brand attribute levels, although some useful guidelines have been put forth to more effectively apply conjoint analysis to brand positioning.[16]

HOLISTIC METHODS

We use comparative methods to approximate specific benefits of brand equity. *Holistic methods* place an overall value on the brand in either abstract utility terms or concrete financial terms. Thus, holistic methods attempt to "net out" various considerations to determine the unique contribution of the brand. The *residual approach* examines the value of the brand by subtracting consumers' preferences for the brand—based on physical product attributes alone—from their overall brand preferences. The *valuation approach* places a financial value on brand equity for accounting purposes, mergers and acquisitions, or other such reasons. After an example from Liz Claiborne, we'll look at each of these approaches.

LIZ CLAIBORNE

A company that found great success selling popular fashions to working women in the 1980s—generating $2 billion in annual sales by the early 1990s—Liz Claiborne found itself in serious trouble two decades later when sales started to cool. A brand transformation that eliminated some slower-selling older lines to focus on younger customers failed to turn the business around. Aging core customers deserted the brand, and department stores began to replace it with their own private labels. The company was posting annual losses by 2006, and sales dropped by half over the next five years. Management decided to retrench in 2011 and focus its resources on its faster-selling brands—Kate Spade, Lucky Brands Jeans, and Juicy Couture. The Claiborne and Monet brands were sold to JCPenney for $288 million, and as part of the sales agreement, Liz Claiborne was given one year to change its name. The firm was making another financial bet on a new brand strategy it hoped would prove more fruitful than the last one, while JCPenney was betting there was life left in the Liz Claiborne brand on which it could capitalize.[17]

Liz Claiborne decided to sell its own brand in order to concentrate on more financially promising brands like Juicy Couture.
Source: Nick Baylis/Alamy

Residual Approaches

The rationale behind residual approaches is the view that brand equity is what remains of consumer preferences and choices after we subtract physical product effects. The idea is that we can infer the relative valuation of brands by observing consumer preferences and choices *if* we take into account as many sources of measured attribute values as possible. Several researchers have defined brand equity as the incremental preference over and above what would result without brand identification. In this view, we can calculate brand equity by subtracting preferences for objective characteristics of the physical product from overall preference.[18]

Scanner Panel.   Some researchers have focused on analysis of brand value based on data sets from supermarket scanners of consumer purchases. In an early study, Kamakura and Russell proposed a measure that employs consumer purchase histories from supermarket scanner data to estimate brand equity through a residual approach.[19] Specifically, their model explains the choices observed from a panel of consumers as a function of the store environment (actual shelf prices, sales promotions, displays), the physical characteristics of available brands, and a residual term dubbed brand equity. By controlling for other aspects of the marketing mix, they estimate that aspect of brand preference that is unique to a brand and not currently duplicated by competitors.

More recently, a variation proposed by Ailawadi, Lehmann, and Neslin employs actual retail sales data to calculate a "revenue premium" as an estimate of brand equity, by calculating the difference in revenues between a brand and a generic or private label in the same category.[20] Sriram, Balachandar, and Kalwani similarly use store-level scanner data to track brand equity and key drivers of brand equity over time.[21]

Choice Experiments. Swait, Erdem, and colleagues have proposed a related approach to measuring brand equity with choice experiments that account for brand names, product attributes, brand image, and differences in consumer sociodemographic characteristics and brand usage.[22] They define the ***equalization price*** as the price that equates the utility of a brand to the utilities that could be attributed to a brand in the category where no brand differentiation occurred. We can consider equalization price a proxy for brand equity.[23]

Multi-Attribute Attitude Models. Srinivasan, Park, and Chang have proposed a comprehensive residual methodology to measure brand equity based on the multiattribute attitude model.[24] Their approach reveals the relative sizes of different bases of brand equity by dividing brand equity into three components: brand awareness, attribute perception biases, and nonattribute preference.

- The ***attribute-perception biased component*** of brand equity is the difference between subjectively perceived attribute values and objectively measured attribute values. Objectively measured attribute values come from independent testing services such as *Consumer Reports* or acknowledged experts in the field.
- The ***nonattribute preference component*** of brand equity is the difference between subjectively perceived attribute values and overall preference. It reflects the consumer's overall appraisal of a brand that goes beyond the utility of individual product attributes.

The researchers also incorporate the effects of enhancing brand awareness and preference on consumer "pull" and the brand's availability. They propose a survey procedure to collect information for estimating these different perception and preference measures.

Dillon and his colleagues have presented a model for decomposing attribute ratings of a brand into two components: (1) brand-specific associations, meaning features, attributes, or benefits that consumers link to a brand; and (2) general brand impressions based on a more holistic view of a brand.[25]

Critique. Residual approaches provide a useful benchmark for interpreting brand equity, especially when we need approximations of brand equity or a financially oriented perspective on it. The disadvantage of residual approaches is that they are most appropriate for brands with a lot of product-related attribute associations, because these measures are unable to distinguish between different types of non-product-related attribute associations. Consequently, the residual approach's diagnostic value for strategic decision making in other cases is limited.

More generally, residual approaches take a fairly static view of brand equity by focusing on consumer *preferences*. This contrasts sharply with the process view advocated by the customer-based brand equity framework. The brand-based and marketing-based comparative approaches stress looking at consumer *response* to the marketing of a brand and attempting to uncover the extent to which that response is affected by brand knowledge.

This distinction is also relevant for the issue of "separability" in brand valuation that various researchers have raised. For example, Barwise and his colleagues note that marketing efforts to create an extended or augmented product, say, with extra features or service plus other means to enhance brand value, "raise serious problems of separating the value of the brand name and trademark from the many other elements of the 'augmented' product."[26] According to customer-based brand equity, those efforts could affect the favorability, strength, and uniqueness of various brand associations, which would, in turn, affect consumer response to *future* marketing activities.

For example, imagine that a brand becomes known for providing extraordinary customer service because of certain policies and favorable advertising, publicity, or word-of-mouth (like Nordstrom department stores or Singapore Airlines). These favorable perceptions of customer service and the attitudes they engender could create customer-based brand equity by affecting consumer response to a price policy (consumers would be willing to pay higher prices), a new ad campaign (consumers would accept an ad illustrating customer satisfaction), or a brand extension (customers would become interested in trying a new type of retail outlet).

Much of the company value of Prada has been attributed to the value of the brand.
Source: Pascal Sittler/REA/ Redux Pictures

Valuation Approaches

An increasingly widely held belief is that much of the corporate value of many companies is wrapped up in intangible assets, including the brand. Many studies have reinforced this point:[27]

- A survey reported by *Fortune* magazine in 2006 suggested that 72 percent of the Dow Jones market cap was made up of intangible assets.
- Accenture estimated that intangibles accounted for almost 70 percent of the value of the S&P 500 in 2007, up from 20 percent in 2007.
- Brand consultancy Brand Finance has estimated that brand value for Nike and Prada made up as much as 84 percent and 73 percent of total company value, respectively, in 2006.

Recognizing that fact, many firms are interested in exactly what that brand value is. The ability to put a specific price tag on a brand's value may be useful for a number of reasons:

- *Mergers and acquisitions:* Both to evaluate possible purchases as well as to facilitate disposal
- *Brand licensing:* Internally for tax reasons and to third parties
- *Fund raising:* As collateral on loans or for sale or leaseback arrangements
- *Brand portfolio decisions:* To allocate resources, develop brand strategy, or prepare financial reports

For example, many companies appear to be attractive acquisition candidates because of the strong competitive positions of their brands and their reputation among consumers.

Unfortunately, the value of the brand assets in many cases is largely excluded from the company's balance sheet and is therefore of little use in determining overall value. It has been argued that adjusting the balance sheet to reflect the true value of a company's brands permits us to take a more realistic view and assess the purchase premium to book value that might be earned from the brands after acquisition. Such a calculation, however, would also require estimates of capital required by brands and the expected after-acquisition return on investment (ROI) of a company.

Separating out the percentage of revenue or profits attributable to brand equity is a difficult task. In the United States, there is no conventional accounting method for doing so.[28] Some of Coca-Cola's experiences with brand valuation are instructive here.

COCA-COLA BRAND VALUATION

Despite the fact that expert analysts estimate the value of the Coca-Cola name in the billions of dollars, due to accounting convention, it appears in the company's books as only $25 *million.* Based on accounting rules, Coca-Cola's assets in 2004 had a book value of $31.3 billion, with various intangible assets assessed at $3.8 billion and a market cap of $100 billion. On June 7, 2007, Coca-Cola acquired Energy Brands, also known as glacéau, maker of enhanced water brands such as vitaminwater, fruit-water, and smartwater, for approximately $4.1 billion. Because these brands were acquired, different accounting rules apply to them. Based upon a preliminary purchase price allocation, approximately $2.8 billion was allocated to trademarks, $2.2 billion to goodwill, $200 million to customer relationships, and $900 million to deferred tax liabilities. At the end of 2007, Coke had trademarks on its balance sheet with a book value of $5.135 billion. Of this figure, about $2.8 billion is associated with Energy Brands.[29]

Although the Coke brand is estimated to be worth billions, for accounting purposes it is on the books for mere millions.
Source: Chen Jianli/ZUMA Press/Newscom

As the Coca-Cola experiences show, market-based estimates of value can differ dramatically from those based on U.S. accounting conventions.[30] Other countries, however, are trying to capture that value. How do we calculate the financial value of a brand? This section, after providing some accounting background and historical perspective, describes several leading brand valuation approaches.[31] The Brand Focus reviews some financial considerations in the relationship of brand equity to the stock market and provides additional perspective on accounting issues in branding.

Accounting Background. The assets of a firm can be either tangible or intangible. *Tangible assets* include property, plant, and equipment; current assets (inventories, marketable securities, and cash); and investments in stocks and bonds. We can estimate the value of tangible assets using accounting book values and reported estimates of replacement costs.

Intangible assets, on the other hand, are any factors of production or specialized resources that permit the company to earn cash flows in excess of the return on tangible assets. In other words, intangible assets augment the earning power of a firm's physical assets. They are typically lumped under the heading of *goodwill* and include things such as patents, trademarks, and licensing agreements, as well as "softer" considerations such as the skill of the management and customer relations.

In an acquisition, the goodwill item often includes a premium paid to gain control, which, in certain instances, may even exceed the value of tangible and intangible assets. In Britain and certain other countries, it has been common to write off the goodwill element of an acquisition against reserves; tangible assets, on the other hand, are transferred straight to the acquiring company's balance sheet.

Historical Perspectives. Brand valuation's more recent past started with Rupert Murdoch's News Corporation, which included a valuation of some of its magazines on its balance sheets in 1984, as permitted by Australian accounting standards. The rationale was that the goodwill element of publishing acquisitions—the difference in value between net

By taking advantage of Australian accounting standards to put brand value on balance sheets, Rupert Murdoch was able to build a media giant with News Corporation.

Source: Jeremy Sutton-Hibbert/Alamy

assets and the price paid—was often enormous and negatively affecting the balance sheet. News Corporation used the recognition that the titles themselves contained much of the value of the acquisition to justify placing them on the balance sheet, improving the debt/equity ratio and allowing the company to get some much-needed cash to finance acquisition of some foreign media companies.

In the United Kingdom, Grand Metropolitan was one of the first British companies to place a monetary value on the brands it owned and to put that value on its balance sheet. When Grand Met acquired Heublein distributors, Pearle eye care, and Sambuca Romana liqueur in 1987, it placed the value of some of its brands—principally Smirnoff—on the balance sheet for roughly $1 billion. In doing so, Grand Met used two different methods. If a company consisted of primarily one brand, it figured that the value of the brand was 75 percent of the purchase price, whereas if the company had many brands, it used a multiple of an income figure.

British firms used brand values primarily to boost their balance sheets. By recording their brand assets, the firms maintained, they were attempting to bring their shareholder funds nearer to the market capitalization of the firm. In the United Kingdom, Rank Hovis McDougal (RHM) succeeded in putting the worth of the company's existing brands as a figure on the balance sheet to fight a hostile takeover bid in 1988. With the brand value information provided by Interbrand, the RHM board was able to go back to investors and argue that the bid was too low, and eventually to repel it.

Accounting firms in favor of valuing brands argue that it is a way to strengthen the presentation of a company's accounts, to record hidden assets so they are disclosed to company's shareholders, to enhance a company's shareholders' funds to improve its earnings ratios, to provide a realistic basis for management and investors to measure a company's performance, and to reveal detailed information on brand strengths so that management can formulate appropriate brand strategies. In practical terms, however, recording brand value as an intangible asset from the firm's perspective is a means to increase the asset value of the firm.

Actual practices have varied from country to country. Brand valuations have been accepted for inclusion in the balance sheets of companies in countries such as the United Kingdom, Australia, New Zealand, France, Sweden, Singapore, and Spain. In the United Kingdom, Martin Sorrell improved the balance sheet of WPP by attaching brand value to its primary assets, including J. Walter Thompson Company, Ogilvy & Mather, and Hill & Knowlton, stating in the annual report that:

> Intangible fixed assets comprise certain acquired separable corporate brand names. These are shown at a valuation of the incremental earnings expected to arise from the ownership of brands. The valuations have been based on the present value of notional royalty savings arising from [ownership] and on estimates of profits attributable to brand loyalty.[32]

In the United States, generally accepted accounting principles (blanket amortization principles) mean that placing a brand on the balance sheet would require amortization of that asset for up to 40 years. Such a charge would severely hamper firm profitability; as a result, firms avoid such accounting maneuvers. On the other hand, certain other countries (including Canada, Germany, and Japan) have gone beyond tax deductibility of brand equity to permit some or all of the goodwill arising from an acquisition to be deducted for tax purposes.

General Approaches. In determining the value of a brand in an acquisition or merger, firms can choose from three main approaches: the cost, market, and income approaches.[33]

The cost approach maintains that brand equity is the amount of money that would be required to reproduce or replace the brand (including all costs for research and development, test marketing, advertising, and so on). One common criticism of approaches relying on historic or replacement cost is that they reward past performance in a way that may bear little relation to future profitability—for example, many brands with expensive introductions have been unsuccessful. On the other hand, for brands that have been around for decades (such as Heinz, Kellogg's, and Chanel), it would be virtually impossible to find out what the investment in brand development was—and largely irrelevant as well.

It is also obviously easier to estimate costs of tangible assets than intangible assets, but the latter often may lie at the heart of brand equity. Similar problems exist with a replacement cost approach; for example, the cost of replacing a brand depends a great deal on how quickly the process would take and what competitive, legal, and logistical obstacles might be encountered.

According to the second approach, the market approach, we can think of brand equity as the present value of the future economic benefits to be derived by the owner of the asset. In other words, it is the amount an active market would allow so that the asset would exchange between a willing buyer and willing seller. The main problems with this approach are the lack of open market transactions for brand name assets, and the fact that the uniqueness of brands makes extrapolating from one market transaction to another problematic.

The third approach to determining the value of a brand, the income approach, argues that brand equity is the discounted future cash flow from the future earnings stream for the brand. Three such income approaches are as follows:

1. Capitalizing royalty earnings from a brand name (when these can be defined)
2. Capitalizing the premium profits that are earned by a branded product (by comparing its performance with that of an unbranded product)
3. Capitalizing the actual profitability of a brand after allowing for the costs of maintaining it and the effects of taxation

For example, as an example of the first income approach, brand consultancy Brand Finance uses a Royalty Relief methodology for brand valuation. Their approach is based on the premise that brand value can be thought of in terms of what a company avoids in paying a license fee from actually owning the trademark. Their rationale is that such an approach has much credibility with accountants, lawyers, and tax experts because it calculates brand values on the basis of comparable third-party transactions. They use publically available information to estimate future, post-tax royalties of a brand and thus its net present value and overall brand value.[34]

The next sections and The Science of Branding 1 describe other income-based valuation approaches.[35]

Simon and Sullivan's Brand Equity Value. In a seminal academic research study, Simon and Sullivan developed a technique for estimating a firm's brand equity derived from financial market estimates of brand-related profits.[37] They define brand equity as the incremental cash flows that accrue to branded products over and above the cash flows that would result from the sale of unbranded products.

To implement their approach, they begin by estimating the current market value of the firm. They assume the market value of the firm's securities to provide an unbiased estimate of the future cash flows attributable to all the firm's assets. Their methodology attempts to extract the value of a firm's brand equity from the value of the firm's other assets. The result is an estimate of brand equity based on the financial market valuation of the firm's future cash flows.

THE SCIENCE OF BRANDING 1

The Prophet Brand Valuation Methodology

Prophet's brand valuation methodology starts with the realization that accountants define an asset as "a resource, under the control of an enterprise, to which future economic benefits will flow." In the context of a brand, a resource is something a company owns that it uses to achieve an end or fulfill a function, namely to identify the company's product or service so that consumers can identify it and attach perceptions to it.

Fundamental to Prophet's approach is that brands generate future economic benefits, in that consumers who know of a brand and prefer it to other choices will spend money buying it now and in the future. The purpose of marketing, according to Prophet, is to find these customers in the first place and keep them over time. Prophet maintains that a credible brand valuation methodology must reflect this definition, which is why it is at the foundation of Prophet's approach.

Prophet's brand valuation methodology is also constructed on the basis of sound corporate finance principles and complies with the standards laid down by the U.S. Marketing Accountability Standards Board (MASB). Specifically, it has four steps:

1. Finance

Economic profit (EP) is the profit a company earns that exceeds its cost of capital.[36] Only firms that have developed sustainable competitive advantages over time are able to earn this class of profit. It is generally acknowledged that brands are a major cause of a company earning and sustaining economic profit. The starting point for any valuation is therefore to extract from the income statement and balance sheet the economic profit earned by the brand being valued.

2. Brand Contribution

The Prophet brand contribution is a procedure that breaks economic profit into a set of drivers and then isolates the portion that is attributable to the brand's equity or strength. The Prophet approach employs a classical qualitative/quantitative technique in the following five steps:

1. Using a modified focus group format, senior company management generates a list of probable EP drivers. These are reduced by various rating and ranking methods to between 10 and 15.

2. A panel of about 50 respondents knowledgeable about the category is assembled, and participants are briefed to participate in a two- or three-round set of quantitative questions. These require them to evaluate the driver set and allocate ratings according to relative importance. Thus the list is reduced still further to between 5 and 9.

3. The respondents are asked to evaluate the market competitiveness of each of the drivers in the set, using market-based asset as the criteria. A score out of 100 indicates each one's relative importance.

4. Finally, respondents are asked to assess each driver's dependence on, or independence from, the brand's external equity.

5. The brand equity scores are multiplied by the driver weightings. The products are summed to produce the percentage that is then applied to economic profit to identify the brand portion or contribution. In the model, this profit is called brand premium profit (BPP).

3. Category Expected Life

The profit a brand can earn is to a large extent dictated by the nature of the category in which it sells. A category might be as broad as financial services, which can be narrowed to banking and insurance, or as precise as toothpaste, which can be expanded to dental care. Within the category, supply and demand pressures will exert an influence on the price range consumers will tolerate, which in turn determines profit margins brand owners can achieve.

The Prophet model uses an evaluation of the category to measure the extent to which the category encourages or inhibits the earning of economic profit for the brands that compete within it. It does this by looking at four variables: how mature is the category; are brand shares stable or volatile; does competitive activity create high barriers to entry or not; and, how vulnerable is the category to external pressures such as government regulation, raw material supply, and changing fashions. The outcome of this evaluation is to set parameters in years of expected economic life for a strong (dominant) and weak (marginal) brand.

4. Brand Knowledge Structure (BKS)

Brand knowledge structure, or BKS, is the bundle of knowledge consumers hold in memory and use to decide what products they need and which of the available brands they will buy. The comparative strength with which this information is held by the category community of users determines the success of the competing brands. It is also a good proxy for risk: the stronger the brand, the more likely consumers are to continue to buy in the future. Brand strength ensures future cash flows. The opposite is equally true. The Prophet method uses market research–based measurements of brand strength and preference to set the number of years in the cash flow projection: the stronger the brand relative to its competitors, the more years in the model.

The Valuation

The model calculates the value of the brand by working out how many years to project the growing part of the cash flows and then the shape and duration of a theoretical decay period. It does this by merging the BKS data with the category expected life results. The value is the resulting capitalized value of the projected cash flows. The discount rate is a classical weighted average cost of capital (WACC), and risk is taken into account by specially constructed probability weightings of the near term cash flows.

Key Differences

A few characteristics distinguish the Prophet brand valuation methodology. Other models typically look at only five years of future cash flows, add a perpetuity based on a discounted sixth year, and simply divide the sixth year by the discount rate. Frequently the perpetuity represents one-quarter to one-third of the total brand value; the five-year discounted cash flow into which most of the work has been invested results in only a small amount of the valuation.

The Prophet approach models the entire expected economic life of the brand in terms of the franchise run (its rise) and decay (its decline). The nature of the brand category (category expected life) and the relative strength of the brand as measured by the BKS determine the total number of years for the present-value calculation. The proportions are reversed compared to many other models, with the major portion of the Prophet valuation located in the early franchise run, which includes the five-year discounted part of the cash flow projection. This makes the valuation sensitive to changes in the BKS and early cash flows.

Also, like most corporate finance valuations, the Prophet approach uses a classically estimated weighted average cost of capital (WACC). It takes specific risk into account in the cash flows, as opposed to the discount rate. Other methodologies use the market risk and beta components of WACC to insert their consumer-driven brand risk premiums.

Source: Based on the research and writings of Prophet's Roger Sinclair whose considerable input is gratefully acknowledged. For more information, visit www.prophet.com.

From these basic premises, Simon and Sullivan derive their methodology to extract the value of brand equity from the financial market value of the firm. The total asset value of the firm is the sum of the market value of common stock, preferred stock, long-term debt, and short-term debt. The value of intangible assets is captured in the ratio of the market value of the firm to the replacement cost of its tangible assets. There are three categories of intangible assets: brand equity, nonbrand factors that reduce the firm's costs relative to competitors like R&D and patents, and industry-wide factors that permit monopoly profits, such as regulation. By considering factors such as the age of the brand, order of entry in the category, and current and past advertising share, Simon and Sullivan then provide estimates of brand equity.

Interbrand's Brand Valuation Methodology. Interbrand is probably the premier brand valuation firm. In developing its brand valuation methodology, Interbrand approached the problem by assuming that the value of a brand, like the value of any other economic asset, was the present worth of the benefits of future ownership. In other words, according to Interbrand, brand valuation is based on an assessment of what the value is today of the earnings or cash flow the brand can be expected to generate in the future.[38]

Because Interbrand's approach looks at the ongoing investment and management of the brand as an economic asset, it takes into account all the different ways in which a brand benefits

According to Simon and Sullivan's analysis, in the highly competitive candy category, Tootsie Roll's brand name was a valuable financial asset.
Source: Tootsie Roll Industries, Inc.

an organization both internally and externally—from attracting and retaining talent to delivering on customer expectations. One advantage of the Interbrand valuation approach is that it is very generalizable and can be applied to virtually any type of brand or product.

Three key components contribute to the brand value assessment: (1) the financial performance of the branded products or services, (2) the role of brand in the purchase decision process, and (3) the strength of the brand.[39] Here's how Interbrand addresses each of these three components.

Brand Financial Performance.   Financial performance for the brand reflects an organization's raw financial return to the investors and is analyzed as economic profit, a concept akin to economic value added (EVA). To determine economic profit, subtract taxes from net operating profit to arrive at net operating profit after tax (NOPAT). From NOPAT, subtract a capital charge to account for the capital used to generate the brand's revenues, yielding the economic profit for each year analyzed. The capital charge rate is set by the industry-weighted average cost of capital (WACC). The financial performance is analyzed for a five-year forecast and for a terminal value. The terminal value represents the brand's expected performance beyond the forecast period. The economic profit that is calculated is then multiplied by the role of brand (a percentage, as described below) to determine the branded earnings that contribute to the valuation total.

Role of Brand.   Role of brand measures the portion of the customer decision to purchase that is attributable to brand—exclusive of other purchase drivers such as price or product features. Conceptually, role of brand reflects the portion of demand for a branded product or service that exceeds what the demand would be for the same product or service if it were unbranded. We can determine role of brand in different ways, including primary research, a review of historical roles of brand for companies in that industry, and expert panel assessment. We multiply the percentage for the role of brand by the economic profit of the branded products or services to determine the amount of branded earnings that contribute to the valuation total.

Brand Strength.   Brand strength measures the ability of the brand to secure the delivery of expected future earnings. Brand strength is reported on a scale of 0–100 based on an evaluation across 10 dimensions of brand activation. Performance in these dimensions is generally judged relative to other brands in the industry. The brand strength inversely determines a discount rate, through a proprietary algorithm. That rate is used to discount branded earnings back to a present value, based on the likelihood that the brand will be able to withstand challenges and deliver the expected earnings.

Summary.   Brand valuation and the "brands on the balance sheet" debate are controversial subjects. There is no one universally agreed-upon approach.[40] In fact, many marketing experts feel it is impossible to reduce the richness of a brand to a single, meaningful number, and that any formula that tries to do so is an abstraction and arbitrary.

The primary disadvantage of valuation approaches is that they necessarily have to make a host of potentially oversimplified assumptions to arrive at one measure of brand equity. For example, Sir Michael Perry, former chairman of Unilever, once objected for philosophical reasons:

> The seemingly miraculous conjuring up of intangible asset values, as if from nowhere, only serves to reinforce the view of the consumer skeptics, that brands are just high prices and consumer exploitation.[41]

Wharton's Peter Fader points out a number of limitations of valuation approaches: they require much judgmental data and thus contain much subjectivity; intangible assets are not always synonymous with brand equity; the methods sometimes defy common sense and lack "face validity"; the financial measures generally ignore or downplay current investments in future equity like advertising or R&D; and the strength of the brand measures may be confounded with the strength of the company.[42]

At the heart of much of the criticism is the issue of separability we identified earlier. An *Economist* editorial put it this way: "Brands can be awkward to separate as assets. With Cadbury's Dairy Milk, how much value comes from the name Cadbury? How much from Dairy Milk? How much merely from the product's (replicable) contents or design?"[43]

To draw a sports analogy, extracting brand value may be as difficult as determining the value of the coach to a team's performance. And the way a brand is managed can have a large effect, positive or negative, on its value. Branding Brief 1 describes several brand acquisitions that turned out unsuccessfully for firms.

As a result of these criticisms, the climate regarding brand valuation has changed. See the Brand Focus for more on how accounting standards have changed to accommodate the concept of brand value.

BRANDING BRIEF 1

Beauty Is in the Eye of the Beholder

Companies make acquisitions because they wish to grow and expand their business. In making acquisitions, a company has to determine what it feels the acquired brands are worth. In some instances, the hoped-for brand value has failed to materialize, serving as a reminder that the value of a brand is partly a function of what you do with it. The booming business environment of the 1990s witnessed many such failures.

A classic example is Quaker Oats's $1.7 billion acquisition of Snapple in 1994. Snapple had become a popular national brand through powerful grassroots marketing and a willingness to distribute to small outlets and convenience stores. Quaker changed Snapple's ad campaign—abandoning the rotund and immensely popular Snapple Lady—and revamped its distribution system. Quaker also changed the packaging by updating the label and putting Snapple in 64-ounce bottles, moves that did not sit well with loyal customers. The results were disastrous: Snapple began losing money and market share, allowing a host of competitors to move in. Unable to revive the foundering brand, Quaker sold the company in 1997 for $300 million to Triarc, which owned other beverages such as Royal Crown Cola and Diet Rite.

Another unsuccessful acquisition occurred when Quality Dining bought Bruegger's Bagels in 1996 with $142 million in stock. Within one year, Quality Dining agreed to sell the bagel chain back to its original owners for $50 million after taking a $203 million charge on the acquisition. Experts blamed an overly ambitious expansion strategy. Quality Dining planned to expand to 2,000 stores within four years, despite the fact that before the acquisition, Bruegger's had posted two consecutive annual losses due to its expansion to 339 stores. The new ownership also set the lofty goal of entering the top 60 domestic markets, which limited the amount of advertising and promotional support each market received. As Bruegger's fortunes turned, competitor Einstein/Noah Bagel overtook the company as the market leader in the United States. One franchisee commented, "[Quality Dining] would have had to stay up pretty late at night to screw up anything more than they did."

More recently, despite much success with its Ford brand, Ford Motor Company could never seem to find the right

A brand is partly worth what you can do with it—a lesson Quaker Oats learned the hard way after it mismanaged the Snapple brand after acquiring it.
Source: Ramin Talaie/Bloomberg via Getty Images

formula for the overseas acquisitions that made up its Premier Automotive Group collection. The company sold the Jaguar and Land Rover brands to India's Tata Motors in March 2008 for $1.7 billion—roughly a third of the price it had paid for the two luxury brands ($2.5 billion in 1989 and $2.7 billion in 2000, respectively). After paying $6.5 billion for Volvo in 1999, Ford sold it to China's Geely for $1.5 billion in 2010. Ford's decision was motivated by a lack of success with its luxury brands and a desire to focus on its more promising Ford brand.

In all these case, despite the best of intentions, brands were sold with an implicit assumption that could be more profitably marketed by someone else.

Sources: "Cadbury Is Paying Triarc $1.45 Billion for Snapple Unit," *Baltimore Sun,* 19 September 2000; Thomas M. Burton, "The Profit Center of the Bagel Business Has Quite a Big Hole," *Wall Street Journal,* 6 October 1997; "Ford Sells Luxury Brands for $1.7 Billion," Associated Press, 26 March 2008; "Ford Sells Volvo to Chinese Carmaker Geely for $1.5 Billion," *New York Daily News,* 3 August 2010. For an interesting academic analyses, see S. Cem Bahadir, Sundar G. Bharadwaj, and Rajendra K. Srivastava, "Financial Value of Brands in Mergers and Acquisitions: Is Value in the Eye of the Beholder?," *Journal of Marketing* 72 (November 2008): 49–64; Michael A. Wiles, Neil A. Morgan, and Lopo L. Rego, "The Effect of Brand Acquisition and Disposal on Stock Returns," *Journal of Marketing,* 2012, in press.

REVIEW

This chapter considered the two main ways to measure the benefits or outcomes of brand equity: comparative methods (a means to better assess the effects of consumer perceptions and preferences on aspects of the marketing program) and holistic methods (attempts to come up with an estimate of the overall value of the brand). Figure 2 summarizes the different but complementary approaches. In fact, understanding the particular range of benefits for a brand on the basis of comparative methods may be useful as an input in estimating the overall value of a brand by holistic methods.

Combining these outcome measures with measures of sources of brand equity as part of the brand value chain can provide insight into the effectiveness of marketing actions. Nevertheless, assessing the ROI of marketing activities remains a challenge.[44] Here are four general guidelines for creating and measuring ROI from brand marketing activities:

1. *Spend wisely—focus and be creative.* To be able to measure ROI, we need to be earning a return to begin with! Investing in distinctive and well-designed marketing activities increases the chance for a more positive and discernible ROI.
2. *Look for benchmarks—examine competitive spending levels and historical company norms.* It is important to get the lay of the land in a market or category in order to understand what we may expect.
3. *Be strategic—apply brand equity models.* Use models such as the brand resonance model and the brand value chain to provide discipline and a structured approach to planning, implementing, and interpreting marketing activity.
4. *Be observant—track both formally and informally.* Qualitative and quantitative insights can help us understand brand performance.

Perhaps the dominant theme of this chapter on measuring sources of brand equity is the importance of using multiple measures and research methods to capture the richness and complexity of brand equity. No matter how carefully we apply them, single measures of brand equity provide at best a one- or two-dimensional view of a brand and risk

Comparative methods: Use experiments that examine consumer attitudes and behavior toward a brand, to more directly assess the benefits arising from having a high level of awareness and strong, favorable, and unique brand associations.

- *Brand-based comparative approaches:* Experiments in which one group of consumers responds to an element of the marketing program when it is attributed to the brand and another group responds to that same element when it is attributed to a competitive or fictitiously named brand.

- *Marketing-based comparative approaches:* Experiments in which consumers respond to changes in elements of the marketing program for the brand or competitive brands.

- *Conjoint analysis:* A survey-based multivariate technique that enables marketers to profile the consumer buying decision process with respect to products and brands.

Holistic methods: Attempt to place an overall value on the brand in either abstract utility terms or concrete financial terms. Thus, holistic methods attempt to "net out" various considerations to determine the unique contribution of the brand.

- *Residual approach:* Examines the value of the brand by subtracting out from overall brand preferences consumers' preferences for the brand based on physical product attributes alone.

- *Valuation approach:* Places a financial value on the brand for accounting purposes, mergers and acquisitions, or other such reasons.

FIGURE 2

Measures of Outcomes of Brand Equity

missing important dimensions of brand equity. Recall the problems encountered by Coca-Cola from its overreliance on blind taste tests.

No single number or measure fully captures brand equity.[45] Rather, we should think of brand equity as a multidimensional concept that depends on what knowledge structures are present in the minds of consumers, and what actions a firm takes to capitalize on the potential that these knowledge structures offer.

There are many different sources of, and outcomes from, brand equity, depending on the marketers' skill and ingenuity. Firms may be more or less able to maximize the potential value of a brand according to the type and nature of their marketing activities. As Wharton's Peter Fader says:

> The actual value of a brand depends on its fit with buyer's corporate structure and other assets. If the acquiring company has manufacturing or distribution capabilities that are synergistic with the brand, then it might be worth paying a lot of money for it. Paul Feldwick, a British executive, makes the analogy between brands and properties on the Monopoly game board. You're willing to pay a lot more for Marvin Gardens if you already own Atlantic and Ventnor Avenues![46]

The customer-based brand equity framework therefore emphasizes employing a range of research measures and methods to fully capture the multiple potential sources and outcomes of brand equity.

DISCUSSION QUESTIONS

1. Choose a product. Conduct a branded and unbranded experiment. What do you learn about the equity of the brands in that product class?
2. Can you identify any other advantages or disadvantages of the comparative methods?
3. Pick a brand and conduct an analysis similar to that done with the Planters brand. What do you learn about its extendability as a result?
4. What do you think of the Interbrand methodology? What do you see as its main advantages and disadvantages?
5. How do you think Young & Rubicam's BrandAsset Valuator relates to the Interbrand methodology? What do you see as its main advantages and disadvantages?

BRAND FOCUS

Branding and Finance

Marketers increasingly must be able to quantify their activities directly or indirectly in financial terms. One important topic that has received increasing academic interest is the relationship between brand equity and brand strategies and stock market information and performance. Another important topic is the accounting implications of branding. We review issues around these two topics in this appendix.

Stock Market Reactions

Several researchers have studied how the stock market reacts to the brand equity and marketing activities for companies and products.

Brand Equity. In a classic study, David Aaker and Robert Jacobson examined the association between yearly stock return and yearly brand changes (as measured by EquiTrend's perceived quality rating of brand equity) for 34 companies during the years 1989–1992.[47] They also compared the accompanying changes in current-term return on investment (ROI).

They found that, as expected, stock market return was positively related to changes in ROI. Interestingly, they also uncovered a strong positive relationship between brand equity and stock return. Firms that experienced the largest gains in brand equity saw their stock return average 30 percent. Conversely, those firms with the largest losses in brand equity saw stock return average a negative 10 percent. The researchers concluded that investors can and do learn about changes in brand equity—not necessarily through EquiTrend studies (which may have little exposure to the financial community) but by learning about a company's plans and programs.[48]

In a follow-up study, using data for firms in the computer industry in the 1990s, Aaker and Jacobson found that changes in brand attitude were associated contemporaneously with stock return and led accounting financial performance.[49]

They also found five factors (new products, product problems, competitor actions, changes in top management, and legal actions) that were associated with significant changes in brand attitudes. Awareness that did not translate into more positive attitudes, however, did little to the stock price (Ameritrade, Juno, and Priceline). The authors conclude, "So it's not the brands customers know, but the brands customers respect, that are ultimately successful." Similarly, using *Financial World* estimates of brand equity, another comprehensive study found that brand equity was positively related to stock return and that this effect was incremental to other accounting variables such as the firm's net income.[50]

Madden, Fehle, and Fournier found that strong brands not only delivered greater returns to stockholders versus a relevant market benchmark, they did so with less risk.[51] Fornell and his colleagues find similar benefits of higher returns and lower risk for satisfied, loyal customers.[52]

Marketing Activities. Adopting an event study methodology, Lane and Jacobson were able to show that stock market participants' response to brand extension announcements, consistent with the trade-offs inherent in brand leveraging, depend interactively and nonmonotonically on brand attitude and familiarity.[53]

Specifically, the stock market responded most favorably to extensions of high-esteem, high-familiarity brands (Hershey, Coke, Norton/Symantec) and to low-esteem, low-familiarity brands (in the latter case, presumably because there was little to risk and much to gain with extensions). The stock market reaction was less favorable (and sometimes even negative!) for extensions of brands for which consumer familiarity was disproportionately high compared with consumer regard and to extensions of brands for which consumer regard was disproportionately high compared with familiarity.

In another event study of 58 firms that changed their names in the 1980s, Horsky and Swyngedouw found that for most of the firms, name changes were associated with improved performance; the greatest improvement tended to occur in firms that produced industrial goods and whose performance prior to the change was relatively poor.[54] Not all changes, however, were successful. The researchers interpreted the act of a name change as a signal that other measures to improve performance (changes in product offerings and organizational changes) will be seriously and successfully undertaken.

Rao and his colleagues analyzed financial performance of 113 firms over a five-year period and found that corporate branding strategies were associated with higher values of Tobin's Q.[55] Tobin's Q is a forward-looking measure of intangible assets and a firm's future profit potential, calculated as the ratio of the market value of the firm to the replacement cost of the firm's assets.

A mixed branding strategy (where a firm used corporate names for some products and individual names for others) was associated with lower values of Tobin's Q. The researchers also concluded that most firms would have been able to improve their Tobin's Q had they adopted a branding strategy different from the one suggested by examining their brand portfolios.

Similarly, Morgan, Rego, and colleagues showed how five brand portfolio characteristics (number of brands owned, number of segments in which they are marketed, degree to which the brands in the firm's portfolio compete with one another, and consumer perceptions of the quality and price of the brands in the firm's portfolio) affected a firm's marketing effectiveness and efficiency and financial performance.[56]

Finally, Mizik and Jacobson found that the stock market reacted favorably when a firm increased its emphasis on value appropriation (extracting profits in the marketplace) over value creation (innovating, producing, and delivering products to the market), although certain qualifying conditions prevailed.[57]

Accounting Perspectives on Brands[58]

In the period following the Second World War, investors used the physical, tangible assets owned by a company to assess its value. Records show that the market value of companies on major stock markets more or less equaled their book value. Any surplus over book value was called goodwill and was considered to be a reflection of relationships the company had built with suppliers and customers and never amounted to much.

Coinciding with the introduction to business of the mainframe computer in the 1970s and the personal computer in the 1980s, the gap started to open. At the peak of the "dot.com" boom, market value was measured at five times book value.

Traditionally, company annual financial accounts were based on "historic cost"—a record on the balance sheet of what was paid for the tangible assets a company needed to operate the business. But the cost and the value of the asset at current market prices often differed. Asset strippers could buy a company based on the historic cost of its assets and then sell off the assets at market value and make a handsome profit. Since the dot.com bust in 2000, the ratio of market to book has dropped sharply to stabilize over the last 10 years at about 2.8.[59] At the time of the 2008 financial crisis, it dropped below 2 before recovering somewhat afterward.

To provide investors with more readily useful information for making investment decisions, the major accounting bodies, the Financial Accounting Standards Board (FASB) in the United States and the International Accounting Standards Board (IASB) representing accountants in the rest of the world, took two steps:

1. They moved from historic cost to fair value, which is the price that would be received if an asset were sold in an orderly market between two market participants, that is, the current market value.

2. They began to develop accounting standards to take account of assets that have no monetary value and no physical substance—that is, intangible assets.

Over the past decade, FASB and the IASB have worked on the following four standards relevant to brands.[60]

IFRS 3 *Business Combinations.* The purpose of this standard is to guide preparers of financial statements in the treatment of companies after a merger or acquisition. A radical aspect of this standard is that it requires acquired goodwill to be allocated to cash generating units. This replaces goodwill as the arithmetic difference between net tangible value and the price paid and calls for it to be broken down into identifiable items. The standard specifies that trademarks and brands will feature among the marketing-based intangibles to be valued and included in the accounts.

IAS 38 *Intangible Assets.* This standard still has a label that indicates it has not been updated. When this happens, it will take on the IFRS appellation. In its current form, it contradicts IFRS 3 in that it states that brands developed by a company do not qualify to be described as assets. They fail to meet the recognition criteria. This is an anomaly that is known and understood by the accounting standard setters. Work had been invested in bringing IAS 38 into line but was delayed as the accounting boards dealt with the financial crisis of 2008 and other matters.[61]

IFRS 13 *Fair Value Measurement.* This standard was issued formally during the course of 2011. As its name implies, it explains in considerable detail how an asset should be measured at its fair value. While it doesn't specify brands, it makes allowance for a class of assets that can be difficult to value because they lack publicly available data. This standard provides substantial guidance on how brands should be valued.

IFRS 36 *Impairment of Assets.* Accounting principles state that an asset should not be held on the balance sheet at its original value if that value no longer applies. IFRS 36 requires assets to be tested annually, and if the value has fallen below what is called the carrying amount, the difference must be treated as a loss in the income statement. That rarely applies to brands, which tend to increase in value over time, yet there is no allowance at this stage for the opposite of impairment, which is accretion. What makes the standard useful to brand owners is the clear explanation of how the annual measurement process should be conducted.

Notes

1. C. B. Bhattacharya and Leonard M. Lodish, "Towards a System for Monitoring Brand Health," *Marketing Science Institute Working Paper Series* (00–111) (July 2000).

2. Richard F. Chay, "How Marketing Researchers Can Harness the Power of Brand Equity," *Marketing Research* 3, no. 2 (1991): 10–30.

3. For an interesting approach, see Martin R. Lautman and Koen Pauwels, "Metrics That Matter: Identifying the Importance of Consumer Needs and Wants," *Journal of Advertising Research* (September 2009): 339–359.

4. Peter Farquhar and Yuji Ijiri have made several other distinctions in classifying brand equity measurement procedures. Peter H. Farquhar, Julia W. Han, and Yuji Ijiri, "Recognizing and Measuring Brand Assets," *Marketing Science Institute Report* (1991): 91–119. They describe two broad classes of measurement approaches to brand equity: separation approaches and integration approaches. Separation approaches view brand equity as the value added to a product. Farquhar and Ijiri categorize separation approaches into residual methods and comparative methods. Residual methods determine brand equity by what remains after subtracting physical product effects. Comparative methods determine brand equity by comparing the branded product with an unbranded product or an equivalent benchmark.

   Integration approaches, on the other hand, typically define brand equity as a composition of basic elements. Farquhar and Ijiri categorize integration approaches into association and valuation methods. Valuation methods measure brand equity by its cost or value as an intangible asset for a particular owner and intended use. Association methods measure brand equity in terms of the favorableness of brand evaluations, the accessibility of brand attitudes, and the consistency of brand image with consumers.

   This chapter considers techniques related to the other three categories of methods.

5. Jennifer E. Breneiser and Sarah N. Allen, "Taste Preference for Brand Name versus Store Brand Sodas," *North American Journal of Psychology* 13, no. 2 (2011): 281–290.

6. Julian Clover, "Virgin Connects Mobile Network with Orange," *Broadband TV News*, 10 October 2011; Chris Martin, "Virgin Media Mobile Customers Will Get Orange Network Coverage," *The Inquirer*, 7 October 2011; www.virginmobile.com.

7. Edgar Pessemier, "A New Way to Determine Buying Decisions," *Journal of Marketing* 24 (1959): 41–46.

8. Björn Höfer and Volker Bosch, "Brand Equity Measurement with GfK Price Challenger, *Yearbook of Marketing and Consumer Research*, Vol. 5 (2007): 21–39.

9. Paul E. Green and V. Srinivasan, "Conjoint Analysis in Consumer Research: Issues and outlook," *Journal of Consumer Research* 5 (1978): 103–123; Paul E. Green and V. Srinivasan, "Conjoint Analysis in Marketing: New Developments with Implications for Research and Practice," *Journal of Marketing* 54 (1990): 3–19; David Bakken and Curtis Frazier, "Conjoint Analysis: Understanding Consumer Decision Making," Chapter 15 in *Handbook of Marketing Research: Uses, Misuses, and Future Advances*, eds. Rajiv Grover and Marco Vriens (Thousand Oaks, CA: Sage Publications, 2006): 288–311.

10. For more details, see Betsy Sharkey, "The People's Choice," *Adweek*, 27 November 1989, MRC 8.

11. Paul E. Green and Yoram Wind, "New Ways to Measure Consumers' Judgments," *Harvard Business Review* 53 (July–August 1975): 107–111.

12. Jerry Wind, Paul E. Green, Douglas Shifflet, and Marsha Scarbrough, "Courtyard by Marriott: Designing a Hotel Facility with Consumer-Based Marketing Models," *Interfaces* 19 (January–February 1989): 25–47.

13. Max Blackstone, "Price Trade-Offs as a Measure of Brand Value," *Journal of Advertising Research* (August/September 1990): RC3–RC6.

14. Arvind Rangaswamy, Raymond R. Burke, and Terence A. Oliva, "Brand Equity and the Extendibility of Brand Names," *International Journal of Research in Marketing* 10 (March 1993): 61–75. See also Moonkyu Lee, Jonathan Lee, and Wagner A. Kamakura, "Consumer Evaluations of Line Extensions: A Conjoint Approach," in *Advances in Consumer Research*, Vol. 23

(Ann Arbor, MI: Association of Consumer Research, 1996), 289–295.

15. Howard Barich and V. Srinivasan, "Prioritizing Marketing Image Goals under Resource Constraints," *Sloan Management Review* (Summer 1993): 69–76.

16. Marco Vriens and Curtis Frazier, "The Hard Impact of the Soft Touch: How to Use Brand Positioning Attributes in Conjoint," *Marketing Research* (Summer 2003): 23–27.

17. Nicholas Rubino, "McComb Played a Bad Hand Well," *Wall Street Journal*," 20 October 2011; Dana Mattiolo, "Liz Claiborne Must Say Adieu to Liz," *Wall Street Journal*, 13 October 2011; Associated Press, "Liz Claiborne to Sell Several Brands, Change Name, *USA Today*, 12 October 2011.

18. V. Srinivasan, "Network Models for Estimating Brand-Specific Effects in Multi-Attribute Marketing Models," *Management Science* 25 (January 1979): 11–21; V. Srinivasan, Chan Su Park, and Dae Ryun Chang, "An Approach to the Measurement, Analysis, and Prediction of Brand Equity and Its Sources," *Management Science* 51, no. 9 (September 2005): 1433–1448.

19. Wagner A. Kamakura and Gary J. Russell, "Measuring Brand Value with Scanner Data," *International Journal of Research in Marketing* 10 (1993): 9–22.

20. Kusum Ailawadi, Donald R. Lehmann, and Scott A. Neslin, "Revenue Premium as an Outcome Measure of Brand Equity," *Journal of Marketing* 67 (October 2003): 1–17. See also Avi Goldfarb, Qiang Lu, and Sridhar Moorthy, "Measuring Brand Value in an Equilibrium Framework," *Marketing Science* 28 (January–February 2009): 69–86; C. Whan Park, Deborah J. MacInnis, Xavier Dreze, and Jonathan Lee, "Measuring Brand Equity: The Marketing Surplus & Efficiency (MARKSURE)–Based Brand Equity Measure," in *Brands and Brand Management: Contemporary Research Perspectives*, eds. Barbara Loken, Rohini Ahluwalia, and Michael J. Houston (London: Taylor and Francis Group Publishing, 2010), 159–188.

21. S. Sriram, Subramanian Balachander, and Manohar U. Kalwani, "Monitoring the Dynamics of Brand Equity Using Store-level Data," *Journal of Marketing* 71 (April 2007): 61–78.

22. Joffre Swait, Tülin Erdem, Jordan Louviere, and Chris Dubelar, "The Equalization Price: A Measure of Consumer-Perceived Brand Equity," *International Journal of Research in Marketing* 10 (1993): 23–45; Tülin Erdem and Joffre Swait, "Brand Equity as a Signaling Phenomenon," *Journal of Consumer Psychology* 7, no. 2 (1998): 131–157; Tülin Erdem, Joffre Swait, and Ana Valenzuela, "Brands as Signals: A Cross-Country Validation Study," *Journal of Marketing* 70 (January 2006): 34–49; Joffre Swait and Tülin Erdem, "Characterizing Brand Effects on Choice Set Formation and Preference Discrimination Under Uncertainty," *Marketing Science* 26 (September–October 2007): 679–697.

23. See also Eric L. Almquist, Ian H. Turvill, and Kenneth J. Roberts, "Combining Economic Analysis for Breakthrough Brand Management," *Journal of Brand Management* 5, no. 4 (1998): 272–282.

24. V. Srinivasan, Chan Su Park, and Dae Ryun Chang, "An Approach to the Measurement, Analysis, and Prediction of Brand Equity and Its Sources," *Management Science* 51 (September 2005): 1433–1448. See also Chan Su Park and V. Srinivasan, "A Survey-Based Method for Measuring and Understanding Brand Equity and Its Extendability," *Journal of Marketing Research* 31 (May 1994): 271–288. See also Na Woon Bong, Roger Marshall, and Kevin Lane Keller, "Measuring Brand Power: Validating a Model for Optimizing Brand Equity," *Journal of Product and Brand Management* 8, no. 3 (1999): 170–184; Randle Raggio and Robert P. Leone, "Producing a Measure of Brand Equity by Decomposing Brand Beliefs into Brand and Attribute Sources," ICFAI Press, 2007.

25. William R. Dillon, Thomas J. Madden, Amna Kirmani, and Soumen Mukherjee, "Understanding What's in a Brand Rating: A Model for Assessing Brand and Attribute Effects and Their Relationship to Brand Equity," *Journal of Marketing Research* 38 (November 2001): 415–429.

26. Patrick Barwise (with Christopher Higson, Andrew Likierman, and Paul Marsh), "Brands as 'Separable Assets,'" *Business Strategy Review* (Summer 1990): 49.

27. "The Battle for the Best," *The Economist*, 16 November 2006; John Gerzema and Edward Lebar, "The Danger of a Brand Bubble," *Market Leader* (Quarter 4, 2009): 30–34; John Gerzema and Edward Lebar, *The Brand Bubble: The Looming Crisis in Brand Value and How to Avoid It* (San Francisco: Jossey-Bass, 2008); www.brandfinance.com.

28. For some accounting perspectives on intangible assets, see Baruch Lev, *Intangibles: Management, Measurement, and Reporting* (Washington, D.C.: Brookings Institution Press, 2001); Leslie A. Robinson and Richard Sansing, "The Effect of 'Invisible' Tax Preferences on Investment and Tax Preference Measures," *Journal of Accounting and Economics* 46 (2008). The helpful input of Richard Sansing on this topic is gratefully acknowledged.

29. Andrew Ross Sorkin and Andrew Martin, "Coca-Cola Agrees to Buy Vitaminwater," *New York Times*, 26 May 2007; "Coca-Cola 2007 Annual Report," www.thecoca-colacompany.com.

30. Bernard Condon, "Gaps in GAAP," *Forbes*, 25 January 1999, 76–80.

31. For a comprehensive and insightful summary of key issues, see Gabriela Salinas, *The International Brand Valuation Manual* (West Sussex, United Kingdom: John Wiley & Sons, 2009), as well as Gabriela Salinas and Tim Ambler, "A Taxonomy of Brand Valuation Practice: Methodologies and Purposes," *Journal of Brand Management* 17 (September 2009): 39–61. Another helpful guide is Jan Lindemann, *The Economy of Brands* (London: Palgrave Macmillan, 2010).

32. Quoted in "What's a Brand Worth? [editorial]," *Advertising Age*, 18 July 1994.

33. Lew Winters, "Brand Equity Measures: Some Recent Advances," *Marketing Research* (December 1991): 70–73; Gordon V. Smith, *Corporate Valuation: A Business and Professional Guide* (New York: John Wiley & Sons, 1988).

34. www.brandfinance.com.

35. The Science of Branding 1 is based on the research and writings of Prophet's Roger Sinclair, whose

considerable input is gratefully acknowledged. For more information, visit www.prophet.com.

36. Investors put capital into a company to ensure it can operate on a day-to-day basis. This money does not come free, as investors expect a return on their investment. While accountants are happy to accept the difference between revenue and expenses as the company's profit, economists believe that true profit is accounting profit less the expected return on the company's capital employed: the investors' funds.

37. Carol J. Simon and Mary W. Sullivan, "Measurement and Determinants of Brand Equity: A Financial Approach," *Marketing Science* 12, no. 1 (Winter 1993): 28–52.

38. Michael Birkin, "Assessing Brand Value," in *Brand Power*, ed. Paul Stobart (Washington Square, NY: New York University Press, 1994).

39. http://www.interbrand.com/en/best-global-brands/best-global-brands-methodology/Overview.aspx; Jan Lindemann, *The Economy of Brands* (London: Palgrave Macmillan, 2010).

40. For example, brand characteristics have been show to improve brand valuation accuracy. See Natalie Mizik and Robert Jacobson, "Valuing Branded Businesses," *Journal of Marketing* 73 (November 2009): 137–153.

41. Diane Summers, "IBM Plunges in Year to Foot of Brand Name Value League," *Financial Times*, 11 July 1994.

42. Peter Fader, course notes, Wharton Business School, University of Pennsylvania, 1998.

43. "On the Brandwagon," *The Economist*, 20 January 1990.

44. Koen Pauwels and Martin Lautman, "What Is Important? Identifying Metrics That Matter," *Journal of Advertising Research* 49 (September 2009), 339–359.

45. For an interesting empirical application, see Manoj K. Agarwal and Vithala Rao, "An Empirical Comparison of Consumer-Based Measures of Brand Equity," *Marketing Letters* 7, no. 3 (1996): 237–247.

46. Fader, course notes.

47. David A. Aaker and Robert Jacobson, "The Financial Information Content of Perceived Quality," *Journal of Marketing Research* 31 (May 1994): 191–201.

48. For a more recent illustration, see Robert A. Peterson and Jaeseok Jeong, "Exploring the Impact of Advertising and R&D Expenditures on Corporate Brand Value and Firm-Level Financial Performance," *Journal of the Academy of Marketing Science* 38, no. 6 (2010): 677–690.

49. David A. Aaker and Robert Jacobson, "The Value Relevance of Brand Attitude in High-Technology Markets," *Journal of Marketing Research* 38 (November 2001): 485–493.

50. M. E. Barth, M. Clement, G. Foster, and R. Kasznik, "Brand Values and Capital Market Valuation," *Review of Accounting Studies* 3 (1998): 41–68.

51. Thomas J. Madden, Frank Fehle, and Susan M. Fournier, "Brands Matter: An Empirical Demonstration of the Creation of Shareholder Value through Brands," *Journal of the Academy of Marketing Science* 34, no. 2 (2006): 224–235; Frank Fehle, Susan M. Fournier, Thomas J. Madden, and David G. Shrider, "Brand Value and Asset Pricing," *Quarterly Journal of Finance & Accounting* 47, no. 1 (2008): 59–82. See also, Lopo L. Rego, Matthew T. Billet, and Neil A. Morgan, "Consumer-Based Brand Equity and Firm Risk," *Journal of Marketing* 73 (November 2009): 47–60.

52. Clas Fornell, Sunil Mithas, Forrest V. Morgeson III, and M. S. Krishnan, "Customer Satisfaction and Stock Prices: High Returns, Low Risk," *Journal of Marketing* 70 (January 2006): 3–14.

53. Vicki Lane and Robert Jacobson, "Stock Market Reactions to Brand Extension Announcements: The Effects of Brand Attitude and Familiarity," *Journal of Marketing* 59 (January 1995): 63–77.

54. Dan Horsky and Patrick Swyngedouw, "Does It Pay to Change Your Company's Name? A Stock Market Perspective," *Marketing Science* (Fall 1987): 320–335.

55. Vithala R. Rao, Manoj K. Agrawal, and Denise Dahlhoff. "How Is Manifested Branding Strategy Related to the Intangible Value of a Corporation?" *Journal of Marketing* 68 (October 2004): 126–141; see also Liwu Hsu, Susan Fournier, and Shuba Srinivasan, "How Brand Portfolio Strategy Affects Firm Value," working paper, 2011, Boston University.

56. Neil A. Morgan and Lopo L. Rego, "Brand Portfolio Strategy and Firm Performance," *Journal of Marketing* 73 (January 2009): 59–74.

57. Natalie Mizik and Robert Jacobson, "Trading Off between Value Creation and Value Appropriation: The Financial Implications of Shifts in Strategic Emphasis," *Journal of Marketing* 67 (January 2003): 63–76; see also V. Kumar and Denish Shah, "Can Marketing Lift Stock Prices?," *MIT Sloan Management Review* (Summer 2011): 24–26.

58. This section based in part on a white paper by Roger Sinclair (www.prophet.com), "The Final Barrier: Marketing and Accounting Converge at the Corporate Finance Interface," as well as his other writings and personal correspondence.

59. http://www.vectorgrader.com/indicators/price-book.html.

60. In February 2006, FASB and IASB signed a memorandum of understanding setting out the relationship priorities that would bring about a harmonization of their respective standards. We refer to the ISAB in this appendix given that the standards involved are largely harmonized.

61. In June 2011, the IASB invited comments on topics that should be included in its three-year research agenda for the period 2012 to 2015. Among others, the Marketing Accountability Standards Board (MASB) submitted a letter arguing that IAS 38 should be on the agenda in order to iron out the variability between the two standards (IFRS 3 and IAS 38). IASB stated that it would reach and announce its decision between March and May 2012. If IAS 38 were to be added to the agenda, experts believe that in all likelihood, brands would be balance sheet items within two to three years regardless of whether they are internally generated or acquired.

CUSTOMER PROFITABILITY

Introduction

Key concepts covered:

Customers, Recency, and Retention

Customer Profit

Customer Lifetime Value

Prospect Value Versus Customer Value

Acquisition Versus Retention Spending

In this chapter, we cover metrics that measure the performance of individual customer relationships. We start with metrics designed to simply count how many customers the firm serves. As this chapter will illustrate, it is far easier to count the number of units sold than to count the number of people or businesses buying those units. Section 2 introduces the concept of customer profit. Just as some brands are more profitable than others, so too are some customer relationships. Whereas customer profit is a metric that summarizes the past financial performance of a customer relationship, customer lifetime value looks forward in an attempt to value existing customer relationships. Section 3 discusses how to calculate and interpret customer lifetime value. One of the more important uses of customer lifetime value is to inform prospecting decisions. Section 4 explains how this can be accomplished and draws the careful distinction between prospect and customer value. Section 5 discusses acquisition and retention spending—two metrics firms track in order to monitor the performance of these two important kinds of marketing spending—spending designed to acquire new customers and spending designed to retain and profit from existing customers.

From Chapter 5 of *Marketing Metrics: The Definitive Guide to Measuring Marketing Performance*, 2/e. Paul W. Farris. Neil T. Bendle. Phillip E. Pfeifer. David J. Reibstein. Copyright © 2010 by Pearson Education. Published by Wharton School Publishing.

	Metric	Construction	Considerations	Purpose
1	Customers	The number of people (businesses) who bought from the firm during a specified time period.	Avoid double counting people who bought more than one product. Carefully define customer as individual/ household/ screen-name/ division who bought/ordered/ registered.	Measure how well the firm is attracting and retaining customers.
1	Recency	The length of time since a customer's last purchase.	In non-contractual situations, the firm will want to track the recency of its customers.	Track changes in number of active customers.
1	Retention Rate	The ratio of customers retained to the number at risk.	Not to be confused with growth (decline) in customer counts. Retention refers only to existing customers in contractual situations.	Track changes in the ability of the firm to retain customers.
2	Customer Profit	The difference between the revenues earned from and the costs associated with the customer relationship during a specified period.	Requires assigning revenues and costs to individual customers.	Allows the firm to identify which customers are profitable and which are not . . . as a precursor to differential treatment designed to improve firm profitability.

	Metric	Construction	Considerations	Purpose
3	Customer Lifetime Value	The present value of the future cash flows attributed to the customer relationship.	Requires a projection of future cash flows from a customer relationship. This will be easier to do in a contractual situation. Formulations of CLV differ with respect to the treatment of the initial margin and acquisition spending.	Customer relationship management decisions should be made with the objective of improving CLV. Acquisition budgeting should be based on CLV.
4	Prospect Lifetime Value	The response rate times the sum of the initial margin and the CLV of the acquired customer minus the cost of the prospecting effort.	There are a variety of equivalent ways to do the calculations necessary to see whether a prospecting effort is worthwhile.	To guide the firm's prospecting decisions. Prospecting is beneficial only if the expected prospect lifetime value is positive.
5	Average Acquisition Cost	The ratio of acquisition spending to the number of new customers acquired.	It is often difficult to isolate acquisition spending from total marketing spending.	To track the cost of acquiring new customers and to compare that cost to the value of the newly acquired customers.
5	Average Retention Cost	The ratio of retention spending to the number of customers retained.	It is often difficult to isolate retention spending from total marketing spending. The average retention cost number is not very useful to help make retention budgeting decisions.	To monitor retention spending on a per-customer basis.

1 Customers, Recency, and Retention

These three metrics are used to count customers and track customer activity irrespective of the number of transactions (or dollar value of those transactions) made by each customer.

A customer is a person or business that buys from the firm.

- **Customer Counts:** *These are the number of customers of a firm for a specified time period.*

- **Recency:** *This refers to the length of time since a customer's last purchase. A six-month customer is someone who purchased from the firm at least once within the last six months.*

- **Retention Rate:** *This is the ratio of the number of retained customers to the number at risk.*

In contractual situations, it makes sense to talk about the number of customers currently under contract and the percentage retained when the contract period runs out.

In non-contractual situations (such as catalog sales), it makes less sense to talk about the *current* number of customers, but instead to count the number of customers of a specified recency.

Purpose: To monitor firm performance in attracting and retaining customers.

Only recently have most marketers worried about developing metrics that focus on individual customers. In order to begin to think about managing individual customer relationships, the firm must first be able to count its customers. Although consistency in counting customers is probably more important than formulating a precise definition, a definition is needed nonetheless. In particular, we think the definition of and the counting of customers will be different in contractual versus non-contractual situations.

Construction

COUNTING CUSTOMERS

In contractual situations, it should be fairly easy to count how many customers are currently under contract at any point in time. For instance, Vodafone Australia,[1] a global mobile phone company, was able to report 2.6 million direct customers at the end of the December quarter.

One complication in counting customers in contractual situations is the handling of contracts that cover two or more individuals. Does a family plan that includes five phones but one bill count as one or five? Does a business-to-business contract with one base fee and charges for each of 1,000 phones in use count as one or 1,000 customers? Does the answer to the previous question depend on whether the individual users pay Vodafone, pay their company, or pay nothing? In situations such as these, the firm must select some standard definition of a customer (policy holder, member) and implement it consistently.

A second complication in counting customers in contractual situations is the treatment of customers with multiple contracts with a single firm. USAA, a global insurance and diversified financial services association, provides insurance and financial services to the U.S. military community and their families. Each customer is considered a member, complete with a unique membership number. This allows USAA to know exactly how many members it has at any time—more than five million at the end of 2004—most of whom avail themselves of a variety of member services.

For other financial services companies, however, counts are often listed separately for each line of business. The 2003 annual report for State Farm Insurance, for example, lists a total of 73.9 million policies and accounts with a pie chart showing the percentage breakdown among auto, homeowners, life, annuities, and so on. Clearly the 73.9 million is a count of policies and not customers. Presumably because some customers use State Farm for auto, home, and life insurance, they get double and even triple counted in the 73.9 million number. Because State Farm knows the names and addresses of all their policyholders, it seems feasible that they could count how many individual customers they serve. The fact that State Farm counts policies and not customers suggests an emphasis on selling policies rather than managing customer relationships.

Finally, we offer an example of a natural gas company that went out of its way to double count customers—defining a customer to be "a consumer of natural gas distributed in any one billing period at one location through one meter. An entity using gas at separate locations is considered a separate customer at each location." For this natural gas company, customers were synonymous with meters. This is probably a great way to view things if your job is to install and service meters. It is not such a great way to view things if your job is to market natural gas.

In non-contractual situations, the ability of the firm to count customers depends on whether individual customers are identifiable. If customers are not identifiable, firms can only count visits or transactions. Because Wal-Mart does not identify its shoppers, its customer counts are nothing more than the number of transactions that go through the cash registers in a day, week, or year. These "traffic" counts are akin to turnstile numbers at sporting events and visits to a Web site. In one sense they count people, but when summed over several periods, they no longer measure separate individuals. So whereas home attendance at Atlanta Braves games in 1993[2] was 3,884,720, the number of people attending one or more Braves games that year was some smaller number.

In non-contractual situations with identifiable customers (direct mail, retailers with frequent shopper cards, warehouse clubs, purchases of rental cars and lodging that require registration), a complication is that customer purchase activity is sporadic. Whereas the *New York Times* knows exactly how many *current* customers (subscribers) it has, the sporadic buying of cataloger L.L.Bean's customers means that it makes no sense to talk about the number of *current* L.L.Bean customers. L.L.Bean will know the number of orders it receives daily, it will know the number of catalogs it mails monthly, but it cannot be expected to know the number of current customers it has because it is difficult to define a "current" customer.

Instead, firms in non-contractual situations count how many customers have bought within a certain period of time. This is the concept of recency —the length of time since the last purchase. Customers of recency one year or less are customers who bought within the last year. Firms in non-contractual situations with identifiable customers will count customers of various recencies.

Recency: *The length of time since a customer's last purchase.*

For example, eBay reported 60.5 million active users in the first quarter of 2005. Active users were defined as the number of users of the eBay platform who bid, bought, or listed an item within the previous 12-month period. They go on to report that 45.1 million active users were reported in the same period a year ago.

Notice that eBay counts "active users" rather than "customers" and uses the concept of recency to track its number of active users across time. The number of active (12-month) users increased from 45.1 million to 60.5 million in one year. This tells the firm that the number of active customers increased due in part to customer acquisition. A measure of how well the firm maintained existing customer relationships is the percentage of the 45.1 million active customers one year ago who were active in the previous 12 months. That ratio measure is similar to retention in that it reflects the percentage of active customers who remained active in the subsequent period.

Retention: Applies to contractual situations in which customers are either retained or not. Customers either renew their magazine subscriptions or let them run out. Customers maintain a checking account with a bank until they close it out. Renters pay rent until they move out. These are examples of pure customer retention situations where customers are either retained or considered lost for good.

In these situations, firms pay close attention to retention rates.

Retention Rate: *The ratio of the number of customers retained to the number at risk.*

If 40,000 subscriptions to *Fortune* magazine are set to expire in July and the publisher convinces 26,000 of those customers to renew, we would say that the publisher retained 65% of its subscribers.

The complement of retention is attrition or churn. The attrition or churn rate for the 40,000 *Fortune* subscribers was 35%.

Notice that this definition of retention is a ratio of the number retained to the number at risk (of not being retained). The key feature of this definition is that a customer must be at risk of leaving in order to be counted as a customer successfully retained. This means that new *Fortune* subscribers obtained during July are not part of the equation, nor are the large number of customers whose subscriptions were set to run out in later months.

Finally, we point out that it sometimes makes better sense to measure retention in "customer time" rather than "calendar time." Rather than ask what the firm's retention rate was in 2004, it may be more informative to ask what percentage of customers surviving for three years were retained throughout year four.

Data Sources, Complications, and Cautions

The ratio of the total number of customers at the end of the period to the number of customers at the beginning of the period is not a retention rate. Retention during the period does affect this ratio, but customer acquisitions also affect the ratio.

The percentage of customers starting the period who remained customers throughout the period is a lot closer to being a retention rate. This percentage would be a true retention rate if all the customers starting the period were at risk of leaving during the period.

Advice on Counting Customers[3]

Defining the customer properly is critical.

Marketers tend to count "customers" in ways that are easy and consequently get the wrong answers. They tend to gloss over the fundamental and critically important step of *defining the customer*. With the wrong definition, counting doesn't matter.

Banks look at "households" because they are "relationship" obsessed (*relationship* being defined as the number of products sold to customers with a common account address). Banks tend to emphasize the number of products sold. No matter that the household may contain a business owner with nearly all the accounts, a spouse who banks mostly elsewhere, and children who do not bank at all. Household in this situation is meaningless. There are at least three "customers" here: business owner (a great customer), spouse (almost a non-customer), and kids (definitely non-customers).

Retailers count transactions or "tickets" (cash register receipts), which may cover stuff sold to Mom, Dad, and the kids, along with Aunt Mary and neighbor Sue. Or, it may reflect a purchase by a spouse who is buying for his or her partner under specific instructions. In this circumstance, the spouse is the real customer, with the other taking on the role of gofer.

Defining the customer is nearly always hard because it requires a clear understanding of both business strategy and buyer behavior.

Not all "customers" are the same.

Attracting and retaining "customers" cannot be measured for management action purposes without understanding the differences between customers. Last year, a major software firm we will call Zapp bought a single copy of a piece of software. Another company we will call Tancat bought 100 copies. Are these both "customers?" Of course not. Tancat is almost certainly a customer that needs to be retained and possibly expanded into other products. Zapp is probably just evaluating the product in order to stay on top of new software concepts and potentially copy it. One option is to follow up with Zapp with their one-copy purchase to see what is really going on. Zapp could become a great "customer" if we understand what motivated their purchase or if we use that purchase to gain a contact base.

Before you count anything, you have to segment your *potential and current* product or service users into groups that can be strategically addressed. Some current buyers like Zapp are actually potential buyers in terms of what you should do about them. You must count buyers and prospects who are *alike* in defined ways.

Where is the "customer?"

Large customers often buy independently from each user location. Is Bank of America the customer, or is each branch office a customer? If Citicorp were to buy centrally, how could you count it as one customer while Bank of America counts as hundreds of customers?

Who is the "customer?"

Defining *who* is the customer is even trickier. Many "customers" are not those who place the order with your salespeople. The real customer is deep within the bowels of the buyer organization, someone who may take a great deal of effort to even identify. The account name may be GM, but the real customer may be Burt Cipher, an engineer in some unknown facility. Or, the Ford buyer may have consolidated orders from several individuals scattered across the country. In this case, Ford is not the customer for anything but billing purposes. So, what do you count?

Even more common is the multi-headed customer. Buying decisions are made by several people. Different people may be central to a decision at different times or for different products. Big companies have sales teams dedicated to selling into such buying groups. Although they may be counted as a single customer, the dynamics of their buying decision is substantially more complicated than decisions made by a single individual.

Apparel retailers who sell pre-teen clothing have at least two customers: Mom and the pre-teen wearer. Do you count one or both as customers? Marketing might want to treat each as a customer for deciding how to design and place ads. The store might treat them both as a single customer or choose the pre-teen as their target.

The key takeaway is that customer definition for counting depends fundamentally on the purpose of the count. You may have to count the same "customer" in different ways for different purposes. There is no universal customer definition.

2   Customer Profit

Customer profit (CP) is the profit the firm makes from serving a customer or customer group over a specified period of time.

Calculating customer profitability is an important step in understanding which customer relationships are better than others. Often, the firm will find that some customer relationships are unprofitable. The firm may be better off (more profitable) without these customers. At the other end, the firm will identify its most profitable customers and be in a position to take steps to ensure the continuation of these most profitable relationships.

Purpose: To identify the profitability of individual customers.

Companies commonly look at their performance in aggregate. A common phrase within a company is something like: "We had a good year, and the business units delivered $400,000 in profits." When customers are considered, it is often using an average such as "We made a profit of $2.50 per customer." Although these can be useful metrics, they sometimes disguise an important fact that not all customers are equal and, worse yet, some are unprofitable. Simply put, rather than measuring the "average customer," we can learn a lot by finding out what each customer contributes to our bottom line.[4]

> **Customer Profitability:** *The difference between the revenues earned from and the costs associated with the customer relationship during a specified period.*

The overall profitability of the company can be improved by treating dissimilar customers differently.

In essence, think of three different tiers of customer:

1. Top Tier customers—**REWARD**: Your most valuable customers are the ones you most want to retain. They should receive more of your attention than any other group. If you lose these guys, your profit suffers the most. Look to reward them in ways other than simply lowering your price. These customers probably value what you do the most and may not be price-sensitive.

2. Second Tier customers—**GROW**: The customers in the middle—with middle to low profits associated with them—might be targeted for growth. Here you have customers whom you may be able to develop into Top Tier customers. Look to the share of customer metrics described in Section 3 to help figure out which customers have the most growth potential.

3. Third Tier customers—**FIRE**: The company loses money on servicing these people. If you cannot easily promote them to the higher tiers of profitability, you should consider charging them more for the services they currently consume. If you can recognize this group beforehand, it may be best not to acquire these customers in the first place.

A database that can analyze the profitability of customers at an individual level can be a competitive advantage. If you can figure out profitability by customer, you have a chance to defend your best customers and maybe even poach the most profitable consumers from your competitors.

Construction

In theory, this is a trouble-free calculation. Find out the cost to serve each customer and the revenues associated with each customer for a given period. Do the subtraction to get profit for the customer and sort the customers based on profit. Although painless in theory, large companies with a multitude of customers will find this a major challenge even with the most sophisticated of databases.

To do the analysis with large databases, it may be necessary to abandon the notion of calculating profit for each individual customer and work with meaningful groups of customers instead.

After you have the sorted list of customer profits (or customer-group profits), the custom is to plot cumulative percentage of total profits versus cumulative percentage of total customers. Given that the customers are sorted from highest to lowest profit, the resulting graph usually looks something like the head of a whale.

Profitability will increase sharply and tail off from the very beginning. (Remember, our customers have been sorted from most to least profitable.) Whenever there are some negative profit customers, the graph reaches a peak—above 100%—as profit per customer moves from positive to negative. As we continue through the negative-profit customers, cumulative profits decrease at an ever-increasing rate. The graph always ends at 100% of the customers accounting for 100% of the total profit.

Robert Kaplan (co-developer of Activity-Based Costing and the Balanced Scorecard) likes to refer to these curves as "whale curves."[5] In Kaplan's experience, the whale curve usually reveals that the most profitable 20% of customers can sometimes generate between 150% and 300% of total profits so that the resulting curve resembles a sperm whale rising above the water's surface. See Figure 2 for an example of a whale curve.

EXAMPLE: A catalog retailer has grouped customers in 10 deciles based on profitability (see Table 1 and Figure 1). (A decile is a tenth of the population, so 0-10% is the most profitable 10% of customers.)

Table 1   Customer Profitability Ranked by Profitability

Customers Decile by Profitability	0–10%	10–20%	20–30%	30–40%	40–50%	50–60%	60–70%	70–80%	80–90%	90–100%
Band ($m) Profitability	$100	$50	$25	$10	$5	$3	$2	$0	($8)	($20)
% of Total Profits	60%	30%	15%	6%	3%	2%	1%	0%	−5%	−12%

Here we have a clear illustration that if they were no longer to serve the least profitable 20% of customers, they would be $28 million better off.

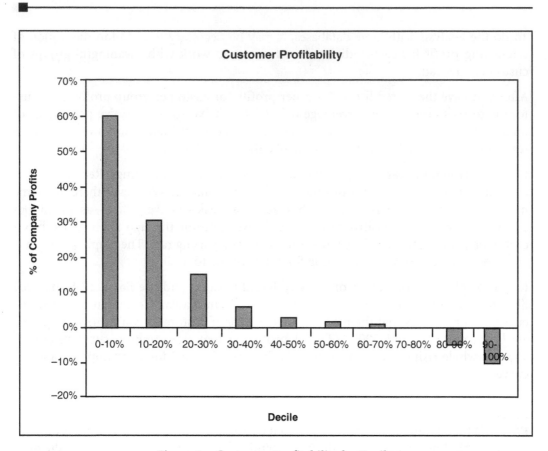

Figure 1   Customer Profitability by Decile

Table 2   Cumulative Profitability Peaks Before All Customers Are Served

Customers Decile by Profitability	0–10%	10–20%	20–30%	30–40%	40–50%	50–60%	60–70%	70–80%	80–90%	90–100%
Cumulative Profits	$100	$150	$175	$185	$190	$193	$195	$195	$187	$167
Cumulative Profits %	59.9	89.8	104.8	110.8	113.8	115.6	116.8	116.8	112.0	100.0

Table 2 presents this same customer information in cumulative form. Cumulative profits plotted across deciles begins to look like a whale with a steeply rising ridge reaching a peak of total profitability above 100% and tapering off thereafter (see Figure 2).

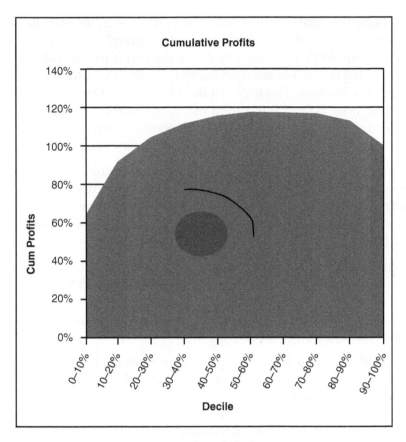

Figure 2   The Whale Curve

Data Sources, Complications, and Cautions

Measuring customer profitability requires detailed information. Assigning revenues to customers is often the easy part; assigning your costs to customers is much harder. The cost of goods sold obviously gets assigned to the customers based on the goods each customer purchased. Assigning the more indirect costs may require the use of some form of activity-based costing (ABC) system. Finally, there may be some categories of costs that will be impossible to assign to the customer. If so, it is probably best to keep these costs as company costs and be content with the customer profit numbers adding up to something less than the total company profit.

When considering the profits from customers, it must be remembered that most things change over time. Customers who were profitable last year may not be profitable this year. Because the whale curve reflects past performance, we must be careful when using it to make decisions that shape the future. For example, we may very well want to continue a relationship that was unprofitable in the past if we know things will change for the better in the future. For example, banks typically offer discount packages to students to gain their business. This may well show low or negative customer profits in the short term. The "plan" is that future profits will compensate for current losses. Customer lifetime value (addressed in Section 3) is a forward-looking metric that attempts to account for the anticipated future profitability of each customer relationship.

When capturing customer information to decide which customers to serve, it is important to consider the legal environment in which the company operates. This can change considerably across countries, where there may be anti-discrimination laws and special situations in some industries. For instance, public utilities are sometimes obligated to serve all customers.

It is also worth remembering that intrusive capturing of customer-specific data can damage customer relationships. Some individuals will be put off by excess data gathering. For a food company, it may help to know which of your customers are on a diet. But the food company's management should think twice before adding this question to their next customer survey.

Sometimes there are sound financial reasons for continuing to serve unprofitable customers. For example, some companies rely on network effects. Take the case of the United States Postal Service—part of its strength is the ability to deliver to the whole country. It may superficially seem profitable to stop deliveries to remote areas. But when that happens, the service becomes less valuable for all customers. In short, sometimes unprofitable customer relationships are necessary for the firm to maintain their profitable ones.

Similarly, companies with high fixed costs that have been assigned to customers during the construction of customer profit must ask whether those costs will go away if they terminate unprofitable customer relationships. If the costs do not go away, ending unprofitable relationships may only serve to make the surviving relationships look even less profitable (after the reallocation of costs) and result in the lowering of company profits. In short, make certain that the negative profit goes away if the relationship is terminated. Certainly the revenue and cost of goods sold will go away, but if some of the other costs do not, the firm could be better off maintaining a negative profit relationship as it contributes to covering fixed cost.

Abandoning customers is a very sensitive practice, and a business should always consider the public relations consequences of such actions. Similarly, when you get rid of a customer, you cannot expect to attract them back very easily should they migrate into your profitable segment.

Finally, because the whale curve examines cumulative *percentage* of total profits, the numbers are very sensitive to the dollar amount of total profit. When the total dollar profit is a small number, it is fairly easy for the most profitable customers to represent a huge *percentage* of that small number. So when you hear that 20% of the firm's customers represent 350% of the firm's profit, one of the first things you should consider is the total dollar value of profits. If that total is small, 350% of it can also be a fairly small number of dollars. To cement this idea, ask yourself what the whale curve would look like for a firm with $0 profit.

3   Customer Lifetime Value

Customer lifetime value is the dollar value of a customer relationship based on the present value of the projected future cash flows from the customer relationship.

When margins and retention rates are constant, the following formula can be used to calculate the lifetime value of a customer relationship:

$$\text{Customer Lifetime Value (\$)} = \text{Margin (\$)} * \frac{\text{Retention Rate (\%)}}{1 + \text{Discount Rate (\%)} - \text{Retention Rate (\%)}}$$

Customer lifetime value (CLV) is an important concept in that it encourages firms to shift their focus from quarterly profits to the long-term health of their customer relationships. Customer lifetime value is an important number because it represents an upper limit on spending to acquire new customers.

Purpose: To assess the value of each customer.

As Don Peppers and Martha Rogers are fond of saying, "some customers are more equal than others."[6] We saw a vivid illustration of this in the last section, which examined the profitability of individual customer relationships. As we noted, customer profit (CP) is the difference between the revenues and the costs associated with the customer relationship during a specified period. The central difference between CP and customer lifetime value (CLV) is that CP measures the past and CLV looks forward. As such, CLV can be more useful in shaping managers' decisions but is much more difficult to quantify. Quantifying CP is a matter of carefully reporting and summarizing the results of past activity, whereas quantifying CLV involves forecasting future activity.

> **Customer Lifetime Value (CLV):** *The present value of the future cash flows attributed to the customer relationship.*

You can think of present value as the discounted sum of future cash flows. We discount (multiply by a carefully selected number less than one) future cash flows before we add them together to account for the fact that there is a time value of money. The time value of money is another way of saying that everyone would prefer to get paid sooner rather than later and everyone would prefer to pay later rather than sooner. This is true for individuals (the sooner I get paid, the sooner I can pay down my credit card balance and avoid interest charges) as well as for firms. The exact discount factors used depend on the discount rate chosen (10% per year as an example) and the number of periods until we receive each cash flow (dollars received 10 years from now must be discounted more than dollars received five years in the future).

The concept of CLV is nothing more than the concept of present value applied to cash flows attributed to the customer relationship. Because the present value of any stream of future cash flows is designed to measure the single lump sum value today of the future stream of cash flows, CLV will represent the single lump sum value today of the customer relationship. Even more simply, CLV is the dollar value of the customer relationship to the firm. It is an upper limit on what the firm would be willing to pay to acquire the customer relationship as well as an upper limit on the amount the firm would be willing to pay to avoid losing the customer relationship. If we view a customer relationship as an asset of the firm, CLV would present the dollar value of that asset.

COHORT AND INCUBATE

One way to project the value of future customer cash flows is to make the heroic assumption that the customers acquired several periods ago are no better or worse (in terms of their CLV) than the ones we currently acquire. We then go back and collect data on a cohort of customers all acquired at about the same time and carefully reconstruct their cash flows over some finite number of periods. The next step is to discount the cash flows for each customer back to the time of acquisition to calculate that customer's sample CLV and then average all of the sample CLVs together to produce an estimate of the CLV of each newly acquired customer. We refer to this method as the "cohort and incubate" approach. Equivalently, one can calculate the present value of the *total* cash flows from the cohort and divide by the number of customers to get the average CLV for the cohort. If the value of customer relationships is stable across time, the average CLV of the cohort sample is an appropriate estimator of the CLV of newly acquired customers.

As an example of this cohort and incubate approach, Berger, Weinberg, and Hanna (2003) followed all the customers acquired by a cruise-ship line in 1993. The 6,094 customers in the cohort of 1993 were tracked (incubated) for five years. The total net present value of the cash flows from these customers was $27,916,614. These flows included revenues from the cruises taken (the 6,094 customers took 8,660 cruises over the five-year horizon), variable cost of the cruises, and promotional costs. The total five-year net present value of the cohort expressed on a per-customer basis came out to be $27,916,614/6,094 or $4,581 per customer. This is the average five-year CLV for the cohort.

> *"Prior to this analysis, [cruise-line] management would never spend more than $3,314 to acquire a passenger . . . Now, aware of CLV (both the concept and the actual numerical results), an advertisement that [resulted in a cost per acquisition of $3 to $4 thousand] was welcomed—especially because the CLV numbers are conservative (again, as noted, the CLV does not include any residual business after five years.)"*[7]

The cohort and incubate approach works well when customer relationships are stationary—changing slowly over time. When the value of relationships changes slowly, we can use the value of incubated past relationships as predictive of the value of new relationships.

In situations where the value of customer relationships changes more rapidly, firms often use a simple model to forecast the value of those relationships. By a model, we mean some assumptions about how the customer relationship will unfold. If the model is simple enough, it may even be possible to find an equation for the present value of our model of future cash flows. This makes the calculation of CLV even easier because it now requires only the substitution of numbers for our situation into the equation for CLV.

Next, we will explain what is perhaps the simplest model for future customer cash flows and the equation for the present value of those cash flows. Although it's not the only model of future customer cash flows, this one gets used the most.

Construction

The model for customer cash flows treats the firm's customer relationships as something of a leaky bucket. Each period, a fraction (1 less the retention rate) of the firm's customers leave and are lost for good.

The CLV model has only three parameters: 1) constant margin (contribution after deducting variable costs including retention spending) per period, 2) constant retention probability per period, and 3) discount rate. Furthermore, the model assumes that in the event that the customer is not retained, they are lost for good. Finally, the model assumes that the first margin will be received (with probability equal to the retention rate) at the end of the first period.

The one other assumption of the model is that the firm uses an infinite horizon when it calculates the present value of future cash flows. Although no firm actually has an infinite horizon, the consequences of assuming one are discussed in the following.

Customer Lifetime Value: The CLV formula[8] multiplies the per-period cash margin (hereafter we will just use the term "margin") by a factor that represents the present value of the expected length of the customer relationship:

$$\text{Customer Lifetime Value (\$)} = \text{Margin (\$)} * \frac{\text{Retention Rate (\%)}}{1 + \text{Discount Rate (\%)} - \text{Retention Rate (\%)}}$$

Under the assumptions of the model, CLV is a multiple of the margin. The multiplicative factor represents the present value of the expected length (number of periods) of the customer relationship. When retention equals 0, the customer will never be retained, and the multiplicative factor is zero. When retention equals 1, the customer is always retained, and the firm receives the margin in perpetuity. The present value of the margin in perpetuity turns out to be Margin/Discount Rate. For retention values in between, the CLV formula tells us the appropriate multiplier.

EXAMPLE: An Internet Service Provider (ISP) charges $19.95 per month. Variable costs are about $1.50 per account per month. With marketing spending of $6 per year, their attrition is only 0.5% per month. At a monthly discount rate of 1%, what is the CLV of a customer?

$$\text{Contribution Margin} = (\$19.95 - \$1.50 - \$6/12) = \$17.95$$
$$\text{Retention Rate} = 0.995$$
$$\text{Discount Rate} = 0.01$$

$$\text{Customer Lifetime Value (CLV)} = \text{Margin} * \frac{\text{Retention Rate (\%)}}{1 + \text{Discount Rate (\%)} - \text{Retention Rate (\%)}}$$

$$\text{CLV} = \$17.95 * [0.995/(1 + 0.01 - 0.995)]$$
$$\text{CLV} = [\$17.95] * [66.33]$$
$$\text{CLV} = \$1,191$$

Data Sources, Complications, and Cautions

The retention rate (and by extension the attrition rate) is a driver of customer value. Very small changes can make a major difference to the lifetime value calculated. Accuracy in this parameter is vital to meaningful results.

The retention rate is assumed to be constant across the life of the customer relationship. For products and services that go through a trial, conversion, and loyalty progression, retention rates will increase over the lifetime of the relationship. In those situations, the model explained here might be too simple. If the firm wants to estimate a sequence of retention rates, a spreadsheet model might be more useful in calculating CLV.

The discount rate is also a sensitive driver of the lifetime value calculation—as with retention, seemingly small changes can make major differences to customer lifetime value. The discount rate should be chosen with care.

The contribution is assumed to be constant across time. If margin is expected to increase over the lifetime of the customer relationship, the simple model will not apply.

Take care not to use this CLV formula for relationships in which customer inactivity does not signal the end of the relationship. In catalog sales, for example, a small percentage of the firm's customers purchase from any given catalog. Don't confuse the percentage of customers active in a given period (relevant for the cataloger) with the retention rates in this model. If customers often return to do business with the firm after a period of inactivity, this CLV formula does not apply.

Customer Lifetime Value (CLV) with Initial Margin: One final source of confusion concerns the timing assumptions inherent in the model. The first cash flow accounted for in the model is the margin received at the end of one period with probability equal to the retention rate. Other models also include an initial margin received at the beginning of the period. If a certain receipt of an initial margin is included, the new CLV will equal the old CLV plus the initial margin. Furthermore, if the initial margin is equal to all subsequent margins, there are at least two ways to write formulas for the CLV that include the initial margin:

$$\text{CLV with Initial Margin (\$)} = \text{Margin (\$)} + \text{Margin (\$)} * \frac{\text{Retention Rate (\%)}}{1 + \text{Discount Rate (\%)} - \text{Retention Rate (\%)}}$$

or

$$= \text{Margin (\$)} * \frac{1 + \text{Discount Rate (\%)}}{1 + \text{Discount Rate (\%)} - \text{Retention Rate (\%)}}$$

The second formula looks just like the original formula with $1 + $ Discount Rate taking the place of the retention rate in the numerator of the multiplicative factor. Just remember that the new CLV formula and the original CLV formula apply to the same situations and differ only in the treatment of an initial margin. This new CLV formula includes it, whereas the original CLV formula does not.

THE INFINITE HORIZON ASSUMPTION

In some industries and companies it is typical to calculate four- or five-year customer values instead of using the infinite time horizon inherent in the previous formulas. Of course, over shorter periods customer retention rates are less likely to be affected by major shifts in technology or competitive strategies and are more likely to be captured by historical retention rates. For managers, the question is "Does it make a difference whether I use the infinite time horizon or (for example) the five-year customer value?" The answer to this question is yes, sometimes, it can make a difference because the value over five years can be less than 70% of the value over an infinite horizon (see Table 3).

Table 3 calculates the percentages of (infinite horizon) CLV accruing in the first five years. If retention rates are higher than 80% and discount rates are lower than 20%, differences in the two approaches will be substantial. Depending on the strategic risks that companies perceive, the additional complexities of using a finite horizon can be informative.

Table 3   Finite-Horizon CLV As a Percentage of Infinite-Horizon CLV

Percent of CLV Accruing in First Five Years

Discount Rates	Retention Rates					
	40%	50%	60%	70%	80%	90%
2%	99%	97%	93%	85%	70%	47%
4%	99%	97%	94%	86%	73%	51%
6%	99%	98%	94%	87%	76%	56%
8%	99%	98%	95%	89%	78%	60%
10%	99%	98%	95%	90%	80%	63%
12%	99%	98%	96%	90%	81%	66%
14%	99%	98%	96%	91%	83%	69%
16%	100%	99%	96%	92%	84%	72%
18%	100%	99%	97%	93%	86%	74%
20%	100%	99%	97%	93%	87%	76%

4   Prospect Lifetime Value Versus Customer Value

Prospect lifetime value is the expected value of a prospect. It is the value expected from the prospect minus the cost of prospecting. The value expected from the prospect is the expected fraction of prospects who will make a purchase times the sum of the average margin the firm makes on the initial purchase and the CLV of the newly acquired customer.

Only if prospect lifetime value is positive should the firm proceed with the planned acquisition spending.

Purpose: To account for the lifetime value of a newly acquired customer (CLV) when making prospecting decisions.

One of the major uses of CLV is to inform prospecting decisions. A prospect is someone whom the firm will spend money on in an attempt to acquire her or him as a customer. The acquisition spending must be compared not just to the contribution from the immediate sales it generates but also to the future cash flows expected from the newly acquired customer relationship (the CLV). Only with a full accounting of the value of the newly acquired customer relationship will the firm be able to make an informed, economic prospecting decision.

Construction

The expected prospect lifetime value (PLV) is the value expected from each prospect minus the cost of prospecting. The value expected from each prospect is the acquisition rate (the expected fraction of prospects who will make a purchase and become customers) times the sum of the initial margin the firm makes on the initial purchases and the CLV. The cost is the amount of acquisition spending per prospect. The formula for expected PLV is as follows:

$$\textbf{Prospect Lifetime Value (\$)} = \textbf{Acquisition Rate (\%)} * [\textbf{Initial Margin (\$)} + \textbf{CLV (\$)}] \\ - \textbf{Acquisition Spending (\$)}$$

If PLV is positive, the acquisition spending is a wise investment. If PLV is negative, the acquisition spending should not be made.

The PLV number will usually be very small. Although CLV is sometimes in the hundreds of dollars, PLV can come out to be only a few pennies. Just remember that PLV applies to prospects, not customers. A large number of small but positive-value prospects can add to a considerable amount of value for a firm.

EXAMPLE: A service company plans to spend $60,000 on an advertisement reaching 75,000 readers. If the service company expects the advertisement to convince 1.2% of the readers to take advantage of a special introductory offer (priced so low that the firm makes only $10 margin on this initial purchase) and the CLV of the acquired customers is $100, is the advertisement economically attractive?

Here Acquisition Spending is $0.80 per prospect, the expected acquisition rate is 0.012, and the initial margin is $10. The expected PLV of each of the 75,000 prospects is

$$PLV = 0.012 * (\$10 + \$100) - \$0.80$$
$$= \$0.52$$

The expected PLV is $0.52. The total expected value of the prospecting effort will be 75,000 * $0.52 = $39,000. The proposed acquisition spending *is* economically attractive.

If we are uncertain about the 0.012 acquisition rate, we might ask what the acquisition rate from the prospecting campaign must be in order for it to be economically successful. We can get that number using Excel's goal seek function to find the acquisition rate that sets PLV to zero. Or we can use a little algebra and substitute $0 in for PLV and solve for the break-even acquisition rate:

$$\text{Break-Even Acquisition Rate} = \frac{\text{Acquisition Spending (\$)}}{\text{Initial Margin (\$)} + \text{CLV (\$)}}$$

$$= \frac{\$0.80}{\$10 + \$100} = 0.007273$$

The acquisition rate must exceed 0.7273% in order for the campaign to be successful.

Data Sources, Complications, and Cautions

In addition to the CLV of the newly acquired customers, the firm needs to know the planned amount of acquisition spending (expressed on a per-prospect basis), the expected success rate (the fraction of prospects expected to become customers), and the average margin the firm will receive from the initial purchases of the newly acquired customers. The initial margin number is needed because CLV as defined in the previous section accounts for only the future cash flows from the relationship. The initial cash flow is not included in CLV and must be accounted for separately. Note also that the initial margin must account for any first-period retention spending.

Perhaps the biggest challenge in calculating PLV is estimating CLV. The other terms (acquisition spending, acquisition rate, and initial margin) all refer to flows or outcomes in the near future, whereas CLV requires longer-term projections.

Another caution worth mentioning is that the decision to spend money on customer acquisition whenever PLV is positive rests on an assumption that the customers acquired would not have been acquired had the firm not spent the money. In other words, our approach gives the acquisition spending "full credit" for the subsequent customers acquired. If the firm has several simultaneous acquisition efforts, dropping one of them might lead to increased acquisition rates for the others. Situations such as these (where one solicitation cannibalizes another) require a more complicated analysis.

The firm must be careful to search for the most economical way to acquire new customers. If there are alternative prospecting approaches, the firm must be careful not to simply go with the first one that gives a positive projected PLV. Given a limited number of prospects, the approach that gives the highest expected PLV should be used.

Finally, we want to warn you that there are other ways to do the calculations necessary to judge the economic viability of a given prospecting effort. Although these other approaches are equivalent to the one presented here, they differ with respect to what gets included in "CLV." Some will include the initial margin as part of "CLV." Others will include both the initial margin and the expected acquisition cost per acquired customer as part of "CLV." We illustrate these two approaches using the service company example.

EXAMPLE: A service company plans to spend $60,000 on an advertisement reaching 75,000 readers. If the service company expects the advertisement to convince 1.2% of the readers to take advantage of a special introductory offer (priced so low that the firm makes only $10 margin on this initial purchase) and the CLV of the acquired customers is $100, is the advertisement economically attractive?

If we include the initial margin in "CLV" we get

$$\text{"CLV" [with Initial Margin (\$)]} = \text{Initial Margin (\$)} + \text{CLV (\$)}$$
$$= \$10 + \$110 = \$110$$

The expected PLV is now

$$\text{PLV (\$)} = \text{Acquisition Rate (\%)} * \text{"CLV" [with Initial Margin (\$)]} - \text{Acquisition Cost (\$)}$$
$$= 0.012 * \$110 - \$0.85 = \$0.52$$

This is the same number as before calculated using a slightly different "CLV"—one that includes the initial margin.

We illustrate one final way to do the calculations necessary to judge the economics of a prospecting campaign. This last way does things on a per-acquired-customer basis using a "CLV" that includes both initial margin and an allocated acquisition spending. The thinking goes as follows: The expected value of a new customer is $10 now plus $100 from future sales, or $110 in total. The expected cost to acquire a customer is the total cost of the campaign divided by the expected number of new customers. This average acquisition cost is calculated as $60,000/(0.012 * 75,000) = 66.67. The expected value of a new customer net of the expected acquisition cost per customer is $110 − $66.67 = 43.33. Because this new "net" CLV is positive, the campaign is economically attractive. Some will even label this $43.33 number as the "CLV" of a new customer.

Notice that $43.33 times the 900 expected new customers equals $39,000, the same total net value from the campaign calculated in the original example as the $0.52 PLV times the 75,000 prospects. The two ways to do the calculations are equivalent.

5   Acquisition Versus Retention Cost

The firm's average acquisition cost is the ratio of acquisition spending to the number of customers acquired. The average retention cost is the ratio of retention spending directed toward a group of customers to the number of those customers successfully retained.

$$\text{Average Acquisition Cost (\$)} = \frac{\text{Acquisition Spending (\$)}}{\text{Number of Customers Acquired (\#)}}$$

$$\text{Average Retention Cost (\$)} = \frac{\text{Retention Spending (\$)}}{\text{Number of Customers Retained (\#)}}$$

These two metrics help the firm monitor the effectiveness of two important categories of marketing spending.

Purpose: To determine the firm's cost of acquisition and retention.

Before the firm can optimize its mix of acquisition and retention spending, it must first assess the status quo. At the current spending levels, how much does it cost the firm (on average) to acquire new customers, and how much is it spending (on average) to retain its existing customers? Does it cost five times as much to acquire a new customer as it does to retain an existing one?

Construction

Average Acquisition Cost: *This represents the average cost to acquire a customer and is the total acquisition spending divided by the number of new customers acquired.*

$$\text{Average Acquisition Cost (\$)} = \frac{\text{Acquisition Spending (\$)}}{\text{Number of Customers Acquired (\#)}}$$

Average Retention Cost: *This represents the average "cost" to retain an existing customer and is the total retention spending divided by the number of customers retained.*

$$\text{Average Retention Cost (\$)} = \frac{\text{Retention Spending (\$)}}{\text{Number of Customers Retained (\#)}}$$

EXAMPLE: During the past year, a regional pest control service spent $1.4 million and acquired 64,800 new customers. Of the 154,890 customer relationships in existence at the start of the year, only 87,957 remained at the end of the year, despite about $500,000 spent during the year in attempts to retain the 154,890 customers. The calculation of average acquisition cost is relatively straightforward. A total of $1.4 million resulted in 64,800 new customers. The average acquisition cost is $1,400/64.8 = $21.60 per customer. The calculation of average retention cost is also straightforward. A total of $500,000 resulted in 87,957 retained customers. The average yearly retention cost is $500,000/87,957 = $5.68. Thus, for the pest control firm, it cost about *four* times as much to acquire a new customer as it did to retain an existing one.

Data Sources, Complications, and Cautions

For any specific period, the firm needs to know the total amount it spent on customer acquisition and the number of new customers that resulted from that spending. With respect to customer retention, the firm needs to measure the total amount spent during the period attempting to retain the customers in existence at the start of the period and the number of the existing customers successfully retained at the end of the period. Notice that retention spending directed at customers acquired within the period is not included in this figure. Similarly, the number retained refers only to those retained from the pool of customers in existence at the start of the period. Thus, the average retention cost calculated will be associated with the length of the period in question. If the period is a year, the average retention cost will be a cost per year per customer retained.

The calculation and interpretation of average acquisition cost is much easier than the calculation and interpretation of average retention cost. This is so because it is often possible to isolate acquisition spending and count the number of new customers that resulted from that spending. A simple division results in the average cost to acquire a customer. The reasonable assumption underlying this calculation is that the new customers would not have been acquired had it not been for the acquisition spending.

Things are not nearly so clear when it comes to average retention cost. One source of difficulty is that retention rates (and costs) depend on the period of time under consideration. Yearly retention is different from monthly retention. The cost to retain a customer for a month will be less than the cost to retain a customer for a year. Thus, the definition of average retention cost requires a specification of the time period associated with the retention.

A second source of difficulty stems from the fact that some customers will be retained even if the firm spends nothing on retention. For this reason it can be a little misleading to call the ratio of retention spending to the number of retained customers the average retention cost. One must not jump to the conclusion that retention goes away if the retention spending goes away. Nor should one assume that if the firm increases the retention budget by the average retention cost that it will retain one more customer. The average retention cost number is not very useful to help make retention budgeting decisions.

One final caution involves the firm's capability to separate spending into acquisition and retention classifications. Clearly there can be spending that works to improve both the acquisition and retention efforts of the firm. General brand advertisements, for example, serve to lower the cost of both acquisition and retention. Rather than attempt to allocate all spending as either acquisition or retention, we suggest that it is perfectly acceptable to maintain a separate category that is neither acquisition nor retention.

References and Suggested Further Reading

Berger, Weinberg, and Hanna. (2003). "Customer Lifetime Value Determination and Strategic Implications for a Cruise-Ship Line," *Database Marketing and Customer Strategy Management,* 11(1).

Blattberg, R.C., and S.J. Hoch. (1990). "Database Models and Managerial Intuition: 50% Model + 50% Manager," *Management Science,* 36(8), 887–899.

Gupta, S., and Donald R. Lehmann. (2003). "Customers As Assets," *Journal of Interactive Marketing,* 17(1).

Kaplan, R.S., and V.G. Narayanan. (2001). "Measuring and Managing Customer Profitability," *Journal of Cost Management,* September/October: 5–15.

Little, J.D.C. (1970). "Models and Managers: The Concept of a Decision Calculus," *Management Science,* 16(8), B-466; B-485.

McGovern, G.J., D. Court, J.A. Quelch, and B. Crawford. (2004). "Bringing Customers into the Boardroom," *Harvard Business Review,* 82(11), 70–80.

Much, J.G., Lee S. Sproull, and Michal Tamuz. (1989). "Learning from Samples of One or Fewer," *Organization Science: A Journal of the Institute of Management Sciences,* 2(1), 1–12.

Peppers, D., and M. Rogers. (1997). *Enterprise One-to-One: Tools for Competing in the Interactive Age* (1st ed.), New York: Currency Doubleday.

Pfeifer, P.E., M.E. Haskins, and R.M. Conroy. (2005). "Customer Lifetime Value, Customer Profitability, and the Treatment of Acquisition Spending," *Journal of Managerial Issues,* 17(1), 11–25.

ENDNOTES

1. "Vodafone Australia Gains Customers," *Sydney Morning Herald*, January 26, 2005.

2. "Atlanta Braves Home Attendance." Wikipedia, the free encyclopedia. http://en.wikipedia.org/wiki/Major_League_Baseball_attendance_records

3. Thanks to Gerry Allan, President, Anametrica, Inc. (developer of Web-based tools for managers) for his work on this section.

4. Pfeifer, P.E., Haskins, M.E., and Conroy, R.M. (2005). "Customer Lifetime Value, Customer Profitability, and the Treatment of Acquisition Spending," *Journal of Managerial Issues*, 25 pages.

5. Kaplan, R.S., and V.G. Narayanan. (2001). "Measuring and Managing Customer Profitability," *Journal of Cost Management*, September/October, 5–15.

6. Peppers, D., and M. Rogers. (1997). *Enterprise One to One: Tools for Competing in the Interactive Age*, New York: Currency Doubleday.

7. Berger, P.D., B. Weinberg, and R. Hanna. (2003). "Customer Lifetime Value Determination and Strategic Implications for a Cruise-Ship Line," *Database Marketing and Customer Strategy Management*, 11(1), 40–52.

8. Gupta and Lehman. (2003). "Customers as Assets," *Journal of Interactive Marketing*, 17(1), 9–24.

SALES FORCE AND CHANNEL MANAGEMENT

Introduction

Key concepts covered:

Sales Force Coverage	Facings and Share of Shelf
Sales Force Goals	Out-of-Stock and Service Levels
Sales Force Results	Inventory Turns
Sales Force Compensation	Markdowns
Pipeline Analysis	Gross Margin Return on Inventory Investment (GMROII)
Numeric Distribution, ACV Distribution, and PCV Distribution	Direct Product Profitability (DPP)

This chapter deals with push marketing. It describes how marketers measure the adequacy and effectiveness of the systems that provide customers with reasons and opportunities to buy their products.

The first sections discuss sales force metrics. Here, we list and define the most common measures for determining whether sales force effort and geographic coverage are adequate. We discuss pipeline analysis, which is useful in making sales forecasts and in allocating sales force effort to different stages of the selling process. Pipeline metrics are used to examine a sequence of selling activities, from lead generation, through follow-up, to conversion and sales. Although the most important of these represents the

From Chapter 6 of *Marketing Metrics: The Definitive Guide to Measuring Marketing Performance,* 2/e.
Paul W. Farris. Neil T. Bendle. Phillip E. Pfeifer. David J. Reibstein. Copyright © 2010 by Pearson Education.
Published by Wharton School Publishing.

percentage of initial leads who ultimately buy, other measures of activity, productivity, efficiency, and cost can be useful at each stage of the selling process.

In further sections of this chapter, we discuss measures of product distribution and availability. For manufacturers who approach their market through resellers, three key metrics provide an indication of "listings"—the percentage of potential outlets that stock their products. These include numeric distribution, which is unweighted; ACV, the industry standard; and PCV, a category-specific measure of product availability.

Marketing logistics tracking metrics are used to measure the operational effectiveness of the systems that service retailers and distributors. Inventory turns, out-of-stocks, and service levels are key factors in this area.

At the retail level, gross margin return on inventory investment (GMROII) and direct product profitability (DPP) offer SKU-specific metrics of product performance, combining movement rates, gross margins, costs of inventory, and other factors.

	Metric	Construction	Considerations	Purpose
1	Workload	Hours required to service clients and prospects.	Prospect numbers may be debatable. Time spent trying to convert prospects can vary by territory, salesperson, and potential client.	To assess the number of sales-people required to service a territory, and to ensure balanced workloads.
1	Sales Potential Forecast	This comprises the number of prospects and their buying power.	Doesn't assess the likelihood of converting "potential" accounts. Definitions of buying power are more an art than a science.	To determine sales targets. Can also help identify territories worthy of an allocation of limited sales resources.

	Metric	Construction	Considerations	Purpose
2	Sales Goal	Individual sales projections may be based on a salesperson's share of forecasted sales, on prior year sales and a share of increased district projections, or on a management-designed weighting system.	Setting individual targets on the basis of prior year sales can discourage optimal performance, as strong performance in one year leads to more aggressive targets in the next.	To set targets for individual salespeople and for territories.
3	Sales Force Effectiveness	Effectiveness metrics analyze sales in the context of various criteria, including calls, contacts, potential accounts, active accounts, buying power of territory, and expenses.	Depends on factors that also affect sales potential and workload.	To assess the performance of a salesperson or team.
4	Compensation	Total payments made to a salesperson, typically consisting of base salary, bonus, and/or commission.	Perceived relationship between incentive reward and controllable activities may vary widely among industries and firms.	To motivate maximum sales effort. To enable salespeople and management to track progress toward goals.
4	Break-Even Number of Employees	Sales revenue, multiplied by margin net of commission, divided by cost per staff member.	Margins may vary across products, time, and salespeople. Sales are not independent of the number of salespeople.	To determine the appropriate personnel level for a projected sales volume.

Continues

	Metric	Construction	Considerations	Purpose
5	Sales Funnel, Sales Pipeline	Portrayal of the number of clients and potential clients at various stages of the sales cycle.	Funnel dimensions depend on type of business and definition of potential clients.	To monitor sales effort and project future sales.
6	Numeric Distribution	Percentage of outlets in a defined universe that stock a particular brand or product.	Outlets' size or sales levels are not reflected in this measure. Boundaries by which distribution universe is defined may be arbitrary.	To assess the degree to which a brand or product has penetrated its potential channels.
6	All Commodity Volume (ACV)	Numeric distribution, weighted by penetrated outlets' share of sales of all product categories.	Reflects sales of "all commodities," but may not reflect sales of the relevant product or category.	To assess the degree to which a brand or product has access to retail traffic.
6	Product Category Volume (PCV)	Numeric distribution, weighted by penetrated outlets' share of sales of the relevant product category.	Strong indicator of share potential, but may miss opportunities to expand category.	To assess the degree to which a brand or product has access to established outlets for its category.
6	Total Distribution	Usually based on ACV or PCV. Sums the relevant measures for each SKU in a brand or product line.	Strong indicator of the distribution of a product *line*, as opposed to an individual SKU.	To assess the extent to which a product line is available.

	Metric	Construction	Considerations	Purpose
6	Category Performance Ratio	The ratio of a PCV to ACV distribution.	Same as for ACV and PCV.	To assess whether a brand's distribution or a particular retailer is performing above or below average for the category.
7	Out-of-Stock	Percentage of outlets that "list" or normally stock a product or brand, but have none available for sale.	Out-of-stocks can be measured in Numeric, ACV, or PCV terms.	To monitor the ability of logistics systems to match supply with demand.
7	Inventories	Total amount of product or brand available for sale in a channel.	May be held at different levels and valued in ways that may or may not reflect promotional allowances and discounts.	To calculate ability to meet demand and determine channel investments.
8	Markdowns	Percentage discount from the regular selling price.	For many products, a certain percentage of markdowns are expected. Too few markdowns may reflect "under-ordering." If markdowns are too high, the opposite may be true.	To determine whether channel sales are being made at planned margins.

Continues

	Metric	Construction	Considerations	Purpose
8	Direct Product Profitability (DPP)	The adjusted gross margin of products, less direct product costs.	Cost allocation is often imprecise. Some products may be intended not to generate profit but to drive traffic.	To identify profitable SKUs and realistically calculate their earnings.
8	Gross Margin Return on Inventory Investment (GMROII)	Margin divided by the average dollar value of inventory held during a specific period of time.	Allowances and rebates must be considered in margin calculations. For "loss leaders" this measure may be consistently negative and still not present a problem. For most products, negative trends in GMROII are signs of future problems.	To quantify return on working capital invested in inventory.

1   Sales Force Coverage: Territories

Sales force territories are the customer groups or geographic districts for which individual salespeople or sales teams hold responsibility. Territories can be defined on the basis of geography, sales potential, history, or a combination of factors. Companies strive to balance their territories because this can reduce costs and increase sales.

Workload (#) = [Current Accounts (#) * Average Time to Service an Active Account (#)]
+ [Prospects (#) * Time Spent Trying to Convert a Prospect into
an Active Account (#)]

Sales Potential ($) = Number of Possible Accounts (#) * Buying Power ($)

Purpose: To create balanced sales territories.

There are a number of ways to analyze territories.[1] Most commonly, territories are compared on the basis of their potential or size. This is an important exercise. If territories differ sharply or slip out of balance, sales personnel may be given too much or too little work. This can lead to under- or over-servicing of customers.

When sales personnel are stretched too thin, the result can be an *under-servicing* of customers. This can cost a firm business because over-taxed salespeople engage in sub-optimal levels of activity in a number of areas. They seek out too few leads, identify too few prospects, and spend too little time with current customers. Those customers, in turn, may take their business to alternate providers.

Over-servicing, by contrast, may raise costs and prices and therefore indirectly reduce sales. Over-servicing in some territories may also lead to under-servicing in others.

Unbalanced territories also raise the problem of unfair distribution of sales potential among members of a sales force. This may result in distorted compensation and cause talented salespeople to leave a company, seeking superior balance and compensation.

Achieving an appropriate balance among territories is an important factor in maintaining satisfaction among customers, salespeople, and the company as a whole.

Construction

In defining or redefining territories, companies strive to

- Balance workloads
- Balance sales potential
- Develop compact territories
- Minimize disruptions during the redesign

These goals can have different effects on different stakeholders, as represented in Table 1.[2]

Before designing new territories, a sales force manager should evaluate the workloads of all members of the sales team. The workload for a territory can be calculated as follows:

**Workload (#) = [Current Accounts (#) * Average Time to Service an Active Account (#)]
+ [Prospects (#) * Time Spent Trying to Convert a Prospect into an Active Account (#)]**

The sales potential in a territory can be determined as follows:

Sales Potential ($) = Number of Possible Accounts (#) * Buying Power ($)

Table 1 Effects of Balancing Sales Territories

		Balance the Workload	Balance Sales Potential	Minimize Disruption	Develop Compact Territories
Customers	Responsiveness	X			X
	Relationships			X	
Salespeople	Earnings opportunities		X		
	Manageable workload	X			X
	Reduced uncertainty			X	
	Control of overnights				X
Firm	Sales results	X	X	X	
	Effort control	X			
	Motivation	X	X	X	X
	Travel cost control				X

Buying power is a dollar figure based on such factors as average income levels, number of businesses in a territory, average sales of those businesses, and population demographics. Buying power indices are generally specific to individual industries.

EXAMPLE: Among the sales prospects in one of its territories, a copier manufacturer has identified six small businesses, eight medium-sized firms, and two large companies. Enterprises of these sizes have historically made annual copier purchases that average $500, $700, and $1,000, respectively. The sales potential for the territory is thus:

$$\text{Sales Potential} = (6 * \$500) + (8 * \$700) + (2 * \$1,000) = \$10,600$$

In addition to workload and sales potential, a third key metric is needed to compare territories. This is size or, more specifically, travel time. In this context, travel time is more useful than size because it more accurately represents the factor that size implies—that is, the amount of time needed to reach customers and potential customers.

As a manager's goal is to balance workload and potential among sales personnel, it can be beneficial to calculate combined metrics—such as sales potential or travel time—in order to make comparisons between territories.

Data Sources, Complications, and Cautions

Sales potential can be represented in a number of ways. Of these, the most basic is population—the number of potential accounts in a territory. In the copier case cited earlier, this might be the number of offices in a territory.

Estimating the size of a territory might involve simply calculating the geographic area that it covers. It is likely, however, that average travel time will also be important. Depending on the quality of roads, density of traffic, or distance between businesses, one may find that territories of equal area entail very different travel time requirements. In evaluating such distinctions, sales force records of the time needed to travel from call to call can be useful. Specialized computer software programs are available for these purposes.

Redefining territories is a famously difficult process. To perform it well, in addition to the metrics cited earlier, disruption of customer relationships and feelings of ownership among sales personnel must also be considered.

2 Sales Force Objectives: Setting Goals

Sales goals are generally needed to motivate salespeople. These can have negative effects, however, if set too high or low. Means of establishing sales goals include the following:

$$\text{Sales Goal (\$)} = \text{Salesperson's Share of Prior-Year Sales in District (\%)} \\ * \text{Forecasted Sales for District (\$)}$$

$$\text{Sales Goal (\$)} = \text{Salesperson's Prior-Year Sales (\$)} + [\text{Forecasted Sales Increase for} \\ \text{District (\$)} * \text{Territory's Share of Sales Potential in District (\%)}]$$

$$\text{Weighted Share of Sales Allotment (\%)} = \{\text{Salesperson's Share of Prior-Year Sales in} \\ \text{District (\%)} * \text{Assigned Weighting (\%)}\} + \\ \{\text{Territory's Share of Sales Potential in District} \\ \text{(\%)} * [1 - \text{Assigned Weighting (\%)}]\}$$

$$\text{Sales Goal (\$)} = \text{Weighted Share of Sales Allotment (\%)} \\ * \text{Forecasted Sales for District (\$)}$$

Many of these approaches involve a combination of historical results and a weighting of sales potential among the territories. This ensures that overall goals will be attained if all salespeople meet their individual goals.

Purpose: To motivate sales personnel and establish benchmarks for evaluating and rewarding their performance.

In setting sales goals, managers strive to motivate their personnel to stretch themselves and generate the most sales possible. But they don't want to set the bar too high. The correct goal levels will motivate all salespeople and reward most of them.

When planning sales goals, certain guidelines are important. Under the SMART strategy recommended by Jack D. Wilner, author of *Seven Secrets to Successful Sales Management*,[3] goals should be **S**pecific, **M**easurable, **A**ttainable, **R**ealistic, and **T**imebound. Goals should be specific to a department, a territory, and even a salesperson. They should be clear and applicable to each individual so that salespeople do not have to derive part of their goal. Measurable goals, expressed in concrete numbers such as "dollar sales" or "percentage increase," enable salespeople to set precise targets and track their progress. Vague goals, such as "more" or "increased" sales, are not effective because they make it difficult to measure progress. Attainable goals are in the realm of possibility. They can be visualized and understood by both the manager and the salesperson. Realistic goals are set high enough to motivate, but not so high that salespeople give up before they even start. Finally, time-bound goals must be met within a precise time frame. This applies pressure to reach them sooner rather than later and defines an endpoint when results will be checked.

Construction

There are numerous ways of allotting a company's forecast across its sales force. These methods are designed to set goals that are fair, achievable, and in line with historic results. Goals are stated in terms of sales totals for individual salespeople. In the following formulas, which encapsulate these methods, a *district* is composed of the individual territories of multiple salespeople.

A sales goal or allocation based on prior-year sales can be calculated as follows:[4]

Sales Goal ($) = Salesperson's Share of Prior-Year Sales in District (%) ∗ Forecasted Sales for District ($)

A sales goal based on prior-year sales *and* the sales potential of a territory can be calculated as follows:

Sales Goal ($) = Salesperson's Prior-Year Sales ($) + [Forecasted Sales Increase for District($) ∗ Territory's Share of Sales Potential in District (%)]

Sales goals can also be set by a combined method, in which management assigns weightings to both the prior-year sales of each salesperson and the sales potential of each territory. These weightings are then used to calculate each salesperson's percentage share of the relevant sales forecast, and percentage shares are used to calculate sales goals in dollar terms.

Weighted Share of Sales Allotment (%) = {Salesperson's Share of Prior-Year Sales in District (%) ∗ Assigned Weighting (%)} + {Territory's Share of Sales Potential in District (%) ∗ [1 − Assigned Weighting (%)]}

Sales Goal ($) = Weighted Share of Sales Allotment (%) ∗ Forecasted Sales for District ($)

EXAMPLE: A salesperson achieved prior-year sales of $1,620, which represented 18% of the sales in her district. This salesperson was responsible for a territory that held 12% of the sales potential in the district. If the salesperson's employer mandates a district sales goal of $10,000 for the coming year—representing an overall increase of $1,000 over prior-year results—then the salesperson's individual sales goal can be calculated in several ways that involve different emphasis on historical sales versus sales potential. Here are four examples:

1. Sales Goal Based on Prior-year Sales = 18% * $10,000 = $1,800

2. Sales Goals Based on Sales Potential = 12% * $10,000 = $1,200

3. Sales Goal Based on Prior-year Sales + Sales Potential * Increase = $1,620 + (12% * $1,000) = $1,740

4. Weighted Share of Sales Allotment, in Which Prior-year Sales and Sales Potential Are Weighted (for Example) by a Factor of 50% Each = (18% * 50%) + (12% * 50%) = 15%. Then...

Sales Goal Based on Weighted Share of Sales Allotment = 15% * $10,000 = $1,500

Data Sources, Complications, and Cautions

Sales goals are generally established by using combinations of bottom-up and top-down procedures. Frequently, top management sets objectives at a corporate level, while the sales manager allocates shares of that overall goal among the various members of the sales force.

Top management generally uses multiple metrics to forecast sales, including prior-year sales of the product in question, total prior-year sales in the relevant market, prior-year sales by competitors, and the company's current market share. After the corporate sales forecast is derived, a sales force manager verifies that these targets are reasonable, pushing back where necessary. The manager then allots the projected sales among the sales force in a district, based at least in part on measures of individual performance from the prior year. Of greatest importance in this calculation are each salesperson's historic percentage of sales and the sales potential of his or her territory.

It is important to re-evaluate sales goals *during* the year to ensure that actual performance is running reasonably close to projections. If, at this checkpoint, it appears that more than 90% or less than 50% of the sales force is on track to achieve their goals, then it may be advisable to alter the goals. This will prevent salespeople from easing off too early because their goals are in sight, or giving up because their goals are unattainable. In setting goals, one possible rule of thumb would be to plan for a success rate of 75%. That would ensure that enough salespeople reach their goal *and* that the goal is sufficiently challenging.

If "rebudgeting" becomes necessary, it is important to ensure that this is properly recorded. Unless care is taken, revised sales goals can slip out of alignment with financial budgets and the expectations of senior management.

3   Sales Force Effectiveness: Measuring Effort, Potential, and Results

By analyzing sales force performance, managers can make changes to optimize sales going forward. Toward that end, there are many ways to gauge the performance of individual salespeople and of the sales force as a whole, in addition to total annual sales.

Sales Force Effectiveness Ratios

$$= \frac{\text{Sales (\$)}}{\text{Contacts with Clients (Calls) (\#)}}$$

$$= \frac{\text{Sales (\$)}}{\text{Potential Accounts (\#)}}$$

$$= \frac{\text{Sales (\$)}}{\text{Active Accounts (\#)}}$$

$$= \frac{\text{Sales (\$)}}{\text{Buying Power (\$)}}$$

$$= \frac{\text{Expenses (\$)}}{\text{Sales (\$)}} \quad \text{(Also Known As Cost of Sales)}$$

Each can also be calculated on a dollar contribution basis.

Purpose: *To measure the performance of a sales force and of individual salespeople.*

When analyzing the performance of a salesperson, a number of metrics can be compared. These can reveal more about the salesperson than can be gauged by his or her total sales.

Construction

An authoritative source lists the following ratios as useful in assessing the relative effectiveness of sales personnel:[5]

$$\frac{\text{Sales (\$)}}{\text{Contacts with Clients (Calls) (\#)}}$$

$$\frac{\text{Sales (\$)}}{\text{Potential Accounts (\#)}}$$

$$\frac{\text{Sales (\$)}}{\text{Active Accounts (\#)}}$$

$$\frac{\text{Sales (\$)}}{\text{Buying Power (\$)}}$$

These formulas can be useful for comparing salespeople from different territories and for examining trends over time. They can reveal distinctions that can be obscured by total sales results, particularly in districts where territories vary in size, in number of potential accounts, or in buying power.

These ratios provide insight into the factors behind sales performance. If an individual's sales per call ratio is low, for example, that may indicate that the salesperson in question needs training in moving customers toward larger purchases. Or it may indicate a lack of closing skills. If the sales per potential account or sales per buying power metric is low, the salesperson may not be doing enough to seek out new accounts. These metrics reveal much about prospecting and lead generation because they're based on each salesperson's *entire* territory, including potential as well as current customers. The sales per active account metric provides a useful indicator of a salesperson's effectiveness in maximizing the value of existing customers.

Although it is important to make the most of every call, a salesperson will not reach his or her goal in just one call. A certain amount of effort is required to complete sales. This can be represented graphically (see Figure 1).[6]

Although one can increase sales by expending more time and attention on a customer, at a certain point, a salesperson encounters diminishing returns in placing more calls to

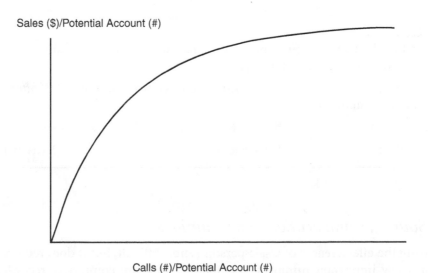

Sales ($)/Potential Account (#)

Calls (#)/Potential Account (#)

Figure 1 Sales Resulting from Calls to Customers

the same customers. Eventually, the incremental business generated by each call will be worth less than the cost of making the call.

In addition to the formulas described earlier, one other important measure of effectiveness is the ratio of expenses to sales. This cost metric is commonly expressed as a percentage of sales and is calculated as follows:

$$\frac{\text{Expenses (\$)}}{\text{Sales (\$)}}$$

If this ratio is substantially higher for one salesperson than for others, it may indicate that the individual in question has poor control of his or her expenses. Examples of poor expense control could include making unnecessary trips to a client, overproducing product pamphlets, or hosting too many dinners. Alternatively, expenses may represent a high percentage of sales if an individual possesses poor closing skills. If a salesperson's expenses are comparable to those of his peers, but his sales are lower, then he may be failing to deliver sales after spending significant money on a potential customer.

A more challenging set of sales force performance metrics involves customer service. Customer service is difficult to measure because there are no concrete numbers representing it, other than repeat rates or customer complaints. Each of those is telling, but how can a sales manager evaluate the service provided to customers who are not repeating, leaving, or complaining? One possibility is to develop a survey, including an itemized scale to help customers quantify their opinions. After enough of these surveys are completed, managers will be able to calculate average scores for different service metrics. By comparing these with sales figures, managers can correlate sales with customer service and grade salespeople on their performance.

EXAMPLE: To translate customers' opinions into a metric, a company might pose survey questions such as the following:

Please circle the level of service your business received from our sales staff after shipment of the products you ordered:

1	2	3	4	5	6	7	8	9	10
Extremely Poor				Satisfactory					Extremely Good

Data Sources, Complications, and Cautions

Calculating the effectiveness of a salesperson is not difficult, but it does require keeping track of a few important numbers. Fortunately, these are commonly recorded in the sales industry.

The most important statistics are the amount of each sale (in dollars) and the contribution generated by that sale. It may also be important to keep track of which items are sold if a salesperson has been instructed to emphasize a certain product line. Additional useful information would include measures of the number of calls made (including both face-to-face and phone meetings), total accounts active, and total accounts in the territory. Of these, the latter two are needed to calculate the buying power of a territory.

The largest problem in performance review is a tendency to rely on only one or two metrics. This can be dangerous because an individual's performance on any one measure may be anomalous. A salesperson who generates $30,000 per call may be more valuable than one who generates $50,000 per call, for example, if he generates greater sales per potential account. A salesperson in a small territory may generate low total contribution but high dollar sales per buying power. If this is true, it may be advisable to increase the size of that person's territory. Another salesperson may show a dramatic increase in dollar sales per active account. If he achieves this simply by eliminating weaker accounts without generating incremental sales, it would not be grounds for reward. In reviewing sales personnel, managers are advised to evaluate as many performance metrics as possible.

Although the customer service survey described earlier is grounded upon a straightforward concept, managers can find it difficult to gather enough data—or sufficiently representative data—to make it useful. This could be because customers hesitate to fill out the surveys, or because they do so only when they encounter a problem. A small sample size or a prevalence of negative responses might distort the results. Even so, some effort to measure customer satisfaction is needed to ensure that salespeople don't emphasize the wrong issues—or neglect issues that have a substantial impact on customers' lifetime value.

4 Sales Force Compensation: Salary/Reward Mix

"The incentive plan needs to align the salesperson's activities with the firm's objectives."[7] Toward that end, an effective plan may be based on the past (growth), the present (comparison with others), or the future (percentage of goal achieved). Key formulas in this area include the following:

$$\text{Compensation (\$)} = \text{Salary (\$)} + \text{Bonus 1 (\$)} + \text{Bonus 2 (\$)}$$

$$\text{Compensation (\$)} = \text{Salary (\$)} + [\text{Sales (\$)} * \text{Commission (\%)}]$$

$$\text{Break-Even Number of Employees (\#)} = \frac{(\text{Sales (\$)} * [\text{Margin (\%)} - \text{Commission (\%)}])}{[\text{Salary (\$)} + \text{Expenses (\$)} + \text{Bonus (\$)}]}$$

Purpose: To determine the mix of salary, bonus, and commission that will maximize sales generated by the sales force.

When designing a compensation plan for a sales force, managers face four key considerations: level of pay, mix between salary and incentive, measures of performance, and performance-payout relationships. The level of pay, or compensation, is the amount that a company plans to pay a salesperson over the course of a year. This can be viewed as a range because its total will vary with bonuses or commissions.

The mix between salary and incentive represents a key allocation within total compensation. Salary is a guaranteed sum of money. Incentives can take multiple forms, including bonuses or commissions. In the case of a bonus, a salesperson will receive a lump sum for reaching certain sales targets. With a commission, the incentive is incremental and is earned on each sale. In order to generate incentives, it is important to measure accurately the role a salesperson plays in each sale. The higher the level of causality that can be attributed to a salesperson, the easier it is to use an incentive system.

Various metrics can be used to measure a salesperson's performance. With these, managers can evaluate a salesperson's performance in the context of past, present, or future comparators, as follows:

- **The past:** Measure the salesperson's percentage growth in sales over prior-year results.

- **The present:** Rank salespeople on the basis of current results.

- **The future:** Measure the percentage of individual sales goals achieved by each salesperson.

Sales managers can also select the organizational level on which to focus an incentive plan. The disbursement of incentive rewards can be linked to results at the company, division, or product-line level. In measuring performance and designing compensation plans along all these dimensions, managers seek to align salespeople's incentives with the goals of their firm.

Lastly, a time period should be defined for measuring the performance of each salesperson.

Construction

Managers enjoy considerable freedom in designing compensation systems. The key is to start with a forecast for sales and a range within which each salesperson's compensation should reside. After these elements are determined, there are many ways to motivate a salesperson.

In a multi-bonus system, the following formula can represent the compensation structure for a salesperson:

$$\text{Compensation (\$)} = \text{Salary (\$)} + \text{Bonus 1 (\$)} + \text{Bonus 2 (\$)}$$

In this system, bonus 1 might be attained at a level approximately halfway to the individual's sales goal for the year. The second bonus might be awarded when that goal is met.

In a commission system, the following formula would represent compensation for a salesperson:

$$\text{Compensation (\$)} = \text{Salary (\$)} + [\text{Sales (\$)} * \text{Commission (\%)}]$$

Theoretically, in a 100% commission structure, salary might be set as low as $0. Many jurisdictions, however, place limits on such arrangements. Managers must ensure that their chosen compensation structures comply with employment law.

Managers can also combine bonus and commission structures by awarding bonuses on top of commissions at certain sales levels, or by increasing the commission rate at certain sales levels.

EXAMPLE: Tina earns a commission of 2% on sales up to $1,000,000, and a 3% commission on sales beyond that point. Her salary is $20,000 per year. If she makes $1,200,000 in sales, her compensation can be calculated as follows:

$$\text{Compensation} = \$20,000 + (.02) * (\$1,000,000) + (.03) * (\$200,000)$$
$$= \$46,000$$

After a sales compensation plan has been established, management may want to re-evaluate the size of its sales force. Based on forecasts for the coming year, a firm may have room to hire more salespeople, or it may need to reduce the size of the sales force. On the basis of a given value for projected sales, managers can determine the break-even number of employees for a firm as follows:

$$\text{Break-Even Number of Employees (\#)} = \frac{\text{Sales (\$)} * [\text{Margin (\%)} - \text{Commission (\%)}]}{[\text{Salary (\$)} + \text{Expenses (\$)} + \text{Bonus (\$)}]}$$

Data Sources, Complications, and Cautions

Measurements commonly used in incentive plans include total sales, total contribution, market share, customer retention, and customer complaints. Because such a plan rewards a salesperson for reaching certain goals, these targets must be defined at the beginning of the year (or other time period). Continual tracking of these metrics will help both the salesperson and the company to plan for year-end compensation.

Timing is an important issue in incentive plans. A firm must collect data in a timely fashion so that both managers and salespeople know where they stand in relation to established goals. The time frame covered by a plan also represents an important consideration. If a company tries to generate incentives through weekly rewards, its compensation program can become too expensive and time-consuming to maintain. By contrast, if the program covers too long a period, it may slip out of alignment with company forecasts and goals. This could result in a sales force being paid too much or too little. To guard against these pitfalls, managers can develop a program that mixes both short- and long-term incentives. They can link some rewards to a simple, short-term metric, such as calls per week, and others to a more complex, long-term target, such as market share achieved in a year.

A further complication that can arise in incentive programs is the assignment of causality to individual salespeople. This can become a problem in a number of instances, including team collaborations in landing sales. In such a scenario, it can be difficult to determine which team members deserve which rewards. Consequently, managers may find it best to reward all members of the team with equal bonuses for meeting a goal.

A last concern: When an incentive program is implemented, it may reward the "wrong" salespeople. To avoid this, before activating any newly proposed program, sales managers are advised to apply that program to the prior year's results as a test. A "good" plan will usually reward the salespeople whom the manager knows to be the best.

5   Sales Force Tracking: Pipeline Analysis

Pipeline analysis is used to track the progress of sales efforts in relation to all current and potential customers in order to forecast short-term sales and to evaluate sales force workload.

Purpose: To forecast upcoming sales and evaluate workload distribution.

A convenient way to forecast sales in the short term and to keep an eye on sales force activity is to create a sales pipeline or sales funnel. Although this concept can be represented graphically, the data behind it are stored electronically in a database or spreadsheet.

The concept of the sales funnel originates in a well-known dynamic: If a sales force approaches a large number of potential customers, only a subset of these will actually make purchases. As salespeople proceed through multiple stages of customer interaction, a number of prospects are winnowed out. At the conclusion of each stage, fewer potential customers remain. By keeping track of the number of potential customers at each stage of the process, a sales force manager can balance the workload within a team and make accurate forecasts of sales.

This analysis is similar to the hierarchy of effects. Whereas the hierarchy of effects focuses on the impact of advertising or mass media, the sales funnel is used to track individual customers (often by name) and sales force efforts. (Note: In some industries, such as consumer packaged goods, the term "pipeline sales" can refer to sales into a distribution channel. Please do not confuse pipeline sales with a sales pipeline.)

Construction

In order to conceptualize a sales funnel or pipeline, it is helpful to draw a diagram showing the stages of the selling process (see Figure 2). At any point in the year, it is likely that all stages of the pipeline will include some number of customers. As Figure 2 illustrates, although there may be a large number of *potential* customers, those who actually make purchases represent only a percentage of these original leads.

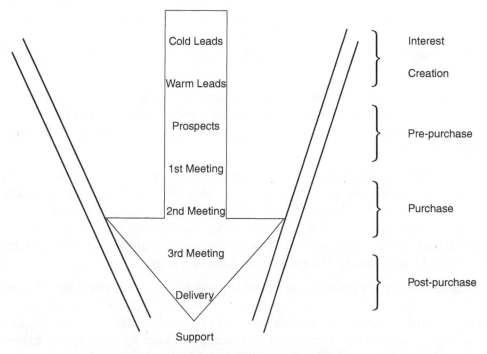

Figure 2   Sales Force Funnel

Interest Creation: This entails building awareness of a product through such activities as trade shows, direct mail, and advertising. In the course of interest creation, salespeople can also generate leads. That is, they can identify targets to add to their pool of potential customers. Two main classifications of leads include cold leads and warm leads.

> **Cold Lead:** *A lead that has not specifically expressed interest. These can be identified through mailing lists, phone books, business listings, and so on.*
>
> **Warm Lead:** *A lead that is expected to be responsive. These potential customers may have registered through a Web site or requested product information, for example.*

Pre-Purchase: This stage involves identifying prospects from among cold and warm leads. Salespeople make this distinction through initial meetings with leads, in which they explain product features and benefits, and cooperate in problem solving with the customer. The desired result of such an early-stage meeting is not a sale but rather the identification of a prospect and the scheduling of another meeting.

> **Prospect:** *A potential customer who has been identified as a likely buyer, possessing the ability and willingness to buy.*[8]

Purchase: After prospects are identified and agree to additional calls, salespeople engage in second and third meetings with them. It is in these sessions that traditional "selling" takes place. Salespeople will engage in persuading, negotiating, and/or bidding. If a purchase is agreed upon, a salesperson can close the deal through a written proposal, contract, or order.

Post-Purchase: After a customer has made a purchase, there is still considerable work to be done. This includes delivery of the product or service, installation (if necessary), collection of payments, and possibly training. There is then an ongoing commitment to customer service.

After salespeople visualize the different stages represented in a sales funnel, they can track their customers and accounts more accurately. They can do this electronically by using a database or spreadsheet. If a sales pipeline file is maintained on a shared drive, any member of a sales force will be able to update the relevant data on a regular basis. This will also enable a sales manager to view the progress of the team at any point in time. Table 2 is an example of a spreadsheet form of a sales funnel.

A manager can use the information stored in such a funnel to prepare for sales in the near future. This is a form of *pipeline analysis*. When a firm faces inventory issues, or when sales goals are being missed, this represents vital information. By applying historical averages, a sales or marketing manager can improve sales forecasts by using the data in a sales funnel. This can be done manually or with specialized software. The underly-

Table 2 Spreadsheet Sales Funnel

| | Interest Creation | | Pre-purchase | | Purchase | Post-purchase | |
| | Cold | Warm | | 1st/2nd | 2nd/3rd | | |
Salesperson	Leads	Leads	Prospects	Meeting	Meeting	Delivery	Support
Sandy	56	30	19	5	8	7	25
Bob	79	51	33	16	4	14	35

ing assumption behind a sales funnel is that failure at any stage eliminates a prospect from the funnel. The following example illustrates how this bottom-up forecasting could be applied.

EXAMPLE: Using the sales funnel from earlier, Sandy and Bob's manager wants to forecast the number of sales that will require fulfillment in the next five months. Toward that end, she applies certain historical averages:

- 2% of cold calls are converted to sales within five months.
- 14% of warm calls are converted to sales within four months.
- 25% of prospects are converted to sales within three months.
- 36% of customers who agree to a pre-purchase meeting are converted to sales within two months.
- 53% of customers who agree to a purchase meeting are converted to sales within one month.

On this basis:

$$\text{Upcoming Sales} = [(56 + 79) * 2\%] + [(30 + 51) * 14\%] + [(19 + 33) * 25\%] + [(5 + 16) * 36\%)] + [(8 + 4) * 53\%] = 41$$

Note: This example applies to only one product. Often, a firm will need multiple sales funnels for different products or product lines. Additionally, a sale may comprise a single item or thousands of items. In the latter case, it would be appropriate to use a metric for "average sale size/customer" in forecasting.

Data Sources, Complications, and Cautions

In order to populate a sales funnel correctly, salespeople must maintain records of all their current and potential customers, and the status of each within the purchase process. Each salesperson must also share this information, which can then be aggregated in a comprehensive database of sales force activities. By applying assumptions to these—including assumptions drawn from historical sales results—a firm can project future sales. For example, if 25% of warm leads are generally converted to sales within two months, and 200 warm leads currently appear in a sales funnel, management can estimate that 50 of these will be converted to sales within two months.

At times, the use of a sales funnel leads to the pitfall of over-prospecting. If the incremental contribution generated by a customer is less than the cost of acquiring that customer, then prospecting for that customer yields a negative result. Salespeople are advised to use customer lifetime value metrics as a guide in deciding the appropriate scale and direction of their prospecting. Increasing pre-purchase sales funnel metrics will not be worthwhile unless that increment leads to improved figures further down the pipeline as well.

Difficulties in the sales cycle can also arise when a salesperson judges that a potential customer may be a prospect because he or she has the willingness and ability to buy. To solidify this judgment, the salesperson must also confirm that the customer possesses the *authority* to buy. When prospecting, salespeople should take the time needed to verify that their contacts can make purchase decisions without approval from another source.

6 Numeric, ACV and PCV Distribution, Facings/Share of Shelf

Distribution metrics quantify the availability of products sold through resellers, usually as a percentage of all potential outlets. Often, outlets are weighted by their share of category sales or "all commodity" sales.

$$\text{Numeric Distribution (\%)} = \frac{\text{Number of Outlets Carrying Brand (\#)}}{\text{Total Number of Outlets (\#)}}$$

$$\text{All Commodity Volume (ACV) Distribution (\%)} = \frac{\text{Total Sales of Outlets Carrying Brand (\$)}}{\text{Total Sales of All Outlets (\$)}}$$

$$\text{Product Category Volume (PCV) Distribution[9] (\%)} = \frac{\text{Total Category Sales of Outlets Carrying Brand (\$)}}{\text{Total Category Sales of All Outlets (\$)}}$$

$$\text{Category Performance Ratio (\%)} = \frac{\text{PCV (\%)}}{\text{ACV (\%)}}$$

For marketers who sell through resellers, distribution metrics reveal a brand's percentage of market access. Balancing a firm's efforts in "push" (building and maintaining reseller and distributor support) and "pull" (generating customer demand) is an ongoing strategic concern for marketers.

Purpose: To measure a firm's ability to convey a product to its customers.

In broad terms, marketing can be divided into two key challenges:

- The first—and most widely appreciated—is to ensure that consumers or end users want a firm's product. This is generally termed *pull* marketing.

- The second challenge is less broadly recognized, but often just as important. *Push* marketing ensures that customers are given opportunities to buy.

Marketers have developed numerous metrics by which to judge the effectiveness of the distribution system that helps create opportunities to buy. The most fundamental of these are measures of product availability.

Availability metrics are used to quantify the number of outlets reached by a product, the fraction of the relevant market served by those outlets, and the percentage of total sales volume in all categories held by the outlets that carry the product.

Construction

There are three popular measures of distribution coverage:

1. Numeric distribution

2. All commodity volume (ACV)

3. Product category volume (PCV), also known as weighted distribution

NUMERIC DISTRIBUTION

This measure is based on the number of outlets that carry a product (that is, outlets that list at least one of the product's stock-keeping units, or SKUs). It is defined as the percentage of stores that stock a given brand or SKU, within the universe of stores in the relevant market.

The main use of numeric distribution is to understand how many physical locations stock a product or brand. This has implications for delivery systems and for the cost of servicing these outlets.

Numeric Distribution: To calculate numeric distribution, marketers divide the number of stores that stock at least one SKU of a product or brand by the number of outlets in the relevant market.

$$\text{Numeric Distribution (\%)} = \frac{\text{Number of Outlets Carrying Product (\#)}}{\text{Total Number of Outlets in the Market (\#)}}$$

EXAMPLE: Alice sells photo albums to gift shops. There are 60 such stores in her area. In order to generate adequate distribution coverage, Alice believes she must reach at least 60% of these. In initiating her relationship with each store, however, Alice must provide the store with $4,000 worth of inventory to build a presence. To attain her distribution goal, how much will Alice need to invest in inventory?

To reach her numeric distribution target of 60%, Alice must build a presence in 36 stores (that is, 0.60 * 60).

She will therefore have to spend at least $144,000 on inventory (36 stores * $4,000 per store).

ALL COMMODITY VOLUME

All commodity volume (ACV) is a weighted measure of product availability, or distribution, based on total store sales. ACV can be expressed as a dollar value or percentage.

All Commodity Volume (ACV): *The percentage of sales in all categories that are generated by the stores that stock a given brand (again, at least one SKU of that brand).*

$$\text{All Commodity Volume (ACV Distribution) (\%)}$$
$$= \frac{\text{Total Sales of Stores Carrying Brand (\$)}}{\text{Total Sales of All Stores (\$)}}$$

All Commodity Volume (ACV Distribution) ($) = Total Sales of Stores Carrying Brand ($)

EXAMPLE: The marketers at Madre's Tortillas want to know the all commodity volume of their distribution network (Table 3).

Table 3 Madre's Tortillas' Distribution

Outlet	All Sales	Tortilla Sales	Madre's Tortillas SKUs Stocked	Padre's Tortillas SKUs Stocked
Store 1	$100,000	$1,000	12 ct, 24 ct	12 ct, 24 ct
Store 2	$75,000	$500	12 ct	24 ct
Store 3	$50,000	$300	12 ct, 24 ct	none
Store 4	$40,000	$400	none	12 ct, 24 ct

Madre's Tortillas are carried by Stores 1-3, but not by Store 4. The ACV of its distribution network is therefore the total sales of Stores 1, 2, and 3, divided by the total sales of all stores. This represents a measure of the sales of all commodities in these stores, not just tortilla sales.

$$\text{Madre's Tortillas ACV (\%)} = \frac{\text{Sales Stores 1} - 3}{\text{All Store Sales}}$$

$$= \frac{(\$100k + \$75k + \$50k)}{(\$100k + \$75k + \$50k + \$40k)}$$

$$= \frac{\$225k}{\$265k} = 84.9\%$$

The principal benefit of the ACV metric, by comparison with numeric distribution, is that it provides a superior measure of customer traffic in the stores that stock a brand. In essence, ACV adjusts numeric distribution for the fact that not all retailers generate the same level of sales. For example, in a market composed of two small stores, one superstore, and one kiosk, numeric distribution would weight each outlet equally, whereas ACV would place greater emphasis on the value of gaining distribution in the superstore. In calculating ACV when detailed sales data are not available, marketers sometimes use the square footage of stores as an approximation of their total sales volume.

The weakness of ACV is that it does not provide direct information about how well each store merchandises and competes in the relevant product category. A store can do a great deal of general business but sell very little of the product category under consideration.

Product Category Volume

Product category volume (PCV)[10] is a refinement of ACV. It examines the share of the relevant product category sold by the stores in which a given product has gained distribution. It helps marketers understand whether a given product is gaining distribution in outlets where customers look for its category, as opposed to simply high-traffic stores where that product may get lost in the aisles.

Continuing our example of the two small retailers, the kiosk, and the superstore, although ACV may lead the marketer of a chocolate bar to seek distribution in the high-traffic superstore, PCV might reveal that the kiosk, surprisingly, generates the greatest volume in snack sales. In building distribution, the marketer would then be advised to target the kiosk as her highest priority.

> **Product Category Volume (PCV):** *The percentage share, or dollar value, of category sales made by stores that stock at least one SKU of the brand in question, in comparison with all stores in their universe.*

$$\text{Product Category Volume (PCV Distribution) (\%)} = \frac{\text{Total Category Sales by Stores Carrying Brand (\$)}}{\text{Total Category Sales of All Stores (\$)}}$$

$$\text{Product Category Volume (PCV Distribution) (\$)} = \text{Total Category Sales of Stores Carrying Brand (\$)}$$

When detailed sales data are available, PCV can provide a strong indication of the market share within a category to which a given brand has access. If sales data are not available, marketers can calculate an approximate PCV by using square footage devoted to the relevant category as an indication of the importance of that category to a particular outlet or store type.

EXAMPLE: The marketers at Madre's Tortillas want to know how effectively their product is reaching the outlets where customers shop for tortillas. Using data from the previous example:

Stores 1, 2, and 3 stock Madre's Tortillas. Store 4 does not. The product category volume of Madre's Tortillas' distribution network can be calculated by dividing total tortilla sales in Stores 1-3 by tortilla sales throughout the market.

$$\text{PCV (\%)} = \frac{(\text{Tortilla Sales of Stores Carrying Madre's})}{(\text{Tortilla Sales of All Stores})}$$

$$= \frac{(\$1,000 + \$500 + \$300)}{(\$1,000 + \$500 + \$300 + \$400)} = \$81.8\%$$

Total Distribution: *The sum of ACV or PCV distribution for all of a brand's stock-keeping units, calculated individually. By contrast with simple ACV or PCV, which are based on the all commodity or product-category sales of all stores that carry at least one SKU of a brand, total distribution also reflects the number of SKUs of the brand that is carried by those stores.*

Category Performance Ratio: *The relative performance of a retailer in a given product category, compared with its performance in all product categories.*

By comparing PCV with ACV, the category performance ratio provides insight into whether a brand's distribution network is more or less effective in selling the category of which that brand is a part, compared with its average effectiveness in selling all categories in which members of that network compete.

$$\text{Category Performance Ratio (\%)} = \frac{\text{PCV (\%)}}{\text{ACV (\%)}}$$

If a distribution network's category performance ratio is greater than 1, then the outlets comprising that network perform comparatively better in selling the category in question than in selling other categories, relative to the market as a whole.

EXAMPLE: As noted earlier, the PCV of Madre's Tortillas' distribution network is 81.8%. Its ACV is 84.9%. Thus, its category performance ratio is 0.96.

Madre's has succeeded in gaining distribution in the largest stores in its market. Tortilla sales in those stores, however, run slightly below the average of all commodity sales in those stores, relative to the market as a whole. That is, outlets carrying Madre's show a slightly weaker focus on tortillas than the overall universe of stores in this market.

Data Sources, Complications, and Cautions

In many markets, there are data suppliers such as A.C. Nielsen, which specialize in collecting information about distribution. In other markets, firms must generate their own data. Sales force reports and shipment invoices provide a place to start.

For certain merchandise—especially low-volume, high-value items—it is relatively simple to count the limited number of outlets that carry a given product. For higher-volume, lower-cost goods, merely determining the number of outlets that stock an item can be a challenge and may require assumptions. Take, for instance, the number of outlets selling a specific soft drink. To arrive at an accurate number, one would have to include vending machines and street vendors as well as traditional grocery stores.

Total outlet sales are often approximated by quantifying selling space (measured in square feet or square meters) and applying this measure to industry averages for sales per area of selling space.

In the absence of specific category sales data, it is often useful to weight ACV to arrive at an approximation of PCV. Marketers may know, for example, that pharmacies, relative to their overall sales, sell proportionally more of a given product than do superstores. In this event, they might increase the weighting of pharmacies relative to superstores in evaluating relevant distribution coverage.

Related Metrics and Concepts

Facing: A facing is a frontal view of a single package of a product on a fully stocked shelf.

Share of Shelf: A metric that compares the facings of a given brand to the total facing positions available, in order to quantify the display prominence of that brand.

$$\text{Share of Shelf (\%)} = \frac{\text{Facings for Brand (\#)}}{\text{Total Facings (\#)}}$$

Store Versus Brand Measures: Marketers often refer to a grocery chain's ACV. This can be either a dollar number (the chain's total sales of all categories in the relevant geographic market) or a percentage number (its share of dollar sales among the universe of stores). A brand's ACV is simply the sum of the ACVs of the chains and stores that stock that brand. Thus, if a brand is stocked by two chains in a market, and these chains have 40% and 30% ACV respectively, then the ACV of that brand's distribution network is 30% + 40%, or 70%.

Marketers can also refer to a chain's market share in a specific category. This is equivalent to the chain's PCV (%). A brand's PCV, by contrast, represents the sum of the PCVs of the chains that stock that brand.

Inventory: This is the level of physical stock held. It will typically be measured at different points in a pipeline. A retailer may have inventory on order from suppliers, at warehouses, in transit to stores, in the stores' backrooms, and on the store shelves.

Breadth of Distribution: This figure can be measured by the number of SKUs held. Typically, a company will hold a wide range of SKUs—a high breadth of distribution—for the products that it is most interested in selling.

Features in Store: The percentage of stores offering a promotion in a given time period. This can be weighted by product or by all commodity volume (ACV).

ACV on Display: Distinctions can be made in all commodity volume metrics to take account of where products are on display. This will reduce the measured distribution of products if they are not in a position to be sold.

AVC on Promotion: Marketers may want to measure the ACV of outlets where a given product is on promotion. This is a useful shorthand way of determining the product's reliance on promotion.

7   Supply Chain Metrics

Marketing logistics tracking includes the following metrics:

$$\text{Out-of-Stocks (\%)} = \frac{\text{Outlets Where Brand or Product Is Listed But Unavailable (\#)}}{\text{Total Outlets Where Brand or Product Is Listed (\#)}}$$

$$\text{Service Levels; Percentage on Time Delivery (\%)} = \frac{\text{Deliveries Achieved in Timeframe Promised (\#)}}{\text{All Deliveries Initiated in the Period (\#)}}$$

$$\text{Inventory Turns (I)} = \frac{\text{Product Revenues (\$)}}{\text{Average Inventory (\$)}}$$

Logistics tracking helps ensure that companies are meeting demand efficiently and effectively.

Purpose: To monitor the effectiveness of an organization in managing the distribution and logistics process.

Logistics are where the marketing rubber meets the road. A lot can be lost at the potential point-of-purchase if the right goods are not delivered to the appropriate outlets on time and in amounts that correspond to consumer demand. How hard can that be? Well, ensuring that supply meets demand becomes more difficult when:

- The company sells more than a few stock keeping units (SKUs).
- Multiple levels of suppliers, warehouses, and stores are involved in the distribution process.
- Product models change frequently.
- The channel offers customer-friendly return policies.

In this complex field, by monitoring core metrics and comparing these with historical norms and guidelines, marketers can determine how well their distribution channel is functioning as a supply chain for their customers.

By monitoring logistics, managers can investigate questions such as the following: Did we lose sales because the wrong items were shipped to a store that was running a promotion? Are we being forced to pay for the disposal of obsolete goods that stayed too long in warehouses or stores?

Construction

Out-of-Stocks: *This metric quantifies the number of retail outlets where an item is expected to be available for customers, but is not. It is typically expressed as a percentage of stores that list the relevant item.*

$$\text{Out-of-Stocks (\%)} = \frac{\text{Outlets Where Brand or Product Is Listed But Unavailable (\#)}}{\text{Total Outlets Where Brand or Product Is Listed (\#)}}$$

Being "listed" by a chain means that a headquarters buyer has "authorized" distribution of a brand, SKU, or product at the store level. For various reasons, being listed does not always ensure presence on the shelf. Local managers may not approve "distribution." Alternatively, a product may be distributed but sold out.

Out-of-stocks are often expressed as a percentage. Marketers must note whether an out-of-stock percentage is based on numeric distribution, ACV, PCV, or the percentage of distributing stores for a given chain.

The in-stock percentage is the complement of the out-of-stock percentage. A 3% out-of-stock rate would be equivalent to a 97% in-stock rate.

PCV Net Out-of-Stocks: *The PCV of a given product's distribution network, adjusted for out-of-stock situations.*

Product Category Volume (PCV), Net Out-of-Stocks: This out-of-stocks measure is calculated by multiplying PCV by a factor that adjusts it to recognize out-of-stock situations. The adjusting factor is simply one minus the out-of-stocks figure.

$$\text{Product Category Volume, Net Out-of-Stocks (\%)} = \text{PCV (\%)} * [1 - \text{Out-of-Stock (\%)}]$$

Service Levels, Percentage On-time Delivery: There are various service measures in marketing logistics. One particularly common measure is on-time delivery. This metric captures the percentage of customer (or trade) orders that are delivered in accordance with the promised schedule.

$$\text{Service Levels, Percentage on Time Delivery (\%)} = \frac{\text{Deliveries Achieved in Timeframe Promised (\#)}}{\text{All Deliveries Initiated in the Period (\#)}}$$

Inventories, like out-of-stocks and service levels, should be tracked at the SKU level. For example, in monitoring inventory, an apparel retailer will need to know not only the brand and design of goods carried, but also their size. Simply knowing that there are 30 pairs of suede hiking boots in a store, for example, is not sufficient—particularly if all those boots are the same size and fail to fit most customers.

By tracking inventory, marketers can determine the percentage of goods at each stage of the logistical process—in the warehouse, in transit to stores, or on the retail floor, for example. The significance of this information will depend on a firm's resource management strategy. Some firms seek to hold the bulk of their inventory at the warehouse level, for example, particularly if they have an effective transport system to ship goods quickly to stores.

Inventory Turns: The number of times that inventory "turns over" in a year can be calculated on the basis of the revenues associated with a product and the level of inventory held. One need only divide the revenues associated with the product in question by the average level of inventory for that item. As this quotient rises, it indicates that inventory of the item is moving more quickly through the process. Inventory turns can be calculated for companies, brands, or SKUs and at any level in the distribution chain, but they are frequently most relevant for individual trade customers. Important note: In calculating inventory turns, dollar figures for both sales and inventory must be stated either on a cost or wholesale basis, or on a retail or resale basis, but the two bases must not be mixed.

$$\text{Inventory Turns (I)} = \frac{\text{Annual Product Revenues (\$)}}{\text{Average Inventory (\$)}}$$

Inventory Days: This metric also sheds light on the speed with which inventory moves through the sales process. To calculate it, marketers divide the 365 days of the year by the number of inventory turns, yielding the average number of days of inventory carried by a firm. By way of example, if a firm's inventory of a product "turned" 36.5 times in a year, that firm would, on average, hold 10 days' worth of inventory of the product. High inventory turns—and, by corollary, low inventory days—tend to increase profitability through efficient use of a firm's investment in inventory. But they can also lead to higher out-of-stocks and lost sales.

$$\text{Inventory Days (\#)} = \frac{\text{Days in Year (365)}}{\text{Inventory Turns (I)}}$$

Inventory days represents the number of days' worth of sales that can be supplied by the inventory present at a given moment. Viewed from a slightly different perspective, this figure advises logistics managers of the time expected to elapse before they suffer a stock-out. To calculate this figure, managers divide product revenue for the year by the value of the inventory days, generating expected annual turns for that inventory level. This can be easily converted into days by using the previous equation.

EXAMPLE: An apparel retailer holds $600,000 worth of socks in inventory January 1, and $800,000 the following December 31. Revenues generated by sock sales totaled $3.5 million during the year.

To estimate average sock inventory during the year, managers might take the average of the beginning and ending numbers: ($600,000 + $800,000)/2 = $700,000 average inventory. On this basis, managers might calculate inventory turns as follows:

$$\text{Inventory Turns} = \frac{\text{Product Revenues}}{\text{Average Inventory}}$$

$$= \frac{\$3,500,000}{\$700,000} = 5$$

If inventory turns five times per year, this figure can be converted to inventory days in order to measure the average number of days worth of stock held during the period.

$$\text{Inventory Days} = \frac{\text{Days in Year (365)}}{\text{Inventory Turns}}$$

$$= \frac{365}{5} = 73 \text{ Days Worth of Inventory}$$

Data Sources, Complications, and Cautions

Although some companies and supply chains maintain sophisticated inventory tracking systems, others must estimate logistical metrics on the basis of less-than-perfect data. Increasingly, manufacturers may also have difficulty purchasing research because retailers that gather such information tend to restrict access or charge high fees for it. Often, the only readily available data may be drawn from incomplete store audits or reports filed by an overloaded sales force. Ideally, marketers would like to have reliable metrics for the following:

- Inventory units and monetary value of each SKU at each level of the distribution chain for each major customer.

- Out-of-stocks for each SKU, measured at both the supplier and the store level.

- Percentage of customer orders that were delivered on time and in the correct amount.

- Inventory counts in the tracking system that don't match the number in the physical inventory. (This would facilitate a measure of shrinkage or theft.)

When considering the monetary value of inventory, it is important to use comparable figures in all calculations. As an example of the inconsistency and confusion that can arise in this area, a company might value its stock on the retail shelf at the cost to the store, which might include an approximation of all direct costs. Or it might value that stock for some purposes at the retail price. Such figures can be difficult to reconcile with the cost of goods purchased at the warehouse and can also be different from accounting figures adjusted for obsolescence.

When evaluating inventory, managers must also establish a costing system for items that can't be tracked on an individual basis. Such systems include the following:

- **First In, First Out (FIFO):** The first unit of inventory received is the first expensed upon sale.

- **Last In, First Out (LIFO):** The last unit of inventory received is the first expensed upon sale.

The choice of FIFO or LIFO can have a significant financial impact in inflationary times. At such times, FIFO will hold down the cost of goods sold by reporting this figure at the earliest available prices. Simultaneously, it will value inventory at its highest possible level—that is, at the most recent prices. The financial impact of LIFO will be the reverse.

In some industries, inventory management is a core skill. Examples include the apparel industry, in which retailers must ensure that they are not left with prior seasons' fashions, and the technology industry, in which rapid developments make products hard to sell after only a few months.

In logistical management, firms must beware of creating reward structures that lead to sub-optimal outcomes. An inventory manager rewarded solely for minimizing out-of-stocks, for example, would have a clear incentive to overbuy—regardless of inventory holding costs. In this field, managers must ensure that incentive systems are sophisticated enough not to reward undesirable behavior.

Firms must also be realistic about what will be achieved in inventory management. In most organizations, the only way to be completely in stock on every product all the time is to ramp up inventories. This will involve huge warehousing costs. It will tie up a great deal of the company's capital in buying stocks. And it will result in painful obsolescence charges to unload over-purchased items. Good logistics and inventory management entails finding the right trade-off between two conflicting objectives: minimizing both inventory holding costs and sales lost due to out-of-stocks.

Related Metrics and Concepts

Rain Checks, or Make-Goods on Promotions: These measures evaluate the effect on a store of promotional items being unavailable. In a typical example, a store might track the incidents in which it offers customers a substitute item because it has run out of stock on a promoted item. Rain checks or make-goods might be expressed as a percentage of goods sold, or more specifically, as a percentage of revenues coded to the promotion but generated by sales of items not listed as part of the promotional event.

Misshipments: This measures the number of shipments that failed arrive on time or in the proper quantities.

Deductions: This measures the value of deductions from customer invoices caused by incorrect or incomplete shipments, damaged goods, returns, or other factors. It is often useful to distinguish between the reasons for deductions.

Obsolescence: This is a vital metric for many retailers, especially those involved in fashion and technology. It is typically expressed as the monetary value of items that are obsolete, or as the percentage of total stock value that comprises obsolete items. If obsolescence is high, then a firm holds a significant amount of inventory that is likely to sell only at a considerable discount.

Shrinkage: This is generally a euphemism for theft. It describes a phenomenon in which the value of actual inventory runs lower than recorded inventory, due to an unexplained reduction in the number of units held. This measure is typically calculated as a monetary figure or as a percentage of total stock value.

Pipeline Sales: Sales that are required to supply retail and wholesale channels with sufficient inventory to make a product available for sale (refer to Section 5).

Consumer Off-Take: Purchases by consumers from retailers, as opposed to purchases by retailers or wholesalers from their suppliers. When consumer off-take runs higher than manufacturer sales rates, inventories will be drawn down.

Diverted Merchandise or Diverted Goods: Products shipped to one customer that are subsequently resold to another customer. For example, if a retail drug chain overbuys vitamins at a promotional price, it may ship some of its excess inventory to a dollar store.

8 SKU Profitability: Markdowns, GMROII, and DPP

Profitability metrics for retail products and categories are generally similar to other measures of profitability, such as unit and percentage margins. Certain refinements have been developed for retailers and distributors, however. Markdowns, for example, are calculated as a ratio of discount to original price charged. Gross margin return on inventory investment (GMROII) is calculated as margin divided by the cost of inventory and is expressed as a "rate" or percentage. Direct product profitability (DPP) is a metric that adjusts gross margin for other costs, such as storage, handling, and allowances paid by suppliers.

$$\text{Markdown (\%)} = \frac{\text{Reduction in Price of SKU (\$)}}{\text{Initial Price of SKU (\$)}}$$

$$\text{Gross Margin Return on Inventory Investment (\%)} = \frac{\text{Gross Margin on Product Sales in Period (\$)}}{\text{Average Inventory Value at Cost (\$)}}$$

$$\text{Direct Product Profitability (\$)} = \text{Gross Margin (\$)} - \text{Direct Product Costs (\$)}$$

By monitoring markdowns, marketers can gain important insight into SKU profitability. GMROII can be a vital metric in determining whether sales rates justify inventory positions. DPP is a theoretically powerful measure of profit that has fallen out of favor, but it may be revived in other forms (for example, activity-based costing).

Purpose: To assess the effectiveness and profitability of individual product and category sales.

Retailers and distributors have a great deal of choice regarding which products to stock and which to discontinue as they make room for a steady stream of new offerings. By measuring the profitability of individual stock keeping units (SKUs), managers develop the insight needed to optimize such product selections. Profitability metrics are also useful in decisions regarding pricing, display, and promotional campaigns.

Figures that affect or reflect retail profitability include markdowns, gross margin return on inventory investment, and direct product profitability. Taking each in turn:

Markdowns are not always applied to slow-moving merchandise. Markdowns in excess of budget, however, are almost always regarded as indicators of errors in product assortment, pricing, or promotion. Markdowns are often expressed as a percentage of regular price. As a standalone metric, a markdown is difficult to interpret.

Gross margin return on inventory investment (GMROII) applies the concept of return on investment (ROI) to what is often the most crucial element of a retailer's working capital: its inventory.

Direct product profitability (DPP) shares many features with activity-based costing (ABC). Under ABC, a wide range of costs are weighted and allocated to specific products through cost drivers—the factors that cause the costs to be incurred. In measuring DPP, retailers factor such line items as storage, handling, manufacturer's allowances, warranties, and financing plans into calculations of earnings on specific product sales.

Construction

Markdown: This metric quantifies shop-floor reductions in the price of a SKU. It can be expressed on a per-unit basis or as a total for the SKU. It can also be calculated in dollar terms or as a percentage of the item's initial price.

$$\text{Markdown (\$)} = \text{Initial Price of SKU (\$)} - \text{Actual Sales Price (\$)}$$

$$\text{Markdown (\%)} = \frac{\text{Markdown (\$)}}{\text{Initial Price of SKU (\$)}}$$

Gross Margin Return on Inventory Investment (GMROII): This metric quantifies the profitability of products in relation to the inventory investment required to make them available. It is calculated by dividing the gross margin on product sales by the cost of the relevant inventory.

$$\text{Gross Margin Return on Inventory Investment (\%)} = \frac{\text{Gross Margin on Product Sales in Period (\$)}}{\text{Average Inventory Value at Cost (\$)}}$$

DIRECT PRODUCT PROFITABILITY (DPP)

Direct product profitability is grounded in a simple concept, but it can be difficult to measure in practice. The calculation of DPP consists of multiple stages. The first stage is to determine the gross margin of the goods in question. This gross margin figure is then modified to take account of other revenues associated with the product, such as promotional rebates from suppliers or payments from financing companies that gain business on its sale. The adjusted gross margin is then reduced by an allocation of direct product costs, described next.

Direct Product Costs: These are the costs of bringing a product to customers. They generally include warehouse, distribution, and store costs.

$$\text{Direct Product Costs (\$)} = \text{Warehouse Direct Costs (\$)} + \text{Transportation Direct Costs (\$)} + \text{Store Direct Costs (\$)}$$

Direct Product Profitability (DPP): Direct product profitability represents a product's adjusted gross margin, less its direct product costs.

As noted earlier, the concept of DPP is quite simple. Difficulties can arise, however, in calculating or estimating the relevant costs. Typically, an elaborate ABC system is needed to generate direct costs for individual SKUs. DPP has fallen somewhat out of favor as a result of these difficulties.

Other metrics have been developed, however, in an effort to obtain a more refined and accurate estimation of the "true" profitability of individual SKUs, factoring in the varying costs of receiving, storing, and selling them. The variations between products in the levels of these costs can be quite significant. In the grocery industry, for example, the cost of warehousing and shelving frozen foods is far greater—per unit or per dollar of sales—than the cost of warehousing and shelving canned goods.

$$\text{Direct Product Profitability (\$)} = \text{Gross Margin (\$)} - \text{Direct Product Costs (\$)}$$

EXAMPLE: The apparel retailer cited earlier wants to probe further into the profitability of its sock line. Toward that end, it assembles the following information. For this retailer, socks generate slotting allowances—in essence, fees paid by the manufacturer to the retailer in compensation for shelf space—in the amount of $50,000 per year. Warehouse costs for the retailer come to $10,000,000 per year. Socks consume 0.5% of warehouse space. Estimated store and distribution costs associated with socks total $80,000.

With this information, the retailer calculates an adjusted gross margin for its sock line.

$$\text{Adjusted Gross Margin} = \text{Gross Margin} + \text{Additional Margin}$$
$$= \$350,000 + \$50,000$$
$$= \$400,000$$

The retailer then calculates direct product costs for its sock line.

$$\text{Direct Product Costs} = \text{Store and Distribution Costs} + \text{Warehouse Costs}$$
$$= \$80,000 + (0.5\% * \$10,000,000)$$
$$= \$80,000 + \$50,000$$
$$= \$130,000$$

On this basis, the retailer calculates the direct product profitability of its sock line.

$$\text{DPP} = \text{Gross Margin} - \text{Direct Product Costs}$$
$$= \$400,000 - \$130,000$$
$$= \$270,000$$

Data Sources, Complications, and Cautions

For GMROII calculations, it is necessary to determine the value of inventory held, at cost. Ideally, this will be an average figure for the period to be considered. The average of inventory held at the beginning and end of the period is often used as a proxy, and is generally—but not always—an acceptable approximation. To perform the GMROII calculation, it is also necessary to calculate a gross margin figure.

One of the central considerations in evaluating direct product profitability is an organization's ability to capture large amounts of accurate data for analysis. The DPP calculation requires an estimate of the warehousing, distribution, store direct, and other costs attributable to a product. To assemble these data, it may be necessary to gather all distribution costs and apportion them according to the cost drivers identified.

Inventory held, and thus the cost of holding it, can change considerably over time. Although one may usually approximate average inventory over a period by averaging the beginning and ending levels of this line item, this will not always be the case. Seasonal factors may perturb these figures. Also, a firm may hold substantially more—or less—inventory during the course of a year than at its beginning and end. This could have a major impact on any DPP calculation.

DPP also requires a measure of the ancillary revenues tied to product sales.

Direct product profitability has great conceptual strength. It tries to account for the wide range of costs that retailers incur in conveying a product to customers, and thus to yield a more realistic measure of the profitability of that product. The only significant weakness in this metric is its complexity. Few retailers have been able to implement it. Many firms continue to try to realize its underlying concept, however, through such programs as activity-based costing.

Related Metrics and Concepts

Shopping Basket Margin: *The profit margin on an entire retail transaction, which may include a number of products. This aggregate transaction is termed the "basket" of purchases that a consumer makes.*

One key factor in a firm's profitability is its capability to sell ancillary products in addition to its central offering. In some businesses, more profit can be generated through accessories than through the core product. Beverage and snack sales at movie theaters are a prime example. With this in mind, marketers must understand each product's role within their firm's aggregate offering—be it a vehicle to generate customer traffic, or to increase the size of each customer's basket, or to maximize earnings on that item itself.

References and Suggested Further Reading

Wilner, J.D. (1998). *7 Secrets to Successful Sales Management: The Sales Manager's Manual*, Boca Raton: St. Lucie Press.

Zoltners, A.A., P. Sinha, and G.A. Zoltners. (2001). *The Complete Guide to Accelerating Sales Force Performance*, New York: Amacom.

ENDNOTES

1. Material in Sections 1–5 is based on a *Note on Sales Force Metrics*, written by Eric Larson, Darden MBA 2005.

2. Zoltners, Andris A., Prabhakant Sinha, and Greggor A. Zoltners. (2001). *The Complete Guide to Accelerating Sales Force Performance*, New York: AMACON.

3. Wilner, Jack D. (1998). *7 Secrets to Successful Sales Management*, Boca Raton, Florida: CRC Press LLC; 35–36, 42.

4. For more on these total allocations, see Zoltners, Andris A., Prabhakant Sinha, and Greggor A. Zoltners. (2001). *The Complete Guide to Accelerating Sales Force Performance*, New York: AMACON.

5. Zoltners, Andris A., Prabhakant Sinha, and Greggor A. Zoltners. (2001). *The Complete Guide to Accelerating Sales Force Performance*, New York: AMACON.

6. Dolan, Robert J., and Benson P. Shapiro. "Milford Industries (A)," Harvard Business School, Case 584-012.

7. Zoltners, Andris A., Prabhakant Sinha, and Greggor A. Zoltners. (2001). *The Complete Guide to Accelerating Sales Force Performance*, New York: AMACON.

8. Jones, Eli, Carl Stevens, and Larry Chonko. (2005). *Selling ASAP: Art, Science, Agility, Performance*, Mason, Ohio: South Western, 176.

9. Product category volume is also known as weighted distribution.

10. The authors use the term product category volume (PCV) for this metric. However, this term is not as widely used in industry as all commodity volume (ACV).

PRICING STRATEGY

Introduction

Key concepts covered:	
Price Premium	Optimal Prices, Linear and Constant Demand
Reservation Price	"Own," "Cross," and "Residual" Price Elasticity
Percent Good Value	
Price Elasticity of Demand	

"The cost of . . . lack of sophistication in pricing is growing day by day. Customers and Competitors operating globally in a generally more complex marketing environment are making mundane thinking about pricing a serious threat to the firm's financial well being."[1]

A full-fledged evaluation of pricing strategies and tactics is well beyond the scope of this text. However, there are certain key metrics and concepts that are fundamental to the analysis of pricing alternatives, and this chapter addresses them.

First we describe several of the more common methods of calculating price premiums—also called relative prices.

Next, we discuss the concepts that form the foundation of price-quantity schedules—also known as demand functions or demand curves. These include reservation prices and percent good value.

In the third section, we explain the definition and calculation of price elasticity, a frequently used index of market response to changes in price. This relatively simple ratio

From Chapter 7 of *Marketing Metrics: The Definitive Guide to Measuring Marketing Performance*, 2/e. Paul W. Farris. Neil T. Bendle. Phillip E. Pfeifer. David J. Reibstein. Copyright © 2010 by Pearson Education. Published by Wharton School Publishing.

of percentage changes in volumes and prices is complicated in practice by variations in measure and interpretation.

For managers, the purpose of understanding price elasticity is to improve pricing. With this in mind, we've devoted a separate section to determining optimal prices for the two main types of demand functions: linear and constant elasticity. The final portion of this chapter addresses the question of whether elasticity has been calculated in a manner that incorporates likely competitive reactions. It explains three types of elasticity—"own," "cross," and "residual" elasticity. Although these may seem at first glance to rest upon subtle or pedantic distinctions, they have major pragmatic implications. The familiar concept of the prisoner's dilemma helps explain their import.

	Metric	Construction	Considerations	Purpose
1	Price Premium	The percentage by which the price of a brand exceeds a benchmark price.	Benchmarks include average price paid, average price charged, average price displayed, and price of a relevant competitor. Prices can be compared at any level in the channel and can be calculated on a gross basis or net of discounts and rebates.	Measures how a brand's price compares to that of its competition.
2	Reservation Price	The maximum amount an individual is willing to pay for a product.	Reservation prices are difficult to observe.	One way to conceptualize a demand curve is as the aggregation of reservation prices of potential customers.
2	Percent Good Value	The proportion of customers who consider a product to be a good value—that is, to have a selling price below their reservation price.	Easier to observe than individual reservation prices.	A second way to conceptualize a demand curve is as the relationship between percent good value and price.

	Metric	Construction	Considerations	Purpose
3	Price Elasticity of Demand	The responsiveness of demand to a small change in price, expressed as a ratio of percentages.	For linear demand, linear projections based on elasticity are accurate, but elasticity changes with price. For constant elasticity demand, linear projections are approximate, but elasticity is the same for all prices.	Measures the responsiveness of quantity to changes in price. If priced optimally, the margin is the negative inverse of elasticity.
4	Optimal Price	For linear demand, optimal price is the average of variable cost and the maximum reservation price. For constant elasticity, optimal price is a known function of variable cost and elasticity. In general, optimal price is the price that maximizes contribution after accounting for how quantity changes with price.	Optimal price formulas are appropriate only if the variable cost per unit is constant, and there are no larger strategic considerations.	Quickly determines the price that maximizes contribution.
5	Residual Elasticity	Residual elasticity is "own" elasticity plus the product of competitor reaction elasticity and cross elasticity.	Rests on an assumption that competitor reaction to a firm's price changes is predictable.	Measures the responsiveness of quantity to changes in price, after accounting for competitor reactions.

1 Price Premium

Price premium, or relative price, is the percentage by which a product's selling price exceeds (or falls short of) a benchmark price.

$$\text{Price Premium (\%)} = \frac{[\text{Brand A Price (\$)} - \text{Benchmark Price (\$)}]}{\text{Benchmark Price (\$)}}$$

Marketers need to monitor price premiums as early indicators of competitive pricing strategies. Changes in price premiums can also be signs of product shortages, excess inventories, or other changes in the relationships between supply and demand.

Purpose: To evaluate product pricing in the context of market competition.

Although there are several useful benchmarks with which a manager can compare a brand's price, they all attempt to measure the "average price" in the marketplace. By comparing a brand's price with a market average, managers can gain valuable insight into its strength, especially if they view these findings in the context of volume and market share changes. Indeed, price premium—also known as relative price—is a commonly used metric among marketers and senior managers. Fully 63% of firms report the Relative Prices of their products to their boards, according to a recent survey conducted in the U.S., UK, Germany, Japan, and France.[2]

Price Premium: *The percentage by which the price charged for a specified brand exceeds (or falls short of) a benchmark price established for a similar product or basket of products. Price premium is also known as relative price.*

Construction

In calculating price premium, managers must first specify a benchmark price. Typically, the price of the brand in question will be included in this benchmark, and all prices in the benchmark will be for an equivalent volume of product (for example, price per liter). There are at least four commonly used benchmarks:

- The price of a specified competitor or competitors.

- Average price paid: The unit-sales weighted average price in the category.

- Average price displayed: The display-weighted average price in the category.

- Average price charged: The simple (unweighted) average price in the category.

   Price of a Specified Competitor: *The simplest calculation of price premium involves the comparison of a brand's price to that of a direct competitor.*

EXAMPLE: Ali's company sells "gO2" mineral water in its EU home market at a 12% premium over the price of its main competitor. Ali would like to know whether the same price premium is being maintained in the Turkish market, where gO2 faces quite different competition. He notes that gO2 mineral water sells in Turkey for 2 (new) Lira per liter, while its main competitor, Essence, sells for 1.9 Lira per liter.

$$\text{Price Premium} = \frac{(2.0\,\text{YTL} - 1.9\,\text{YTL})}{1.9\,\text{YTL}}$$

$$= \frac{0.1\,\text{YTL}}{1.9\,\text{YTL}} = 5.3\%\ \text{Premium Versus Essence}$$

When assessing a brand's price premium vis à vis multiple competitors, managers can use as their benchmark the average price of a selected group of those competitors.

> **Average Price Paid:** *Another useful benchmark is the average price that customers pay for brands in a given category. This average can be calculated in at least two ways: (1) as the ratio of total category revenue to total category unit sales, or (2) as the unit-share weighted average price in the category. Note that the market Average Price Paid includes the brand under consideration.*

Note also that changes in unit shares will affect the average price paid. If a low-price brand steals shares from a higher-priced rival, the average price paid will decline. This would cause a firm's price premium (calculated using the average price paid as a benchmark) to rise, even if its absolute price did not change. Similarly, if a brand is priced at a premium, that premium will decline as it gains share. The reason: A market share gain by a premium-priced brand will cause the overall average price paid in its market to rise. This, in turn, will reduce the price differential between that brand and the market average.

EXAMPLE: Ali wants to compare his brand's price to the average price paid for similar products in the market. He notes that gO2 sells for 2.0 Lira per liter and has 20% of the unit sales in market. Its up-market competitor, Panache, sells for 2.1 Lira and enjoys 10% unit market share. Essence sells for 1.9 Lira and has 20% share. Finally, the budget brand, Besik, sells for 1.2 Lira and commands 50% of the market.

Ali calculates the weighted Average Price Paid as $(20\% * 2) + (10\% * 2.1) + (20\% * 1.9) + (50\% * 1.2) = 1.59$ Lira.

$$\text{Price Premium (\%)} = \frac{(2.00 - 1.59)}{1.59}$$

$$= \frac{0.41}{1.59}$$

$$= 25.8\%$$

To calculate the price premium using the average price paid benchmark, managers can also divide a brand's share of the market in value terms by its share in volume terms. If value and volume market shares are equal, there is no premium. If value share is greater than volume share, then there is a positive price premium.

$$\text{Price Premium (\%)} = \frac{\text{Revenue Market Share (\%)}}{\text{Unit Market Share (\%)}}$$

Average Price Charged: *Calculation of the average price paid requires knowledge of the sales or shares of each competitor. A much simpler benchmark is the average price charged—the simple unweighted average price of the brands in the category. This benchmark requires knowledge only of prices. As a consequence, the price premium calculated using this benchmark is not affected by changes in unit shares. For this reason, this benchmark serves a slightly different purpose. It captures the way a brand's price compares to prices set by its competitors, without regard to customers' reactions to those prices. It also treats all competitors equally in the calculation of the benchmark price. Large and small competitors are weighted equally when calculating average price charged.*

EXAMPLE: Using the previous data, Ali also calculates the average price charged in the mineral water category as $(2 + 2.1 + 1.9 + 1.2)/4 = 1.8$ Lira.

Using the average price charged as his benchmark, he calculates gO2's price premium as

$$\text{Price Premium (\%)} = \frac{(2.0 - 1.8)}{1.8}$$

$$= \frac{0.2}{1.8}$$

$$= 11.1\% \text{ Premium}$$

Average Price Displayed: *One benchmark conceptually situated between average price paid and average price charged is the average price displayed. Marketing managers who seek a benchmark that captures differences in the scale and strength of brands' distribution might weight each brand's price in proportion to a numerical measure of distribution. Typical measures of distribution strength include numeric distribution, ACV (%), and PCV (%).*

EXAMPLE: Ali calculates the average price displayed using numeric distribution.

Ali's brand, gO2, is priced at 2 Lira and is distributed in 500 of the 1,000 stores that carry bottled water. Panache is priced at 2.1 Lira and stocked by 200 stores. Essence is priced at 1.9 Lira and sold through 400 stores. Besik carries a price of 1.2 Lira and has a presence in 900 stores.

Ali calculates relative weighting on the basis of numeric distribution. The total number of stores is 1,000. The weightings are therefore, for gO2, 500/1,000 = 50%; for Panache, 200/1,000 = 20%; for Essence, 400/1,000 = 40%; and for Besik, 900/1,000 = 90%. As the weightings thus total 200%, in calculating average price displayed, the sum of the weighted prices must be divided by that figure, as follows:

$$\text{Average Price Displayed} = \frac{[(2 * 50\%) + (2.1 * 20\%) + (1.9 * 40\%) + (1.2 * 90\%)]}{200\%}$$

$$= 1.63 \text{ Lira}$$

$$\text{Price Premium (\%)} = \frac{(2.00 - 1.63)}{1.63}$$

$$= \frac{0.37}{1.63}$$

$$= 22.7\% \text{ premium}$$

Data Sources, Complications, and Cautions

There are several practical aspects of calculating price premiums that deserve mention. Managers may find it easier to select a few leading competitors and focus their analysis and comparison on these. Often, it is difficult to obtain reliable data on smaller competitors.

Managers must exercise care when interpreting price premiums. Different benchmarks measure different types of premiums and must be interpreted accordingly.

Can a price premium be negative? Yes. Although generally expressed in terms that imply only positive values, a price premium can be negative. If one brand doesn't command a positive premium, a competitor will. Consequently, except in the unlikely event that all prices are exactly equal, managers may want to speak in terms of *positive* premiums. When a given brand's price is at the low end of the market, managers may want to say that the competition holds a price premium of a certain value.

Should we use retail, manufacturer, or distributor pricing? Each is useful in understanding the market dynamics at its level. When products have different channel margins, their price premiums will differ, depending on the channel under consideration. When stating a price premium, managers are advised to specify the level to which it applies.

Prices at each level can be calculated on a gross basis, or net of discounts, rebates, and coupons. Especially when dealing with distributors or retailers, there are likely to be substantial differences between manufacturer selling prices (retail purchase prices), depending on whether they are adjusted for discounts and allowances.

Related Metrics and Concepts

Theoretical Price Premium: *This is the price difference that would make potential customers indifferent between two competing products. It represents a different use of the term "price premium" that is growing in popularity. The theoretical price premium can also be discovered through a conjoint analysis using brand as an attribute. The theoretical price premium is the point at which consumers would be indifferent between a branded and an unbranded item, or between two different brands. We have termed this a "theoretical" price premium because there is no guarantee that the price premiums observed in the market will take this value.*

2   Reservation Price and Percent Good Value

The reservation price is the value a customer places on a product. It constitutes an individual's maximum willingness to pay. Percent good value represents the proportion of customers who believe a product is a "good value" at a specific price.

These are useful metrics in marketers' evaluation of pricing and customer value.

Purpose

Reservation prices provide a basis for estimating products' demand functions in situations where other data are not available. They also offer marketers insight into pricing latitude. When it is not possible or convenient to ask customers about their reservation prices, percent good value can provide a substitute for that metric.

Construction

Reservation Price: *The price above which a customer will not buy a product. Also known as the maximum willingness to pay.*

Percent Good Value: *The proportion of customers who perceive a product to represent a good value, that is, to carry a selling price at or below their reservation price.*

By way of example, let's posit a market consisting of 11 individuals with reservation prices for a given product of $30, $40, $50, $60, $70, $80, $90, $100, $110, $120, and $130. The manufacturer of that product seeks to decide upon its price. Clearly, it might do better than to offer a single price. For now, however, let's assume tailored prices are impractical. The variable cost to produce the product is $60 per unit.

With these reservation prices, the manufacturer might expect to sell 11 units at $30 or less, 10 units at a price greater than $30 but less than or equal to $40, and so on. It would make no sales at a unit price greater than $130. (For convenience, we have assumed that people buy at their reservation price. This assumption is consistent with a reservation price being the *maximum* an individual is willing to pay.)

Table 1 shows this price-quantity relationship, together with the contribution to the firm at each possible price.

Table 1 Price-Quantity Relationship

Price	% Good Value	Quantity	Total Contribution
$20	100.00%	11	−$440
$30	100.00%	11	−$330
$40	90.91%	10	−$200
$50	81.82%	9	−$90
$60	72.73%	8	$0
$70	63.64%	7	$70
$80	54.55%	6	$120
$90	45.45%	5	$150
$100	36.36%	4	$160
$110	27.27%	3	$150
$120	18.18%	2	$120
$130	9.09%	1	$70
$140	0.00%	0	$0
$150	0.00%	0	$0

Variable Cost is $60 per unit.

A table of quantities expected at each of several prices is often called a demand schedule (or curve). This example shows that one way to conceptualize a demand curve is as the accumulation of individual reservation prices. Although it will clearly be difficult in practice to measure individual reservation prices, the point here is simply to illustrate the use of reservation prices in pricing decisions. In this example, the optimal price—that is, the price that maximizes total contribution—is $100. At $100, the manufacturer expects to sell four units. Its contribution margin is $40, yielding a total contribution of $160.

This example also illustrates the concept of consumer surplus. At $100, the manufacturer sells three items at a price point below customers' reservation prices. The consumer with the reservation price of $110 enjoys a surplus of $10. The consumer with the reservation price of $120 receives a surplus of $20. Finally, the consumer with the highest reservation price, $130, receives a surplus of $30. From the manufacturer's perspective, the total consumer surplus—$60—represents an opportunity for increased contribution if it can find a way to capture this unclaimed value.

Data Sources, Complications, and Cautions

Finding reservation prices is no easy matter. Two techniques that are frequently used to gain insight into this metric are as follows:

- **Second-price auctions:** In a second-price auction, the highest bidder wins but pays only the second-highest bid amount. Auction theory suggests that when bidding on items of known value in such auctions, individuals have an incentive to bid their reservation prices. Certain survey techniques have been designed to mimic this process. In one of these, customers are asked to name their prices for an item, with the understanding that these prices will then be subjected to a lottery. If the price drawn in the lottery is less than the price named, the respondent gains an opportunity to purchase the item in question at the drawn price.

- **Conjoint analysis:** In this analytical technique, marketers gain insight into customer perceptions regarding the value of any set of attributes through the trade-offs they are willing to make.

Such tests can, however, be difficult to construct and impractical in many circumstances. Consequently, as a fallback technique, marketers can measure percent good value. Rather than seeking to learn each customer's reservation price, they may find it easier to test a few candidate prices by asking customers whether they consider an item a "good value" at each of those prices.

Linear Demand

The quantity-price schedule formed by an accumulation of reservation prices can take a variety of shapes. When the distribution of reservation prices is uniform—when reservation prices are equally spaced, as in our example—the demand schedule will be linear (see Figure 1). That is, each increment in price will reduce quantity by an equal amount. As the

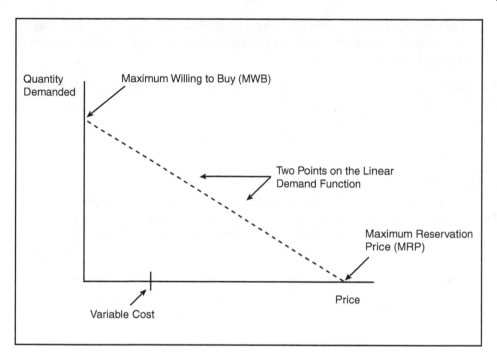

Figure 1   Maximum Willing to Buy and Maximum Reservation Price

linear function is by far the most commonly used representation of demand, we provide a description of this function as it relates to the distribution of underlying reservation prices.

It takes only two points to determine a straight line. Likewise, it takes only two parameters to write an equation for that line. Generally, that equation is written as $Y = mX + b$, in which m is the slope of the line and b is its Y-intercept.

A line, however, can also be defined in terms of the two points where it crosses the axes. In the case of linear demand, these crossing points (intercepts) have useful managerial interpretations.

The quantity-axis intercept can be viewed as a representation of the maximum willing to buy (MWB). This is the total number of potential customers for a product. A firm can serve all these customers only at a price of zero. Assuming that each potential customer buys one unit, MWB is the quantity sold when the price is zero.

The price-axis intercept can be viewed as the maximum reservation price (MRP). The MRP is a number slightly greater than the highest reservation price among all those willing to buy. If a firm prices its product at or above MRP, no one will buy.

Maximum Reservation Price: *The lowest price at which quantity demanded equals zero.*

Maximum Willing to Buy (MWB): *The quantity that customers will "buy" when the price of a product is zero. This is an artificial concept used to anchor a linear demand function.*

In a linear demand curve defined by MWB and MRP, the equation for quantity (**Q**) as a function of price (**P**) can be written as follows:

$$Q = (MWB) * [1 - \frac{P}{MRP}]$$

EXAMPLE: Erin knows that the demand for her soft drink is a simple linear function of price. She can sell 10 units at a price of zero. When the price hits $5 per unit, demand falls to zero. How many units will Erin sell if the price is $3 (see Figure 2)?

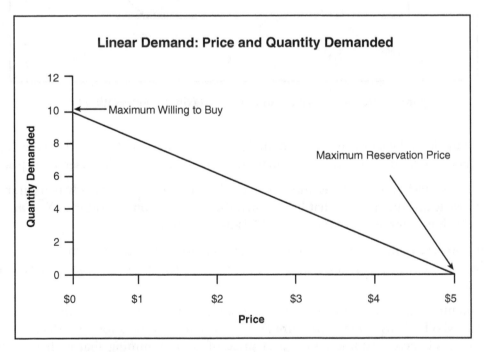

Figure 2   Simple Linear Demand (Price-Quantity) Function

For Erin's soft drink, the MRP (Maximum Reservation Price) is $5 and the MWB (Maximum Willing to Buy) is 10 units. At a price of $3, Erin will sell 10 * (1 − $3/$5), or 4 units.

When demand is linear, any two points on the price-quantity demand function can be used to determine **MRP** and **MWB**. If P_1 and Q_1 represent the first price-quantity point on the line, and P_2 and Q_2 represent the second, then the following two equations can be used to calculate **MWB** and **MRP**.

$$MWB = Q_1 - \left(\frac{Q_2 - Q_1}{P_2 - P_1}\right) * P_1$$

$$MRP = P_1 - \left(\frac{P_2 - P_1}{Q_2 - Q_1}\right)$$

EXAMPLE: Early in this chapter, we met a firm that sells five units at a price of $90 and three units at a price of $110. If demand is linear, what are **MWB** and **MRP**?

$$MWB = 5 - (-2/\$20) * \$90$$
$$= 5 + 9$$
$$= 14$$
$$MRP = \$90 - (\$20/-2) * 5$$
$$= \$90 + \$50$$
$$= \$140$$

The equation for quantity as a function of price is thus:

$$Q = 14 * \left(1 - \frac{P}{\$140}\right)$$

The market in this example, as you may recall, comprises 11 potential buyers with reservation prices of $30, $40, . . . , $120, $130. At a price of $130, the firm sells one unit. If we set price equal to $130 in the previous equation, our calculation does indeed result in a quantity of one. For this to hold true, the MRP must be a number slightly higher than $130.

A linear demand function often yields a reasonable approximation of actual demand only over a limited range of prices. In our 11-person market, for example, demand is linear only for prices between $30 and $130. To write the equation of the linear function that describes demand between $30 and $130, however, we must use an MWB of 14 and an MRP of $140. When we use this linear equation, we must remember that it reflects actual demand only for prices between $30 and $130, as illustrated in Figure 3.

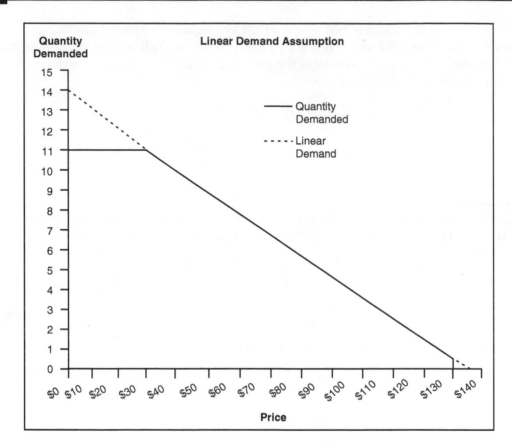

Figure 3   Example of Linear Demand Function

3   Price Elasticity of Demand

Price elasticity measures the responsiveness of quantity demanded to a small change in price.

$$\text{Price Elasticity (I)} = \frac{\text{Change in Quantity (\%)}}{\text{Change in Price (\%)}}$$

Price elasticity can be a valuable tool, enabling marketers to set an optimal price.

Purpose: To understand market responsiveness to changes in price.

Price elasticity is the most commonly employed measure of market responsiveness to changes in price. Many marketers, however, use this term without a clear understanding of what it entails. This section will help clarify some of the potentially dangerous details associated with estimates of price elasticity. This is challenging material but is well worth the effort. A strong command of price elasticity can help managers set optimal prices.

> **Price Elasticity:** *The responsiveness of demand to a small change in price, expressed as a ratio of percentages. If price elasticity is estimated at −1.5, for example, then we expect the percentage change in quantity to be approximately 1.5 times the percentage change in price. The fact that this number is negative indicates that when price rises, the quantity demanded is expected to decline, and vice versa.*

Construction

If we raise the price of a product, do we expect demand to hold steady or crash through the floor? In markets that are unresponsive to price changes, we say demand is inelastic. If minor price changes have a major impact on demand, we say demand is elastic. Most of us have no trouble understanding elasticity at a qualitative level. The challenges come when we quantify this important concept.

CHALLENGE ONE: QUESTIONS OF SIGN.

The first challenge in elasticity is to agree on its sign. Elasticity is the ratio of the percentage change in quantity demanded to the percentage change in price, for a small change in price. If an increase in price leads to a decrease in quantity, this ratio will be negative. Consequently, by this definition, elasticity will almost always be a negative number.

Many people, however, simply assume that quantity goes down as price goes up, and jump immediately to the question of "by how much." For such people, price elasticity answers that question and is a positive number. In their eyes, if elasticity is 2, then a small percentage increase in price will yield twice that percentage decrease in quantity.

In this book, under that scenario, we would say price elasticity is −2.

CHALLENGE TWO: WHEN DEMAND IS LINEAR, ELASTICITY CHANGES WITH PRICE.

For a linear demand function, the slope is constant, but elasticity is not. The reason: Elasticity is not the same as slope. Slope is the change in quantity for a small change in price. Elasticity, by contrast, is the *percentage* change in quantity for a small *percentage* change in price.

EXAMPLE: Consider three points on a linear demand curve: ($8, 100 units), ($9, 80 units), and ($10, 60 units) (see Figure 4). Each dollar change in price yields a 20-unit change in quantity. The slope of this curve is a constant −20 units per dollar.

As price rises from $8 to $9 (a 12.5% increase), quantity declines from 100 to 80 (a 20% decrease). The ratio of these percentages is 20%/12.5%, or −1.6. Similarly, as price rises from $8 to $10 (a 25% increase), quantity declines from 100 to 60 (a 40% decrease). Once again, the ratio (40%/25%) is −1.6. It appears that the ratio of percentage change in quantity to percentage change in price is −1.6, regardless of the size of the change made in the $8 price.

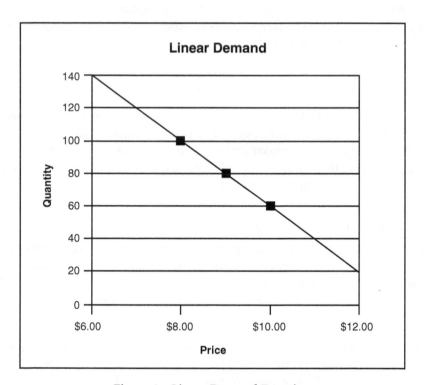

Figure 4   Linear Demand Function

Consider, however, what happens when price rises from $9 to $10 (an 11.11% increase). Quantity declines from 80 to 60 (a 25% decrease). The ratio of these figures, 25%/11.11%, is now −2.25. A price decline from $9 to $8 also yields an elasticity ratio of −2.25. It appears that this ratio is −2.25 at a price of $9, regardless of the direction of any change in price.

Exercise: Verify that the ratio of percentage change in quantity to percentage change in price at the price of $10 is −3.33 for every conceivable price change.

For a linear demand curve, elasticity changes with price. As price increases, elasticity gains in magnitude. Thus, for a linear demand curve, the absolute unit change in quantity for an absolute dollar change in price (slope) is constant, while the percentage change in quantity for a percentage change in price (elasticity) is not. Demand becomes more elastic—that is, elasticity becomes more negative—as price increases.

For a linear demand curve, the elasticity of demand can be calculated in at least three ways:

$$Elasticity\ (P_1) = \frac{\dfrac{Q_2 - Q_1}{Q_1}}{\dfrac{P_2 - P_1}{P_1}}$$

$$= \frac{Q_2 - Q_1}{P_2 - P_1} * \left(\frac{P_1}{Q_1}\right)$$

$$= Slope * \left(\frac{P_1}{Q_1}\right)$$

To emphasize the idea that elasticity changes with price on a linear demand curve, we write "*Elasticity (P),*" reflecting the fact that elasticity is a function of price. We also use the term "point elasticity" to cement the idea that a given elasticity applies only to a single point on the linear demand curve.

Equivalently, because the slope of a linear demand curve represents the change in quantity for a given change in price, price elasticity for a linear demand curve is equal to the slope, multiplied by the price, divided by the quantity. This is captured in the third equation here.

EXAMPLE: Revisiting the demand function from earlier, we see that the slope of the curve reflects a 20-unit decline in demand for each dollar increase in price. That is, slope equals -20.

The slope formula for elasticity can be used to verify our earlier calculations. Calculate price/quantity at each point on the curve, and multiply this by the slope to yield the price elasticity at that point (see Table 2).

For example, at a price of $8, quantity sold is 100 units. Thus:

$$Elasticity\ (\$8) = -20 * (8/100)$$

$$= -1.6$$

Table 2 Elasticities at a Point Calculated from the Slope of a Function

Price	Quantity Demanded	Price/Quantity	Slope	Price Elasticity at Point
$8.00	100	0.08	(20.00)	(1.60)
$9.00	80	0.11	(20.00)	(2.25)
$10.00	60	0.17	(20.00)	(3.33)

In a linear demand function, point elasticities can be used to predict the percentage change in quantity to be expected for any percentage change in price.

EXAMPLE: Xavi manages the marketing of a toothpaste brand. He knows the brand follows a linear demand function. At the current price of $3.00 per unit, his firm currently sells 60,000 units with an elasticity of −2.5. A proposal is floated to raise the price to $3.18 per unit in order to standardize margins across brands. At $3.18, how many units would be sold?

The proposed change to $3.18 represents a 6% increase over the current $3 price. Because elasticity is −2.5, such an increase can be expected to generate a decrease in unit sales of 2.5 * 6, or 15%. A 15% reduction in current sales of 60,000 units would yield a new quantity of 0.85 * 60,000, or 51,000.

Constant Elasticity: Demand Curve with a Constantly Changing Slope

A second common form of function used to estimate demand entails constant elasticity.[3] This form is responsible for the term "demand curve" because it is, indeed, curved. In contrast with the linear demand function, the conditions in this scenario are reversed: Elasticity is constant, while the slope changes at every point.

The assumption underlying a constant elasticity demand curve is that a small percentage change in price will cause the same percentage change in quantity, regardless of the value of the initial price. That is, the rate of change in quantity versus price, expressed as a ratio of percentages, is equal to a constant throughout the curve. That constant is the elasticity.

In mathematical terms, in a constant elasticity demand function, slope multiplied by price divided by quantity is equal to a constant (the elasticity) for all points along the curve (see Figure 5). The constant elasticity function can also be expressed in an equation that is easily calculated in spreadsheets:

$$Q(P) = A * P^{ELAS}$$

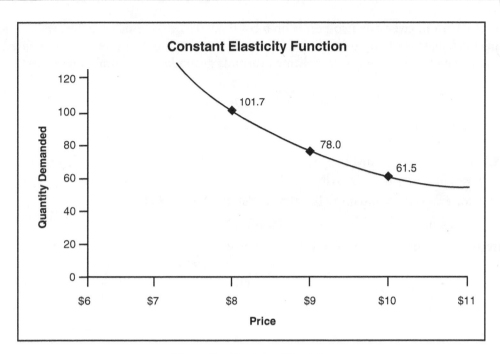

Figure 5 Constant Elasticity

In this equation, *ELAS* is the price elasticity of demand. It is usually a negative number. *A* is a scaling factor. It can be viewed as the quantity that would be sold at a price of $1 (assuming that $1 is a reasonable price for the product under consideration).

EXAMPLE: Plot a demand curve with a constant elasticity of −2.25 and a scaling factor of 10,943.1. For every point on this curve, a small percentage increase in price will yield a percentage decrease in quantity that is 2.25 times as great. This 2.25 ratio holds, however, only for the very smallest percentage changes in price. This is because the slope changes at every point. Using the 2.25 ratio to project the results of a finite percentage increase in price is always approximate.

The curve traced in this example should look like the constant elasticity curve in Figure 5. More exact figures for demand at prices $8, $9, and $10 would be 101.669, 78.000, and 61.538 units.

In its way, constant elasticity is analogous to the continuous compounding of interest. In a constant elasticity function, every small percentage increase in price generates the same percentage decrease in quantity. These percentage decreases compound at a constant rate, leading to an overall percentage decrease that does not precisely equal the continuous rate.

For this reason, given any two points on a constant elasticity demand curve, we can no longer calculate elasticity using finite differences as we could when demand was linear. Instead, we must use a more complicated formula grounded in natural logarithms:

$$ELAS = \frac{\ln(Q_2/Q_1)}{\ln(P_2/P_1)}$$

EXAMPLE: Taking any two points from the previous constant elasticity demand curve, we can verify that elasticity is -2.25.

At \$8, for example, the quantity is 101.669. Call these P_1 and Q_1.

At \$9 the quantity is 78.000. Call these P_2 and Q_2.

Inserting these into our formula, we determine that

$$ELAS = \frac{\ln(78.000/101.669)}{\ln(9/8)}$$

$$= \frac{-0.265}{0.118}$$

$$= -2.25$$

If we had set P_2 equal to \$8, and P_1 equal to \$9, we would have arrived at the same figure for elasticity. In fact, regardless of which two points we select on this constant elasticity curve, and regardless of the order in which we consider them, elasticity will always be -2.25.

In summary, elasticity is the standard measure of market responsiveness to changes in price. In general, it is the "percentage slope" of the demand function (curve) obtained by multiplying the slope of the curve for a given price by the ratio of price to quantity.

$$\textit{Elasticity}(P) = \textit{Slope} * \left(\frac{P}{Q}\right)$$

Elasticity can also be viewed as the percentage change in quantity for a small percentage change in price.

In a linear demand function, the slope is constant, but elasticity changes with price. In this scenario, marketers can use elasticity estimates to calculate the result of an anticipated price change in either direction, but they must use the elasticity that is appropriate for their initial price point. The reason: In a linear demand function, elasticity varies across price points, but projections based on these elasticities are accurate.

In a constant elasticity demand function, elasticity is the same at all price points, but projections based on these elasticities will be approximate. Assuming they are estimated with precision, using the constant elasticity demand function itself to make sales projections on the basis of price changes will be more accurate.

Data Sources, Complications, and Cautions

Price elasticity is generally estimated on the basis of available data. These data can be drawn from actual sales and price changes observed in the market, conjoint studies of customer intentions, consumer surveys about reservation prices or percent good value, or test-market results. In deriving elasticity, price-quantity functions can be sketched on paper, estimated from regressions in the form of linear or constant elasticity equations, or estimated through more complex expressions that include other variables in the marketing mix, such as advertising or product quality.

To confirm the validity and usefulness of these procedures, marketers must thoroughly understand the implications of the resulting elasticity estimate for customer behavior. Through this understanding, marketers can determine whether their estimate makes sense or requires further validation. That done, the next step is to use it to decide on pricing.

4   Optimal Prices and Linear and Constant Demand Functions

The optimal price is the most profitable price for any product. In a linear demand function, the optimal price is halfway between the maximum reservation price and the variable cost of the product.

$$\text{Optimal Price for a Linear Demand Function (\$)} = \frac{[\text{Maximum Reservation Price (\$)} + \text{Variable Cost (\$)}]}{2}$$

Generally, the gross margin on a product at its optimal price will be the negative inverse of its price elasticity.

$$\text{Gross Margin at Optimal Price (\%)} = \frac{-1}{\text{Elasticity (I)}}$$

Although it can be difficult to apply, this relationship offers a powerful insight: In a constant elasticity demand function, optimal margin follows directly from elasticity. This greatly simplifies the determination of the optimal price for a product of known variable cost.

Purpose: To determine the price that yields the greatest possible contribution.

Although "optimal price" can be defined in a number of ways, a good starting point is the price that will generate the greatest contribution by a product after deducting its variable cost—that is, the most profitable price for the product.

If managers set price too low, they forego revenue from customers who would willingly have paid more. In addition, a low price can lead customers to value a product less than they otherwise might. That is, it causes them to lower their reservation prices.

By contrast, if managers set price too high, they risk losing contribution from people who could have been served profitably.

Construction

For linear demand, the optimal price is the midpoint between the maximum reservation price and the variable cost of the product.

In linear demand functions, the price that maximizes total contribution for a product is always precisely halfway between the maximum reservation price (MRP) and the variable cost to produce that product. Mathematically, if **P*** represents the optimal price of a product, **MRP** is the X-intercept of its linear demand function, and **VC** is its variable cost per unit:

$$P^* = (MRP + VC)/2$$

EXAMPLE: Jaime's business sells goods that cost $1 to produce. Demand is linear. If priced at $5, Jaime believes he won't sell anything. For every dollar decrease in price, Jaime believes he will sell one additional unit.

Given that the variable cost is $1, the maximum reservation price is $5, and the demand function is linear, Jaime can anticipate that he'll achieve maximum contribution at a price midway point between VC and MRP. That is, the optimal price is ($5 + $1)/2, or $3.00 (see Figure 6).[4]

In a linear demand function, managers don't need to know the quantity of a product demanded in order to determine its optimal price. For those who seek to examine Jaime's contribution figures, however, please find the details in Table 3.

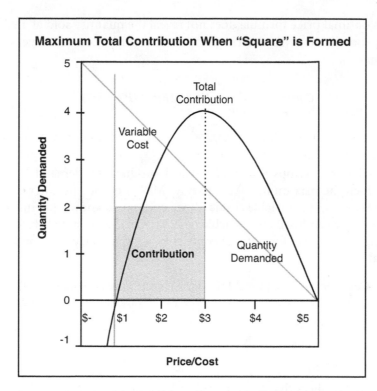

Figure 6   Optimal Price Midway Between Variable Cost and MRP

Table 3   Optimal Price = $\frac{1}{2}$ (MRP + Variable Cost)

Price	Quantity Demanded	Variable Cost per Unit	Contribution per Unit	Total Contribution
$0	5	$1	($1)	($5)
$1	4	$1	$0	$0
$2	3	$1	$1	$3
$3	**2**	**$1**	**$2**	**$4**
$4	1	$1	$3	$3
$5	0	$1	$4	$0

The previous optimal price formula does not reveal the quantity sold at a given price or the resulting contribution. To determine optimal contribution, managers can use the following equation:

$$Contribution^* = (MWB/MRP) * (P^* - VC)^2$$

EXAMPLE: Jaime develops a new but similar product. Its demand follows a linear function in which the maximum willing to buy (MWB) is 200 and the maximum reservation price (MRP) is $10. Variable cost is $1 per unit. Jaime knows that his optimal price will be midway between MRP and variable cost. That is, it will be ($1 + $10)/2 = $5.50 per unit. Using the formula for optimal contribution, Jaime calculates total contribution at the optimal price:

Contribution at Optimal Price for a Linear Demand Function ($)
= [MWB (#)/MRP ($)] * [Price ($) − Variable Costs ($)] ^ 2

= (200/10) * ($5.50 − $1) ^ 2

= 20 * $4.5 ^ 2

= $405

Jaime builds a spreadsheet that supports this calculation (see Table 4).

Table 4   Contribution Maximized at the Optimal Price

Price	Variable Costs	Quantity Demanded	Contribution per Unit	Total Contribution
$6	$1	80	$5.00	$400
$5.50	**$1**	**90**	**$4.50**	**$405**
$5	$1	100	$4.00	$400
$4	$1	120	$3.00	$360
$3	$1	140	$2.00	$280
$2	$1	160	$1.00	$160
$1	$1	180	$0.00	$0

This relationship holds across all linear demand functions, regardless of slope. For such functions, it is therefore possible to calculate the optimal price for a product on the basis of only two inputs: variable cost per unit and the maximum reservation price.

EXAMPLE: Brands A, B, and C each have a variable cost of $2 per unit and follow linear demand functions as shown in Table 5.

Table 5   The Optimal Price Formula Applies to All Linear Demand Functions

Price	Demand Brand A	Demand Brand B	Demand Brand C
$2	12	20	16
$3	10	18	15
$4	8	16	14
$5	6	14	13
$6	4	12	12
$7	2	10	11
$8	0	8	10
$9	0	6	9
$10	0	4	8
$11	0	2	7
$12	0	0	6

On the basis of these inputs, we can determine the maximum reservation price—the lowest price at which demand is zero. For Brand C, for example, we know that demand follows a linear function in which quantity declines by one unit for each dollar increase in price. If six units are demanded at $12, then $18 will be the lowest price at which no one will buy a single unit. This is the maximum reservation price. We can make similar determinations for Brands A and B (see Table 6).

Table 6   In Linear Demand Functions, the Determination of
Optimal Price Requires Only Two Inputs

	Brand A	Brand B	Brand C
Maximum Reservation Price	$8	$12	$18
Variable Costs	$2	$2	$2
Optimal Price	$5	$7	$10

To verify that the optimal prices so determined will generate the maximum attainable contribution, please see Table 7.

Table 7   The Optimal Prices for Linear Demand Functions Can Be Verified

Price	Variable costs	Unit Contribution = P - VC	Demand Brand A (Given)	Total Contribution Brand A	Demand Brand B (Given)	Total Contribution Brand B	Demand Brand C (Given)	Total Contribution Brand C
P	VC	UC	Q	Q*UC	Q	Q*UC	Q	Q*UC
$2	$2	$0	12	$0	20	$0	16	$0
$3	$2	$1	10	$10	18	$18	15	$15
$4	$2	$2	8	$16	16	$32	14	$28
$5	$2	$3	**6**	**$18**	14	$42	13	$39
$6	$2	$4	4	$16	12	$48	12	$48
$7	$2	$5	2	$10	**10**	**$50**	11	$55
$8	$2	$6	0	$0	8	$48	10	$60
$9	$2	$7	0	$0	6	$42	9	$63
$10	$2	$8	0	$0	4	$32	**8**	**$64**
$11	$2	$9	0	$0	2	$18	7	$63
$12	$2	$10	0	$0	0	$0	6	$60

Because slope doesn't influence optimal price, all demand functions with the same maximum reservation price and variable cost will yield the same optimal price.

EXAMPLE: A manufacturer of chair cushions operates in three different markets—urban, suburban, and rural. These vary greatly in size. Demand is far higher in the city than in the suburbs or the country. Variable cost, however, is the same in all markets at $4 per unit. The maximum reservation price, at $20 per unit, is also the same in all markets. Regardless of market size, the optimal price is therefore $12 per unit in all three markets (see Figure 7 and Table 8).

The optimal price of $12 is verified by the calculations in Table 9.

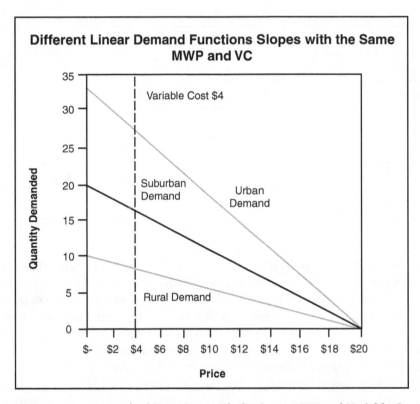

Figure 7   Linear Demand Functions with the Same MRP and Variable Cost

Table 8   The Slope Doesn't Influence Optimal Price

Maximum Reservation Price	$20
Variable Cost	$4
Optimal Price	$12

Table 9   Linear Demand Functions with Different Slopes

Price	Contri-bution	Suburban Demand	Rural Demand	Urban Demand	Suburban Contri-bution	Rural Contri-bution	Urban Contri-bution
$0	($4)	20	10	32	($80)	($40)	($128)
$2	($2)	18	9	29	($36)	($18)	($58)
$4	$0	16	8	26	$0	$0	$0
$6	$2	14	7	22	$28	$14	$45
$8	$4	12	6	19	$48	$24	$77
$10	$6	10	5	16	$60	$30	$96
$12	*$8*	*8*	*4*	*13*	*$64*	*$32*	*$102*
$14	$10	6	3	10	$60	$30	$96
$16	$12	4	2	6	$48	$24	$77
$18	$14	2	1	3	$28	$14	$45
$20	$16	—	—	—	—	—	—

In this example, it might help to think of the urban, suburban, and rural markets as groups of people with identical, uniform distributions of reservation prices. In each, the reservation prices are uniform between $0 and the maximum reservation price (MRP). The only difference between segments is the number of people in each. That number represents the maximum willing to buy (MWB). As might be expected, the *number* of people in a segment doesn't affect optimal price as much as the *distribution* of reservation prices in that segment. As all three segments here show the same distribution of reservation prices, they all carry the same optimal price.

Another useful exercise is to consider what would happen if the manufacturer in this example were able to increase everyone's reservation price by $1. This would raise the optimal price by half that amount, or $0.50. Likewise, the optimal price would rise by half the amount of any increase in variable cost.

Optimal Price in General

When demand is linear, we have an easy-to-use formula for optimal price. Regardless of the shape of the demand function, there is a simple relationship between gross margin and elasticity at the optimal price.

Optimal Price, Relative to Gross Margin: *The optimal price is the price at which a product's gross margin is equal to the negative of the reciprocal of its elasticity of demand.*[5]

$$\text{Gross Margin at Optimal Price (\%)} = \frac{-1}{\text{Elasticity at Optimal Price}}$$

A relationship such as this, which holds at the optimal price, is called an optimality condition. If elasticity is constant, then we can easily use this optimality condition to determine the optimal price. We simply find the negative of the reciprocal of the constant elasticity. The result will be the optimal gross margin. If variable costs are known and constant, then we need only determine the price that corresponds to the calculated optimal margin.

EXAMPLE: The manager of a stall selling replica sporting goods knows that the demand for jerseys has a constant price elasticity of -4. To price optimally, she sets her gross margin equal to the negative of the reciprocal of the elasticity of demand. (Some economists refer to the price-cost margin as the Lerner Index.)

$$\text{Gross Margin at Optimal Price} = \frac{-1}{-4}$$

$$= 25\%$$

If the variable cost of each jersey is \$5, the optimal price will be \$5/(1 − 0.25), or \$6.67.

The optimal margins for several price elasticities are listed in Table 10.

Table 10   Optimal Margins for Sample Elasticities

Price Elasticity	Gross Margin
−1.5	67%
−2	50%
−3	33%
−4	25%

Thus, if a firm's gross margin is 50%, its price will be optimal only if its elasticity at that price is −2. By contrast, if the firm's elasticity is −3 at its current price, then its pricing will be optimal only if it yields a gross margin of 33%.

This relationship between gross margin and price elasticity at the optimal price is one of the principal reasons that marketers take such a keen interest in the price elasticity of demand. Price elasticities can be difficult to measure, but margins generally are not. Marketers might now ask whether their current margins are consistent with estimates of price elasticity. In the next section, we will explore this issue in greater detail.

In the interim, if elasticity changes with price, marketers can use this optimality condition to solve for the optimal price. This condition applies to linear demand functions as well. Because the optimal price formula for linear demand is relatively simple, however, marketers rarely use the general optimality condition in this instance.

Data Sources, Complications, and Cautions

The shortcuts for determining optimal prices from linear and constant elasticity demand functions rest on an assumption that variable costs hold constant over the range of volumes considered. If this assumption is not valid, marketers will likely find that a spreadsheet model will offer the easiest way to determine optimal price.

We have explored these relationships in detail because they offer useful perspectives on the relationship between margins and the price elasticity of demand. In day-to-day management, margins constitute a starting point for many analyses, including those of price. One example of this dynamic would be cost-plus pricing.

Cost-plus pricing has received bad press in the marketing literature. It is portrayed not only as internally oriented, but also as naïve, in that it may sacrifice profits. From an alternate perspective, however, cost-plus pricing can be viewed as an attempt to maintain margins. If managers select the correct margin—one that relates to the price elasticity of demand—then pricing to maintain it may in fact be optimal if demand has constant elasticity. Thus, cost-plus pricing can be more customer-oriented than is widely perceived.

Related Metrics and Concepts

Price Tailoring—a.k.a. Price Discrimination: Marketers have invented a variety of price discrimination tools, including coupons, rebates, and discounts, for example. All are designed to exploit variations in price sensitivity among customers. Whenever customers have different sensitivities to price, or different costs to serve, the astute marketer can find an opportunity to claim incremental value through price tailoring.

EXAMPLE: The demand for a particular brand of sunglasses is composed of two segments: style-focused consumers who are less sensitive to price (more inelastic), and value-focused consumers who are more sensitive to price (more elastic) (see Figure 8). The style-focused group has a maximum reservation price of $30 and a maximum willing to buy of 10 units. The value-focused group has a maximum reservation price of $10 and a maximum willing to buy of 40 units.

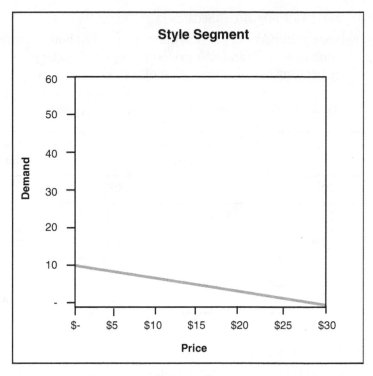

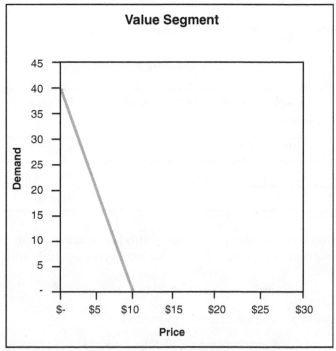

Figure 8   Two Segments Form Demand

■

ALTERNATIVE A: ONE PRICE FOR BOTH SEGMENTS

Suppose the sunglasses manufacturer plans to offer one price to both segments. Table 11 shows the contribution of several candidate prices. The optimal single price (to the nearest cent) is $6.77, generating a total contribution of $98.56.

Table 11   Two Segments: One Price for Both Segments

Single Price	Value Quantity Demanded	Style Quantity Demanded	Total Demand	Total Contribution
$5	20	8.33	28.33	$85.00
$6	16	8.00	24.00	$96.00
$6.77	**12.92**	**7.74**	**20.66**	**$98.56**
$7	12	7.67	19.67	$98.33
$8	8	7.33	15.33	$92.00

ALTERNATIVE B: PRICE PER SEGMENT

If the manufacturer can find a way to charge each segment its own optimal price, it will increase total contribution. In Table 12, we show the optimal prices, quantities, and contributions attainable if each segment pays a distinct optimal price.

Table 12   Two Segments: Price Tailoring

	MRP	Variable Costs	Optimal Price	Quantity	Revenue	Contribution
Style	$30	$2	$16	4.67	$74.67	$65.33
Value	$10	$2	$6	16	$96.00	$64.00
Total				20.67	$170.67	**$129.33**

These optimal prices were calculated as the midpoints between maximum reservation price (MRP) and variable cost (VC). Optimal contributions were calculated with the formula

$$\text{Contribution}^* = (\text{MWB/MRP}) * (P^* - \text{VC})^2$$

In the style-focused segment, for example, this yields

$$\text{Contribution}^* = (10/30) * (\$16 - \$2)^2$$
$$= (1/3) * (14^2) = \$65.33$$

Thus, through price tailoring, the sunglasses manufacturer can increase total contribution from \$98.56 to \$129.33 while holding quantity constant.

Where variable costs differ between segments, as in an airline's costs of service in business class versus economy class, the fundamental calculations are the same. To determine optimal prices, marketers need only change the variable cost per unit in each segment to correspond to actual costs.

Caution: Regulation

In most industrial economies, governments have passed regulations concerning price discrimination. In the United States, the most important of these is the Robinson-Patman Act. According to Supreme Court interpretations of this statute (as of mid-2009), Robinson-Patman forbids price discrimination *only to the extent that it threatens to injure competition.* There are two main types of injury contemplated by the Act:

1. **Primary line competitive injury**: Price discrimination might be used as a predatory tactic. That is, a firm might set prices below cost to certain customers in order to harm competition at the supplier level. Anti-trust authorities apply this standard to predatory pricing claims under the Sherman Act and the Federal Trade Commission Act in order to evaluate allegations of price discrimination.

2. **Secondary line competitive injury**: A seller that charges different prices to competing buyers of the same commodity, or that discriminates in providing "allowances"—such as compensation for advertising or other services—may be violating the Robinson-Patman Act. Such discrimination can impair competition by awarding favored customers an edge that has nothing to do with superior efficiency.

In the United States, price discrimination is often lawful, particularly if it reflects different costs of dealing with diverse buyers, or if it results from a seller's attempts to meet a competitor's prices or services.[6] Clearly, this is not intended to be a legal opinion, however. Legal advice should be sought for a company's individual circumstances.

5 "Own," "Cross," and "Residual" Price Elasticity

The concept of residual price elasticity introduces competitive dynamics into the pricing process. It incorporates competitor reactions and cross elasticity. This, in turn, helps explain why prices in daily life are rarely set at the optimal level suggested by a simpler view of elasticity. Marketers consciously or unconsciously factor competitive dynamics into their pricing decisions.

Residual Price Elasticity (I) = Own Price Elasticity (I) + [Competitor Reaction Elasticity (I) ⋆ Cross Elasticity (I)]

The greater the competitive reaction anticipated, the more residual price elasticity will differ from a company's own price elasticity.

Purpose: To account for both customers' price elasticity and potential competitive reactions when planning price changes.

Often, in daily life, price elasticity doesn't quite correspond to the relationships discussed in the prior section. Managers may find, for example, that their estimates of this key metric are not equal to the negative of the reciprocal of their margins. Does this mean they're setting prices that are not optimal? Perhaps.

It is more likely, however, that they're including competitive factors in their pricing decisions. Rather than using elasticity as estimated from current market conditions, marketers may estimate—or intuit—what elasticity *will be* after competitors respond to a proposed change in price. This introduces a new concept, residual price elasticity—customers' elasticity of demand in response to a change in price, *after* accounting for any increase or decrease in competitors' prices that may be triggered by the initial change.

Residual price elasticity is the combination of three factors:

1. **"Own" price elasticity**—The change in units sold due to the reaction of a firm's *customers* to its changes in price.

2. **"Competitor reaction" elasticity**—The reaction of *competitors* to a firm's price changes.

3. **"Cross" price elasticity**—The reaction of a firm's customers to price changes by its competitors.

These factors and their interactions are illustrated in Figure 9.

> **Own Price Elasticity:** *How customers in the market react to our price changes.*
>
> **Competitive Reaction Elasticity:** *How our competitors respond to our price changes.*
>
> **Cross Elasticity:** *How our customers respond to the price changes of our competitors.*

The distinction between own and residual price elasticity is not made clear in the literature. Some measures of price elasticity, for example, incorporate past competitive reactions and thus are more indicative of residual price elasticity. Others principally reflect

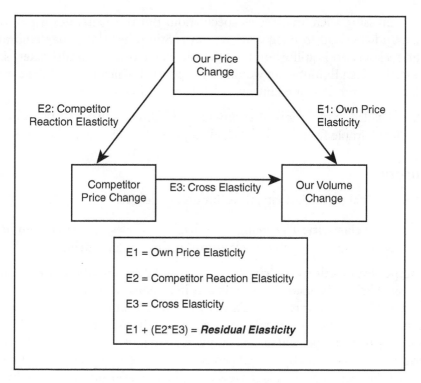

Figure 9   Residual Price Elasticity

own price elasticity and require further analysis to determine where sales and income will ultimately settle. The following sequence of actions and reactions is illustrative:

1. A firm changes price and observes the resulting change in sales. As an alternative, it may track another measure correlated with sales, such as share of choice or preference.

2. Competitors observe the firm's change in price and its increase in sales, and/or their own decrease in sales.

3. Competitors decide whether and by how much to change their own prices. The market impact of these changes will depend on (1) the direction and degree of the changes, and (2) the degree of cross elasticity, that is, the sensitivity of the initial firm's sales quantity to changes in competitors' prices. Thus, after tracking the response to its own price change, the initial firm may observe a further shift in sales as competitors' price changes take effect in the market.

Due to this dynamic, if a firm measures price elasticity only through customer response to its initial actions, it will miss an important potential factor: competitive reactions and their effects on sales. Only monopolists can make pricing decisions without regard to competitive response. Other firms may neglect or decline to consider competitive reactions, dismissing such analyses as speculation. But this generates a risk of short-sightedness and can lead to dangerous surprises. Still other firms may embrace game theory and seek a Nash Equilibrium to anticipate where prices will ultimately settle. (In this context, the Nash Equilibrium would be the point at which none of the competitors in a market have a profit-related incentive to change prices.)

Although a detailed exploration of competitive dynamics is beyond the scope of this book, we offer a simple framework for residual price elasticity next.

Construction

To calculate residual price elasticity, three inputs are needed:

1. **Own price elasticity**: The change in a firm's unit sales, resulting from its initial price change, assuming that competitors' prices remain unchanged.

2. **Competitor reaction elasticity**: The extent and direction of the price changes that are likely to be made by competitors in response to a firm's initial price change. If competitor reaction elasticity is 0.5, for example, then as a firm reduces its prices by a small percentage, competitors can be expected to reduce their own prices by half that percentage. If competitor reaction elasticity is −0.5, then as a firm reduces its prices by a small percentage, competitors will *increase* their prices by half that percentage. This is a less common scenario, but it is possible.

3. **Cross elasticity with regard to competitor price changes**: The percentage and direction of the change in the initial firm's sales that will result from a small percentage change in competitors' prices. If cross elasticity is 0.25, then a small percentage increase in competitors' prices will result in an increase of one-fourth that percentage in the initial firm's sales. Note that the sign of cross elasticity is generally the reverse of the sign of own price elasticity. When competitors' prices rise, a firm's sales will usually increase, and vice versa.

Residual Price Elasticity (I) = Own Price Elasticity (I) + [Competitor Reaction Elasticity (I) ∗ Cross Elasticity (I)]

The percentage change in a firm's sales can be approximated by multiplying its own price change by its residual price elasticity:

Change in Sales from Residual Elasticity (%) = Own Price Change (%) ∗ Residual Price Elasticity (I)

Forecasts of any change in sales to be generated by a price change thus should take into account the subsequent competitive price reactions that can be reasonably expected, as well as the second-order effects of those reactions on the sales of the firm making the initial change. The net effect of adjusting for such reactions might be to amplify, diminish, or even reverse the direction of the change in sales that was expected from the initial price change.

EXAMPLE: A company decides to reduce price by 10% (price change = −10%). It has estimated its own price elasticity to be −2. Ignoring competitive response, the company would expect a 10% price reduction to yield an approximately 20% increase in sales (−2 ∗ −10%). (Note: As observed in our earlier discussion of elasticity, projections based on point elasticity are accurate only for linear demand functions. Because this example does not specify the shape of the demand function, the projected 20% increase in sales is an approximation.)

The company estimates competitor reaction elasticity to be 1. That is, in response to the firm's action, competitors are expected to shift pricing in the same direction and by an equal percentage.

The company estimates cross elasticity to be 0.7. That is, a small percentage change in competitors' prices will result in a change in the firm's own sales of 0.7 percent. On this basis,

$$\text{Residual Elasticity} = \text{Own Price Elasticity} + (\text{Competitor Reaction Elasticity} \\ \ast \text{Cross Elasticity})$$

$$= -2 + (1 \ast 0.7)$$

$$= -2 + 0.7$$

$$= -1.3$$

$$\text{Sales Increase} \approx \text{Change in Price} \ast \text{Residual Elasticity}$$

$$= -10\% \ast -1.3$$

$$= 13\% \text{ Increase in Sales}$$

Competitor reactions and cross elasticity are expected to reduce the firm's initially projected sales increase from 20% to 13%.

Data Sources, Complications, and Cautions

Accounting for potential competitive reactions is important, but there may be simpler and more reliable methods of managing price strategy in a contested market. Game theory and price leadership principles offer some guidance.

It is important for managers to distinguish between price elasticity measures that are inherently unable to account for competitive reactions and those that may already incorporate some competitive dynamics. For example, in "laboratory" investigations of price sensitivity—such as surveys, simulated test markets, and conjoint analyses—consumers may be presented with hypothetical pricing scenarios. These can measure both own price elasticity and the cross elasticities that result from specific combinations of prices. But an effective test is difficult to achieve.

Econometric analysis of historical data, evaluating the sales and prices of firms in a market over longer periods of time (that is, annual or quarterly data), may be better able to incorporate competitive changes and cross elasticities. To the extent that a firm has changed price somewhat randomly in the past, and to the extent that competitors have reacted, the estimates of elasticity that are generated by such analyses will measure residual elasticity. Still, the challenges and complexities involved in measuring price elasticity from historical data are daunting.

By contrast, short-term test market experiments are unlikely to yield good estimates of residual price elasticity. Over short periods, competitors might not learn of price changes or have time to react. Consequently, elasticity estimates based on test markets are much closer to own price elasticity.

Less obvious, perhaps, are econometric analyses based on transactional data, such as scanner sales and short-term price promotions. In these studies, prices decline for a short time, rise again for a longer period, decline briefly, rise again, and so forth. Even if competitors conduct their own price promotions during the study period, estimates of price elasticity derived in this way are likely to be affected by two factors. First, competitors' reactions likely will not be factored into an elasticity estimate because they won't have had time to react to the initial firm's pricing moves. That is, their actions will have been largely motivated by their own plans. Second, to the extent that consumers stock up during price deals, any estimates of price elasticity will be higher than would be observed over the course of long-term price changes.

Prisoner's Dilemma Pricing

Prisoner's dilemma pricing describes a situation in which the pursuit of self-interest by all parties leads to sub-optimal outcomes for all. This phenomenon can lead to stability at prices above the expected optimal price. In many ways, these higher-than-optimal prices have the appearance of cartel pricing. But they can be achieved without explicit collusion, provided that all parties understand the dynamics, as well as their competitors' motivations and economics.

The prisoner's dilemma phenomenon derives its name from a story illustrating the concept. Two members of a criminal gang are arrested and imprisoned. Each prisoner is placed in solitary confinement, with no means of speaking to the other. Because the police don't have enough evidence to convict the pair on the principal charge, they plan to sentence both to a year in prison on a lesser charge. First, however, they try to get one or both to confess. Simultaneously, they offer each prisoner a Faustian bargain. If the prisoner testifies against his partner, he will go free, while the partner is sentenced to three years in prison on the main charge. But there's a catch . . . If *both* prisoners testify against each other, *both* will be sentenced to two years in jail.[7] On this basis, each prisoner reasons that he'll do best by testifying against his partner, regardless of what the partner does.

For a summary of the choices and outcomes in this dilemma, please see Figure 10, which is drawn in the first person from the perspective of one of the prisoners. First-person outcomes are listed in bold. Partner outcomes are italicized.

My partner refuses to testify	3 years	1 year
	I go free	**1 year**
My partner testifies	2 years	My partner goes free
	2 years	**3 years**
	I testify	**I refuse to testify**

Figure 10   Prisoner's Dilemma Pay-off Grid

Continuing the first-person perspective, each prisoner reasons as follows: If my partner testifies, I'll be sentenced to two years in prison if I testify as well, or three years if I don't. On the other hand, if my partner refuses to testify, I'll go free if I testify, but serve one year in prison if I don't. In either case, I do better if I testify. But this raises a dilemma. If I follow this logic and testify—and my partner does the same—we end up in the lower-left cell of the table, serving two years in prison.

Figure 11 uses arrows to track these preferences—a dark arrow for the first-person narrator in this reasoning, and a light arrow for his partner.

The dilemma, of course, is that it seems perfectly logical to follow the arrows and testify. But when both prisoners do so, they both end up worse off than they would have if they'd both refused. That is, when both testify, both are sentenced to two years in prison. If both had refused, they both could have shortened that term to a single year.

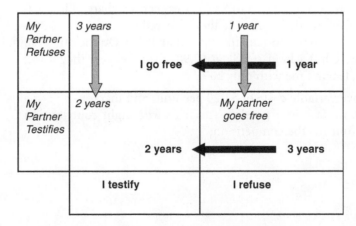

Figure 11   Pay-off Grid with Arrows Representing Preferences for Prisoners

Admittedly, it takes a good deal of time to grasp the mechanics of the prisoner's dilemma, and far longer to appreciate its implications. But the story serves as a powerful metaphor, encapsulating a wide range of situations in which acting in one's own best interest leads to outcomes in which everyone is worse off.

In pricing, there are many situations in which a firm and its competitors face a prisoner's dilemma. Often, one firm perceives that it could increase profits by reducing prices, regardless of competitors' pricing policies. Simultaneously, its competitors perceive the same forces at work. That is, they too could earn more by cutting prices, regardless of the initial firm's actions. If *both* the initial firm and its competitors reduce prices, however—that is, if all parties follow their own unilateral best interests—they will, in many situations, all end up worse off. The industry challenge in these situations is to keep prices high despite the fact that each firm will benefit by lowering them.

Given a choice between high and low prices a firm faces a prisoner's dilemma pricing situation when the following conditions apply:

1. Its contribution is greater at the low price when selling against both high and low competitor prices.

2. Competitors' contribution is greater at their low price when selling against both the high and low prices of the initial firm.

3. For both the initial firm and its competitors, however, contribution is lower if all parties set their price low than it would have been if all parties had priced high.

EXAMPLE: As shown in Table 13, my firm faces one main competitor. Currently my price is $2.90, their price is $2.80, and I hold a 40% share of a market that totals 20 million units. If I reduce my price to $2.60, I expect my share will rise to 55%—unless, of course, they also cut their price. If they also reduce price by $0.30—to $2.50—then I expect our market shares to remain constant at 40/60. On the other hand, if my competitor cuts its price but I hold steady at $2.90, then I expect they'll increase their market share to 80%, leaving me with only 20%.

If we both have variable costs of $1.20 per unit, and market size remains constant at 20 million units, we face four possible scenarios with eight contribution figures—four for my firm and four for the competition:

Table 13   Scenario Planning Pay-off Table

Pricing Scenario	My Price	My Volume (m)	My Sales ($m)	My Variable Costs ($m)	My Contribution ($m)
My Firm High. Competition High.	$2.90	8	$23.2	$9.6	$13.6
My Firm High. Competition Low.	$2.90	4	$11.6	$4.8	$6.8
My Firm Low. Competition Low.	$2.60	8	$20.8	$9.6	$11.2
My Firm Low. Competition High.	$2.60	11	$28.6	$13.2	$15.4

Pricing Scenario	Their Price	Their Volume (m)	Their Sales ($m)	Their Variable Costs ($m)	Their Contribution ($m)
My Firm High. Competition High.	$2.80	12	$33.6	$14.4	$19.2
My Firm High. Competition Low.	$2.50	16	$40.0	$19.2	$20.8
My Firm Low. Competition Low.	$2.50	12	$30.0	$14.4	$15.6
My Firm Low. Competition High.	**$2.80**	**9**	**$25.2**	**$10.8**	**$14.4**

Are we in a prisoner's dilemma situation?

Figure 12 shows the four contribution possibilities for both my firm and my competitor.

Their Price = $2.80 High	$14.4 $15.4	$19.2 $13.6
Their Price = $2.50 Low	$15.6 $11.2	$20.8 $6.8
	My Price = $2.60 Low	My Price = $2.90 High

Figure 12   Pay-off Grid with Expected Values (Values Are in the Millions of Dollars)

Let's check to see whether the conditions for the prisoner's dilemma are met:

1. My contribution is higher at the low price for both high and low competitor prices ($15.4m > $13.6m, and $11.2m > $6.8m). No matter what my competitor does, I make more money at the low price.

2. My competitor's contribution is higher at the low price, regardless of my price ($15.6m > $14.4m, and $20.8m > $19.2m). They, too, are better off at the low price, regardless of my price.

3. For both my firm and my competitor, however, contribution is lower if we both price low than it would be if we both price high ($15.6m < $19.2m, and $11.2m < $13.6m).

The conditions for the prisoner's dilemma are met (see Figure 13).

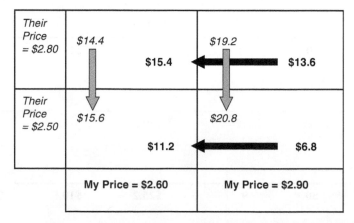

Figure 13   Pay-off Grid with Expected Values and Preference Arrows (Values Are in the Millions of Dollars)

The implication for my firm is clear: Although it is tempting to lower my price, seeking increased share and a $15.4 million contribution, I must recognize that my competitor faces the same incentives. They, too, have an incentive to cut price, grab share, and increase their contribution. But if they lower their price, I'll probably lower mine. If I lower my price, they'll probably lower theirs. If we both reduce our prices, I'll earn only $11.2m in contribution—a sharp decline from the $13.6m I make now.

Managerial Note: To determine whether you face a prisoner's dilemma situation, project the dollar contributions for both your firm and your competition at four combinations of high and low prices. Projections may require assumptions about your competitors' economics. These, in turn, will require care. If competitors' economics differ greatly from your projections, they may not face the decisions or motivations ascribed to them in your model. Additionally, there are a number of reasons why the logic of the prisoner's dilemma won't always hold, even if all assumptions are correct.

1. **Contribution may not be the sole criterion in decision-making:** In our example, we used contribution as the objective for both firms. Market share, however, may have importance to one or more firms, above and beyond its immediate, direct effect on contribution. Whatever a firm's objective may be, if it is quantifiable, we can place it in our table to better understand the competitive situation.

2. **Legal issues:** Certain activities designed to discourage competition and maintain high prices are illegal. Our purpose here is to help managers understand the economic trade-offs involved in competitive pricing. Managers should be aware of their legal environment and behave accordingly.

3. **Multiple competitors:** Pricing becomes more complicated when there are multiple competitors. The test for a multi-party prisoner's dilemma is the logical extension of the test described earlier. A major difference, however, arises in practice. As a general principle, the greater the number of independent competitors, the more difficult it will be to keep prices high.

4. **Single versus repeated play:** In our original story, two prisoners decide whether to testify in a single investigation. In game theory terms, they play the game a single time. Experiments have shown that in a single play of a prisoner's dilemma, the likely outcome is that both prisoners will testify. If the game is played repeatedly, however, it is more likely that both prisoners will refuse to testify. Because pricing decisions are made repeatedly, this evidence suggests that high prices are a more likely outcome. Most businesses eventually learn to live with their competition.

5. **More than two possible prices:** We have examined a situation in which each player considers two prices. In reality, there may be a wide range of prices under

consideration. In such situations, we might extend our analysis to more boxes. Once again, we might add arrows to track preferences. Using these more complex views, one sometimes finds areas within the table in which a prisoner's dilemma applies (usually at the higher prices), and others where it does not (usually at the lower prices). One might also find that the arrows lead to a particular cell in the middle of the table called the equilibrium. A prisoner's dilemma situation generally applies for prices higher than the set of equilibrium prices.

Applying the lessons of the prisoner's dilemma, we see that optimal price calculations based on own price elasticity may lead us to act in our own unilateral best interest. By contrast, when we factor residual price elasticity into our calculations, competitive response becomes a key element of our pricing strategy. As the prisoner's dilemma shows, over the long term, a firm is not always best served by acting in its apparent unilateral best interest.

References and Suggested Further Reading

Dolan, Robert J., and Hermann Simon. (1996). *Power Pricing: How Managing Price Transforms the Bottom Line*, New York: Free Press, 4.

Roegner, E.V., M.V. Marn, and C.C. Zawada. (2005). "Pricing," *Marketing Management*, 14(1), 23–28.

ENDNOTES

1. Dolan, Robert J., and Hermann Simon. *Power Pricing: How Managing Price Transforms the Bottom Line*, New York: The Free Press, 4.

2. Barwise, Patrick, and John U. Farley, "Which Marketing Metrics Are Used and Where?" Marketing Science Institute, (03-111) 2003, working paper, Series issues two 03-002.

3. Constant elasticity functions are also called log linear because they can be expressed as: log Q = log A + elasticity x log (p).

4. In graphing such relationships, economists often plot price on the vertical axis and quantity demanded on the horizontal axis. When reviewing a graph, managers are advised to always check the axis definitions.

5. If price elasticity is expressed in shorthand as a positive number, then we do not need the negative sign in the formula that follows.

6. Poundstone, William. (1993). *Prisoner's Dilemma*, New York: Doubleday, 118.

PROMOTION

Introduction

Key concepts covered:

Baseline Sales, Incremental Sales, and Promotional Lift

Percent Sales on Deal, Percent Time on Deal, and Average Deal Depth

Redemption Rates for Coupons/Rebates

Pass-Through and Price Waterfall

Price promotions can be divided into two broad categories:

- Temporary price reductions.

- Permanent features of pricing systems.[1]

With both of these, firms seek to change the behavior of consumers and trade customers in ways that increase sales and profits over time, though a promotion's short-term effect on profits will often be negative. There are multiple routes to sales and profit growth and many potential reasons for offering price promotions. Such programs might be aimed at affecting the behavior of end users (consumers), trade customers (distributors or retailers), competitors, or even a firm's own salespeople. Although the goal of a promotion is often to increase sales, these programs can also affect costs. Examples of specific, short-term promotional objectives include the following:

- To acquire new customers, perhaps by generating trial.

- To appeal to new or different segments that are more price-sensitive than a firm's traditional customers.

From Chapter 8 of *Marketing Metrics: The Definitive Guide to Measuring Marketing Performance*, 2/e. Paul W. Farris. Neil T. Bendle. Phillip E. Pfeifer. David J. Reibstein. Copyright © 2010 by Pearson Education. Published by Wharton School Publishing.

- To increase the purchase rates of existing customers; to increase loyalty.

- To gain new trade accounts (that is, distribution).

- To introduce new SKUs to the trade.

- To increase shelf space.

- To blunt competitive efforts by encouraging the firm's customers to "load up" on inventory.

- To smooth production in seasonal categories by inducing customers to order earlier (or later) than they ordinarily would.

In this chapter, we focus on metrics for monitoring the acceptance of price promotions and their effects on sales and profits.

The most powerful framework for evaluating temporary price promotions is to partition sales into two categories: baseline and incremental. Baseline sales are those that a firm would have expected to achieve if no promotion had been run. Incremental sales represent the "lift" in sales resulting from a price promotion. By separating baseline sales from incremental lift, managers can evaluate whether the sales increase generated by a temporary price reduction compensates for the concomitant decrease in prices and margins. Similar techniques are used in determining the profitability of coupons and rebates.

Although the short-term effect of a price promotion is almost invariably measured by its increase in sales, over longer periods management becomes concerned about the percentage of sales on deal and the percentage of time during which a product is on deal. In some industries, list price has become such a fiction that it is used only as a benchmark for discussing discounts.

Average deal depth and the price waterfall help capture the depth of price cuts and explain how one arrives at a product's net price (pocket price) after accounting for all discounts. There are often major differences between the discounts offered to trade customers and the extent to which those discounts are accepted. There may also be a difference between the discounts received by the trade and those that the trade shares with its customers. The pass-through percentage and price waterfall are analytic structures designed to capture those dynamics and thus to measure the impact of a firm's promotions.

	Metric	Construction	Considerations	Purpose
1	Baseline Sales	Intercept in regression of sales as function of marketing variables. Baseline Sales = Total Sales, less incremental sales generated by a marketing program or programs.	Marketing activities also contribute to baseline.	To determine the extent to which current sales are independent of specific marketing efforts.
1	Incremental Sales, or Promotional Lift	Total sales, less baseline sales. Regression coefficient to marketing variables cited above.	Need to consider competitive actions.	To determine short-term effects of marketing effort.
2	Redemption Rates	Coupons redeemed divided by coupons distributed.	Will differ significantly by mode of coupon distribution.	Rough measure of coupon "lift" after adjusting for sales that would have been made without coupons.
2	Costs for Coupons and Rebates	Coupon face amount plus redemption charges, multiplied by the number of coupons redeemed.	Does not consider margins that would have been generated by those willing to buy product without coupon.	Allows for budgeting of coupon expense.
2	Percentage Sales with Coupon	Sales via coupon, divided by total sales.	Doesn't factor in magnitude of discount offered by specific coupons.	A measure of brand dependence on promotional efforts.

Continues

	Metric	Construction	Considerations	Purpose
3	Percent Sales on Deal	Sales with temporary discounts as a percentage of total sales.	Does not make distinction for depth of discounts offered.	A measure of brand dependence on promotional efforts.
3	Pass-Through	Promotional discounts provided by the trade to consumers, divided by discounts provided to the trade by the manufacturer.	Can reflect power in the channel, or deliberate management or segmentation.	To measure the extent to which a manufacturer's promotions generate promotional activity further along the distribution channel.
4	Price Waterfall	Actual average price per unit divided by list price per unit. Can also be calculated by working backward from list price, taking account of potential discounts, weighted by the frequency with which each is exercised.	Some discounts may be offered at an absolute level, not on a per-item basis.	To indicate the price actually paid for a product, and the sequence of channel factors affecting that price.

1 Baseline Sales, Incremental Sales, and Promotional Lift

Estimates of baseline sales establish a benchmark for evaluating the incremental sales generated by specific marketing activities. This baseline also helps isolate incremental sales from the effects of other influences, such as seasonality or competitive promotions. The following equations can be applied for defined periods of time and for the specific element of the marketing mix that is used to generate incremental sales.

$$\text{Total Sales (\$,\#)} = \text{Baseline Sales (\$,\#)} + \text{Incremental Sales from Marketing (\$,\#)}$$

$$\text{Incremental Sales from Marketing (\$,\#)} = \text{Incremental Sales from Advertising (\$,\#)}$$
$$+ \text{Incremental Sales from Trade Promotion (\$,\#)}$$
$$+ \text{Incremental Sales from Consumer Promotion (\$,\#)}$$
$$+ \text{Incremental Sales from Other (\$,\#)}$$

$$\text{Lift (from Promotion) (\%)} = \frac{\text{Incremental Sales (\$,\#)}}{\text{Baseline Sales (\$,\#)}}$$

$$\text{Cost of Incremental Sales (\$)} = \frac{\text{Marketing Spending (\$)}}{\text{Incremental Sales (\$,\#)}}$$

The justification of marketing spending almost always involves estimating the incremental effects of the program under evaluation. However, because some marketing costs are often assumed to be fixed (for example, marketing staff and sales force salaries), one rarely sees incremental sales attributed to these elements of the mix.

Purpose: To select a baseline of sales against which the incremental sales and profits generated by marketing activity can be assessed.

A common problem in marketing is estimating the sales "lift" attributable to a specific campaign or set of marketing activities. Evaluating lift entails making a comparison with baseline sales, the level of sales that would have been achieved without the program under evaluation. Ideally, experiments or "control" groups would be used to establish baselines. If it were quick, easy, and inexpensive to conduct such experiments, this approach would dominate. In lieu of such control groups, marketers often use historical sales adjusted for expected growth, taking care to control for seasonal influences. Regression models that attempt to control for the influence of these other changes are often used to improve estimates of baseline sales. Ideally, both controllable and uncontrollable factors, such as competitive spending, should be included in baseline sales regression models. When regression is used, the intercept is often considered to be the baseline.

Construction

In theory, determining incremental sales is as simple as subtracting baseline sales from total sales. Challenges arise, however, in determining baseline sales.

> **Baseline Sales:** *Expected sales results, excluding the marketing programs under evaluation.*

In reviewing historical data, total sales are known. The analyst's task then is to separate these into baseline sales and incremental sales. This is typically done with regression analysis. The process can also involve test market results and other market research data.

$$\text{Total Sales (\$,\#)} = \text{Baseline Sales (\$,\#)} + \text{Incremental Sales (\$,\#)}$$

Analysts also commonly separate incremental sales into portions attributable to the various marketing activities used to generate them.

$$\text{Incremental Sales (\$,\#)} = \text{Incremental Sales from Advertising (\$,\#)} + \text{Incremental Sales from Trade Promotion (\$,\#)} + \text{Incremental Sales from Consumer Promotion (\$,\#)} + \text{Incremental Sales from Other (\$,\#)}$$

Baseline sales are generally estimated through analyses of historical data. Firms often develop sophisticated models for this purpose, including variables to adjust for market growth, competitive activity, and seasonality, for example. That done, a firm can use its model to make forward-looking projections of baseline sales and use these to estimate incremental sales.

Incremental sales can be calculated as total sales, less baseline sales, for any period of time (for example, a year, a quarter, or the term of a promotion). The lift achieved by a marketing program measures incremental sales as a percentage of baseline sales. The cost of incremental sales can be expressed as a cost per incremental sales dollar or a cost per incremental sales unit (for example, cost per incremental case).

$$\text{Incremental Sales (\$,\#)} = \text{Total Sales (\$,\#)} - \text{Baseline Sales (\$,\#)}$$

$$\text{Lift (\%)} = \frac{\text{Incremental Sales (\$,\#)}}{\text{Baseline Sales (\$,\#)}}$$

$$\text{Cost of Incremental Sales (\$)} = \frac{\text{Marketing Spending (\$)}}{\text{Incremental Sales (\$,\#)}}$$

EXAMPLE: A retailer expects to sell $24,000 worth of light bulbs in a typical month without advertising. In May, while running a newspaper ad campaign that cost $1,500, the store sells $30,000 worth of light bulbs. It engages in no other promotions or non-recurring events during the month. Its owner calculates incremental sales generated by the ad campaign as follows:

$$\text{Incremental Sales (\$)} = \text{Total Sales (\$)} - \text{Baseline Sales (\$)}$$
$$= \$30,000 - \$24,000 = \$6,000$$

The store owner estimates incremental sales to be $6,000. This represents a lift (%) of 25%, calculated as follows:

$$\text{Lift (\%)} = \frac{\text{Incremental Sales (\$)}}{\text{Baseline Sales (\$)}}$$
$$= \frac{\$6,000}{\$24,000} = 25\%.$$

The cost per incremental sales is $0.25, calculated as follows:

$$\text{Cost of Incremental Sales (\$)} = \frac{\text{Marketing Spending (\$)}}{\text{Incremental Sales (\$)}}$$
$$= \frac{\$1,500}{\$6,000} = 0.25$$

Total sales can be analyzed or projected as a function of baseline sales and lift. When estimating combined marketing mix effects, one must be sure to determine whether lift is estimated through a multiplicative or an additive equation. Additive equations combine marketing mix effects as follows:

Total Sales ($,#) = Baseline Sales + [Baseline Sales ($,#) * Lift (%) from Advertising]
+ [Baseline Sales ($,#) * Lift (%) from Trade Promotion]
+ [Baseline Sales ($,#) * Lift (%) from Consumer Promotion]
+ [Baseline Sales ($,#) * Lift (%) from Other]

This additive approach is consistent with the conception of total incremental sales as a sum of the incremental sales generated by various elements of the marketing mix. It is equivalent to a statement that

Total Sales ($,#) = Baseline Sales + Incremental Sales from Advertising + Incremental Sales from Trade Promotion + Incremental Sales from Consumer Promotion + Incremental Sales from Other

Multiplicative equations, by contrast, combine marketing mix effects by using a multiplication procedure, as follows:

Total Sales ($,#) = **Baseline Sales ($,#)** * (1 + **Lift (%) from Advertising**) * (1 + **Lift (%) from Trade Promotion**) * (1 + **Lift (%) from Consumer Promotion**) * (1 + **Lift (%) from Other**)

When using multiplicative equations, it makes little sense to talk about the incremental sales from a single mix element. In practice, however, one may encounter statements that attempt to do exactly that.

EXAMPLE: Company A collects data from past promotions and estimates the lift it achieves through different elements of the marketing mix. One researcher believes that an additive model would best capture these effects. A second researcher believes that a multiplicative model might better reveal the ways in which multiple elements of the mix combine to increase sales. The product manager for the item under study receives the two estimates shown in Table 1.

Table 1   Expected Returns to Marketing Spending

	Additive			Multiplicative		
Spending	Advertising Lift	Trade Promotion Lift	Consumer Promotion Lift	Advertising Lift	Trade Promotion Lift	Consumer Promotion Lift
$0	0%	0%	0%	1	1	1
$100k	5.5%	10%	16.5%	1.05	1.1	1.15
$200k	12%	24%	36%	1.1	1.2	1.3

Fortunately, both models estimate baseline sales to be $900,000. The product manager wants to evaluate the following spending plan: advertising ($100,000), trade promotion ($0), and consumer promotion ($200,000). He projects sales using each method as follows:

Additive:

$$\text{Projected Sales (\$)} = \$900,000 + [\$900,000 * 5.5\%] + [\$900,000 * 0] + [\$900,000 * 36\%]$$
$$= \$900,000 + \$49,500 + \$0 + \$324,000$$
$$= \$1,273,500$$

Multiplicative:

$$\text{Projected Sales} = \text{Baseline} * \text{Advertising Lift} * \text{Trade Promotion Lift}$$
$$* \text{Consumer Promotion Lift}$$
$$= \$900,000 * 1.05 * 1 * 1.3$$
$$= \$1,228,500$$

Note: Because these models are constructed differently, they will inevitably yield different results at most levels. The multiplicative method accounts for a specific form of interactions between marketing variables. The additive method, in its current form, does not account for interactions.

When historic sales have been separated into baseline and incremental components, it is relatively simple to determine whether a given promotion was profitable *during the period under study*. Looking forward, the profitability of a proposed marketing activity can be assessed by comparing projected levels of profitability with and without the program:

Profitability of a Promotion (\$) = Profits Achieved with Promotion (\$)
− Estimated Profits without Promotion
(that is, Baseline) (\$)[2]

EXAMPLE: Fred, the VP of Marketing, and Jeanne, the VP of Finance, receive estimates that sales will total 30,000 units after erecting special displays. Because the proposed promotion involves a considerable investment (\$100,000), the CEO asks for an estimate of the incremental profit associated with the displays. Because this program involves no change in price, contribution per unit during the promotion is expected to be the same as at other times, \$12.00 per unit. Thus, total contribution during the promotion is expected to be 30,000 * \$12, or \$360,000. Subtracting the incremental fixed cost of specialized displays, profits for the period are projected to be \$360,000 − \$100,000, or \$260,000.

Fred estimates that baseline sales total 15,000 units. On this basis, he calculates that contribution without the promotion would be \$12 * 15,000 = \$180,000. Thus, he projects that the special displays can be expected to generate incremental profit of \$360,000 − \$180,000 − \$100,000 = \$80,000.

Jeanne argues that she would expect sales of 25,000 units without the promotion, generating baseline contribution of \$12 * 25,000 = \$300,000. Consequently, if the promotion is implemented, she anticipates an incremental *decline* in profits from \$300,000 to \$260,000. In her view, the promotion's lift would not be sufficient to cover its incremental fixed costs. Under this promotion, Jeanne believes that the firm would be spending

$100,000 to generate incremental contribution of only $60,000 (that is, 5,000 units * $12 contribution per unit).

The baseline sales estimate is a crucial factor here.

EXAMPLE: A luggage manufacturer faces a difficult decision regarding whether to launch a new promotion. The firm's data show a major increase in product sales in November and December, but its managers are unsure whether this is a permanent trend of higher sales or merely a blip—a successful period that can't be expected to continue (see Figure 1).

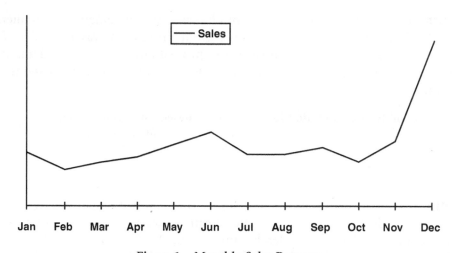

Figure 1   Monthly Sales Patterns

The firm's VP of Marketing strongly supports the proposed promotion. He argues that the increased volume can't be expected to continue and that the firm's historic baseline (26,028 units) should be used as the level of sales that can be anticipated without the promotion. In addition, the Marketing VP argues that only the variable cost of each sale should be considered. "After all, the fixed costs will be with us whatever we do," he says. On this basis, the relevant cost per unit subject to analysis would be $25.76.

The CEO hires a consultant who has a very different opinion. In the consultant's view, the November-December sales increase was more than a blip. The market has grown, she says, and the strength of the firm's brand has grown with it. Consequently, a more appropriate estimate of baseline sales would be 48,960 units. The consultant also points out that in the long term, no costs are fixed. Therefore, for purposes of analysis, fixed costs should be allocated to the cost of the product because the product must ultimately generate a return after such expenses as factory rent are paid. On this basis, the full cost of each unit, $34.70, should be used as the cost of incremental sales (see Table 2).

Table 2 Baseline Matters When Considering Profitability

| | Consultant | | VP Marketing | |
	Promotion	Baseline	Promotion	Baseline
Price	$41.60	$48.00	$41.60	$48.00
Cost	$34.70	$34.70	$25.76	$25.76
Margin	$6.90	$13.30	$15.84	$22.24
Sales	75,174	48,960	75,174	26,028
Profit	$518,701	$651,168	$1,190,756	$578,863
Profitability of Promotion	($132,467)		$611,893	

The Marketing VP and the consultant make very different projections of the profitability of the promotion. Once again, the choice of the baseline matters. Also, we can see that establishing a shared understanding of costs and margins can be critical.

Data Sources, Complications, and Cautions

Finding a baseline estimate of what a company can be expected to sell, "all things being equal," is a complex and inexact process. Essentially, the baseline is the level of sales that can be expected without significant marketing activities. When certain marketing activities, such as price promotions, have been employed for several periods, it can be especially difficult to separate "incremental" and "baseline" sales.

In many companies, it is common to measure sales performance against historic data. In effect, this sets historic sales as the baseline level for analysis of the impact of marketing spending. For example, retailers can evaluate their performance on the basis of same store sales (to remove differences caused by the addition or removal of outlets). Further, they can compare each current period to the same period in the prior year, in order to avoid seasonality biases and to ensure that they measure periods of special activity (such as sales events) against times of similar activity.

It is also common practice to adjust the profitability of promotions for longer-term effects. These effects can include a decline in sales levels in periods immediately following a promotion, as well as higher or lower sales in related product categories that are associated with a promotion. Adjustments can be negative or positive.

LONG-TERM EFFECTS OF PROMOTIONS

Over time, the effects of promotions may be to "ratchet" sales up or down (see Figures 2 and 3). Under one scenario, in response to one firm's promotions, competitors may also increase their promotional activity, and consumers and trade customers in the field may learn to wait for deals, increasing sales for no one.

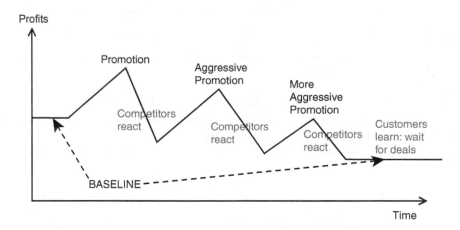

Figure 2   Downward Spiral—Promotional Effectiveness

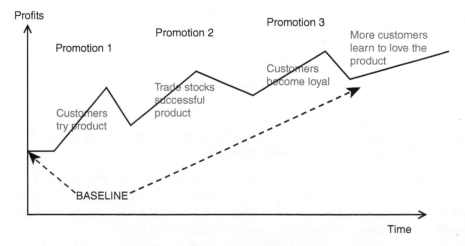

Figure 3   Successful Promotion with Long-Term Benefits

Under a different, more heartening scenario, promotions can generate trial for new products, build trade distribution, and encourage loyalty, thus raising the long-term level of baseline sales.

2 Redemption Rates, Costs for Coupons and Rebates, Percent Sales with Coupon

Redemption rate is the percentage of distributed coupons or rebates that are used (redeemed) by consumers.

$$\text{Coupon Redemption Rate (\%)} = \frac{\text{Coupons Redeemed (\#)}}{\text{Coupons Distributed (\#)}}$$

$$\text{Cost per Redemption (\$)} = \text{Coupon Face Amount (\$)} + \text{Redemption Charges (\$)}$$

$$\text{Total Coupon Cost (\$)} = [\text{Cost per Redemption (\$)} * \text{Coupons Redeemed (\#)}] + \text{Coupon Printing and Distribution Cost (\$)}$$

$$\text{Percentage Sales with Coupon (\%)} = \frac{\text{Sales with Coupon (\$)}}{\text{Sales (\$)}}$$

The redemption rate is an important metric for marketers assessing the effectiveness of their coupon distribution strategy. It helps determine whether coupons are reaching the customers who are motivated to use them. Similar metrics apply to mail-in rebates.

Cost per redemption ($) measures variable costs per coupon redeemed. Coupon distribution costs are usually viewed as fixed costs.

Purpose: To track and evaluate coupon usage.

Some people hate coupons. Some like them. And some say they hate coupons, but really like them. Businesses often say they hate coupons but continue to use them. Coupons and rebates are used to introduce new products, to generate trial of existing products by new customers, and to "load" consumers' pantries, encouraging long-term consumption.

Almost all of the interim objectives discussed in the introduction to this chapter can apply to coupons and rebates. Coupons can be used to offer lower prices to more price-sensitive consumers. Coupons also serve as a form of advertising, making them dual-purpose marketing vehicles. Coupon clippers will see a brand name and pay closer attention to it—considering whether they desire the product—than would an average consumer exposed to an advertisement without a compelling offer. Finally, both rebates and coupons can serve as focus points for retailer promotions. To generate traffic, retailers can double or even triple coupon amounts—generally up to a declared limit. Retailers also often advertise prices "after rebates" in order to promote sales and perceptions of value.

Construction

$$\text{Coupon Redemption Rate (\%)} = \frac{\text{Coupons Redeemed (\#)}}{\text{Coupons Distributed (\#)}}$$

$$\text{Cost per Redemption (\$)} = \text{Coupon Face Amount (\$)} + \text{Redemption Charges (\$)}$$

Total Coupon Cost: *Reflects distribution, printing,[3] and redemption costs to estimate the total cost of a coupon promotion.*

$$\text{Total Coupon Cost (\$)} = [\text{Coupons Redeemed (\#)} * \text{Cost per Redemption (\$)}] + \text{Coupon Printing and Distribution Cost (\$)}$$

$$\text{Total Cost per Redemption (\$)} = \frac{\text{Total Coupon Cost (\$)}}{\text{Coupons Redeemed (\#)}}$$

$$\text{Percentage Sales with Coupon (\%)} = \frac{\text{Sales with Coupon (\$,\#)}}{\text{Sales (\$,\#)}}$$

To determine the profitability of coupons and rebates, managers require approaches similar to those used in estimating baseline and incremental sales, as discussed in the previous section of this chapter. By themselves, redemption rates are not a good measure of success. Under certain circumstances, even low redemption rates can be profitable. Under other circumstances, by contrast, high redemption rates can be quite damaging.

EXAMPLE: Yvette is the Manager of Analysis for a small regional consumer packaged goods firm. Her product has a dominant share of the retail distribution in a narrow geographic area. Her firm decides to launch a coupon campaign, and Yvette is charged with reporting on the program's success. Her assistant looks at the figures and realizes that of the 100,000 coupons distributed in the local paper, 5,000 were used to buy product. The assistant is excited when he calculates that this represents a 5% redemption rate—a much higher figure than the company has ever previously seen.

Yvette, however, is more cautious in judging the promotion a success. She checks the sales of the relevant product and learns that these increased by only 100 units during the promotion period. Yvette concludes that the vast majority of coupon use was by customers who would have bought the product anyway. For most customers, the sole impact of the coupon was to reduce the price of the product below the level they would have willingly paid. Until she conducts a full profitability analysis, evaluating the profit generated by the 100 incremental sales and comparing this to coupon costs and the value lost on most coupon sales, Yvette can't be sure that the program made an overall loss. But she feels certain that she should curtail the celebrations.

Data Sources, Complications, and Cautions

To calculate coupon redemption rates, managers must know the number of coupons placed in circulation (distributed) as well as the number redeemed. Companies generally engage distribution services or media companies to place coupons in circulation. Redemption numbers are usually derived from the invoices presented by coupon clearinghouses.

Related Metrics and Concepts

MAIL-IN REBATES

The rebate, in effect, is a form of coupon that is popular with big-ticket items. Its usage dynamics are straightforward: Customers pay the full price for a product, enabling retailers to meet a specific price point. The customer then exercises the rebate and receives back a specified dollar amount.

By using rebates, marketers gain information about customers, which can be useful in remarketing and product control. Mail-in rebates also reduce the effective price of an item for customers who are sufficiently price-conscious to take advantage of them. Others pay full price. The "non-redemption rates" for rebates are sometimes called "breakage."

> **Breakage:** *The number of rebates not redeemed by customers. The breakage rate is the percentage of rebates not redeemed.*

EXAMPLE: A cell phone company sold 40,000 handsets in one month. On each purchase, the customer was offered a $30 rebate. Thirty thousand rebates were successfully claimed.

In volume terms, the rebate redemption rate can be calculated by dividing the number of rebates successfully claimed (30,000) by number offered (40,000):

$$\text{Redemption Rate (in volume terms)} = \frac{30,000}{40,000} = 75\%$$

Managers often balk at the cost of distributing coupons. Because promotions rely on adequate distribution, however, it is inadvisable to create arbitrary cutoffs for distribution costs. The total cost of incremental sales generated would represent a better metric to evaluate coupon efficiency—and thus to determine the point at which diminishing returns make further coupon distribution unattractive.

In evaluating a coupon or rebate program, companies should also consider the overall level of benefit provided to consumers. Retailers commonly increase the value of coupons, offering customers a discount of double or even triple the coupons' face value. This enables retailers to identify price-sensitive customers and offer them additional savings. Of course, by multiplying the savings afforded consumers, the practice of doubling or tripling coupons undoubtedly raises some redemption rates.

3   Promotions and Pass-Through

Of the promotional value provided by a manufacturer to its retailers and distributors, the pass-through percentage represents the portion that ultimately reaches the consumer.

$$\text{Percentage Sales on Deal (\%)} = \frac{\text{Sales with any Temporary Discount (\$,\#)}}{\text{Total Sales (\$,\#)}}$$

$$\text{Pass-Through (\%)} = \frac{\text{Value of Temporary Promotional Discounts Provided to Consumers by the Trade (\$)}}{\text{Value of Temporary Discounts Provided to Trade by Manufacturer (\$)}}$$

Manufacturers offer many discounts to their distributors and retailers (often called "the trade") with the objective of encouraging them to offer their own promotions, in turn, to their customers. If trade customers or consumers do not find promotions attractive, this will be indicated by a decline in percentage sales on deal. Likewise, low pass-through percentages can indicate that too many deals—or the wrong kinds of deals—are being offered.

Purpose: To measure whether trade promotions are generating consumer promotions.

Pass-Through: *The percentage of the value of manufacturer promotions paid to distributors and retailers that is reflected in discounts provided by the trade to their own customers.*

"Middlemen" are a part of the channel structure in many industries. Companies may face one, two, three, or even four levels of "resellers" before their product reaches the ultimate consumer. For example, a beer manufacturer may sell to an exporter, who sells to an importer, who sells to a local distributor, who sells to a retail store. If each channel adds its own margin, without regard for how others are pricing, the resulting price can be higher than a marketer would like. This sequential application of individual margins has been referred to as "double marginalization."[4]

Construction

Percentage Sales on Deal: *Measures the percentage of company sales that are sold with a temporary trade discount of some form. Note: This usually would not include standard discounts such as those for early payment or cooperative advertising allowances (accruals).*

$$\text{Percentage Sales on Deal (\%)} = \frac{\text{Sales with Any Temporary Discount (\#,\$)}}{\text{Total Sales (\#,\$)}}$$

Promotional discount represents the total value of promotional discounts given throughout the sales channel.

$$\text{Promotional Discount (\$)} = \text{Sales with Any Temporary Discount (\$)}$$
$$* \text{ Average Depth of Discount As Percent of List (\%)}$$

$$\text{Depth of Discount As Percent of List} = \frac{\text{Unit Discount (\$)}}{\text{Unit List Price (\$)}}$$

Pass-through is calculated as the value of discounts given by the trade to their customers, divided by the value of temporary discounts provided by a manufacturer to the trade.

$$\text{Pass-Through (\%)} = \frac{\text{Promotional Discounts Provided by the Trade to Consumers (\$)}}{\text{Discounts Provided to Trade by Manufacturer (\$)}}$$

Data Sources, Complications, and Cautions

Manufacturers often compete with one another for the attention of retailers, distributors, and other resellers. Toward that end, they build special displays for their products, change assortments to include new offerings, and seek to elicit increasing attention from resellers' sales personnel. Significantly, in their effort to increase channel "push," manufacturers also offer discounts and allowances to the trade. It is important to understand the rates and amounts of discounts provided to the trade, as well as the proportions of those discounts that are passed along to the resellers' customers. At times, when resellers' margins are thin, manufacturers' discounts are designed to enhance them. Market leaders often worry that trade margins are too thin to support push efforts. Other manufacturers may be concerned that retail margins are too high, and that too few of their discounts are being passed along. The metrics discussed in this chapter should be interpreted with these thoughts in mind.

Resellers may decide that optimizing an entire product line is more important than maximizing profits on any given product. If a reseller stocks multiple competing lines, it can be difficult to find an overall solution that suits both that reseller and its suppliers. Manufacturers strive to motivate resellers to market their goods aggressively and to grow their shared sales through such programs as incentives for "exclusivity," or rebates based on increasing shares of category sales or on year-to-year growth in sales.

Resellers learn to adapt their buying and selling practices to take advantage of manufacturer pricing incentives. In this area, marketers must pay special attention to the law of unforeseen consequences. For example, resellers have been known to

- Buy larger quantities of a product than they can sell—or want to sell—in order to qualify for volume discounts. The excess goods are then sold (diverted) to other retailers, stored for future sales, or even destroyed or returned to the manufacturer for "credit."

- Time their purchases at the ends of accounting periods in order to qualify for rebates and allowances. This results in "lumpy" sales patterns for manufacturers, making forecasting difficult, increasing problems with out-of-date products and returns, and raising production costs.

In some instances, a particularly powerful channel "captain" can impose pricing discipline on an entire channel. In most cases, however, each "link" in the distribution chain can coordinate only its own pricing. A manufacturer, for example, may work out appropriate pricing incentives for wholesalers, and the wholesalers in turn may develop their own pricing incentives for retailers.

In many countries and industries, it is illegal for suppliers to dictate the selling prices of resellers. Manufacturers can't dictate wholesaler selling prices, and wholesalers can't dictate retail prices. Consequently, members of the channel seek indirect methods of influencing resellers' prices.

4   Price Waterfall

The price waterfall is a way of describing the progression of prices from published list price to the final price paid by a customer. Each drop in price represents a drop in the "water level." For example:

100
List Price

    Dealer Discount

      90

      Cash Discount

        85

        Annual Rebate

          82

          Co-op Advertising

            Net Price $80

$$\text{Price Waterfall (\%)} = \frac{\text{Net Price per Unit (\$)}}{\text{List Price per Unit (\$)}}$$

In this structure, the average price paid by customers will depend on the list price of a product, the sizes of discounts given, and the proportion of customers taking advantage of those discounts.

By analyzing the price waterfall, marketers can determine where product value is being lost. This can be especially important in businesses that allow the sales channel to reduce prices in order to secure customers. The price waterfall can help focus attention on deciding whether these discounts make sense for the business.

Purpose: To assess the actual price paid for a product, in comparison with the list price.

In pricing, the bad news is that marketers can find it difficult to determine the right list price for a product. The good news is that few customers will actually pay that price anyway. Indeed, a product's net price—the price actually paid by customers—often falls between 53% and 94% of its base price.[5]

Net Price: *The actual price paid for a product by customers after all discounts and allowances have been factored in. Also called the pocket price.*

List Price: *The price of a good or service before discounts and allowances are considered.*

Invoice Price: *The price specified on the invoice for a product. This price will typically be stated net of some discounts and allowances, such as dealer, competitive, and order size discounts, but will not reflect other discounts and allowances, such as those for special terms and cooperative advertising. Typically, the invoice price will therefore be less than the list price but greater than the net price.*

Price Waterfall: *The reduction of the price actually paid by customers for a product as discounts and allowances are given at various stages of the sales process. Because few customers take advantage of all discounts, in analyzing a product's price waterfall, marketers must consider not only the amount of each discount but also the percentage of sales to which it applies.*

As customers vary in their use of discounts, net price can fall into a wide range relative to list price.

Construction

To assess a product's price waterfall, one must plot the price a customer will pay at each stage of the waterfall, specifying potential discounts and allowances in the sequence in which those are usually taken or applied. For example, broker commissions are generally applied *after* trade discounts.

> **Net Price:** *The actual average price paid for a product at a given stage in its distribution channel can be calculated as its list price, less discounts offered, with each discount multiplied by the probability that it will be applied. When all discounts are considered, this calculation yields the product's net price.*

Net Price (\$) = List Price (\$) − [Discount A (\$) ∗ Proportion of Purchases on which Discount A is Taken (%)] − [Discount B (\$) ∗ Proportion of Purchases on which Discount B is Taken (%)] and so on . . .

$$\text{Price Waterfall Effect (\%)} = \frac{\text{Net Price per Unit (\$)}}{\text{List Price per Unit (\$)}}$$

EXAMPLE: Hakan manages his own firm. In selling his product, Hakan grants two discounts or allowances. The first of these is a 12% discount on orders of more than 100 units. This is given on 50% of the firm's business and appears on its invoicing system. Hakan also gives an allowance of 5% for cooperative advertising. This is not shown on the invoicing system. It is completed in separate procedures that involve customers submitting advertisements for approval. Upon investigation, Hakan finds that 80% of customers take advantage of this advertising allowance.

The invoice price of the firm's product can be calculated as the list price (50 Dinar per unit), less the 12% order size discount, multiplied by the chance of that discount being given (50%).

Invoice Price = List Price − [Discount ∗ Proportion of Purchases on Which Discount Is Taken]
= 50 Dinar − [(50 ∗ 12%) ∗ 50%]
= 50 Dinar − 3 Dinar = 47 Dinar

The net price further reduces the invoice price by the average amount of the cooperative advertising allowance granted, as follows:

Net Price = List Price − [Discount ∗ Proportion of Purchases on Which Discount Is Taken]
− [Advertising Allowance ∗ Proportion of Purchases on Which Ad Allowance Is Taken] = 50 Dinar − [(50 ∗ 12%) ∗ 50%] − [(50 ∗ 5%) ∗ 80%] = 50 − 3 − 2
= 45 Dinar

To find the effect of the price waterfall, divide the net price by the list price.

$$\text{Price Waterfall (\%)} = \frac{45}{50} = 90\%$$

Data Sources, Complications, and Cautions

To analyze the impact of discounts, allowances, and the overall price waterfall effect, marketers require full information about sales, in both revenue and unit volume terms, at an individual product level, including not only those discounts and allowances that are formally recorded in the billing system, but also those granted without appearing on invoices.

The major challenge in establishing the price waterfall is securing product-specific data at all of these various levels in the sales process. In all but the smallest businesses, this is likely to be quite difficult, particularly because many discounts are granted on an off-invoice basis, so they might not be recorded at a product level in a firm's financial system. Further complicating matters, not all discounts are based on list price. Cash discounts, for example, are usually based on net invoice price.

Where discounts are known in theory, but the financial system doesn't fully record their details, the problem is determining how to calculate the price waterfall. Toward that end, marketers need not only the amount of each discount, but also the percentage of unit sales for which customers take advantage of that discount.

The typical business offers a number of discounts from list prices. Most of these serve the function of encouraging particular customer behaviors. For example, trade discounts can encourage distributors and resellers to buy in full truckloads, pay invoices promptly, and place orders during promotional periods or in a manner that smoothes production. Over time, these discounts tend to multiply as manufacturers find it easier to raise list price and add another discount than to eliminate discounts altogether.

Problems with discounts include the following:

- Because it's difficult to record discounts on a per-item basis, firms often record them in aggregate. On this basis, marketers may see the total discounts provided but have difficulty allocating these to specific products. Some discounts are offered on the total size of a purchase, exacerbating this problem. This increases the challenge of assessing product profitability.

- Once given, discounts tend to be sticky. It is hard to take them away from customers. Consequently, inertia often leaves special discounts in place, long after the competitive pressures that prompted them are removed.

- To the extent that discounts are not recorded on invoices, management often loses track of them in decision-making.

As the Professional Pricing Society advises, when considering the price of a product, "Look past the invoice price."[6]

Related Metrics and Concepts

Deductions: Some "discounts" are actually deductions applied by a customer to an invoice, adjusting for goods damaged in shipment, incorrect deliveries, late deliveries, or in some cases, for products that did not sell as well as hoped. Deductions might not be recorded in a way that can be analyzed, and they often are the subject of disputes.

Everyday Low Prices (EDLP): EDLP refers to a strategy of offering the same pricing level from period to period. For retailers, there is a distinction between buying at EDLP and selling at EDLP. For example, some suppliers offer constant selling prices to retailers but negotiate periods during which a product will be offered on deal with display and other retail promotions. Rather than granting temporary price discounts to retailers, suppliers often finance these programs through "market development funds."

HI-LO (High-Low): This pricing strategy constitutes the opposite of EDLP. In HI-LO pricing, retailers and manufacturers offer a series of "deals" or "specials"—times during which prices are temporary decreased. One purpose of HI-LO pricing and other temporary discounts is to realize price discrimination in the economic—not the legal—sense of the term.

PRICE DISCRIMINATION AND TAILORING

When firms face distinct and separable market segments with different willingness to pay (price elasticities), charging a single price means that the firm will "leave money on the table"—not capture the full consumer value.

There are three conditions for price tailoring to be profitable:

- Segments must have **different elasticities** (willingness to pay), and/or marketers must have different costs of serving the segments (say shipping expenses) and the incremental volume must be sufficiently large to compensate for the reduction in margin.

- Segments must be **separable**—that is, charging different prices does not just result in transfer between segments (for example, your father cannot buy your dinner and apply the senior citizen discount).

- The **incremental profit from price tailoring exceeds the costs** of implementing multiple prices for the same product or service.

Price tailoring is clearly a euphemism for price discrimination. However, the latter term is loaded with legal implications, and marketers understandably use it with caution.

When facing a total demand curve composed of identifiable segments with different demand slopes, a marketer can use optimal pricing for each segment recognized, as opposed to using the same price based upon aggregate demand. This is usually done by

- **Time:** For example, subways or movie theaters charging a higher price during rush or peak hour or products that are launched at a high price in the beginning, "skimming" profits from early adopters.

- **Geography:** Such as international market divisions—different prices for different regions for DVDs, for example.

- **Tolerable discrimination:** Identifying acceptable forms of segmentation, such as discriminating between students or senior citizens and the general public.

Price differences cause gray markets; goods are imported from low-price to high-price markets. Gray markets are common in some fashion goods and pharmaceuticals.

Caution: Regulations

Most countries have regulations that apply to price discrimination. As a marketer, you should understand these regulations. In the U.S., the most important regulation is the Robinson-Patman Act. It is mainly intended to control price differences that might injure competition.[7] We encourage you to visit the Federal Trade Commission's Web site (www.ftc.gov) for more information.

References and Suggested Further Reading

Abraham, M.M., and L.M. Lodish. (1990). "Getting the Most Out of Advertising and Promotion," *Harvard Business Review*, 68(3), 50.

Ailawadi, K., P. Farris, and E. Shames. (1999). "Trade Promotion: Essential to Selling Through Resellers," *Sloan Management Review*, 41(1), 83–92.

Christen, M., S. Gupta, J.C. Porter, R. Staelin, and D.R. Wittink. (1997). "Using Market-level Data to Understand Promotion Effects in a Nonlinear Model," *Journal of Marketing Research (JMR)*, 34(3), 322.

"Roegner, E., M. Marn, and C. Zawada. (2005). "Pricing," *Marketing Management*, Jan/Feb, Vol. 14 (1).

ENDNOTES

1. In this context, we use the term "permanent" with some flexibility, recognizing that even long-term arrangements must be subject to change in response to market and industry dynamics.

2. Often, contribution can be used as a proxy for profits.

3. Distribution for coupons is used in the sense of postage and insertion costs, rather than retail and inventory logistics.

4. For a richer discussion, see Ailawadi, Farris, and Shames, *Sloan Management Review*, Fall 1999.

5. Roegner, E., M. Marn, and C. Zawada. (2005). "Pricing," *Marketing Management*, Jan/Feb, Vol. 14 (1).

6. "How to Fix Your Pricing if it is Broken," by Ron Farmer, CEO, Revenue Technologies for The Professional Pricing Society: http://www.pricingsociety.com/htmljournal/ 4thquarter2003/article1.htm. Accessed 03/03/05.

7. The following are the two main types of injury contemplated by the Act: (a): Price discrimination might be used as a predatory pricing tactic, setting prices below cost to certain customers to harm competition at the supplier's level. Anti-trust authorities use the same standards applied to predatory pricing claims under the Sherman Act and the FTC Act to evaluate allegations of price discrimination used for this purpose. (b) Secondary Line competitive injury: A seller charging competing buyers different prices for the same "commodity" or discriminating in the provision of "allowances" such as compensation for advertising and other services may be violating the Robinson-Patman Act. This kind of price discrimination can hurt competition by giving favored customers an edge in the market that has nothing to do with their superior efficiency. However, in the U.S., price discrimination is generally lawful, particularly if it reflects the different costs of dealing with diverse buyers or results from a seller's attempts to meet a competitor's prices or services. Clearly this is not intended to be a legal opinion, and legal advice should be sought for a company's individual circumstances.

ADVERTISING MEDIA AND WEB METRICS

Introduction

Key concepts covered:

Advertising: Impressions, Gross Rating Points, and Opportunities-to-See

Cost per Thousand Impressions (CPM) Rates

Reach/Net Reach and Frequency

Frequency Response Functions

Effective Reach and Effective Frequency

Share of Voice

Impressions, Pageviews, and Hits

Rich Media Display Time

Rich Media Interaction Rate

Clickthrough Rates

Cost per Impression, Cost per Click, and Cost of Acquisition

Visits, Visitors, and Abandonment

Bounce Rate

Friends/Followers/Supporters

Downloads

Advertising is the cornerstone of many marketing strategies. The positioning and communications conveyed by advertising often set the tone and timing for many other sales and promotion efforts. Advertising is not only the defining element of the marketing mix, but it is also expensive and notoriously difficult to evaluate. This is because it is not easy to track the incremental sales associated with advertising decisions. For many marketers, media metrics are particularly confusing. A command of the vocabulary involved in this field is needed to work with media planners, buyers, and agencies. A strong understanding of media metrics can help marketers ensure that advertising budgets are spent efficiently and directed toward a specific aim.

In the first part of this chapter, we discuss media metrics that reveal how many people may be exposed to an advertising campaign, how often those people have an

■

From Chapter 9 of *Marketing Metrics: The Definitive Guide to Measuring Marketing Performance*, 2/e.
Paul W. Farris. Neil T. Bendle. Phillip E. Pfeifer. David J. Reibstein. Copyright © 2010 by Pearson Education.
Published by Wharton School Publishing.

opportunity to see the ads, and the cost of each potential impression. Toward that end, we introduce the vocabulary of advertising metrics, including such terms as impressions, exposures, OTS, rating points, GRPs, net reach, effective frequency, and CPMs.

In the second part of this chapter, we focus on metrics used in Web-based marketing efforts. The Internet increasingly provides valuable opportunities to augment traditional "broadcast" advertising with interactive media. In fact, many of the same advertising media terms, such as impressions, are used to describe and evaluate Web-based advertising. Other terms, such as clickthrough, are unique to the Web. Certain Web-specific metrics are needed because the Internet, like direct mail, serves not only as a communications medium, but also as a direct sales channel that can provide real-time feedback on the effectiveness of advertising in generating customer interest and sales.

	Metric	Construction	Considerations	Purpose
1	Impressions	An impression is generated each time an advertisement is viewed. The number of impressions achieved is a function of an ad's reach (the number of people seeing it), multiplied by its frequency (number of times they see it).	As a metric, impressions do not account for quality of viewings. In this regard, a glimpse will have less effect than a detailed study. Impressions are also called exposures and opportunities-to-see (OTS).	To understand how many times an advertisement is viewed.
1	Gross Rating Points (GRPs)	Impressions divided by the number of people in the audience for an advertisement.	Impressions expressed in relation to population. GRPs are cumulative across media vehicles, making it possible to achieve GRPs of more than 100%. Target Rating Points (TRPs) are measured in relation to defined target populations.	To measure impressions in relation to the number of people in the audience for an advertising campaign.

	Metric	Construction	Considerations	Purpose
2	Cost per Thousand Impressions (CPM)	Cost of advertising divided by impressions generated (in thousands).	CPM is a measure of cost per advertising impression, reckoning impressions in thousands. This makes it easier to work with the resulting dollar figures than would be possible on the basis of cost per single impression.	To measure the cost-effectiveness of the generation of impressions.
3	Net Reach	The number of people who receive an advertisement.	Equivalent to reach. Measures unique viewers of an advertisement. Often best mapped on a Venn diagram.	To measure the breadth of an advertisement's spread across a population.
3	Average Frequency	The average number of times that an individual receives an advertisement, given that he or she is indeed exposed to the ad.	Frequency is measured only among people who have in fact seen the advertisement under study.	To measure how strongly an advertisement is concentrated on a given population.
4	Frequency Response Functions	Linear: All advertising impressions are equally impactful. Threshold: A certain number of impressions are needed before an advertising message will sink in. Learning curve: An advertisement has little impact at first but gains force with repetition and then tails off as saturation is achieved.	Linear model is often unrealistic, especially for complex products. Threshold model is often used, as it is simple and intuitive. Learning curve models often hypothesized, but difficult to test for accuracy. Simpler models often work as well.	To model the reaction of a population to exposure to an advertisement.

Continues

	Metric	Construction	Considerations	Purpose
5	Effective Reach	Reach achieved among individuals who are exposed to an advertisement with a frequency greater than or equal to the effective frequency.	The effective frequency rate constitutes a crucial assumption in the calculation of this metric.	To measure the portion of an audience that is exposed to an advertisement enough times to be influenced.
5	Effective Frequency	The number of times an individual must see an advertisement in order to register its message.	As a rule of thumb in planning, marketers often use an effective frequency of 3. To the extent that it promises to have a significant impact on campaign results, this assumption should be tested.	To determine optimal exposure levels for an advertisement or campaign, trading the risk of over-spending against the risk of failing to achieve the desired impact.
6	Share of Voice	Quantifies the advertising "presence" of a brand, campaign, or firm in relation to total advertising in a market.	Market definition is central to meaningful results. Impressions or ratings represent a conceptually strong basis for share of voice calculations. Often, however, such data are unavailable. Consequently, marketers use spending, an input, as a proxy for output.	To evaluate the relative strength of advertising program within its market.
7	Pageviews	The number of times a Web page is served.	Represents the number of Web pages served. Hits, by contrast, represent pageviews multiplied by the number of files on a page, making it as much a metric of page design as of traffic.	To provide a top-level measure of the popularity of a Web site.

	Metric	Construction	Considerations	Purpose
8	Rich Media Display Time	The average time that rich media are displayed per viewer.	Can be heavily influenced by unusually long display times. How data is gathered is an important consideration.	To measure average viewing time of rich media.
9	Rich Media Interaction Rate	Provides fraction of viewers interacting with the rich media.	The definition of interaction should exclude actions unrelated to the rich media (a mouse crossing the rich media to reach another part of the screen).	Measures relative attractiveness of rich media and ability to generate viewer engagement.
10	Clickthrough Rate	Number of clickthroughs as a fraction of the number of impressions.	An interactive measure of Web advertising. Has great strengths, but clicks represent only a step toward conversion and are thus an intermediate advertising goal.	To measure the effectiveness of a Web advertisement by counting those customers who are sufficiently intrigued to click through it.
11	Cost per Click	Advertising cost, divided by number of clicks generated.	Often used as a billing mechanism.	To measure or establish the cost-effectiveness of advertising.
11	Cost per Order	Advertising cost, divided by number of orders generated.	More directly related to profit than cost per click, but less effective in measuring pure marketing. An advertisement may generate strong clickthrough but yield weak conversion due to a disappointing product.	To measure or establish the cost-effectiveness of advertising.

Continues

	Metric	Construction	Considerations	Purpose
11	Cost per Customer Acquired	Advertising cost, divided by number of customers acquired.	Useful for purposes of comparison to customer lifetime value. Helps marketers determine whether customers are worth the cost of their acquisition.	To measure the cost-effectiveness of advertising.
12	Visits	The number of unique viewings of a Web site.	By measuring visits relative to pageviews, marketers can determine whether viewers are investigating multiple pages on a Web site.	To measure audience traffic on a Web site.
12	Visitors	The number of unique Web site viewers in a given period.	Useful in determining the type of traffic generated by a Web site—a few loyal adherents, or many occasional visitors. The period over which this metric is measured can be an important consideration.	To measure the reach of a Web site.
12	Abandonment Rate	The rate of purchases started but not completed.	Can warn of weak design in an e-commerce site by measuring the number of potential customers who lose patience with a transaction process or are surprised and put off by "hidden" costs revealed toward its conclusion.	To measure one element of the close rate of Internet business.

	Metric	Construction	Considerations	Purpose
13	Bounce Rate	Fraction of Web site visitors who view a single page.	Requires a clear definition of when a visit ends. Usually considers bounce rate with respect to visits rather than visitors.	Often used as an indicator of site's relevance and ability to generate visitor interest.
14	Friends/ Followers/ Supporters	Number of individuals joining a social network.	Success depends on target group and the social nature of the product. This metric is unlikely to reflect the ultimate aim of a marketing campaign.	To measure size of social network, but unlikely to measure engagement.
15	Downloads	Number of times an application or file is downloaded.	Counts the times a file was downloaded, not the number of customers who downloaded a file. It is often useful to monitor downloads started but not completed.	To determine effectiveness in getting applications out to users.

1 Advertising: Impressions, Exposures, Opportunities-To-See (OTS), Gross Rating Points (GRPs), and Target Rating Points (TRPs)

Advertising impressions, exposures, and opportunities-to-see (OTS) all refer to the same metric: an estimate of the audience for a media "insertion" (one ad) or campaign.

Impressions = OTS = Exposures. In this chapter, we will use all these terms. It is important to distinguish between "reach" (number of unique individuals exposed to certain advertising) and "frequency" (the average number of times each such individual is exposed).

Rating Point = Reach of a media vehicle as a percentage of a defined population (for example, a television show with a rating of 2 reaches 2% of the population).

> **Gross Rating Points (GRPs)** = **Total Ratings** achieved by multiple media vehicles expressed in rating points (for example, advertisements on five television shows with an average rating of 30% would achieve 150 GRPs).
>
> Gross rating points are impressions expressed as a percentage of a defined population, and often total more than 100%. This metric refers to the defined population reached rather than an absolute number of people. Although GRPs are used with a broader audience, the term target rating points (TRPs) denotes a narrower definition of the target audience. For example, TRPs might consider a specific segment such as youths aged 15 to 19, whereas GRPs might be based on the total TV viewing population.

Purpose: To measure the audience for an advertisement.

Impressions, exposures, and opportunities-to-see (OTS) are the "atoms" of media planning. Every advertisement released into the world has a fixed number of planned exposures, depending on the number of individuals in its audience. For example, an advertisement that appears on a billboard on the Champs-Élysées in central Paris will have an estimated number of impressions, based on the flow of traffic from visitors and locals. An advertisement is said to "reach" a certain number of people on a number of occasions, or to provide a certain number of "impressions" or "opportunities-to-see." These impressions or opportunities-to-see are thus a function of the number of people reached and the number of times each such person has an opportunity to see the advertisement.

Methodologies for estimating opportunities-to-see vary by type of media. In magazines, for example, opportunities-to-see will not equal circulation because each copy of the magazine may be read by more than one person. In broadcast media, it is assumed that the quantified audience comprises those individuals available to hear or see an advertisement. In print and outdoor media, an opportunity-to-see might range from a brief glance to a careful consideration. To illustrate this range, imagine you're walking down a busy street. How many billboard advertisements catch your eye? You may not realize it, but you're contributing to the impressions of several advertisements, regardless of whether you ignore them or study them with great interest.

When a campaign involves several types of media, marketers may need to adjust their measures of opportunities-to-see in order to maintain consistency and allow for comparability among the different media.

Gross rating points (GRPs) are related to impressions and opportunities-to-see. They quantify impressions as a percentage of the population reached rather than in absolute numbers of people reached. Target rating points (TRPs) express the same concept but with regard to a more narrowly defined target audience.

Construction

Impressions, Opportunities-to-See (OTS), and Exposures: *The number of times a specific advertisement is delivered to a potential customer. This is an estimate of the audience for a media "insertion" (one ad) or a campaign. Impressions = OTS = Exposures.*

Impressions: The process of estimating reach and frequency begins with data that sum all of the impressions from different advertisements to arrive at total "gross" impressions.

$$\text{Impressions (\#)} = \text{Reach (\#)} * \text{Average Frequency (\#)}$$

The same formula can be rearranged as follows to convey the average number of times that an audience was given the opportunity to see an advertisement. Average frequency is defined as the average number of impressions per individual "reached" by an advertisement or campaign.

$$\text{Average Frequency (\#)} = \frac{\text{Impressions (\#)}}{\text{Reach (\#)}}$$

Similarly, the reach of an advertisement—that is, the number of people with an opportunity to see the ad—can be calculated as follows:

$$\text{Reach (\#)} = \frac{\text{Impressions (\#)}}{\text{Average Frequency (\#)}}$$

Although reach can thus be quantified as the number of individuals exposed to an advertisement or campaign, it can also be calculated as a percentage of the population. In this text, we will distinguish between the two conceptualizations of this metric as reach (#) and reach (%).

The reach of a specific media vehicle, which may deliver an advertisement, is often expressed in rating points. Rating points are calculated as individuals reached by that vehicle, divided by the total number of individuals in a defined population, and expressed in "points" that represent the resulting percentage. Thus, a television program with a rating of 2 would reach 2% of the population.

The rating points of all the media vehicles that deliver an advertisement or campaign can be summed, yielding a measure of the aggregate reach of the campaign, known as gross rating points (GRPs).

Gross Rating Points (GRPs): *The sum of all rating points delivered by the media vehicles carrying an advertisement or campaign.*

EXAMPLE: A campaign that delivers 150 GRPs might expose 30% of the population to an advertisement at an average frequency of 5 impressions per individual (150 = 30 * 5). If 15 separate "insertions" of the advertisement were used, a few individuals might be exposed as many as 15 times, and many more of the 30% reached would only have 1 or 2 opportunities-to-see (OTS).

$$\text{Gross Rating Points (GRPs) (\%)} = \text{Reach (\%)} * \text{Average Frequency (\#)}$$

$$\text{Gross Rating Points (GRPs) (\%)} = \frac{\text{Impressions (\#)}}{\text{Defined Population (\#)}}$$

Target Rating Points (TRPs): *The gross rating points delivered by a media vehicle to a specific target audience.*

EXAMPLE: A firm places 10 advertising insertions in a market with a population of 5 people. The resulting impressions are outlined in the following table, in which "1" represents an opportunity-to-see, and "0" signifies that an individual did not have an opportunity to see a particular insertion.

Insertion	Individual					Impressions	Rating Points (Impressions/ Population)
	A	B	C	D	E		
1	1	1	0	0	1	3	60
2	1	1	0	0	1	3	60
3	1	1	0	1	0	3	60
4	1	1	0	1	0	3	60
5	1	1	0	1	0	3	60
6	1	0	0	1	0	2	40
7	1	0	0	1	0	2	40
8	1	0	0	0	0	1	20
9	1	0	0	0	0	1	20
10	1	0	0	0	0	1	20
Totals	**10**	**5**	**0**	**5**	**2**	**22**	**440**

In this campaign, the total impressions across the entire population = 22.

As insertion 1 generates impressions upon three of the five members of the population, it reaches 60% of that population, for 60 rating points. As insertion 6 generates impressions upon two of the five members of the population, it reaches 40% of the population, for 40 rating points. Gross rating points for the campaign can be calculated by adding the rating points of each insertion.

$$\text{Gross Rating Points (GRPs)} = \text{Rating Points of Insertion 1} + \text{Rating Points of Insertion 2} + \text{etc.} = 440$$

Alternatively, gross rating points can be calculated by dividing total impressions by the size of the population and expressing the result in percentage terms.

$$\text{Gross Rating Points (GRPs)} = \frac{\text{Impressions}}{\text{Population}} * 100\% = \frac{22}{5} * 100\% = 440$$

Target rating points (TRPs), by contrast, quantify the gross rating points achieved by an advertisement or campaign among targeted individuals within a larger population. For purposes of this example, let's assume that individuals A, B, and C comprise the targeted group. Individual A has received 10 exposures to the campaign; individual B, 5 exposures; and individual C, 0 exposures. Thus, the campaign has reached two out of three, or 66.67% of targeted individuals. Among those reached, its average frequency has been 15/2, or 7.5. On this basis, we can calculate target rating points by either of the following methods.

$$\text{Target Rating Points (TRPs)} = \text{Reach (\%)} * \text{Average Frequency}$$

$$= 66.67\% * \frac{15}{2}$$

$$= 500$$

$$\text{Target Rating Points (TRPs)} = \frac{\text{Impressions (\#)}}{\text{Targets (\#)}} = \frac{15}{3} = 500$$

Data Sources, Complications, and Cautions

Data on the estimated audience size (reach) of a media vehicle are typically made available by media sellers. Standard methods also exist for combining data from different media to estimate "net reach" and frequency. An explanation of these procedures is beyond the scope of this book, but interested readers might want to consult a company dedicated to tracking rating points, such as Nielsen (www.nielsen.com), for further detail.

Two different media plans can yield comparable results in terms of costs and total exposures but differ in reach and frequency measures. In other words, one plan can expose a larger audience to an advertising message less often, while the other delivers more exposures to each member of a smaller audience. For an example, please see Table 1.

Table 1   Illustration of Reach and Frequency

	Reach	Average Frequency*	Total Exposures (Impressions, OTS)
Plan A	250,000	4	1,000,000
Plan B	333,333	3	1,000,000

*Average frequency is the average number of exposures made to each individual who has received at least one exposure to a given advertisement or campaign. To compare impressions across media, or even within classes of media, one must make a broad assumption: that there is some equivalency between the different types of impressions generated by each media classification. Nonetheless, marketers must still compare the "quality" of impressions delivered by different media.

Consider the following examples: A billboard along a busy freeway and a subway advertisement can both yield the same number of impressions. Whereas the subway advertisement has a captive audience, however, members of the billboard audience are generally driving and concentrating on the road. As this example demonstrates, there may be differences in the quality of impressions. To account for these differences, media optimizers apply weightings to different media vehicles. When direct response data are available, they can be used to evaluate the relative effectiveness and efficiency of impression purchases in different media. Otherwise, this weighting might be a matter of judgment. A manager might believe, for example, that an impression generated by a TV commercial is twice as effective as one made by a magazine print advertisement.

Similarly, marketers often find it useful to define audience sub-groups and generate separate reach and frequency statistics for each. Marketers might weight sub-groups differently in the same way that they weight impressions delivered through different media.[1] This helps in evaluating whether an advertisement reaches its defined customer groups.

When calculating impressions, marketers often encounter an overlap of people who see an advertisement in more than one medium.

2   Cost per Thousand Impressions (CPM) Rates

Cost per thousand impressions (CPM) is the cost per thousand advertising impressions. This metric is calculated by dividing the cost of an advertising placement by the number of impressions (expressed in thousands) that it generates.

$$\text{Cost per Thousand Impressions (CPM) (\$)} = \frac{\text{Advertising Cost (\$)}}{\text{Impressions Generated (\# in Thousands)}}$$

CPM is useful in comparing the relative efficiency of different advertising opportunities or media and in evaluating the costs of overall campaigns.

Purpose: To compare the costs of advertising campaigns within and across different media.

A typical advertising campaign might try to reach potential consumers in multiple locations and through various media. The cost per thousand impressions (CPM) metric enables marketers to make cost comparisons between these media, both at the planning stage and during reviews of past campaigns.

Marketers calculate CPM by dividing advertising campaign costs by the number of impressions (or opportunities-to-see) that are delivered by each part of the campaign. As the impression counts are generally sizable, marketers customarily work with the CPM impressions. Dividing by 1,000 is an industry standard.

> **Cost per Thousand Impressions (CPM):** *The cost of a media campaign, relative to its success in generating impressions or opportunities-to-see.*

Construction

To calculate CPM, marketers first state the results of a media campaign (gross impressions) in thousands. Second, they divide that result into the relevant media cost:

$$\text{Cost per Thousand Impressions (CPM) (\$)} = \frac{\text{Advertising Cost (\$)}}{\text{Impressions Generated (\# in Thousands)}}$$

EXAMPLE: An advertising campaign costs $4,000 and generates 120,000 impressions. On this basis, CPM can be calculated as follows:

$$\text{Cost per Thousand Impressions} = \frac{\text{Advertising Cost}}{\text{Impressions Generated (thousands)}}$$

$$= \frac{\$4,000}{(120,000/1,000)}$$

$$= \frac{\$4,000}{120} = \$33.33$$

Data Sources, Complications, and Cautions

In an advertising campaign, the full cost of the media purchased can include agency fees and production of creative materials, in addition to the cost of media space or time. Marketers also must have an estimate of the number of impressions expected or delivered in the campaign at an appropriate level of detail. Internet marketers (see Section 7) often can easily access these data.

CPM is only a starting point for analysis. Not all impressions are equally valuable. Consequently, it can make good business sense to pay more for impressions from some sources than from others.

In calculating CPM, marketers should also be concerned with their ability to capture the full cost of advertising activity. Cost items typically include the amount paid to a creative agency to develop advertising materials, amounts paid to an organization that sells media, and internal salaries and expenses related to overseeing the advertisement.

Related Metrics and Concepts

Cost per Point (CPP): *The cost of an advertising campaign, relative to the rating points delivered. In a manner similar to CPM, cost per point measures the cost per rating point for an advertising campaign by dividing the cost of the advertising by the rating points delivered.*

3 Reach, Net Reach, and Frequency

Reach is the same as net reach; both of these metrics quantify the number or percentage of individuals in a defined population who receive at least one exposure to an advertisement. Frequency measures the average number of times that each such individual sees the advertisement.

Impressions (#) = Reach (#) * Frequency (#)

Net reach and frequency are important concepts in describing an advertising campaign. A campaign with a high net reach and low frequency runs the danger of being lost in a noisy advertising environment. A campaign with low net reach but high frequency can over-expose some audiences and miss others entirely. Reach and frequency metrics help managers adjust their advertising media plans to fit their marketing strategies.

Purpose: To separate total impressions into the number of people reached and the average frequency with which those individuals are exposed to advertising.

To clarify the difference between reach and frequency, let's review what we learned in Section 1. When impressions from multiple insertions are combined, the results are often called "gross impressions" or "total exposures." When total impressions are expressed as a percentage of the population, this measure is referred to as gross rating points (GRPs). For example, suppose a media vehicle reaches 12% of the population. That vehicle will have a single-insertion reach of 12 rating points. If a firm advertised in 10 such vehicles, it would achieve 120 GRPs.

Now, let's look at the composition of these 120 GRPs. Suppose we know that the 10 advertisements had a combined net reach of 40% and an average frequency of 3. Then their gross rating points might be calculated as 40 * 3 = 120 GRPs.

EXAMPLE: A commercial is shown once in each of three time slots. Nielsen keeps track of which households have an opportunity to see the advertisement. The commercial airs in a market with only five households: A, B, C, D, and E. Time slots 1 and 2 both have a rating of 60 because 60% of the households view them. Time slot 3 has a rating of 20.

Time Slot	Households with Opportunity-to-See	Households with no Opportunity-to-See	Rating Points of Time Slot
1	A B E	C D	60
2	A B C	D E	60
3	A	B C D E	20
		G R P	140

$$GRP = \frac{\text{Impressions}}{\text{Population}} = \frac{7}{5} = 140\ (\%)$$

The commercial is seen by households A, B, C, and E, but not D. Thus, it generates impressions in four out of five households, for a reach (%) of 80%. In the four households reached, the commercial is seen a total of seven times. Thus, its average frequency can be calculated as 7/4, or 1.75. On this basis, we can calculate the campaign's gross rating points as follows:

$$GRP = \text{Reach (\%)} * \text{Average Frequency (\#)} = \frac{4}{5} * \frac{7}{4} = 80\% * 1.75 = 140\ (\%)$$

Unless otherwise specified, simple measures of overall audience size (such as GRPs or impressions) do not differentiate between campaigns that expose larger audiences fewer times and those that expose smaller audiences more often. In other words, these metrics do not distinguish between reach and frequency.

Reach, whether described as "net reach" or simply "reach," refers to the unduplicated audience of individuals who have been exposed at least once to the advertising in question. Reach can be expressed as either the number of individuals or the percentage of the population that has seen the advertisement.

Reach: *The number of people or percent of population exposed to an advertisement.*

Frequency is calculated by dividing gross impressions by reach. Frequency is equal to the average number of exposures received by individuals who have been exposed to at least one impression of the advertising in question. Frequency is calculated *only* among individuals who have been exposed to this advertising. On this basis: Total Impressions = Reach * Average Frequency.

Average Frequency: *The average number of impressions per reached individual.*

Media plans can differ in reach and frequency but still generate the same number of total impressions.

Net Reach: *This term is used to emphasize the fact that the reach of multiple advertising placements is not calculated through the gross addition of all individuals reached by each of those placements. Occasionally, the word "net" is eliminated, and the metric is called simply reach.*

EXAMPLE: Returning to our prior example of a 10-insertion media plan in a market with a population of five people, we can calculate the reach and frequency of the plan by analyzing the following data. As previously noted, in the following table, "1" represents an opportunity-to-see, and "0" signifies that an individual did not have an opportunity to see a particular insertion.

Insertion	Individual					Impressions	Rating Points (Impressions/ Population)
	A	B	C	D	E		
1	1	1	0	0	1	3	60
2	1	1	0	0	1	3	60
3	1	1	0	1	0	3	60
4	1	1	0	1	0	3	60
5	1	1	0	1	0	3	60
6	1	0	0	1	0	2	40
7	1	0	0	1	0	2	40
8	1	0	0	0	0	1	20
9	1	0	0	0	0	1	20
10	1	0	0	0	0	1	20
Totals	**10**	**5**	**0**	**5**	**2**	**22**	**440**

Reach is equal to the number of people who saw at least one advertisement. Four of the five people in the population (A, B, D, and E) saw at least one advertisement. Consequently, reach (#) = 4.

$$\text{Average Frequency} = \frac{\text{Impressions}}{\text{Reach}} = \frac{22}{4} = 5.5$$

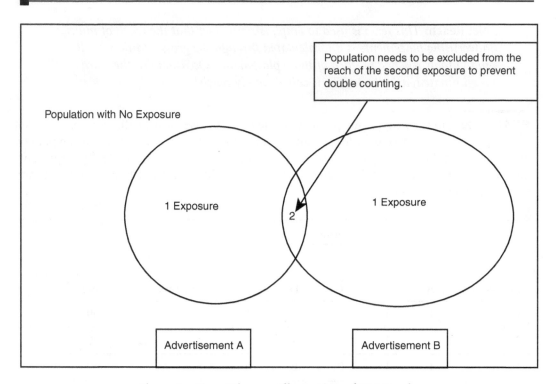

Figure 1   Venn Diagram Illustration of Net Reach

When multiple vehicles are involved in an advertising campaign, marketers need information about the overlap among these vehicles as well as sophisticated mathematical procedures in order to estimate reach and frequency. To illustrate this concept, the following two-vehicle example can be useful. Overlap can be represented by a graphic known as a Venn diagram (see Figure 1).

EXAMPLE: As an illustration of overlap effects, let's look at two examples. *Aircraft International* magazine offers 850,000 impressions for one advertisement. A second magazine, *Commercial Flying Monthly*, offers 1 million impressions for one advertisement.

Example 1: Marketers who place advertisements in both magazines should not expect to reach 1.85 million readers. Suppose that 10% of *Aircraft International* readers also read *Commercial Flying Monthly*. On this basis, net reach = (850,000 * .9) + 1,000,000 = 1,765,000 unique individuals. Of these, 85,000 (10% of *Aircraft International* readers) have received two exposures. The remaining 90% of *Aircraft International* readers have received only one exposure. The overlap between two different media types is referred to as external overlap.

Example 2: Marketers often use multiple insertions in the same media vehicle (such as the July and August issues of the same magazine) to achieve frequency. Even if the estimated audience size is the same for both months, not all of the same people will read the magazine each month. For purposes of this example, let's assume that marketers place insertions in two different issues of *Aircraft International*, and that only 70% of readers of the July issue also read the August issue. On this basis, net reach is not merely 850,000 (the circulation of each issue of *Aircraft International*) because the groups viewing the two insertions are not precisely the same. Likewise, net reach is not 2 * 850,000, or 1.7 million, because the groups viewing the two insertions are also not completely disparate. Rather, net reach = 850,000 + (850,000 * 30%) = 1,105,000.

The reason: Thirty percent of readers of the August issue did not read the July issue and so did not have the opportunity to see the July insertion of the advertisement. These readers—and only these readers—represent incremental viewers of the advertisement in August, and so they must be added to net reach. The remaining 70% of August readers were exposed to the advertisement twice. Their total represents internal overlap or duplication.

Data Sources, Complications, and Cautions

Although we've emphasized the importance of reach and frequency, the impressions metric is typically the easiest of these numbers to establish. Impressions can be aggregated on the basis data originating from the media vehicles involved in a campaign. To determine net reach and frequency, marketers must know or estimate the overlap between audiences for different media, or for the same medium at different times. It is beyond the capability of most marketers to make accurate estimates of reach and frequency without access to proprietary databases and algorithms. Full-service advertising agencies and media buying companies typically offer these services.

Assessing overlap is a major challenge. Although overlap can be estimated by performing customer surveys, it is difficult to do this with precision. Estimates based on managers' judgment occasionally must suffice.

4   Frequency Response Functions

Frequency response functions help marketers to model the effectiveness of multiple exposures to advertising. We discuss three typical assumptions about how people respond to advertisements: linear response, learning curve response, and threshold response.

In a linear response model, people are assumed to react equally to every exposure to an advertisement. The learning curve response model assumes that people are initially slow to respond to an advertisement and then respond more quickly for a time, until ultimately they reach a point at which their response to the message tails off. In a threshold response function, people are assumed to show little response until a critical frequency level is reached. At that point, their response immediately rises to maximum capacity.

Frequency response functions are not technically considered metrics. Understanding how people respond to the frequency of their exposure to advertising, however, is a vital part of media planning. Response models directly determine calculations of effective frequency and effective reach, metrics discussed in Section 5.

Purpose: To establish assumptions about the effects of advertising frequency.

Let's assume that a company has developed a message for an advertising campaign, and that its managers feel confident that appropriate media for the campaign have been selected. Now they must decide: How many times should the advertisement be placed? The company wants to buy enough advertising space to ensure that its message is effectively conveyed, but it also wants to ensure that it doesn't waste money on unnecessary impressions.

To make this decision, a marketer will have to make an assumption about the value of frequency. This is a major consideration: What is the assumed value of repetition in advertising? Frequency response functions help us to think through the value of frequency.

> **Frequency Response Function:** *The expected relationship between advertising outcomes (usually in unit sales or dollar revenues) and advertising frequency.*

There are a number of possible models for the frequency response functions used in media plans. A selection among these for a particular campaign will depend on the product advertised, the media used, and the judgment of the marketer. Three of the most common models are described next.

> **Linear Response:** *The assumption behind a linear response function is that each advertising exposure is equally valuable, regardless of how many other exposures to the same advertising have preceded it.*

> **Learning Curve Response:** *The learning or S curve model rests on the assumption that a consumer's response to advertising follows a progression: The first few times an advertisement is shown, it does not register with its intended audience. As repetition occurs, the message permeates its audience and becomes more effective as people absorb it. Ultimately, however, this effectiveness declines, and diminishing returns set in. At this stage, marketers believe that individuals who want the information already have it and can't be influenced further; others simply are not interested.*

> **Threshold Response:** *The assumption behind this model is that advertising has no effect until its exposure reaches a certain level. At that point, its message becomes fully effective. Beyond that point, further advertising is unnecessary and would be wasted.*

These are three common ways to value advertising frequency. Any function that accurately describes the effect of a campaign can be used. Typically, however, only one function will apply to a given situation.

Construction

Frequency response functions are most useful if they can be used to quantify the effects of incremental frequency. To illustrate the construction of the three functions described in this section, we have tabulated several examples.

Tables 2 and 3 show the assumed incremental effects of each exposure to a certain advertising campaign. Suppose that the advertisement will achieve maximum effect (100%) at eight exposures. By analyzing this effect in the context of various response functions, we can determine when and how quickly it takes hold.

Under a linear response model, each exposure below the saturation point generates one-eighth, or 12.5%, of the overall effect.

The learning curve model is more complex. In this function, the incremental effectiveness of each exposure increases until the fourth exposure and declines thereafter.

Under the threshold response model, there is no effect until the fourth exposure. At that point, however, 100% of the benefit of advertising is immediately realized. Beyond that point, there is no further value to be obtained through incremental advertising. Subsequent exposures are wasted.

The effects of these advertising exposures are tabulated cumulatively in Table 3. In this display, maximum attainable effectiveness is achieved when the response to advertising reaches 100%.

Table 2   Example of the Effectiveness of Advertising

Exposure Frequency	Linear	Learning or S Curve	Threshold Value
1	0.125	0.05	0
2	0.125	0.1	0
3	0.125	0.2	0
4	0.125	0.25	1
5	0.125	0.2	0
6	0.125	0.1	0
7	0.125	0.05	0
8	0.125	0.05	0

Table 3   Assumptions: Cumulative Advertising Effectiveness

Exposure Frequency	Linear	Learning or S Curve	Threshold Value
1	12.5%	5%	0%
2	25.0%	15%	0%
3	37.5%	35%	0%
4	50.0%	60%	100%
5	62.5%	80%	100%
6	75.0%	90%	100%
7	87.5%	95%	100%
8	100.0%	100%	100%

We can plot cumulative effectiveness against frequency under each model (see Figure 2). The linear function is represented by a simple straight line. The Threshold assumption rises steeply at four exposures to reach 100%. The cumulative effects of the learning curve model trace an S-shaped curve.

Frequency Response Function; Linear: *Under this function, the cumulative effect of advertising (up to the saturation point) can be viewed as a product of the frequency of exposures and effectiveness per exposure.*

Frequency Response Function; Linear (I) = Frequency (#) * Effectiveness per Exposure (I)

Frequency Response Function; Learning Curve: *The learning curve function can be charted as a non-linear curve. Its form depends on the circumstances of a particular campaign, including selection of advertising media, target audience, and frequency of exposures.*

Frequency Response Function; Threshold: *The threshold function can be expressed as a Boolean "if" statement, as follows:*

Frequency Response Function; Threshold Value (I) = If (Frequency (#) ≥ Threshold (#), 1, 0)

Stated another way: In a threshold response function, if frequency is greater than or equal to the threshold level of effectiveness, then the advertising campaign is 100% effective. If frequency is less than the threshold, there is no effect.

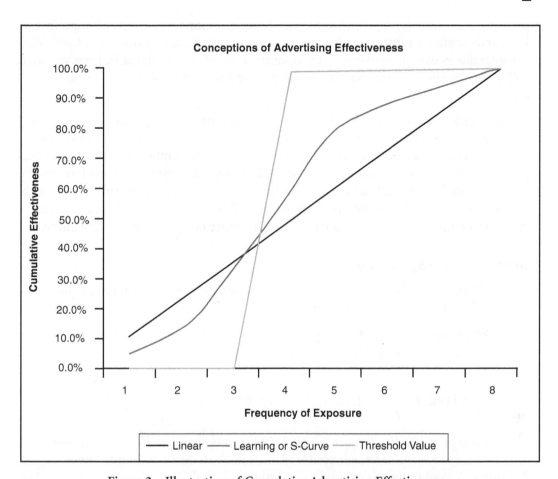

Figure 2   Illustration of Cumulative Advertising Effectiveness

Data Sources, Complications, and Cautions

A frequency response function can be viewed as the structure of assumptions made by marketers in planning for the effects of an advertising campaign. In making these assumptions, a marketer's most useful information can be derived from an analysis of the effects of prior ad campaigns. Functions validated with past data, however, are most likely to be accurate if the relevant circumstances (such as media, creative, price, and product) have not significantly changed.

In comparing the three models discussed in this section, the linear response function has the benefit of resting on a simple assumption. It can be unrealistic, however, because it is hard to imagine that every advertising exposure in a campaign will have the same effect.

The learning curve has intuitive appeal. It seems to capture the complexity of life better than a linear model. Under this model, however, challenges arise in defining and predicting an advertisement's effectiveness. Three questions emerge: At what point does the curve begin to ramp up? How steep is the function? When does it tail off? With considerable research, marketers can make these estimates. Without it, however, there will always be the concern that the learning curve function provides a spurious level of accuracy.

Any implementation of the threshold response function will hinge on a firm's estimate of where the threshold lies. This will have important ramifications. If the firm makes a conservative estimate, setting the tipping point at a high number of exposures, it may pay for ineffective and unneeded advertising. If it sets the tipping point too low, however, it may not buy enough advertising media, and its campaign may fail to achieve the desired effect. In implementation, marketers may find that there is little practical difference between using the threshold model and the more complicated learning curve.

Related Metrics and Concepts

Wear-in: *The frequency required before a given advertisement or campaign achieves a minimum level of effectiveness.*

Wear-out: *The frequency at which a given advertisement or campaign begins to lose effectiveness or even yield a negative effect.*

5 Effective Reach and Effective Frequency

The concept of effective frequency rests on the assumption that for an advertisement or campaign to achieve an appreciable effect, it must attain a certain number of exposures to an individual within a specified time period.

Effective reach is defined as the number of people or the percentage of the audience that receives an advertising message with a frequency equal to or greater than the effective frequency. That is, effective reach is the population receiving the "minimum" effective exposure to an advertisement or campaign.

Purpose: To assess the extent to which advertising audiences are being reached with sufficient frequency.

Many marketers believe their messages require repetition to "sink in." Advertisers, like parents and politicians, therefore repeat themselves. But this repetition must be monitored for effectiveness. Toward that end, marketers apply the concepts of effective frequency and effective reach. The assumptions behind these concepts run as follows: The first few times people are exposed to an ad, it may have little effect. It is only when more exposures are achieved that the message begins to influence its audience.

With this in mind, in planning and executing a campaign, an advertiser must determine the number of times that a message must be repeated in order to be useful. This number is the effective frequency. In concept, this is identical to the threshold frequency in the threshold response function discussed in Section 4. A campaign's effective frequency will depend on many factors, including market circumstances, media used, type of ad, and campaign. As a rule of thumb, however, an estimate of three exposures per purchase cycle is used surprisingly often.

Effective Frequency: *The number of times a certain advertisement must be exposed to a particular individual in a given period to produce a desired response.*

Effective Reach: *The number of people or the percentage of the audience that receives an advertising message with a frequency equal to or greater than the effective frequency.*

Construction

Effective reach can be expressed as the number of people who have seen a particular advertisement or the percentage of the population that has been exposed to that advertisement at a frequency greater than or equal to the effective frequency.

$$\text{Effective Reach } (\#, \%) = \text{Individuals Reached with Frequency Equal to or} \\ \text{Greater Than Effective Frequency}$$

EXAMPLE: An advertisement on the Internet was believed to need three viewings before its message would sink in. Population data showed the distribution in Table 4.

Table 4 Number of Views of Advertisement

Number of Views	Population
0	140,000
1	102,000
2	64,000
3	23,000
4 or more	11,000
Total	**340,000**

Because the effective frequency is 3, only those who have seen the advertisement three or more times have been effectively reached. The effective reach is thus 23,000 + 11,000 = 34,000.

In percentage terms, the effective reach of this advertisement is 34,000/340,000 = 10% of the population.

Data Sources, Complications, and Cautions

The Internet has provided a significant boost to data gathering in this area. Although even Internet campaigns can't be totally accurate with regard to the number of advertisements served to each customer, data on this question in Web campaigns are far superior to those available in most other media.

Where data can't be tracked electronically, it's difficult to know how many times a customer has been in a position to see an advertisement. Under these circumstances, marketers make estimates on the basis of known audience habits and publicly available resources, such as TV ratings.

Although test markets and split-cable experiments can shed light on the effects of advertising frequency, marketers often lack comprehensive, reliable data on this question. In these cases, they must make—and defend—assumptions about the frequency needed for an effective campaign. Even where good historical data are available, media planning should not rely solely on past results because every campaign is different.

Marketers must also bear in mind that effective frequency attempts to quantify the *average* customer's response to advertising. In practice, some customers will need more information and exposure than others.

6 Share of Voice

Share of voice quantifies the advertising "presence" that a specific product or brand enjoys. It is calculated by dividing the brand's advertising by total market advertising, and it is expressed as a percentage.

$$\text{Share of Voice (\%)} = \frac{\text{Brand Advertising (\$, \#)}}{\text{Total Market Advertising (\$, \#)}}$$

For purposes of share of voice, there are at least two ways to measure "advertising": in terms of dollar spending; or in unit terms, through impressions or gross rating points (GRPs). By any of these measures, share of voice represents an estimate of a company's advertising, as compared to that of its competitors.

Purpose: To evaluate the comparative level of advertising committed to a specific product or brand.

Advertisers want to know whether their messages are breaking through the "noise" in the commercial environment. Toward that end, share of voice offers one indication of a brand's advertising strength, relative to the overall market.

There are at least two ways to calculate share of voice. The classic approach is to divide a brand's advertising dollar spend by the total advertising spend in the marketplace.

Alternatively, share of voice can be based on the brand's share of GRPs, impressions, effective reach, or similar measures (see earlier sections in this chapter for more details on basic advertising metrics).

Construction

Share of Voice: *The percentage of advertising in a given market that a specific product or brand enjoys.*

$$\text{Share of Voice (\%)} = \frac{\text{Brand Advertising (\$, \#)}}{\text{Total Market Advertising (\$, \#)}}$$

Data Sources, Complications, and Cautions

When calculating share of voice, a marketer's central decision revolves around defining the boundaries of the market. One must ensure that these are meaningful to the intended customer. If a firm's objective is to influence savvy Web users, for example, it would not be appropriate to define advertising presence solely in terms of print media. Share of voice can be computed at a company level, but brand- and product-level calculations are also common.

In executing this calculation, a company should be able to measure its total advertising spend fairly easily. Determining the ad spending for the market as a whole can be fraught with difficulty, however. Complete accuracy will probably not be attainable. It is important, however, that marketers take account of the major players in their market. External sources such as annual reports and press clippings can shed light on competitors' ad spending. Services such as leading national advertisers (LNA) can also provide useful data. These services sell estimates of competitive purchases of media space and time. They generally do not report actual payments for media, however. Instead, costs are estimated on the basis of the time and space purchased and on published "rate cards" that list advertised prices. In using these estimates, marketers must bear in mind that rate cards rarely cite the discounts available in buying media. Without accounting for these discounts, published media spending estimates can be inflated. Marketers are advised to deflate them by the discount rates they themselves receive on advertising.

A final caution: Some marketers might assume that the price of advertising is equal to the value of that advertising. This is not necessarily the case. With this in mind, it can be useful to augment a dollar-based calculation of share of voice with one based on impressions.

7 Impressions, Pageviews, and Hits

As noted in Section 1, impressions represent the number of opportunities that have been presented to people to see an advertisement. The best available measures of this figure use technology in an effort to judge whether a given advertisement was actually seen. But this is never perfect. Many recorded impressions are not actually perceived by the intended viewer. Consequently, some marketers refer to this metric as opportunities-to-see.

In applying this concept to Internet advertising and publishing, pageviews represent the number of opportunities-to-see for a given Web page. Every Web page is composed of a variety of individual objects and files, which can contain text, images, audio, and video. The total number of these files requested in a given period is the number of hits a Web site or Web server receives. Because pages composed of many small files generate numerous hits per pageview, one must take care not to be overly impressed by large hit counts.

Purpose: To assess Web site traffic and activity.

To quantify the traffic a Web site generates, marketers monitor pageviews—the number of times a page on a Web site is accessed.

In the early days of e-commerce, managers paid attention to the number of hits a Web site received. Hits measure file requests. Because Web pages are composed of numerous text, graphic, and multimedia files, the hits they receive are a function not only of pageviews, but also of the way those pages were composed by their Web designer.

As marketing on the Internet has become more sophisticated, better measures of Web activity and traffic have evolved. Currently, it is more common to use pageviews as the measure of traffic at a Web location. Pageviews aim to measure the number of times a page has been displayed to a user. It thus should be measured as close to the end user as possible. The best technology counts pixels returned to a server, confirming that a page was properly displayed. This pixel[2] count technique yields numbers closer to the end user than would a tabulation of requests to the server, or of pages sent from the server in response to a request. Good measurement can mitigate the problems of inflated counts due to servers not acting on requests, files failing to serve on a user's machine, or users terminating the serving of ads.

> **Hits:** *A count of the number of files served to visitors on the Web. Because Web pages often contain multiple files, hits is a function not only of pages visited, but also of the number of files on each page.*

> **Pageviews:** *The number of times a specific page has been displayed to users. This should be recorded as late in the page-delivery process as possible in order to get as close as possible to the user's opportunity to see. A page can be composed of multiple files.*

For marketing purposes, a further distinction needs to be made as to how many times an advertisement was viewed by unique visitors. For example, two individuals entering a Web page from two different countries might receive the page in their respective languages and might not receive the same ad. One example of an advertisement that changes with different visitors is an embedded link with a banner ad. Recognizing this potential for variation, advertisers want to know the number of times that their specific advertisement was displayed to visitors, rather than a site's number of pageviews.

With this in mind, Internet advertisers often perform their analyses in terms of impressions—sometimes called ad impressions or ad views. These represent the number of times an advertisement is served to visitors, giving them opportunities to see it. (Many of the concepts in this section are in line with the terms covered in the advertising section, Section 1.)

For a single advertisement served to all visitors on a site, impressions are equal to the number of pageviews. If a page carries multiple advertisements, the total number of all ad impressions will exceed the number of pageviews.

Construction

Hits: The number of hits on a Web site is a function of the number of pageviews multiplied by the number of files comprising each page. Hit counts are likely to be more relevant to technicians responsible for planning server capacity than to marketers interested in measuring visitor activity.

$$\text{Hits (\#)} = \text{Pageviews (\#)} * \text{Files on the Page (\#)}$$

Pageviews: The number of pageviews can be easily calculated by dividing the number of hits by the number of files on the page.

$$\text{Pageviews (\#)} = \frac{\text{Hits (\#)}}{\text{Files on the Page (\#)}}$$

EXAMPLE: There are 250,000 hits on a Web site that serves five files each time a page is accessed. Pageviews = 250,000/5 = 50,000.

If the Web site served three files per page and generated 300,000 pageviews, then hits would total 3 * 300,000 = 900,000.

Data Sources, Complications, and Cautions

Pageviews, page impressions, and ad impressions are measures of the responses of a Web server to page and ad requests from users' browsers, filtered to remove robotic activity and error codes prior to reporting. These measures are recorded at a point as close as possible to the user's opportunity to see the page or ad.[3]

A count of ad impressions can be derived from pageviews if the percentage of pageviews that contain the ad in question is known. For example, if 10% of pageviews receive the advertisement for a luxury car, then the impressions for that car ad will equal 10% of pageviews. Web sites that serve the same advertisement to all Web users are much easier to monitor because only one count is required.

These metrics quantify opportunities-to-see without taking into account the number of ads actually seen or the quality of what is shown. In particular, these metrics do not account for the following:

- Whether the message appeared to a specific, relevant, defined audience.
- Whether the people to whom the pages appeared actually looked at them.
- Whether those who looked at the pages had any recall of their content, or of the advertising messages they contained, after the event.

Despite the use of the term impression, these measures do not tell a business manager about the effect that an advertisement has on potential customers. Marketers can't be sure of the effect that pageviews have on visitors. Often, pageview results will consist of data that include duplicate showings to the same visitor. For this reason, the term gross impressions might be used to suggest a key assumption—that opportunities-to-see can be delivered to the same viewer on multiple occasions.

8   Rich Media Display Time

Marketers use the rich media display time metric to monitor how long their advertisements are holding the attention of potential customers.

$$\text{Average Rich Media Display Time (\#)} = \frac{\text{Total Rich Media Display Time (\#)}}{\text{Total Rich Media Impressions (\#)}}$$

Rich media display time represents an important way of tracking the success of Internet advertising.

Purpose: To determine how long an advertisement is viewed.

Rich media is a term used for interactive media that allows consumers to be more actively engaged than they might be with a billboard, a TV advertisement, or even a traditional display Web advertisement. Rich media metrics, or Audience Interaction Metrics, are very similar in principle to other advertising metrics. Marketers want to track whether the advertisement is effective at grabbing and maintaining the attention of potential customers and so they track how long people spend "viewing" the advertisement as a proxy for how interested they are in the content of the advertisement. The rich media display time shows how long, on average, people spend engaged with the rich media.

Construction

Rich media display time is simply the average time that viewers spent with the rich media of an advertisement. For this the marketer will need the total amount of time spent with the rich media and the total number of times that the rich media was displayed. It is a simple matter to create an average time in seconds spent with the rich media by dividing the total amount of time in seconds spent by the total number of impressions.

$$\text{Average Rich Media Display Time (\#)} = \frac{\text{Total Rich Media Display Time (\#)}}{\text{Total Rich Media Impressions (\#)}}$$

Data Sources, Complications and Cautions

As with many Web-based metrics, data often seem abundant to marketers who come from the offline world. However, there are several measurement issues the marketer must address in order to convert the abundance of data into useful metrics. For example, marketers usually cut display times off at some upper bound, that is, if the piece of rich media has been displayed for five minutes, it is safe to assume the viewer has probably gone to make a cup of coffee or been otherwise distracted. The question of how long a displayed piece of rich media was actually viewed is similar to the question offline marketers face with respect to *whether* an offline advertisement was viewed. A slight advantage here goes to the rich online media in that most displays of rich media begin because of an active request of the viewer…whereas no such action is required offline.

This metric, because it usually deals with short periods of time, can be influenced by unusual events. Take a simplified example: If five people see the rich media display for one second each and one person sees it for 55 seconds, the (average) rich media display time is ten seconds. There is no way to distinguish this average display time from the average time generated by six moderately interested viewers each viewing the advertisement for ten seconds. Such is the case with any average.

Marketers should be clear that they understand how the data were gathered and be especially aware of any changes in the way the data were gathered. Changes in the way the data were gathered and the metric constructed may be necessary for technological reasons, but will limit the usefulness of the metric as longitudinal comparisons are no longer valid. At a minimum, the marketer must be aware of and account for measurement changes when interpreting the metric.

9 Rich Media Interaction Rate

Marketers use the rich media interaction rate to assess the effectiveness of a single rich media advertisement in generating engagement from its viewers.

$$\text{Rich Media Interaction Rate (\%)} = \frac{\text{Total Rich Media Impressions with Interactions (\#)}}{\text{Total Rich Media Impressions (\#)}}$$

Rich media interaction rate represents an important way of tracking the success of Internet advertising in that it monitors the fraction of impressions that generate interaction on the part of the viewer.

Purpose: To measure and monitor active involvement with an advertisement.

The rich media interaction rate tracks how actively involved potential consumers are with an advertisement. The big advantage of rich media is the ability of viewers to interact with it. Marketers using rich media can have a much better idea of potential customers' reactions to an advertisement simply because these interactions are counted. They can monitor whether potential customers are simply passively "viewing" the media on their screen or are actively engaged by taking some traceable action. A user who interacts is showing evidence of being more actively engaged and is thus probably more likely to move toward purchase.

Construction

This metric is the number of impressions of an advertisement that were interacted with divided by the total number of impressions of that advertisement. It tells the marketers how successful any advertisement was at getting potential customers to engage with it in some way, (mouse rollover, click on, etc.). As an example, a rich media advertisement that was displayed 100 times with an interaction rate of 15% would mean that 15 of the impressions resulted in some kind of interaction whereas 85 resulted in no interaction.

$$\text{Rich Media Interaction Rate (\%)} = \frac{\text{Total Rich Media Impressions with Interactions (\#)}}{\text{Total Rich Media Impressions (\#)}}$$

Data Sources, Complications and Cautions

Data for this metric will typically be available. Indeed the metric itself might be reported as part of a standard reporting package. One important decision that has to be made in generating the metric is what counts as an interaction. This will depend upon the potential actions that the viewers could take, which in turn depends upon the precise form of the advertisement. What counts as an interaction will usually have some lower bound. For example, an interaction is only counted if the visitor spends more than one second with his mouse over the impression. (This is designed to exclude movements of the mouse unrelated to the advertisement such as moving the mouse to another part of the page.)

As is true of any advertising, marketers should not forget the goal of their advertising. Interaction is unlikely to be an end in itself. As such, a larger interaction rate, which might be secured by gimmicks that appeal to people who will never buy the product, may be no better than a smaller rate if the larger rate doesn't move the visitor closer to a sale (or some other high order objective).

Related Metrics

Rich Media Interaction Time: This metric captures the total amount of time that a visitor spends interacting with an advertisement. This is an accumulation of the total time spent interacting per visit on a single page. So on a visit to a page a user might interact with the rich media for two interactions of two seconds each and so have an interaction time of four seconds.

Video Interactions: Video metrics are very similar to rich media metrics. Indeed video can be classified as rich media depending upon the way it is served to the viewer. Similar principles apply, and the marketer should track how long viewers engage with the video (the amount of time the video plays), what viewers do with the video (pause it, mute it), and the total and specific interactions with the video (which show evidence of attention to the video). Such metrics are then summarized across the entire pool of visitors, (for instance the average visit led to the video being played for 12 seconds).

10   Clickthrough Rates

Clickthrough rate is the percentage of impressions that lead a user to click on an ad. It describes the fraction of impressions that motivate users to click on a link, causing a redirect to another Web location.

$$\text{Clickthrough Rate (\%)} = \frac{\text{Clickthroughs (\#)}}{\text{Impressions (\#)}}$$

Most Internet-based businesses use clickthrough metrics. Although these metrics are useful, they should not dominate all marketing analysis. Unless a user clicks on a "Buy Now" button, clickthroughs measure only one step along the path toward a final sale.

Purpose: To capture customers' initial response to Web sites.

Most commercial Web sites are designed to elicit some sort of action, whether it be to buy a book, read a news article, watch a music video, or search for a flight. People generally don't visit a Web site with the intention of viewing advertisements, just as people rarely watch TV with the purpose of consuming commercials. As marketers, we want to know the reaction of the Web visitor. Under current technology, it is nearly impossible to fully quantify the emotional reaction to the site and the effect of that site on the firm's brand. One piece of information that is easy to acquire, however, is the clickthrough rate. The clickthrough rate measures the proportion of visitors who initiated action with respect to an advertisement that redirected them to another page where they might purchase an item or learn more about a product or service. Here we have used "clicked their mouse" on the advertisement (or link) because this is the generally used term, although other interactions are possible.

Construction

Clickthrough Rate: *The clickthrough rate is the number of times a click is made on the advertisement divided by the total impressions (the times an advertisement was served).*

$$\text{Clickthrough Rate (\%)} = \frac{\text{Clickthroughs (\#)}}{\text{Impressions (\#)}}$$

Clickthroughs: *If you have the clickthrough rate and the number of impressions, you can calculate the absolute number of clickthroughs by multiplying the clickthrough rate by the impressions.*

Clickthroughs (#) = Clickthrough Rate (%) ∗ Impressions (#)

EXAMPLE: There are 1,000 clicks (the more commonly used shorthand for clickthroughs) on a Web site that serves up 100,000 impressions. The clickthrough rate is 1%.

$$\text{Clickthrough Rate} = \frac{1,000}{100,000} = 1\%$$

If the same Web site had a clickthrough rate of 0.5%, then there would have been 500 clickthroughs:

$$\text{Clickthrough Rate} = 100,000 \ast 0.5\% = 500$$

If a different Web site had a 1% clickthrough rate and served up 200,000 impressions, there would have been 2,000 clicks:

$$\text{\# of Clicks} = 1\% \ast 200,000 = 2,000$$

Data Sources, Complications, and Cautions

The number of impressions is a necessary input for the calculation. On simpler Web sites, this is likely to be the same as pageviews; every time the page is accessed, it shows the same details. On more sophisticated sites, different advertisements can be shown to different viewers. In these cases, impressions are likely to be some fraction of total pageviews. The server can easily record the number of times the link was clicked (see Figure 3).

First, remember that clickthrough rate is expressed as a percentage. Although high clickthrough rates might in themselves be desirable and help validate your ad's appeal, companies will also be interested in the total number of people who clicked through. Imagine a Web site with a clickthrough rate of 80%. It may seem like a highly successful Web site until management uncovers that only a total number of 20 people visited the site with 16 clicking through compared with an objective of 500 visitors.

Also remember that a click is a very weak signal of interest. Individuals who click on an ad might move on to something else before the new page is loaded. This could be because the person clicked on the advertisement by accident or because the page took too long to load. This is a problem that is of greater significance with the increase in richer media advertisements. Marketers should understand their customers. Using large video files is likely to increase the number of people abandoning the process before the ad is served, especially if the customers have slower connections.

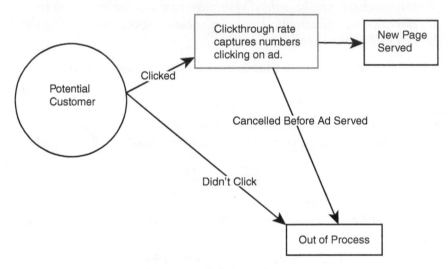

Figure 3   Clickthrough Process

As with impressions, try to ensure that you understand the measures. If the measure is of clicks (the requests received from client machines to the server to send a file), then there may be a number of breakage points between the clickthrough rate and the impressions of the ad generated from a returned pixel count. Large discrepancies should be understood—is it technical (the size/design of the advertisement) or weak interest from clickers?

Clicks are the number of times the advertisement was interacted with, not the number of customers who clicked. An individual visitor can click on an ad several times—either in a single session or across multiple sessions. Only the most sophisticated Web sites control the number of times they show a specific advertisement to the same customer. This means that most Web sites can only count the number of times the ad was clicked, not the number of visitors who clicked on an ad. Finally, the clickthrough rate must be interpreted relative to an appropriate baseline. Clickthrough rates for banner ads are very low and continue to fall. In contrast, clickthrough rates for buttons that simply take visitors to the next page on a site should be much higher. An analysis of how click-through rates change as visitors navigate through various pages can help identify "dead end" pages that visitors rarely move beyond.

11 Cost per Impression, Cost per Click, and Cost per Order

These three metrics measure the average cost of impressions, clicks, and customers. All three are calculated in the same way—as the ratio of cost to the number of resulting impressions, clicks, or customers.

$$\text{Cost per Impression} = \frac{\text{Advertising Cost (\$)}}{\text{Number of Impressions (\#)}}$$

$$\text{Cost per Click (\$)} = \frac{\text{Advertising Cost (\$)}}{\text{Number of Clicks (\#)}}$$

$$\text{Cost per Order (\$)} = \frac{\text{Advertising Cost (\$)}}{\text{Orders (\#)}}$$

These metrics are the starting point for assessing the effectiveness of a company's Internet advertising and can be used for comparison across advertising media and vehicles and as an indicator of the profitability of a firm's Internet marketing.

Purpose: To assess the cost effectiveness of Internet marketing.

In this section, we present three common ways of measuring the cost effectiveness of Internet advertising. Each has benefits depending upon the perspective and end goal of the advertising activity.

Cost per Impression: *The cost to offer potential customers one opportunity to see an advertisement.*

Cost per Click: *The amount spent to get an advertisement clicked.*

Cost per click has a big advantage over cost per impression in that it tells us something about how effective the advertising was. Clicks are a way to measure attention and interest. Inexpensive ads that few people click on will have a low cost per impression and a high cost per click. If the main purpose of an ad is to generate a click, then cost per click is the preferred metric.

Cost per Order: *The cost to acquire an order.*

If the main purpose of the ad is to generate sales, then cost per order is the preferred metric.

Once a certain number of Web impressions are achieved, the quality and placement of the advertisement will affect clickthrough rates and the resulting cost per click (see Figure 4).

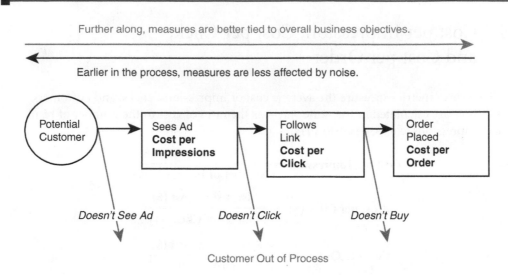

Figure 4   The Order Acquisition Process

Construction

The formulas are essentially the same for the alternatives; just divide the cost by the appropriate number, for example, impressions, clicks, or orders.

Cost per Impression: This is derived from advertising cost and the number of impressions.

$$\text{Cost per Impression (\$)} = \frac{\text{Advertising Cost (\$)}}{\text{Number of Impressions (\#)}}$$

Remember that cost per impression is often expressed as cost per thousand impressions (CPM) in order to make the numbers easier to manage (for more on CPM, refer to Section 2).

Cost per Click: This is calculated by dividing the advertising cost by the number of clicks generated by the advertisement.

$$\text{Cost per Click (\$)} = \frac{\text{Advertising Cost (\$)}}{\text{Clicks (\#)}}$$

Cost per Order: This is the cost to generate an order. The precise form of this cost depends on the industry and is complicated by product returns and multiple sales channels. The basic formula is

$$\text{Cost per Order (\$)} = \frac{\text{Advertising Cost (\$)}}{\text{Orders Placed (\#)}}$$

EXAMPLE: An Internet retailer spent $24,000 on online advertising and generated 1.2 million impressions, which led to 20,000 clicks, with 1 in 10 clicks resulting in a purchase.

$$\text{Cost per Impression} = \frac{\$24,000}{1,200,000} = \$0.02$$

$$\text{Cost per Click} = \frac{\$24,000}{20,000} = \$1.20$$

If 1 in 10 of the clicks resulted in a purchase

$$\text{Cost per Order} = \frac{\$24,000}{2,000} = \$12.00$$

This last calculation is also called "cost per purchase."

Data Sources, Complications, and Cautions

The Internet has provided greater availability of advertising data. Consequently, Internet advertising metrics are likely to rely on data that is more readily obtainable than data from conventional channels. The Internet can provide more information about how customers move through the system and how individual customers behave at the purchase stage of the process.

For advertisers using a mix of online and "offline" media, it will be difficult to categorize the cause and effect relationships between advertising and sales from both online and offline sources. Banner ads might receive too much credit for an order if the customer has also been influenced by the firm's billboard advertisement. Conversely, banner ads might receive too little credit for offline sales.

The calculations and data we have discussed in this section are often used in contracts compensating advertisers. Companies may prefer to compensate media and ad agencies on the basis of new customers acquired instead of orders.

SEARCH ENGINES

Search engine payments help determine the placement of links on search engines. The most important search engine metric is the cost per click, and it is generally the basis for establishing the search engine placement fee. Search engines can provide plenty of data to analyze the effectiveness of a campaign. In order to reap the benefits of a great Web site, the firm needs to get people to visit it. In the previous section, we discussed how firms *measure* traffic. Search engines help firms *create* that traffic.

Although a strong brand helps drive traffic to a firm's site, including the firm's Web address in all of its offline advertising might not increase traffic count. In order to generate additional traffic, firms often turn to search engines. It was estimated that over $2.5 billion was spent on paid search marketing, which made up approximately 36% of total online spending of $7.3 billion in 2003.[4] Other online spending was composed of the following categories: 50% as impressions, 12% as banner ads, and 2% as email advertising.

Paid search marketing is essentially paying for the placement of ads on search engines and content sites across the Internet. The ads are typically small portions of text (much like newspaper want ads) made to look like the results of an unpaid or organic search. Payment is usually made only when someone clicks on the ad. It is sometimes possible to pay more per click in return for better placement on the search results page. One important subset of paid search is keyword search in which advertisers can bid to be displayed whenever someone searches for the keyword(s). In this case, companies bid on the basis of cost per click. Bidding a higher amount per click gets you placed higher. However, there is an added complexity, which is if the ad fails to generate several clicks, its placement will be lowered in comparison to competing ads.

The measures for testing search engine effectiveness are largely the same as those used in assessing other Internet advertising.

Cost per Click: The most important concept in search engine marketing is cost per click. Cost per click is widely quoted and used by search engine companies in charging for their services. Marketers use cost per click to build their budgets for search engine payments.

Search engines ask for a "maximum cost per click," which is a ceiling whereby the marketer imposes the maximum amount they are willing to pay for an individual click. A search engine will typically auction the placement of links and only charge for a click at a rate just above the next highest bid. This means the maximum cost per click that a company would be willing to pay can be considerably higher than the average cost per click they end up paying.

Marketers often talk about the concept of daily spend on search engines—just as it sounds, this is the total spent on paid search engine advertising during one day. In order to control spending, search engines allow marketers to specify maximum daily spends. When the maximum is reached, the advertisement receives no preferential treatment.

The formula is the multiple of average cost per click and the number of clicks:

Daily Spend ($) = Average Cost per Click ($) ∗ Number of Clicks (#)

EXAMPLE: Andrei, the Internet marketing manager of an online music retailer, decides to set a maximum price of $0.10 a click. At the end of the week he finds that the search engine provider has charged him a total of $350.00 for 1,000 clicks per day.

His average cost per click is thus the cost of the advertising divided by the number of clicks generated:

$$\text{Cost per Click} = \frac{\text{Cost per Week}}{\text{Clicks per Week}}$$

$$= \frac{\$350}{7,000}$$

$$= \$0.05 \text{ a Click}$$

Daily spend is also calculated as average cost per click times the number of clicks:

$$\text{Daily Spend} = \$0.05 * 1,000$$

$$= \$50.00$$

ADVICE FOR SEARCH ENGINE MARKETERS

Search engines typically use auctions to establish a price for the search terms they sell. Search engines have the great advantage of having a relatively efficient market; all users have access to the information and can be in the same virtual location. They tend to adopt a variant on the second price auction. Buyers only pay the amount needed for their requested placement.

Cost per Customer Acquired: *Similar to cost per order when the order came from a new customer.*

12   Visits, Visitors, and Abandonment

Visits measures the number of sessions on the Web site. Visitors measures the number of people making those visits. When an individual goes to a Web site on Tuesday and then again on Wednesday, this should be recorded as two visits from one visitor. Visitors are sometimes referred to as "unique visitors." Visitors and unique visitors are the same metric.

Abandonment usually refers to shopping carts. The total number of shopping carts used in a specified period is the sum of the number abandoned and the number that resulted in complete purchases. The abandonment rate is the ratio of the number of abandoned shopping carts to the total.

Purpose: To understand Web site user behavior.

Web sites can easily track the number of pages requested. As we saw earlier in Section 7, the pageviews metric is useful but far from complete. In addition to counting the number of pageviews a Web site delivers, firms will also want to count the number of times someone visits the Web site and the number of people requesting those pages.

Visits: *The number of times individuals request a page on the firm's server for the first time. Also known as sessions.*

The first request counts as a visit. Subsequent requests from the same individual do not count as visits unless they occur after a specified timeout period (usually set at 30 minutes).

Visitors: *The number of individuals requesting pages from the firm's server during a given period. Also known as unique visitors.*

To get a better understanding of traffic on a Web site, companies attempt to track the number of visits. A visit can consist of a single pageview or multiple pageviews, and one individual can make multiple visits to a Web site. The exact specification of what constitutes a visit requires an accepted standard for a timeout period, which is the number of minutes of inactivity from the time of entering the page to the time of requesting a new page.

In addition to visits, firms also attempt to track the number of individual visitors to their Web site. Because a visitor can make multiple visits in a specified period, the number of visits will be greater than the number of visitors. A visitor is sometimes referred to as a unique visitor or unique user to clearly convey the idea that each visitor is only counted once.

The measurement of users or visitors requires a standard time period and can be distorted by automatic activity (such as "bots") that classify Web content. Estimation of visitors, visits, and other traffic statistics are usually filtered to remove this activity by eliminating known IP addresses for "bots," by requiring registration or cookies, or by using panel data.

Pageviews and visits are related. By definition, a visit is a series of pageviews grouped together in a single session, so the number of pageviews will exceed the number of visits.

Consider the metrics as a series of concentric ovals as shown in Figure 5. In this view, the number of visitors must be less than or equal to the number of visits, which must be less than or equal to the number of pageviews, which must be equal to or less than the number of hits. (Refer to Section 7 for details of the relationship between hits and pageviews.)

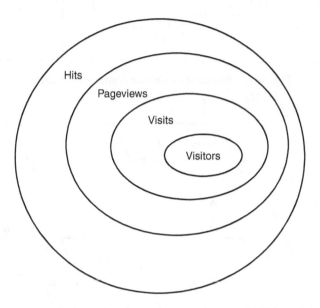

Figure 5   Relationship of Hits to Pageviews to Visits to Visitors

Another way to consider the relationship between visitors, visits, pageviews, and hits is to consider the following example of one visitor entering a Web site of an online newspaper (see Figure 6). Suppose that the visitor enters the site on Monday, Tuesday, and Friday. In her visits she looks at a total of 20 pageviews. Those pages are made up of a number of different graphic files, word files, and banner ads.

The ratio of pageviews to visitors is sometimes referred to as the average pages per visit. Marketers track this average to monitor how the average visit length is changing over time.

It is possible to dig even deeper and track the paths visitors take within a visit. This path is called the clickstream.

Clickstream: *The path of a user through the Internet.*

The clickstream refers to the sequence of clicked links while visiting multiple sites. Tracking at this level can help the firm identify the most and least appealing pages (see Figure 7).

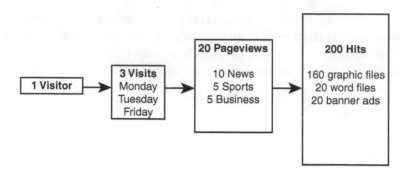

Figure 6   Example of Online Newspaper Visitor

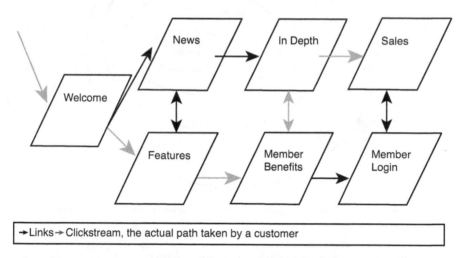

→Links→ Clickstream, the actual path taken by a customer

Figure 7   A Clickstream Documented

The analysis of clickstream data often yields significant customer insights. What path is a customer most likely to take prior to purchase? Is there a way to make the most popular paths even easier to navigate? Should the unpopular paths be changed or even eliminated? Do purchases come at the end of lengthy or short sessions? At what pages do sessions end?

A portion of the clickstream that deserves considerable attention is the subset of clicks associated with the use of shopping carts. A shopping cart is a piece of software on the server that allows visitors to select items for eventual purchase. Although shoppers in brick and mortar stores rarely abandon their carts, abandonment of virtual shopping carts is quite common. Savvy marketers count how many of the shopping carts used in a specified period result in a completed sale versus how many are abandoned. The ratio of the number of abandoned shopping carts to the total is the abandonment rate.

Abandonment Rate: *The percentage of shopping carts that are abandoned.*

To decide whether a visitor is a returning visitor or a new user, companies often employ cookies. A cookie is a file downloaded onto the computer of a person surfing the Web that contains identifying information. When the person returns, the Web server reads the cookie and recognizes the visitor as someone who has been to the Web site previously. More advanced sites use cookies to offer customized content, and shopping carts make use of cookies to distinguish one shopping cart from another. For example, Amazon, eBay, and EasyJet all make extensive use of cookies to personalize the Web views to each customer.

Cookie: *A small file that a Web site puts on the hard drive of visitors for the purpose of future identification.*

Construction

Visitors: Cookies can help servers track unique visitors, but this data is never 100% accurate (see the next section).

Abandoned Purchases: *The number of purchases that were not completed.*

EXAMPLE: An online comics retailer found that of the 25,000 customers who loaded items into their electronic baskets, only 20,000 actually purchased:

$$\text{Purchases Not Completed} = \text{Purchases Initiated Less Purchases Completed}$$

$$= 25{,}000 - 20{,}000 = 5{,}000$$

$$\text{Abandonment Rate} = \frac{\text{Not Completed}}{\text{Customer Initiation}} = \frac{5{,}000}{25{,}000}$$

$$= 20\% \text{ Abandonment Rate}$$

Data Sources, Complications, and Cautions

Visits can be estimated from log file data. Visitors are much more difficult to measure. If visitors register and/or accept cookies, then at least the computer that was used for the visit can be identified.

Meaningful results are difficult to get for smaller or more narrowly focused Web sites.

It is possible to bring in professionals in competitive research and user behavior. Nielsen, among other services, runs a panel in the U.S. and a number of major economies.[5]

13   Bounce Rate

Bounce Rate is a measure of the effectiveness of a Web site in encouraging visitors to continue their visit. It is expressed as a percentage and represents the proportion of visits that end on the first page of the Web site that the visitor sees.

$$\text{Bounce Rate (\%)} = \frac{\text{Visits That Access Only a Single Page (\#)}}{\text{Total Visits (\#) to the Web site}}$$

High bounce rates typically indicate that the Web site isn't doing a good job of attracting the continuing interest of visitors.

Purpose: To determine the effectiveness of the Web site at generating the interest of visitors.

Bounce rate is a commonly reported metric that reflects the effectiveness of Web sites at drawing the continuing attention of visitors. The assumption behind the usefulness of the metric is that the owner of the Web site wants visitors to visit more than just the landing page. For most sites this is a reasonable assumption. For example, sites that are seeking to sell goods want visitors to go to other pages to view the goods and ultimately make a purchase. Bounce rate is also a measure of how effective the company is at generating relevant traffic. The more the Web site is relevant to the traffic coming to it, the lower will be the bounce rate. This becomes particularly important when traffic is generated through paid search. Money spent to generate traffic for whom the Web site is not relevant (as reflected in a high bounce rate) is money wasted. The bounce rate is a particularly useful measure in respect of the entry pages to Web sites. An entry page with a very low bounce rate is doing its job of driving traffic to other pages. As Google analytics explains; "The more compelling your landing pages, the more visitors will stay on your site and convert."[6]

Having a low bounce rate is often a prerequisite of having a successful e-commerce presence.

Construction

Bounce Rate: The number of visits that access only a single page of a Web site divided by the total number of visits to the Web site.

$$\text{Bounce Rate (\%)} = \frac{\text{Visits that Access Only a Single Page (\#)}}{\text{Total Visits (\#) to the Web site}}$$

Data Sources, Complications and Cautions

Data to construct this metric, or even the metric itself, will usually come from the Web site's host as part of the normal reporting procedure. Given how common it is that bounce rate is reported by default, it is a metric that is difficult to ignore. Construction of the metric requires a precise definition of when a visit ends. Leaving the site may come from closing the window, entering a new URL, clicking on a link off the site, hitting the Back button or being timed out. After a timeout a new session is usually started if the visitor returns to the Web site. A lower timeout period results in increased bounce rates, all else equal.

Reports may use the term visitors instead of visits. You should be clear what data is actually reported. Visits are much easier to track because when the same visitor makes return visits, especially to different entry pages, it can be difficult to connect the return visit to the original visitor. As such visits, rather than visitors, are most likely used to calculate bounce rates.

This metric can also be defined and constructed for individual pages rather than the site as a whole. Indeed the bounce rate for each page allows for more precise diagnosis of problem areas on a Web site. One must interpret page bounce rates, however, in light of the purpose of the page. For some pages, such as directions pages, a high bounce rate is to be expected. The value of this metric will depend upon the objective of the organization. Informational sites may develop a strong bond with their users through frequent short interaction, such as checking sports scores. The organization may be comfortable if many users do not visit other parts of the site, and may not be too concerned about high bounce rates. However, most companies will probably want low bounce rates and will actively monitor this important metric.

14 Friends/Followers/Supporters

Friends/Followers/Supporters is a very simple metric that measures the number of individuals who join an organization's social network.

Friends (#) = Number of friends of the entity registered on a social networking page (#)

A high number of friends signifies an active interest in the owner of the page. If a brand has a high number of friends, this indicates a stronger brand with a loyal customer base.

Purpose: To determine the effectiveness of a social networking presence.

We use the term friends to encompass followers, supporters, and other similar concepts. Friends are members of a social networking site who register that they know, like and/or support the owner of the social networking page. For instance a strong brand may have many customers who want to publicly signal their love of the brand. Social networking sites hold great benefits in allowing companies to develop customer relationships and can help a company identify and communicate with committed customers.

Construction

> **Friends (#) = Number of friends of the entity registered on a social networking page (#)**

Data Sources, Complications, and Cautions

Success in recruiting friends is likely to depend heavily on the group of people who identify with the entity (e.g., individuals, brands, companies, or other groups). In the case of brands, some customer segments are more reluctant to reveal their brand loyalty than others, and as such two brands of equivalent strength may have very different levels of social network presence. Similarly the product involved is likely to influence the likelihood of registering as a friend at the social networking site. It is easy to think of some vitally important but more private products that are relied upon by their users but are less likely to gain public expressions of support than brands that are more related to public consumption.

It is very hard to objectively judge the effectiveness of social networking activities. Generally having more followers is an excellent sign of customer engagement. The more customers who have an ongoing relationship with a brand that they are willing to publicly support, the more likely the brand is to have strong customer awareness and loyalty. It is worth noting, however, that Friends, as with many metrics, is most often an intermediate metric rather than an aim of the organization itself. It is unlikely that most organizations exist with the explicit objective of generating friends. As such it is rarely sufficient to report the number of friends as a successful outcome of a marketing strategy without any additional information. It is often appropriate to construct metrics around the downstream outcomes and cost effectiveness of such strategies. A marketer would be well advised to pay attention to the costs and ultimate benefits of social networking presence as well as the clear potential to engage with customers.

Cost per Friend: The cost to the organization per friend recruited.

$$\text{Cost per Friend} = \frac{\textbf{Total Cost to Provide Social Networking Presence (\$)}}{\textbf{Number of Friends (\#)}}$$

Often the direct costs of having a social networking site are very low. This should not, however, lead the marketer to conclude the cost is effectively zero. Sites have to be designed, staff have to update the site, and marketers have to devise strategies. Remember when calculating the cost of having a social network presence that the costs should include all costs incurred in the provision of the social network presence.

Outcomes Per Friend: A similar attempt might be made to clarify the precise downstream outcomes gained by the presence of friends. ("Did we sell more ketchup?") It is often very hard to track outcomes to specific social networking actions. This does not mean that an active social networking presence is not a vital part of an Internet marketing strategy, but when designing a presence the ultimate objective of the company needs to be borne in mind. For example, friends are often recruited to "vote" in polls. The percentage of friends participating is a simple example of an "outcome per friend" metric but probably not the ultimate objective.

15   Downloads

Monitoring downloads is a way of tracking engagement with the organization.

Downloads (#) = Number of times that an application or file is downloaded (#)

Downloads reflect the success of organizations at getting their applications distributed to users.

Purpose: To determine effectiveness in getting applications out to users.

Downloads are a common way for marketers to gain a presence with consumers. This includes applications for mobile phones, for MP3-style devices, and computers.

Apps for iPhones, software trials, spreadsheets, ring tones, white papers, pictures, and widgets are examples of downloads. These downloads typically provide a benefit to the consumer in return for a presence on the device of the user. For instance a weather app might be branded with the Web site of the weather channel and provide updates on atmospheric conditions. A consumer packaged goods company might supply an app that suggests recipes that could use its products in novel ways.

Construction

Downloads (#) = Number of times that an application or file is downloaded (#)

Data Sources, Complications, and Cautions

Downloads is a simple count of the number of times an application or file is downloaded, regardless of who requested the download. It does not distinguish 10 identical downloads to a given individual from 10 separate downloads to 10 separate individuals, although these two situations may have dramatically different consequences for the company. In this way downloads is akin to impressions where a given number of impressions can be obtained by a variety of combinations of reach and frequency (see section 3).

A consideration in the counting of downloads is how to handle downloads that are started but not completed. The alternative to keeping track of both (allowing the construction of a bounce-rate-like metric with respect to downloads) is to pick one or the other (starts or completions). As always, it is imperative for the user to know which convention was used in construction of the download metric.

References and Suggested Further Reading

Farris, Paul W., David Reibstein, and Ervin Shames. (1998). "Advertising Budgeting: A Report from the Field," monograph, New York: American Association of Advertising Agencies.

Forrester, J.W. (1959). "ADVERTISING: A Problem in Industrial Dynamics," *Harvard Business Review*, 37(2), 100.

Interactive Advertising Bureau. (2004). Interactive Audience Measurement and Advertising Campaign Reporting and Audit Guidelines. United States Version 6.0b.

Lodish, L.M. (1997). "Point of View: J.P. Jones and M.H. Blair on Measuring Ad Effects: Another P.O.V," *Journal of Advertising Research*, 37(5), 75.

Net Genesis Corp. (2000). E-metrics Business Metrics for the New Economy. Net Genesis and Target Marketing of Santa Barbara.

Tellis, G.J., and D.L. Weiss. (1995). "Does TV Advertising Really Affect Sales? The Role of Measures, Models, and Data Aggregation," *Journal of Advertising*, 24(3), 1.

ENDNOTES

1. Farris, Paul W. (2003). "Getting the Biggest Bang for Your Marketing Buck," *Measuring and Allocating Marcom Budgets: Seven Expert Points of View*, Marketing Science Institute Monograph.

2. Known as client-side tagging, beacon, and 1 × 1 clear pixel technology.

3. The Interactive Advertising Bureau gives the following definition of ad impression: "A measurement of responses from an ad delivery system to an ad request from the user's browser, which is filtered from robotic activity and is recorded at a point as late as possible in the process of delivery of the creative material to the user's browser—therefore closest to actual opportunity to see by the user." Interactive Audience Measurement and Advertising Campaign Reporting and Audit Guidelines. September 2004, United States Version 6.0b.

4. The spending data is taken from "Internet Weekly," Credit Suisse First Boston, 14 September 2004, 7–8.

5. http://www.nielsen-netratings.com/. Accessed 06/11/2005.

6. http://www.google.com/support/googleanalytics/bin/answer.py?answer=81986&cbid=gbo1sdrurcrz&src=cb&lev=answer

Evaluating an Integrated Marketing Program

From Chapter 15 of *Integrated Advertising, Promotion, and Marketing Communications,* Seventh Edition. Kenneth E. Clow, Donald Baack.

Evaluating an Integrated Marketing Program

Chapter Objectives

After reading this chapter, you should be able to answer the following questions:

1 What are the three broad categories of evaluation tools used to evaluate IMC systems?

2 How do marketing teams match evaluation methods with IMC objectives?

3 What forms of message evaluations can be conducted to assess IMC programs?

4 Which evaluation criteria are suggested by the positioning advertising copytesting (PACT) system?

5 How do online evaluation systems assist advertising managers in assessing the quality of a firm's internet activities?

6 What types of behavioral evaluations can be employed to assess IMC programs?

7 What criteria should be used to assess the overall IMC program?

8 How are evaluation programs adjusted to match international operations?

Overview

John Wanamaker, a well-known nineteenth-century department store owner, was among the first to use advertising to attract customers to his store. He once remarked, "I know half the money I spend on advertising is wasted, but I can never find out which half." Evaluating the effectiveness of advertising has become increasingly difficult. In today's environment, company executives demand measurable results because of the high costs of advertising campaigns. The challenge for advertising account executives and others who prepare ads continues to be offering evidence that those campaigns are successful.

To meet the growing insistence for accountability, research and media experts spend time and energy seeking to develop new and accurate measures of success. These measures, known as **metrics**, attempt to accurately portray the effectiveness of a marketing communications plan, which may not be easy.

SANDS RESEARCH, INC.

Neuromarketing on the Cutting Edge

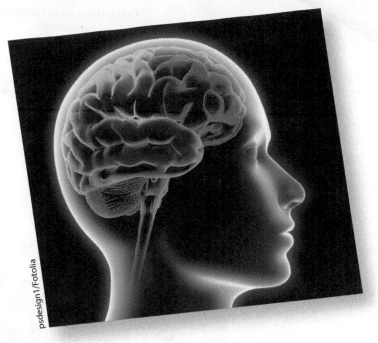

psdesign1/Fotolia

If any one theme emerges from the interviews with members of the various advertising agencies featured in this text, it would be that company executives demand clear and convincing evidence that marketing and advertising actually work. Tangible measures such as increases in store traffic, website hits, coupon redemptions, and sales provide behavioral evidence. Many times other factors influence these outcomes, and a lag occurs between the time the advertisement was run until any corresponding behavior resulted.

Advertising agencies continue to look for methods to refine the development and delivery of marketing messages. Several techniques exist, including recall tests and studies of brand perceptions and loyalty. Finding real-time data suggesting that an advertisement has captured and kept a viewer's attention is what remains.

Sands Research, Inc., led by its chairman and chief science officer, Dr. Steve Sands, is a leading neuromarketing firm. The company pioneered developments in applications that draw on cognitive neuroscience technology to provide unique insights into consumer responses to television and print advertisements, product packaging, and digital media. By combining its technology with before-and-after-questionnaires, Sands Research provides a comprehensive, objective analysis of the viewer's engagement in the marketing material presented by an advertiser.

Recently, Dr. Sands announced a breakthrough in the rapidly growing area of applying neuroscience to market research. Sands Research uses high-density arrays of EEG (electroencephalograph) sensors to capture brainwave activity across the full brain at 10,000 times a second, per sensor. In essence, this means the firm has the ability to study the impact a message has on capturing a person's attention and track times of peak interest as the person stays engaged with that message.

Traditional methods designed to analyze the impact of an advertisement with rating statements and open-ended questions tend to be verbally biased. They may also fail to completely measure the impact of the nonverbal components of commercials, including music and visuals. Creative people have long suspected that traditional research approaches, such as recall testing, unfairly reward overly rational advertising and penalize emotional executions.

Research suggests that when commercials quickly capture attention, they tend to generate more "peak" moments during the run. Peak moments of attention increase positive feelings toward commercials and potentially influence recall. Peaks are likely to occur when:

- Important news is provided; for example, the announcement of a strong price promotion.
- Inciting incidents appear, typically those involving a moment strongly charged with negative emotion to set up a joke or storyline.
- Surprising moments or turning points in stories take place.
- The delivery of climatic moments or punch lines occurs.

The value of these new techniques may be enhanced through the understanding that three different memory systems may be involved in developing a person's view of a brand: knowledge memories, emotion or episodic memories, and action or procedural memories of bodily experiences and physical sensations. Evidence from these studies suggests that these memories might be stored in different parts of the brain. Consequently, a rational and verbal memory might be reported, but emotional or episodic memories may not. This would explain the underreporting of the impact of musical and visual cues in advertisements.

The full impact of these new technologies has yet to be realized. At the least, Sands Research suggests the company can help an advertiser create an advertisement with the greatest potential for capturing attention from storyboard to the run of the commercial. And, an exciting new era in marketing measurement may be well underway.[1]

MASTER YOUR WORKLOAD.

New Holland WORKMASTER™ 75 tractors deliver dependable power, versatility and simple operation. Best of all, they're easy to afford.

$349/month

with 625TL Loader

SCOTT EQUIPMENT

NEW HOLLAND AGRICULTURE

www.newholland.com/na

Courtesy French Creative

This chapter considers the methods available for evaluating components of an IMC program. Three broad categories of evaluation tools can be used to evaluate IMC systems: message evaluations, online evaluations, and respondent behavior evaluations.

Evaluation Metrics

Three primary metrics may be used to evaluate marketing communications (see Figure 1). **Message evaluation techniques** examine the message and the physical design of the advertisement, coupon, or direct marketing piece. Message evaluation procedures include the study of actors in advertisements as well as the individuals who speak in radio ads. A message evaluation program reviews the cognitive components associated with an ad, such as recall and recognition, as well as emotional, attitudinal, and behavioral intention responses.

Online evaluation metrics examine online advertising and marketing campaigns. The internet provides a unique set of metrics and techniques that are not available for traditional media. In addition to click-throughs, marketers can track such metrics as dwell rate and dwell time. The internet provides highly accurate, real-time measures of consumer reactions.

Respondent behavior evaluations address visible customer actions, including store visits, inquiries, or actual purchases. This category contains evaluation technique measures that feature numbers such as the amount of coupons redeemed, hits on a website, and changes in sales.

The emphasis on providing compelling proof that advertising actually works has led to a greater emphasis on respondent behaviors. Higher sales, increases in store traffic, a greater number of daily hits on a website, and other numbers-based outcomes appeal to many managers. At the same time, message evaluations, online metrics, and behavioral responses help the marketing manager and advertising team build short-term results and achieve long-term success.

Matching Methods with IMC Objectives

Marketers choose methods of evaluation that match the objectives to be measured.[2] An advertising campaign with the objective of increasing customer interest in and recall of a brand will be assessed using the level of customer awareness as the metric. Normally, this means the marketing team measures awareness before, during, and after the ads have run. At other times, objectives focus on customer actions. Redemption rates can measure the success of a campaign featuring coupons.

Several levels are used to analyze an advertising or IMC program. They include:

* Short-term outcomes (sales, redemption rates)
* Long-term results (brand awareness, brand loyalty, or brand equity)
* Product- and brand-specific awareness
* Awareness of the overall company
* Affective responses (liking the company and a positive brand image)

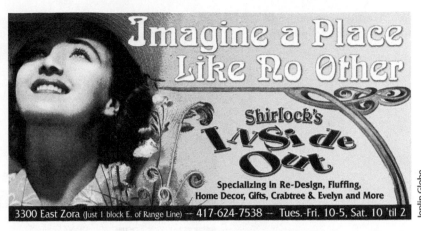

▲ A number of extraneous events might affect the impact of this ad for Shirlock's Inside Out advertisement.

The temptation sometimes arises to overemphasize the first factor, short-term outcomes, without considering the long-term impact of a campaign or marketing program. The company's marketing team endeavors to maintain a voice that carries across campaigns over time.

In light of the overall marketing and advertising goals, the marketing manager then considers the various options for evaluating advertising. Selection of evaluation procedures takes place prior to launching a campaign. An advertisement placed in a trade journal can contain a code number, a special telephone number, or a special internet microsite to track responses. For coupons, premiums, and other sales promotions, code numbers are printed on each item to identify the source.

In general, careful planning prior to initiating an IMC program allows the evaluation of the campaign to be easier and more accurate. At the same time, the evaluation of a specific advertisement or marketing piece may be difficult, because many factors can affect the outcome being measured. For instance, a retailer may run a series of newspaper and radio ads to boost store traffic. In order to measure the impact of the ads, the retailer keeps records of store traffic before, during, and after the campaign. Unfortunately, the traffic count might be affected by various factors, even something as simple as the weather. If it rains for two days, the traffic count will be lower. Further, the store's chief competitor may run a special sale during the same time period, which also affects traffic. A TV program, such as the season finale of a major series, or even a special program at the local high school (commencement, school play), could have an impact. In other words, many extraneous factors could affect results. When reviewing an advertising program, marketing professionals consider these factors.

Performing one analysis normally does not adequately assess the influence of the impact of marketing communications on a company's image. Even though store traffic was low, the ad may have been stored in the buyer's long-term memory, which may make a difference later. Conversely, the same ad may have been awkward or offensive in some way. The store owner might believe the weather affected the outcome instead of a poor advertising design. Consequently, company leaders consider short- and long-term implications when assessing an IMC program.

Message Evaluations

Evaluation or testing of advertising communications occurs at every stage of the development process. This includes the concept stage before an advertisement is produced. Testing at that stage often involves soliciting the opinions of a series of experts or from "regular" people. Ads can be tested after completion of the design stage but prior to development. Advertising creatives often design television commercials using a storyboard such as the one shown on the next page for Interstate Batteries. Print ads can be analyzed using artist sketches.

objective 3
What forms of message evaluations can be conducted to assess IMC programs?

◀ A storyboard for an Interstate Batteries television advertisement.

Jane Koenecke/Interstate Batteries

Although ads and marketing pieces can be tested prior to production, most advertising agencies perform a small amount of pretesting, primarily due to the lack of reliable test results. Elena Petukhova from The Richards Group advertising agency notes that, "We really don't trust the results of pretests using boards because the format makes a difference. Consumers are used to seeing the finished product, so when you show them a mockup or sketch, they tend not to see it very positively. It is difficult for them to make the transition to what the ad will look like after production, and in their minds they compare it to finished ads, which produce low evaluation scores. Whenever possible, we wait until after production to test ads."[3]

As shown in Figure 2, individual companies and advertising agencies employ three primary methods to evaluate advertising campaign messages: advertising tracking research, copytesting, and emotional reaction tests. Each fits differing circumstances, advertising methods, and IMC objectives. For the future, a promising method of advertising evaluation involves cognitive neuroscience.

Advertising Tracking Research

One common method of evaluation involves tracking an advertisement by one of the major advertising research firms, such as Nielsen IAG or Millward Brown. Tracking research examines ads that have launched. This in-market research method monitors a brand's performance and advertising effectiveness. Tests are performed at specific times or intervals or continuously. Ad tracking provides a general measure of the effect of the

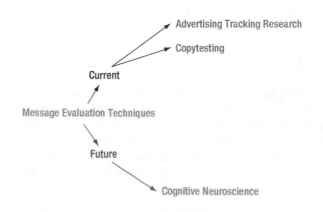

▶ **FIGURE 2**
Evaluating Advertising Messages

media weight (i.e., spending level), the effectiveness of the media buys, and the quality of the ad's message and execution. Ad tracking examines the relative impact of a message compared to the competition and over time.

Nielsen IAG provides ad tracking. The company offers a syndicated database of real-time brand and ad performance tracking based on more than 210,000 television program episodes and 250,000 commercials. In addition to television ads, the service applies to the evaluation of internet ads and in-cinema campaigns. Nielsen conducts thousands of surveys daily measuring viewer engagement with TV programs and the effectiveness of each advertisement on network and cable television channels.[4]

Ad Tracking Methodology With ad tracking, research respondents are usually shown a brief portion of an advertisement or a few stills from a TV ad with the brand name removed or not visible. Researchers ask respondents if they recognize the company, which measures brand and ad recognition. Subjects are then asked to identify the brand being advertised, which measures unaided brand awareness. Those that cannot correctly identify the sponsor are given a list of brands and asked to identify the correct brand, which measures aided brand awareness. In addition to recognition and unaided and aided brand awareness, tracking research also measures:

- Memorability
- Likeability
- Unaided and aided message recall
- Unaided and aided campaign recall

Marketers for Maxwell House coffee might take advantage of ad tracking research to measure the success of the "Stay Grounded" ad campaign.

Similar techniques are available for magazines. Mediamark Research & Intelligence's AdMeasure tracks recall and response to advertisements in every issue of 200 magazine titles. Affinity offers a competing service, the American Magazine Study Print Ad Ratings, which contains ad measurements across 125 magazine titles.[5]

When the mcgarrybowen agency created a campaign for Burger King, employees engaged in ad tracking to measure the brand's impression score. Both Burger King and its primary rival were measured with YouGov Brandindex's impression score which asks respondents, "Do you have a general positive feeling about the brand?" Prior to the campaign launch, Burger King's impression score was 24.4 compared to McDonald's score of 48.9. During the campaign, Burger King's score rose to a high of 45.1 then dropped at the end to 38.4. At the same time, McDonald's impression score fell to 34.8. By assessing these results before, during, and after the campaign, marketers from Burger King and mcgarrybowen were able to obtain more accurate measures of the campaign's effectiveness in creating a more positive impression of the restaurant chain.[6]

Report Cards and Benchmarks Dave Snell of The Richards Group reported the information provided by Nielsen IAG offers a continuous "report card" as well as a "benchmark." During the second or third week of a new campaign, ad tracking research provides two types of information about a new advertisement's performance. First, it shows how the new ad performs in comparison to the brand's competitors. Second, it indicates how well the advertisement performed in relation to those from previous campaigns.

Nielsen IAG also builds a benchmark for a company as it measures ad performance over months and years. These benchmark data are especially valuable when a new campaign

Lunches, made.

Backpacks, ready.

Hair, braided.

Shoes, tied.

Moment, to savor.

pheel
the joy

KRAFT
PHILADELPHIA
REGULAR

pheel the moment

Kirtan Patel/Philadephia Cream Cheese

▲ Ad tracking can help marketers for Philadelphia Cream Cheese detect when wear out begins to occur.

launches. Advertisers compare new messages to previous ones along various dimensions to ensure the commercials performed as expected. The benchmark from previous ads provides a better indicator of performance than comparisons with competitors or ads for similar products.

Tracking services also "help us to know when wearout is beginning to set in," says Dave Snell. Measuring the advertisement's effectiveness on a biweekly basis and graphing those measures indicate when an advertisement starts to lose its impact. At that point, the agency and client can switch to a new campaign, bring back a previous ad, or modify the current commercial.

The Richards Group's Elena Petukhova notes that ad tracking includes the disadvantage of failing to provide any diagnostics. The data indicate how the ad performs in relation to the competition, against previous ads, and over time. They do not yield information regarding the reasons an advertisement did not perform well. Other types of research explore the reasons why an advertisement failed. In essence, ad tracking research indicates when an advertisement has worn out or is not performing, but it does not tell the agency what to do.

Copytesting

The second form of message evaluation, **copytests**, assesses the finished marketing piece or one in the final stages of development. Copytesting elicits responses to the main message of the advertisement as well as the presentation format. Television and print ads have long been evaluated using copytesting procedures. Online print and video ads were seldom copytested, but that trend is changing. According to Jeff Cox, CEO of ARS Group which performs copytesting, about 75 percent of the firm's clients now test at least some of their digital ads during development.[7]

Common copytesting techniques include portfolio tests, theater tests, and online tests. A **portfolio test** displays a set of print ads containing the one being evaluated. A **theater test** displays a set of television ads, including the one being studied. The individuals who participate do not know which piece is under scrutiny. Both techniques mimic reality in the sense that consumers normally are exposed to multiple messages, such as when a radio or television station plays a series of commercials in a row or when a set of newspaper ads appears on a single page. The tests also allow researchers to compare the target piece with other marketing messages. For these approaches to produce the optimal findings, all of the marketing pieces shown must be in the same stage of development, such as preproduction ads or finished ads.

Internet copytesting can replace both the portfolio and theater tests. Online copytesting costs less and provides more immediate results. The Millward Brown advertising firm features online testing procedures, including copytesting. Typically, an agency client performs copytests five to eight times per year. The tests deliver information regarding the in-depth potential of an ad under ideal circumstances. When they are conducted online, consumers pay more attention to the ad than they would for a television show, radio program, or while reading a magazine. Therefore, copytesting results offer a measure of the advertisement's potential when it receives the viewer's complete attention.

Copytesting follows finished ads that have already been launched. Millward Brown typically studies the ad using 150 respondents. Quantitative questions address issues such as:

- Breakthrough ability
- The brand message and image

- The level of the ad and brand memory
- Levels of enjoyment
- What the ad communicates
- How well the intended message was communicated
- Potential responses (i.e., likelihood of making a purchase)
- Persuasive power of the advertisement
- Engagement of the viewer with the ad and brand

Testing Emotional Reactions   In addition to these measures, Millward Brown prepares a second-by-second emotional reaction chart that indicates how viewers feel about an advertisement to be shown on television. As they watch the commercial on a computer screen, respondents move the computer mouse to indicate their feelings—one direction for positive feelings and the other direction for negative feelings. By superimposing these 150 emotional reaction tests onto one graph, the client sees how the feelings and emotions of the respondents change throughout the commercial. This information has value because it indicates points at which emotions turn. Although the test does not measure the level of emotion but rather changes in emotion, these data provide sufficient evidence for the agency to develop hypotheses or best practice ideas to assist in making future advertisements.

Verbatim Comments   The final pieces of information provided to clients by Millward Brown and other

JD Bank

▲ Emotional reaction tests provide valuable information to advertising agencies and brand managers.

agencies are the verbatim comments of the respondents. Each respondent presents, in his or her own words, thoughts about the advertisement. According to Dave Snell from The Richards Group, "These verbatim comments are extremely valuable to us because they provide a written commentary on what people think about the ad and what thoughts are foremost from watching the ad."[8] Millward Brown asks a number of open-ended questions to engage respondents and gain a deeper understanding of their thought processes. The research team also requests respondents to tell the story of the ad, which provides additional valuable insights. The Richards Group's Elena Petukhova commented that, "It can tell you a lot about the ad, both positive and negative. It tells you what the customer sees and thinks and how the ad story came across to them."[9]

As noted previously, ad tracking does not generate information regarding the reasons an ad did not perform well or what to do to correct it. Copytesting procedures can generate some of this information. Advertising creatives can then determine what to do next. By using continuous ad tracking and copytesting, an agency builds a benchmark for a particular client on an advertisement's performance. The agency also gains insights into what works and what does not work for consumers for that particular product category and brand.

Copytesting Controversies   Controversies regarding copytesting remain. A number of advertisers and marketers strongly believe the method favors rational approaches over affective and conative (action-inspiring) methods. To correct this potential deficiency, some research firms add emotional tests to copytesting procedures.

Further, some marketers believe copytesting prior to production stifles the creativity needed to produce ads that will stand out in the clutter. Recently, creatives working for brands—including Nike, Volkswagen, Budweiser, and Target—have been allowed to skip the copytesting phase of advertising design and move straight into production. When the agency Wieden + Kennedy created "the man your man could smell like" campaign for Old Spice cologne, the brand's parent firm Procter & Gamble allowed Wieden to skip the concept testing stage completely. Also, the approval process for the Old Spice campaign was streamlined to just one P&G executive.[10]

Unless the client insists on preproduction copytests, agencies now move directly into production and perform the tests after the ad launches. Many advertisers believe copytests are likely to lead creatives to design ad messages about the product benefits that are believable and understandable to members of a focus group or panel. Many consumers in focus groups know little, if anything, about how to create an effective advertisement. Most creatives believe it does not make sense to have them serve as final judges of an advertisement's quality.

Although a number of marketing professionals do not favor using copytests at all, the majority believe they are necessary, primarily due to accountability issues. Jeff Cox, CEO of copytesting agency ARS Group, argues that, "Copytesting can squelch creative, but the marketplace and the world's largest advertisers see value in doing this."[11] When the time comes to support a decision for a high-dollar advertising campaign, advertising agency and company executives want evidence that supports the investment. Also, advertising agencies can use the results of copytesting to perfect future ads and campaigns by understanding what works and what does not work in a given marketplace.

▼ Emotional reaction tests provide valuable information to advertisers, such as Progressive Bank.

Think finances for community projects get in shape on their own?

Think again.

Helping build a better community and a brighter future is something all of us have a stake in.

Meet Michele Thaxton, Senior Vice President, Chief Financial Officer and 10-year member of our ProTeam. She watches over all financial aspects of Progressive Bank to ensure we continue to grow as a strong, vibrant institution, fulfilling our mission every day as a committed and caring community bank.

She also works out in the community as a volunteer on the finance committees and boards of entities like

United Way and the Northeast Louisiana Soccer Association. An avid health enthusiast, Michele is equally dedicated to helping keep the financial matters of these key community organizations in shape and running smoothly.

Community service like this does a community good. And you can take that to the bank.

Get to know Michele better – call her at 318-812-5226.

PROGRESSIVE BANK
Banking *reinvented.*

(318) 398-9772 • progressivebank.com
Monroe • West Monroe • Winnsboro • Bossier City • 7 Locations • 31 Convenient ATM Locations

French Creative

Emotional Reaction Tests

Many advertisements seek to elicit emotional responses from consumers. Emotional ads are based on the concept that messages eliciting positive feelings are more likely to be remembered. Also, consumers who have positive attitudes toward ads develop more favorable attitudes regarding the product. This, in turn, should result in increased purchases.[12]

Measuring the emotional impact of an advertisement can be difficult. The simplest method involves asking about an individual's feelings and emotions after viewing a marketing communication piece. An alternative method, a **warmth monitor**, relies on the notion that feelings of warmth are positive when they are directed toward an ad or a product. To measure warmth, subjects are asked to manipulate a joystick or the mouse on a computer while watching a commercial, moving one direction for warmer and another for cooler.[13]

Members of the faculty at the University of Hawaii developed the first warmth meter. Individuals viewed advertisements in a theater-type lab featuring a big-screen television. Those who felt negatively about what they were watching pulled a joystick downward. Those who felt more positively pushed the joystick in the opposite direction. As they watched a commercial, the subjects constantly moved the joystick, thereby conveying their feelings during every moment of the ad. The results of the 20 participants were tallied into one graph and then placed over the commercial. This technology allowed the advertiser to see the parts of the message that elicited positive emotions and which parts elicited negative emotions.[14]

Reactions and Opinions designed a similar technology for use on the internet. The company can easily poll 1,000 or more people who view an advertisement online. As individuals watch the ad on streaming video, the participants use a mouse to move a tab on a sliding scale from 1 to 10. When they like what they see, they slide the tab toward the 10. Those who do not like what they see slide the tab toward the 1. After the data have been collected, a graph will be superimposed over the advertisement to indicate the likable and dislikable parts of the message. The internet offers the advantage of allowing subjects to provide ratings at their convenience. If the agency needs a focus group to discuss the ad, subjects can be selected from the participants. The focus group session can also be held online.[15]

Another approach to measuring emotional reactions, **biometric research**, involves measuring physiological reactions to advertisements and marketing messages. The Innerscope company specializes in biometric research. Carl Marci, CEO and chief science officer stated that, "Innerscope strongly believes that unconscious emotional responses direct attention, enhance learning, and memory, and ultimately drive behaviors that our clients care about." Innerscope puts test subjects in a living room setting. A device on the television tracks eye movement to track the subject's attention to stimuli. At the same time, a special belt worn by the subject collects data regarding the person's heartbeat, perspiration levels, respiration, and body movements. By integrating all of these biological measures, Innerscope measures the level of emotional engagement of viewers during every second of the ad via their emotional, unconscious responses to what they see.[16]

Time Warner built a 9,600-square-foot media lab in Manhattan for its own operation but also leases to clients for biometric research. The cost ranges from $50,000 for basic focus groups to $120,000 for research featuring biometrics. The company makes biometric belts available to measure physiological reactions to ads. Cameras measure eye movements and two-way mirrors allow for client observation.[17] Rather than rely on consumers telling researchers how they are reacting via some type of warmth meters, biometrics measure actual emotional reactions. Individuals can lie about how they feel with a warmth meter, but bodily reactions to ads are more difficult to fake.

Cognitive Neuroscience

In recent years, significant advances have occurred in **cognitive neuroscience**, a brain-image measurement process that tracks brain activity. As noted in the opening vignette for this chapter, it tracks the flow and movement of electrical currents in the brain. One study using cognitive neuroscience (psychophysiology) demonstrated that the currents in a subject's brain indicated a preference for Coke or Pepsi that are the same as for the product a person chooses in a blind taste test. According to neuroscientist Justin Meaux, "Preference has measurable correlates in the brain; you can see it." Richard Siberstein, an Australian neuroscientist, took physiological measurements of the brain to show that successful ads tend to generate higher levels of emotional engagement and long-term memory coding.[18]

Consider a sexually provocative advertisement under development. Individual members of a focus group may enjoy the ad but cover up these feelings by saying it was sexist and inappropriate. Their responses may be due to the desire for social acceptance. In a copytest for the same ad, a respondent may also offer socially acceptable answers even though he is not face-to-face with the researcher. The individual may not move the computer mouse to report his true feelings in a study using an emotional monitor. The negative stigma attached to sex in advertising often affects self-reported reactions. A physiological arousal test, such as cognitive neuroscience, might provide a better indicator of a person's true response. Many advertising researchers believe physiological arousal tests provide more accurate information than emotional reaction tests, because physiological arousal is more genuine.[19]

◀ Cognitive neuroscience is likely to produce a more accurate assessment of this billboard than a copytest.

The most recent research in this area has been undertaken by companies such as EmSense, Neuro-Focus, Sands Research, and OTX Research. These companies experiment with portable devices that measure both brain waves and biologic data. Coca-Cola employed this methodology to select ads to run on the Super Bowl. Coke produced a dozen ads that were evaluated by the EmSense device. The EmSense device measures brain waves and monitors breathing, heart rates, blinking, and skin temperatures as consumers watch ads. Through these physiological measurements, Coca-Cola researchers determined which ads to use. Some Super Bowl commercials were modified to produce higher levels of emotions.[20]

Frito-Lay engaged in neuroscience to test product packaging. Company marketers discovered that matte beige bags of potato chips picturing potatoes and other healthier ingredients did not trigger anterior cingulated cortex activity (the area of the brain associated with guilt) as much as shiny potato chip bags.

Frito-Lay's chief marketing officer, Ann Mukherjee, said, "Brain-imaging tests can be more accurate than focus groups." After a focus group rejected a Cheetos advertisement, Frito-Lay tested the commercial using neuroscience methods. The ad featured a woman taking revenge on someone in a Laundromat by putting orange snack food in a dryer that was full of white clothes. The focus group participants felt the prank made Frito-Lay look mean-spirited. The neuroscience test indicated that women loved the commercial.[21]

Cognitive neuroscience reveals physiological reactions to a message. It shows where brain activity occurs and, to some extent, the level of activity. It can identify times when a test subject becomes enthralled with a message. It also indicates when the person merely focuses on the logo or an attractive woman in the commercial. The methodology identifies positive and negative emotions and the intensity of the emotions by the amount of neurons firing. This methodology enables scientists (and marketers) to understand the information being processed, where it is being processed, and how the individual reacted to the ad or marketing piece. Although still in its infancy, cognitive neuroscience offers great potential for evaluating advertising and marketing.

Evaluation Criteria

objective 4

Which evaluation criteria are suggested by the positioning advertising copytesting (PACT) system?

Each of the evaluation programs mentioned thus far require quality evaluation criteria. One helpful program, **positioning advertising copytesting (PACT)**, was created by 21 leading U.S. advertising agencies to help evaluate television ads.[22] Even though PACT examines the issues involved in copytesting television ads, the principles apply to any type of message evaluation system and all types of media. Figure 3 lists the nine main principles to follow when testing a written or verbal marketing communication piece.

Any advertising procedure should be *relevant to the advertising objective being tested*. For a coupon promotion designed to stimulate trial purchases, marketers should evaluate the coupon's copy in order to determine its ability to stimulate those purchases. An evaluation of attitudes toward a brand requires a different instrument.

- Testing procedure should be relevant to the advertising objectives.
- In advance of each test, researchers should agree on how the results will be used.
- Multiple measures should be used.
- The test should be based on some theory or model of human response to communication.
- Tha testing procedure should allow for more than one exposure to the advertisement, if necessary.
- In selecting alternate advertisements to include in the test, each should be at the same stage in the process as the test ad.
- The test should provide controls to avoid biases.
- The sample used for the test should be representative of the target sample.
- The testing procedure should demonstrate reliability and valldity.

▶ **FIGURE 3**
Copytesting Principles of PACT

Researchers should agree about how the results are going to be used when selecting test instruments. They should also agree on the design of the test in order to obtain the desired results. This becomes especially important during the preparation stage of an advertisement's development because many tests are used to determine whether the advertisement eventually will be created.

The research team should select a *cutoff score* to be used following the test. This prevents biases from affecting findings about the ad's potential effectiveness. Many advertising agencies use test markets for new advertisements before they are launched in a larger area. A recall method used to determine if people in the target market remember seeing the ad should contain a prearranged cutoff score. In other words, the acceptable percentage may be established so that 25 percent of the sample should remember the ad in order to move forward with the campaign. An advertisement that does not achieve the percentage has failed the test.

Using multiple measures allows for more precise evaluations of ads and campaigns. A well-designed ad may fail one particular testing procedure yet score higher on others. Consumers and business buyers who are the targets of marketing communications are complex human beings. Various people perceive individual ads differently. As a result, advertisers usually try to develop more than one measure to be certain greater agreement can be reached about whether the ad or campaign will succeed and reach its desired goals.

The test to be used should be *based on some theory or model of human response to communication*, which makes it more likely that the test will accurately predict the human response. Enhancing the odds that the communication will produce the desired results (going to the website, visiting the store, or making a purchase) when an ad launches becomes the objective.

Many testing procedures are based on a single exposure. Although in many cases this may be sufficient for research purposes, sometimes *multiple exposures* are necessary to obtain reliable test results. For complex ads, more than one exposure may be needed. The human mind comprehends only so much information in one viewing. The marketing team should make sure a person can and will comprehend the message to determine whether it achieve the desired effects.

Often ads are tested in combination with other ads to disguise the one being examined. Placing the test marketing piece in with others means the test subjects do not know which one is being evaluated. This prevents personal biases from affecting judgments. To ensure valid results, *the alternative ads should be in the same stage of process development*. When ad copy is being tested prior to ad development, the alternative ads should also be in the ad copy development stage.

Next, adequate controls are put in place to *prevent biases and external factors from affecting results*. To help control external factors, researchers often utilize experimental designs. When conducting experiments, researchers hold as many things as constant as possible and manipulate one variable at a time. With a theater test, the temperature, time of day, room lighting, television program, and ads shown should all be the same. Then, the researcher may display the program and ads to an all-male audience followed by an all-female audience. Changing a single variable (gender) makes it possible to see if the ad, in a controlled environment, was perceived differently by men as opposed to women.

Field tests can also be effective. Testing marketing communications in real-world situations offers value, because they approximate reality. When conducting field tests, such as mall intercepts, those performing the testing seek to control as many variables as possible. Thus, the same mall, same questions, and same ads are shown. Then, researchers manipulate age, gender, or other variables one at a time.

Tracey Altman/Fresherized Foods

▲ This advertisement for Wholly Guacamole includes a coupon and offer for free potato tots, which means the message evaluation could focus on its ability to stimulate purchases.

Courtesy of Joplin Globe.

▲ Using PACT principles helps ensure a better evaluation of this advertisement for Chic Shaque.

As with any research procedure, sampling procedures are important. The *sample being used should be representative of the target population*. A print ad designed for Spanish-speaking Hispanic Americans should be tested using a Spanish questionnaire or interview format.

Finally, researchers continually try to make tests *reliable and valid*. Reliable means "repeatable." In other words, if the same test were given five times to the same person, the individual should respond in the same way each time. If a respondent is "emotional" on one iteration of a warmth test and "neutral" when the ad is shown a second time, the research team will wonder if the test is reliable.

Valid means "generalizable." Valid research findings can be generalized to other groups. For instance, when a focus group of women finds an ad to be funny, and then a group of men reacts in the same way, the finding that the humor was effective becomes more valid. This would be an increasingly valuable outcome if the results were generalizable to people of various ages and races. Many times an ad may be reliable, or repeatable in the same group, but not valid or generalizable to other groups of consumers or business buyers.

The PACT principles have value when agencies design tests of short-term advertising effectiveness. They also help when marketers seek to understand larger and more long-term issues such as brand loyalty and identification with the company. Generating data documenting that what a company is doing works should be the objective. When this occurs, the company and its advertising team have access to valuable information.

Online Evaluation Metrics

objective 5

How do online evaluation systems assist advertising managers in assessing the quality of a firm's internet activities?

To evaluate digital marketing communications from the internet, a number of metrics are available that provide hard and soft data. Figure 4 identifies methods of measuring digital marketing and the percentage of companies using each method.

Click-throughs remain the primary method used to measure the impact of online advertising. The number of click-throughs provides an idea of how many people see an

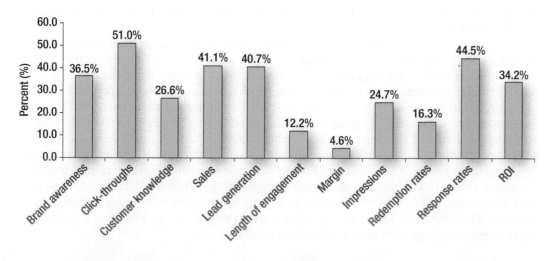

▶ **FIGURE 4**
Measuring Effectiveness of Digital Marketing

online ad, click it, and go to the website. Once there, additional metrics, such as length of engagement, dwell rate, dwell time, redemption rates, response rates, and sales, become available.

▲ Click-throughs offer a common metric used to measure the impact of banner ads, such as this one for Sonic and Wholly Guacamole.

Redemption rates and response rates occur when visitors to the site take an action. Sales occur when the individual makes the purchase online. *Dwell rate* measures the proportion of ad impressions that resulted in a user engaging with the ad, such as clicking it or just mousing over it. *Dwell time* measures the amount of time users spend engaged with a particular advertisement. *Length of engagement*, a newer metric, measures how long the person stays at a website. It offers a surrogate of a person's interest in the product and the site being visited.

AdKnowledge introduced an online management tool called MarketingMatch Planner to evaluate internet advertising campaigns. MarketingMatch Planner software includes two components: Campaign Manager and Administrator. Campaign Manager records traffic to a site and performs postpurchase analysis. Administrator integrates web ad-buy data and performance analysis with the firm's accounting and billing systems. In addition, MarketingMatch Planner can integrate third-party data, including audience demographics, from the following sources:

- MediaMetrix for basic demographics
- NetRatings for gross rating points (GRP) and other ratings instruments
- Psychographic data from SRI Consulting
- Website ratings and descriptions from NetGuide
- Web traffic audit data from BPA Interactive[23]

Marketers view digital data results in light of the company's IMC objectives. An IMC objective of building brand awareness requires something other than online sales data to be assessed. An internet ad might bring awareness to a brand but not lead to an online purchase. This may occur when a consumer or business uses the internet to gather information but then makes the actual purchase at a retail store or by telephone. In that situation, the analysis of an internet advertising campaign may not reflect all of the brand awareness or sales that the campaign generated.

▼ A number of different metrics can be used to evaluate websites, such as this one for DuPage Medical Group.

One of the newest forms of online evaluations is measuring and monitoring *web chat*. A company called WiseWindow developed software (Mass Opinion Business Intelligence, MOBI) that can swiftly analyze large numbers of opinions on the web, blogs, Twitter, and social networking sites such as Facebook. MOBI provides continuous, real-time information concerning consumer sentiment about a brand, business, or advertising campaign from millions of sites virtually instantaneously. Companies including Kia, Best Buy, Viacom, Cisco Systems, and Intuit utilize the software to analyze how customers, employees, and investors feel.

Gaylord Hotels applied sentiment analysis software called Clarabridge to determine how customers feel about the company's network of upscale resorts. From the sentiment analysis, Gaylord concluded that the first 20 minutes of a guest's visit were the most

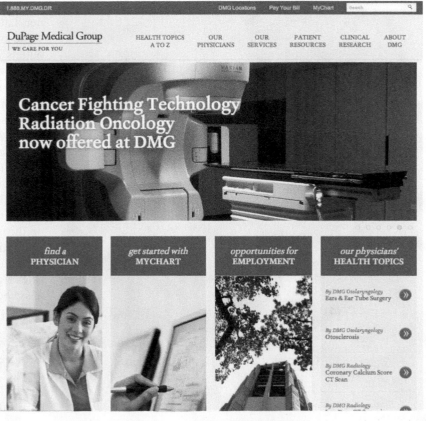

critical and there were five ways the company could increase the likelihood that guests would recommend the hotel to others. For instance, the web chat analysis revealed it was important to take a new guest to a location rather than just point out where it was or show them on a map. Before this sentiment analysis, Gaylord believed the company had to do 80 things. David C. Kloeppel, chief operating officer for Gaylord Hotels, stated, "We learned that the first 20 minutes of the hotel experience was of vital importance to our guests. Our hypothesis became, if we could perfect the first 20 minutes of the experience, we could drive positive overall guest satisfaction."[24]

objective 6

What types of behavioral evaluations can be employed to assess IMC programs?

- Sales
- Response rates
- Redemption rates
- Test markets
- Purchase simulation tests

▲ **FIGURE 5**
Behavioral Measures

▼ This Scott Equipment advertising campaign resulted in an increase in sales.

Bobbie Williams/Scott Equipment

Behavioral Evaluations

The first part of this chapter regarding message evaluations focuses on insights into what people think and feel. Some marketers contend that sales represent the only valid evaluation criterion. An advertisement may be fun and enjoyable, but if sales do not increase, it was ineffective. The same reasoning applies to other marketing communication tools, such as consumer promotions, trade promotions, and direct marketing tactics.

While it may be true that tangible results should be the bottom line of any marketing program, not all communication objectives can be measured using sales figures. Leaders of companies with low brand awareness may be most interested in the visibility and memorability aspects of a communication plan, even though a marketing program designed to boost brand awareness does not result in immediate sales.

Measuring the results of a consumer promotion campaign featuring coupons using sales figures is easier than measuring the results of a television advertising campaign. Consequently, effective promotions evaluations involve the study of both message and behavioral elements. This section describes behavioral measures shown in Figure 5.

Sales and Response Rates

Measuring changes in sales following a marketing campaign is relatively simple. Retailers collect information from universal product codes (UPCs) and scanner data. These data are available on a weekly and, in some situations, daily basis for each store. Many retail outlets have access to real-time sales information that can be accessed at any point during the day.

Scanner data make it possible for company leaders to monitor sales and help both the retailer and the manufacturer discover the impact of a particular marketing program. At the same time, extraneous factors can affect sales. In a multimedia advertising program, it would be difficult to know which advertisement moved the customer to action. A company featuring a fall line of jackets may be affected by a cold snap. If so, what caused the customer to buy—the ad or the weather? Firms utilizing trade and consumer promotion programs must account for the impact of both the promotion and the advertising when studying sales figures. Sales provide one indicator of effectiveness; however, they may be influenced by additional factors.

As highlighted in Figure 6, advertisements may be the most difficult component of the IMC program to evaluate, for several reasons. As just noted, distinguishing *the effects of advertising from other factors* may be difficult. Advertisements create short- and long-term effects, and consumers and businesses see them in many different contexts. The direct impact of one advertisement or one campaign on sales will be difficult to decipher.

Advertising often has a delayed impact. Many times, consumers encounter ads and are persuaded to purchase the product but will not actually make the purchase until later when they actually need the item. A woman may be convinced that she wants to buy a new pair of jeans in response to a sexy and effective advertisement by Calvin Klein. Still, rather than buying them herself, she leaves several well-placed hints for her husband before her next birthday, which could be several months later. The problem could be that her husband purchased another brand or a different gift. So, she either waits for another special occasion for her husband to buy the jeans or she makes the purchase herself at a later time.

Consumers often decide to make purchases based on an advertisement but *change their minds when they arrive at the retail store*. A competing brand may be on sale, the store could be out of the desired brand, or the salesperson could persuade the customer that another brand is better. In each case, the ad was successful on one level but another factor interfered before the purchase was made.

Further, *the brand being advertised may not be part of the consumer's evoked set*. Upon hearing or seeing the ad, however, the brand moves into the evoked set. Thus, even when an individual does not consider the brand at first, it will be in the future when the need arises or when the consumer becomes dissatisfied with a current option.

Advertising helps generate brand awareness and brand equity. Although sales may not be the result immediately, *the ad may build brand equity*, which, in turn, influences future purchases.

A wide variety of responses to marketing communications programs are available besides sales. Figure 7 lists some of the responses that can be tracked.

Promotions   Measuring the effects of trade and consumer promotions, direct marketing programs, and personal selling on actual sales is relatively easy. Manufacturers study the impact of trade promotions by observing changes in sales to the retailers at the time the company offers promotions. The same holds true for consumer promotions, such as coupons, contests, and point-of-purchase displays. Many manufacturers' representatives push hard to get retailers to prominently place the company's point-of-purchase displays. At the same time, the retailer might be more interested in the effects of the display on sales. Using scanner data, both the retailer and the manufacturer can measure the impact of a display. Retailers normally prefer point-of-purchase displays that have demonstrated the ability to boost sales.

Toll-Free Numbers   One method of measuring the impact of an advertisement, direct mail piece, TV direct offer, or price-off discount to a business customer involves assigning a toll-free number to each marketing piece. A great deal of information can be collected during an inbound call. Sales data can be recorded and demographic information gathered. Psychographic information may then be added by contacting various commercial services.

In business-to-business situations, a toll-free number provides contact names to help the vendor discover who performs the various functions in the buying center. As a result, a toll-free number provides sales data to determine which marketing program would be best and generate valuable information that can be tied to the sales data. Knowing who responds to an offer helps marketers better understand customers and develop the right approach for each target group.

QR Codes and Facebook Likes   Two new methods of evaluation are QR code responses and Facebook likes. Many ads include QR codes consumers can access with their mobile phones. Some link to a company's website, while others offer special deals or information. The advertisement for Kraft Parmesan Cheese on the next page includes a QR code. The marketing department counts how many individuals access the code. They also gather information about individuals who accessed the QR code.

With the increased popularity of Facebook, a new measure of a brand's popularity is the number of individuals who "like" a brand. Employees count the number of likes

- Influence of other factors
- Delayed impact of the ads
- Consumers changing their minds while in the store
- Whether the brand is in the consumer's evoked set
- Level of brand equity

▲ **FIGURE 6**
Factors that Make Advertising Difficult to Evaluate

- Changes in sales
- Telephone inquiries
- Response cards
- Internet responses
- Direct-marketing responses
- Redemption rate of sales promotion offers—coupons, premiums, contests, sweepstakes

▲ **FIGURE 7**
Tracking Marketing Responses

▶ One Measure of effectiveness of this O'Nealgas advertisement is the increase in the number of phone calls made for pricing and scheduling.

▼ Kraft Foods' marketing team can measure how many individuals accessed the QR code contained in the ad for for Parmesan cheese.

and correlate the likes to special offers that are made on the brand's Facebook. Many marketers consider fans "liking" a brand or something a brand does as a surrogate for word-of-mouth endorsement.

Response Cards Response cards collect customer information as the forms are filled out at the time of an inquiry. Response cards carry the disadvantage of providing less data. Consequently, commercial sources are needed to obtain additional demographic and psychographic information, because response cards solicited from current customers contain information the firm may already have in its database.

Internet Responses Internet responses provide quality behavioral measures. By using cookies, a marketing team obtains considerable information about the person or business making the inquiry. In addition, many times the person or business responding voluntarily provides a great deal of helpful information. Responses to direct advertising through internet views may also be tracked.

The Canadian Tourism Commission tested direct-response ads placed on television, radio, direct mail, and online. Each ad used a different URL for viewers to access for additional information. To the tourist, there was no perceivable difference, because each URL took the person to the designated Canadian Tourism site. The Tourism Commission could track which ad the person viewed and which URL the person used. This made it possible to count the number of visitors from each of the direct-response advertisements.[25]

◀ Wholly Guacamole's marketers can evaluate this brand alliance campaign with Disney using the redemption rate for the mail-in rebate.

Redemption Rates   Marketers study various kinds of redemption rates to measure behavioral effectiveness. Employees code coupons, premiums, rebates, contests, sweepstakes, and direct-mail pieces and record redemption rates. Comparing a current campaign with previous campaigns makes it possible to examine changes made in the design or advertisement's execution. The marketing team reviews the results in light of positive or negative changes in redemption rates.

Immediate changes in sales and redemptions offer another form of behavioral evaluation. An advertiser or company may use them but fail to see "the forest for the trees." One campaign, advertisement, or promotions program should be viewed in the context of all other marketing efforts. Behavioral measures work best when the team sees them as part of the bigger picture.

Test Markets

Test markets allow company leaders to examine the effects of a marketing effort on a small scale before launching a national or international campaign. The marketing team is able to examine several elements of a marketing communication program in one setting. If the test market achieves success, then the likelihood that the national campaign will be effective improves. Test markets measure the effects of a campaign in a new country before launching a full-scale international effort. Test market programs are used to assess:

- Advertisements
- Consumer and trade promotions
- Pricing tactics
- New products

Test markets provide cost-effective methods to analyze and then make changes in marketing efforts before millions of dollars are spent on something that might not accomplish its objectives. Advertisements can be modified, promotions revised, and pricing policies revisited before undertaking a more widespread program. For example, McDonald's tested new ads that touted cleaner restaurants and friendlier service. The goal of the commercials was to test a campaign emphasizing McDonald's effort to improve in-store and drive-through service. Two television spots and one radio spot were produced and aired in Tampa and Seattle. Reactions from the test markets provided McDonald's marketing team and the advertising agency with information about the impact of the ad campaign, the parts of the message that should be modified, and whether the campaign should be launched nationally.[26]

Test markets hold the advantage of resembling an actual purchasing situation more than any of the other tests. Making sure the site selected for the test market strongly resembles the target population becomes the key. A product targeted toward senior citizens should be studied in an area with a high concentration of seniors.

SHAPING THE
FUTURE OF TEXAS

Weaver is the firm of choice for companies and individuals with dreams
and goals as big as Texas. And bigger.

AUSTIN | DALLAS | FORT WORTH | HOUSTON | MIDLAND | ODESSA | SAN ANTONIO
MORE AT WEAVER.COM

weaver
Assurance · Tax · Advisory

Katie Mcgee

▲ A test market can be used to evaluate various aspects of an advertising campaign for Weaver before it is launched in the seven cities where offices are located.

▼ Rather than field test markets, researchers can use simulated shopping exercises.

Yuri Arcurs/Fotolia

A test market campaign should resemble the national or full marketing plan, if possible. A lengthy time lapse may cause a company to experience differing results. Marketers try to make sure the test market provides a mirror image of the actual marketing program.

A test market might be as short as a few days or as long as two to three years. A test that is too short may yield less reliable results. If the test market is too long, the national market situation may change and the test market may no longer be a representative sample. The greater drawback is that the competition can study what is going on, which gives them time to react to the proposed marketing campaign.

Competitive Responses   Competing companies often respond to test market programs in one of two ways. First, some introduce a special promotion in the test market area in order to confound the results. This may reduce sales for the tested product, making the campaign appear to be less attractive than it actually was. The second approach involves not intervening in the test market, but instead using the time to prepare a countermarketing campaign. Firms that use this tactic are ready when the national launch occurs, and the impact may be that the test market results are not as predictive of what will happen.

Scanner Data   Scanner data make it possible for results from test market campaigns to be made quickly available. The figures help determine the acceptability of test market results. A firm can design several versions of a marketing campaign in different test markets. Scanner data assist marketers in comparing the sales from each test market to determine which version works best. For example, in one test market the firm may present an advertising campaign only. In the second test market, coupons may be added to the ad program. In the third test market, a premium will be combined with advertising. The results from each area help the marketing team understand which type of marketing campaign fared best.

Test markets provide the opportunity to test communication ideas in more true-to-life settings. Test markets examine trade and consumer promotions, direct marketing, and other marketing communication tools. They are not quite as accurate when assessing advertising, because changes in sales take longer and the test market program may not be long enough to measure the full impact. In any case, test markets offer valuable instruments to examine specific marketing features and more general communications campaigns.

Purchase Simulation Tests

Instead of test markets, marketing researchers employ purchase simulation tests. *Simulated purchase tests* present a cost-effective approach to examine purchase behaviors. Research Systems Corporation (RSC) specializes in purchase simulation studies. RSC tests the impact of commercials by studying consumer behaviors in a controlled laboratory environment.

Consumers are asked if they would be willing to buy products in a variety of ways, using various methods. They might be asked about purchase intentions at the end of a laboratory experiment. In this situation, however, intentions are self-reported and may be a less accurate predictor of future purchase behaviors. RSC does not request consumer opinions, ask them to describe their attitudes, or even ask if they plan to purchase the product. Instead, RSC creates a simulated shopping experience. Subjects choose from a variety of products they would see on a store shelf. After completing a simulated shopping exercise, the subjects are seated and watch a television preview containing various commercials. The participants are asked to view the TV program as they would watch any TV show at home. The test ad is placed in with other ads, and the subjects do not know which ad is being tested.

After completing the preview, the subjects participate in a second shopping exercise. Researchers then compare the products chosen in the first shopping trip to those selected in the second. Shifts in brand choices are at least partly due to the effectiveness of the advertisement, because it was the only variable that changed.

This methodology provides the advantage of using test procedures that do not rely on opinions and attitudes. Among other things, this means that RSC's procedure would work in international markets as well as domestic markets.[27] In some cultures, subjects tend to seek to please the interviewer who asks questions about opinions and attitudes. As a result, the answers are polite and socially acceptable. The same subjects may also seek to provide answers they think the interviewer wants to hear. By studying purchases instead of soliciting opinions, subjects are free to respond in a more forthright fashion.

Any methodology designed to tap into behaviors rather than emotions and feelings features a built-in advantage. Opinions and attitudes change and may be quickly affected by other variables. Observing behaviors and changes in behaviors gets more quickly to the point of the experiment, which is whether the buyer can tangibly be influenced by a marketing communications tool.

In summary, the systems available to examine respondent behaviors are response rates, online metrics, test markets, and purchase simulation tests. Marketers employ programs in conjunction with one another and also with the message evaluation techniques described earlier. None of these approaches is used in a vacuum. Instead, the data generated and findings revealed are tested across several instruments and with numerous groups of subjects. In that manner, the marketing department manager and the advertising agency can try to heighten the odds that both short- and long-term goals can be reached through the ads, premiums, coupons, and other marketing communications devices used. Even then, the job of evaluation is not complete.

Evaluating the Overall IMC Program

As has been noted throughout this text, the expenditures companies make for marketing communications has led CEOs and other executives to push for greater accountability. These individuals, as well as stockholders and boards of directors, want to know what type of return results when a firm spends a large sum of money on an advertising campaign or other marketing activity. They seek to discover the *return on investment (ROI)* of an advertising and promotions program.

Little agreement exists regarding what "ROI" means when applied to a marketing program. No consensus takes place regarding how to measure marketing ROI. In one study, more than 70 percent of marketers said it would be difficult to measure the impact of advertising and marketing on sales. The same number predicted that it would be extremely difficult for the marketing industry to reach any agreement on what constitutes ROI for marketing. The most common are behavioral responses, such as incremental sales, total sales, and market share.[28]

This confusion will likely continue, even as company executives try to justify advertising and marketing expenditures. Consequently, those in the marketing profession keep trying to identify ways to measure the impact of marketing communications, ultimately in dollars and cents.

objective 7

What criteria should be used to assess the overall IMC program?

- Market share
- Innovation
- Productivity
- Physical and financial resources
- Profitability
- Manager performance and development
- Employee performance and attitudes
- Social responsibility

▲ **FIGURE 8**
Overall Health of a Company

Many years ago, Peter Drucker outlined a series of goal areas that indicate organizational health. These goals (listed in Figure 8) match well with the objectives of an IMC program.[29] As marketers struggle to find a way to measure the ROI of marketing communication expenditures, understanding the various measures of overall health of an organization can provide valuable insight on how marketing communications contributes.

Market share has long been linked to profitability. It demonstrates consumer acceptance, brand loyalty, and a strong competitive position. The IMC planning process should help the marketing team understand both market share and the relative strengths and weaknesses of the competition. IMC programs are designed to hold and build market share.

Innovation includes finding new and different ways to achieve objectives. This applies to many marketing activities, including new and unusual trade and consumer promotions, public relations events and sponsorships, e-commerce and social media programs, and the firm's advertising efforts.

Productivity reflects the industry's increasing emphasis on results. IMC experts are being asked to demonstrate tangible results from IMC campaigns. Both short- and long-term measures of the effects of advertisements and promotions demonstrate the "productivity" of the organization in terms of gaining new customers, building recognition in the marketplace, determining sales per customer, and through other measures.

Physical and financial resources are important to an IMC program. Physical resources include the most up-to-date computer and internet capabilities. The firm must provide sufficient financial resources to reach this goal. Communication devices that keep the firm in contact with consumers constitute vital elements in the long-term success of an IMC plan.

Profitability remains vitally important to the marketing department and the overall organization. Many IMC managers know that more than sales are at issue when assessing success. Sales must generate profits in order for the company to survive and thrive.

Manager performance and development may be an overlooked part of an IMC program. Effective marketing departments and advertising agencies should develop pipelines of new, talented creatives, media buyers, promotions managers, webmasters, and others in order to succeed in the long term. Also, new people should be trained and prepared for promotion for more important roles.

Employee performance and attitudes reflect not only morale within the marketing department, but also relations with other departments and groups. An effective IMC plan consists of building bridges with internal departments so that everyone is aware of the thrust and theme of the marketing program. Satisfied and positive employees help the firm promote its image.

Social responsibility can be linked to the long-term well-being of an organization. Brand equity and loyalty are hurt when the firm is known for illegal or unethical actions. Therefore, marketing leaders should encourage all of the members of an organization to act in ethically and socially responsible ways.

When these goals are reached, the firm's IMC program works well. Beyond these targets, IMC plans should continually emphasize the evolving nature of relationships with customers. Retail consumers and business-to-business buyers should be constantly contacted to find out how the company can best serve their needs.

Simply stated, this text implies a series of key performance targets for IMC programs that can guide the actions of the marketing department and the advertising agency both in the short term and for the long term. Firms that are able to maintain one clear voice in a cluttered marketplace stand the best chance of gaining customer interest and attention as well as developing long-term bonds with all key publics and stakeholders. An effective IMC program helps set the standards and measure performance and, in the end, becomes the model for marketing success for the entire organization.

International Implications

objective 8

How are evaluation programs adjusted to match international operations?

Many of the techniques described in this chapter are available worldwide. IMC programs should be assessed in several ways, including domestic results, results in other countries, and as an overall organization.

Individual advertisements and promotional programs are examined within the countries in which they appear. Due to differing standards regarding advertising content, they must be evaluated in light of local cultures and purchasing habits.

Many times, advertising and promotional programs are assessed across national boundaries. For example, a campaign launched in Europe leads to evaluations in individual countries including France, Spain, and Italy, but also as a collective, such as the European Union. Measures of attitudes are difficult to collect. Sales are easier to assess due to the use of the Euro in all of these nations; however, inflation rates and other statistics are affected by local conditions.

It is advisable to contract with local advertising agencies to discover which techniques are most viable in other countries. In some nations, using coupons may be viewed as a sign of poverty, and users are either secretive or embarrassed about redeeming them. In those situations, it helps to study results in light of cultural norms.

Numerous multinational conglomerates assess advertising and promotional efforts through regional offices. Pacific Rim information will be combined with information from Europe, Africa, and other places. The goal is to make sure an overall image and theme is projected worldwide.

Summary

Assessing an IMC program often involves examining the effects of individual advertisements. These efforts are conducted in three major ways: message evaluations, online evaluation metrics, and evaluating respondent behaviors. Numerous techniques are available. Most of the time, marketing managers and advertisement agencies apply several different methods in order to get the best picture of an ad's potential for success. Advertisements are studied before they are developed, while they are being developed, and after they have been released or launched.

The guiding principles for any marketing tool include agreement on how test results will be used, pre-establishing a cutoff score for a test's results, employing multiple measures, basing studies on models of human behaviors, creating multiple exposures, testing marketing instruments that are in the same stage of development, and preventing as many biases as possible while conducting the test. Many times, certain members of the marketing team may not be objective, especially when they had the idea for the ad or campaign. In these instances, companies retain an outside research agency to study the project.

Message evaluations take place at every stage of the development process. Methods that may be employed include advertising tracking research, copytesting, emotional reaction tests, and cognitive neuroscience.

Positioning advertising copytesting (PACT) is primarily used to evaluate television advertisements. Nine key principles are involved. The principles may be applied to any type of message evaluation system and all types of media.

Online evaluation metrics include the use of click-throughs, dwell rates, dwell time, and length of engagement. Interactive data are carefully evaluated in light of the company's IMC objectives. The newest form of evaluation is measuring and monitoring web chat.

Behavioral evaluations consist of sales and response rates, toll-free number responses, response cards, internet responses, and redemption rates. Test markets assess advertisements, consumer and trade promotions, pricing tactics, and acceptance of new products. Purchase simulation tests offer cost-effective methods to analyze the impact of advertising and promotion on immediate consumer purchase responses.

IMC plans guide the entire company. Therefore, more general and long-term criteria should be included in any evaluation of an IMC program. When the IMC theme and voice are clear, the company is achieving its long-range objectives, the principles stated in this book are applied efficiently and effectively, and the company is in the best position to succeed at all levels, including in all international operations.

Key Terms

metrics Measures designed to accurately portray the effectiveness of a marketing communications plan

message evaluation techniques Methods used to examine the creative message and the physical design of an advertisement, coupon, or direct marketing piece

online evaluation metrics Methods used to examine online advertising and marketing campaigns

respondent behavior evaluations Methods used to examine visible customer actions, including making store visits, inquiries, or actual purchases

copytests Tests used to evaluate a marketing piece that is finished or in its final stages prior to production

portfolio test A test of an advertisement using a set of print ads, one of which is the ad being evaluated

theater test A test of an advertisement using a set of television ads, including the one being evaluated

warmth monitor A method to measure emotional responses to advertisements

biometric research A method to measure physiological reactions to advertisements and marketing messages

cognitive neuroscience A brain-image measurement process that tracks brain activity

positioning advertising copytesting (PACT) Principles to use when assessing the effectiveness of various messages

MyMarketingLab

Go to **mymktlab.com** to complete the problems marked with this icon .

Review Questions

1. What are the three categories of evaluation tools that can be used to evaluate IMC systems?

2. What common IMC objectives are matched with methods of evaluation?

3. What are message evaluations?

4. What is advertising tracking research? What does it help the marketing team assess?

5. Describe the use of portfolio tests and theater tests in copytesting programs.

6. Describe a warmth monitor and biometric research. What do they measure?

7. Describe the advantages and uses of cognitive neuroscience as a method for evaluating advertising and marketing programs.

8. What are the positioning advertising copytesting principles that help advertisers prepare quality ads and campaigns?

9. Define the terms click-throughs, dwell rate, dwell time, and length of engagement. How are these measures used to evaluate marketing communications?

10. What are the primary forms of behavioral evaluations that can be used to test advertisements and other marketing pieces?

11. How are behavioral responses to marketing messages measured?

12. What items can be evaluated using test markets?

13. Describe a purchase simulation test.

14. Name and describe the criteria that can be used to assess the impact of the overall IMC program, as noted in this chapter.

15. What differences occur when international marketing programs are assessed?

Critical Thinking Exercises

DISCUSSION QUESTIONS

16. Create an advertising approach for one of the following products. Describe your idea in three or four sentences. Organize a small focus group of four other students in class. Ask the group to evaluate your advertising concept. What did you learn from the exercise?
    a. Retail pet store
    b. Baseball caps
    c. Computers
    d. Sweaters
    e. Watches

17. Pick five print advertisements. Organize a small focus group of four or five other students in your class or individuals you know. Ask the group to discuss the ads. What do they like? What do they dislike? Write a summary of the evaluation of the ad and the process you used.

18. Form a group of five other students or individuals. Ask each person to write down two advertisements they enjoyed and their reasons. Ask individuals to write down two advertisements they dislike and their reasons. Finally, ask them to write down an advertisement they believe is offensive and their reasons.

Ask each student to read his or her list comparing ads that were liked, disliked, or those considered offensive. What common elements did you find in each category? What were the differences?

19. Are sales figures important when evaluating integrated marketing communications? How should hard data such as redemption rates and store traffic be used in the evaluation of marketing communications? In terms of accountability, how important are behavioral measures of IMC effectiveness?

20. From the viewpoint of a marketing manager of a large sporting goods manufacturer, what types of measures of effectiveness would you want from the $5 million you pay to an advertising agency for an advertising campaign? Knowing that evaluations cost money, how much of the $5 million would you be willing to spend to measure effectiveness? What type of report would you prepare for your supervisor?

21. A clothing manufacturer spends $6 million on trade promotions and $3 million on consumer promotions. How would you measure the impact of these

expenditures? If an agency was hired to manage these expenditures, what type of measures would you insist the company utilize?

22. Examine a current magazine. Make a record of how many advertisements include methods for measuring responses. That is, how many list a code number, a toll-free number, or a website? Listing a toll-free number or a website does not ensure that the agency or firm will know where the customer obtained that information. How can the advertising agency or firm track the responses from a specific advertisement in the magazine you examined?

23. In some Asian countries, it is improper to talk about oneself. Therefore, people often are too embarrassed to answer questions about feelings and emotions. Those who do answer the questions would tend to provide superficial answers. Explain the advantages of a simulated purchasing test methodology in this situation. What other methods of evaluating feelings and emotions could an agency use in Asian countries?

Integrated Learning Exercises

24. Pick three print advertisements that include website URLs. Visit each site. Was the website a natural extension of the advertisement? What connection or similarities did you see between the website and the advertisement? Do you think your response was tracked? How can you tell?

25. Decision Analysts, Inc. is a leading provider of advertising and marketing research. Access the company's website at **www.decisionanalyst.com** and investigate the various services the company offers. Examine the advertising research services available. Write a short report about how advertising research services provided by Decision Analysts could be used.

26. Ipsos-ASI (**www.ipsos-asi.com**) is an advertising research firm with a high level of expertise in ad testing and measurements. Access the company's products and services. What services are offered? When would the various services be used? How would each be used?

27. AdKnowledge is a firm that excels at measuring internet traffic and internet advertising. Access the website at **www.adknowledge.com**. What services does the company offer? Describe a research project you feel this company could do successfully to assist in advertising or internet research.

28. ComScore is a firm that measures internet traffic and internet advertising. Access the website at **www.comscore.com**. What services does the company offer? Describe a research project you feel this company could do successfully to assist in advertising or internet research.

29. Millward Brown provides marketing and advertising evaluations. Access the company's website at **www.millwardbrown.com**. Describe the various services offered by the company. Suppose you want to evaluate an advertising campaign for Forever 21 clothes. Identify and discuss the Millward Brown tools you would use.

Student Project

CREATIVE CORNER

After leaders at PepsiCo and Starbucks became concerned about the diminishing supply of fresh, clean water, the companies teamed together to sell Ethos Water. The product's

distribution has expanded, and it is now sold in major grocery stores, convenience stores, and drug stores. The goal of Ethos Water is to ensure that children throughout the world have clean water.

Access the Ethos Water website at **www.ethoswater.com**. After reviewing the site, design a print ad for a magazine aimed at college students in your area. When you have finished designing the ad, trade your ad with another student or ask him or her to show it to 10 students not enrolled in this class. Explain to the student how to conduct a copytest to gather attitudes and opinions about the ad. Before conducting the copytest, make a list of questions you want to ask. Some suggestions are:

30. Have you ever heard of Ethos Water?

31. What do you think is the primary message of this advertisement?

32. Does the copy make sense? Is it understandable?

33. Does the visual attract your attention?

34. What types of feelings does the ad elicit?

35. How likely would you be to access the Ethos Water website for more information?

36. What is your overall evaluation of the advertisement?

It is important that someone else conduct the copytest for you to gain honest answers. Respondents are less likely to be honest, especially about any negative feedback, if you show them the advertisement and they know you designed it.

CASE 1 BREAKFAST WARS

Each year, Americans spend $32 billion on fast-food breakfast, and McDonalds holds nearly one-third of the market share.[30] Seeing a major opportunity, the management team at Taco Bell launched a line of breakfast sandwiches, each of which can be held in one hand, similar to the famous McDonald's Egg McMuffin.

Beyond sheer sales figures, other elements came into play. For one, the 2008 recession's impact on spending may have lingered. Consumers discovered that the cheapest fast-food meal can be breakfast. Many fast-food chains recognized that while breakfast revenues were increasing, lunch and dinner had begun to decline slightly. In the case of McDonald's, nearly $10 billion in profits resulted from morning sales in 2013.

Taco Bell undertook a major assault on the breakfast food market. Along with a new line of sandwiches, the company developed new coffee products to fill out the morning menu. "The message is we're here to stay in breakfast," said Taco Bell's chief marketing officer Chris Brandt. "The whole reason we're doing this is we just thought breakfast was really boring and so we wanted to break up the boring, shake up the routine."[31]

To support these new offerings, Taco Bell launched a major advertising campaign designed to create consumer awareness and encourage brand switching. One early commercial depicts a man abandoning old habits, including his mullet, and then starting new ones, including buying a smart phone and giving up on his daily Egg McMuffin, with "Old MacDonald" playing as background music. Then, another group of ads featured individuals named Ronald McDonald, each indicating a strong preference for the new Taco Bell line of breakfast sandwiches.

McDonald's response was nearly immediate, due to the buzz created by the campaign. One commercial shows the Ronald McDonald mascot kneeling down to pet the Taco Bell Chihuahua with the words, "imitation is the sincerest form of flattery." The chain offered free cups of McCafe coffee to customers during breakfast hours for two weeks. The company also instigated a flash mob event in Chicago and sponsored a free concert in New York's Times Square to ramp up support.

Clutter played a role in the Taco Bell launch. Dunkin Donuts also entered the breakfast sandwich business, as did Starbucks.

Slavomir Pancevac/Fotolia

▲ Taco Bell undertook a major assault on the breakfast food market.

In the following months and years, history will judge whether these new competitors are able to establish breakfast programs to compete with the longstanding giant of the morning fast-food world.

37. What message evaluation techniques could be used in evaluating the Taco Bell breakfast program advertising campaign? Be specific.

38. Describe how advertising tracking research could be used to evaluate the Taco Bell advertising program.

39. Describe how cognitive neuroscience could be used in developing and evaluating the Taco Bell advertising campaign.

40. What IMC objectives match McDonald's response to the Taco Bell launch? Justify your selection.

41. Which evaluating techniques should marketers for McDonald's use in analyzing the company's response to the Taco Bell launch?

42. Which behavioral evaluations would be most useful for Taco Bell and McDonald's during this time period? Explain how the evaluation technique should be used and why it should be used.

CASE 2 ▶ SPYCH MARKET ANALYTICS

A new age of marketing communication evaluation may be under way. Spych Marketing Analytics, which was founded in 2008, provides innovative solutions for companies seeking a better understanding of the future market environments, including the Gen Y and Millennial consumer segments, the advancement of technology, and the quickly evolving world of customer experience. The company tries to delve into the insights and emotions of these groups, providing an innovative portal into the psyches of these markets through its program called Empathic Youth Research and other mixed methodological approaches to consumer insights. CEO Benjamin Smithee argues that, "You have to look at the foundations and fundamentals of the advertising industry, and right now we are seeing a dramatic paradigm shift in the ways marketing communications are delivered and consumed." The media include traditional advertising venues, public relations, but also social media and mobile technologies, utilized by an evolving set of consumers.

Company employees work to enhance every aspect of the market research process. On its website, the organization proclaims, "… we create natural environments for our respondents, evoking rich insights and opinions that surface only through truly natural and empathic interactions." Further, "The Spych Experience maximizes the return your team obtains from each project overcoming fallacies often associated with traditional youth research."

To achieve these ideals, the company employs innovative concepts regarding marketing metrics and consumer understanding. The concepts are based on the importance of going

▲ **FIGURE 9**
Moving from Message to Buying/Sharing

beyond simply engaging customers to include "re-advertising." CEO Benjamin Smithee notes a new model in which "sharing" becomes a second important outcome from a marketing effort as shown in Figure 9.

Spych seeks to identify levels of engagement in terms of "intensity," in which a message is shared with friends and others. The concepts of "share-ability" and "virality" take on particular importance in Spych parlance. As Spych Marketing Analytics brand strategist Landon Ledford notes, "We ask the question, does this pass the traditional advertising test and then lead to sharing?" He notes that in previous times, an ad might be shared with one or two other people, such as when a person would tear an advertisement out of a newspaper or magazine and give it to a friend. Now, a message can quickly be re-posted to 200-plus Facebook friends.

In essence, Spych bases its conclusions regarding a message's success with "engagement" with an advertisement being

◀ Spych Brand Strategist Landon Ledford and CEO Ben Smithee.

measured first by "click commitment," which is the willingness of a person to click on an ad on a medium such as Twitter, making that decision in three seconds or less, and second by "socialization," or passing the advertisement on to others.

Taking the next step, new technologies allow for tracking of shares and targeted marketing capabilities unlike anything we have ever possessed. Beyond simply counting the number of times a marketing message has been passed along to others, the company can examine the "social profiles" of those receiving re-advertisements and focus on the influences most relevant to a brand, rather than the generic traditional means of targeting. The reasoning behind such tracking goes to the heart of the target market. A new generation of consumer shops in a new manner, communicates through channels that have not been previously available, and responds to companies and marketing messages in ways we have never seen.

The ultimate goals of these measures and concepts remain the same as in any traditional marketing effort. Return visits to various vendors, repeat purchases, word-of-mouth endorsements, and feeling a connection (brand loyalty) with a company, all of which lead to increased sales over time suggest that a marketing program has achieved success. Re-advertising and sharing with others enhance the prospects of reaching the right audience, sending the right message, and creating long term relationships with the company. As CEO Smithee summarized, "The more layers you can seamlessly integrate, the better chance of getting something sticky."

43. Would the concepts used to measure marketing success match with the message evaluation methods presented in this chapter? Why or why not?

44. Compare the concepts used by Spych with the terms "behavioral response" and "attitudinal response."

45. What roles do "emotions" and "logic" play in the Spych approach to marketing communications?

46. What roles do social media and hand-held technologies such as smart phones play in today's marketing environment? How will they evolve in the future?

MyMarketingLab

Go to **mymktlab.com** for Auto-graded writing questions as well as the following Assisted-graded writing questions:

47. Are sales figures important when evaluating integrated marketing communications? How should hard data such as redemption rates and store traffic be used in the evaluation of marketing communications? In terms of accountability, how important are behavioral measures of IMC effectiveness?

48. ComScore is a firm that measures internet traffic and internet advertising. Access the website at **www. comscore.com**. What services does the company offer? Describe a research project you feel this company could do successfully to assist in advertising or internet research.

Endnotes

1. http://www.sandsresearch.com/, accessed September 14, 2010.

2. Gordon A. Wyner, "Narrowing the Gap," *Marketing Research* 16, no. 1 (Spring 2004), pp. 6–7.

3. Interview with Elena Petukhova, The Richards Group, May 17, 2010, by Kenneth E. Clow.

4. "Nielsen IAG" (http://en-us.nielsen.com/tab/product_families/iag, accessed May 19, 2010).

5. Lucia Moses, "Publishers Offer TV-Like Metrics, But Will Buyers Bite?" *Mediaweek*, (**www.mediaweek. com/mw/content_display/news/magazines-newspapers/e3ieea0d35**), January 17, 2010.

6. "Has Burger King's First Mcgarrybowen Ad Helped the Brand?" *Advertising Age*, September 19, 2011, http://adage.com/print229832.

7. "Copy Testing Coming to Digital Marketing," *Advertising Age*, February 27, 2011, http://adage.com/print/149100.

8. Interview of David Snell by Kenneth E. Clow, May 17, 2010.

9. Interview with Elena Petukhova, The Richards Group, May 17, 2010, by Kenneth E. Clow.

10. Andrew McMains, "P&G Does Dan Wieden's Bidding," *Adweek*, June 27, 2011, www.adweek.com/print/132903.

11. "Copy Testing Coming to Digital Marketing," *Advertising Age*, February 27, 2011, http://adage.com/print/149100.

12. Steven P. Brown and Douglas M. Stayman, "Antecedents and Consequences of Attitude Toward the Ad: A Meta-Analysis," *Journal of Consumer Research* 19 (June 1992), pp. 34–51.

13. Douglas M. Stayman and David A. Aaker, "Continuous Measurement of Self-Report or Emotional Response," *Psychology and Marketing* 10 (May–June 1993), pp. 199–214.

14. Freddie Campos, "UH Facility Test Ads for $500," *Pacific Business News* 35, no. 23 (August 18, 1997), pp. A1–A2.

15. Patricia Riedman, "Discover Why Tests TV Commercials Online," *Advertising Age* 71, no. 13 (March 27, 2000), pp. 46–47.

16. Jon Lafayette, "Biometric Study: Broadcast Ads Make Web Work Better," May 9, 2011, www.broadcasting-cable.com/article/print/467935.

17. Amy Chozick, "These Lab Specimens Watch 3-D Television," *The New York Times*, January 24, 2012, www.nytimes.com/2012/01/25/business/media/a-media-lab-will-test-consumers-reactions.

18. Bruce F. Hall, "On Measuring the Power of Communications," *Journal of Advertising Research* 44, no. 2 (June 2004), pp. 181–88.

19. Hall, "On Measuring the Power of Communications."

20. John Capone, "Microsoft and Initiative Strive for Better Advertising Through Neuroscience," *Online Media Daily*(**www.mediapost.com/publications/?fa=Articles.printFriendly&art_aid=118835**), December 9, 2009; Steve McClellan, "Mind Over Matter: New Tools Put Brands in Touch with Feelings," *Adweek* (http://www.adweek.com/aw/content_display/news/media/e3i-975331243e08d74c5b66f857ff12cfd5), February 18, 2008.

21. Laurie Burkitt, "Battle for the Brain," *Forbes* 184, no. 9 (November 16, 2009), pp. 76–78.

22. Based on PACT document published in *Journal of Marketing* 11, no. 4 (1982), pp. 4–29.

23. http://www.adknowledge.com/usa/index.php, accessed September 14, 2010.

24. Rachel King, "Sentiment Analysis Gives Companies Insights into Consumer Opinion," *Bloomberg Business*, March 1, 2011, www.businessweek.com/print/technology/content/feb2011/tc20110228_366762.htm.

25. Chris Dillabough, "Web Lets Canadian Tourism Test Media Effectiveness," *New Media Age* (October 31, 2002), p. 12.

26. Kate MacArthur, "McDonald's Tests Ads That Focus on Service," *Advertising Age* 74, no. 1 (January 6, 2003), p. 3.

27. Tim Triplett, "Researchers Probe Ad Effectiveness Globally," *Marketing News* 28, no. 18 (August 29, 1994), pp. 6–7.

28. Paul J. Cough, "Study: Marketers Struggle to Measure Effectiveness," *Shoot* 45, no. 29 (August 20, 2004), pp. 7–8.

29. Peter Drucker, *Management: Tasks, Responsibilities, Practices* (New York: Harper & Row, 1974).

30. Linzie Janis, Chris James, and Lauren Effron, "Breakfast Wars: Taco Bell Aims to Devour McDonald's Morning Menu Empire," ABC News, http://abcnews.go.com/Business/breakfast-wars-taco-bell-aims-devour-mcdonalds-morning/story?id=23295904, retrieved April 26, 2014.

31. Ibid

MARKETING AND FINANCE

Introduction

Key concepts covered:

Net Profit and Return on Sales (ROS)   Project Metrics: Payback, NPV, IRR

Return on Investment (ROI)   Return on Marketing Investment

Economic Profit (aka, EVA®)

As marketers progress in their careers, it becomes increasingly necessary to coordinate their plans with other functional areas. Sales forecasts, budgeting, and estimating returns from proposed marketing initiatives are often the focus of discussions between marketing and finance. For marketers with little exposure to basic finance metrics, a good starting point is to gain a deeper understanding of "rate of return." "Return" is generally associated with profit, or at least positive cash flow. "Return" also implies that something has left—cash outflow. Almost all business activity requires some cash outflow. Even sales cost money that is only returned when bills are paid. In this chapter we provide a brief overview of some of the more commonly employed measures of profitability and profits. Understanding how the metrics are constructed and used by finance to rank various projects will make it easier to develop marketing plans that meet the appropriate criteria.

The first section covers net profits and return on sales (ROS). Next, we look at return on investment (ROI), the ratio of net profit to amount of investment. Another metric that accounts for the capital investment required to earn profits is economic profits (also known as economic value added—EVA), or residual income. Because EVA and ROI provide snapshots of the per-period profitability of firms, they are not appropriate for valuing projects spanning multiple periods. For multi-period projects, three of the

From Chapter 10 of *Marketing Metrics: The Definitive Guide to Measuring Marketing Performance*, 2/e. Paul W. Farris. Neil T. Bendle. Phillip E. Pfeifer. David J. Reibstein. Copyright © 2010 by Pearson Education. Published by Wharton School Publishing.

most common metrics are payback, net present value (NPV), and internal rate of return (IRR).

The last section discuses the frequently mentioned but rarely defined measure, return on marketing investment (ROMI). Although this is a well-intentioned effort to measure marketing productivity, consensus definitions and measurement procedures for "marketing ROI" or ROMI have yet to emerge.

	Metric	Construction	Considerations	Purpose
1	Net Profit	Sales revenue less total costs.	Revenue and costs can be defined in a number of ways leading to confusion in profit calculations.	The basic profit equation.
1	Return on Sales (ROS)	Net profit as a percentage of sales revenue.	Acceptable level of return varies between industries and business models. Many models can be described as high volume/low return or vice versa.	Gives the percentage of revenue that is being captured in profits.
1	Earnings Before Interest, Taxes, Depreciation, and Amortization (EBITDA)	Earnings Before Interest, Taxes, Depreciation, and Authorization.	Strips out the effect of accounting and financing polices from profits. Ignores important factors, such as depreciation of assets.	Rough measure of operating cash flow.
2	Return on Investment (ROI)	Net profits over the investment needed to generate the profits.	Often meaningless in the short term. Variations such as return on assets and return on investment capital analyze profits in respect of different inputs.	A metric that describes how well assets are being used.

	Metric	Construction	Considerations	Purpose
3	Economic Profit (aka EVA®, Economic Value Added)	Net operating profit after tax (NOPAT) less the cost of capital.	Requires a cost of capital to be provided/calculated.	Shows profit made in dollar terms. Gives a clearer distinction between the sizes of returns than does a percentage calculation.
4	Payback	The length of time taken to return the initial investment.	Will favor projects with quick returns more than long-term success.	Simple return calculation.
4	Net Present Value (NPV)	The value of a stream of future cash flows after accounting for the time value of money.	The discount rate used is the vital consideration and should account for the risk of the investment too.	To summarize the value of cash flows over multiple periods.
4	Internal Rate of Return (IRR)	The discount rate at which the NPV of an investment is zero.	IRR does not describe the magnitude of return; $1 on $10 is the same as $1 million on $10 million.	An IRR will typically be compared to a firm's hurdle rate. If IRR is higher than hurdle rate, invest; if lower, pass.
5	Return on Marketing Investment (ROMI); Revenue	Incremental revenue attributable to marketing over the marketing spending.	Marketers need to establish an accurate Baseline to be able to meaningfully state what revenue is attributable to marketing.	Compares the sales generated in revenue terms with the marketing spending that helped generate the sales. The percentage term helps comparison across plans of varying magnitude.

1   Net Profit and Return on Sales

Net profit measures the profitability of ventures after accounting for all costs. Return on sales (ROS) is net profit as a percentage of sales revenue.

$$\textbf{Net Profit (\$) = Sales Revenue (\$) − Total Costs (\$)}$$

$$\textbf{Return on Sales—ROS (\%)} = \frac{\textbf{Net Profit (\$)}}{\textbf{Sales Revenue (\$)}}$$

$$\textbf{EBITDA (\$) = Net Profit (\$) + Interest Payments (\$) + Taxes (\$) +}$$
$$\textbf{Depreciation and Authorization Charges (\$)}$$

ROS is an indicator of profitability and is often used to compare the profitability of companies and industries of differing sizes. Significantly, ROS does not account for the capital (investment) used to generate the profit.

Earnings Before Interest, Taxes, Depreciation, and Amortization (EBITDA) is a rough measure of operating cash flow, which reduces the effect of accounting, financing, and tax polices on reported profits.

Purpose: To measure levels and rates of profitability.

How does a company decide whether it is successful or not? Probably the most common way is to look at the net profits of the business. Given that companies are collections of projects and markets, individual areas can be judged on how successful they are at adding to the corporate net profit. Not all projects are of equal size, however, and one way to adjust for size is to divide the profit by sales revenue. The resulting ratio is return on sales (ROS), the percentage of sales revenue that gets "returned" to the company as net profits after all the related costs of the activity are deducted.

Construction

Net profit measures the fundamental profitability of the business. It is the revenues of the activity less the costs of the activity. The main complication is in more complex businesses when overhead needs to be allocated across divisions of the company (see Figure 1). Almost by definition, overheads are costs that cannot be directly tied to any specific product or division. The classic example would be the cost of headquarters staff.

Net Profit: *To calculate net profit for a unit (such as a company or division), subtract all costs, including a fair share of total corporate overheads, from the gross revenues.*

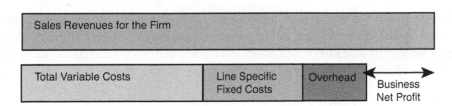

Simple View of Business – Revenues and Costs

Figure 1   Profits = Revenues Less Costs

Net Profit ($) = Sales Revenue ($) − Total Costs ($)

Return on Sales (ROS): *Net profit as a percentage of sales revenue.*

$$\text{Return on Sales (\%)} = \frac{\text{Net Profit (\$)}}{\text{Sales Revenue (\$)}}$$

Earning before interest taxes, depreciation, and amortization (EBITDA) is a very popular measure of financial performance. It is used to assess the "operating" profit of the business. It is a rough way of calculating how much cash the business is generating and is even sometimes called the "operating cash flow." It can be useful because it removes factors that change the view of performance depending upon the accounting and financing policies of the business. Supporters argue it reduces management's ability to change the profits they report by their choice of accounting rules and the way they generate financial backing for the company. This metric excludes from consideration expenses related to decisions such as how to finance the business (debt or equity) and over what period to depreciate fixed assets. EBITDA is typically closer to actual cash flow than is NOPAT (discussed later in the chapter).

EBITDA can be calculated by adding back the costs of interest, depreciation, and amortization charges and any taxes incurred.

EBITDA ($) = Net Profit ($) + Interest Payments ($) + Taxes Incurred ($) + Depreciation and Amortization Charges ($)

Data Sources, Complications, and Cautions

Although it is theoretically possible to calculate profits for any sub-unit, such as a product or region, often the calculations are rendered suspect by the need to allocate overhead costs. Because overhead costs often don't come in neat packages, their allocation among the divisions or product lines of the company can often be more art than science.

For return on sales, it is worth bearing in mind that a "healthy" figure depends on the industry and capital intensity (amount of assets per sales dollar). Return on sales is similar to margin (%), except that ROS accounts for overheads and other fixed costs that are often ignored when calculating margin (%) or contribution margin (%).

Related Metrics and Concepts

Net operating profit after tax (NOPAT) deducts relevant income taxes but excludes some items that are deemed to be unrelated to the main ("operating") business.

2 Return on Investment

Return on investment is one way of considering profits in relation to capital invested.

$$\text{Return on Investment—ROI (\%)} = \frac{\text{Net Profit (\$)}}{\text{Investment (\$)}}$$

Return on assets (ROA), return on net assets (RONA), return on capital (ROC), and return on invested capital (ROIC) are similar measures with variations on how "investment" is defined.

Marketing not only influences net profits but also can affect investment levels too. New plants and equipment, inventories, and accounts receivable are three of the main categories of investments that can be affected by marketing decisions.

Purpose: To measure per period rates of return on dollars invested in an economic entity.

ROI and related metrics (ROA, ROC, RONA, and ROIC) provide a snapshot of profitability adjusted for the size of the investment assets tied up in the enterprise. Marketing decisions have obvious potential connection to the numerator of ROI (profits), but these same decisions often influence assets usage and capital requirements (for example, receivables and inventories). Marketers should understand the position of their company and the returns expected. ROI is often compared to expected (or required) rates of return on dollars invested.

Construction

For a single period review just divide the return (net profit) by the resources that were committed (investment):

$$\text{Return on Investment (\%)} = \frac{\text{Net Profit (\$)}}{\text{Investment (\$)}}$$

Data Sources, Complications, and Cautions

Averaging the profits and investments over periods such as one year can disguise wide swings in profits and assets, especially inventories and receivables. This is especially true for seasonal businesses (such as some construction materials and toys). In such businesses it is important to understand these seasonal variations to relate quarterly and annual figures to each other.

Related Metrics and Concepts

Return on assets (ROA), return on net assets (RONA), return on capital employed (ROCE), and return on invested capital (ROIC) are commonly used variants of ROI. They are also calculated using net profit as the numerator, but they have different denominators. The relatively subtle distinctions between these metrics are beyond the scope of this book. Some differences are found in whether payables are subtracted from working capital and how borrowed funds and stockholder equity are treated.

3   Economic Profit—EVA

Economic profit has many names, some of them trademarked as "brands." Economic value added (EVA) is Stern-Stewart's trademark. They deserve credit for popularizing this measure of net operating profit after tax adjusted for the cost of capital.

Economic Profit (\$) = Net Operating Profit After Tax (NOPAT) (\$) − Cost of Capital (\$)

Cost of Capital (\$) = Capital Employed (\$) ∗ WACC (%)

Unlike percentage measures of return (for example, ROS or ROI), Economic profit is a dollar metric. As such, it reflects not only the "rate" of profitability, but also the size of the business (sales and assets).

Purpose: To measure dollar profits while accounting for required returns on capital invested.

Economic profit, sometimes called residual income, or EVA, is different from "accounting" profit—in that economic profit also considers the cost of invested capital—the opportunity cost (see Figure 2). Like the discount rate for NPV calculations, this charge should also account for the risk associated with the investment. A popular (and proprietary) way of looking at economic profit is economic value added.[1]

Increasingly, marketers are being made aware of how some of their decisions influence the amount of capital invested or assets employed. First, sales growth almost always requires additional investment in fixed assets, receivable, or inventories. Economic profit and EVA help determine whether these investments are justified by the profit earned. Second, the marketing improvements in supply chain management and channel coordination often show up in reduced investments in inventories and receivables. In some cases, even if sales and profit fall, the investment reduction can be worthwhile. Economic profit is a metric that will help assess whether these trade-offs are being made correctly.

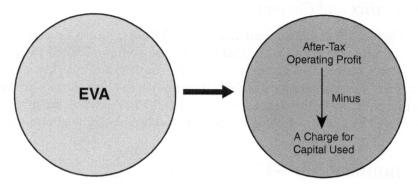

Figure 2   EVA Is After-Tax Profit Minus a Charge for Capital Usage

Construction

Economic profit/economic value added can be calculated in three stages. First, determine NOPAT (net operating profit after tax). Second, calculate the cost of capital by multiplying capital employed by the weighted average cost of capital.[2] The third stage is to subtract the cost of capital from NOPAT.

Economic Profit ($) = Net Operating Profit After Tax (NOPAT) ($) − Cost of Capital ($)

Cost of Capital ($) = Capital Employed ($) ∗ WACC (%)

Economic Profit: *If your profits are less than the cost of capital, you have lost value for the firm. Where economic profit is positive, value has been generated.*

EXAMPLE: A company has profits—NOPAT—of $145,000.

They have a straightforward capital structure, half of which is supplied by shareholders. This equity expects a 12% return on the risk the shareholders are taking by investing in this company. The other half of the capital comes from a bank at a charge of 6%:

Weighted average cost of capital (WACC) therefore

$$= \text{Equity } (12\% * 50\%) + \text{Debt } (6\% * 50\%) = 9\%$$

The company employs total capital of $1 million. Multiplying the capital employed by the weighted average cost for the capital employed will give us an estimate of the profit (return) required to cover the opportunity cost of capital used in the business:

$$\text{Cost of Capital} = \text{Capital Employed} * \text{WACC}$$
$$= \$1,000,000 * 9\%$$
$$= \$90,000$$

Economic profit is the surplus of profits over the expected return to capital.

$$\text{Economic Profit} = \text{NOPAT} - \text{Cost of Capital}$$
$$= \$145,000 - \$90,000$$
$$= \$55,000$$

Data Sources, Complications, and Cautions

Economic profit can give a different ranking for companies than does return on investment. This is especially true for companies such as Wal-Mart and Microsoft that have experienced (achieved) high rates of growth in sales. Judging the results of the giant U.S. retailer Wal-Mart by many conventional metrics will disguise its success. Although the rates of return are generally good, they hardly imply the rise to dominance that the company achieved. Economic profit reflects both Wal-Mart's rapid sales growth and its adequate return on the capital invested. This metric shows the magnitude of profits after the cost of capital has been subtracted. This combines the idea of a return on investment with a sense of volume of profits. Simply put, Wal-Mart achieved the trick of continuing to gain decent returns on a dramatically increasing pool of capital.

4   Evaluating Multi-period Investments

Multi-period investments are commonly evaluated with three metrics.

**Payback (#) = The number of periods required to "pay back"
or "return" the initial investment.**

**Net Present Value (NPV) ($) = The discounted value of future cash flows
minus the initial investment.**

Internal Rate of Return (IRR) (%) = The discount rate that results in an NPV of zero.

These three metrics are designed to deal with different aspects of the risk and returns of multi-period projects.

Purpose: To evaluate investments with financial consequences spanning multiple periods.

Investment is a word business people like. It has all sorts of positive connotations of future success and wise stewardship. However, because not all investments can be pursued, those available must be ranked against each other. Also, some investments are not attractive even if we have enough cash to fund them. In a single period, the return on any investment is merely the net profits produced in the time considered divided by the capital invested. Evaluation of investments that produce returns over multiple periods requires a more complicated analysis—one that considers both the magnitude and timing of the returns.

Payback (#): *The time (usually years) required to generate the (undiscounted) cash flow to recover the initial investment.*

Net Present Value—NPV ($): *The present (discounted) value of future cash inflows minus the present value of the investment and any associated future cash outflows.*

Internal Rate of Return—IRR (%): *The discount rate that results in a net present value of zero for a series of future cash flows after accounting for the initial investment.*

Construction

Payback: *The years required for an investment to return the initial investment.*

Projects with a shorter payback period by this analysis are regarded more favorably because they allow the resources to be reused quickly. Also, generally speaking, the shorter the payback period, the less uncertainty is involved in receiving the returns. Of course the main flaw with payback period analysis is that it ignores all cash flows after the payback period. As a consequence, projects that are attractive but that do not produce immediate returns will be penalized with this metric.

EXAMPLE: Harry is considering buying a small chain of hairdressing salons. He estimates that the salons will produce a net income of $15,000 a year for at least five years. Harry's payback on this investment is $50,000/$15,000, or 3.33 years.

NET PRESENT VALUE

Net present value (NPV) is the discounted value of the cash flows associated with the project.

The present value of a dollar received in a given number of periods in the future is

$$\text{Discounted Value (\$)} = \frac{\text{Cash Flow (\$) * 1}}{[(1 + \text{Discount Rate (\%)}) \wedge \text{Period (\#)}]}$$

This is easiest to see when set out in spreadsheet form.

A 10% discount rate applied to $1 received now and in each of the next three years reduces in value over time as shown in Table 1.

Table 1 Discounting Nominal Values

	Year 0	Year 1	Year 2	Year 3
Discount Formula	1	1/(1+10%)^1	1/(1+10%)^2	1/(1+10%)^3
Discount Factor	1	90.9%	82.6%	75.1%
Undiscounted Cash Flows	$1.00	$1.00	$1.00	$1.00
Present Value	$1.00	$0.91	$0.83	$0.75

Spreadsheets make it easy to calculate the appropriate discount factors.

EXAMPLE: Harry wants to know the dollar value of his business opportunity. Although he is confident about the success of the venture, all future cash flows have a level of uncertainty. After receiving a friend's advice, he decides a 10% discount rate on future cash flows is about right.

He enters all the cash flow details into a spreadsheet (see Table 2).[3] Harry works out the discount factor using the formula and his discount rate of 10%:

$$\text{Discounted Value} = \frac{\text{Cash Flow} * 1}{[(1 + \text{Discount Rate}) \wedge \text{Year}]}$$

$$\text{For Year 1 Cashflows} = \frac{\$15,000 * 1}{[(1 + 10\%) \wedge 1)]} = \frac{\$15,000 * 1}{110\%}$$

$$= \$15,000 * 90.9\% = 13,636$$

Table 2   Discounted Cashflow (10% Discount Rate)

	Year 0	Year 1	Year 2	Year 3	Year 4	Year 5	Total
Investment	($50,000)						($50,000)
Income		$15,000	$15,000	$15,000	$15,000	$15,000	$75,000
Undiscounted Cashflow	($50,000)	$15,000	$15,000	$15,000	$15,000	$15,000	$25,000
Discount Formula	$1/(1+DR)^0$	$1/(1+DR)^1$	$1/(1+DR)^2$	$1/(1+DR)^3$	$1/(1+DR)^4$	$1/(1+DR)^5$	
Discount Factor	100.0%	90.9%	82.6%	75.1%	68.3%	62.1%	
Present Value	($50,000)	$13,636	$12,397	$11,270	$10,245	$9,314	$6,862

The NPV of Harry's project is $6,862. Of course the NPV is lower than the sum of the undiscounted cash flows. NPV accounts for the fact that on a per-dollar basis, cash flows received in the future are less valuable than cash in the hand.

INTERNAL RATE OF RETURN

The internal rate of return is the percentage return made on the investment over a period of time. The internal rate of return is a feature supplied on most spreadsheets and thus is relatively easy to calculate.

Internal Rate of Return (IRR): *The discount rate for which the net present value of the investment is zero.*

The IRR is especially useful because it can be compared to a company's hurdle rate. The hurdle rate is the necessary percentage return to justify a project. Thus a company might decide only to undertake projects with a return greater than 12%. Projects that have an IRR greater than 12% get the green light; all others are thrown in the bin.

EXAMPLE: Returning to Harry, we can see that IRR is an easy calculation to perform using a software package. Enter the values given in the relevant periods on the spreadsheet (see Table 3).

Year 0—now—is when Harry makes the initial investment; each of the next five years sees a $15,000 return. Applying the IRR function gives a return of 15.24%.

Table 3   Five-Year Cashflow

Cell ref	A	B	C	D	E	F	G
1		Year 0	Year 1	Year 2	Year 3	Year 4	Year 5
2	Cashflows	($50,000)	$15,000	$15,000	$15,000	$15,000	$15,000

In Microsoft Excel, the function is = IRR(B2:G2)

which equals 15.24%.

The cell references in Table 3 should help in re-creating this function. The function is telling Excel to perform an IRR on the range B2 (cashflow for year 0) to G2 (cashflow for year 5).

IRR and NPV Are Related

The internal rate of return is the percentage discount rate at which the net present value of the operation is zero.

Thus companies using a hurdle rate are really saying that they will only accept projects where the net present value is positive at the discount rate they specify as the hurdle rate. Another way to say this is that they will accept projects only if the IRR is greater than the hurdle rate.

Data Sources, Complications, and Cautions

Payback and IRR calculations require estimates of cash flows. The cash flows are the monies received and paid out that are associated with the project per period, including the initial investment. Topics that are beyond the scope of this book include the time frame over which forecasts of cash flows are made and how to handle "terminal values" (the value associated with the opportunity at the end of the last period).[4] Net present value calculations require the same inputs as payback and IRR, plus one other: the *discount rate*. Typically, the discount rate is decided at the corporate level. This rate has a dual purpose to compensate for the following:

- The time value of money
- The risk inherent in the activity

A general principle to employ is that the riskier the project, the greater the discount rate to use. Considerations for setting the discounts rates are also beyond the scope of this book. We will simply observe that, ideally, separate discount rates would be assessed for each individual project because risk varies by activity. A government contract might be a fairly certain project—not so for an investment by the same company in buying a fashion retailer. The same concern occurs when companies set a single hurdle rate for all projects assessed by IRR analysis.

> **Cashflows and Net Profits:** *In our examples cash flow equals profit, but in many cases they will be different.*

A Note for Users of Spreadsheet Programs

Microsoft Excel has an NPV calculator, which can be very useful in calculating NPV. The formula to use is NPV(rate,value1,value2, etc.) where the rate is the discount rate and the values are the cash flows by year, so year 1 = value 1, year 2 = value 2, and so on.

The calculation starts in period one, and the cash flow for that period is discounted. If you are using the convention of having the investment in the period before, i.e. period 0, you should not discount it but add it back outside the formula. Therefore Harry's returns discounted at 10% would be

$$= \text{NPV(Rate, Value 1, Value 2, Value 3, Value 4, Value 5)}$$

$$= \text{NPV(10\%, 15000, 15000, 15000, 15000, 15000)} \text{ or } \$56,861.80 \text{ less the initial investment of } \$50,000.$$

This gives the NPV of $6,861.80 as demonstrated fully in the example.

---

5   Return on Marketing Investment

Return on marketing investment (ROMI) is a relatively new metric. It is not like the other "return-on-investment" metrics because marketing is not the same kind of investment. Instead of moneys that are "tied" up in plants and inventories, marketing funds are typically "risked." Marketing spending is typically expensed in the current period. There are many variations in the way this metric has been used, and although no authoritative sources for defining it exist, we believe the consensus of usage justifies the following:

$$\text{Return on Marketing Investment (ROMI) (\%)} = \frac{[\text{Incremental Revenue Attributable to Marketing (\$)} * \text{Contribution Margin \%} - \text{Marketing Spending (\$)}]}{\text{Marketing Spending (\$)}}$$

The idea of measuring the market's response in terms of sales and profits is not new, but terms such as marketing ROI and ROMI are used more frequently now than in past periods. Usually, marketing spending will be deemed as justified if the ROMI is positive.

Purpose: To measure the rate at which spending on marketing contributes to profits.

Marketers are under more and more pressure to "show a return" on their activities. However, it is often unclear exactly what this means. Certainly, marketing spending is not an "investment" in the usual sense of the word. There is usually no tangible asset and often not even a predictable (quantifiable) result to show for the spending, but marketers still want to emphasize that their activities contribute to financial health. Some might argue that marketing should be considered an expense and the focus should be on whether it is a necessary expense. Marketers believe that many of their activities generate lasting results and therefore should be considered "investments" in the future of the business.[5]

> **Return on Marketing Investment (ROMI):** *The contribution attributable to marketing (net of marketing spending), divided by the marketing "invested" or risked.*

Construction

A necessary step in calculating ROMI is the estimation of the incremental sales attributable to marketing. These incremental sales can be "total" sales attributable to marketing or "marginal." The following example, in Figure 3, should help clarify the difference:

$$Y_0 = \text{Baseline Sales (with \$0 Marketing spending)},$$

$$Y_1 = \text{Sales at Marketing spending level } X_1, \text{ and}$$

$$Y_2 = \text{Sales at Marketing spending level } X_2,$$

where the difference between X_1 and X_2 represents the cost of an incremental marketing budget item that is to be evaluated, such as an advertising campaign or a trade show.

1. **Revenue Return to Incremental Marketing** $= (Y_2 - Y_1)/(X_2 - X_1)$: The additional revenue generated by an incremental marketing investment, such as a specific campaign or sponsorship, divided by the cost of that marketing investment.

2. **Revenue Attributable to Marketing** $= Y_2 - Y_0$: The increase in sales attributable to the entire marketing budget (equal to sales minus baselines sales).

3. **Revenue Return to Total Marketing** $= (Y_2 - Y_0)/(X_2)$: The revenue attributable to marketing divided by the marketing budget.

4. **Return on Marketing Investment (ROMI)** $= [(Y_2 - Y_0) * \text{Contribution Margin (\%)} - X_2]/X_2$: The additional net contribution from all marketing activities divided by the cost of those activities.

5. **Return on Incremental Marketing Investment (ROIMI)** $= [(Y_2 - Y_1) * \text{Contribution Margin (\%)} - (X_2 - X_1)]/(X_2 - X_1)$: The incremental net contribution due to the incremental marketing spending divided by the amount of incremental spending.

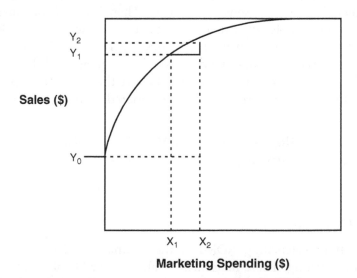

Figure 3   Evaluating the Cost of an Incremental Marketing Budget Item

EXAMPLE: A farm equipment company was considering a direct mail campaign to remind customers to have tractors serviced before spring planting. The campaign is expected to cost $1,000 and to increase revenues from $45,000 to $50,000. Baseline revenues for tractor servicing (with no marketing) were estimated at $25,000. The direct mail campaign was in addition to the regular advertising and other marketing activities costing $6,000. Contribution on tractor servicing revenues (after parts and labor) averages 60%.

For some industries the revenue-based metrics might be useful, but for most situations these metrics are liable to be very misleading. ROMI or ROIMI (see following examples) are generally more useful. However, for most situations this metric is liable to be very misleading. There is no point in spending $20,000 on advertising to generate $100,000 of sales—a respectable 500% return to revenue—if high variable costs mean the marketing only generates a contribution of $5,000.

$$\text{Return on Marketing Investment} = \frac{[\text{Revenue Attributable to Marketing} * \text{Contribution Margin (\%)} - \text{Marketing Cost (\$)}]}{\text{Marketing Cost (\$)}}$$

EXAMPLE: Each of the metrics in this section can be calculated from the information in the example.

$$\text{Revenue Return to Incremental Marketing} = \frac{(\$50,000 - \$45,000)}{(\$7,000 - \$6,000)}$$

$$= \frac{\$5,000}{\$1,000} = 500\%$$

Revenue Attributable to Marketing = $50,000 - $25,000 = $25,000 [Note this figure applies if the additional direct mail campaign is used; otherwise it would be $20,000 ($45,000 - $25,000).]

Revenue Returns to Total Marketing = $25,000/$7,000 = 357% [Or, if the direct mail campaign is not used ($20,000/$6,000), 333%.]

Return on Marketing Investment (ROMI) = ($25,000 * 60% - $7,000)/$7,000 = 114% [Or, if the direct mail campaign is not used ($20,000 * .6 - $6,000)/$6,000 = 100%.]

$$\text{Return on Incremental Marketing Investment (ROIMI)} = \frac{(\$5,000 * 60\% - \$1,000)}{\$1,000} = 200\%$$

Data Sources, Complications, and Cautions

The first piece of information needed for marketing ROI is the cost of the marketing campaign, program, or budget. Although defining which costs belong in marketing can be problematic, a bigger challenge is estimating the incremental revenue, contribution, and net profits attributable to marketing.

A further complication of estimating ROMI concerns how to deal with important interactions between different marketing programs and campaigns. The return on many marketing "investments" is likely to show up as an increase in the responses received for other types of marketing. For example, if direct mail solicitations show an increase in response because of television advertising, we could and should calculate that those incremental revenues had something to do with the TV campaign. As an interaction, however, the return on advertising would depend on what was being spent on other programs. The function is not a simple linear return to the campaign costs.

For budgeting, one key element to recognize is that maximizing the ROMI would probably reduce spending and profits. Marketers typically encounter diminishing returns, in which each incremental dollar will yield lower and lower incremental ROMI, and so low levels of spending will tend to have very high return rates. Maximizing ROMI might lead to reduced marketing and eliminating campaigns or activities that are, on balance, profitable, even if the return rates are not as high. This issue is similar to the distinction between ROI (%) and EVA ($) discussed in Sections 2 and 3. Additional marketing activities or campaigns that bring down average percentage returns but increase overall profits can be quite sensible. So, using ROMI or any percentage measure of profit to determine overall budgets is questionable. Of course, merely eliminating programs with a negative ROMI is almost always a good idea.

The previous discussion intentionally does not deal with carryover effect, that is, marketing effects on sales and profits that extend into future periods. When marketing spending is expected to have effects beyond the current period, other techniques will be needed. These include payback, net presented value, and internal rate of return. Also, see customer lifetime value for a more disaggregated approach to evaluating marketing spending designed to acquire long-lived customer relationships.

Related Metrics

Media Exposure Return on Marketing Investment: In an attempt to evaluate the value of marketing activities such as sponsorships, marketers often commission research to gauge the number and quality of media exposures achieved. These exposures are then valued (often using "rate cards" to determine the cost of equivalent advertising space/time) and a "return" is calculated by dividing the estimated value by the costs.

$$\text{Media Exposure Return on Marketing Investment} - \text{(MEROMI) (\%)} = \frac{\begin{array}{c}\text{(Estimated Value of Media Exposures Achieved (\$)}\\ - \text{ Cost of Marketing Campaign, Sponsorship,}\\ \text{or Promotion (\$))}\end{array}}{\begin{array}{c}\text{Cost of Marketing Campaign, Sponsorship,}\\ \text{or Promotion (\$)}\end{array}}$$

This is most appropriate where there isn't a clear market rate for the results of the campaign and so marketers want to be able to illustrate the equivalent cost for the result for a type of campaign that has an established market rate.

EXAMPLE: A travel portal decides to sponsor a car at a Formula 1 event. They assume that the logo they put on the car will gain the equivalent of 500,000 impressions and will cost 10,000,000 yen. The cost per impression is thus 10 million yen/500,000 = or 20 yen per impression. This can be compared to the costs of other marketing campaigns.

References and Suggested Further Reading

Hawkins, D. I., Roger J. Best, and Charles M. Lillis. (1987). "The Nature and Measurement of Marketing Productivity in Consumer Durables Industries: A Firm Level Analysis," *Journal of the Academy of Marketing Science*, 1(4), 1–8.

ENDNOTES

1. Economic value added is a trademark of Stern Stewart Consultants. For their explanation of EVA, go to http://www.sternstewart.com/evaabout/whatis.php. Accessed 03/03/05.

2. The weighted average cost of capital, a.k.a. the WACC, is just the percentage return expected to capital sources. This finance concept is better left to specialist texts, but to give a simple example, if a third of a firm's capital comes from the bank at 6% and two-thirds from shareholders who expect a 9% return, then the WACC is the weighted average 8%. The WACC will be different for different companies, depending on their structure and risks.

3. Excel has a function to do this quickly, which we explain at the end of the section. However, it is important to understand what the calculation is doing.

4. A terminal value in a simple calculation might be assumed to be zero or some simple figure for the sale of the enterprise. More complex calculations consider estimating future cashflows; where this is done, ask about assumptions and importance. If the estimated terminal value is a significant area of the analysis, why have you curtailed the full analyses at this point?

5. Hawkins, Del I., Roger J. Best, and Charles M. Lillis. (1987). "The Nature and Measurement of Marketing Productivity in Consumer Durables Industries: A Firm Level Analysis," *Journal of Academy of Marketing Science*, Vol. 1, No. 4, 1–8.

APPENDIX—SURVEY OF MANAGERS' USE OF METRICS

Job Title _____ Industry Market _____

Q1. Which best describes what your business sells?

☐ Products

☐ Services

☐ Relatively even mix of both products and services

☐ Other

Q2. Purchase relationship with customers can best be defined as

☐ Contractual for a specified period which customers can renew (e.g., magazines)

☐ Contractual for an indefinite period which customers can cancel (e.g., newspapers)

☐ Frequent purchases (e.g., consumables, restaurant meals)

☐ Infrequent purchase with little/no service/repair/supplies (e.g., digital cameras)

☐ Infrequent purchase with service/repair/supplies relationship (e.g., automobiles, printers)

Q3. Are your customers best understood as

☐ Consumers (e.g., breakfast cereal)

☐ Business or other organizational buying units (e.g., steel)

☐ Relatively even mix of both consumers and business customers (e.g., UPS)

Q4. How does your business go to market?

Q5. What are the major influencers of the purchase decision?

☐ Individual choice, little in the way of group dynamics (e.g., soft drinks, express services)

☐ Consumers rely heavily on recommendations of professionals (e.g., doctors, plumbers)

☐ Separate buying organization with multiple influences (e.g., corporate purchasing organizations)

☐ Other (please explain)

Q6. Total sales of your company are

☐ Below $10 million ☐ $10-$100 million ☐ $101-$500 million
☐ $501 million–$1 billion ☐ Over $1 billion

Q7. Over the last three years, the growth rate in sales at my company has been

☐ Below 1% ☐ 1-3% ☐ 3-10% ☐ Over 10%

For the following questions, please tell us how useful you find each of the metrics below in managing and monitoring your business.

Q8.1. How useful in managing and monitoring your business are the following Market Share Measures?

Choices: Very Useful, Somewhat Useful, Not at All Useful, Don't Know, N/A

1. Dollar (revenue) market share

2. Unit market share

3. Relative market share

4. Brand development index

5. Category development index

6. Market penetration

7. Brand penetration

8. Penetration share

9. Share of requirements

10. Heavy usage index

11. Hierarchy of effects

Q8.2. How useful in managing and monitoring your business are the following Hierarchy of Effect Metrics? (Consumer awareness, attitude, belief, trial, repeat, etc. of product)

Choices: Very Useful, Somewhat Useful, Not at All Useful, Don't Know, N/A

1. Brand awareness
2. Top of mind
3. Ad awareness
4. Consumer knowledge
5. Consumer beliefs
6. Purchase intentions
7. Purchase habits
8. Loyalty
9. Likeability
10. Willingness to recommend
11. Net promoter score
12. Customer satisfaction
13. Willingness to search

Q8.3. How useful in managing and monitoring your business are the following Margins and Cost Metrics?

Choices: Very Useful, Somewhat Useful, Not at All Useful, Don't Know, N/A

1. Unit margin
2. Margin %
3. Channel margin
4. Average price per unit
5. Price per statistical unit
6. Variable and fixed costs
7. Marketing spending
8. Contribution per unit
9. Contribution margin %
10. Break-even sales

Q8.4. How useful in managing and monitoring your business are the following Forecasting and New Product Metrics?

Choices: Very Useful, Somewhat Useful, Not at All Useful, Don't Know, N/A

1. Target volumes
2. Target revenues
3. Trial volume
4. Repeat volume
5. Penetration
6. Volume projections
7. Annual growth %
8. Growth CAGR
9. Cannibalization rate
10. Brand equity metrics
11. Conjoint utilities
12. Conjoint utilities & volume projection

Q8.5. How useful in managing and monitoring your business are the following Customer Metrics?

Choices: Very Useful, Somewhat Useful, Not at All Useful, Don't Know, N/A

1. Customers #
2. Recency
3. Retention rate
4. Customer profit
5. Customer lifetime value
6. Prospect lifetime value
7. Average acquisition cost
8. Average retention cost

Q8.6. How useful in managing and monitoring your business are the following Sales Force Metrics?

Choices: Very Useful, Somewhat Useful, Not at All Useful, Don't Know, N/A

1. Workload
2. Sales potential forecast
3. Sales total
4. Sales force effectiveness
5. Compensation
6. Break-even number of employees
7. Sales funnel, sales pipeline

Q8.7. How useful in managing and monitoring your business are the following Distribution and Retail Metrics?

Choices: Very Useful, Somewhat Useful, Not at All Useful, Don't Know, N/A

1. Numeric distribution (%)
2. All commodity volume
3. Product category volume
4. Total distribution
5. Facings
6. Out of stock %
7. Inventories
8. Markdowns
9. Direct product profitability
10. GMROII

Q8.8. How useful in managing and monitoring your business are the following Pricing and Promotion Metrics?

Choices: Very Useful, Somewhat Useful, Not at All Useful, Don't Know, N/A

1. Price premium
2. Reservation price

3. Percent good value

4. Price elasticity

5. Optimal price

6. Residual elasticity

7. Baseline sales

8. Incremental sales, or promotional lift

9. Redemption rates

10. Cost of coupons/rebates

11. Percentage sales with coupon

12. Percentage sales on deal

13. Percent time on deal

14. Average deal depth

15. Pass-through

Q8.9. How useful in managing and monitoring your business are the following Advertising Media and Web Metrics?

Choices: Very Useful, Somewhat Useful, Not at All Useful, Don't Know, N/A

1. Impressions

2. Gross rating points

3. Cost per thousand impressions

4. Net reach

5. Average frequency

6. Effective reach

7. Effective frequency

8. Share of voice

9. Pageviews

10. Clickthrough rate

11. Cost per click

12. Cost per order

13. Cost per customer acquired

14. Visit (# Web site views)

15. Visitors (# Web site viewers)

16. Abandonment rate

Q8.10. How useful in managing and monitoring your business are the following Finance and Profitability Metrics?

Choices: Very Useful, Somewhat Useful, Not at All Useful, Don't Know, N/A

1. Net profit

2. Return on sales

3. Return on investment

4. Economic profit (EVA)

5. Payback

6. Net present value

7. Internal rate of return

8. Return on marketing investment ROMI

BIBLIOGRAPHY

Aaker, David A. (1996). *Building Strong Brands*, New York: The Free Press.

Aaker, David A. (1991). *Managing Brand Equity*, New York: The Free Press.

Aaker, David A., and Kevin Lane Keller. (1990). "Consumer Evaluations of Brand Extensions," *Journal of Marketing*, V54 (Jan), 27.

Aaker, David W., and James M. Carman. (1982). "Are You Over Advertising?" *Journal of Advertising Research*, 22, 57–70.

Abela, Andrew, Bruce H. Clark, and Tim Ambler. "Marketing Performance Measurement, Performance, and Learning," working paper, September 1, 2004.

Abraham, Magid H., and Leonard M. Lodish. (1990). "Getting the Most Out of Advertising and Promotion," *Harvard Business Review*, May–June, 50–58.

Ailawadi, Kusum, Donald Lehmann, and Scott Neslin (2003). "Revenue Premium as an Outcome Measure of Brand Equity," *Journal of Marketing*, Vol. 67, No. 4, 1-17.

Ailawadi, Kusum, Paul Farris, and Ervin Shames. (1999). "Trade Promotion: Essential to Selling through Resellers," *Sloan Management Review*, Fall.

Ambler, Tim, and Chris Styles. (1995). "Brand Equity: Toward Measures That Matter," working paper No. 95-902, London Business School, Centre for Marketing.

Barwise, Patrick, and John U. Farley. (2003). "Which Marketing Metrics Are Used and Where?" Marketing Science Institute, (03-111), working paper, Series issues two 03-002.

Berger, Weinberg, and Hanna. (2003). "Customer Lifetime Value Determination and Strategic Implications for a Cruise-Ship Line," *Database Marketing and Customer Strategy Management*, 11(1).

Blattberg, Robert C., and Stephen J. Hoch. (1990). "Database Models and Managerial Intuition: 50% Model + 50% Manager," *Management Science*, 36, No. 8, 887–899.

Borden, Neil H. (1964). *Journal of Advertising Research*, 4, June: 2-7.

Brady, Diane, with David Kiley and Bureau Reports. "Making Marketing Measure Up," *Business Week*, December 13, 2004, 112–113.

Bruno, Hernan, Unmish Parthasarathi, and Nisha Singh, Eds. (2005). "The Changing Face of Measurement Tools Across the Product Lifecycle," in *Does Marketing Measure Up? Performance Metrics: Practices and Impact*, Marketing Science Conference Summary, No. 05-301.

Christen, Markus, Sachin Gupta, John C. Porter, Richard Staelin, and Dick R. Wittink. (1994). "Using Market-Level Data to Understand Promotion Effects in a Nonlinear Model," *Journal of Marketing Research*, August, Vol. 34, No. 3, 322–334.

Clark, Bruce H., Andrew V. Abela, and Tim Ambler. "Return on Measurement: Relating Marketing Metrics Practices to Strategic Performance," working paper, January 12, 2004.

Dekimpe, Marnik G., and Dominique M. Hanssens. (1995). "The Persistence of Marketing Effects on Sales," *Marketing Science*, 14, 1–21.

Dolan, Robert J., and Hermann Simon. *Power Pricing: How Managing Price Transforms the Bottom Line*, New York: The Free Press, 4.

Farris, Paul W., David Reibstein, and Ervin Shames. (1998). "Advertising Budgeting: A Report from the Field," New York: American Association of Advertising Agencies.

Forrester, Jay W. (1961). "Advertising: A Problem in Industrial Dynamics," *Harvard Business Review*, March–April, 110.

Forrester, Jay W. (1965), "Modeling of Market and Company Interactions," Peter D. Bennet, ed. *Marketing and Economic Development, American Marketing Association*, Fall, 353–364.

Gregg, Eric, Paul W. Farris, and Ervin Shames. (revised, 2004). "Perspective on Brand Equity," Darden School Technical Notes, UVA-M-0668.

Greyser, Stephen A. (1980). "Marketing Issues," *Journal of Marketing*, 47, Winter, 89-93.

Gupta and Lehman. (2003). "Customers As Assets," *Journal of Interactive Marketing*, 17(1), 9–24.

Harvard Business School: Case Nestlé Refrigerated Foods Contadina Pasta & Pizza (A) 9-595-035. Rev Jan 30 1997.

Hauser, John, and Gerald Katz. (1998). "Metrics: You Are What You Measure," *European Management Journal*, Vo. 16, No. 5, 517–528.

Interactive Advertising Bureau. Interactive Audience Measurement and Advertising Campaign Reporting and Audit Guidelines, September 2004, United States Version 6.0b.

Kaplan, R. S., and V.G. Narayanan. (2001). "Measuring and Managing Customer Profitability." *Journal of Cost Management*, September/October: 5–15.

Keiningham, Timothy, Bruce Cooil, Tor Wallin Andreassen, and Lerzan Aksoy (2007). "A Longitudinal Examination of Net Promoter and Firm Revenue Growth." *Journal of Marketing*, Volume 71, July.

Little, John D.C. (1970). "Models and Managers: The Concept of a Decision Calculus," *Management Science*, 16, No. 8, b-466—b-484.

Lodish, Leonard M. (1997). "J.P. Jones and M.H. Blair on Measuring Advertising Effects "Another Point of View," *Journal of Advertising Research*, September–October, 75–79.

McGovern, Gail J., David Court, John A. Quelch, and Blair Crawford. (2004). "Bringing Customers into the Boardroom," *Harvard Business Review*, November, 70–80.

Meyer, Christopher (1994), How the Right Measures Help Teams Excel, Harvard Business Review, May–June, pp. 95–103.

Much, James G., Lee S. Sproull, and Michal Tamuz. (1989). "Learning from Samples of One or Fewer," *Organizational Science*, Vol. 2, No. 1, February, 1–12.

Murphy, Allan H., and Barbara G. Brown. (1984). "A Comparative Evaluation of Objective and Subjective Weather Forecasts in the United States," *Journal of Forecasting*, Vol. 3, 369–393.

Net Genesis Corp. (2000). *E-Metrics: Business Metrics for the New Economy.* Net Genesis & Target Marketing of Santa Barbara.

Peppers, D., and M. Rogers. (1997). *Enterprise One to One: Tools for Competing in the Interactive Age*, New York: Currency Doubleday.

Pfeifer, P.E., Haskins, M.E., and Conroy, R.M. (2005). "Customer Lifetime Value, Customer Profitability, and the Treatment of Acquisition Spending," *Journal of Managerial Issues*, 25 pages.

Poundstone, William. (1993). *Prisoner's Dilemma*, New York: Doubleday, 118.

Reichheld, Frederick F., and Earl W. Sasser, Jr. (1990). "Zero Defections: Quality Comes to Services," *Harvard Business Review*, September–October, 105–111.

Reichheld, Fred. (2006). *The Ultimate Question: Driving Good Profits and True Growth.* Boston: Harvard Business School Publishing Corporation.

Roegner, E., M. Marn, and C. Zawada. (2005). "Pricing," *Marketing Management*, Jan/Feb, Vol. 14 (1).

Sheth, Jagdish N., and Rajendra S. Sisodia. (2002). "Marketing Productivity Issues and Analysis," *Journal of Business Research*, 55, 349–362.

Tellis, Gerald J., and Doyle L. Weiss. (1995). "Does TV Advertising Really Affect Sales? The Role of Measures, Models, and Data Aggregation," *Journal of Marketing Research*, Fall, Vol. 24-3.

Wilner, Jack D. (1998). *7 Secrets to Successful Sales Management*, Boca Raton, Florida: CRC Press LLC; 35–36, 42.

Zellner, A., H. Kuezenkamp, M. McAleer, Eds. (2001). "Keep It Sophisticatedly Simple." *Simplicity, Inference and Econometric Modeling*. Cambridge University Press, Cambridge, 242–262.

Zoltners, Andris A., and Prabhakant Sinha, and Greggor A. Zoltners. (2001). *The Complete Guide to Accelerating Sales Force Performance*, New York: AMACON.

Index